Power and Everyday Practices

Power and Everyday Practices

SECOND EDITION

Deborah Brock, Aryn Martin, Rebecca Raby, and Mark P. Thomas

UNIVERSITY OF TORONTO PRESS

Toronto Buffalo London
utorontopress.com
Printed in Canada

Library and Archives Canada Cataloguing in Publication

Title: Power and everyday practices / Deborah Brock, Rebecca Raby, Mark P. Thomas, Aryn Martin.
Names: Brock, Deborah R. (Deborah Rose), 1956– editor. | Raby, Rebecca, 1968– editor. | Thomas, Mark P. (Mark Preston), 1969– editor. | Martin, Aryn E., 1973– editor.
Description: Second edition. | Includes bibliographical references and index.
Identifiers: Canadiana 20190099119 | ISBN 9781487588236 (hardcover) | ISBN 9781487588229 (softcover)
Subjects: LCSH: Equality. | LCSH: Power (Social sciences)
Classification: LCC HN49.P6 P69 2019 | DDC 303.3—dc23

We welcome comments and suggestions regarding any aspect of our publications—please feel free to contact us at news@utorontopress.com or visit our internet site at utorontopress.com.

North America
5201 Dufferin Street
North York, Ontario, Canada, M3H 5T8

2250 Military Road
Tonawanda, New York, USA, 14150

ORDERS PHONE: 1–800–565–9523
ORDERS FAX: 1–800–221–9985
ORDERS E-MAIL: utpbooks@utpress.utoronto.ca

UK, Ireland, and continental Europe
NBN International
Estover Road, Plymouth, PL6 7PY, UK
ORDERS PHONE: 44 (0) 1752 202301
ORDERS FAX: 44 (0) 1752 202333
ORDERS E-MAIL: enquiries@nbninternational.com

This book is printed on acid-free paper.

University of Toronto Press acknowledges the financial assistance to its publishing program of the Canada Council for the Arts and the Ontario Arts Council, an agency of the Government of Ontario.

Canada Council for the Arts
Conseil des Arts du Canada

ONTARIO ARTS COUNCIL
CONSEIL DES ARTS DE L'ONTARIO
an Ontario government agency
un organisme du gouvernement de l'Ontario

Funded by the Government of Canada
Financé par le gouvernement du Canada

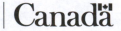

For Mary Jo Nadeau
Teacher, Scholar, Activist, Inspiration

Figures

Text Boxes

Preface

We are pleased to present you with this second edition of *Power and Everyday Practices* (*PEP*). We have prepared an unconventional textbook: one that takes up sociological theory and methods in the context of everyday objects and practices.

One objective of this text is to enrich students' appreciation of the uses of theory for exploring the everyday world. A second objective is to "trouble" normative assumptions about the everyday world; to question the seemingly taken for granted, common-sense social relations that shape our lives. We ask students to explore not only *why* questions, but also *how* questions; to make visible not only why things are as they are, but how they have come to be organized historically, socially, and culturally. A third objective of this text is to enhance students' ability to be critical consumers of information, and to explore the links between the production of knowledge and the circulation of power in contemporary Western societies.

The themes, topics, and organization of this text owe much to an undergraduate foundations course in sociology at York University in Toronto, "Social Organization/ Social Order" (now titled "Power and Everyday Life"). The course turns an analytic lens toward sites of privilege and the production of power. So, for example, rather than focusing on particular groups as objects of empirical investigation (such as the impact of racism on people of colour, the marginalization of gay, lesbian, and transgendered people, or the problems of the poor), we interrogate the centrality of whiteness, heterosexuality, and consumption practices in contemporary Western societies. Students think about how that cup of coffee they are drinking was produced, how their own deeply personal efforts at self-improvement are connected to a particular therapeutic ethos that characterizes our time and place, and why so many people now list "shopping" as one of their favourite activities. We have been consistently pleased with the high level of enthusiasm for the course—and for the first edition of *PEP*—among students, teaching assistants, and colleagues. The first edition has been read in a wide variety of courses across Canada. Our aim with this second edition is to build upon *PEP1's* successes by expanding the range of topics and chapters covered, so as to deepen the analysis of bodies, genders, and sexualities. We have also reconfigured the text so that it is accessible for a range of course levels. For example, course directors can build on the analytic content by assigning more attention to material contained in the ancillaries, such as the glossary, text boxes, and instructor's manual. Finally, we have attempted, however modestly, to address some aspect of Indigenous knowledge and experience in every chapter, as a simple matter of recognition of Indigenous peoples, and in recognition of the ongoing reality of colonialism in Canada.

Features of the Text

There are three major parts to *Power and Everyday Practices*:

- **Part I** introduces you to the thematic, theoretical, and methodological approaches of the textbook.
- **Part II** is organized to deepen your comprehension of some key thematic concepts of the book: the centre, normalization, and power. The students' appreciation of these concepts is gained through an exploration of bodies, genders, sexualities, whiteness, capitalism and class relations, age, and citizenship and borders.
- **Part III** shifts the analytic lens to a selection of everyday images and practices. Here the students engage with the meanings of scientific knowledge, the pervasiveness of therapeutic culture, consumption practices, and the logic of finance for Western industrialized societies. As well, we make links between everyday images and practices in the West and global relations of power. Here students examine the power relations embedded in a cup of coffee, the social construction of the "Indian" in the West, and the significance of tourism and the tourist experience both for local and global economies and for tourists themselves.

Each chapter concludes with a series of exercises and questions that will assist students with their review and comprehension of the material. Some of these exercises and questions are designed for students to undertake on their own, and some are designed for groups. Accompanying each chapter is a bibliography of sources that were important to its construction.

Throughout the text, key concepts are shown in **bold text** the first time they are mentioned in each chapter. Often you will find the concept explained in the chapter, and you will always find it in the glossary at the end of the book. Keep in mind, however, that the definitions are abbreviated versions of the explanations provided by our authors, and they are not a substitute for the fuller explanation and analyses to be found in the chapters themselves. Some authors may take up the same concepts in somewhat different ways, so it is important to understand the meaning and context for concepts in relation to specific chapters and issues.

Acknowledgements

We wish to express our heartfelt thanks to the many people who provided the labour, support, guidance, and inspiration that made this textbook possible. In particular, the anonymous reviewers took on an enormous job in reading numerous iterations of the manuscript and advising us on how to do the best job possible for students and colleagues. It is a task that is carried out with little acknowledgement and no reward, other than knowing that they are being excellent colleagues.

Alix Holtby, a TA for a few versions of the course and a chapter author, provided indispensable and down-to-the-wire editorial assistance for this edition of *Power and Everyday Practices*. Huge thanks to Alix!

Hundreds of past students at York University provided enthusiastic feedback along the way that ultimately convinced us to produce a first, and then second, edition of this textbook. Big thanks to all of them! We would similarly like to thank past teaching assistants for their pedagogical commitment to the course on which this book is based, and to teaching with this textbook and making it work so well. Special mention goes to former TAs Rob Teixeira, Andie Noack, Rebecca Raby, Lachlan Story, Mary-Jo Nadeau, Dan Irving, Alix Holtby, Kritee Ahmed, Shelagh Ois, Kristen Hardy, and Jenna Meguid.

Our biggest thank you goes to Mary-Jo Nadeau, to whom this book is dedicated. Like Lachlan, Andie, and Rebecca, Mary-Jo taught this book before it was a book. When the book was "born," Mary-Jo immediately put it to use in a course that she was teaching at the University of Toronto, providing valuable feedback for the second edition. Most importantly, Mary-Jo has been an inspiration in everything that she does, as a teacher, an activist and labour organizer, and a craft beer lover. Mary-Jo's steadfast commitment to critical thinking and her unceasing dedication to making the world a more just place truly reflect the spirit in which this book is written.

We want to acknowledge the contributions of UTP staff in crafting the transition from manuscript to book. There are many people working behind the scene to whom we extend our gratitude. Our biggest thanks go to our editor, Anne Brackenbury, who has been a terrific source of support since the inception of the second edition. And now for personal thanks from each of us.

Deborah Brock: Big thanks to my fine colleagues at York University, for whom doing sociology and socio-legal studies are also commitments to making the world more equitable. I am very fortunate to have had a number of wide-ranging and wonderful places to work on this book: Artscape Gibraltar Point on Toronto Islands; the International Institute for the Sociology of Law in Oñati, Spain; the "sunflower room" in Utrecht, The Netherlands; and my trailer park life in southwestern Ontario. I am enormously grateful to my sister, Janet Brock, for everything that she does for me. I am grateful also to my late brother-in-law, Ian Clark, for showing me the complexities of working-class masculinity, mixed with a lot of love. Big, warm thanks to my partner, Gerard de Witt, and the network of friends and family, both in Canada and the Netherlands, who sustain me and help make my life such a wonderful adventure. Gezellig!

Rebecca Raby: Thank you to my social justice colleagues at Brock University, especially those in the Social Justice Research Institute. Thank you to child studies scholars around the world who have been doing such tremendous work engaging empirically and theoretically with childhood (and with implications for adulthood) in thoughtful and innovative ways. Thank you also to Holly Patterson for her unflagging support.

Mark P. Thomas: I would like to thank David Camfield for very helpful comments on an earlier version of Chapter 7, as well as the community of scholars at the Global Labour Research Centre at York University for being a constant source of insight and inspiration.

Aryn Martin: Thanks to Debi, Mark, and Rebecca for the trust and generosity they exhibited in bringing me on board to a collaboration already well underway. I came into York's Sociology Department as a Science and Technology Studies scholar, and teaching the first edition of this book made me a Sociologist. Students, especially graduate students, have shaped my contributions to this project, and I'm delighted that two of them (Kelly Fritsch and Alix Holtby) have contributed chapters to this volume. Eric, Asher, Max, and Scout just keep putting the love on me.

We wish to acknowledge the financial support of the Faculty of Liberal Arts and Professional Studies at York University.

Power and Everyday Practices

Introduction: Unpacking the Centre

DEBORAH BROCK, ARYN MARTIN, REBECCA RABY, and MARK P. THOMAS

Jasmine is sprawled on her bed, surrounded by her sociology course books and notes, ready to prepare her assignment. Her laptop has a number of pages open, including her sociology course syllabus, an almost empty Word document, her email account, and her favourite online shopping site. But Jasmine is on her smartphone, quickly shifting between texting and social media feeds.

Jas admits that she has a weakness for the clickbait quizzes that pop up on her social media feeds, even though she knows that they are unreliable. She has already completed two of them today: one to rate her self-esteem about her body image, and the other to assess how guys rate her sexual attractiveness. She has searched online for a new fall jacket, finally deciding to wait to make the purchase until Saturday, when she goes to the outlet mall with her friends. Jas is satisfied, though, as she has managed to buy a dream-catcher online for her mom's birthday, because her mom is really into dream-catchers and hangs them throughout their suburban home. Luckily Jas was able to apply for her own credit card on the first day of classes, when the bank on campus offered free bonus travel reward points with every application.

Mainly, though, Jasmine has been texting throughout the day with her friend, Mandy, who is getting married in the summer and is planning a big white wedding, followed by an "exotic" honeymoon on a Caribbean island. Mandy is posting wedding dress ideas on Snapchat and wants to know immediately what Jas thinks of them. Jas has not been to such a wedding, so the preparation is intriguing, and now she is accumulating travel reward points every time she uses her credit card so that she can participate in the big day.

Jasmine finally notices the time … it is almost midnight. She has barely been out of her room all day, and should have been asleep an hour ago. She has no time now to make a lunch to take to school tomorrow. Oh well. She will have to buy something in the morning (again!) when she picks up her daily latte on the way to class. But she has still not decided the topic for her sociology assignment, which is due in less than two weeks. Jasmine needs to select an everyday object or practice and discuss how it is part of the organization and flow of **power relations**. What can she possibly select, she wonders, that is interesting from her own routine, everyday life?

Jasmine's story is fictional, but in it we can find many **everyday practices** that are familiar and that might, at first glance, seem benign: online shopping, using a credit card, buying a cup of coffee, even taking an online quiz. By "everyday" we mean the practices that are a part of people's commonplace and taken-for-granted activities. But people's everyday activities reflect, reproduce, and sometimes challenge a wide range of power relations. Through this textbook we will encourage you to ask questions about these kinds of practices. We ask *how*: How are everyday occurrences connected to the social organization of power? How are **gender**, **class**, **race**, **citizenship**, and **age** shaped and reflected in many such taken-for-granted practices? How are the goods we buy produced, and by whom? How do practices such as travelling, shopping, and getting a credit card reflect and reproduce power, even create our very sense of who we are? We also address the *why* questions that these examples will no doubt bring to mind: Why are certain patterns of consumption encouraged and facilitated? And who benefits from these patterns?

For example, even that café latte some cherish as an everyday ritual reflects a geography, history, and economy of power relations. These relations become visible when we begin to study where coffee beans come from, who grows and harvests them, how they come to be ground and sold in drinks, and how they are marketed to the North American consumer. Chapter 14 thus explores how the choice to buy a cup of coffee—including what kind of coffee and where it is bought—is a practice embedded in a global web of power relations. The places we shop, the products we buy, and the websites we visit are all part of a system of consumption that links us to people, places, and things that seem very distant from our own lives.

Another of Jasmine's everyday practices is to seek out fashion tips and self-improvement advice. The magazines and other popular media she consults are embedded in power relations: selling certain kinds of images, promoting individualized self-improvement, cultivating desires that support a consumer **culture**, and, through these practices, reproducing power relations of race, gender, heterosexuality, ability, and a narrow concept of beauty. The quiz she takes could just have easily been about her fashion style, maturity, likeability, fitness routine, money management, or dating success. In any of these cases, part of the imperative within the quiz is to encourage Jasmine to reflect upon herself and to try to shape herself to better fit a presumed ideal.

The chapters in this textbook address the diverse power relations embedded in such everyday objects and practices. They complicate objects and practices that many of us take for granted and offer new, sometimes unsettling ways of thinking about them. They illustrate how a cup of coffee is never *just* a cup of coffee and why a quiz is never *just* a quiz. When we begin to examine everyday objects and practices in this way, we also begin a process of "unpacking the centre."

Unpacking the Centre

Most sociological textbooks do not directly investigate what we will refer to here as **the centre**. It is much more common for them to analyze social **deviance** through the lens of the normative social order, or to focus on what happens to people who exist at the margins: the **racialized**, the colonized, the so-called sexual "minorities," the poor, and so on. Some scholars have instead focused on studying the centre in order to develop a more comprehensive understanding of how power relations are organized. They "unpack" the centre—just like taking apart a piece of mechanical equipment—in order to find out how it works. To focus almost exclusively on the deviant or the marginalized without interrogating the centre is to risk reproducing a pattern that defines the margins as the location of *the problem*.

For example, we think it imperative to conduct sociological research on same-gender **sexuality** in order to document the forms of systemic and attitudinal **inequality** that marginalize people because of their sexual desires and practices. However, when scholars focus on same-gender sexuality while ignoring the social construction of **heterosexuality**, we continue to name same-gender attraction, including being gay, lesbian or bisexual, as, in effect, the *problem* for sociological inquiry, even though our **objective** may be to explain why these forms of sexuality should not be considered problems. Heterosexuality is able to maintain its privileged position as the **normal** and natural form of sexual expression. The **binary**, **two-gender system** is another way in which our relation to ourselves and others is normatively, and narrowly, organized. Yet this system delegitimates or erases a vast array of possibilities for living one's life. Why the insistence that there are only two genders, when that limits possibilities for so many of us and substantial numbers of people refuse to be contained by them? **Whiteness** is another social characteristic that occupies the centre. Academic and public accounts of **racism** commonly focus on the impact of racism on people of colour, and ignore the social construction of whiteness and the relations of power and privilege connected to whiteness. The social organization of whiteness, however, is an important part of practices of **racialization** and the problems of racism. Racism is also perpetuated when those who occupy the centre fail to acknowledge systematic historic and current racial and cultural ideas and practices that are deeply connected to **colonialism** and the marginalization of **Indigenous** peoples.

This approach to studying the social organization of everyday objects and practices draws attention to what sociologists have long referred to as patterns of **social inequality**. We are interested in power primarily because of the ways it produces and sustains inequalities between social groups. We do not, however, simply focus on patterns of social inequality as the outcome of power. While themes of inequality are certainly present in the chapters in this book, our approach seeks to understand the social organization of dominant power relations in terms of the ways in which these power relations shape *both* broad patterns of inequality *and* everyday experiences. In other words, we do not simply aim to document different levels of socio-economic **status**, as stratification theorists often do (Aronowitz, 2003); rather, we are interested in the social relations that produce and reproduce the "normal," the dominant, and the "centre." This means our analysis focuses on understanding relationships between social processes, social groups, *and* individuals as they live their daily lives. For example, in Chapter 7 Mark P. Thomas writes about the need to understand class as a social relation rather than a social position. This means seeking out the ways the economic system we live in—**capitalism**—brings people into social relationships with one another shaped by the distribution and control of economic resources. In order to understand "class" we need to look not simply at one's income level, but at the deeper social organization of the "everyday experience" of going to work.

To unpack the centre is to explore the taken-for-granted features of dominant forms of social organization. It is the most difficult to see that a centre exists when you occupy it—for example, when you are white, **heterosexual**, a citizen, or someone with an ample secure income. It is not so difficult when you are an Indigenous person, a non-citizen, do not identify as straight, are racialized, or are in some way minoritized. We want you to become particularly aware of the ways in which centuries of colonization have placed the descendants of colonizers in a position of assumed ownership of the homelands of Indigenous peoples, for which they typically never ceded title. Finally, the experiences of **migrant** workers reveal how citizenship and national belonging are part of the centre, even while migrants might wish such acceptance for themselves. In *Power and Everyday Practices* we aim to show how these active and ongoing social processes are integral to everyday life.

To further understand the centre, it is helpful to borrow from Ruth Frankenberg's (1993) description of whiteness, a topic which you will read more about in Chapter 6, by Melanie Knight. Frankenberg explored how whiteness is

- a position of social advantage;
- a standpoint from which those who occupy the centre see the world; and
- sustained through what are typically unmarked and unnamed cultural practices.

Yet this analysis is not as simple as naming some people as insiders and others as outsiders. For example, while we might occupy the centre in one respect (such as through an identification as white), we might not in others (such as an identification as **queer**), as we all have many dimensions and attachments. Furthermore, we are always negotiating and sometimes even reframing these, according to the distinct composition of various social locations we occupy. As a result, we might simultaneously occupy the centre and the margins. This is a somewhat different approach than building an **intersectional analysis**, a concept developed by Kimberlé Crenshaw (1989, 1991) to understand the multiple and interwoven ways in which Black women experience social marginalization and exclusion. We ask you to explore how marginalized identities and social locations intersect and reinforce one another, consistent with Crenshaw's original intention. However, we ask you to do this while continually returning to our main focus for *Power and Everyday Practices*: the "problem" that is the centre.

When any of us, regardless of our social position, negotiate multiple social locations and forces, we exercise **agency**: a capacity to make choices within the frames of reference and possibilities available to us and to act on those choices. So, we are not one-dimensional people leading prepackaged lives. We are not simply stamped from a mold by processes of **socialization** to be cookie-cutter people created by powerful **social institutions**. Indeed, we would argue that "socialization" should only be used as a verb, to describe a practice of social learning; it should not imply a rigid predetermination by larger social forces of who we are. We are complex and thinking subjects. At the same time, *who* we are, and how we know ourselves to be, is very much linked to power: the power relations that shape our everyday practices, create the centre, and also create our notions of what is normal. Occupying the centre is a lot like being considered normal. Both are largely taken for granted by the people who occupy the centre, and both reproduce the kinds of comparisons, hierarchies, and exclusions between groups of people that are examined throughout this textbook and that invariably reflect and reproduce relations of power.

Thinking About Power

What comes to mind when you think about power? A corporate boardroom? Political office? A raised fist? A gun? A nuclear weapon? Less often does the everyday social world come to mind. How did that T-shirt make its way to your favourite shopping website or local outlet mall? What does it mean to be responsible for your own economic well-being? How do you come to celebrate national holidays such as Canada Day? Why do you prefer to kiss women rather than men (or vice versa) and why does it matter? Comprehending power, not only in significant world events or in schoolyard fights, but in our everyday, often mundane social worlds, is an important task and is central to this textbook. And because the mundane language and activities of everyday life often reproduce the centre, those who are at the centre often do not see power at work.

Usually we only think of power when it involves visible coercion. For example, sociologist Max Weber (1947, p. 152) defined power as "the probability that one actor in a social relationship will be in a position to carry out his [*sic*] will despite resistance." Yet power is also being exercised when we are so entrenched within a particular way of "seeing" that we cannot imagine alternatives to it. It is exercised when our thoughts, preferences, and acceptance of ourselves have been established within the taken-for-granted order of things. We might think that this way has been designed by God or by the natural order and is therefore unchangeable. Yet power includes the ability of a person, group, organization, **discourse**, etc., to put into place the definition of a situation. This entails establishing the terms through which events will be understood and through which we can discuss the pertinent issues. Also, power involves the creation of ideals which people and organizations then try to achieve. In this way power often includes the ability to define what is considered moral and good, and what isn't (McDowell & Sharp, 1999). In examining these complexities of power, part of our task is to explore how power is socially organized, who is advantaged or disadvantaged, what factors need to be in place for this to happen, when and where the exercise of power is most likely to occur, and, ultimately, why power happens. It is also necessary to explore why and how dominant power relations come to be challenged, contested, or resisted, and how such resistance can, in turn, create new social relations and organization. These are daunting tasks, because power is one of the most complex concepts in the social sciences.

When we mention "society" or the social (as in social organization or social relations), we do not mean that it is in opposition to "nature" or the physical world around us. Instead, we will show that in most instances, facts of nature and physical things are tangled up in social worlds, and vice versa. And power is implicated in how facts and things come to be. Hence, social entities (power, laws, family relations, etc.) require elements of built and natural worlds, just as natural things (equations, weather, genes, and fish) cannot be isolated from human social patterns. The minute we try to capture nature in itself—through description, measurement, and experiment (aka "**science**")—we introduce humans into the mix. In a famous example, Emily Martin showed that it is impossible to render a "pure" description of egg and sperm cells without seeing them through the lens of gender (1991). But it is equally impossible to produce a (believable, replicable, convincing) description of egg and sperm cells without attending to their material[1] being. This is true not just of nature but of things that humans build (aka "technology"). For example, computer code is written by humans who have beliefs and interests that get built into the code. But the material properties of hardware (tangible parts of computing technology) and software (data, such as 1s and 0s in binary code) introduce constraints on what can be done by social actors, and "code" can act in ways that are unanticipated by its designers. Feminist physicist Karen Barad describes these constraints by saying "the world kicks back" (1998, p. 112).

One way of expressing this relationship is by saying that the natural/technical (on one hand) and the social/cultural (on the other) are *mutually* ***constituted***. The facts of nature, painstakingly arrived at through the labour and language of human scientists, carry the marks of social beings embedded in their time and place (see Chapter 10), but this does not mean facts are purely social; they are not "made up" by humans or naked reflections of whoever is in power. Instead, **matter** in the world participates in science, too, shaping what can and can't be plausibly said about it. Scientific facts are **nature-cultures.**[2] In what follows, we will see that this is true of disease categories, growth charts, movie cameras, brain scans, and so on.

Let's think about three very different examples of how power works, each of which will be examined further in this book. We'll begin with a discussion of medical science, which one would think is foremost engaged with identifying and explaining naturally occurring phenomena. What is the relation between power and the professional knowledge of medical science? If your answer is that medical experts are powerful, you will find that this textbook requires you to dig much deeper. Scientists and physicians do not simply discover and name diseases that affect human populations; they also make decisions within certain contexts (explored in Chapter 10) about what it means to be sick or healthy (explored in Chapter 11). Such decisions can, in turn, categorize entire groups of people. The implications of this are enormously significant. Certain populations of people (for example, HIV-positive people, sex workers, and "lepers") become associated with contagion, regardless of their individual likelihood to transmit disease. These populations then become a source of public anxiety, and at times are subject to social rejection and isolation. Heidi Rimke and Deborah Brock develop this topic in Chapter 11, where they address the rise of **therapeutic culture**.

Another example of how power works can be found in Chapter 13, "Are You Financially Fit?," by Mary-Beth Raddon. Discussions of "the market" have dominated the public agenda for decades, and are commonly framed as if market forces have a self-regulating logic of their own. Adam Smith (1723–1790) first introduced this notion of the "invisible hand" in his treatise on the birth of capitalism, *The Wealth of Nations* (1776), where he argued that social good is best achieved through the pursuit of individual self-interest through exchanges in a **free market**. **Neoliberal** rationalities similarly attribute to the market the dimensions of a natural force, existing independent of human activity. Problems with this conceptualization of the market became clear in the financial crisis of 2008, when global markets that had been most vigorously pursuing the neoliberal agenda began to unravel. Not only did this crisis require the rapid intervention of **nation-states** in order to save their national economies from bankruptcy; it also exposed something of the organization of power behind the myth of the self-regulating market. Despite this exposure, the neoliberal conceptualization of social life as governed by natural economic rationalities remains in place and permeates our everyday financial decisions and practices, as Chapter 13 explores.

Finally, another notable example of the workings of power can be seen in the way Indigenous people have been represented and treated in Canada and other societies that were founded on colonialism. When colonists first came to North America, numerous thriving peoples and cultures were already living here on **Turtle Island**, and yet colonialists claimed to have "discovered" this new land, naming territories, mountains, and rivers after European explorers and rulers. Sometimes Indigenous people were respected and valued for their knowledge and their alliances, but overall, as colonizers claimed their lands, they were seen and treated as problems to be dealt with. European scientists at the time played a role in rendering this justifiable to the colonizers by pointing to racial hierarchies supposedly dictated by nature (Schiebinger, 1993). Indigenous peoples were confined to reserves, denied self-government, and forced into **residential schools**. As one of the key residential school architects, Duncan Campbell Scott, stated, "our object is to continue until there is not a single **Indian** in Canada that has not been absorbed into the body politic" (Truth and Reconciliation Commission of Canada, 2015, p. 3). The legacy of these and other injustices continues to have effects on all of our lives: in Canada, most Canadians live on unceded Indigenous lands, we are governed by a political system and laws reflecting a European heritage, and prejudices against Indigenous people prevail. Meanwhile, reserves are systematically under-resourced, Indigenous communities are seldom consulted about important decisions affecting land, and the soul-destroying legacy of residential schools continues to haunt many Indigenous communities and individuals.

Indigenous scholar Glen Coulthard (2014, pp. 6–7) describes these processes as a "settler-colonial relationship," which arises from discursive, material, and institutional forms of power (which you will read more about shortly) that serve to "facilitate the dispossession of Indigenous peoples of their lands and self-determining authority." This **settler colonialism** (a concept that will be discussed further in Chapter 1 by Deborah Brock and problematized in Chapter 9 by Nandita Sharma) is sustained by multiple and interconnected dynamics of capitalism, **patriarchy**, **white supremacy**, and **state** power, with access to, and control over, territory being a central outcome. Recently, the Canadian government has tried to address some of this legacy through the Truth and Reconciliation Commission, which was established to uncover and recognize the history and impacts of the residential school system. However, as Coulthard makes clear, we need to move far beyond a politics of recognition because "recognition" does not disrupt the centre, and so does not fundamentally challenge prevailing colonial power relations, in Canada and beyond. For Coulthard, what is needed is a movement of decolonization that would challenge and overturn the structural basis of the settler-colonial relationship.

In this textbook, we do *not* intend to provide a comprehensive survey of the study of power in the social sciences. However, we do want to provoke you to think more about how power works and to complicate your perceptions of what power is, where it comes from, how it is expressed, and how it is resisted. We offer you some clues, debates, and examples in order to get you started in your own thinking about power. The chapters that follow engage with a range of sociological theorists and perspectives that will assist you in thinking about power in relation to everyday practices. While you will encounter a variety of approaches to the study of power and everyday practices in this book, the works of Karl Marx and Michel Foucault are particularly influential to our overall approach, as Deborah Brock explains in detail in Chapter 1.

Karl Marx (1818–1883) was a German political economist who spent his life writing about the economics of capitalism. His aim was to understand both its social organization and the ways in which it could be transformed. For Marx, capitalism is an economic system inherently defined by antagonistic class relations between two fundamental groups—the **capitalist class** and the **working class**. He understood class as primarily defined by ownership of and control over economic resources within society, such as capital and business infrastructure (which he termed the **means of production**). Those who own these resources—the capitalist class—are able to generate more capital (profits) by exploiting those who do not—the working class. For Marx, power in capitalist society stems from these fundamental relationships of control over economic resources. The class system of capitalism—in Marx's terms—is explored by Mark P. Thomas in Chapter 7. Marx's ideas about power are reflected in chapters that connect individual everyday objects and practices—for example, drinking a cup of coffee—to broader economic processes rooted in the **exploitation** of labour that produced that cup of coffee. Marx was not only interested in understanding capitalism. He was also committed to an analysis that would advance social change, arguing that the exploitation he identified as inherent to capitalism must be countered by social movements that aim to create an economic system based on democratic control over economic production. This being so, various chapters in this text examine alternative social movements and politics, including **slow money** (Chapter 13) and fair trade purchasing (Chapter 14). Marx's ideas are also reflected in the analysis of settler colonialism that runs through the book. Using Marx's concept of **primitive accumulation** (see Chapter 7), Coulthard (2014) points out that the settler-colonial relationship in Canada is itself built through the dispossession of the land and resources that have sustained Indigenous societies. Coulthard argues that this practice of dispossession is not simply an historical act: it is ongoing and persistent. Mainstream representations of First Nations people as part of Canada's *past* foster an orientation to these groups as extinct or endangered, and thus continue to erase the lives of contemporary peoples and cultures. In terms of the analysis of "the centre" in this book, the settler-colonial relationship plays a key role in normalizing both whiteness and the construction of the Canadian nation-state.

Michel Foucault (1926–1984) was a French social theorist who believed that one of the most pervasive forms of power in contemporary societies comes through processes of **normalization**. Foucault was interested in how we come to understand what is considered to be "normal." This is not an innocent or random process; for Foucault, the "normal" is a form of social **regulation** that pervades institutions and everyday practices. Following Foucault, chapters in this book seek to understand ways in which discourses about "normal" behaviour (for example, sexual orientation or age) are connected to the power relations that reproduce "the centre." We employ the definition of discourse provided by Mary Louise Adams: "Organized systems of knowledge that make possible what can be spoken about, and how one can speak about it" (Adams, 1997, p. 6). The concept of discourse is important for making sense of power and everyday practices; you will encounter it frequently throughout this text.

In shaping our lives through these discourses, by governing ourselves in accordance with principles of "normal" behaviour, we contribute to the reproduction of social inequality. Foucault's approach—explained in more detail in Chapter 1—helps us understand both the connections between discourse and power and how dominant discourses serve to shape our understanding of the "normal," hiding alternative ways of seeing the world. Far from regarding this as an iron cage of **social control**, Foucault also explored some of the ways in which counter-discourses emerged to produce social change and new understandings of social life.

We find that combining the approaches of Foucault and Marx can provide valuable insights into the social organization of power in any specific occurrence. For example, throughout this textbook you will find frequent references to **neoliberalism**.

Here we will see Marx's ideas about power expressed in analyses of neoliberalism as the now-dominant economic rationality for Western capitalism. We will also see how Foucault's ideas about discourse, power, and knowledge are helpful for understanding the production of meaning, so that neoliberalism comes to appear as the normal and natural approach to organizing economies. Both approaches therefore assist us in understanding how political institutions and social policies come to prioritize economic logic over the social welfare of people, in ways that normalize this economic logic as "the centre."

As you can see from the example of neoliberalism, the study of Marx and Foucault reveals very different approaches to how power may operate in and through social relations: one focusing on material production and the other on normalizing practices. It is at times a challenge to bring these frameworks into alignment with one another. In order to develop a more integrative approach—one that brings together analyses of discourses (building from Foucault) and analyses of material conditions (building from Marx)—we can also look to the work of social theorists who have themselves sought such integration, such as Stuart Hall. Hall developed his analysis of "the West and the rest" in order to understand how forms of economic and political exploitation inherent to European colonialism were both connected to *and made possible by* discourses of Western cultural superiority. This book aims to build on this kind of theoretical integration. The aim of *Power and Everyday Practices* is not to resolve all the tensions that may exist between these different perspectives, but rather to draw from them so as to help us understand the many ways power is produced, reproduced, and contested in relation to a wide range of everyday practices. While individual chapters utilize different aspects of these approaches, the overarching analysis of the textbook is brought together through the focus on unpacking the centre, particularly the everyday practices and processes so often unquestioned and therefore taken for granted as "normal."

What Is to Come

The book is divided into three sections. In Part I, "Foundations," we present the general theoretical and methodological approach of this textbook. In Part II, "The Centre, Normalization, and Power," we outline key social relationships that we see as constitutive of "the centre": whiteness, the middle class, **normative gender** and sexuality, the idealized body, adulthood, and citizenship—and we identify the ways all are present and reinforced within many everyday practices. The chapters in this section explore the connections of these social relations to the production and reproduction of "normal" through dominant discourses and through the social relations of contemporary capitalism. Building from C.W. Mills's idea of the "**sociological imagination**," which connects individuals to the wider social context within which they live, the authors in this section introduce ways of making connections between our everyday social locations and the larger events that shape the social world by revealing how the centre is created and reproduced. These chapters frame the case studies of "the everyday" that follow.

In Part III, "Everyday Practices," we introduce examples of practices that illustrate these social relations at work in everyday contexts. These include the pervasive influence of both scientific and economic discourses, strategies for self-improvement, and our acts of everyday consumption, including buying a coffee. While this is a diverse collection of case studies, one of the threads running through them is how experts, or **expert knowledge**, shape how we see ourselves and act in the world. Our reliance on experts is sometimes well recognized, such as when we hire a financial advisor to help "get our house in order." In such cases, we may seek expert advice to make sense of the world. Other times, however, this advice may be invisible and unwanted, for example in the strategically designed layout of a big box retailer that requires you to navigate an entire store before finding the checkout and exit. In deferring to experts to help plan our lives, or in accepting the road map of the shopping mall or big box store, we are enmeshed in relations of power that may in many ways reproduce the centre. Chapters in this section also discuss how such expertise has been challenged through alternative histories, discourses, and social movements. Our purpose here is expressly *not* to invite assertions that all scientific knowledge is simply relative, or to promote uninformed personal opinion over decades of training and investigation. We instead provide you with some tools to become more informed and critical consumers of information, to better understand why you do what you do, and to grasp the causes, consequences, and alternatives associated with individual and collective action.

This section also discusses how many everyday practices tie the everyday to the dynamics of international **political economy,** through economic systems, representations of Indigenous peoples, the **commodification** of produce such as coffee, and the production of the tourist experience. As part of this discussion we introduce Stuart Hall's writing on "the West and the rest," using Hall's work as a way to study how discourse, systems of **representation**, and political economy connect with one another in organizing power and shaping everyday practices. Following Hall, we see that discourses produce knowledge by shaping how we understand the world, but discourses cannot be separated from economic and political institutions in the production of systems of power. For example, the "escape" to an "exotic" location promoted through all-inclusive vacation packages is produced by both a discourse of "the other" (for example, exotic people in an exotic location) *and* a political economy of poverty and global inequality that enables some to *become* tourists while others *serve* tourists. Of course—as Margot Francis reminds us in her chapter "Imagining Indians"—"the West and the rest" is not just about the global economy; the discursive production of "the other" links as well to histories of colonialism in Canada, through the marginalization of Indigenous populations in North America. Thus, although Hall did not coin the term, through his exploration of the West and the rest we see varied examples of the production of power through everyday practices in local, national, and global settings.

Conclusion

We conclude this chapter by returning you to the everyday world of Jasmine, who has managed to catch five hours of sleep after a final desperate attempt to identify and explain a topic for her sociology paper. She set her smartphone alarm to ring early enough to allow time to have a quick shower with her favourite invigorating soap, arrange her hair, and dig through her overflowing closet for the right outfit for the day ahead, before leaving for class. Many of the possessions that now give Jasmine pleasure will soon seem dated and will be discarded. Her smartphone is already three versions behind the latest release. The café latte that Jasmine purchases on the way to class is quickly consumed and forgotten. In other words, Jasmine's taken-for-granted daily routines are ripe for the study of the power relations that shape our seemingly mundane everyday decisions and action, as Rebecca Solnit reminds us in "The Silence of the Lambswool Cardigans" (2007, p. 323).

There was a time not so long ago when everything was recognizable not just as a cup or a coat, but as a cup made by so-and-so out of clay from this bank on the local river or a coat woven by the guy in that house out of wool from the sheep visible on the hills. Then, objects were not purely material, mere commodities, but signs of processes, human and natural, pieces of a story, and both the story and the stuff sustained life. It's as though every object spoke—some of them must have sung out—in a language everyone could hear, a language that surrounded every object in an aura of its history.

Solnit's purpose is not to suggest that we must return to a more perfect and simple past. Like us, she seeks to foster in you the skills and vision to explore everyday objects, lives, and practices, and to recognize your part in shaping and reshaping social life. Understanding power begins to make that possible.

Notes

1 Following scientists, theorists in the field of science and technology studies ("STS") use the term "matter" to mean everything with a physical presence in the world—objects that have weight and take up space. This includes trees, water, bodies, molecules, planets, desks, machines, and so on.

2 This concept was introduced by Donna Haraway (2003) to counter the deeply entrenched habit of treating nature and culture as though they are opposites.

References

Adams, M.L. (1997). *The trouble with normal: Postwar youth and the making of heterosexuality.* Toronto, ON: University of Toronto Press.

Aronowitz, S. (2003). *How class works: Power and social movement.* New Haven, CT: Yale University Press.

Barad, K. (1998). Getting real: Technoscientific practices and the materialization of reality. *Differences: A Journal of Feminist Cultural Studies, 10*(2), 87–128.

Coulthard, G. (2014). *Red skin, white masks: Rejecting the colonial politics of recognition*. Minneapolis, MN: University of Minnesota Press.

Crenshaw, K. (1989). Demarginalizing the intersection of race and sex: A black feminist critique of antidiscrimination doctrine, feminist theory, and antiracist politics. *University of Chicago Legal Forum, 14*, 538–554.

Crenshaw, K. (1991). Mapping the margins: Intersectionality, identity politics, and violence against women of color. *Stanford Law Review, 43*(6), 1241–1299.

Frankenberg, R. (1993). *White women, race matters: The social construction of whiteness*. Minneapolis, MN: University of Minnesota Press.

Haraway, D. (2003). *The companion species manifesto: Dogs, people, and significant otherness*. Chicago, IL: Prickly Paradigm Press.

Marx, K. (1976). *Capital: A critique of political economy* (Vol. 1, B. Fowkes, Trans.). Harmondsworth, UK: Penguin.

Martin, E. (1991). The egg and the sperm: How science has constructed a romance based on stereotypical male-female roles. *Signs, 16*(3), 485–501.

McDowell, L., & Sharp, J. (1999). *A feminist glossary of human geography*. London, UK: Arnold.

Schiebinger, L. (1993). *Nature's body: Gender in the making of modern science*. Boston, MA: Beacon Press.

Smith, A. (1776). The *wealth of nations*. London, UK: W. Strahan and T. Cadell.

Solnit, R. (2007). The silence of the lambswool cardigans. In *Storming the gates of paradise: Landscapes for politics* (pp. 323–327). Berkeley, CA: University of California Press.

Truth and Reconciliation Commission of Canada. (2015). *Honouring the truth, reconciling for the future: Summary of the final report of the truth and reconciliation commission of Canada*. Winnipeg, MB: Truth and Reconciliation Commission of Canada.

Weber, M. (1947). Sociological categories of economic action. In *The theory of social and economic organization* (pp. 158–323). New York, NY: Oxford University Press.

PART ONE
Foundations

DEBORAH BROCK, ARYN MARTIN, REBECCA RABY, and MARK P. THOMAS

Part I introduces students to an innovative approach to comprehending the flows of power in everyday life. It introduces you to the thematic, theoretical, and methodological approaches of the textbook, in what we believe is an accessible style that does not compromise scholarly rigour. We want you to appreciate the importance of theory and methodology for social research and analysis, and to develop the skills to conduct informed, critical, and smart thinking. We also want to spark an interest in digging deeper whenever you engage with research, the news, social media, and everyday activities that are typically taken for granted. Most of all, we want to help equip you with the skills to confront social inequalities and injustices and to participate in movements for social change. This may seem like a lot to take on. However, we are confident that, by the end of your reading, you will have learned much more than you had believed possible.

In this section, you will be introduced to many concepts that will help to guide you through the text. Three key terms are **the centre**, **normalization**, and **power**. **Concepts** enable us to grasp the idea of something by giving it a name or a symbol that we can incorporate into our thinking. They help us to capture that which is beyond our own observation or experience. While concepts are **representations** of ideas (you will be learning more about representations shortly) and can therefore seem pretty abstract, they are really helpful for us to understand and describe specific social phenomena. They also help us to make links between phenomena that may appear to be disconnected from one another. Concepts give us a context for understanding the many people, objects, experiences, and events we encounter every day, whether that be in our own lives, in popular culture, or in our intellectual work.

Concepts are the basic building blocks of theory; thinking with theory is the topic of Chapter 1. Theories are ways that we think about and explain the world around us.

In this chapter we will introduce you to theoretical perspectives that are critical, and also sometimes in tension with each other, with a particular focus on the theoretical perspectives of Karl Marx and Michel Foucault. These perspectives can be tough, so take your time as you read this chapter and reflect on it.

Methodology addresses the logic and decision-making around our research methods, or how we do research. You will find that methodology is linked to theory, because there are connections between what we choose to study and why, how we study it, and the concepts we build on or challenge when we study it. In Chapter 2, our tool kit will provide you with some essential ideas for thinking methodologically when you are engaged in academic study, but also when you are moving through your life, observing the world around you. This chapter is quite different than what you will find in most sociology textbooks, so do not be intimidated by the thought of reading it. Just dive in and see where it takes you.

Before you move forward with the chapters, keep in mind that analysis and reasoning require critical thought. A critical approach is not simply a negative evaluation, an attack, a finding of fault, or a complaint. Good critical thinking can also have a positive or ambivalent character. It moves us beyond dualisms of positive and negative to capture the complexities of knowledge and experience. The critical thinker is open to new ideas and interpretations, and to challenging their own ideas, beliefs, and values. Through the process of critical thinking, we evaluate information, claims, and arguments, and develop the means to formulate and defend our own positions through logical argument with evidence. Moreover, critical thinking requires that we ask informed, analytic questions and that we are prepared to engage with the analysis that is opened up through this questioning process. Heads up: The assertion of a personal opinion is not an acceptable substitute for critical thinking; in this textbook you will find the tools and learn the skills to engage in meaningful social analysis that is grounded in evidence-based research.

1 Thinking About Power

DEBORAH BROCK

The first wisdom of sociology is this: Things are not what they seem.

Peter Berger, *Invitation to Sociology* (1963, p. 34)

As you read in the introduction to this volume, we want you to find something surprising and enlightening in seemingly mundane everyday activities, such as paying your bills and your taxes, reading self-help advice, drinking a cup of coffee, or applying for a passport. Yet it is also important to look beyond our own lives and experiences for clues about the organization of the social world. In other words, we want you to connect your everyday experiences to larger social, political, and economic processes. We want you to gain an appreciation for the uses of theory in making sense of your everyday world, while encouraging you to develop the skills of abstract and critical thinking to take you beyond the bounds of your actual everyday lives. These are important steps to make your **sociological imagination** flourish. This chapter encourages you to interrogate your own practices of looking, listening, and thinking. You will learn more about different approaches to knowledge, how to be critical in your consumption of information, and how to familiarize yourself with some strategies for undertaking analytic work.

Sociological theories often appear to be abstract and far removed from the world that we know. But it is the theorists—those people who develop the concepts—who help to make the social world more visible, from the everyday activities that people engage in to analyses of historic events. In this chapter, we give particular attention to how some prominent theorists conceptualize the organization of power. Our aim is to offer a way of understanding where power comes from, how it is expressed, and how it is resisted.

In the introduction, you learned a basic definition of power. However, this definition does not explain how power is socially organized, who is advantaged or disadvantaged, what factors need to be in place for this to happen, when and where the exercise of power is most likely to occur, or why power happens. You were also introduced to three examples for thinking about how power works in contemporary Western industrialized societies: (1) the organization and significance of medical **science**, (2) financial markets, and (3) everyday colonialism. You learned that there are different ways theorists can analyze these social practices. These approaches are not necessarily incompatible, because the key theories that inform this textbook are closely related in some ways, most notably in that theory is being used as a tool for making visible the workings of power and **social inequality**. And no single theory or theorist is adequate to the task of explaining everything. As such, we will look for the ways that theories can work together, rather

FIGURE 1.1a Karl Marx

FIGURE 1.1b Antonio Gramsci. World History Archive/Alamy.

FIGURE 1.1c Michel Foucault. Photo by Josee Lorenzo/INA via Getty Images.

FIGURE 1.1d Stuart Hall. Reproduced by permission of Angus Mill.

FIGURE 1.1e Leanne Simpson. Reproduced by permission of Leanne Simpson and Nadya Kwandibens/Red Works Photography.

than focusing on what divides them. In this chapter, we'll have another look at some of the ideas of Karl Marx and then move on to some of the contributions of Michel Foucault. [More detailed information about these and other theorists can be found in text boxes that follow this chapter.] We will also think about how other theorists and approaches have engaged with, built on, and challenged some of their ideas, especially in relation to **colonialism**, **postcolonialism**, and **Indigenous knowledges**. We will then consider how we can use these ideas to think differently about **neoliberalism**, which now occupies the centre of political and economic life in most Western industrialized nations.

Marx, Foucault, and Power

Nineteenth-century philosopher Karl Marx (1818–1883) was deeply concerned about the vast economic inequalities that he saw emerging in the context of the growth of early **capitalism**. This influenced his perspective on power as something that some people have and other people do not. When we analyze power as Marx understood it, we see that it is maintained through a system of domination, in which control is exercised by the **ruling class** over land, labour, and capital. Power therefore rests most fundamentally in the possession of economic resources, which in turn leads to the maintenance and intensification of economic inequality. To exercise power in capitalism is an act of **social control**, because power means having the ability to organize social, economic, and political relations in a way that benefits the possessors of power (in this case those who control economic wealth), and disadvantages those who do not hold it. This means that within a capitalist economy, the **state** (that is, the political and administrative apparatus that claims legitimacy to manage or rule the affairs of a geographical and political territory) is fundamentally a capitalist state. It ultimately works in the interest of preserving a particular economic order that benefits foremost the owners of economic wealth.

Given that the owners of economic wealth make up a small fraction of the population, you would be right to question how a system based on social inequality could be maintained, as it works against the best interests of the majority of people. Yet despite resistance (such as protests) and large-scale economic crises like the global financial crisis of 2008, capitalism persists. To many it appears to be the best economic system that we can hope for. Understanding this persistence is a major concern for our study of power. Antonio Gramsci (1891–1937) introduced the **concept** of **hegemony** to explain how cultural, intellectual, and moral leadership organize society in a way that does not upset the influence of the dominant group. This leadership instead influences the ideas and practices of the people who are being led, in a way that favours rather than threatens the dominant group, as those who are ruled come to regard their interests as being the same as those who rule (Gramsci, 1971). Gramsci explained that through hegemony, people consent to capitalist rule.

The concept of hegemony offers something of a bridge between Karl Marx's conceptualization of power and an alternative approach to power offered by Michel Foucault that we will explore next, because Foucault identifies a complex, diffuse, and dynamic network of power in capitalist societies.[1]

Before we move on, however, it is important to note that all ideas are shaped and constrained by the time and location of their development and often by the interests of their proponents. Marx, for example, was a typical **modernist** theorist because he believed that scientific knowledge could expose the truth of **exploitation**, and ultimately would lead people to challenge the false belief systems that enabled exploitative rule over them. Other modernists had a more conservative faith in science, but similarly believed in a scientific truth that would improve society. Few of the premises of early modernist thought—freedom and equality, for example—were extended beyond the lives of European men, however. Instead, many early thinkers problematically proposed a "natural" hierarchy that justified colonial expansion, slavery, and other means of subordinating non-European peoples as lesser or non-people. Even seemingly progressive modernist thinkers like Marx, who challenged these unequal conditions, assumed that European capitalist societies were more advanced than other forms of economic and social organization. You will read more about the legacy of these modernist beliefs and processes throughout this book, as well as some challenges to them. As an intellectual who was involved with the French Left during the 1960s, Foucault was concerned about social marginalization and inequality, and how domination is accomplished. However, he was not satisfied with the analysis of power provided by a Marxist approach that focused on economic domination. Instead, he regarded domination as an effect, or outcome, of power. He believed that power in contemporary Western societies is omnipresent, multifaceted, complicated, and difficult to detect, making it more effective in accomplishing domination than Marx's conceptualization of power as something possessed by the ruling class.

In order to better understand Foucault's notion of power and how it works today, we need to trace his history of different forms of power. We will first encounter sovereign power and **juridical power**, then disciplinary power, biopolitics and biopower, and, finally, governmental power, the form that Foucault finds most evident in contemporary Western industrialized societies.[2]

The Many Faces of Power: Sovereign, Disciplinary, and Biopower

Foucault referred to the oldest and most immediately recognizable form of power as sovereign power. **Sovereign power** is top-down, exercised through direct political rule, most notably the rule over subjects by a monarch (king or queen) or representatives of the monarch. When we consider historical examples of the exercise of sovereign power, we see how expansive it can be, to the point of total control. For example, prior to the emergence of liberal democracies in the West, monarchs had direct control over the life and death of their subjects, whether by ordering armies into battle, by inflicting torture to punish and bend the will of another, or by condemning a person to death. Foucault referred to this as "the right to *take* life or *let* live" (Foucault, 1978, p. 136). There was a risk to exercising sovereign power, however, as public spectacles such as executions risked shifting sympathy to the person condemned to die and away from the sovereign.

Sovereign power has not been limited to monarchs. It has also been applied to describe other asymmetrical relationships, including wherever men have been able to exercise **patriarchal** control over their wives, children, and servants. It may also be enforced juridically through the rule of law, in legislation, edicts, and other codes and commands. Contemporary sovereign power can be best described as negative or prohibitive forms of rule over individuals and groups, where, like a king, those in charge have the ability to command what people must not do. Because it is highly visible, sovereign power is also easy to identify in action and potentially to resist.

The French Revolution (1789–1799) was the first significant **radical** challenge in Europe to monarchical rule as the old feudal order began to give way to a new economic system—capitalism—and a new system of political thought and action—democracy through **liberalism**. Marx's investigation of capitalism looked at how this new historical epoch replaced one system of domination with another through the emergence of the class system (discussed in Chapter 7). Foucault's attention, however, was drawn to intricacies of power that were coming into being through the art of governing. He described the rise of **disciplinary power** through the surveillance and correction of the bodies and conduct of individual people, alongside biopolitics,[3] or the **constitution** of **populations** as targets for **regulation**.

Together, this twofold process of discipline and regulation (which he sometimes also referred to as **biopower**) produced the **disciplinary society**. The disciplinary society was characterized by strategies to administer to and regulate populations and individuals through observation, examination, judgement, and direction. It favoured **normalization** (discussed below) and correction over punishment, and reform over revenge. Power, in the disciplinary society, gradually took the form of being indirectly exercised and bound with the production of knowledge, rather than enforced through overt forms of social control. Foucault famously applied the **metaphor** of the **panopticon** in his book *Discipline and Punish: The Birth of the Prison* (1995). The model of the panopticon (see Figure 1.2) was created by Jeremy Bentham in late 18th-century England, just as the power of the sovereign was beginning to diminish. Bentham believed that a panopticon model of a prison would be economical to operate because the prison guards could not be seen and so—regardless of whether they were present or not—would always be presumed by the inmates to be present and watching them. Unlike the dungeon, which enclosed people, deprived them of light, and hid them from view, the panopticon simultaneously enclosed and made the prisoner more visible to scrutiny. Visibility was ultimately more effective than darkness in altering the prisoner. Through the panopticon, external surveillance became self-surveillance and self-regulation. The panopticon thereby not only constrained prisoners' bodies but also reconfigured their minds, as they were compelled to become self-disciplining subjects.

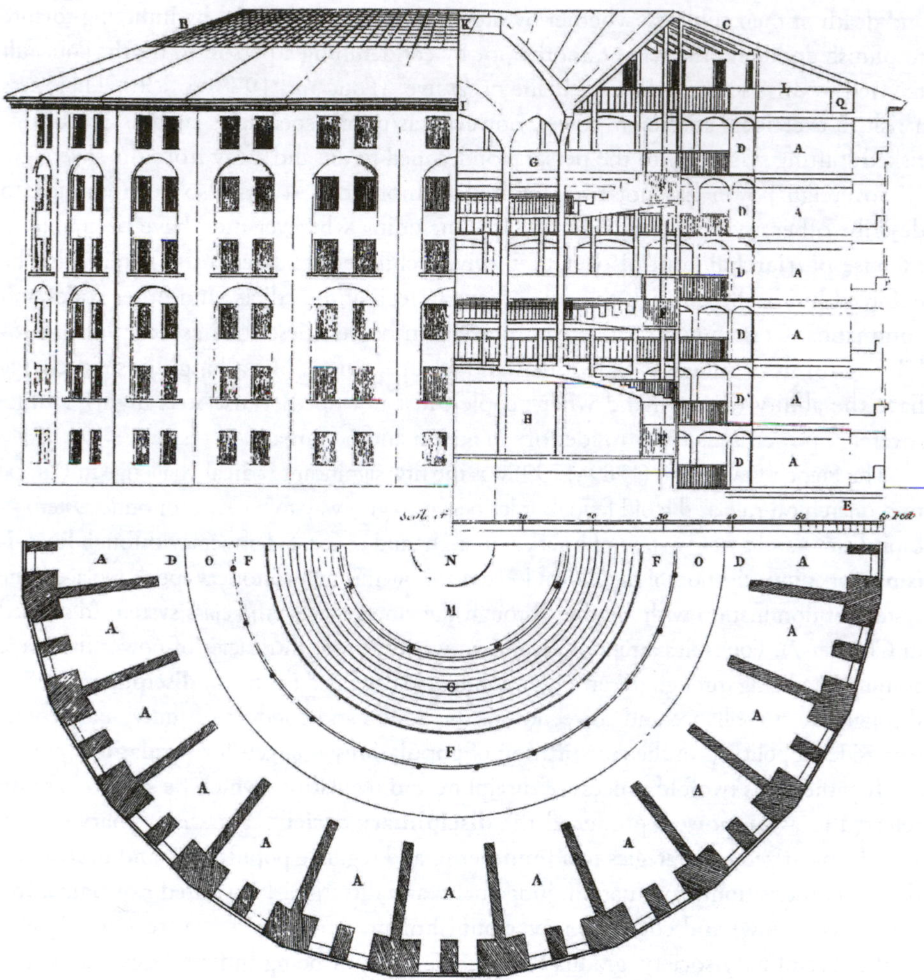

FIGURE 1.2 The Panopticon.

Foucault used the model of the panopticon to explore the disciplinary power emerging not just in prisons but factories, schools, the military, and other hierarchical institutions that were developing by the 19th century. Prisoners could be reformed, patients treated, students instructed, workers supervised, and so on, to be lawful and conformist. Foucault believed the shaping of "docile bodies" through "the gaze" of surveillance and through normalizing judgement (a topic we will return to shortly) helped to make the development of capitalist industry possible. It produced bodies amenable to schooling, work in factories, participation in the military, and so on in ways that would make the emerging economic system—capitalism—possible. In contrast, Marx noted that capitalism forced people off the land (for example, through a series of Land Enclosure Acts in 18th-century England), compelled people to find employment as **wage labourers** by depriving them of other means to make a living, and punished wageless people as vagrants and vagabonds. Recalling that no one theory explains everything, we can think about these processes as simultaneous and mutually reinforcing.

The governance of social life that gradually developed in Western Europe between the 17th and 19th centuries involved the proliferation of techniques for managing and administering individuals and populations. These were crucial to the emergence of the modern state. For example, state administrators began to compile **statistics** on births, deaths, patterns of illness, income, education, employment, housing, family size, and so on, all for the management of life and administering to the health of individual bodies and of populations. Statistics provided a means of quantifying, measuring, and assessing people and **classifying** them into populations, determining how people were to be known and understood, with the aim of correction and improvement. It was statistical measurement that led to the idea of the norm as an identification of the typical or the average, against which variations from the norm should be investigated[4] (see Chapter 3). By the 19th century, such similar institutions as prisons, asylums, and factories all aimed at "correct training" and the management and administration of life. Power was thus diffused through expanding fields of knowledge and expertise in the physical and social sciences, and through institutional application of that knowledge and expertise. As the idea of the norm took hold, the outcome was the **classification** of people into distinct categories, determining what it meant to be, for example, healthy, ill, **normal**, or deviant, as well as what it meant to be a man or a woman, a **racialized person**, a sexual being, and so on. Through these processes, people were **constituted** as human kinds (became known as having a particular make-up or shared characteristics). How they were sorted determined how they were studied, managed, treated, and potentially corrected. Moreover, specific populations were co-constituted in pairings, such that what it meant to be a certain kind could only be understood in relation to the other element in the **binary** (e.g., woman/man; Black/white; **heterosexual/homosexual**).

If you look up the definition of "normal" in a dictionary, you find it is associated with conformity, good health, or the maintenance of a natural state of being. Normal must be understood in relation to its opposite: deviant. **Deviance** refers to any form of conduct that violates social **norms**, rules, or laws. To designate a person or a group as deviant is a proscriptive act; that is to say, it is to cast a negative judgement that places those who are labelled deviant outside what is considered acceptable, right, and proper. One purpose of this designation, then, is to define and regulate differences. It also creates and rewards what is considered normal. We can see how Michel Foucault provided a more critical analytic account that linked normalization to power. He investigated how **normalizing power** compares and differentiates between people, beliefs, and practices, organizing them into a hierarchy of value in which some are considered more important, normal, accepted, and so on, than others. Some may be considered "abnormal" or deviant, and subject to normalizing intervention and exclusion[5] (Foucault, 1982). If we follow the logic of Foucault's analysis, normalizing power is therefore a **dividing practice**, because it clearly involves the making of value-laden distinctions between people, thereby dividing them from one another. These dividing practices are invariably linked to social inequality. As **gender** theorist Judith Butler comments, "How shall I know you?" implies "How shall I treat you?" (Butler, 2004). For example, early Canadian politicians established the *Indian Act* in 1876 to define who would officially be a "**status**" **Indian** and to administer the daily life and treatment of Indigenous people. To be Indigenous in Canada meant, in effect, to be a ward of the Canadian state, deprived of the independence that is a formal right of Canadian **citizenship**. A very different contemporary example is how the category of "the obese" both marks particular bodies as non-normative, in contrast to a not-obese or normal population, and creates a binary value-laden distinction between people who actually exist on a continuum. But because dividing practices are linked to social inequality, they can also create affinities among those who are considered outside normal, which leads to resistance, as counter-discourses and actions are inspired by shared experiences of subjugation.[6] You can see, however, how disciplinary power is much less visible than the exercise of sovereign power, and therefore much more difficult to identify and to resist.

Introducing Governmentality

As you have seen, by the 18th century in Western Europe new forms of power were beginning to displace sovereign power. This shift included the rise of the modern state through the emergence of governments as political institutions and profound economic changes linked to the growth of capitalism. The modern state still included features of sovereign power, particularly through law, policing, and the military. However, state power also became more diffuse, as it became increasingly reliant on a widening array of professional and administrative knowledges and expertise, from the psychiatric expert who judged the mental competency of the accused, to the financial analyst who advised on economic affairs, to the town planner who suggested how people should be housed, schooled, and fed (Miller & Rose, 2008). This means that governmentality is an approach distinct from the idea of the state as government. Foucault's approach instead addresses the shaping of human minds, desires, and conduct (think Govern-Mentality) by a wide range of **expert knowledges** and **truth claims**. Governmental power entails, foremost, the production and organization of knowledge, or how we come to know what we know, and the techniques and strategies that make governance possible.

These create what governmentality researchers refer to as the arts of government, with particular attention to the relation between power and knowledge (**power-knowledge**) and **subjectification** (the formation of subjects). When Foucault talked about the relation between power and knowledge he did not suggest that "knowledge is power." Instead, he believed that power and knowledge exist in a circular relationship, as power-knowledge (Foucault, 1995). For example, in his examination of the history of **sexuality**, Foucault investigated how notions of "truth" are created through **discourses** about sexuality, and how the ability to define truth is inevitably a practice of power. Psychologists, psychiatrists, and other doctors developed systems of classification to sort what was considered the "normal" from the "perverse" and the "pathological." **Heterosexuality** was invented at the same time as its counterpart **homosexuality**, with the latter marked as a medical disorder (see Chapter 5). This kind of **taxonomy** (system of scientific classification) became the basis for the diagnosis and treatment of an expanding array of perceived illnesses.

People's bodies, then, came to be understood in new ways, and these new knowledges—new "truths"—in turn would produce new discourses and forms of power, such as the multiplication of ways of classifying and treating people. The example of sexuality above illustrates how contemporary power operates through the production of meaning and truth, and the shaping of conduct, rather than as a coercive force. Instead, power in liberal societies is most effective when it has a positive character in that it is productive of new ways of knowing, being, and acting, thereby making use of people's capacities for **agency** and action. Where "negative" forces (for example, the power of the sovereign) suppress, punish, incarcerate, and otherwise curtail freedom of subjects, positive power creates rather than simply stifles ways of being. For example, **psy discourses** have been productive, or creative, of new identities, and so can be considered discourses associated with positive forms of power. Those identities may have good associations (being well) or bad ones (being ill), yet both are examples of positive forms of power, because of their creative and productive character. The identity of the consumer, for whom shopping is an act of exercising many choices, is another example of positive power. It is a practice that was created through the rise of capitalism, whose seemingly limitless capacity to produce new products requires consumers to purchase those products. While shopping is a kind of freedom, you will read in Chapter 12 about the ways in which shopping can also be a condition of unfreedom for both the producers and consumers of the goods that we purchase. So a word of caution: "Positive" does not necessarily mean good.

We find requisites of freedom, choice, and responsibility in the most taken-for-granted aspects of our everyday lives, from deciding on our future career to engaging in self-improvement projects to produce "our own best selves." These practices of freedom (Rose, 1999) are simultaneously disciplinary practices, because of how our conduct is influenced, even in ways that appear to bring us pleasure. Contemporary governmental power is therefore at its most effective when people experience themselves as free; indeed, we are compelled to be free through the expectation that we will be self-reflective, responsible, and entrepreneurial. These are the conditions originally established by liberal states, for whom democracy is predicated on the notion of freedom. Neoliberalism has intensified the requisite for individual freedom, in conditions where measures to achieve greater equality are clearly absent.

In summary, we can see that, for Foucault, contemporary dynamics of power are not simply about the control of one individual over others or one group or class over others.

Foucault is not concerned with who has power, because for him governmental power is not something anyone can possess and exercise over others. While Marx concerned himself with the state, law, and social classes as sources *of* power, and how power moves through these sources, Foucault instead identified how institutions, identities, relations, practices, and so on are *created through* the circulation of power. The most pervasive form of power today, governmental power, is occurring when we are no longer aware of power's effects, because we have already embraced it, and we reproduce it in relation to governing ourselves and others. Instead of the absolute power of a king, we are willingly acted on by, for example, a desire to be successful, or a number on a bathroom scale. Power is "a multiplicity of force relations" (Foucault, 1978, p. 92) that is produced from moment to moment, point to point. In other words, it circulates like blood through a capillary system. As Foucault famously summarized:

> Power is everywhere; not because it embraces everything, but because it comes from everywhere … power is not an institution, and not a structure; neither is it a certain strength that we are endowed with; it is the name that one attributes to a complex strategical situation in a particular society. (1978, p. 93)

Governance is not simply a top-down process; we are indeed governed, but we also govern others and govern ourselves (Dean, 1999). This distinguishes governmental societies from strictly disciplinary ones. However, Foucault importantly noted that sovereign, disciplinary, and governmental power do co-exist in the same societies; they have not merely replaced one another in a linear succession (Foucault, 1991). Moreover, while Foucault directs us away from the notion that power is intrinsically bad or good, we must be aware that power can indeed be dangerous, because techniques of power can look neutral when they are not, and the political ramifications can be hard to detect (Faubion, 2000, p. xv).

While valuing the distinct lenses of Marx and Foucault, in this text we also seek to build links between their approaches. How can we do so? There are many ways that we could approach this, but we will begin with the work of Stuart Hall and then turn to a brief consideration of postcolonial and Indigenous thought.

Stuart Hall and the Politics of Representation

Stuart Hall (1934–2014) deepened our appreciation for the importance of **culture** in the reproduction of inequality. While Hall's early work was influenced by Marx's focus on class relations within capitalism, he was very interested in the politics of **race**, systems of representation, and how social relations of race and class intersected.[7] He ultimately found a traditional Marxist analysis inadequate to understand these phenomena. Like Foucault, Hall believed that discourses produce and transmit knowledge, which always occurs in relation to the production of power. A discourse produces "meaningful knowledge" about a subject, thereby limiting "other ways in which the topic can be constructed" (Hall, 1996, p. 201). Moreover, Hall suggested it is not useful to focus on the distinction between true and false because a discourse that becomes dominant can have real effects whether it is "true" or not: "people act on them believing that they are true, and so their actions have real consequences" (p. 203). This is what he meant by stating that discourses are *effective*.

While emphasizing the role of discourse, however, Hall also recognized the importance of material conditions. For Hall, the effects of discourse could not be detached from social relationships connected to control over economic resources and political institutions. He thus argued that discourses and material conditions are both *produced and productive* of one another. Discourse has real effects: it enables people to know or speak of certain things in certain ways and thereby not only legitimates but also constitutes forms of power. Further, discourse cannot be separated from economic and political institutions in the production of power—for example, those institutions that facilitate the appropriation of resources (the state) and the exploitation of labour (the corporation).

A notable accomplishment in Hall's intellectual biography was his close analysis of the **politics of the image**, which is also known as the **politics of representation**. For Hall, representation is "the way in which meaning is being given to the things being represented" (1997). It is here that Foucault's influence becomes more apparent, particularly through Hall's contributions to media studies. Hall urged us to interrogate how knowledge and power intersect within representations, especially media representations.

Hall explained that while some media studies attempt to locate an underlying "true" meaning in visual representations of events, they do not have a true, fixed meaning. Rather, meaning depends on what people make of something, which in turn depends on how events and images are represented to them. Representation therefore enters into the constitution of the event. This may seem like fairly abstract analysis, so let's bring it back to the intersection of knowledge and power. Because meaning is always contextual, it is always open to contestation. Meaning is struggled over, and potentially changed. Power, however, tries to claim that one way of seeing something is true. Think about the influence of **stereotypes**, which attempt to fix, or narrowly close off, the meanings attributed to certain groups, but which are also challenged and resisted. There is an ongoing struggle over meaning. *We must examine images to reveal who made them and why, who, or what is present in the depiction and who or what is missing.* We can, as Hall does, deconstruct them. For example, we can challenge binaries that structure representations and organize knowledge, such as white signifies good and black signifies bad. If we don't do this, such representations become naturalized and taken for granted as true, and indeed we encounter them frequently enough in everyday life (in fairy tales, Hollywood movies, morality tales, etc.) to make them seem so.

As Hall notes, there is much at stake. Because representation shapes our knowledge of the world, "opening up representation allows for new kinds of knowledge to be produced, and new kinds of **subjectivity** to be explored. It makes possible new kinds of representation that have not been foreclosed by the systems of power in operation" (Hall, 1997). You will learn more about representation and discourse in Chapter 2.

At the same time, material conditions impact the formulation of discourses, as they set the limits of what is possible for people in particular social, economic, spatial (geographic), and historical locations. For example, the flag could not represent rule over a colonized territory without conditions of colonial control (including economic and military) being established in that territory. All of these—material conditions, discourses, and knowledge formation—are interconnected in a complex web of **power relations.**

In summary, Stuart Hall draws on the approaches to power found in both Marx and Foucault, because he is able to demonstrate the simultaneous importance of discourse and material conditions for shaping meaning and for delimiting possibilities for people. His work draws attention to the complexities of power in contemporary Western societies, while demonstrating how these complexities secure relations of domination and subordination that divide people from one another. At the same time, he provides an entry point into our next areas of theory and analysis: postcolonial and Indigenous knowledges.

Postcolonial and Indigenous Knowledges

Part of the rationale for contesting **grand narratives** about history and society (the stories that occupy a privileged centre in the production of ideas) is to account for what Foucault referred to as **subjugated knowledges** (Foucault, 1989): ideas that are hidden, disqualified, or masked by dominant knowledges. Subjugated knowledges are found among those who are socially positioned as other, including the racialized, the colonized, and the sexually marginalized. They offer different knowledge claims, but also raise questions about how such knowledge claims are produced. Such challenges to grand narratives remind us that theory is not simply something that exists over and above us, as "big" ideas that are removed from our lives. Rather, theory is created when people try to make sense of their worlds, and draw upon their histories and ways of knowing. These ideas are shared, compared, tested, and revised continually. You will see in the next chapter that we can apply a similar approach to the use of methodology.

While there is no agreed-upon definition of postcolonialism, it is generally used to describe critical, scholarly research about the history and legacy of European colonialism, most typically by scholars with origins within those former colonies. Postcolonialism is in some ways a misnomer that postcolonial theorists are well aware of. Colonialism is not a thing of the past. Instead, it can be argued that new forms of colonialism (sometimes called **neocolonialism**) have emerged alongside the continuation of historical forms, not through direct political and military control but through economic domination. The first task of postcolonial theory has been to complicate and disrupt **Enlightenment** and modernist narratives, particularly those that assume the ascendancy and superiority of European thought and activity.

Indigenous perspectives in North America and Australia remind us that Indigenous epistemologies and ontologies were passed down through storytelling for centuries, and through "place-based practices—practices that require land" (Simpson, 2017, p. 50). Many Indigenous scholars honour these histories while working with European-based social thought to expose the histories and dimensions of ongoing colonial rule. Dene scholar Glen Coulthard employs a Marxist analysis to reveal ties between the dispossession of Indigenous land and the demands of capitalism, while briefly noting the relevance of Foucault's work for understanding how domination can be challenged (Coulthard, 2014). For example, Foucault suggested that dominant discourses could be turned back on themselves to "disrupt a **hegemonic** field of power" through using the colonial legal system to fight for rights, for example (Coulthard, 2014, p. 214, n49).[8]

The late Mohawk lawyer and scholar Patricia Monture-Angus did much to challenge the marginalization of Indigenous women in the courts. Through her writing and her activism (Monture-Angus, 1995, 1999; Monture-Angus & Mcguire, 2009), she worked to restore inherent rights that Indigenous women had been deprived of by patriarchal colonial authorities. While a necessary tactic, Indigenous scholars agree that using the legal systems of the colonizer to challenge colonial relationships is not a sufficient means of confronting colonial rule. Other Indigenous scholars, such as Nishnaabeg scholar and activist Leanne Betasamosake Simpson, avoid direct engagement with European social systems and ideas. Simpson instead draws on traditional storytelling, poetry, and spoken word to demolish colonial narratives. She reveals some of the history of anti-capitalist ideas and practices in Indigenous thought and communities, and speaks of the need for a "**radical resurgence**"—or "an extensive, rigorous, and profound reorganizing of things" (Simpson, 2017, pp. 48–49) commensurate with Indigenous life as a way of knowing and living.[9] This is just a small sample of Indigenous researchers who develop theory as a way of knowing who we are, where we are, and what we do, whoever that "we" may be. These are more than self-affirmations about identity and belonging; they must be in place for any challenge to social domination and inequality.

Consider, for example, the places where we live, work, and study. Some of us who are involved in *Power and Everyday Practices* teach at York University in Toronto, Canada. York University was founded in 1959, yet its name was chosen to reflect the colonial origins of Canada as part of Great Britain. Such ongoing naming of places and institutions in Canada honours and reproduces the history of colonial relations and obscures what made this possible. York University has recently begun to acknowledge that it is built on the traditional territory of the Mississaugas of the New Credit First Nation. We ask you to "unpack the centre" by thinking about the erasure of Indigenous lives and ways of knowing that has occurred in the places where you live, work, and study, and consider what next steps should be taken to unsettle the everydayness of colonial power.

Liberalism, Neoliberalism, and Power

You have now been introduced, however briefly, to an impressive array of ideas from a number of theoretical approaches. Our task in this textbook, extending well beyond the remainder of this chapter, is to think about how these approaches can contribute to unpacking the West's now-dominant approach to the organization of social and economic life—neoliberalism—and how it has been sustained, despite its obvious disastrous consequences. **Neoliberalism** is a philosophy and a practice that is best known for its economic dimensions, including support of the **free market** through the deregulation of businesses and the financial sector, and for **free trade**, minimizing corporate taxation, and the privatization of public services. However, it now also governs social life through the application of market principles well beyond anything previously experienced. All of the theorists we have considered thus far can help us understand and critique the organization of power in the neoliberal period we are in. We should be vigilant about the intensification of capital in the hands of the few (Marx), about the kinds of subjects it produces (Foucault), and about the deepening of global inequalities following the same patterns laid down by colonial expansion.

While it is a phenomenon of late 20th-century capitalism, the origins of neoliberalism can be found in the philosophy of liberalism and in the development of capitalism in Europe in the 17th century. The liberal approach to power is very much tied to the rise of both capitalism and the political philosophy and practice that accompanied it—democracy. It is also linked to the modernist and humanist traditions, although clearly it is leagues away from the approach of Karl Marx. While Marx believed that the transition from the feudal order to capitalism in the West replaced one system of domination with another, the liberal approach describes this shift quite differently. Liberals found that the development of capitalism and democratic ideals opened the possibility of greater freedom for those who had been relegated by birth to the status of landless peasants (that is, the vast majority of the population) under **feudalism**. With the transition from the feudal order to capitalism, the aristocracy began to lose their almost exclusive control of land and wealth. Merchants, traders, and craftspeople began to accumulate wealth of their own, and consequently began to demand political rights as well. The development of parliamentary systems in Western Europe was a direct outcome of this growing demand for a political voice among the emerging propertied class.

Over the course of the next two centuries, the right to political inclusion was gradually extended first to non-property-owning white men, then to white women, to non-white people, and eventually to Indigenous peoples. For example, in Canada, the right to vote federally was not accorded to **Inuit** people until 1950, and not to status

Indians until 1960. Full citizenship, political participation, and formal legal equality only gradually came to be considered rights, and only as a result of demands for inclusion by the excluded groups themselves. Non-citizens continue to be excluded from political participation, as discussed in Chapter 9, as do children (see Chapter 8).

In liberal philosophy, all adult citizens who reside within a nation have the right to political participation and to accumulate private property if they can. While liberalism is now premised on the belief that all adult citizens have these rights, it does not assume that everyone has (or should have) the same economic rewards. Rather, liberalism is predicated on the belief that Western, capitalist, democratic nations are systems that "provide equal opportunity to compete for unequal rewards" (Forcese, 1986, p. 72). Those who accumulate wealth, prestige, and power are thought to do so largely because they maximized the social and economic opportunities made available to them by capitalism, a self-serving discourse called **meritocracy**.

Liberal philosophy drew upon scientific and social scientific research from the Enlightenment period in order to naturalize capitalism's economic premises, particularly **competitive individualism**. Herbert Spencer (1820–1903) coined the term "survival of the fittest" in his hypothesis that economic principles were similar to evolutionary principles that Darwin explored in his theory of natural selection (Spencer, 1864). His approach came to be known as **Social Darwinism**, although its links to Darwin's theory of evolution are flawed. Social Darwinists promoted a system of hierarchical racial classification, lending dubious scientific support for European colonial expansion and rule. Not surprisingly, persons of their own racial classification, gender, class, and geographical location (white, male, bourgeois Europeans) were determined to be the most highly evolved of all. The historical extent of Social Darwinist ideas exposes the myth that liberalism was a political system based on social equality. The perspectives of Marx, Foucault, and Hall, among countless others, unmask these knowledge systems as practices of domination.

The liberal approach to power assumes that equality is a reality, because all citizens have the same political rights and the same economic opportunities. If social inequality exists, it is not the fault of the system, but of the individual. It is assumed that power is available to those who seek to achieve it, and that it is possible for everyone in a democratic society to have their interests addressed. It is the role of the **nation-state** to ensure that citizens have the same access to formal political rights and to free markets, so that they might participate in this system. Yet here we see a contradiction within liberal states because their overriding purpose is to defend a capitalist, neoliberal economic order that is premised on inequality.

Unpacking the centre requires us to "trouble" capitalism and the liberal philosophy that supports it, as we seek to understand the rise of neoliberalism. Neoliberalism was popularized in the late 1970s by the endorsement of Ronald Reagan (Republican party) in the United States and Margaret Thatcher (Conservative party) in Britain, both of whom went on to form governments of their respective nations. The election of these political leaders was key to the rapid expansion of what was then called the New Right (see the text box on Stuart Hall's work), which actively sought to undo progressive social policies that had been underway since the mid-20th century. Advocates of neoliberalism argue that a fully competitive economy must allow unfettered access to national and global markets (the so-called free market), without competition from the state in the form of public resources, such as publicly funded health and education systems or public corporations managing national resources. It has led to economic **globalization**, privatization of public resources, and provision of the same legal rights to corporations as to individual citizens, all of which have contributed to growing global inequality (Harvey, 2005). We saw the outcome of these processes in the historic near-collapse of global financial markets in 2008. This failure is in some way a fitting irony of the "survival of the fittest" philosophy, although neoliberalism has far from disappeared as a result of this crisis, and, indeed, the enormous concentration of wealth and growing economic inequality supported by neoliberalism continued in the years following the 2008 crisis (see, most notably, Piketty, 2014).

Moreover, the neoliberalism of the present day continues to deepen and intensify economic and social inequality through what David Harvey (2005) refers to as its "**financialization** of everything," as the logics of the marketplace are extended to virtually every sphere of life, transforming us all into **human capital**, a concept first developed by Gary Becker (1964). As human capital, we must continually build and maintain our value (Brown, 2015a), as if our worth as human beings is dependent on it. As you read the chapters that follow, we would like you to think about the implications of neoliberalism for your everyday lives, given its profound effects, big and small. Neoliberalism informs the policies and economies of Western capitalist nations, drives worrisome changes in health and education, and shapes our own behaviours, attitudes, and sense of self.

The financial crisis that unfolded in 2008 had far-reaching effects on people's lives and left many wondering how neoliberalism could be sustained. One means by which neoliberalism survived was through the rise of both **economic nationalism**[10]—the protection of domestic industries and workers against foreign competition—and right-wing **populist** politicians and movements in Europe and North and South America. To fuel their rise to power, these populist movements have sought to mobilize economic insecurities and **racism** to promote policies that are economic nationalist and anti-immigration. These tactics partially address the puzzle of how neoliberalism can continue to retain the support of so many, despite its obvious anti-democratic effects. Gramsci's concept of hegemony is also helpful in making sense of how people can come to identify with interests that actually work against them. A governmentality approach allows us to dig deeper still, because it shows how a specifically neoliberal subject is created. This subject is highly individualistic and entrepreneurial, and is motivated by self-management, self-improvement, achievement, and consumption-oriented goals.

Neoliberal values now saturate everyday life as neoliberalism has become a **governing rationality** (Brown, 2015b). For example, in Chapter 13 Mary-Beth Raddon shows how the individual has come to be considered solely responsible for their financial position and outcomes. Whether you were born into poverty or experienced systemic discrimination in the education system and labour force are seemingly of no consequence (in spite of decades of sociological evidence to the contrary). In neoliberalism, it is all up to you. What makes neoliberalism distinct from classical liberalism is that in neoliberal times our understanding of ourselves as human capital and as active participants in the capitalist marketplace extends well beyond our economic activity. Our entrepreneurialism can be found in the time and money we spend cultivating diet and fitness routines and reading self-improvement and self-help manuals, in order to enhance our own value. It can be found in the enormous increase in costly cosmetic and bodily enhancement techniques and in how we represent ourselves through social media sites. Never before has the notion of **the self** been more important or more expensive, as Rimke and Brock discuss in Chapter 11.

The assumption of seemingly unlimited human agency permeates everyday discourses and practices, and we are compelled to be better, more successful, and happier people. Our individual decisions and actions seem personal and not particularly consequential for anyone but ourselves. However, when we observe the larger picture, the extent of social change becomes clearer. A new kind of person has emerged—one who is expected to rely on neither the state nor the community, but their own self. In this sense, neoliberalism is an excellent example of biopower in practice, because it is a rationality that disciplines the bodies and lives of individuals, while simultaneously managing and administering populations. As you read the chapters that follow, we invite you to explore the constitution of neoliberal subjectivity and to reflect upon how you might embody and reproduce many of these principles.

Conclusion

It is important to keep in mind that not every social theorist shares our view that divergent theoretical perspectives can be reconciled. For example, some, indeed many, claim that the works of Marx and Foucault are fundamentally incompatible, largely because Marx is rooted in what became known, long after his death, as the modernist tradition, while Foucault made a significant contribution to the development of **postmodern** and **poststructural** thinking. We have previously discussed how these approaches challenge the belief that there is an underlying social reality that can be discovered and controlled. Postmodern and poststructural theorists reject the belief that through scientific exploration we can measure and understand not only the natural environment, but also human behaviour. This is a key reason why these theorists are considered to be fundamentally at odds with **modernism**. Yet we think that fruitful bridges exist between these kinds of theoretical perspectives. That is why we have prepared for you a textbook that reflects our belief that thinking sociologically entails an openness to a range of approaches to intellectual inquiry, so that we might better understand the world and our everyday lives.

These chapters emphasize the importance of knowledge and discourse for shaping the way that the world is, in addition to material forces and effects. You will find that some of the authors of these chapters integrate more than one approach to power, while others are more definitively influenced by the approach to power exemplified in the work of Marx, Foucault, or other scholars. That said, one might argue that many current sociologists have been in some way influenced by the foundational approaches of both Marx and Foucault, as these approaches to power have in various ways influenced contemporary scholarship, including feminist, anti-racist, **queer**, crip, postcolonial, and Indigenous thought, as well as some new ideas that you will be introduced to in the next chapter. Many contemporary theorists resist placing themselves in a distinct theoretical "camp" such as modernism or postmodernism, because they consider such divisions to be less significant than in the past. Rather, emerging forms of inquiry are open to a range of voices and ideas, including the **subaltern**, the Indigenous, and the queer. Many are developing new forms of **materialist** analysis that also account for the importance of discourses, spiritual worlds, bodily experiences, and community life.

What unifies the contributors to this textbook is the insistence that knowledge and power are indeed interconnected, that ideas are, in the words of Sut Jhally (1997), "worth struggling over," and that with these ideas we can more fully become participants in processes of social change. Crucial to such engagements, we need to know about how power works in Western capitalist societies, and how domination is challenged by Marx, Foucault, Hall, and the numerous other critical theorists whose influence can be found in *Power and Everyday Practices*. We ask what gets left out when we do not investigate the relation between knowledge and power. This is why we begin with the idea of unpacking the centre, and why we have chosen certain theoretical and methodological tools to help us with our digging. The chapters that follow demonstrate how subsequent theorists and researchers in areas such as feminist, critical race, postcolonial, Indigenous, gender, and queer studies have taken up, integrated, and moved beyond the foundational ideas of Marx and Foucault.

In the next chapter, you will add to your tool kit of concepts as Andrea Noack and Aryn Martin deepen your comprehension of representation, discourse, what counts as knowledge, and how we learn about the world. You will be instructed in how to become better critical consumers of information, as you unpack discourses and representations. You will then be prepared for an analytic engagement with the everyday world in the subsequent chapters, where you will discover within our everyday beliefs and practices the links to some of the key issues of our time.

Study Questions

1. Compare and contrast the approaches to power suggested by Karl Marx and Michel Foucault.
2. Foucault suggests that normalization is an effective means of social regulation in contemporary Western societies. Discuss.

3 How has neoliberalism's emphasis on the autonomous competitive individual influenced how you think about your own life? How does a governmentality approach either complement or challenge your beliefs and assumptions?
4 How do postcolonial, neocolonial, and Indigenous perspectives unpack the centre to expose systems of domination in knowledge production and in the making of material life?

Exercises

1 Adopt a concept. Select one of the concepts highlighted in Chapters 1 and 2, and in your own words explain its meaning to other students in your study group. In the process of explaining this concept, provide your own examples of how the concept can be applied to studies of power and everyday practices. As you continue reading this textbook, look for other instances in which this concept is used or in which you think it might be appropriately applied.
2 Keep a record of all of your activities over the course of a single day. Think about all the ways you take your everyday practices for granted, so that they are in effect normalized. Then connect these everyday practices to Marx, Foucault, and Hall's conceptualizations of power.

Notes

1 Thanks to Ruthann Lee for her discussion of hegemony (Lee, 2010).
2 This means that we need to take considerably more time in this chapter to introduce Foucault's approaches to power, because his work can appear to be more complicated and unfamiliar.
3 As you encounter the concept of biopolitics in the course of your studies, you will need to be aware of how specific authors define the concept, as it is used quite variably. Even Foucault's application of the concept was far from consistent.
4 In sociology, the concept of norms is widely used to indicate social expectations about attitudes, beliefs, and values.
5 You will find a deeper engagement with the concept of normal in Chapter 3.
6 We will return to a discussion of dividing practices in Chapter 11.
7 Thanks to Mark P. Thomas for preparing the following comments about Stuart Hall's work.
8 Much more influential on Coulthard, however, is the work of anti-colonial theorist Frantz Fanon (1925–1961), whose book *Black Skin, White Masks* (first published in 1952), on the psychological effects of colonization on the colonized, provided the inspiration for Coulthard's own analysis and book title.

9 The need for a radical resurgence inspired her participation in **Idle No More** and her support for queer and **gender fluid** embodiment. Sovereignty and self-governance (in the Indigenous rather than Foucauldian uses of the concepts, to indicate self-determination) must begin with our own bodies.

10 Co-editor Mark P. Thomas adds that economic nationalism is the principle of supporting government intervention in the economy in ways that are deemed to be in the national interest. This often involves developing economic policies that aim to protect domestic industries and workers against foreign competition in a global economy. Economic nationalism may be motivated by feelings of patriotism and/or xenophobia. In practice, it produces systems of trade barriers and tariffs, restrictions on immigration, and other forms of exclusions related to economic activities.

References

Becker, G.S. (1964). *Human capital: A theoretical and empirical analysis, with special reference to education*. Chicago, IL: University of Chicago Press.

Berger, P. (1963). *Invitation to sociology*. New York, NY: Doubleday.

Brown, W. (2015a, May 14). Neoliberalism's stealth revolution. *An Interview by Sam Seder for Majority Report*. Retrieved from http://majority.fm/2015/05/12/512-wendy-brown-neoliberalisms-stealth-revolution/

Brown, W. (2015b). *Undoing the demos: Neoliberalism's stealth revolution*. New York, NY: Zone Books.

Butler, J. (2004). *Precarious life: Powers of mourning and violence*. London, UK: Verso.

Coulthard, G.S. (2014). *Red skin, white masks: Rejecting the colonial politics of recognition*. Minneapolis, MN: University of Minneapolis Press.

Dean, M. (1999). *Governmentality: Power and rule in modern society*. London, UK: Sage Publications.

Fanon, F. (1952). *Black skin, white masks* (R. Philcox, Trans.). New York, NY: Grove Press.

Faubion, J. (Ed.). (2000). *Essential works of Foucault 1954–1984: Vol. 3. Power*. New York, NY: New Press.

Forcese, D. (1986). *The Canadian class structure* (3rd ed.). Toronto, ON: McGraw-Hill Ryerson.

Foucault, M. (1978). *The history of sexuality: An introduction* (Vol. 1). New York, NY: Random House.

Foucault, M. (1982). The subject and power. *Critical Inquiry*, *4*(8), 777–795.

Foucault, M. (1989). *The order of things*. New York, NY: Routledge.

Foucault, M. (1991). Governmentality. In G. Burchell, C. Gordon, & P. Miller (Eds.), *The Foucault effect: Studies in governmentality* (pp. 87–104). Chicago, IL: University of Chicago Press.

Foucault, M. (1995). *Discipline and punish: The birth of the prison*. New York, NY: Vintage Books.

Gramsci, A. (1971). *The prison notebooks*. New York, NY: International Publishers.

Hall, S. (1996). The West and the rest: Discourse and power. In S. Hall, D. Held, D. Hubert, & K. Thompson (Eds.), *Modernity: An introduction to modern societies* (pp. 184–228). Oxford, UK: Blackwell Publishers.

Hall, S. (1997). *Representation: Cultural representations and signifying practices*. London, UK: Open University Press.

Harvey, D. (2005). *A brief history of neoliberalism*. London, UK: Oxford University Press.

Jhally, S. (1997). Introduction. In S. Hall, *Representation and the media* [Video]. London, UK: Open University Press.

Lee, R. (2010). *The production of racialized masculinities in contemporary North American popular culture* (Unpublished doctoral dissertation). Department of Sociology, York University, Toronto, ON.

Miller, P., & Rose, N. (2008). Political power beyond the state: Problematics of government. In *Governing the present: Administering economic, social and personal life* (pp. 53–83). Cambridge, UK: Polity Press.

Monture-Angus, P. (1995). *Thunder in my soul: A Mohawk woman speaks*. Halifax, NS: Fernwood Publishing.

Monture-Angus, P. (1999). *Journeying forward: Dreaming First Nations' independence*. Halifax, NS: Fernwood Publishing.

Monture-Angus, P., & Mcguire, P. (Eds.). (2009). *First voices: An Aboriginal women's reader*. Toronto, ON: Inanna Publications.

Piketty, T. (2014). *Capital in the twenty-first century*. Cambridge, MA: Harvard University Press.

Rose, N. (1999). *Powers of freedom: Reframing political thought*. New York, NY: Cambridge University Press.

Simpson, L.B. (2017). *As we have always done: Indigenous freedom through radical resistance*. Minneapolis, MN: University of Minnesota Press.

Spencer, H. (1864). *Principles of biology* (Vol. 1). London, UK: Williams and Norgate.

Karl Marx: Historical Materialism and the Class System

Nineteenth-century philosopher Karl Marx (1818–1883) was a typical modernist theorist because he believed that scientific knowledge could lead to the exposure of truth and, ultimately, to people challenging the false belief systems that ruled over them. It also opened the way for scientific critiques of the material and ideological conditions that sustained emerging systems of power, as Karl Marx's work did.

Marx is best known for his critique of capitalism as an economic and social system. He is also known for his expectation (and hope) that capitalism would eventually be replaced by a more egalitarian system (first by socialism and then by pure communism), in which class inequalities and inequalities between nations would be eliminated. This new revolutionary phase of history would usher in a more just distribution of wealth and social resources. But how was this to be achieved? Marx believed that it is the responsibility of people not only to understand the world, but also to change it. Power, particularly as exercised through the domination of one class over others, must be made visible, critiqued, resisted, and transformed. For Marx, power must be challenged, and widespread social, political, and economic change must be the goal:

> The history of all hitherto existing society is the history of class struggles.
>
> Freeman and slave, patrician and plebian, lord and serf, guild-master and journeyman, in a word, oppressor and oppressed, stood in constant opposition to one another, carried on an uninterrupted, now hidden, now open fight, a fight that each time ended, either in a revolutionary reconstitution of society at large, or in the common ruin of the contending classes.... The modern bourgeois society that has sprouted from the ruins of feudal society has not done away with class antagonisms. It has but established new classes, new conditions of oppression, new forms of struggle in place of the old ones.
>
> – from Karl Marx and Friedrich Engels, *The Communist Manifesto* (1848)

Marx developed a theory and a methodology called **historical materialism**, which he considered to be a scientific study of the stages of human history and development. Historical materialism was based on two essential beliefs, which together reveal the foundations for his approach to power. First, the word "historical" suggests that social structures, social relationships, and social change can only be understood in historical context. While Marx regarded conflict and struggle, such as those between classes, as present throughout human history, he believed that the specific form these social relationships may take varied considerably across different historical periods. Second, he believed that to understand this, we must study how humans produce and reproduce themselves through their labour (Marx & Engels, 1969). As you read in the introduction, it was from this starting point that Marx developed his analysis of the specific class relations within capitalism.

Marx maintained that the class relations of capitalism are characterized by struggle and resistance. This is most visible during strikes or mass protests. Often people question or protest when they are aware of ordinary everyday problems. For example, sharp increases in the price of bread, a staple food of the **working class** and poor, has prompted women to take to the streets in protest. Such resistance to the rising cost of bread (which has also been referred to, perhaps erroneously, as "bread riots") was a contributing factor to the French Revolution. Similar actions by women have been documented in Boston during the early 18th century, in Britain during the late 18th century, in the American South during the 1860s, and in other times and places. Anger about food shortages led to public protests around the world again in 2008. For example, a sharp increase in the price of bread, accompanied by rising energy and water costs, led to riots in Mozambique, where hunger and acute malnutrition are common among the nation's poor (Kollewe, 2010; Patel, 2010).

While Marx predicted that capitalism would eventually produce the conditions leading to revolution and the emergence of a new economic system that would significantly improve people's daily lives, this kind of fundamental social transformation has yet to happen globally. As illustrated through the chapters in this book, Marx's work has been taken up, adapted, and extended through feminist, anti-racist, postcolonial, and poststructural thought, indicating that his framework is, if anything, more influential than ever. And as we will see, his analysis of capitalism as an economic and social system is enormously relevant for the contemporary period and urgently needs to be engaged with, just as the investigative tools developed by Foucault and Foucauldians help us to make sense of capitalism's perseverance despite economic crises. You will learn more about class analysis in Chapter 7.

Kollewe, J. (2010, September 5). UN calls special meeting to address food shortages amid predictions of riots. *The Guardian*. https://www.theguardian.com/business/2010/sep/05/commodities-food-drink-industry

Marx, K. (1969). Preface to *A contribution to a critique of political economy*. In K. Marx & F. Engels, *Selected works* (Vol. 1, pp. 502–506). Moscow, Russia: Progress Publishers.

Marx, K., & Engels, F. (1848). *The communist manifesto*. Harmondsworth, UK: Penguin.

Patel, R. (2010, September 5). Mozambique's food riots: The true face of global warming. *The Guardian*. https://www.theguardian.com/commentisfree/2010/sep/05/mozambique-food-riots-patel

Antonio Gramsci

Italian social theorist Antonio Gramsci (1891–1937) offered further insight into how capitalism has managed to persist despite gross social and economic inequalities. Clearly, people sometimes do rise up in protest when they perceive that they are being oppressed. Such protests have almost always been quelled, sometimes through violent means and sometimes through a renegotiation of the terms between, for example, capitalists and labourers. In Western capitalist nations, power is still maintained through coercion when nation-states, acting in the interests of preserving the economic order, suppress resistance in such ways. Evidence of this is seen in the militaristic approach to policing that has been present at anti-globalization protests in many Western countries, as well as in the policing tactics used to confront the Black Lives Matter demonstrations in North America. The use of police and military forces to counter the movements of Indigenous peoples asserting land rights, as was seen in the protests against the Dakota Access Pipeline in North Dakota in 2016–17, provide perhaps the starkest example of how the coercive power of the state is used to protect the capitalist social order against the rights and demands of the people.

Why do protests not happen more often? Is it only because of police and military forces? Gramsci said no. Writing between World Wars I and II in his prison cell in Italy, where he was jailed by the ruling fascist government, Gramsci proposed that this was because power is not derived from overt social control alone. Instead, power works most effectively through the **organization of consent** to capitalist rule. In the Marxist tradition, Gramsci asserted that the state is the source of political power for the ruling class in capitalist society. He argued, however, that the **capitalist class** maintains its rule through hegemony—systems of cultural, intellectual, and moral leadership that take into account and shape "the interests and tendencies of the groups over which hegemony is exercised" but that do not ultimately threaten the rule of the dominant group (Gramsci, 1971, p. 57). Hegemony thus refers to the construction of "common sense" where those who are ruled come to regard their interests as being the same as those who rule. Through this concept, Gramsci identified a range of cultural practices that served to keep the class structure in place by organizing consent to capitalist rule, which is why you will also find hegemony referred to as **cultural hegemony**.

Through the concept of hegemony, Gramsci reveals how domination can be accomplished *without* direct authoritarian rule, also making it more difficult and complex to challenge the dominance of the capitalist class. For example, your decision to apply for a certain job is at once presumably in your own best interests and a surrender to a wage labour economy that you have little control over. But rather than a perfect and total scheme, Gramsci also saw the maintenance of hegemony as uneven and difficult, and thus his notion of hegemony also suggests possibilities for resistance through the emergence of **counter-hegemonic** forces that challenge dominant economic, political, and cultural institutions and practices (Gramsci, 1971).

Gramsci, A. (1971). *The prison notebooks*. New York, NY: International Publishers.

Michel Foucault

At the beginning of this chapter, you will have noticed a staple formula for intellectual investigation: Who? What? When? Where? Why? How? *How* questions have risen to the forefront in recent years, as some scholars have questioned grand theories or grand narratives that attempt to explain the world through sweeping claims about history and the condition of social and material life, such as those developed by Christianity, positivist science, or the theorists of political and economic systems such as capitalism and socialism. That does not mean we have to dismiss the often groundbreaking research of theorists whose work is given to grand narratives. The foundational work of Karl Marx, which we have just explored, is a case in point.

While Marx's approach to power can be said to focus mainly on addressing *why* questions, Michel Foucault (1926–1984) insisted on shifting the analytic lens to *how* questions. Foucault avoids making universal claims, for example, that there is such a thing as "truth" or "human nature." Instead, he looks at how we come to believe in universal claims, and how particular discourses come to be regarded as "truth." Foucault's purpose is not to replace one set of truth claims with another, but to use his **genealogical method**[1] to carefully uncover how we come to know what we know.

Foucault's method challenges the modernist belief that history and society follow a rational and inevitable course of development. Far from revealing a linear course toward progress, as Marx had charted in his mapping of historical stages, Foucault's genealogical method presents history as fractured, discontinuous, and **contingent** on a broad array of circumstances and possibilities. He called this the **history of the present**. What counts as knowledge and common sense in the present did not necessarily have to be, and it will continue to change, as it always has.

Foucault's work contributed to the development of **postmodernism** and **post-structuralism**, because he suggested that researchers should pursue smaller-scale, localized studies in order to piece together the history of ideas, events, institutions, and objects rather than making claims about broad swathes of human history and consciousness through the construction of grand narratives. Similarly, Foucault posed a challenge to **humanism** because humanism claims that there are essential, inviolable truths about people, most notably that individual will and consciousness shape human understanding and action. He refused the idea that there are core truths or laws that can be applied to all people or specific groups of people (for example, racialized groups). In this, he supported the idea that people are made up, or constituted, through the social relations of their time and place in a continuous but often fragmented process.

At the same time, Foucault's work was compatible with Marx because he acknowledged the ongoing importance of sovereign power and its links to violence. As well, while Foucault sees power as less tangible than Marx does, it does have material effects. Specifically, it creates real things, people, and actions. One effect is the making of a particular kind of subject, acting in particular ways. We can extend the definition of material life to include, for example, physical bodies, and explore the relation between power and the production and disciplining of bodies. We can also insist that discourses are about much more than the production of language, as Stuart Hall's work demonstrates, because they give meaning to the material world that Marx so aptly described.

---

1 For example, in Chapter 11 you will find an example of how Foucault's genealogical approach can be applied to the history of madness and mental illness.

Stuart Hall

Stuart Hall (1934–2014) was one of the founders of cultural studies in England during the 1970s, an approach that blended Marx's materialism with the study of culture. Hall's work included a highly influential analysis of how many people came to support the rise of the New Right that was taking hold in England in the late 1970s, even if it did not support their interests. The **New Right** combined neoliberal economics with conservative social values in order to dismantle the welfare state and replace it with a more punitive, individualistic approach toward both citizens and non-citizens. Hall laid bare the cultural and policing mechanisms that supported the rise of **authoritarian populism** (Hall, 1988). One could argue that there are significant parallels between this period in English history and the outcome of the US elections in 2016.[1]

Hall devoted particular attention to how racial representations were constructed and anti-Black and anti-immigration sentiments were mobilized as a strategy for the validation of the conservative agenda in the 1970s (Hall et al., 1978). Hall continued to advance cultural studies inquiry into racial representations throughout his career.

Like Foucault, Stuart Hall emphasizes the importance of discourse for the linking of knowledge and power. Hall insists that "nothing meaningful exists outside of discourse" because it is through language that meaning is communicated. This is not to deny the importance of the material world and material objects. Rather, discourse helps us to make "meaningful sense" of the world. Hall invites us to think about an object as simple as a football, which "only makes sense within the context of the rules of the game" of football. It is discourses that allow us to think about what is to be done with that round or (in North America) blimp-shaped object. We might apply the same kind of analysis to a wedding ring, which typically represents legal union, fidelity, commitment, and so on, none of which can be discerned from the object itself. Or we might consider how a nation's flag represents rule over a territory, patriotism, and belonging. It can also symbolize who does not belong, such as non-citizens and undocumented workers (see Chapter 9).

---

1 At the time, both Prime Minister Margaret Thatcher of England and President Ronald Reagan of the United States won political office through a backlash against "permissiveness" in their respective countries and their shared endorsement of a neoliberal agenda.

Hall, S. (1988). *The hard road to renewal: Thatcherism and the crisis of the left*. London, UK: Verso.

Hall, S., Critcher, C., Jefferson, T., Clarke, J., & Roberts, B. (1978). *Policing the crisis: Mugging, the state, and law and order*. Teaneck, NJ: Holmes and Meier.

Postcolonialism

Postcolonial and neocolonial theory expose and challenge Western European forms of knowledge and claims to truth, showing how this knowledge production serves the advancement of European thought and colonial power. For instance, postcolonial theorists might challenge the centre by exploring histories of thought that provide alternatives to, and often predate, European theory. Yet many lands never became free from direct colonial rule, as the experiences of Indigenous peoples demonstrate. Some theorists of Indigeneity reject the label of postcolonial, since it is such an obvious misrepresentation of their continued existence under colonial rule, and they further question postcolonial scholarship's ability to fully address Indigenous peoples' experiences of violence and ongoing dispossession from their territories, cultures, and languages (Soldatic & Grech, 2016).

Postcolonial scholars use **deconstruction** to unpack the language and practices of colonialism and their material consequences for societies and for people's lives. For example, Edward Said (1978) introduced the study of **orientalism**, which has some similarities to the work of Stuart Hall in that it critiques systems of representation: orientalism is concerned with how the West understands and represents the East. Scholars such as Gayatri Spivak prioritize the voices of those traditionally silenced by colonialism (Spivak, 1988). Spivak asks how the subaltern (those who have been subordinated by European colonial power and the subsequent spread of economic **imperialism**) and the knowledges that they carry can speak and be heard in the context of European theory. Using deconstruction, Spivak takes apart histories and discourses of European thought that produce colonial relationships and imperial power that cast the subaltern to the margins. She draws on the traditions of Marxism and feminism to challenge dominant narratives, while subjecting these traditions to critique for their own exclusions. Trinh T. Minh-ha, among others, similarly challenges assumptions behind generalized categories such as "women" that cannot fully speak to the experiences of women as **other**. In her writing and film-making, Minh-ha explains the subjugation of women in postcolonial contexts through a combination of imperial and patriarchal powers (Amoko, 2006; Minh-ha, 1989). She calls this **double colonization**. Other postcolonial theorists, such as Homi K. Bhabha, are interested in spaces of **hybridity**, where dominant and marginalized forms of knowledge mix and transform into new ways of being (Bhabha, 1994). For example, Indigneous people may attempt to hold on to traditional forms of knowledge while being part of contemporary Western systems. As such, postcolonial theorists have contributed significantly to the development of poststructuralist thought by introducing multiple and counter narratives that describe and challenge the ongoing effects of colonial rule.

As well, neocolonial thought explores how new kinds of colonialism have emerged alongside the continuation of historical forms, not through direct political and military control, but through economic domination.

Amoko, A. (2006). Race and postcoloniality. In S. Malpas & P. Wake (Eds.), *The Routledge companion to critical theory* (pp. 127–140). New York, NY: Routledge.

Bhabha, H.K. (1994). *The location of culture*. London, UK: Routledge.

Minh-ha, T.T. (1989). *Woman, native, other: Postcoloniality and feminism*. Bloomington, IN: Indiana University Press.

Said, E. (1978). *Orientalism*. London, UK: Routledge.

Soldatic, K., & Grech, S. (2016). *Disability and colonialism: (Dis)encounters and anxious intersectionalities*. New York, NY: Routledge.

Spivak, G.C. (1988). Can the subaltern speak? In C. Nelson & L. Grossberg (Eds.), *Marxism and the interpretation of culture* (pp. 271–316). Champaign, IL: University of Illinois Press.

2 Assembling Our Tool Kit: Interrogating Representations and Discourses

ANDREA M. NOACK and ARYN MARTIN

How can we study our everyday assumptions? As you learned in the introduction, it can be hard to be critical about things that are a part of our "**normal**" lives. Often, we don't notice that we are making assumptions, because they are completely embedded in the way that we, and those around us, understand the world. There are some methodological tools, however, that we can use to help us step outside of our common-sense understandings of the world. This chapter introduces you to some strategies for interrogating **representations** and **discourses**. You can use these strategies to "unpack the **centre**" and to identify some of the ways that **power** operates in your everyday life.

This chapter is theoretically informed by the work of both Michel Foucault and Stuart Hall. Following Foucault, we maintain that our sense of ourselves and of the everyday world is shaped by larger social discourses. Stuart Hall's theories extend these ideas by helping us to think about how our understandings of the world reflect our participation in a shared **culture**. The ideas of both Foucault and Hall help us to see how the representations and discourses that circulate within a culture are connected to **power relations**.

We encourage you to think about the strategies introduced in this chapter as elements of a "tool kit" that you can draw on in order to help you interpret the world around you. You can use these tools to investigate portrayals in your everyday life and in the media you encounter. You can also use these tools as part of a more structured research project in which you analyze texts or interview transcripts, or to interpret field observations. Some of these tools can be used to critique academic journal articles, research reports, or policy documents. Many of these strategies can be used to critically analyze everyday conversations. In general, learning to use these strategies and tools will help you to become a critical thinker and savvy about the ways in which knowledge is produced and circulated.

What Counts as Knowledge?

The chapters in this book encourage you to question how society is organized. They prompt you to think about the social groups and attributes that occupy "the centre," those on "the margins," and the strategies that are used to create and maintain a divide between them. By identifying these **dividing practices** you can begin to see how power works on an everyday basis. A good place to start is by questioning which knowledges are considered real or true or legitimate and which knowledges are considered fake or fictional or illegitimate. The study of what constitutes knowledge and how we come to know things is part of a branch of philosophy called **epistemology**. Epistemologies tell us what counts as "evidence," what criteria must be met to develop new knowledge, and how knowledge is related to morals or values.

Epistemologies—or ways of knowing—vary across time and cultures. **Indigenous knowledges** are fundamentally connected to the land—a physical place—and the interrelationships between the beings who live in it. Knowledge is informed by ongoing relationships with the material world, and is premised on the idea that all aspects of the world have life and spirit and humans have an obligation to learn the rules of relating to the world with respect (Castellano, 2004, p. 104). In describing Nishnaabeg knowledge, Simpson (2014) explains that it is intimate and relational, taking place in the context of family and community, and noting that "meaning is derived … through a compassionate web of interdependent relationships" (p. 11).

European epistemologies are shaped by the developments that occurred during the period we now call the **Enlightenment**, which began in the mid-1600s. Whereas **truth claims** had previously been justified by appealing to a wisdom of a higher power—God or a king or queen—during the Enlightenment period **positivism** became the dominant epistemological approach. A positivist epistemological approach emphasizes systematically collecting information using the five human senses, and then aggregating those observations to generate new knowledge. Instead of appealing to "God's will," scientists provide explanations for the world based on systematic research, experimentation, and logical reasoning. Positivist approaches are typically associated with quantitative research methods, such as experiments, surveys, or the analysis of secondary data (such as administrative data). The rise of positivism was related to **modernist** ideas about the value of using scientific and secular techniques to systematically create a better society. For instance, as you learned in Chapter 1, modern **nation-states** relied on the systematic collection and aggregation of statistical information about populations in efforts to govern social life. In the context of **settler colonialism**, this process often involved either a disregard for or an active erasure of Indigenous ways of knowing and being.

Positivists generally adopt a **realist** perspective; that is, they believe in a single reality that exists independent of society and that is governed by universal, natural laws. In contrast to Indigenous ways of knowing, the search for universal laws results in knowledge that is disconnected from the land or places. Positivists also strive to be **objective** or value-free in their work, arguing that any person doing the same research should come to the same conclusion. It should come as no surprise, however, that the practice of **science** is also influenced by power relations (see Chapter 10). Positivist approaches to knowledge have become idealized as "superior" ways of knowing, largely as a result of European colonializing practices, which violently imposed their worldviews on non-European and Indigenous societies, and treated non-European and Indigenous people as objects of study instead of as knowledge holders/producers in their own right.

Is positivism still a dominant **ideology**? In recent decades, we have seen many more knowledge contestations around the value of scientific inquiry and its results. An example of this can be found in the highly politicized debates about whether or not climate change is occurring and whether or not human actions are contributing to this change. Particularly in the US, alliances between the religious right and fossil fuel capitalists have legitimated a surge in anti-science rhetoric and policy, and an interest in "alternative science." Uncertainty about the value of scientific evidence has also been signalled by elected governments in both Canada and the US, who at times have reduced public funding for scientific inquiry, downsized science-oriented government agencies, constrained the ability of government scientists to report results, and limited data collection. In response to these developments, a pro-science social movement has taken shape, holding regular protests and marches in support of science (see Figure 2.1). The approach in this book is neither "for" nor "against" science per se, but argues instead that this dichotomy is too tidy and ultimately unsatisfying.

The social sciences provide some alternatives to positivist ways of knowing. **Interpretivism** and social constructionism became prominent during the 1970s and 1980s. Interpretivists argue that studying people is not the same as studying the material world, because people interpret and respond to their environment in different ways, and then act on these interpretations. For interpretivists, the goal of social science research is to find out how people's varying understandings of the world affect how they behave. Interpretivist approaches are often associated with qualitative research methods, such as ethnography, in-depth interviews, or the analysis of cultural texts. Interpretivists generally adopt a **social constructionist** perspective on reality, arguing that what people understand as reality is constructed by culture and **social institutions**. Sociologists Peter Berger and Thomas Luhmann introduced the notion of social construction (1966), noting that as humans move through the world they are mostly guided by a set of rules that are dictated not by God or nature, but by patterns of action set in place by collectives of human predecessors. Small innovations and exceptions happen all the time, but in general, order is achieved by copying and repeating what those around us do. An example is the practice of driving a car: while driving we follow an unspoken code developed and held in place by humans, with reasonable success. The ordered

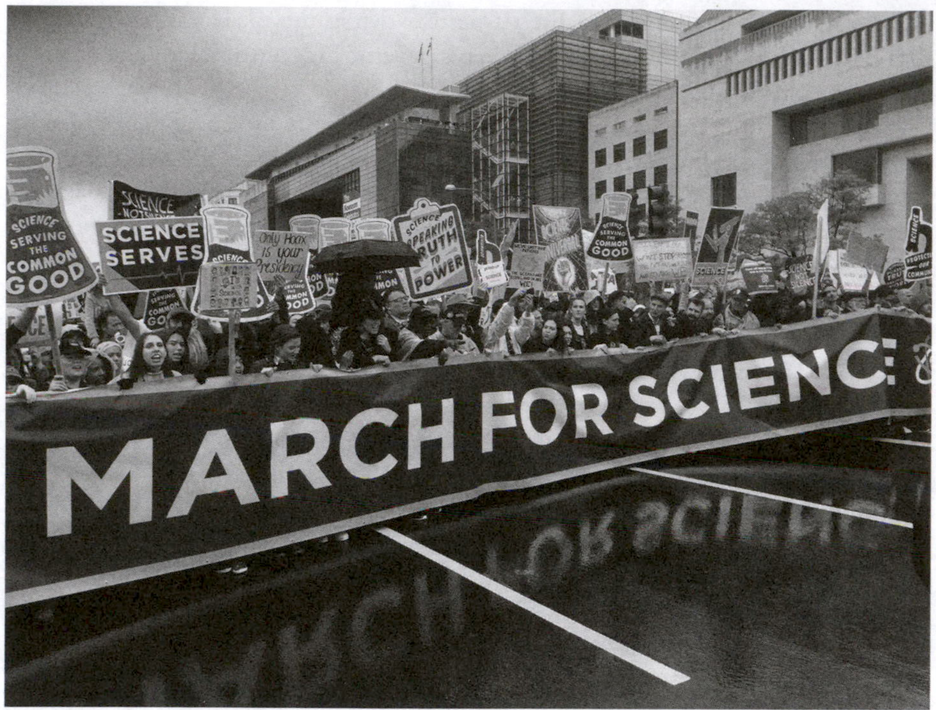

FIGURE 2.1 March for Science. CC BY SA 2.0/Becker1999.

reality we encounter on the highway is thus a socially constructed reality, though not all participants in upholding it are human (think of stoplights and medians, for example). On a grander scale, realities in which human groups dwell vary dramatically in different historical times and geographic places. That is, what we understand to be "real" depends on the ideas, behaviours, and customs of our culture.

A strict positivist would contend that the patterned actions described above (like driving) could, in theory, reflect some discernable laws of nature. To explain human behaviour, they might point to evolutionary psychology and/or genetics. For interpretivists and social constructionists, efforts to explain human social behaviour through genetics encounter (at least) two big problems. The first is the utter complexity of the social world, and the (thus far) inadequacy of scientific tools to develop predictive or comprehensive accounts of love, religion, **gender**, or even something closer to the biological body like depression. The second limiting feature of scientific accounts of social activity is that, however ingenious and useful, scientific "facts" are social products because humans make them. Like a highway, a laboratory is a highly patterned rule-bound social setting where history, geography, and social relationships matter (see Chapter 10). It turns out that scientists in any time and place have inescapable convictions about human nature, and these convictions are reflected in the questions they ask, the results they get, and the ways these results are interpreted. It is easy to find examples of once-true science that reflected what the practitioners wanted to believe of the world—like the fact that a mother's imagination could cause malformations in a growing fetus (16th and 17th centuries), sperm cells contain tiny, fully formed humans (17th and 18th centuries), or that criminals can be identified by the shape of their earlobes (19th century). Indeed, throughout European history, **scientific racism**—such as ranking human types—has been used to justify **colonial** expansion and **genocide** (see Chapter 6).

Instead of presuming that science is a charmed method that uniquely offers up truths about the world *or* that scientists sit back and say whatever they want about nature, feminist scientists like Donna Haraway argue that we should think of science as **situated knowledge**. Every individual researcher, and even every knowledge-making practice (like experimentation or measurement), is situated in a specific and identifiable location. Knowledge has roots in a particular time, place, set of conventions, believable explanations, instruments, and more. Instead of the "view from nowhere" promised by traditional **objectivity**, as though the human scientist was irrelevant to the outcome, situated knowledge is a "view from somewhere" (Haraway, 1991). The facts come along with an acknowledgement of the particular set of experiences and expectations (or **subjectivity**) the researcher brings. This situatedness does not discount the knowledge, but should be recognized. A knower who is situated—as all knowers are—is capable only of **partial perspective**. This **concept** has a double meaning: partial as in biased or not impartial, and partial as in incomplete or only part of the story. Haraway also offers us a way to understand the material world—nature and **matter**—without losing sight of the social context of science. Although human scientists have **agency** in the making of knowledge, so too do the non-human actors in the worlds that scientists study. Genes, cells, hearts, trees, mountains—all are active participants in the scientific method, participating through refusals and compromises, dots on graphs and failed experiments. The world is not easily disciplined, and no scientist can convincingly say whatever they want about nature and have it stick for long. Understanding science as situated knowledge, in which non-human actors have agency, brings knowledge-making practices developed from European societies closer to Indigenous epistemologies.

This quick journey through epistemology sets the stage for understanding the strategies presented in the remainder of this chapter. In general, we adopt a social constructionist lens—understanding that meanings, facts, and technologies are actively made by humans—with the caveat that the world around us is not passive. The key to understanding knowledge and how it is caught up with power is to ask where it comes from, how it gets made, who benefits from it, and what is missing from the story.

How Do We Learn About the World?

Take a moment to think about how you personally learned about the world and the people in it. We learn about some things because we experience them ourselves. You learned how to ride a bicycle or how to swim by physically doing these activities, although you probably had someone helping you as well. You might know what it feels like to win a competition or to be discriminated against. The things we learn through our personal experiences tend to be somewhat haphazard, as they depend on the situations we have encountered in our life, which are in turn affected by power relationships. Whether you recognize it or not, aspects of your identity such as your gender, social **class**, racial or ethnic affiliation, age, Indigenous status, religion, disability status, or sexual orientation have all influenced the types of situations you have personally been in. Ever been to a mosque? A gay bar? A tourist resort? A smudging ceremony? Not only does your identity affect the situations you have encountered, your experience within each of these situations is framed by whether your identity situates you at the "centre" or on the "margins" of the interactions.

Most people strongly believe in the lessons they have learned through their personal experiences, because they are meaningful to them. Yet we tend to overestimate how similar our experiences are to those of others. It's not reasonable to claim that racism does not exist in Canada just because you have never experienced racism. It is also not enough to find out whether your friends have had the same experiences as you, because we tend to be friends with people who are similar to us. At the same time, there are patterns in people's experiences, and understanding these will help you understand how society is organized. The key is to be able to determine how **generalizable** your own experiences are. Generalizable knowledge is knowledge that can be extended to understand a group of people (or population) larger than the group from whom information was collected. People regularly—and problematically—extend their claims beyond what is justified by their evidence. For instance, a parent might assert that the characteristics of their child are representative of all children; similarly, American youth researchers often suggest that their findings are applicable to youth everywhere in the world. In order to learn how relevant your own experiences are to everyone in a society, you need more information.

Most of what we know and believe was not learned through direct personal experience. Instead, we learned it from people in positions of authority, such as teachers, parents, or religious leaders. We believe what these people say because of their credentials or because of their role in our lives. Sometimes, though, people in positions of authority make claims about things they are not experts in. For instance, if your sociology professor tells you what brand of car is the best, you should be skeptical. It can be difficult to be critical of people in positions of authority, however, because they often hold some sort of power over us. Even if people do have expertise in the area they are making claims about, you should still maintain a critical mind; in many cases "**expert knowledge**" is conflicting and contradictory. We often see examples of this phenomenon in health research, when different scientists report contradictory findings about the effectiveness of a treatment or procedure. It can be difficult to determine what to believe when we encounter contradictory information from experts. Some of the strategies described below can be useful for helping to sort out the claims experts make.

Another way we tend to learn things is through "common sense." Instead of collecting and assessing information for ourselves, we make choices and form opinions on the basis of what "everybody knows." Appeals to common sense are based on the idea that we all agree about what is "sensible," but this is clearly not the case. Even if we could all agree about what is sensible, many widely accepted common-sense beliefs have been disproved. For instance, many parents tell their children to wait up to an hour after eating before going swimming based on the notion that your muscles will compete with your stomach to get enough oxygen, and you will get cramps. Digestive health researchers assert, however, that unless you are a competitive swimmer, your body has more than enough oxygen to go around and there is no need to wait to go swimming after eating ("No eating," 2005). A critical approach to knowledge suggests that widely believed things do not necessarily reflect the "truth"—rather, these shortcuts work to maintain the dominant power structure at the expense of those with less power. For instance, racial profiling by police officers and border officials is often presented as a "common-sense" shortcut for making traffic stops or security screenings more efficient. In this case, common sense prompts people to systematically discriminate against groups of people. It serves them right, one might think, if they were breaking the law when profiled. The point is that people who don't fit the profile may be just as likely to be breaking the law, but they will not be caught or punished. This is systemic privilege. Many of the chapters in this book encourage you to question common-sense ideas about the world, and challenge the things that "everybody knows." This is a first step toward "unpacking the centre" and revealing the underlying power relations.

One way that "everybody" can come to know something is through mass media, a category that includes all types of communication to a "mass" audience: newspapers, books, podcasts, television shows, music, art, graffiti, posters, websites, social media, and more. Mass media often provide us with information that we could not get through personal experience. Textbooks teach us about history, Twitter tells us what is happening right now in other places across the world, and nursery rhymes teach us moral lessons. But mass media can also direct our attention to some events and stories and, in doing so, direct our attention away from other events and stories. The most prominent forms of media tend to be under corporate control, and ownership is concentrated in a few large conglomerate companies. These media conglomerates shape our ideas about what is important, what is "normal," what is "dangerous," and what is "in the centre." In recent decades, mass media have become increasingly polarized, such that the same event may be presented in radically different ways, influenced by the political orientation of the media outlet. This trend is exacerbated by social media algorithms, which direct people toward media that are likely to coincide with their worldview. Indeed, some people have started to characterize news reporting that does not coincide with their worldview as "fake news." At the same time, news that is demonstrably fake—by all collective standards—is quickly spread through social media and can be hard to detect. Indeed, the business model of many websites is oriented around generating advertising revenue by enticing people to click on outlandish, misleading, or completely unsupported headlines (commonly called clickbait). Mass media both reflect and reinforce power relations.

Which Knowledge Should I Trust?

If some information is "fake" and all knowledge is situated knowledge, then each time you are presented with a knowledge claim (a fact, an argument, an advertisement, a political statement, a statistic, etc.), it makes sense to ask: Where did it come from? What materials and ideologies went into its construction? This chapter describes some questions you might ask when you are presented with information about the world. It is easiest to start asking these questions whenever you encounter new information, but as you become more proficient, we encourage you to use these same strategies to question things that you have known for a long time.

Who Benefits if the Information Is Believed to Be True?

Our knowledge shapes how we behave, how we perceive other people, and how we understand ourselves. Often, some group of people systematically benefits when some information is believed to be true and other information is believed to be false. One way to begin assessing who might benefit from information is to critically assess its source, and how that source is positioned in a larger knowledge landscape. For instance, in Canada, research done by the Fraser Institute—a right-wing think tank—tends to promote **free markets**, less government intervention, and more personal responsibility. In contrast, research done by the Canadian Centre for Policy Alternatives—a left-wing think tank—tends to promote a more "progressive" approach to issues of social and economic justice and equality. Both groups routinely present the results of their research in the media, make competing claims about how to understand a situation or event, and recommend different types of solutions for social problems. Whenever you encounter information, consider how political motivations or power relationships might be at work, and how they might shape the knowledge that is being presented.

How Is It Trying to Make You Feel?

Not all knowledge claims try to make you feel something, but many do. Advertisements, obviously, are trying to make you spend your money in one particular way. Political messages often aim to arouse fear in the voting public (whether or not it is warranted) in order to encourage people to vote in a way that makes them feel safe. Many kinds of writing, imaging, and speech are designed to *persuade*. The intent of the creator or conveyer of information should not (necessarily) disqualify the statement from becoming part of your store of beliefs, but it may affect the weight that you give it, and it often provides a clue as to how you might go about discrediting a claim if it aims to do harm or consolidate privilege.

What Concepts and Systems of Classification Does the Information Rely On?

All information implicitly relies on concepts and systems of classification. A concept is a mental representation that groups together things that are similar in some way. Concepts enable us to cognitively hold on to the idea of something by giving it a name or a symbol that we can incorporate into our thinking. They also give us a context for understanding the many people, objects, and events we encounter every day: she's another student, that's a chair, they are having an argument. We often use concepts to designate specific types of people ("human kinds") in our society: terrorists, refugees, or the mentally ill. These designations are based on the presumption that we have a shared cultural understanding about who belongs in these groups and what their characteristics are. Using Foucault's **history of the present** approach, however, we know that every discursive category fixed to some humans and not others grew out of a human social group at a particular time and place, and often because of some political or administrative need or a desire to discipline or constrain people. Philosopher Ian Hacking uses the term "making up people" to describe this invention of human categories. Instead of having clear cut, easily discernable boundaries, decisions about whether someone is in or out of a category often depend on the ideas and biases of the one who is doing the **classifying**. Moreover, because of labelling or **looping effects**, when they are classified and treated a certain way, humans change themselves; in Hacking's words, "people spontaneously come to fit their categories" (1986, p. 223). In an important way, the person or thing is **constituted** by its naming, and did not exist in quite the same way prior to naming.

Systems of classification extend our models of the social world by placing concepts in relation to one another; they tell us what types of things are alike, and what types of things are different. For instance, in science class you might have learned about the Linnaean **taxonomy**, a system that groups all life into domains, kingdoms, phyla, classes, orders, families, genera, and species. We also rely on complex systems of classification in the social world, though we rarely explicitly list the elements of these classifications. For example, the idea of "**race**" relies on a **system of classification** based on many criteria, including skin colour, facial structure, hair type and colour, language, cultural background, and geographic origin. Just like taxonomies of the natural world, systems of classification for the social world are created by people and change over time. They are often sustained by "common-sense" knowledge and media portrayals.

Upon scrutiny, many of our concepts and systems of classification break down. When the dividing practices used to sustain categories of people and position them relative to others are identified and interrogated, it becomes evident that many concepts and categories are unsustainable. For example, upon looking more closely, the instability of the concept of "race" becomes apparent, as the idea of "races" with clear distinctions between them falls apart. Critically analyzing these systems of classification helps us to "unpack the centre" by questioning how the boundaries between the "centre" and the "margins" are created and maintained.

What Types of Evidence Are Provided?

Always ask questions to learn more about the type of evidence used to support each claim that you encounter: is it based on someone's personal experience? Hearsay? A scientific study that was completed? If it is a study, ask who funded and/or published the research. The type of evidence will influence how much weight you give to a claim, or how much value you assign to the information.

People often tend to assign more weight to information that is quantitative, statistical, or presented in numbers. Media outlets often report **official statistics** that are collected or compiled by government agencies, like Statistics Canada. Like other types of information, however, official statistics should be critically examined. Official statistics are typically only available about topics, people, and categories that government or other statistical agencies perceive to be important. Thus, it's no surprise that much of the information collected and disseminated by Statistics Canada relates to economic issues, such as unemployment rates and GDP. It is much harder to find official statistics about people's sense of civic engagement or willingness to participate in protests. As well, some people are routinely excluded from official statistical accounts. For instance, Indigenous people living on reserves, people living in Canada's three territories, and members of the armed forces are typically excluded from government surveys. In addition, some categories of people are rendered invisible in statistical data because they are not captured in the official categories used to measure society. For example, until 2018 Statistics Canada did not distinguish between **sex** and gender, essentially assuming that all people are **cisgender**, all men are male and all women are female. It was not possible to use statistical information to know anything about transgender people or those with non-**binary** gender identities.

Some knowledge claims rely on **documentary evidence** such as news reports, policy papers, or letters. As with official statistics, you should critically examine these types of sources. Some epistemological traditions—like those of many Indigenous people—rely primarily on oral knowledge transmission, and thus documentary evidence of knowledge is not available. Where documentary evidence is available, it often reflects the views of those who have power or status. For example, in historical studies it is typically much easier to locate and access the diaries and letters of people from the upper class than from the working or servant classes, partly because of limited literacy among the lower classes, but also because their ideas were less likely to be considered important and thus less likely to be preserved. Documentary evidence may be conflicting within itself, and may also conflict with other forms of evidence. For instance, in some cases, there are substantial discrepancies between the written treaty agreements recorded by European settlers in Canada and the corresponding records of Indigenous people, captured in wampum belts and their accompanying narratives. Always consider how power relations have influenced the existence and content of documentary evidence that is used to support a knowledge claim.

Analyzing Language and Representations

In contemporary North American society, spoken and written language are one of the main ways we communicate with each other. Language is a complex **symbolic system**, that is, an interconnected group of symbols (such as letters in a specific sequence) that have acquired a cultural meaning that is widely understood. Many of our other symbolic systems are visually based (like the iconography of road signs), but we also assign relatively complex cultural meanings to smells (such as fresh-baked cookies) or sounds (such as a gentle harp).

In **semiotic** terms, we refer to the symbol that represents a concept or idea as a **signifier**, which means a symbol that calls up our conceptual understanding of an object, category, experience, feeling, or action. For example, think about the Nike swoosh. The actual shape of the symbol is meaningless, but we have learned that that particular shape symbolizes the Nike brand. Often, there can be different signifiers for a single concept. For example, the words "dog" and "chien" and "Hund" all refer to the same category of domestic animals. There are even more English language variations that refer to the same thing: doggie, pooch, and so on. The concept or idea represented by a signifier is called the **signified**. In the examples above, the Nike brand and the concept of a dog are the things that are signified. There is no guarantee that every person will interpret a signifier in the same way. If you ask a group of people to imagine what a dog looks like, each person will have a slightly different conceptual image: a Labrador retriever, a poodle, a Chihuahua, a greyhound. There will be shared features between the dogs that people imagine—four legs, a barking sound, and possibly a tail—because we have a shared cultural understanding of what constitutes a dog. The less overlap there is between people's cultures, the more divergent their interpretation of signifiers will be. The signifier of the Nike swoosh represents something completely different to the North American consumer than it does to a worker who makes below-poverty-level wages manufacturing Nike products. The idea of **polysemy** refers to the fact that a single **sign** can have more than one meaning or be interpreted in multiple ways.

Signs can be thought of as having three levels (or orders) of signification. The "clapping hands" emoji can help us to illustrate these three levels (see Figure 2.2). The first level of signification refers to what is explicitly shown by the signifier. The emoji signifier shows two human hands with the palms pressed together, with three small triangles above them. The second level of signification refers to the cultural meaning of what is explicitly shown. This emoji conveys the action of clapping the hands together to make

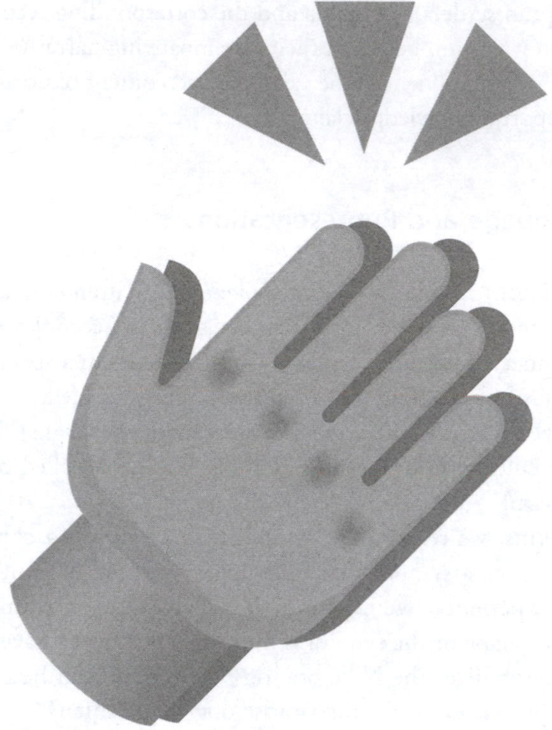

FIGURE 2.2 The "clapping hands" emoji. davidcreacion/iStock.

noise, often occurring in rapid sequence to create applause. Collectively, we understand that clapping or applauding is a gesture used to signal approval or appreciation. (This cultural signifier is not universal, however; for instance, in Deaf communities holding the hands in the air at shoulder height, with fingers apart, and twisting them back and forth is used to signal approval or appreciation.) The third level of signification refers to how the signifier is related to larger cultural expectations. At this level, signifiers and what they refer to are associated with a larger social consensus or understanding of the world (Deacon, Pickering, Goldring, & Murdock, 2007). The skin tone in most emoji signifiers is coded as white (although it's typically a yellow-orange colour). Depending on the messaging system, often only white emojis are available, or white emojis are the default that "skin tone modifiers" can be applied to, or white emojis are situated first in each sequence of matching emoji. All of these practices situate **whiteness** in the "centre" of the symbolic system in our culture. The hands are also those of a young, able-bodied person: free of blemishes, deformities, and wrinkles (and even free of fingernails). This configuration gives us insight into our understanding of the features of whom we imagine to be a "normal" or "universal" person.

Signs and signifiers are the building blocks for practices of representation, a concept introduced in the previous chapter. The traditional way of thinking about representation is as a re-presentation of something that has already happened (Hall, 1999). You might also think about representation as "standing in" for something. So, for example, members of Parliament are supposed to represent or "stand in" for us in the House of Commons (Hall, 1999). In contrast to these traditional ways of thinking about representation, cultural theorists such as Stuart Hall argue that we should think about a representation as being constitutive of an event (1999). Hall argues that there can be multiple interpretations of events. Because there is no single correct interpretation of any event, the practice of representation is more than just a simple re-presentation of something that is already there. Instead, the representation of an event becomes part of the event itself. It is through the process of representation that an event is given meaning in the context of our shared culture. Often, we only know about an event through its representation in the mass media. If we have not experienced an event personally, the media representation of the event effectively becomes the event for us. For example, most people can describe what happens on New Year's Eve in Times Square and explain what the meaning of the event is, even if they have not personally been in New York City on December 31. For them, the media representation of the event has become the event. The ability to represent and thus shape our shared understanding of people, objects, and events is a substantial source of power.

Representations are necessary for the process of "making up people" and classifying "human kinds": they determine the range of identities available to us and our perceptions of the characteristics associated with those identities. Some identities are simply unavailable to us, because there is no concept or representation for that group of people in our culture. For example, we have a word for the group of people who collect stamps (philatelists) and some cultural **stereotypes** about the characteristics of those people (obsessive, detail-oriented). We have no word for people who collect, say, matchbooks, and no corresponding cultural notion of their general characteristics. People who claim an identity—like being a philatelist, or a mom, or a student—learn to compare themselves and are compared by others to representations of that social group. For instance, people are often surprised upon meeting scientists who are women, because they don't conform to our cultural representations of what a scientist looks like (although these representations are slowly changing).

Together, representations and identities work as a form of **social regulation** by constraining how people are perceived and understood in our culture. People who challenge representations often face explicit or subtle punishments from others in their community. Representations affect our own ideas about normal or acceptable behaviour for someone like us. Even if we do not or cannot conform to the behaviour expected, our actions are still interpreted and understood in relation to the cultural norm we are defying.

Language and representations are the building blocks of the discourses that we use to give meaning to the material world and our social interactions in that world. A concrete material world that exists "out there" only becomes knowable and meaningful to humans using things such as words and graphs and numbers. What's more, the material properties of nature—human bodies, for example—change in response to the dominant discourses in a given time and place. For example, while muscle tissue is a material with particular tangible properties and possibilities, masculinity is a discourse. Muscle and masculinity become unified in practices of weight-lifting and ingesting substances (food, steroids, supplements) to produce a new beefed-up reality we can consider a **natureculture** (Haraway, 2003). This term signifies that something is made up of both material and cultural elements that are so tightly connected they cannot be disentangled.

We are surrounded by (and embedded in) multitudes of discourses in our everyday lives—about race, class, gender, economics, health, disability, immigration, religion, crime, and much more. Discourses emerge, change, and disappear over time. Some scholars use a military **metaphor** to talk about how discourses are "deployed" in a society. Discourses are often deployed in mass media, but they become entrenched in our everyday social interactions and our bodies. Whenever we use certain types of language or rely on specific representations to talk about the world in a particular way, we become part of the process of producing meaning through discourse. It is in this way that our **everyday practices** become part of the system that legitimizes and maintains the dominant system of power relations. It may surprise you to think you have unknowingly supported the exercise of power through your everyday practices. But the maintenance of power through language and discourse means we can also challenge the dominant power structure by conscientiously changing how we speak and think about the world. As more people begin to do this, new discourses emerge.

Even though signifiers and representations are polysemous (that is, they can have multiple meanings), one dominant meaning often prevails. The ability to fix and limit the meanings people assign to representations reflects the dominant systems of power in a society (Hall, 1997). Often there are "official" and "alternative" explanations for events or outcomes. For instance, medical practitioners typically argue that heart attacks are the result of individual lifestyle factors, such as smoking, inactivity, and genetic predispositions. This is the dominant discourse around heart disease and heart health in Canadian society. An alternative discourse is presented by researchers who adopt a social determinants of health approach. They argue that heart attacks are the result of social factors such as poverty, social exclusion, and income **inequality** (Raphael, 2002). In the example of heart disease, the medicalized dominant discourse reflects our culture's emphasis on individualism and personal responsibility, features of the prevailing **neoliberal** ideology (see Chapter 13 on **financial fitness** to learn more). Indeed, much of this textbook focuses on identifying dominant discourses, articulating how they relate to power relations and ideologies, and presenting alternative ways of thinking.

Interrogating Representations and Discourses

In this section, we introduce a series of strategies for developing a critical analysis of representations and discourses. It might be useful to think about this process as an interrogation. The typical meaning of "interrogating" is to ask hard questions, like a police officer would ask a suspect (Hall, 1997). Interrogating representations and discourses is also about asking hard questions. Unlike in police interrogations, though, our questions are not necessarily directed to finding the "truth"; instead, we are interested in finding out how representations and discourses constitute people, events, and objects in a particular way.

You might start by using these strategies to analyze conversations, news reports, social media posts, or advertisements that you encounter in your everyday life. You can also use these approaches in the context of a more structured social science research project that uses qualitative research methods. These strategies can be used to analyze spoken language, written transcripts, or any other types of communication that rely on language or symbols. The strategies and questions we list below are not intended to be exhaustive, but rather they are intended to be a launch pad for your own critical interrogation strategies.

Which Representations and Discourses Are Prominent?

One of the easiest ways to begin analyzing the representations and discourses that you encounter is to look for patterns. To start, identify the representations and discourses that are most prominent. Ask questions about why they are so prominent: When did they become part of our cultural knowledge? How do they influence people's everyday practices and knowledge? How do they reflect the larger power relationships? You may need to do some research to find satisfactory answers to these questions. Cross-cultural comparisons might make it easier to identify what is unique about the discourses in your own society or culture. Similarly, historical research can provide insight into how representations and discourses emerge and become dominant (or fade) over time. For example, Karen Dubinsky uses the history of **tourism** at Niagara Falls to investigate how the idea of the honeymoon became part of our discourses about **heterosexual** marriage in the post-World War II period (1999). By investigating which discourses are prominent in specific times and places, you can begin to theorize about how different forms of social organization are related to economic, political, and other social changes.

Once you have identified the most prominent representations and discourses, look for representations and discourses that are presented as "alternatives." Consider how these "alternatives" might reflect different political orientations, ideological positions, or power relations. Pay close attention to how different types of language and symbols are used to make one representation seem more plausible than others, that is, the dividing practices used to separate "legitimate" representations and explanations from their "alternatives."

How Are Identities Represented and Positioned Relative to Each Other?

As a next step, ask how people and identities are portrayed in representations and discourses. One way to do this is to think about the identities or social roles established by a discourse as characters in a story. For instance, crime stories (and discourses about crime) usually identify a victim, a perpetrator, a person with legal authority, and sometimes a witness. Each of these subjects is framed differently by the discourse and is expected to have different experiences, ways of speaking, and interpretations of the event. Discourses also position these people and roles in relation to each other: some are authoritative actors while others are framed as victims of circumstance; some are situated at "the centre" while others are on "the margins." This positionality is often signalled using words like "our," "we," and "us" for those in the centre, compared to words like "your," "they," and "them" for those on the margins.

Social psychologists tell us that people develop a sense of identity or subjectivity based on the interpretive repertoires they use. An **interpretive repertoire** is a cluster of terms, descriptions, metaphors, and figures of speech that people use to understand the world around them. They provide a framework that people use to locate their own position in the world relative to other people, and thus a subjectivity that they use to give meaning to their experiences. When we say things like "I'm a Capricorn" or "I'm a shopaholic" to provide an explanation for our behaviour or actions, we are drawing on complex interpretive repertoires. Representations and discourses inevitably shape the interpretive repertoires that are available to people in a society.

Sometimes, representations of people, objects, or events are clustered together in a way that affects how we understand the people or things that are being represented. For example, until the rise of the gay and lesbian liberation movement, representations of homosexuals were often paired with representations of pedophilia. Although the two phenomena are not related, the proximity of these representations in the media helped to reinforce the idea in popular culture that **homosexuality** was deviant and immoral. By looking at how representations are clustered, we can begin to understand how people and things are positioned at the "centre" or on the "margins" by association.

What Is Absent or Missing from a Representation or Discourse?

All representations and discourses inevitably privilege one partial version of reality to the exclusion of many others. A useful strategy for interrogating representations and discourses is to read "against the grain" in order to assess what is absent or missing, and why. The things that are absent from a representation signify just as much as (and sometimes more than) what is present in a representation (Hall, 1997). Take a moment to close your eyes and imagine an elite hockey player. You likely imagined a young, white man, because this corresponds with the images of hockey players that are routinely circulated in our culture. Now, look at the hockey player in Figure 2.3. When we interpret this representation, we implicitly compare it to what we expected

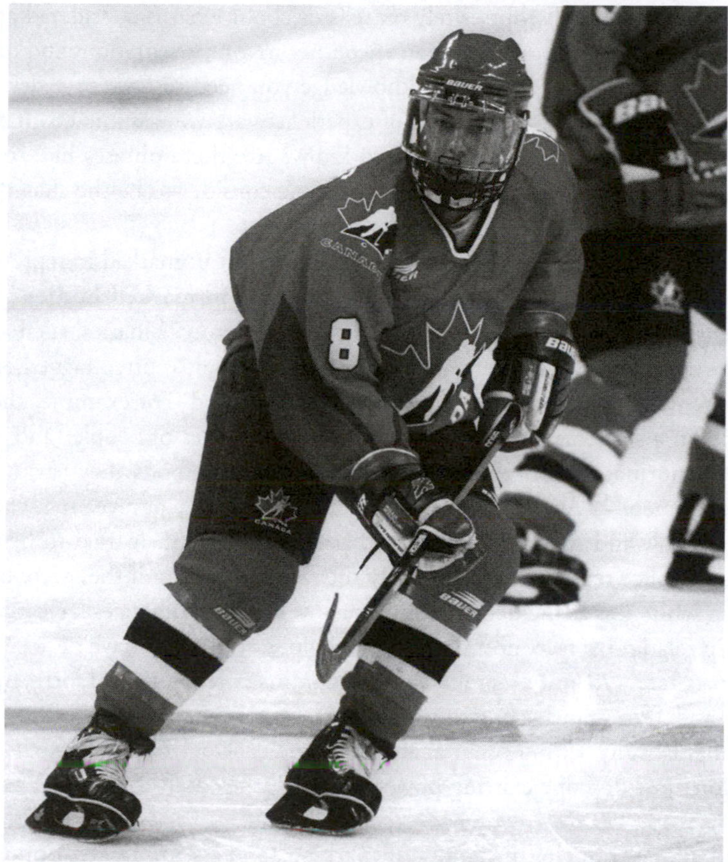

FIGURE 2.3 Angela James, elite hockey player. © Scott Grant Photography.

to see, which is influenced by our pre-existing ideas of what a hockey player looks like. (This image is of Angela James, one of the first two women and the second Black player inducted into the Hockey Hall of Fame.) When we assess what is absent in a representation or discourse, we are forced to assess our expectations, think about how they were established, and then consider how they are or are not met in that particular instance. This can be a difficult skill to learn, but once you have mastered it, it is an exceptionally useful strategy for understanding how representations and discourses shape our social reality.

What Is Framed as "Normal" or Left Unmarked?

The ability to frame something as "normal" in a society is a powerful tool, because it also designates that which is deviant or unusual (or not normal). Chapter 3 will delve further into the power of normal. Critically assessing the "common-sense" knowledge that representations and discourses rely on tells us about what is considered an uncontested element of the social order. As you encounter new representations and discourses, think about what type of background knowledge you need to have in order for them to be culturally intelligible. What types of experiences are you assumed to have? What types of things are you already expected to know? Are there phrases like "of course" or "as usual"? These signifiers illustrate what people consider to be the shared stock of knowledge in a society.

It is common for things considered "normal" to be left unmarked in representations and discourses. The distinction between **marked and unmarked bodies** is a useful way to identify (and contest) hierarchical binaries. In identity binaries, such as citizen/immigrant, the marginal or lesser-valued element in the pair is often tagged or marked in some way while the dominant identity is left unmarked. For example, the "ethnic foods" label in a supermarket implicitly sets out some types of people (and the foods they eat) as "normal" and other types of people (and the foods they eat) as "other." Even a compliment—"Asian babies are sooo cute!"—is a way of revealing what counts as a regular baby, and what baby is marked as being different. It used to be common for news and police reports to only identify the race of a person if they were not white, positioning whiteness as the default condition. While these practices have become less common in relation to race, non-dominant religious affiliations have become marked. News reports rarely identify members of the dominant religions in North America—Catholics and Protestants—but those who are Muslim or Sikh are often identified as such, linguistically setting them apart from "the centre." These marked/unmarked binaries don't just describe existing power relations, they actively inscribe and sustain them.

Beyond simply noticing instances of marking (and its unmarked opposite), one strategy used to resist discourses is to disrupt this dynamic. During World War II, Nazi authorities mandated that Jews in occupied countries wear a yellow Star of David to identify them as such. In Denmark, unlike in most other occupied territories, non-Jewish citizens stood by their Jewish neighbours—and while Jews in Denmark were never forced to wear yellow stars, King Christian wrote in his diary, "If such a demand is made, we would best meet it by all wearing the Star of David." Such an act of solidarity interrupts the function that marking is meant to serve.

What Rhetorical Devices and Organization Patterns Are Used?

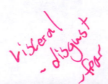

The study of rhetoric focuses on how language is structured and used to persuade. **Rhetorical devices** are linguistic techniques used to promote a particular understanding of a person, object, or event. Metaphors, alliteration, and hyperbole are commonly used rhetorical devices. An easy way to start looking for rhetorical devices in a discourse is by looking at the word choices. What other words or phrasing could have been used, and how might these alternatives have changed your understanding? For example, these three US news headlines from 15 May 2018 reference the same event: the protests in response to the US government's decision to move their embassy to Jerusalem from Tel Aviv, signalling that Jerusalem is being treated as the capital of Israel:[1]

- Over 50 Palestinians in massive protest are killed by Israeli military (ABC News; Hunter, Atta, & Hutchinson, 2018)
- Gaza protests: Dozens of Palestinians killed as US Embassy opens (CNN; Lee, Qiblawi, & Salman, 2018)
- Chaos as US Embassy opens (*Wall Street Journal*; Schwartz & Jones, 2018)

The first headline situates the identities of both those killed (Palestinians) and those doing the killing (the Israeli military), but does not reference the event being protested. Although the second and third headlines elevate the importance of the embassy opening, they simultaneously illustrate how passive language can be used to obscure agency and conceal power relations. For instance, the second headline indicates that Palestinians were killed, but does not indicate who did the killing. The third headline—from the politically and financially conservative *Wall Street Journal*—references no actors at all, implying that a building opened itself and chaos ensued. These linguistic strategies—omitting an active **subject** and assigning agency to things that cannot independently act (such as embassies)—work to conceal power relations.

The first two headlines above also illustrate differing approaches to enumeration. The articles that accompany both headlines indicate that more than 50 people were killed. The first headline highlights the volume of deaths by presenting the number as "over 50" people killed. In contrast, the second headline downplays the number of killings and emphasizes the uncertainty in the death toll by using the less precise language of "dozens." Another common rhetorical strategy used in media enumerations is to report that something has "doubled" or "tripled" without reporting the original incidence, a practice that creates the impression of rapid change or an increase in severity, when it may not be warranted. This strategy is often used in healthcare (and especially health scare) reporting (Gwyn, 1999). For example, the oft-reported statistic that belly sleeping in infants doubles the rate of sudden death obscures the fact that it doubles from a very small number to another very small number.

The organizational structure of narratives can also influence people's understanding of an event, and how its elements are related. Sometimes, cause-and-effect relationships are implied by the sequence in which events are presented. For instance, a government report might discuss both rising unemployment and changing immigration policies in Canada. Depending on how the report is organized, you might be led to believe that either changing immigration policies has led to rising unemployment or that rising unemployment has led the government to change its immigration policies. As you critically assess representations and discourses, consider how the sequence of a narrative affects your interpretation, and ask whether that interpretation would change if the sequence changed.

Conclusion

Taken together, these strategies and tools provide you with a starting point for interrogating representations and discourses in both your everyday environment or in the context of a formal research project. By asking hard questions about how things are represented, we can start to question and critically assess our everyday assumptions about the world and how it works. Our identities, our behaviours, and our perceptions of the world around us are shaped by representations and discourses, which is one way that power influences our everyday practices. As we begin to unpack these representations and discourses, we can start to see alternative ways of being, acting, and thinking that challenge dominant assumptions and power relationships.

In this chapter, we outlined how signifiers, representations, and discourses are central to how we come to know the world around us, and how they ultimately constitute social reality. The fixing or limiting of representations or discourses can be understood as acts of power. We began the chapter by describing how we acquire knowledge and introducing the idea that all knowledge is situated. Although you should undertake a systematic study if you want to make defensible generalizations about the world, we encourage you to develop the habit of interrogating representations and discourses as you encounter them in your everyday lives. The ability to critically analyze representations and discourses is a "craft" that becomes easier with practice. Learning to routinely use these strategies in your everyday life will help you to identify how power works and develop strategies for resisting it.

Study Questions

1 Explain what it means to say that signifiers are *polysemous*. What implications does this have?
2 In your own words, explain what a discourse is and why discourses are useful for understanding the organization of the social world.
3 Explain what it means to say that "absence" is also a signifier.
4 Identify two different rhetorical devices that can be used to affect the interpretation of a text. Give an example of each device.

Exercises

1 Choose an emoji that you regularly use in your communication. Research the history of the emoji (Is it one of the original 176 emojis released in 1999 or a later addition? What prompted the addition?) and record all of the meanings that can be or have been associated with it. Describe how the meaning of the emoji might change depending on the context it is used in.

2 Select an article from the front page of your local newspaper or news website. Read the article carefully, and critically assess what representations and discourses are being mobilized by the writer. Think about how the story might have been written differently and speculate about how this might have changed people's understanding of the news.

3 Find a video display that includes a running text of the news at the bottom. Over a period of time (ideally over several days), observe which stories and information are included in these feeds, and notice which stories and information are excluded. Based on your observations, speculate about the intended audience of this ambient news and its purpose. Using several concepts from this chapter, describe how the information that is included and excluded reflects power relations.

Note

1 Even this is a rhetorical strategy, since the US embassy in Tel Aviv was not moved; it remains open as a branch of the "main" Jerusalem embassy.

References

Berger, P., & Luhmann, T. (1966). *The social construction of reality: A treatise in the sociology of knowledge*. Garden City, NY: Anchor Books.

Castellano, M.B. (2004). Ethics of Aboriginal research. *Journal of Aboriginal Health*, *1*(1), 98–114.

Deacon, D., Pickering, M., Goldring, P., & Murdock, G. (2007). *Researching communications: A practical guide to methods in media and cultural analysis* (2nd ed.). London, UK: Hodder Arnold.

Dubinsky, K. (1999). *The second greatest disappointment: Honeymooning and tourism at Niagara Falls*. Toronto, ON: Between the Lines Press.

Gwyn, R. (1999). Killer bugs, silly buggers and politically correct pals: Competing discourses in health scare reporting. *Health*, *3*(3), 335–345.

Hacking, I. (1986). Making up people. In T.C. Heller, M. Sosna, & D.E. Wellbey (Eds.), *Reconstructing individualism: Autonomy, individuality and the self in Western thought* (pp. 222–236). Stanford, CA: Stanford University Press.

Hall, S. (1997). *Representation: Cultural representation and signifying practices*. Thousand Oaks, CA: Sage Publications.

Hall, S. (1999). *Representation and the media* [Video]. Northampton, MA: Media Education Foundation.

Haraway, D. (1991). Situated knowledges: The science question in feminism and the privilege of partial perspective. In *Simians, cyborgs, and women: The reinvention of nature* (pp. 183–201). New York, NY: Routledge.

Haraway, D. (2003). *The companion species manifesto: Dogs, people, and significant otherness*. Chicago, IL: Prickly Paradigm Press.

Hunter, M., Atta, N., & Hutchinson, B. (2018, May 15). Over 50 Palestinians in massive protest are killed by Israeli military, bloodiest day in Gaza since 2014 war. *ABC News*. Retrieved from https://abcnews.go.com/International/dead-hundreds-injured-palestinians-protest-opening-us-embassy/story?id=55143043

Lee, I., Qiblawi, T., & Salman, A. (2018, May 15). Dozens of Palestinians killed in Gaza clashes as US Embassy opens. *CNN News*. Retrieved from https://www.cnn.com/2018/05/14/middleeast/gaza-protests-intl/index.html

No eating before a swim rule holds no water. (2005, June 30). *CBC News*. Retrieved from http://www.cbc.ca/news/technology/no-eating-before-a-swim-rule-holds-no-water-1.525259

Raphael, D. (2002). *Social justice is good for our hearts: Why societal factors—not lifestyles—are major causes of heart disease in Canada and Elsewhere*. Toronto, ON: CSJ Foundation for Research and Education.

Schwartz, F., & Jones, R. (2018, May 15). Chaos as U.S. embassy opens. *Wall Street Journal*. Retrieved from http://online.wsj.com/public/resources/documents/print/WSJ_-A001-20180515.pdf

Simpson, L. B. (2014). Land as pedagogy: Nishnaabeg intelligence and rebellious transformation. *Decolonization: Indigeneity, Education and Society*, *3*(3), 1–25.

PART TWO
The Centre, Normalization, and Power

DEBORAH BROCK, ARYN MARTIN, REBECCA RABY, and MARK P. THOMAS

We begin this section of *Power and Everyday Practices* by introducing you to a theorist who has been a major influence on the practice of thinking and doing sociology. C. Wright Mills published *The Sociological Imagination* in 1959, yet his analysis has not lost its relevance. Indeed, it might be said to be more relevant than ever. His work inspires us to take up sociology not only as an intellectual vocation (regardless of whether or not one has "sociologist" in one's job description) but also as a political practice. Thinking sociologically will lead us to do sociology in our everyday lives, and to make connections between our everyday lives and the larger events shaping the social world.

Having read thus far, you have already begun to engage your sociological imagination. You have probably reflected on your own life, and the lives of your family members and friends. In other words, you have made the connection between the personal and the social. So what is the sociological imagination? Mills (1959) described it this way:

> a quality of mind that will help men [*sic*] to use information and to develop reason in order to achieve lucid summations of what is going on in the world and what may be happening within themselves. (p. 5)

For Mills, the "first fruit" of the sociological imagination is that individuals can only understand themselves and their experiences by locating these within their own historical time, geographical location, and political context. They can judge their own chances in life only through awareness of the chances of people in a similar position. For Mills, "The sociological imagination enables us to grasp history and biography and the relations between the two" (1959, p. 6). Far from positioning people as mere passive effects of social processes, Mills (like the other theorists that we have discussed so far) believes that people can be active participants in making history, particularly if we are cognizant of the social forces at work around us and are able to develop, along with others, a plan of action for shaping that history. We do indeed participate in the making of the social world at the same time that the social world shapes who we are.

In this section, we begin to build upon the framework that we established in Part I, as we deepen our engagement with unpacking the centre, identifying practices of normalization, and comprehending power. The chapter themes you will encounter are rooted in sociology's enduring interest in the causes and effects of **social inequality**. In modern liberal democracies, like ours, there is a central paradox that is ripe for the sociological imagination: we say that all are created equal and have equal opportunity to access life chances, and yet we (sociologists, pollsters, journalists, etc.) consistently find that some categories of people—women, people with disabilities, **racialized** and **Indigenous** people, transgendered people, immigrants, the elderly, and so on—are likelier to suffer ill health, experience poverty, and become victims of violence. How does this happen? How can this mismatch in life chances be explained without a circular appeal to innate inferiority? That is the story of Part II.

Discrimination—including **racism**, sexism, and other "isms"—is important, yes, but in this textbook we prioritize instead the stealth ways in which social and material structures are deliberately made to favour some identity categories. Importantly, Mills's emphasis on connecting history to biography allows us to move from the "big picture" to individual lives and back again. On the one hand, speaking about entire huge groups of people as having or being a certain way is always an overgeneralization at best and a stereotype at worst. There will always be exceptions—the Oprah Winfreys—who are pointed to by naysayers as though they refute a sociological observation about a shared, group-level experience. On the other hand, empirical research methods allow us to measure group effects—the difference between men's and women's pay, for example, or the proportion of CEOs from any given group. While it might not make sense to think and speak in terms of social groups or identities in every context, in most cases we will see their importance. The identification, marking, diagnosis, and separation of a subjugated grouping by a dominant group typically precedes that subjugated group's self-identification, and an identity is then created as a matter of survival, solidarity, and resistance.

The following chapters are loosely organized in a way that moves from physical bodies and their meanings to social identifications, like **class** and **citizenship**, though in every case physical bodies (flesh, skin, behaviours) and meanings (clothing, status, laws) are closely intertwined. In Chapter 3, "Fashioning the Normal Body," Kelly Fritsch and Anne McGuire set the stage with a further look at the idea of "the normal," including where it came from and how it insidiously shapes external and internal judgements we make. They show how certain kinds of bodies are rewarded while disabled, fat, and other unruly bodies are excluded, policed, and otherwise acted on by constant subtle (and not so subtle) social forces.

In Chapter 4, "Trans/gender," Dan Irving reveals the social and historical construction of what are usually taken to be simply natural and normal ways of being boys and girls or men and women. As you read this chapter, we want you to think about how Western **culture** (including **science**) has produced a dualism of two **sexed** bodies (female and male), and two **genders** (woman and man), and has made these attributes much more fundamental to being human than they need to be.

In Chapter 5, "Thinking 'Straight,'" Alix Holtby invites you to consider the historical construction of a **heterosexual-homosexual binary**, and its relation to the sex-gender system. You will see that the idea of **heterosexuality** is remarkably recent in the big scheme of things, and emerged as a result of **pathologizing** same-sex desires and activities.

In Chapter 6, "Whiteness Invented," Melanie Knight redirects our analytic lens to the legal and scientific invention of **race**, its service of **whiteness**, and its embeddedness in words and logics of contemporary Canada. As you read through this chapter, we would like you to consider how "race" is always **contingent** on the social context that gives it meaning. We want you to explore the everyday experiences of **racialization** and racial ordering that are part of your own life, perhaps in ways that you do not normally notice, especially if you are read as white and accommodated accordingly.

In Chapter 7, "Being 'Middle Class'?," Mark P. Thomas explores the social relations of **capitalism** and the economic interests that have propelled it (and with it, most of us) into a financially precarious time. He situates his analysis within a more general introduction to how capitalism works, the integral place of a class structure for capitalism's functioning, and the significance of **state** processes for the maintenance of this economic system. The chapter suggests that, while not always visible, class remains a central social relationship—and a central aspect of social organization—in contemporary society. It asks you to consider the relation between class and power, and how class is a feature of your everyday life.

In Chapter 8, "Growing Up, Growing Old," Rebecca Raby challenges the widely accepted model of the **life course** by revealing how it has been socially and historically organized into stages, in a manner that privileges the stage of adulthood. She asks: How do we define adulthood and how are conceptualizations of childhood, adolescence, and old age pivotal to that definition? How have these age-based categories been produced historically, and how do they reflect relations of power and inequality?

Finally, in Chapter 9, "Citizenship and Borders," Nandita Sharma examines the making of **borders** and nationalities both historically and in contemporary Canada. She shows us that the lines on maps are accomplishments meant to consolidate certain kinds of power. **Nationalism** creates certain kinds of subjects, and in many ways patriotism has had ugly effects in the world. But borders, and their sometimes devastating impacts on individual biographies, are anything but inevitable or fixed.

These chapters reveal how a normative centre is created and reproduced often through the demarcation of its **others**. In a classic manoeuvre of powerful groups to conserve that power, experts of various stripes attribute this distinction (normal vs. not normal) to nature or God, yet its origin is more accurately human. Harkening back to Mills, what is made by humans can be unmade or remade. Each and every one of us is a social actor making decisions every day about upholding or resisting consequential **dividing practices**.

While we have presented these topics like an identity buffet with separate dishes, bear in mind the ways that identities intersect in particular human beings. Particular intersections—for Black women or racialized transgendered youth, for example—have played out differently in specific times and places, often in ways that amplify the oppressions experienced or exclude certain people from an already-subjugated identity group. You will find that the topics of these chapters—bodies, genders, sexualities, racialization, age, class, and citizenship—are very much linked and interdependent in the making of **normativity** and its opposites.

Reference

Mills, C.W. (1959). *The sociological imagination*. London, UK: Oxford University Press.

3 Fashioning the Normal Body

ANNE MCGUIRE and KELLY FRITSCH

"Dress Normal," commands a Gap clothing advertisement. Featuring actress Elizabeth Moss, the advertisement (Figure 3.1) depicts a young, tall, slender, able-bodied, white woman strolling along a sunny, sandy beach, with seagulls and a pier visible in the background. The image captures Moss mid-step. She is glancing casually over her shoulder and smiling, her right hand raised slightly, as if she's in conversation with someone outside of the frame. Echoing the lightness of her physical stance and windblown hair, the clothing she wears is also casual: a white button-up shirt and black fitted slacks, a light grey wool topcoat, and black ballet flats. "Dress like no one's watching," reads the pale pink text situated to the right of the frame. The Gap logo appears on the left, also in pale pink and, beneath it, "Dress Normal." So pale is the text that the logo and its attendant directives almost disappear into the background of the peaceful seaside scene.

This image is, at once, an instruction, an invocation, and a command. In one sense, the Gap ad is pedagogical—it teaches the viewer about what **normal** is: how it looks, how it moves, which bodies can and do embody its definitional confines (and, by extension, which do not). The image suggests that looking and dressing like Moss is "normal" and that this normal is at once both desirable and mundane: normal is business casual, a dab of lip gloss, coolly strolling along a sunny beach. In addition to the normal standards of dress and beauty presented in the ad, the ad also presents us with other markers of **normativity**. As normal is localized in the body of Moss—an actress famous for her portrayal of the "girl next door" Peggy Olsen on AMC's *Mad Men* and June Osborne on Hulu's *The Handmaid's Tale*—the category of normal implicitly confirms its association with privilege. At the same time as it shows the viewer what *is* normal, the ad also instructs its viewer to *be* normal. Part of unpacking this latter demand is to question how normal became normal in the first place, a query that takes us to the heart of the **everyday practices** of **power**.

FIGURE 3.1 Collection of advertisements focused on normal dress.

Credit: Anne McGuire and Kelly Fritsch

In this chapter, we examine the idea of normal as something that, at the same time, is contextually specific and produces a range of material effects on the bodies and minds of people. We examine the historical underpinnings of the emergence of the category normal in the contemporary West and trace the ways in which this category has changed and continues to change alongside changing social, economic, and geopolitical landscapes. Looking to recent, 21st-century shifts in the concept of normal under globalized **neoliberalism**, we challenge the common assumption that we need only to include more people in the category of normal. Instead, we reveal how non-normative embodied differences, like disability, offer an important critique of the violence of the normal and push for different forms of embodied relations under contemporary conditions of power.

The Normal as Natural

The word "normal" circulates pervasively. It is often used to refer to a statistical and/or medical state of a body (e.g., "normal blood pressure," "normal development"). It is also routinely deployed as a way of categorizing, evaluating, or judging people (e.g., "normal person"). The present-day prevalence of "the normal"—or this idea of a normal typology—might lure us into imagining that this concept is universal and transhistorical: "after all," writes Lennard Davis (1995), "people seem to have an inherent desire to compare themselves to others" (p. 1). "Inherent" here implies natural and inevitable: that this desire to compare ourselves to others is somehow built into people rather than being a result of the ways we have been socialized. Often, in comparing ourselves to others, we find ourselves deficient or lacking and seek to remedy this perceived lack through consumption. Thus, consumer advertisements like the Gap's Dress Normal ad are often rich sites through which we might analyze the normal body and the everyday conditions of its production.

As is evident in the Gap ad specifically, but also more broadly across Western **culture**, the normal is often conflated with the natural. What is normal seems straightforwardly evident; the normal is the status quo, the usual, just the way things are. "Normal" is not fat bodies or wrinkled skin. "Normal" is not wheelchair users or someone hand flapping. Ideas about normal and not normal types are, for many, simply a matter of common sense. Yet, determinations of who or what is "obviously normal" rely on an intricate network of values, beliefs, interpretations, assumptions, and **power relations**. According to Rod Michalko (2002), the persistent contemporary cultural association between the normal and the natural involves a process of camouflage. "Normalcy blends into what is conceived of as 'naturally given,'" he writes, "and the only way to sustain this camouflage is to avoid any attention" (p. 82). Taken to be natural (and thus neutral), the normal appears only to disappear into the background order of everyday life.

The sense of normal as conceptually universal and politically neutral is key to the logic of the Gap ad. The ad presents Moss's body (i.e., her physique and her stance, as well as her clothes and accessories) as simultaneously classic and neutral. Her look, in other words, is not meant to betray any particular or specific presentation of self (i.e., we are told she dresses "like no one's watching"). Classed as normal, her bodily appearance is framed as typical, timeless, and universal—just the way things are and, indeed, have always been. The category normal blends bodily description and bodily evaluation: **norms** thus have the power to "bridge the fact/value distinction," as Ian Hacking (1990) argues, "whispering in your ear that what is normal is also all right" (p. 160). Describing a normal body as one that is, for example, youthful, thin, white, or able-bodied is not only a description of a body but also a judgement or evaluation of those characteristics as positive, good, ideal, and acceptable: the best or even the only possible way to (properly) be. The normal body thus also becomes understood as a body we should all want to have and strive to attain. Endowed with cultural value and social privilege, the category of normal is therefore infused with considerable power, the effects of which, as we shall see, are not evenly distributed across groups of people or populations.

The ways in which the normal camouflages as natural conceals its own foundation as a historically particular, ideologically mediated, political, and cultural phenomenon. If, following the methodology of Michel Foucault, we examine the historical **genealogy** of the concept of the normal—that is, if we trace the development of the concept through culture and history—we discover that the normal presents itself as a given truth or fact when it is actually a specific cultural value judgement. As Peter Cryle and Elizabeth Stephens (2017) argue, the normal "is in no sense historically ubiquitous, and does not deserve to be considered a timeless idea" (p. 3). Neither should it be considered a universal idea. Indeed, notes Davis (1995), "the idea of a norm is less a condition of human nature than it is a feature of a certain kind of society" (p. 24). This idea of normal as a condition of a given society goes beyond a mere recognition that normal varies in different societies, locales, or historical eras (although surely it does). What Davis seems to be suggesting here is that *the very idea that there is a normal is specific to a particular society and time.*

In the Gap ad, Moss's embodied "look" is, of course, most certainly highly curated. The idea of "normal dress" is made sensible, for example, by way of a calculated advertising strategy, one that is reliant upon classed, raced, and gendered trends in fashion, as well as culturally and historically specific norms of bodily desirability, ability, and beauty. Further, as we shall explore later in the chapter, the capacity to "dress normal" in the Global North is only made possible by camouflaging and naturalizing unjust social relations of **colonialism**, **imperialism**, **capitalism**, and ability in the Global South—for example, by way of the debilitation of garment industry workers labouring in hazardous factory conditions. The normal is fashioned literally in the Gap clothing ad in the sense that this is an ad for a particular normative style of fashion. The normal is also fashioned figuratively in the ad insofar as it relies on a culturally particular idea of what normal is, an idea that is made or put together (i.e., fashioned) through a network of cultural values and inequitable social relations.

Because normalcy's cultural power rests in part on its invisibility, or its capacity to blend into the background order of the everyday, Michalko (2009) contends that perhaps the most abnormal thing we might do is "atten[d] to its production" (p. 91). Put differently, we must **denaturalize** normal, or treat it as a **contingent** site of meaning-making **constituted** in and through power relations. This kind of cultural inquiry requires us to **historicize** cultural understandings of the normal, to observe its shifts and adaptations across time and through space, to attend to the particular socio-political conditions that render it intelligible at a given time. It also requires us to observe and analyze normalcy's very real, material effects. While the social relations of normalcy impact all of our bodies, they do so in different ways and with differing outcomes. A key theme of this chapter is that the normative measures of the good, right, normal, healthy, and able human body/mind have provided the grounds for so much social injustice, such as with the **medicalization** of disabled, **queer**, and trans bodies; the rise of eugenic **science** and **scientific racism**; the sense of presumed "goodness" or "rightness" of **colonial** and imperial interventions and occupations; the **regulation** of women's bodies by the **state**; the institutionalization of disabled and mad people; the proliferation of the weight-loss and beauty industry, and so on. The move to historicize (and thus denaturalize) normalcy can enable us to better understand how social categories (i.e., **race**, **class**,

gender, ability, etc.) and systems of oppression (i.e., racism, classism, sexism, ableism) intermingle and interact to produce the everyday understandings that some bodies are better, fitter, or more desirable than others.

It is important to note that in drawing out the power relations that support and sustain normalcy, we are not arguing to broaden what or who is included within the bounds of normal. We are not claiming, in other words, that disabled people, for example, or trans people, or fat people, are normal *too*. Rather, we want to expose the damaging logic of a system that includes some while leaving others perpetually excluded. To borrow from disability justice activist Mia Mingus (2011), "we don't want to simply join the ranks of the privileged; we want to dismantle those ranks and the systems that maintain them." The ways in which some bodies bump up against the rules, expectations, and common sense of what is considered normal allows us to notice the exclusionary ways in which our society is organized. It also invites us to think about and critique how those exclusions become common sense, enabling us to imagine and engage with normalcy differently.

Historicizing Normal

Despite its common usage, and thus its clear significance to the contemporary order of things, the normal is a relatively recent invention. As has been described by Davis (1995), Cryle and Stephens (2017), and a great many other cultural historians (e.g., Hacking, 1990; Warman, 2010), the word "normal"—in its current usage denoting "usual," "typical," or "common"—does not make a formal appearance until as late as 1848. The meaning of the word continued to remain obscure for some time. Prior to the late 19th century, the normal circulated in the realm of geometry, meaning "perpendicular," "right-angled," or "orthogonal" (Hacking, 1990). It was derived from the Latin word *norma*—for a measurement device or T-square used in carpentry, masonry, and drafting to reproduce right angles—and, throughout the 18th century, it became commonplace to use normal in reference to something that was standard, "right by rule, made by the square or Rule" (as defined by Blounts's 1656 *Glossographia*). While normal is no longer commonly associated with geometry, the idea of the norm as a tool of right measurement has endured. By the mid to late 19th century, the normal had become an important concept underpinning a new style of measurement: **statistics** (Cryle & Stephens, 2017; Davis, 1995; Hacking, 1990). At this time, Western Europe saw the introduction of the "normal curve" or "normal distribution"—which describes a law of mathematics positing that the further a given variance is from the mean, the less frequently it will occur in nature (Stephens, 2014). The notion of normal was utilized to mark out a limited numerical range: the middle of the bell curve. The normal, in other words, became synonymous with average.

The statistical norm was not the only conception of normal in circulation in the 19th century, however. While statistics gave us normal by the numbers, 19th-century medicine introduced the somewhat different understanding of normal as a dynamic biological state (Canguilhem, 1991; Cryle & Stephens, 2017; Hacking, 1990). An organ or bodily system could be deemed medically "normal" only in the absence of "**pathology**"—the one state anticipated and required the other. The work of Georges Canguilhem (1991) shows how the biomedical normal at once names the body's "habitual state" and its "ideal" (p. 152). The normal state, he writes, is "that which is such that it ought to be" (p. 125).

While the statistical norm gives rise to the possibility of an outlier (or that which is outside of the normal range), the medical norm similarly gives birth to a **pathologized** category of the abnormal (Canguilhem, 1991; Foucault, 2003). Indeed, according to Cryle and Stephens (2017), it was only through this intermingling of statistical and medical understandings of normal that "that the word came to acquire its current cultural authority, moving from its specialist use in scientific discourses 'into the sphere of—almost—everything'" (p. 4). In this way, the statistical and medical roots of the concept of the normal provide an effective means of **classifying** and ordering all modes of human and non-human variation: as Hacking notes, "people, behaviour, states of affairs, diplomatic relations, molecules: all these may be normal or abnormal" (1990, p. 160). Yet, as you learned in Chapter 1, any act of categorization is also a mode of governance. Through normalcy as a mode of governance, normal has become "indispensable" because it has created scientific and medical ways of being "**objective**" about bodies (Hacking, 1990, p. 160). Statistical/biomedical notions of normal were soon recognized to be an efficient means of measuring, monitoring, and modifying the bodily shapes and comportments of individuals and whole populations in accordance with particular white, Western European idealizations of the human.

A great many early statisticians in 19th-century Europe were also eugenicists (Davis, 1995). This association between statistics and **eugenics** ought not surprise us. As Davis (1995) cautions, "the next step in conceiving of the **population** as norm and non-norm is for the state to attempt to norm the nonstandard—the aim of eugenics" (p. 30). Perhaps the most prominent of the 19th-century eugenicists was Francis Galton, whose foundational work on the development of the statistical sciences cannot be separated from his expansive writing on the superiority of normal or "pure" heredities and, relatedly, on the need for the eugenic elimination of abnormal outliers, so-called "degenerates." Widely adopted in 19th- and 20th-century North America and Europe, eugenics implemented social engineering by incentivizing the reproduction of "fit" families and decreasing or prohibiting reproduction of those deemed abnormal or "unfit." In practice, this included a variety of state-sponsored measures as drastic as forced sterilization, removal of children from their families, and **genocide**. Eugenic normalcy was raced white and its oppositional category—i.e., abnormal degeneracy—grouped together a wide swath of bodies that did not conform to the heavily policed white Western European colonial ideals of bourgeois respectability (e.g., the poor and/or non-white body, the queer, trans, or otherwise "sexually deviant" body, the "cripple," "insane," or "feebleminded," the "alcoholic," the Semitic, and so on).

This distinctively eugenic desire to know, count, classify, order, and control the reproduction of human characteristics in terms of normal or abnormal traits had everything to do with the **ideologies** and practicalities of both colonial and capitalist rule. Characterized as a uniquely "fit" body (i.e., as physically and intellectually strong, virile, and white), the eugenic normal was also, and not coincidentally, considered fit for the idealized work of empire-building. Colonial and imperial politics, alongside the rise of capitalist industrialization in continental Europe and North America, also played a role in the development of eugenic logics of standardization. For example, as the art of war became more and more reliant on mass-produced machines, the idea of a normal soldier body—a body that might easily interface with standard-issue technologies of war—became increasingly important to the overall efficiency of colonial military operatives, which included territorial acquisition and military expansion (Hacking, 1990). Equally important to the efficiency of empire was the body of the citizen-worker at home. As you will learn in Chapter 7, and as Karl Marx's work so clearly shows, the rise of industrialization both required and produced a highly valued homogenized, efficient, able-bodied, citizen-labourer. As the human body began to interface with technologies of production, or, indeed, as the body became an essential part of the machinery of production, there emerged new—and equally mechanical—means of governing and conditioning the body through **disciplinary power**.

The Power of Normalization

In *Discipline and Punish*, Foucault (1979) describes the disciplinary process of **normalization** as "one of the great instruments of power" (p. 184). Whereas some forms of power are overt, mandating that bodies comply with an explicit rule or law—e.g., we might make the conscious decision to show up at work at the required time because we know that this is a formal rule and that not complying will result in an undesirable consequence, such as being fired—the disciplinary technique of normalization that took hold in the 19th century operates more covertly. As we have discussed, the rules of normalcy are often unwritten, concealed as implicit, or naturalized. Yet, while the rules of normalcy do seem to "emanat[e] from everywhere and nowhere," they are nonetheless "compulsory" (McRuer, 2006, p. 8). Just because a given norm is not formally written into state law does not mean that it is any less mandatory. As bodies and minds move outside of the naturalized limits of social norms, these transgressions are nonetheless keenly, and sometimes violently, felt at the level of the body. For example, as a body moves outside of the (raced, classed, gendered) norms of dress—such as when a masculine-appearing person wears pink clothing or a dress in contexts rigidly defined by norms of gender and (hetero)sexuality, or when a Black youth appears wearing a hoodie in spaces ruled by the politics of white respectability—this transgression will be met with a variety of social punishments, which might range from **microaggressions** (e.g., a disgusted or nervous side glance from a stranger passing by) to more overt forms of structural or physical violence (e.g., being made a target for "random" carding by police, physical assault, etc.). Yet, "in discipline," writes Foucault, "punishment is only one element of a double system: gratification-punishment" (1979, p. 180). This means that as a body conforms to social norms of, for example, dress—a white-presenting woman wearing a white button-up shirt and black fitted slacks for example, as is featured in the Dress Normal ad—such compliance is met with a variety of associated rewards: a complimentary look or comment from a friend or stranger, a successful job interview, the ability to pass through airport security without hassle, or seeing one's body positively reflected in the popular media.

Foucault's work thus shows us that normalization does not simply work by extolling individuals to "be more normal" (as the Gap ad suggests). Indeed, the suggestion that normal is merely an autonomous choice asks us to look away from the powerful disciplinary structures through which power comes to shape bodies; disciplinary power encourages or incentivizes particular ways of being, while discouraging or forbidding others. To take another example, let us think for a moment about the disciplinary function of public transportation. We can learn much about the shape of the imagined or assumed "normal rider of public transportation" from the design and placement of bus and subway seats. By examining the height, width, and depth of the standard bus seat, as well as its placement in proximity to other seats, we can come to better understand how the seat itself anticipates a particular kind of body (e.g., a body that will not spill over into the next seat, a body that will be able to stand up and sit down at a particular seat height without any difficulty, and so on). What is more, the standard bus seat not only anticipates the normal body, it also works to ensure it. For example, people who do not easily or comfortably fit into public seating frequently receive hostile comments or stares from others for "taking up too much space." Roxane Gay (2018) notes that she has felt pressure from society to lose weight in order to "fit more peacefully into a world that is not at all interested in accommodating a body like [hers]." She comments, "As a fat person, I am supposed to *want* to lose weight. I am supposed to be working on the problem of my body. I am supposed to apply discipline to physical unruliness." As Gay's statement makes clear, the body is not only disciplined by external rules, structures, and relations (i.e., the seats that don't quite fit, or an aggravated glance by a fellow bus rider), normalization also affects our personal feelings about our bodies, compelling us to discipline and govern ourselves toward social norms.

Similarly, someone who has difficulty balancing or getting in or out of their seat may be subject to pitying looks from other riders, may be chastised for "holding up" the bus, or may become the recipient of unsolicited suggestions from strangers about how to fix or cure their unruly or non-normative bodies so that they would better fit in normative spaces. As disability activist Harriet McBryde Johnson notes, such people "think they know everything there is to know just by looking at me" (2005, p. 2). Eli Clare (2003) similarly speaks to the violence of having his dynamic, disabled, and gender nonconforming body dissected, reduced, and disciplined by the stares of strangers:

> when first a pair of eyes caught me, held me in their vise grip, tore skin from muscle, muscle from bone. Those eyes always shouted, "Freak, retard, cripple," demanding an answer for tremoring hands, a tomboy's bold and unsteady gait I never grew out of. It started young, anywhere I encountered humans. Gawking, gaping, staring seeped into my bones, became the marrow. (p. 257)

Uncomfortable and even physically and/or emotionally harmful, such squeezes, sighs, and stares work to make riding public transportation difficult or even dangerous for people whose bodies deviate from the norm. Meanwhile, those who do the staring fail to recognize that the ease they experience in this built environment is not "natural" but tailor-made for them.

The disciplinary norm serves not only as an ideal toward which the individual must always strive but against which they will inevitably fail. Just because a body might readily approximate a particular set of socio-cultural rules or norms at one time or in a particular space does not mean that this body will always pass as normal. To inhabit the normal is always tenuous, ever dependent upon a constellation of relations between bodies and their discursive and material contexts. Because of this, the normal-passing body is always susceptible to betraying the signs of abnormalcy, and thus is always under threat of being expelled from the normal. To better understand this, we might imagine a scenario wherein an apparently normal child is at play in the school playground. In this particular moment and space, this child passes easily into the category of normal; that is to say, the child plays in conformity with received norms of gender, age, development, and so on. Yet, as we have discussed, the body's claim to normal is precarious. As the recess bell rings, we might imagine this same child, now in the classroom, noticeably shifting in their desk. Perhaps they are bored, or excited, or having difficulty understanding or paying attention to the teacher's lesson. Perhaps the movements of their body are expressive or communicative movements. Or perhaps there is no single or specific cause for this non-normative classroom behaviour: maybe this is simply how this student "does" being a student. Nevertheless, the student who moments earlier on the playground passed easily into the category of "normal-child-at-play" is now experiencing difficulty aligning their body and mind with the decidedly different rules and expectations of classroom conduct. Because of this, their body shifts between categories, classed as normal in one context and abnormal in another.

This scenario is no doubt further complicated if we look at it through an **intersectional** lens: the student's embodied attributes such as race, class, gender, **sexuality**, disability, and **citizenship** inform identity and cannot be separated from one another. While it is true that most people, no matter how hard they try or what choices they make, can never inhabit the category of normal—at least not fully or completely or without the threat of failure—we must nonetheless account for how some bodies are positioned farther away from the normal than others. This has everything to do with power: with historically constituted interlocking systems of privilege and oppression. In her discussion of the school-to-prison pipeline, Nirmala Erevelles (2014) reminds us that while there are no apolitical acts of "labelling" non-normative behaviour in the classroom, power imbalances are made particularly explicit at the intersection of race, class, and disability, where non-normative behaviour is so often criminalized. To return to our example of classroom comportment, if the student in this scenario were, say, a white, female, middle-class six-year-old, their non-normative behaviours may be interpreted differently than if they were a low-income, racialized, male youth.

While our discussion here has been premised on an imaginary scenario, the stakes of embodying the normal are very real. Norms influence which bodies are made to naturally appear as more or less worthy of social protections and freedoms or even of life itself. Attending to the disciplinary workings of normalization can thus help to explain how, following Alexis Shotwell (2017), "norms contribute to the death and degradation of people who fall outside currently normative bounds" (p. 156). What is more, in considering the material impacts of multiple, intersecting embodied non-normativities, Shotwell importantly notes, "the further outside the normal—the closer to death" (p. 156). Intersectional understandings of norms and normativity are acutely salient, for example, in contemporary discussions of anti-Black racism and police brutality, particularly when considering that up to half of all people killed by police in the United States are disabled (Perry & Carter-Long, 2016; Ritchie, 2017). As Andrea Ritchie (2017) notes: "Actual or perceived disability, including mental illness, has … served as a primary driver of surveillance, policing, and punishment for women and gender-nonconforming people of color throughout US history" (p. 91). Indeed, Ritchie continues, "police are more likely to criminalize and use excessive force against people of color with psychiatric disabilities through a process that law professor Camille A. Nelson terms the 'disabling of race and the racing of disability'" (p. 93).

Because the stakes of passing as normal are so high, and because the normal is only ever inhabited tenuously, normalcy requires continuous upkeep. Normal is therefore not a finite state of being (i.e., something we are or are not in any definitive sense) but, rather, it is a *doing* (i.e., a practice or performance reliant on the constant repetition of historically and politically constituted gendered, classed, racialized, and ability norms of comportment). In this way, norms "keep us in our places by helping us know how to be ourselves properly and establishing internal and external monitoring systems" (Spade & Wilse, 2016, p. 554). Disciplinary norms, as suggested by Foucault, "make individuals"; they influence how we perceive and ascribe meaning to the bodies of others, and they also influence how we understand and manage our own bodies.

As is demonstrated by many of the examples from this section, the disabled body in the contemporary West is routinely understood as, at once, abnormal and problematic: the student whose body betrays non-normative behaviours or movements in the classroom; the public transit rider whose body takes longer to get up or sit down; the person of colour with psychiatric disabilities who is detained, incarcerated, or made the victim of police violence. In each of these examples, we can see how the disabled body is read not only as different (i.e., non-normative) but also as deficient and thus as disruptive to the normal/natural (i.e., good) functioning of the social whole. What these examples also show us is that the seemingly neutral cultural association between disabled non-normativity and abnormal deficiency is neither natural nor neutral. As the breadth of scholarship and activism in the field of **disability studies** makes clear, the disabled body is produced through politically and historically constituted cultural norms and their attendant relations of power. Applying Foucault's theories of power to a discussion of the body of the citizen-worker under industrial capitalism, we can develop a better sense of how normalizing discipline works to determine which bodies are made to fit within a given socio-historical context and which are cast out as unfit. We turn our attention now, and for the remainder of this chapter, to the making of the disabled body under the historically specific socio-economic conditions of capitalism and neoliberalism. Often thought to be natural and thus unassailable, contemporary Western understandings of normal/non-disabled and abnormal/disabled bodies are in fact historically produced through the conditions of industrial and post-industrial labour.

Not a Normal Worker: The Creation of Disability as Abnormality

As industrial capitalism developed, one of the objects of the disciplinary enclosure of the factory was to train the bodies of workers to match the rhythm and demands of the factory. Workers were subjected to a uniform set of requirements regarding punctuality, the number of hours and days worked, and the application of effort. These imperatives were enforced through a variety of disciplinary penalties: strict time-keeping; fines for lateness, disobedience, and slow work; and the careful observance of performance. Intensive surveillance required that the worker adapt their body to the shape and rhythms of the machine. Under these particular structural and material conditions, and against the broader social backdrops of colonialism, imperialism, and eugenics, we find that the normative body that is fashioned through the demands of industrialized labour is that of a young, male, able-bodied worker. The industrialization-era version of the normal worker informed not only how much rates of production could be increased, but also influenced the architecture of buildings, urban planning, modes of transportation, the length of the working day, the way in which home and family life were organized, and what was required for labour-power to reproduce itself through sufficient subsistence required for the "normal state as a working individual" (Marx, 1990, p. 275). These normal states, structures, and systems continue to profoundly influence normal conditions in the West to this day (e.g., schools continue to be organized around a factory model, with work periods punctuated by break periods) even though factory work is no longer the norm in Western countries.

The disciplinary regime of the factory shaped and transformed this "normal" working individual. Against this normative able-bodied labouring **subject**, disabled bodies came to be understood as bodies that could not produce, or could not produce at an average acceptable rate. As Marx (1990) points out, industrialization and urbanization necessarily produced an "incapable" social stratum that could not sell its labour-power at the average rate of production, a group that was not able to adapt their bodies to the new modes of production that resulted from the change in the division of labour. This left individuals whose bodies did not conform to the unique labour demands of the industrial economy to suffer from the consequences of being excluded from the market: poverty, ill-health, brevity of life, social marginalization, and dependence upon the informal economy (p. 797). This group included not only the "sickly" but also the "mutilated," the elderly, and "victims of industry" (p. 797). These people form what Marx calls "the dead weight of the industrial reserve army," the incidental expenses of capitalist production (p. 797). Yet, as Marx shows us, capital is nonetheless adept at offsetting its expenses, transferring liability "from its own shoulders to those of the **working class** and the petty bourgeoisie" (p. 797). By the late 19th century, many of those deemed "incapable" were incarcerated in workhouses, hospitals, asylums, and "crippleages" (Gleeson, 1999, p. 108). "Disability" as a category thus emerged historically as a "produc[t] of a society invested in denying the variability of the body" so as to invest in, and profit from, the standardized productivity of the normative able-bodied worker (Davis, 1995, p. xv).

Indeed, the 1834 British *Poor Law* made a strict legal distinction between the able-bodied poor who should be compelled to work and the disabled poor, who were considered objects of charity (Gleeson, 1999). Such objects of charity were to be placed in the new national system of workhouses. As Émile Durkheim has noted, "the insane and the sick of certain types, who were heretofore dispersed, [were] banded together from every province and every department into a single enclosure" (1964, p. 188). Higgins further notes that the workhouse was a "pen of inutility": "The workhouse, the true shrine of the work ethic, was a sort of concentration camp in which were incarcerated, and held up as an example, those who admitted their inutility to capital—the sick, the mad, the handicapped, the unemployed—and in conditions which were even more monstrous than in the factories" (quoted in Gleeson, 1999, p. 105). While the enclosure of the disabled in workhouses was never universal, the subsequent establishment of a network of state-run and charitable hospitals, asylums, and other dedicated institutions for disabled and mad people would, notes Gleeson, "considerably extend the landscape of social dependency" (1999, p. 105). Much of the cultural authority that medicine gained throughout the 19th century was a result of normalizing discourses around the labouring body. That is, medicine, in relation with the emergent discipline of statistics, worked to explain that the inability to labour efficiently under capitalist relations was a natural consequence of physical, intellectual, and psychiatric **deviance**.

Not only did capital disable bodies in excluding them from the valorized workforce, it also created physical impairments in labourers who would have been previously classed as able-bodied. Friedrich Engels (1968) describes the debilitation of labourers in *The Condition of the Working Class in England*, where he writes: "A number of cripples gave evidence before the Commission, and it was obvious that their physical condition was due to their long hours of work" (p. 171). He further writes that "it is easy to identify such cripples at a glance, because their deformities are all exactly the same. They are knock-kneed and deformed and the spinal column is bent either forwards or side-ways" (p. 173). Engels explicitly connects such bodily anomalies to the conditions of industrial labour, arguing that miners' "splayed feet, spinal deformities and other physical defects" could be attributed to "the fact that their constitutions have been weakened and they are nearly always forced to work in a cramped position" (Engels, 1968, p. 280). The workers' increased dependency on, or indeed their enmeshment with, the machinery of industry led to an increase in the destruction of the fleshly body.

Yet, the fact that capital creates disability does not faze capital *as* capital. At the same time as capital consumes the bodies of its workers (i.e., absorbs their **labour power**, life-energies), it also marginalizes those it cannot incorporate, seeing them as abnormal. Therefore, with the rise of **commodity** relations, new forms of labour changed the desired make-up of the social body. More specifically, the political and economic shift lessened the ability of disabled people to make meaningful contributions to their households as their bodies and minds were considered deficient and abnormal. As households became more and more dependent on their members' competitive sale of labour-power, their ability to host "slow" or "dependent" members was greatly reduced. And so, in the 19th century, the enclosure of work within factories became defined and built in relation to the idealized worker body of the non-disabled male, while women, children, and disabled people increasingly shared a common social status of non-labour, even while women, children, and disabled people frequently participated in certain kinds of factory work as well as low-paid piecework at home.

Now, for many in the Global North, labour no longer predominantly takes the form of factory work, and contemporary forms of discipline and power have also shifted. To return to the Dress Normal ad, the image of Moss is not that of a factory labourer, although she does wear the fruits of that labour. Rather, the image frames Moss as a contemporary neoliberal subject—a productive, competitive, entrepreneurial, freelance, flexible subject, who labours continuously to optimize herself, thereby ensuring her value as **human capital**. Her carefree style in the image masks the attendant credit card debt of continuous consumption, and the self-care she performs—a leisurely walk along the beach—is a kind of optimization of the self that is meant to bolster her resilience. In this image of Moss, we encounter a model of neoliberal flexibility and efficiency. Her "normal" business casual attire might entice us to imagine that she has just popped out of the office, or perhaps, as a mobile freelance worker, this seaside pier is her office. We might imagine her sitting down in the sand, work and play intermingling as she orders her groceries online, answers work emails, and posts to social media.

As we have seen, the development of industrial capitalism played a key role in the production of an "incapable" class wherein those bodies and minds that did not fit within the standardized confines of the factory—e.g., the crippled, the maimed, the weak, the sick, the mad—became disabled and, thus, abnormal. With this history in mind, we can, perhaps, better appreciate the ways in which contemporary neoliberal social and economic conditions also anticipate the emergence of a new kind of "incapable" body/mind, one that, moreover, seems to blur long-held categorical distinctions between "normal" and "abnormal" bodies. As Jasbir Puar (2012) compellingly argues, under neoliberalism "the distinctions of normative and nonnormative, disabled and nondisabled do not hold up as easily" (p. 154). Instead, she contends, there "are variegated aggregates of **capacity** and **debility**" (p. 154). Therefore, the key question of the normal body in the 21st century is not "Is this a normal body or not?" but rather "*How* normal is this body; how amenable is it to normative enhancements or optimization?" This means that the 21st-century neoliberal normal is, on the one hand, more inclusive than, say, the normal under industrialization: we might, for example see evidence of the normative inclusion of bodies previously classed as abnormal in the mainstream media or in social policy (e.g., racialized bodies, disabled bodies, women's bodies, queer bodies, etc.). On the other hand, however, this "new" normal is not as inclusive as it would seem at first blush. Participation in the neoliberal entrepreneurial economy normalizes the functions of global capital that require that some bodies be enhanced or capacitated at the expense of others. For Moss to "dress like nobody is watching" requires the exact process of normalization that erases the historical and political conditions that bring this norm into being in the first place. We turn now to a consideration of the (labour) conditions through which some bodies—including, we note, a minority of highly privileged disabled bodies—are incorporated into neoliberal norms and discuss how such inclusions work to normalize the exclusion of other, often multiply marginalized, bodies.

The Capacitation and Debilitation of Bodies under Neoliberalism

Like the Gap ad, the Tommy Hilfiger ad also in Figure 3.1 is another example of how normalcy is fashioned. Here again, we see bodies being fashioned as normal in ways that are, at once, literal (i.e., via normative fashion or style of dress) and figural (i.e., via specific cultural, political, and economic values). What makes this Hilfiger ad particularly interesting to us is how it includes the disabled body in the category of normal: the Hilfiger ad depicts two laughing, fashionably dressed white disabled subjects—a woman with a futuristic high-tech prosthetic arm and a man using a wheelchair. This normative inclusion appears in stark relief against, as we have seen throughout this chapter, a long history of disability exclusion; it marks a clear departure from the everyday assumption that the mark of disability disqualifies a body from participating in narratives of normalcy. A closer look at the Hilfiger ad can teach us something about the increased porousness and flexibility of the neoliberal normal and the distinctive ways it governs, controls, and hierarchizes bodies.

The ad is selling "Tommy Adaptive," Tommy Hilfiger's adaptive clothing line, which promises both "iconic design" and "easy dressing" (usa.tommy.com/en/tommy-adaptive). This collection showcases clothes designed with a variety of access features—e.g., magnetic zippers, Velcro closures, adjustable hems, and so on—that promise to make it easier, according to Tommy Hilfiger himself, for "differently abled adults" to "express themselves for fashion" while also—as is required of any good neoliberal body—to do so independently. Says Hilfiger, "inclusivity and the democratization of fashion have always been at the core of my brand's **DNA**" (Bash, 2017). In the ad, we can see how the intersections of gender, disability, race, and class work together to produce some embodied subjects as seemingly naturally deserving of normative inclusions, while leaving others outside of normalcy's protective embrace. Of course, far from being democratic, this kind of high-end adaptive clothing produces classed (and thus also raced and gendered) divisions within disability communities in the Global North. The Hilfiger line marks out for inclusion those few disabled subjects who can have access to costly normalizing clothing from the majority of disabled people, who, in this era of neoliberal austerity, remain underhoused, underemployed, underinsured, and underserviced, and who are therefore unlikely to have "easy" access to designer pants and sweaters (McRuer, 2018; Puar, 2017). What is more, at the same time as it creates divisions within the category of disability in the Global North, the ready-made garment industry anticipates the production of disability in the Global South.

In April 2013, Rana Plaza, an eight-story garment factory just outside of Dhaka, Bangladesh, which made clothing for Joe Fresh and other "fast-fashion" brands, collapsed, trapping thousands of workers inside. Just one day after the building was declared unsafe due to the discovery of large cracks in the walls, the Rana Plaza collapse killed 1,138 people and injured over 2,600, making it the worst garment factory disaster and among the most significant industrial disasters in recent memory. It can be argued that such fast-fashion factory disasters represent a particularly neoliberal kind of problem. In keeping with the market demands of a globalized, neoliberal economy, North American and Western European chains such as Gap, H&M, and Tommy Hilfiger rely on various shortcuts and subcontracts to facilitate garment production that is both quick and cheap. For example, large garment industry corporations in Dhaka often focus on quick turnaround and strict delivery deadlines—taking fashion from the catwalk to the everyday consumer in mere weeks—putting increased pressure on suppliers that have led to safety shortcuts, such as those that occurred with Rana Plaza.

Despite years of public shaming and a variety of post-Rana Plaza safety agreements and labour reforms, the $28 billion apparel industry in Bangladesh remains a long way from being safe. It is estimated that there are 5,000–6,000 garment factories and facilities in Bangladesh, making it the second largest garment manufacturer in the world, employing over 4 million people, mostly women. Of these facilities, it is estimated that as many as 2,000 are unregistered, unregulated, and "so far removed from oversight and operate on such small margins" that they are unlikely to be affected by "inspection and remediation regimes" (Labowitz & Baumann-Pauly, 2014, pp. 22–23) even if they were offered. Because of these ongoing hazardous labour conditions, in addition to producing cheap clothes in narrow timeframes, the fast-fashion industry also produces, in its workers, various kinds of bodily debilitations. Many studies have tracked the range of adverse health effects brought on by garment factory conditions, citing depression, vision disorders, musculoskeletal disorders, and respiratory abnormalities as bodily conditions commonly experienced by garment industry workers (Villanueva, Fitch, Quadir, Sagiraju, & Alamgir, 2017). Indeed, in Bangladesh, it is estimated that occupational injuries account for more than 8 per cent of all disabilities in the population (Villanueva et al., 2017).

While neither Tommy Hilfiger nor Gap were directly linked to the Rana Plaza factory disaster, these companies both regularly produce their products in unsafe garment factories in Bangladesh, where wages remain the lowest in the world (a normal wage for a garment worker is US$68 per month). Indeed, both Gap and Hilfiger were among a group of manufacturers whose clothing was being produced at the site of a 2010 fire in the Ashulia industrial zone just outside of Dhaka that claimed nearly 30 lives and left over 100 injured. The fire broke out on the 10th floor of the factory, which did not have proper fire escapes, forcing many of the workers to break windows and jump out of the building in an attempt to escape the blaze. We argue that the Hilfiger adaptive line exemplifies and reproduces "neoliberalism's heightened demands for bodily capacity, even as this same neoliberalism marks out populations for what Lauren Berlant has described as 'slow death'—the debilitating ongoingness of structural **inequality** and suffering" (Puar, 2017, p. 149). The fact that a minority of disabled people (typically white, wealthy people living in the Global North) can afford to buy products that (may) help them to bring their bodies closer to the requirements of neoliberal normativity does not address the significant and harmful social and structural inequities that flow from compulsory normativity. These kinds of fast, flexible, consumer-based social enhancements are, at best, a tenuous solution: they leave the included minority in a position of precarity, dependent on acts of consumption as a means of securing social worth. They also, as we have seen, work dangerously to normalize the debilitation and perpetual exclusion of the disabled majority (typically non-white, low-income people living in the Global South).

As with all forms of power, **normalizing power** invariably works to cultivate cultures of resistance. On 24 April 2014, thousands of workers and their unions rallied across Bangladesh to mark the one-year anniversary of the Rana Plaza disaster, demanding fair wages, safe working conditions, and compensation for injured workers. Among these protesters were the disabled survivors of the Rana collapse and other factory disasters, the vast majority of whom, due to inaccessible workplace environments or bodily limitations, are unable to work and/or receive disability supports (Fitch et al., 2015; Villanueva et al., 2017). In Figure 3.2 we encounter a photograph of a picketer attending a one-year anniversary rally. Holding up a protest sign with the handwritten words "I don't want to die for fashion," she stares confidently at the camera with an expression that seems to tether outrage with defiance. Recalling Michalko (2002),

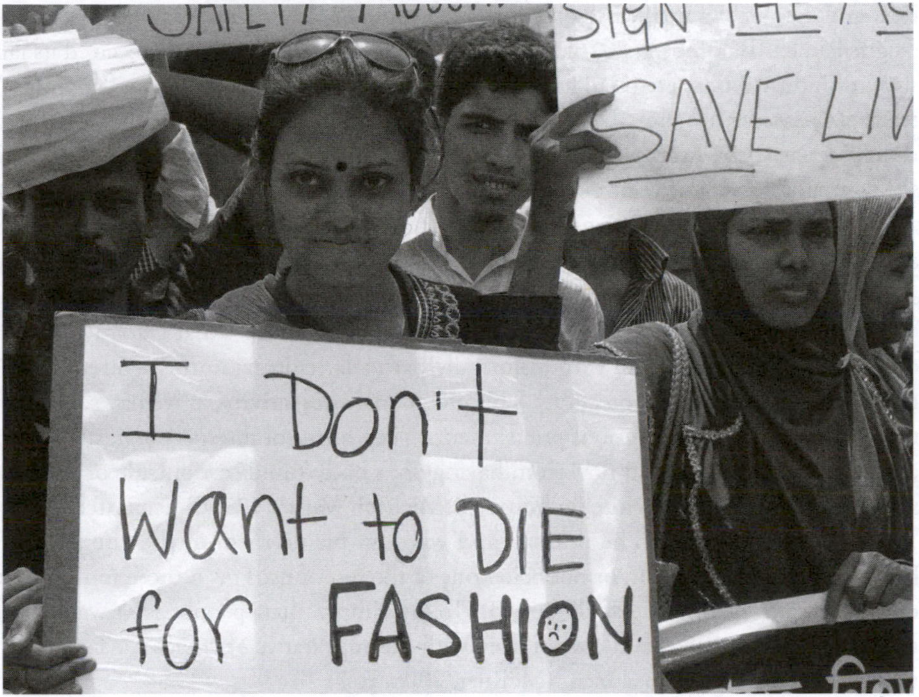

FIGURE 3.2 2014 photograph of a demonstrator attending a rally on the one-year anniversary of the Rana Plaza factory disaster.

Credit: Solidarity Center/Sifat Sharmin Amita.

normalcy's cultural power depends on a process of camouflage. Therefore, Michalko (2009) reminds us, any attempt to disrupt the violence of normativity must first "look" at normal and "atten[d] to its production" (p. 91). In contrast to Gap's appeal to a neoliberal normalcy that is invisible and unseen, and against the backdrop of normative neoliberal practices that derive cultural power from their invisibility, this protester—and the thousands of garment workers with whom she forms a collective—looks directly at the normal conditions of labouring bodies in the Global South. This act of looking marks out the normal ways some lives are rendered less valuable or more disposable, and names the **relational**, material violence of this debilitation.

Conclusion: Normative Failures

Gap's "Dress Normal" campaign turned out to be a spectacular failure: the brand's sales dropped between 4 and 5 per cent in the weeks and months following the launch of the campaign. Stores were forced to offer massive discounts on merchandise in their "normal" line, and Gap's chief marketing officer left the company less than a year after the campaign's launch (Bloomberg, 2016). Not surprisingly, the marketing failure received its fair share of industry ridicule. "Gap faces a world that doesn't want to be normal anymore," reads a *Bloomberg* headline (Bhasin, 2016). "There is such thing as too much of a meh thing," reports Isha Aran, writing for *Jezebel*. "People don't want to actually *be* normal," she contends, "they just want to lay claim to the 'normal' aesthetic" (Aran, 2014).

It is certainly easy, at first glance, to interpret the failure of the Gap campaign as an indication that consumers just don't want to dress or be normal. However, as we've seen throughout this chapter, the cultural power of normal extends well beyond the realm of personal choice. To occupy the position of the normal—that is to say, to have one's body and mind cohere with historically particular cultural norms—offers a great many rewards and social protections. This provisional **subjectivity**, as we have explored, functions to stave off the various punishments—i.e., forms of interpersonal, state, and/or structural violence—that flow from having one's body/mind cast outside of the normative frames of cultural intelligibility. As Michael Warner (2000) accurately notes, "nearly everyone wants to be normal, and who can blame them, if the alternative is being abnormal, or deviant, or not being one of the rest of us? Put in those terms, there doesn't seem to be a choice at all" (p. 53). To say, simply, that "people don't want to be normal" is to "produc[e] and cove[r] over, with the appearance of choice … a system in which there actually is no choice" (McRuer, 2006, p. 7).

In his search for how we might subvert this system of compulsory normativity, Robert McRuer (2006) turns to the work of Judith Butler. "There is no guarantee that exposing the naturalized status of [the normal] will lead to its subversion," warns Butler (quoted in McRuer, 2006, p. 30). With this in mind, the failure of the Gap campaign is not so much that the company merely "missed the mark" on consumer desires or fashion trends (O'Reilly, 2014). Rather, we contend, the campaign's principal failure flows from its failure to sustain normalcy's camouflage. In other words, the Gap ad invites consumers not only to look more normal but also, and because of this, to look at the normal, a form of visibility that works to undermine normalcy's cultural authority and power. Over the course of this chapter, we have mobilized normalcy's failure to camouflage so as to expose normal for what it is: situated, contingent, material, relational, and deeply political. We do this with the hope that this might, following Butler, "work the weakness of the norm" so we can collectively move toward more capacious understandings of human bodies and human value (quoted in McRuer, 2006, p. 30).

Study Questions

1 Explain in your own words how the Gap ad both shows the viewer what *is* normal and also instructs its viewer to *be* normal.
2 Why do the authors suggest that it is not enough to include more kinds of people or different forms of embodiment in the category of the normal?

3 Why do you think normal is so difficult to notice? How can the non-normative body help us to better perceive a camouflaged normalcy and therefore learn about the social conditions of power?
4 Think of a variety of historical or contemporary examples where the category of normal has been used to govern and control the bodies and minds of people. How might a critique of the normal provide a basis for intersectional coalition building?

Exercises

1 Situate yourself in a public space. What strikes you as normal and abnormal? How did you come to think of what you perceived as being normal or abnormal?
2 Choose an object from your everyday life (e.g., your cell phone or computer, a favourite article of clothing, a childhood toy, a chair in your classroom, a course syllabus). What particular body or mind does the object anticipate as its "normal" user? How does the object reflect cultural understandings of desirable/undesirable bodies? For an example of how objects anticipate and shape normal and abnormal bodies, see the authors' discussion of the ways bus seat size and arrangement produce normative and non-normative bodies. *Follow up question:* How might your object be used in different, unexpected, or non-normative ways?
3 This exercise asks you to think critically about the selfie—or the self-taken photograph—as a cultural artefact worthy of analysis. Look back at two or three selfies that you have taken in the past (or take several new images), and reflect on the selfie as a presentation of self. How have you chosen to fashion your body in and through your images? What bodily norms do these selfies reproduce? How does your body show up in the images in ways that are beyond your choosing? *Follow up question:* Do you think selfies can open up new and non-normative ways of making bodies visible? Why or why not?

References

Aran, I. (2014, October 22). Gap's blah "dress normal" campaign doesn't get the irony of normcore. *Jezebel*. Retrieved from https://jezebel.com/gaps-blah-dress-normal-campaign-doesnt-get-the-irony-o-1649345286

Bash, N. (2017, October 20). Tommy Hilfiger has designed a fashion line for people with disabilities. *Fortune Magazine*. Retrieved from http://fortune.com/2017/10/20/tommy-hilfiger-disabilities-clothing-line/

Bhasin, K. (2016). Gap faces a world that doesn't want to be normal anymore. *Bloomberg*. Retrieved from https://www.bloomberg.com/news/articles/2016-08-19/gap-faces-a-world-that-doesn-t-want-to-be-normal-anymore

Bloomberg. (2016). Gap shoppers don't want to "dress normal." *Business of Fashion*. Retrieved from https://www.businessoffashion.com/articles/news-analysis/gap-faces-a-world-that-does-not-want-to-be-normal-anymore

Canguilhem, G. (1991). *The normal and the pathological*. New York, NY: Zone Books. (Original work published 1966)

Clare, E. (2003). Gawking, gaping, staring. *GLQ: A Journal of Lesbian and Gay Studies*, *9*(1), 257–261.

Cryle, P., & Stephens, E. (2017). *Normality: A critical genealogy*. Chicago, IL: University of Chicago Press.

Davis, L. (1995). *Enforcing normalcy: Disability, deafness and the body*. New York, NY: Verso.

Durkheim, É. (1964). *The division of labour in society*. New York, NY: The Free Press.

Engels, F. (1968). *The condition of the working class in England*. Palo Alto, CA: Stanford University Press. (Original work published 1845)

Erevelles, N. (2014). Crippin' Jim Crow: Disability, dis-location, and the school-to-prison pipeline. In L. Ben-Moshe, C. Chapman, & A. Carey (Eds.), *Disability incarcerated: Imprisonment and disability in the United States and Canada* (pp. 81–100). New York, NY: Palgrave MacMillan.

Fitch, T., Moran, J., Villanueva, G., Sagiraju, H.K.R., Quadir, M.M., & Alamgir, H. (2017). Prevalence and risk factors of depression among garment workers in Bangladesh. *International Journal of Social Pyschiatry*, *63*(3), 244–254.

Fitch, T., Villanueva, G., Quadir, M.M., Sagiraju, H.K., & Alamgir, H. (2015). The prevalence and risk factors of post-traumatic stress disorder among workers injured in Rana Plaza building collapse in Bangladesh. *American Journal of Industrial Medicine*, *58*(7), 756–763.

Foucault, M. (1979). *Discipline and punish: The birth of the prison*. New York, NY: Vintage Books.

Foucault, M. (2003). *Abnormal: Lectures at the collège de france, 1974–1975*. London, UK: Verso.

Gay, R. (2018). What fullness is. *Medium*. Retrieved from https://medium.com/s/unrulybodies/the-body-that-understands-what-fullness-is-f2e40c40cd75

Gleeson, B. (1999). *Geographies of disability*. New York, NY: Routledge.

Hacking, I. (1990). The normal state. In *The taming of chance* (pp. 160–169). Cambridge, UK: Cambridge University Press.

Johnson, H.M. (2005). *Too late to die young: Nearly true tales from a life*. New York, NY: Picador.

Labowitz, S., & Baumann-Pauly, D. (2014). *Business as usual is not an option: Supply chains and sourcing after Rana Plaza*. New York, NY: NYU Stern Center for Business and Human Rights.

Marx, K. (1990). *Capital: A critique of political economy* (Vol. 1, B. Fowkes, Trans.). New York, NY: Penguin Books in Association with New Left Review. (Original work published 1867)

McRuer, R. (2006). *Crip theory: Cultural signs of queerness and disability*. New York, NY: New York University Press.

McRuer, R. (2018). *Crip times: Disability, globalization, resistance*. New York, NY: New York University Press.

Michalko, R. (2002). *The difference that disability makes.* Philadelphia, PA: Temple University Press.

Michalko, R. (2009). Coming face-to-face with suffering. In T. Titchkosky & R. Michalko (Eds.), *Rethinking normalcy: A disability studies reader* (pp. 91–114). Toronto, ON: Canadian Scholars' Press.

Mingus, M. (2011, February 12). Changing the framework: Disability justice. *Leaving Evidence.* Retrieved from https://leavingevidence.wordpress.com/2011/02/12/changing-the-framework-disability-justice/

O'Reilly, L. (2014, December 6). People don't want to 'dress normal.' *Slate Magazine.* Retrieved from https://slate.com/business/2014/12/gap-sales-down-4-percent-after-dress-normal-campaign-failure.html

Perry, D., & Carter-Long, L. (2016). *The Ruderman white paper on media coverage of law enforcement use of force and disability.* Retrieved from https://rudermanfoundation.org/white_papers/media-coverage-of-law-enforcement-use-of-force-and-disability/

Puar, J. (2012). Coda: The cost of getting better: Suicide, sensation, switchpoints. *GLQ, 18*(1), 149–158.

Puar, J. (2017). *The right to maim: Debility, capacity, disability.* Durham, NC: Duke University Press.

Ritchie, A. (2017). *Invisible no more: Police violence against black women and women of color.* Boston, MA: Beacon Press.

Shotwell, A. (2017). *Against purity: Living ethically in compromised times.* Minneapolis, MN: University of Minnesota Press.

Spade, D., & Willse, C. (2016). Norms and normalization. In L. Disch & M. Hawkesworth (Eds.), *The Oxford handbook of feminist theory* (pp. 551–571). Oxford, UK: Oxford University Press.

Stephens, E. (2014). Normal. *Transgender Studies Quarterly, 1*(1), 141–145.

Villanueva, G., Fitch, T., Quadir, M.M., Sagiraju, H.K.R., & Alamgir, H. (2017). Self-efficacy, disability level and physical strength in the injured workers: Findings from a major factory disaster in Bangladesh. *Disability & Rehabilitation, 39*(7), 677–683.

Warman, C. (2010). From pre-normal to abnormal: The emergence of a concept in late eighteenth-century France. *Psychology & Sexuality, 1*(3), 200–213.

Warner, M. (2000). *The trouble with normal: Sex, politics and the ethics of queer life.* Cambridge, MA: Harvard University Press.

4 Trans/gender

DAN IRVING

Introduction: Everyday Gender Performances

If you showered after waking up this morning, did you have any feelings or reactions about your body? When you picked out the clothes you are wearing today, did you think about which article of clothing will accentuate your best features or hide particular areas you consider "flawed," or did you just grab what was clean? What were your embodied and emotional experiences as you traversed public spaces as you made your way to class? Is your **gender identity** a constant preoccupation that prevents you from concentrating during class or while working on assignments? Do you strategize about how to get to the single stall washroom in record time so you do not miss any of the lecture after the break?

These questions are intended to direct attention toward some of the ways that **gender** factors into the most mundane aspects of our daily routines, as well as the activities structuring our lives, such as taking public transit and attending university classes. What were you thinking as you answered these questions? How did they make you feel? Your emotional responses and bodily reactions reveal a lot about your gender identity and how it is affected by **power relations** and inequalities. Those of you whose masculinity or femininity adheres to what is socially accepted as proper may have felt these questions to be intrusive, while others felt validated because particular barriers they face in their lives were acknowledged.

This chapter focuses on trans/gender subjectivities, understood through an **intersectional analysis**, to explore some the ways that gender as a "regulatory regime" governs North American society (Butler, 2004). The objectives for this chapter are (1) to define the **sex/gender binary** and unpack the ways that this dualistic logic governs society,

(2) to interrogate **hegemonic masculinity** as a **ruling** category, (3) to introduce **trans*** subjectivities and demonstrate how trans-analysis extends a glimpse into how gender is constructed and challenged, and (4) to broaden and deepen an understanding of how sex and gender as power relations function discursively. As you may recall from this book's introduction, **discourse** refers to organized systems of knowledge that produce and circulate meaning throughout society. Discourses enable a greater comprehension of the ways that particular language and expressions are reflective of the material socio-economic, political, and cultural relations out of which they emerge. The final **objective** for this chapter is to engage in an intersectional analysis, to illustrate how sex/gender are mediated by other systemic relations of power, including settler colonialism and **whiteness**.

Bound by the Binary?

Western societies are organized according to a narrow and rigid binary comprehension of **sex** and gender. Binary thinking is dualistic, meaning that sex and gender are understood in either/or terms. To unpack how the sex/gender binary functions to organize society, it is important to explore sex and gender as separate but interconnected categories.

Contemporary understandings of sex privilege biological determinist discourses and produce two categories—male *or* female. Sex is defined in terms of chromosomes (i.e., males as XY *or* females as XX), genitals, and secondary sex characteristics (e.g., breast development and menstruation for females or facial hair and lowered voices for males). Secondary sex characteristics are related to hormones that activate physical changes associated with puberty. Hormones are also frequently associated with certain behaviours.

Biological determinism refers to the belief that the body and its functions are natural and produce behaviours over which individuals have little control. For example, the common expression "boys will be boys" dismisses rough, domineering, and reckless behaviour as inevitable because it is assumed to be linked to testosterone. It is assumed that boys and men are physiologically hardwired, so to speak, to act in aggressive ways. Privileging biology in this way diverts critical attention away from social relations, institutions, and practices that contribute to understanding men and boys as aggressive beings.

Returning to our definition of sex, it is widely accepted that sex is determined in utero and is unchangeable. In other words, the prevalent societal understanding is that individuals are born either male or female. Sex is attached to the physical body and produced through physiological processes. Typically, the role of medical professionals is not viewed as contributing to producing sex because the dominant belief is that sex is natural. As a result of the definitive characteristics of sex being rooted within chromosomes and other biological determinants, many assume that one cannot legitimately change their sex. While many trans* identified individuals undergo sex reassignment surgeries and hormone replacement therapy, their identification as male or female is dismissed as inauthentic because they were not born as such. As will be reflected in the section addressing trans*, the phrase "sex is assigned at birth" disrupts this hegemonic knowledge concerning sex as a solely biological phenomenon.

What is implied by the counter-assertion that sex is socially constructed? How can material bodies—chromosomes, hormones, muscular structures, and facial hair be constructions? Referring back to discussions of Stuart Hall and Foucault in the introduction and Chapter 1, **social constructionist** approaches to sex do not discount the physical existence of bodies. Social constructionist analysis of sex/gender explores the co-constitutive nature between physical bodies and socio-economic, political, and cultural relations. In other words, "nature" and "nurture" are not considered to be mutually exclusive categories. Rather, a series of dynamic social processes and practices produce the sexed body and conversely, the sexed body contributes to shaping the social environment (Fausto-Sterling, 2005).

Unpacking sex/gender reveals how meaning concerning these governing categories is socially constructed. Why is there only one body acknowledged as male and one as female, when other sexes exist? How is meaning concerning sex circulated throughout society and who benefits from such a rigid comprehension of sex? How does such a narrow meaning of sex mold and sculpt people's bodies? How can the increasing visibility of sex/gender diversity produce alternative understandings of sex and gender?

Dualistic categories of sex represent meanings that are historically and culturally specific. Not all societies have been organized according to a binary notion of sex; for instance, ancient Greek society was organized according to a one-sex model. Males were recognized as the only legitimate sex whereas females were seen as a defect (Laqueur, 1992). Many non-Western cultures, both historically and currently, do not adhere to the gender binary. For example, the kothi and hijras in Western Bengal, eastern India (Dutta & Roy, 2014), and the waria in Indonesia (Hegarty, 2017) are examples of non-binary genders. However, in order to understand the cultural significance of these examples, we need to also engage in critical scholarship that foregrounds **postcolonial** and anti-imperialist analyses, which is discussed in Chapter 9.

Scientific discourse plays a significant role in shaping dominant knowledge concerning binary sex. Medicine and health services, for instance, frequently produce normative categorizations of male or female through **pathologizing** other sexes. Intersex people, for example, are represented as having problematic or abnormal characteristics that require fixing. While there are multiple manifestations of intersexuality, one of the most recognized concerns is around individuals born with ambiguous genitalia. If an infant is born with genitals that cannot be classified easily as male or female, they are diagnosed as having ambiguous genitalia. Medical experts often recommend surgeries to fix ambiguous genitals by constructing a vagina (the most common procedure) or a penis. This invasive surgical procedure scars intersex individuals physically and emotionally. Furthermore, medical professionals recommend that parents adhere strictly to raising their children as either boys or girls (Fausto-Sterling, 2000). Binary notions of sex and gender are thus constructed through interactions between medical experts and the families of intersex children, and through the **politics of invisibility**. The politics of invisibility refers to deliberate actions, in this case on the part of medical experts, the families of intersex individuals, and the media to stifle awareness concerning intersexuality and the multiple manifestations of bodily sex. Such actions include refusal to acknowledge invasive surgeries performed on intersex people during infancy, not making medical records readily available to intersexed individuals, and a sensationalist media portrayal of intersex individuals. The lack of **representation** of variations of sex beyond the binary, as well as the derogatory ways that intersexed people are posited as freaks of nature, reproduce rigid approaches to sex.

Intersex scholars and activists such as Morgan Holmes (2016), Emi Koyama (2003), and Hida Viloria (2015) struggle to challenge the pathologization of intersex people and the subjugation of non-normative bodies to nonconsensual and unnecessary medical interventions. They have made considerable progress, and some parents of infants born with ambiguous genitalia will elect not to subject their child to surgery.

Popular knowledge concerning sex is produced in multiple locations. In addition to scientific and medical discourses, social events also contribute to providing biological determinist and binary knowledge of sex. Baby showers and gender reveal parties exemplify how meaning concerning binary sex is produced and legitimized through everyday social interactions. Traditionally and aligned with gender practices discussed later in the chapter, it is common practice in Canada and the US for baby showers to be thrown for the "mother-to-be" during the latter stages of pregnancy to celebrate the anticipated arrival of the baby. Attended exclusively by women, the décor at this social gathering is usually pink and/or blue, and the games and gifts reflect an attentiveness to gender.

Gender reveal parties are becoming popular amongst couples who wish to announce the gender of their baby with their friends and families. Similar to baby showers, these more contemporary events focus extensively on the baby's sex. Medical technology, such as sonograms used during prenatal visits to the doctor or midwife, capture an image of the fetus. Expectant parents often request to be told the sex of the baby, which is decided based on whether a penis or vagina is visible on the sonogram.

Websites such as parenting.com (https://www.parents.com/pregnancy/my-baby/gender-prediction/how-to-host-a-gender-reveal-party/) and babycenter.com (https://www.babycenter.com/0_7-hot-ideas-for-your-gender-reveal-party_10365580.bc), as well as social media sites such as Pinterest, demonstrate the overwhelming interest and priority individuals place on binary sex in their everyday lives. There is no shortage of ideas for hosts of gender reveal parties to creatively engage guests in guessing whether the fetus is a boy or a girl. The highlight of the gender reveal party comes when the sex of the infant is announced to all the guests.

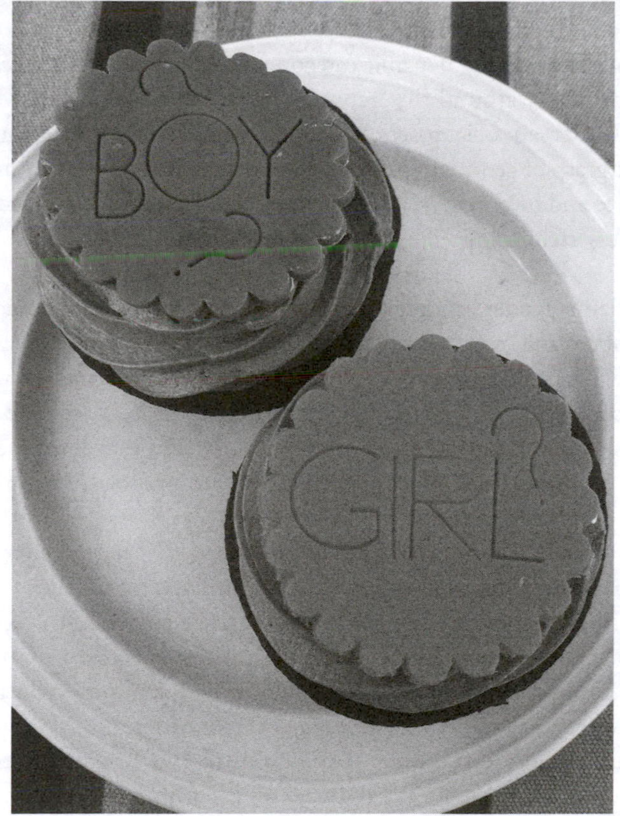

FIGURE 4.1 Normalizing gender through party decor.

Credit: (a) Reproduced by permission of Nicole Folsom. (b) CC BY SA 2.0/kgroovy.

Defining Gender

Gender functions as a binary category as well. While gender is typically accepted as a social phenomenon, the lines between gender and biologically determined sex are blurred. There is a societal expectation that individuals assigned to the male sex will be socialized as masculine to become men. Conversely, individuals assigned to the female sex are expected to be socialized as feminine to become women. Dominant discourses concerning gender associate particular physical and emotional characteristics with masculinity and femininity. If asked to define masculinity, what traits would you list? The most common responses include rationality, strength, courage, assertiveness, independence, and intelligence. If asked to brainstorm about femininity, what identifying features immediately come to mind? Chances are you define femininity as emotional, weak(er), nurturing, passive, dependent, and irrational.

Doing Gender

Similar to sex, gender refers to dynamic categories (i.e., masculinity and femininity) that are organized primarily around the "reproductive arena" (Connell & Messerschmidt, 2005, p. 68). Gender is a social practice. Think of gender as a verb (i.e., an action word) to gain a better grasp of gender as practice. Masculinity and femininity are constructed through "creative and inventive … actions taken" that "respond to particular situations" (Connell & Messerschmitt, p. 72) and reflect specific cultural contexts, locations, and time periods.

Conceptualizing gender as a phenomenon constructed through social interactions allows us to understand masculinity and femininity in a way that moves beyond gender roles. Knowledge that frames gender in terms of roles or characteristics reproduces a static and essentialist approach to gender. In other words, masculine and feminine appearances, as well as behaviours, are normalized in ways that foreclose upon understandings that emphasize how gender is produced through social relations within particular institutions and communities.

The gender binary system is hierarchical, meaning that masculinity and femininity are not separate but equal categories. Masculinity is an idealized way of being, while femininity is degraded as a subpar existence in comparison. To demonstrate this, return to the paragraph above where the traits associated with manhood and womanhood are listed. The characteristics defining masculinity reflect what society holds in high esteem, whereas the defining features of femininity are undervalued. Such an inequitable understanding of masculinity and femininity that is part of hegemonic gendered discourses is produced and legitimized through various **state** laws, institutional policies, and **everyday practices** throughout society. I will expand upon gender **inequality** following a more theoretical discussion of gender as a governing system.

Gender Performativity

Judith Butler's theory of **gender performativity** is currently the most influential theorization of gender embodiment and social practice among other poststructural feminists, **queer** theorists, and critical scholars across inter/disciplinary fields. Gender performativity refers to: "acts and gestures, articulated and enacted desires [to] create the illusion of an interior and organizing gender core" (1999, p. 173). Gender performativity challenges gender **essentialism** by explaining how masculinity and femininity are not ahistorical, preformed, or fixed concepts. In other words, there is no original, true, or authentic form of masculinity or femininity that has always existed throughout time.

Gender performativity differs from the idea of a performance because masculinity or femininity is not always presented through deliberate acts. Do you think about pitching your voice higher or lower to sound masculine or feminine? Do you actively choose to demonstrate your identification as a man or woman through desiring the opposite sex? Or are these embodied behaviours, or behaviours felt in the body, and desires enacted unconsciously? The **borders** between our psyches and the external social world are porous: our innermost thoughts, feelings, and desires are shaped through social relations.

Hegemonic Masculinity

Theorizing gender as performative allows us to discover how gender categories, such as **hegemonic masculinity**, are being constantly produced, and how they function as governing relations. Hegemonic masculinity refers to the ideal bodily aesthetics, characteristics, and behaviours associated with manhood that are produced by various social interactions and "guarantees (or is taken to guarantee) the dominant position of men and the subordination of women" (Connell & Messerschmidt, 2005, p. 77). Hegemonic masculinity reflects **patriarchal** and racialized discourses about what it means to be a man. As discussed in the latter sections of the chapter, hegemonic masculinity within a Western context is defined primarily in terms of whiteness, middle-class social location, and physical, emotional, and **financial fitness** (Connell & Messerschmidt, 2005). This dominant form of masculinity is indicative of a standard of perfection or an untenable **status** that is elusive even for upper- and middle-class white men.

Hegemonic masculinity denotes a hierarchy between masculinity and femininity, and within masculinity as a gender category itself. Masculinity is valued over all expressions of femininity. While multiple expressions of masculinity exist in every society, they are treated unequally. **Indigenous** men, men of colour, dis/abled men, queer or trans* men, unemployed or homeless men, as well as expressions of "female masculinity" (Halberstam, 1998) exist within contemporary Canadian society but are devalued as non-normative.

Gender is something that one does, or performs, rather than being innately something that one is (West & Zimmerman, 1987) and, for men, recognition—as successful, competent, responsible, and rational—is achieved through the policing of **self**, competition with others, and the exclusion of the other men and masculinities mentioned above, as well as women. Everyone is complicit in reproducing hegemonic masculinity through our everyday speech and interactions with each other. For example, in her study of male high school students, C.J. Pascoe argues that young men attempted to secure their own recognition as properly masculine through the use of the word "fag" to configure other boys as effeminate and incompetent (2005).

While men who are able to achieve particular ideals are privileged by hegemonic masculinity, these ideals do not reflect men's actual lives (Connell & Messerschmidt, 2005). For example, many young, white, middle-class men graduate with a university degree but cannot secure a good job, carry large student loan debts, and have their physical and mental health compromised by life's struggles. Measured against the impossible standards of hegemonic masculinity, however, adverse material circumstances such as increased indebtedness and the decline of stable full-time employment are not considered as the reason for men's misfortune. Individual men are configured as personally responsible, and the negative circumstances within which many find themselves are seen as a matter of failed masculinity.

Failure to achieve all of what hegemonic masculinity requires—complete independence, a steady and well-paying job, physical fitness, and emotional resilience—is inevitable. Regardless of the inevitability of not being able to live up to a fantasy of perfection, the emotional consequences of feeling like an inadequate man are real. Michael Kimmel's **concept** of "aggrieved entitlement" addresses the rise of violent behaviours among white working- and middle-class youth (Kimmel, 2008) and adult men as they try to attain and maintain elusive, hegemonic masculinity (Kimmel, 2013). During these austere times when there are no guarantees of a stable income or living comfortable lives regardless of how hard they work, many men are becoming increasingly angry as they face uncertain futures.

Part of this rage stems from the fact that whiteness and hegemonic masculinity are destabilized while dominant expectations stemming from these categories remain. White middle-class men face expectations that they cannot attain and have not had to develop the psycho-social tools to handle particular kinds of adversity (DiAngelo, 2011), so while many men—including Indigenous men, men of colour, and men with disabilities—may be fearful and depressed because they cannot find stable employment and a livable wage, their lived experiences of masculinity create different expectations from society.

Structural Gender Inequalities

Hegemonic masculinity and aggrieved entitlement provide an entry point into further acknowledging and discussing ongoing gender inequality and the violence framing women's lives. Hegemonic masculinity contributes to knowledge and practices that create significant barriers for women to be able to realize their full potential. For example, young girls within the public schooling system are often dissuaded from developing or pursuing an interest in **science**, technology, engineering, and mathematics (STEM). This example demonstrates the gendered logic of approaches to education that are geared more toward fostering boys' success in STEM subjects by attributing rationality and intellect to masculinity. Recently, feminist educators and advocates have resisted such masculinist approaches to education by developing curriculum that encourages girls' education in these areas, which prepare them for postsecondary study and careers in STEM fields.

The gender pay gap, referring to the difference between the lower amount that women are paid in comparison to men, also demonstrates women's structural gender inequality as a result of masculinity being dominant and privileged. Gender-based discourses tether women to their bodies and specifically their (presumed) reproductive capacity by characterizing them as emotional, nurturing, and dependent beings. Such logic supported the male as breadwinner model of work and family that framed post-World War II society. Men's role was to earn a "family wage" to support the household while women performed unpaid reproductive, or domestic, labour at home (i.e., mothering, cooking, and cleaning).

Beginning in the 1970s, significant numbers of middle-class women joined the workforce. Despite having the same credentials and performing the same jobs, women were not paid the same as men. While the gender pay gap has narrowed, particularly for women with the same postsecondary education and professional training as men, issues concerning pay equity continue. In 2015, women earned an average of $26.11 per hour compared to the average of $29.86 that men earned. This translates to women earning 0.87 cents for every dollar men earn (Moyser, 2017).

The hierarchical nature of the sex/gender binary in which masculinity is celebrated and femininity is degraded produce grounds for violence against women (VAW). VAW includes physical, emotional, sexual violence, harassment in real life and online, and financial violence (i.e., control over and/or preventing access to monetary resources). Women are particularly vulnerable to intimate partner violence (IPV), which includes physical, emotional, and/or sexual abuse by spouses or individuals that one is dating or has dated in the past. According to Statistics Canada, "In 2011, 8 in 10 victims of police-reported intimate partner violence were women. Overall, there were about 78,000 female victims of intimate partner violence, representing a rate of 542 victims per 100,000 women aged 15 years and older. This compares to a rate of 139 male victims per 100,000 population" (Sinha, 2013). Such violence is debilitating and creates further barriers that prevent women from living a good life, such as mental health issues, substance use, and social isolation (Status of Women Canada, 2018).

Trans* Gender Analysis

Derived from Latin and meaning "to move across," trans* refers to gender identities that challenge the sex/gender binary system. As discussed earlier, normative discourse concerning the relationship between sex and gender is as follows: males are socialized as masculine to become men while females are socialized as feminine to become women (i.e., males-masculinity-men or females-femininity-women). Trans* identities disrupt this binary logic by decoupling sex and gender. As detailed in the discussion below, trans* encompasses individuals who identify as the sex opposite of the one assigned at birth (e.g., individuals designated as male at birth but identify as female). Trans* also helps to define individuals who transgress the gender binary such as feminine men and masculine women.

The asterisk after trans* was introduced to reflect an important lesson learned by transgender scholars and activists. Imagine this scenario: a coalition against gender-based violence on campus plans to host a fundraiser. Organizers create an event page on Facebook and, in an effort to be inclusive, list various identities that are welcome (e.g., transfeminine, non-binary individuals, **two-spirit** people). Despite their best intentions, the organizers alienate other gender nonconforming people because lists cannot be comprehensive. The asterisk gestures toward sex/gender as flexible and changeable categories and signifies the desire to include all trans identities within a critical gender praxis and efforts to achieve social justice (Tompkins, 2014).

When defining trans*, it is also necessary to recognize the importance of self-identification, as illustrated in this experience of an imaginary student. While grappling with the definition of trans*, they think: "Oh, I get it. Like my roommate's cousin who I just met, she looked and acted just like a guy—she must be trans*." While their roommate's cousin's gender performance may not conform to masculine **norms**, it is wrong to assume that they are a trans* person. Trans* as a specific identity must be self-declared and not assigned by others.

While often included within the LGBTQ acronym, trans* is a gender identity and must not be conflated with **sexuality**. Similar to other individuals within society, trans* people may identify as **heterosexual**, gay, lesbian, queer, asexual. Trans* is an umbrella term encompassing many subjectivities. **Subjectivity** refers to the ways that individual identity is constructed through interaction with systemic power relations.

Transsexual individuals identify with the sex opposite to the one they were assigned at birth. Transsexual women, such as Janet Mock, Laverne Cox, and Caitlyn Jenner, are individuals who identify as women despite being assigned male at birth and being socialized as masculine/men. Transsexual men, such as model and social media personality Aydian Dowling, identify as men despite being assigned female at birth. Transsexual subjects often desire medical treatments such as hormone replacement therapy and "gender reaffirming" surgeries to make their bodies reflect their gender identities. Medical transition processes, however, are not definitive of transsexuality because they are inaccessible to many trans* people for health or financial reasons, and are refused by other transsexual people for cultural or religious reasons.

Trans* also includes transgender people. Transgender subjectivities challenge the sex/gender binary by disrupting the taken-for-granted connection between sex and gender performance. Many transgender individuals, such as bigender-identified people, choose to honour their more feminine or masculine sides while not dis-identifying with their femaleness or maleness as assigned sex.

Non-binary identities are one of the most prevalent trans* subjectivities in North America, especially among youth (for example see Pyne, 2014). Non-binary gender performances challenge the rigid binary, as well as the containment of transgender identities to those that shift between two sexes (i.e., from male to female and vice versa) and two genders (from masculine to feminine and vice versa). Some non-binary people understand their gender identity as genderblending while others prefer to move flexibly between masculinity and femininity within various contexts and times (i.e., **gender fluid**). Agender (i.e., no gender) represents another non-binary identity where gender is refused as a defining factor of oneself.

The Trans* Politics of Resisting Erasure

In the late 1990s and early 2000s, trans* communities mobilized in major cities throughout Canada, the United States, and Western Europe to fight for the social recognition of gender nonconforming populations, as well as against trans* oppression. Part of these struggles has been to make trans* people's lives and struggles known to the **cissexed** or **cisgender** public. Cissexual and cisgender refers to people whose sex assigned at birth, and the gender associated with that sex, coincides with who they understand themselves to be. Cisgender people are the majority of the population, and their privilege stems from the **normalization** of their gender identity within sex/gender binary logic.

The sex/gender binary "erases" trans* identities and experiences (Namaste, 2000). Most governments, for example, do not gather vital statistics concerning trans-identified people on the census, nor is there a trans* or third gender option on birth certificates, driver's licenses, or passports in most countries (Australia, Ireland, India, Nepal, and Canada recently began to offer third gender options on passports). When documentation only allows for M or F sex designation, it is impossible for trans* people to exist categorically. The governance, in the Foucauldian sense of the term, of populations occurs through methods of inclusion and exclusion. Their gender identity as trans men, trans women, or non-binary individuals is either recorded erroneously to reflect the sex/gender assigned at birth or (if permissible) recorded to reflect their medicalized transition. If a transsexual woman transitioned from male to female and was born in a Canadian province that, for example, permits changes to the sex designation on birth certificates, her birth certificate and other government-issued identification could read female—her trans* identity and experiences would be erased.

Systemic erasure of trans* bodies occurs within general healthcare and trans*-specific healthcare. Imagine going to the doctor with a health concern and having them respond, "I don't know, I have never treated someone like you before," or going to the emergency room with a general concern and being treated as an enigma (Bauer et al.,

2011). More shocking are the cases where trans* people have been denied care in hospital emergency rooms (Bauer & Scheim, 2015) or received compromised care because their bodies and appearances did not match the sex designation on their health card or other government-issued ID (Welsh, 2015). In terms of physical health, trans* people experience difficulty obtaining a general practitioner who is willing to treat them, as well as medical experts who are knowledgeable concerning medicalized transitions. Medical school, nursing school, and programs to train paramedics often have little or no trans* content. This invisibility of trans identities, medicalized transitioning procedures, and an unfamiliarity with trans* health puts the well-being and the lives of trans* people at risk.

Think also about the language that is used to describe people as gendered beings. The erasure of trans* people in the healthcare system (and beyond!) also occurs through language, such as chosen names and preferred pronouns. For example, it is extremely uncomfortable to have to make one's way from waiting room to treatment room when summoned by a healthcare practitioner who uses one's birth name instead of chosen name, or when the doctor uses the wrong pronoun constantly when speaking with nurses.

Can you find the answers to how to best protect yourself against STIs, or do you disregard the educational material because it does not reflect your bodily sex or gender identity? Medical and public health professionals produce discourses reflecting the sex/gender binary by using the word penis when referring to males and vagina for females. This normalized assumption that bodies with penises are male and bodies with vaginas are female does not adequately reflect the experiences of many trans* people, whose anatomy may differ from their gender. Such discourses can be very upsetting for trans* people, whose right to gender self-determination is denied by it being assigned by someone else. Moreover, many trans*-identified people are uncomfortable with these terms and prefer other terminology.

Medicalized transition procedures also naturalize the sex/gender binary by pathologizing trans* people. To be eligible for gender-reaffirming surgery, trans* individuals must be diagnosed as suffering from gender dysphoria, a mental illness listed in the *Diagnostic and Statistical Manual-V* used by mental health professionals worldwide. Trans* individuals are argued to be dysphoric or confused concerning their gender, and therefore in need of treatment. Trans* activists, such as Dean Spade, argue that the discomfort that trans* people experience is not the result of an individual psychological or physiological malady; rather, the confusion stems from living in a society that adheres to essentialized and dualistic knowledge of sex and gender (Spade, 2006).

Essential social services are another societal location where trans* people are erased. Housing and shelter represent arenas where trans* activists have struggled for years for trans* inclusion. The violence against women (VAW) sector is one of the locations where struggles for recognition for trans* women are the most contentious. Despite being vulnerable to multiple forms of violence, including intimate partner violence and sexual assault, trans* women have been regularly denied access to emergency housing, longer-term shelters, and rape crisis centres. The *Nixon v. Vancouver Rape Relief* case encapsulates this struggle. Kimberley Nixon was denied the opportunity to continue training as a volunteer peer counsellor for Vancouver Rape Relief (VRR) upon being outed as a trans* women. In 2003, VRR argued its right to freedom of association as a private non-profit organization with a mandate and funding to serve women. In 2005, the BC Court of Appeals agreed that VRR has the right to define and limit its membership (Vancouver Rape Relief, 2009).

The Nixon case polarized many feminists into two camps—the trans exclusionary radical feminist (TERF) camps versus trans* feminists. The Nixon case reveals the ways that major theoretical tenets of radical feminism can lend themselves to justifying the exclusion of trans* women from women's spaces. Radical feminists' arguments are rooted primarily in biological determinism. Womanhood is defined for them by the interconnection between genitalia and other visible signifiers of female embodiment, and gender **socialization** as women. Radical feminists understand women's lives through vulnerability to the persistent threat of violence definitive of heteropatriarchy. Heteropatriarchy denotes how heteronormativity and **patriarchy** are interconnected governing systems that regulate women's bodies and sexualities, particularly in relation to reproduction. Women's bodies are not their own because young girls and women are sexually objectified, and this subordinate position impacts their lives, including their vulnerability to various forms of physical, emotional, financial, and sexual violence. It is this combination of biological determinism and the experience of growing up and living within a **culture** that naturalizes the objectification, control of, and violence against women's bodies that results in a subset of radical feminists adopting a TERF's argument against including trans* women within women's service organizations such as VRR. Different ideas and approaches exist among those who subscribe to radical feminism; in other words, not all radical feminists are TERFS.

Trans* feminists argue that female embodiment and gender socialization beginning at birth are not necessarily definitive of womanhood. Many trans* women knew they were girls at a young age, while others struggled because their gender identity did not fit the binary (Serano, 2007). As a result, they were often confused and injured by being socialized as male. Many trans* women tried to repress their feminine gender identities and lived closeted or conflicted lives, while others faced constant bullying due to the ways that masculinity is attained through the degradation of the feminine. Recall from earlier discussions that hegemonic masculinity performance is secured through competition with and the exclusion of others. Men often attain validation for their own expression of masculinity through differentiating and distancing themselves from women, as well as through violence against effeminate men.

Trans* feminists argue that trans* women are among the most susceptible to gender-based violence and are in need of services geared toward women. While data on violence against trans* people remain sparse, the US-based National Coalition of Anti-Violence Programs reported that, in 2013, trans* women comprised 72 per cent of hate violence homicides and were 1.8 times more likely to be subject to sexual violence than other survivors of sexual violence (Anti-Violence Project, n.d.). The Trans Pulse Project, a community-based research initiative that surveyed 433 trans* peoples residing in Ontario, reports that a quarter of participants reported experiencing physical violence and/or police harassment. Egale Canada (Canada's largest LGBTQ non-profit organization) launched its "Draw the Line: Against Transphobia Violence" campaign to provide multimedia education to address transphobic violence, especially against trans* women.[1]

Employment relations also privilege the sex/gender binary. When you apply for a job, do you worry about the name on your résumé not matching your legal name? Are you afraid that your former employer will use the wrong pronouns when providing a reference for you? Does your personal appearance match the sex designations on government-issued IDs and attached to your social insurance number? Trans* people are often unemployed because of the ways that normative sex and gender function as a qualification for employment. Trans* individuals are also frequently underemployed (i.e., working in a job that does not reflect their qualifications). The Trans Pulse Project surveyed 433 trans* people residing in Ontario and found that 71 per cent of respondents had at least some college or university education, yet half of them earned $15,000 or less a year (Bauer et al., 2011).

Employability is also dependent on employers' assessments of whether or not job applicants can perform the **affective labour** that produces positive feelings for consumers in post-industrial service economies (Lazzarato, 1996). Individuals whose appearance and personality represent the ideals of hegemonic masculinity and femininity are more likely to be hired for jobs that involve public relations. People who do not look, sound, or act like a "proper" man or woman will often not be hired at all (Irving, 2015). Gender norms also impact racialized workers whose hair (e.g., dreadlocks), accents, and tone of voice often marginalize them from employment (Newman, 2009).

Intersectional Analysis of Trans/gender

Critical trans/gender analysis involves intersectional analysis through uncovering the ways that sex and gender are inseparable from other power relations that we are exploring in this book: settler colonialism and whiteness. I organized this chapter intentionally to demonstrate the ways that even critical knowledge produced within Western universities can reproduce discourses legitimizing settler colonialism and whiteness. The chapter begins unpacking gender through an examination of the binary system governing gender and, indeed, many of our social relations. While important, the focus on this binary system that is characteristic of most gender analysis simultaneously obscures other relations of settler colonialism and whiteness. This invisibility is, interestingly, a form of privileging, because these power relations are obscured and therefore allowed to continue doing what they do. The rest of this chapter reaches back to some of the previous discussions to demonstrate the interconnectedness of gender with other systems of power.

Decolonizing Gender in Pedagogy and Praxis

Critical reading and analysis are political acts. To contribute to the decolonization of gender theory in the Western academy, we need to return to the sex/gender binary and the ways that gendered subjectivities are constructed. Prior to colonization, Indigenous cultures had their own knowledge of sex and gender that emerged from their "land-based communities" (Miranda, 2010, p. 266). Gender was understood in terms of the work one performs in society rather than identity or who they are as people. Roles were based on practicality (i.e., what needs to be done). Women cared for children, gathered and prepared food, managed the communities, and often assigned men their tasks. Men provided food and protection for their communities. Contrary to European patriarchal societies, masculinity and femininity were not understood hierarchically. Difference existed, but men were not believed to be better than women, and women were respected for their significant contributions to Indigenous societies (Simpson, 2011).

Many Indigenous cultures also had third or fourth gender-based categories for those who understood themselves as neither female or male, or as a blend of both. Gender was flexible and individuals could shift between performing men's roles or women's roles. Currently, Indigenous scholars and activists refer to such individuals as two-spirit (Driskill, 2011) or twin-spirit (Wesley, 2014). Like women, two-spirit people were respected within Indigenous communities and often played important roles in ceremonies, as healers, and as educators. Two-spirit or twin-spirit is an intersectional subjectivity that refers to Indigenous-identified individuals whose gender identification is both masculine and feminine, gender fluid, or non-binary; however, two-spirit also refers to Indigenous-identified people whose sexual subjectivity is non-normative (e.g., what is referred to as gay, lesbian, bisexual, queer, or pansexual within English-speaking settler society).

Settler Colonialism and Gendercide

The sex/gender binary system and discourses governing **normative gender** performance are integral to **settler colonialism**. As you read elsewhere in this book, settler colonialism is the physical settlement of land and the enactment of genocidal logic (Wolfe, 2006) to terminate Indigenous cultures and people. Colonizers engaged in physical and cultural violence against Indigenous societies and, as Scott Morgensen explains, "gender and sexuality appear not incidental but instrumental to the colonization of Indigenous peoples" (2015, p. 39). In fact, colonization occurred in significant part through acts of "**gendercide**" (Miranda, 2010, p. 259). The gendercidal nature of settler colonialism crucially involves a cultural component: attacks against Indigenous knowledge and cultures. **Residential schools**, for example, functioned as a site where Indigenous children removed from their communities were taught how to perform masculinity and femininity (Anderson, Innes, & Swift, 2012; Knockwood, 2001) according to Western binary logic and Christianity.

The normative discourses of gender that privileged European colonizers were shaped through colonizers' projections of their own fears onto Indigenous peoples (McClintock, 1995; Morgensen, 2015). Two-spirit people were often the first to be physically eliminated by colonizers. Colonizers would witness Indigenous people whose bodies shimmered between genders and label them as perverse, according to Christianity and patriarchal discourses. The elimination of such Indigenous gender identities functioned to annihilate what colonizers believed to be perversions "among or within themselves" (Morgensen, 2015, p. 45).

These acts of gendercide demonstrate that gender categories have contested meanings that have to be secured continuously to maintain their legitimacy. Alternative performances of sex and gender needed to be discredited to eliminate viable competing knowledge. Constructing the supremacy of white, property-owning males within settler-colonialist societies in North America, therefore, involved an attack on Indigenous masculinities and femininities. White colonial administrators and settlers were understood to be rational, intellectual, moral, and hard-working men, and this served as a justification for occupying Indigenous lands to build the white settler **nation**. This idealized version of white settler masculinity was not only formed in relation to its binary opposite (subordinated white settler femininity); it also established a racial hierarchy between men. White settler masculinities were **constituted** (came into being) by degrading Indigenous men and their practices of masculinity (their way of being men). Indigenous men were understood as savages, as the history of "westerns" (Hollywood movies that continually play out a battle between cowboys and Indians) attest; they were represented as violent, sexually aggressive beasts who had to be contained and assimilated into Western Christian values, if possible. And if not possible, physical elimination was justified.

There is an interconnection between settler colonialism, gender as an ongoing and dynamic process, and hegemonic masculinity as an idealized form of patriarchal masculinity. Western patriarchy is based on a hierarchical understanding of gender in which men are understood as superior to women and dominant over women, children, and the natural world. The imposition of Western patriarchal understandings of masculinity were devastating to Indigenous familial and community relations. Male dominance within politics, the economy, and spirituality erodes Indigenous cultures, which are rooted in equity and mutual respect for community members of all ages, genders, and sexualities (Anderson et al., 2012).

Traditionally based Indigenous masculinities were attacked through various colonial means that served to simultaneously weaken Indigenous men and their communities. Thievery of Indigenous lands enacted gendercide against Indigenous masculinity because Indigenous manhood is tied to the role of protector of the land and community, as well as the "sacredness of providing responsibilities" (Anderson et al., 2012, p. 272). Indigenous men lost their ability to protect the land and provide for their communities when treaties were enacted prohibiting them from using guns or horses, and placing Indigenous people on rations. Many Indigenous men were, and continue to be, placed on welfare and imprisoned (Anderson et al., 2012, p. 274).

Settler-colonialist gendered relations framing contemporary society continue to ensure the supremacy of white hegemonic masculinity. The acquittal of Saskatchewan farmer Gerald Stanley, who shot a 22-year-old Indigenous man, Colten Boushie, in the back of the head, serves as an example (Quenneville, 2018). Stanley's legal defence claimed that he was defending his family and property against a small group of intoxicated Indigenous teenagers who, Stanley alleges, tried to steal his ATV after the tire on their SUV went flat. Despite leaning into the front seat and shooting Boushie at close range with a handgun, Stanley was not understood by a jury to be a murderer. He was represented largely as a family man protecting his property from unruly Indigenous youth who trespassed onto his property with intent to steal. Centuries of Indigenous men being represented as unlawful, immoral, intoxicated, and violent (Boyden et al., 2014) permeate the facts of this case. More insidious, however, is the existence of the white Prairie masculinity, supported by the history of representations of Indigenous peoples discussed above, that makes Stanley's action "common sense." According to James McNinch, "we live in a binary world of heroes and villains, that honest hard work has defined Canada, and that Saskatchewan settlers 'pulled themselves up by the bootstraps' and 'became White.' (So why can't or doesn't everyone else?)" (2008, p. 95).

Indigenous women are consistently under attack within settler-colonialist society. Degrading Indigenous femininity and the vital roles that Indigenous women played in traditional Indigenous societies works to ensure white male supremacy and to privilege white femininity. Indigenous women are constructed as improper women who are immoral and dirty and whose bodies are vectors of disease (Razack, 2000). Such disparaging knowledge of Indigenous women works to produce a feminine ideal situated within whiteness, respectability (including sexual morality and proper motherhood), and middle-class professionalism. Similar to hegemonic masculinity, this idealized expression of femininity governs white settler women through its unattainability; even women with **race** and class privilege can never be good, hard-working, nurturing, proper, or attractive enough. This idealized category of the white female settler-subject is produced through being juxtaposed to the creation of the Indigenous woman as the dark, savage, and salacious Other. Such colonial knowledge that degrades Indigenous women illustrates the ways that violence against Indigenous women is not exceptional; rather, it functions as part of settler-colonial gendercidal relations.

Campaigns to draw attention to missing and murdered Indigenous women (MMIW) demonstrate particular forms of decolonial resistance to the ways that Indigenous women and cultures are systemically devalued within Canada as a settler-colonialist state. The fact that police have been slow to investigate reports of MMIW, as well as the failure of the Canadian state to launch an inquiry into this particular manifestation of gender-based violence prior to 2016, illustrates how the sex/gender binary is upheld through interconnected power relations including gender, whiteness, and colonialism.

Racialized Trans/Gender

Building on Achille Mbembe's concept of necropolitics, *queer* necropolitics engages with the ways that queer, racialized bodies are predominantly viewed by members of Western societies as inhuman and monstrous and are thus marked for death (Haritaworn, Kuntsman, & Posocco, 2014). Such understandings work on two registers: to naturalize white masculinity and femininity as **normal** and proper while, at the same time, degrading racialized men, women, and trans* people.

Normative gender processes are also interconnected with whiteness, Islamophobia, and anti-Arab **racism**. Post-9/11 discourses perpetuating the "War on Terror" illuminate the need for intersectional gender-based analysis. Reflective of a long history of Islamophobia and anti-Arab racism in North America, War on Terror discourses produce white masculinity as rational, moral, progressive, and strong while Arab and/or Muslim men (or anyone thought to be Arab or Muslim men) are seen as the mirror opposite—violent, primitive or backward, and weak. White masculinity is produced as heroic (e.g., New York City firefighters—see Carroll, 2011), while Arab masculinity is produced as villainous and terrorizing (Puar & Rai, 2002). Post-9/11 discourses also construct proper femininity through discourses of whiteness, **modernity**, and freedom through a juxtaposition that fabricates Arab or Muslim women as victims of Muslim men, trapped within their cultures and religion (i.e., in need of saving). Conversely, Muslim women are also constructed as terrorists whose covered bodies are held as suspect.

Discourses concerning blackness also contribute to constructing normative gender vis-à-vis whiteness and the nation. Political and socio-economic systems such as slavery objectified Black men and women in the true sense of the word—they were stripped of their humanity and understood as objects that white people could buy and sell (Harris, 1993). Meanings about Black men emerged from multiple sites, including scientific discourses such as pseudo-scientific studies that problematically argued that Black men's brains were smaller than white men's brains, making them therefore intellectually inferior. Other discourses produced the belief that Black men were physically aggressive, untrustworthy, immoral, and violent.

The #BlackLivesMatter movement makes important connections between the historical context and contemporary manifestation of racialized gender-based violence. In Canada, Black men such as Jermaine Carby and Andrew Luko continue to be viewed as violent and uncontrollable, and are therefore targeted by the police (Maynard, 2017). Additionally, in the United States, the murder of Trayvon Martin in 2012 by George Zimmerman, himself a racialized man, demonstrates the way that whiteness and hegemonic masculinity are secured by individuals within everyday life situations. Zimmerman, a resident of an affluent gated community and a volunteer for a neighbourhood watch association, believed Martin—young and Black—to fit the profile of those who are up to no good (Hancock, 2012). Zimmerman shot and killed Martin because Martin did not fit his understanding of the kind of young man belonging to his community.

The experiences of many white trans people, compared to racialized trans* people, also uncovers the interconnectivity between gender and race. Unlike Trayvon Martin, a cisgender young Black man, white trans* men have freedom of mobility and can traverse public space with relative ease. There are certain contexts where white trans* men are vulnerable if they are suspected of being trans*—for example, within change rooms in the gym, if they undergo medical transition on the job, or while crossing a border carrying a passport reflecting the "female" sex they were assigned at birth. Nevertheless, white masculinity extends much credibility to white trans* men and does not make them immediately suspect in the same way that racist discourses configure cisgender and trans* Black men as threatening.

Earlier in the chapter, I discussed how different locations such as healthcare, employment, and public spaces are sites where binary gender is reproduced. The case of Tyra Hunter illustrates an intersectional analysis of aspects of how governing discourses of healthcare determine whose bodies are validated as properly gendered and whose are produced as unhuman, undeserving of care, and disposable. Hunter, a Black trans* woman living in Washington, DC, was involved in a car crash while on her way to work. Members of the fire department, as first responders, began to treat the victims of the crash. When Hunter's pants were cut to treat her injuries, the firefighter cried out in front of a crowd of onlookers: "This bitch ain't no girl … It's a nigger, he got a dick" (Snorton & Haritaworn, 2013, p. 69). Not only did firefighters refuse Hunter further treatment, so did the doctor at the hospital who failed to order a necessary blood transfusion and did not insert a chest tube she required. Hunter died in hospital later that day (Snorton & Haritaworn, 2013). The firefighter's public outcry reveals the way that Hunter's unruly racialized and transgender body was marked for death. Critical scholars refuse to reduce her death to transphobia because her blackness also translates into the undervaluing of her femininity.

Conclusion

The sex/gender binary exists as a governing relation within North American society. Gender contributes to how we come to understand our selves and others, as well as institutions, social practices, and everyday interactions. While shifting over time and across space, hegemonic masculinity and femininity function as ideal forms of gendered embodiment and behaviours. As ideals, these prescriptive and naturalized forms of being in the world represent the values produced by patriarchy, settler colonialism, and the nation. These valued, hierarchical gendered categories are not innate or natural. Individuals are recognized as either belonging within the accepted understanding of what constitutes a proper man or woman, or not. As demonstrated in particular through discussions of trans* subjectivities and oppression, the gendered politics of belonging extend into healthcare, housing, and accessing public spaces.

While gender is often isolated for analysis, the ways that gender functions to order our everyday life experiences is mediated by other inequalities. We do not embody or experience gender without it being mediated by whiteness, settler colonialism, and the nation. These intersections produce significant differences within and between gender classificatory categories. Intersectional analysis and praxis, or putting theory into practice, is an important component of any resistance efforts or movements based in equity and social justice.

Study Questions

1 The case of Tyra Hunter exemplifies the necessity of doing intersectional analysis when discussing ways that racialized gender is replicated within healthcare and other social institutions. Discuss the death of Tyra Hunter in relation to the ways that femininity is mediated by other intersections of inequality.

2 Gender reveal parties are discussed in the chapter to demonstrate how knowledge concerning sex is produced through everyday life events. Using concepts such as naturalization and normalization, how does an anticipatory event such as the "big reveal" reproduce binary understandings of sex and gender?

Exercises

1 Google Jermaine Carby and Andrew Luko. Applying intersectional analysis, discuss how Black masculinity and Black male bodies are constructed as non-normative and threatening. How does the othering of Black masculinity trouble understandings of male privilege in patriarchal society? How is such knowledge reproduced by state violence and media representation?

2 This chapter highlights ways that individuals are implicated in reproducing the sex/gender binary, as well as ways that hegemonic masculinity and femininity are mediated by whiteness and other governing relations. Brainstorm how resistance occurs within our everyday lives.

3 Watch the documentary produced by Egale Canada addressing violence against trans* women and critique the video using concepts discussed in this chapter. https://egale.ca/portfolio/draw-the-line/

Note

1 For more, see https://egale.ca/portfolio/draw-the-line/.

References

Anderson, K., Innes, R., & Swift, J. (2012). Indigenous masculinities: Carrying the bones of the ancestors. In C. Greig & W. Martino (Eds.), *Canadian men and masculinities: Historical and contemporary perspectives* (pp. 266–284). Toronto, ON: Canadian Scholars' Press.

Anti-Violence Project. (n.d.). *Hate violence against transgender communities*. Retrieved from https://avp.org/wp-content/uploads/2017/04/ncavp_transhvfactsheet.pdf

Bauer, G.R., Nussbaum, N., Travers, R., Munro, L., Pyne, J., & Redman, N. (2011). We've got work to do: Workplace discrimination and employment challenges for trans people in Ontario. *Trans PULSE E-Bulletin*, *2*(1), 1–3. Retrieved from http://transpulseproject.ca/wp-content/uploads/2011/05/E3English.pdf

Bauer, G.R., & Scheim, A.I. (2015). *Transgender people in Ontario, Canada: Statistics to inform human rights policy*. London, ON: University of Western Ontario.

Bauer, G.R., Zong, X., Scheim, A.I., Hammond, R., & Thind, A. (2015). Factors impacting transgender patients' discomfort with their family physicians: A respondent-driven sampling survey. PLoS One, *10*(12), e0145046.

Boyden, J., Maracle, L., Sinclair, N.J., Johnston, B.H., Claxton, D., Moses, D.D., ... Thrasher, T.K. (2014). *Masculindians: Conversations about indigenous manhood*. Winnipeg, MB: University of Manitoba Press.

Butler, J. (1999). *Gender trouble: Feminism and the subversion of identity*. New York, NY: Routledge.

Butler, J. (2004). *Undoing gender*. New York, NY: Routledge.

Carroll, H. (2011). *Affirmative reaction: New formations of white masculinity*. Durham, NC: Duke University Press.

Connell, R.W. (1995). *Masculinities*. Berkeley, CA: University of California Press.

Connell, R.W., & Messerschmidt, J.W. (2005). Hegemonic masculinity: Rethinking the concept. *Gender & Society*, *19*(6), 829–859.

DiAngelo, R. (2011). White fragility. *International Journal of Critical Pedagogy*, *3*(3), 54–70.

Driskill, Q.L. (Ed.). (2011). *Queer Indigenous studies: Critical interventions in theory, politics, and literature*. Tucson, AZ: University of Arizona Press.

Dutta, A., & Roy, R. (2014). Decolonizing transgender in India: Some reflections. *Transgender Studies Quarterly*, *1*(3), 320–337.

Fausto-Sterling, A. (2000). *Sexing the body: Gender politics and the construction of sexuality*. New York, NY: Basic Books.

Fausto-Sterling, A. (2005). The bare bones of sex: Part 1: Sex and gender. *Signs: Journal of Women in Culture and Society*, *30*(2), 1491–1527.

Halberstam, J. (1998). *Female masculinity*. Durham, NC: Duke University Press.

Hancock, A. (2012). Trayvon Martin, intersectionality, and the politics of disgust. *Theory & Event*, *15*(3). Retrieved from muse.jhu.edu/article/484428

Haritaworn, J., Kuntsman, A., & Posocco, S. (2014). *Queer necropolitics*. Abingdon, UK: Routledge.

Harris, C.I. (1993). Whiteness as property. *Harvard Law Review*, *106*(8), 1707–1791.

Hegarty, B. (2017). The value of transgender: Waria affective labor for transnational media markets in Indonesia. *Transgender Studies Quarterly*, *4*(1), 78–95.

Holmes, M. (Ed.). (2016). *Critical intersex*. Abingdon, UK: Routledge.

Irving, D. (2015). Performance anxieties: Trans women's un(der)-employment experiences in post-Fordist society. *Australian Feminist Studies*, *30*(83), 50–64.

Kimmel, M. (2008). *Guyland: The perilous world where boys become men*. New York, NY: Harper.

Kimmel, M. (2013). *Angry white men: American masculinity at the end of an era*. New York, NY: Nation Books.

Knockwood, I. (2001). *Out of the depths*. Lockport, NS: Roseway Publishing.

Koyama, E. (2003). *Introduction to intersex activism* (2nd ed.). Portland, OR: Intersex Initiative Portland. Retrieved from http://www.intersexinitiative.org/publications/pdf/intersex-activism2.pdf

Laqueur, T. (1992). *Making sex: Body and gender from the Greeks to Freud*. Cambridge, MA: Harvard University Press, 1992.

Lazzarato, M. (1996). Immaterial labor. In *Radical thought in Italy: A potential politics* (pp. 133–147). Minneapolis, MN: University of Minnesota Press.

Maynard, R. (2017). *Policing black lives: State violence in Canada from slavery to the present*. Black Point, NS: Fernwood Publishing.

McClintock, A. (1995). *Imperial leather: Race, gender and sexuality in the colonial contest*. New York, NY: Routledge.

McNinch, J. (2008). Queer eye on straight youth: Homoerotics and racial violence in the narrative discourse of white settler masculinity. *Journal of LGBT Youth*, *5*(2), 87–107.

Miranda, D.A. (2010). Extermination of the Joyas: Gendercide in Spanish California. *GLQ: A Journal of Lesbian and Gay Studies*, *16*(1–2), 253–284.

Morgensen, S.L. (2015). Cutting to the roots of colonial masculinity. In *Indigenous men and masculinities: Legacies, identities, regeneration* (pp. 38–61). Winnipeg, MB: University of Manitoba Press.

Moyser, M. (2017). Women and paid work. *Statistics Canada*. Retrieved from http://www.statcan.gc.ca/pub/89-503-x/2015001/article/14694-eng.htm

Namaste, V.K. (2000). *Invisible lives: The erasure of transsexual and transgendered people*. Chicago, IL: University of Chicago Press.

Newman, K.S. (2009). *No shame in my game: The working poor in the inner city*. Toronto, ON: Vintage.

Pascoe, C.J. (2005). "Dude, you're a fag": Adolescent masculinity and the fag discourse. *Sexualities*, *8*(3), 329–346.

Puar, J.K., & Rai, A. (2002). Monster, terrorist, fag: The war on terrorism and the production of docile patriots. *Social Text*, *20*(3), 117–148.

Pyne, J. (2014). Gender independent kids: A paradigm shift in approaches to gender nonconforming children. *Canadian Journal of Human Sexuality*, *23*(1), 1–8.

Quenneville, G. (2018, February 6). What happened on Gerald Stanley's farm the day Colten Boushie was shot, as told by witnesses. *CBC News*. Retrieved from http://www.cbc.ca/news/canada/saskatoon/what-happened-stanley-farm-boushie-shot-witnesses-colten-gerald-1.4520214

Razack, S. (2000). Gendered racial violence and spatialized justice: The murder of Pamela George. *Canadian Journal of Law and Society*, *15*(2), 91–130.

Serano, J. (2007). *Whipping Girl: A Transsexual Woman on Sexism and the Scapegoating of Femininity*. Emeryville, CA: Seal Press.

Simpson, L. (2011). *Dancing on our turtle's back: Stories of Nishnaabeg re-creation, resurgence and a new emergence*. Winnipeg, MB: Arbeiter Ring.

Sinha, M. (2013). Measuring violence against women: Statistical trends. *Statistics Canada*. Retrieved from http://www.statcan.gc.ca/pub/85-002-x/2013001/article/11766/11766-1-eng.htm#a43

Snorton, C.R., & Haritaworn, J. (2013). Trans necropolitics: A transnational reflection on violence, death, and the trans of color afterlife. *Transgender Studies Reader*, *2*, 66–76.

Spade, D. (2006). Mutilating gender. In S. Stryker & S. Whittle (Eds.), *The transgender studies reader* (pp. 315–332). Abingdon, UK: Routledge.

Status of Women Canada. (2018). *About gender-based violence*. Retrieved from https://cfc-swc.gc.ca/violence/knowledge-connaissance/about-apropos-en.html

Tompkins, A. (2014). Asterisk. *Transgender Studies Quarterly*, *1*(1–2), 26–27.

Vancouver Rape Relief. (2009). *Chronology of events in Kimberly Nixon vs Vancouver Rape Relief Society*. Retrieved from https://www.rapereliefshelter.bc.ca/learn/resources/chronology-events-kimberly-nixon-vs-vancouver-rape-relief-society

Viloria, H. (2015). Promoting health and social progress by accepting and depathologizing benign intersex traits. *Narrative Inquiry in Bioethics*, *5*(2), 114–117.

Welsh, A. (2015). Transgender experience in the ER: I was a Freak Show. *CBS News*. Retrieved from https://www.cbsnews.com/news/transgender-experience-in-the-er-i-was-a-freak-show/

Wesley, S. (2014). Twin-spirited woman: Sts' iyóye smestíyexw slhá: li. *Transgender Studies Quarterly*, *1*(3), 338–351.

West, C., & Zimmerman, D.H. (1987). Doing gender. *Gender & Society*, *1*(2), 125–151.

Wolfe, P. (2006). Settler colonialism and the elimination of the Native. *Journal of Genocide Research*, *8*(4), 387–409.

5 Thinking "Straight"

ALIX HOLTBY

We're used to thinking about **sexuality** as a private, natural aspect of ourselves that we share with only those closest to us. But do you wear a wedding ring? Would you? Do you have ideas of what you want your wedding to look like (or what it did look like)? Do you ever talk with your friends about who you find attractive? If you've ever signed up for a dating service, did you state your **sexual identity**? All of these are practices through which we create and share an idea of what sexuality is. This chapter will focus on the last question—sexual identity. The goal of this chapter is to **denaturalize** the concept of sexual identity—instead of seeing sexuality as an intrinsic, inborn part of ourselves, I argue that our current understanding of sexuality is the result of certain historical and social processes.

We begin with the invention of the clinical concepts of **heterosexuality** and **homosexuality**, discovering that these are remarkably new ways of understanding sexuality that place an emphasis on gendered attraction as opposed to procreation. We then turn our attention to the active promotion of these categories that allowed them to grow from esoteric terms within scientists' textbooks in the early 1900s to culturally **hegemonic** ways that people came to understand themselves by the 1950s. We will observe how the late-20th-century debate on what "causes" homosexuality makes the category of "**heterosexual**" an unmarked **centre**: heterosexuality is actively produced and centred through **heteronormative** institutions and rituals (such as white weddings), and sexual identities are actively produced through our own thoughts and actions. Finally, we will consider the push from some gay, lesbian, and bisexual people to be included within these institutions, and consider whether some of their tactics reinforce rather than challenge the existing **power** structures in our discussion of the concept of homonormativity.

First, a note about terminology. Language regarding sexuality has changed considerably over the last century and is still in flux. As Irving discussed in the previous chapter, sex, gender, and sexuality are deeply interwoven concepts. Within this chapter, I use the term "**sex**" to refer to erotic practices, "sexual identity" to refer to how a person understands their erotic interests (often categorized as straight, gay, lesbian, bisexual, queer, and asexual, among others), and "sexuality" to refer to social meaning that is associated with erotic practices and identities. I will examine the origin and use of terms that were developed by Western scientists to label sexualities (e.g., heterosexual, homosexual), as well as those used as self-identification within North America (e.g., straight, gay, lesbian, bisexual, queer). The terms used to self-identify sexual interest in the same gender have varied over time: terms used in the early 1900s included "queer" and "fairy," while terms like "gay" and "lesbian" became more popular by mid-century. The term "**queer**" fell out of favour in the mid-20th century but was revived in the 1990s as a way of identifying **gender identity** and/or sexual identity that rejects the **sex/gender binary**.[1] While this chapter will focus on sexual identity, we will address some overlaps with gender identity, particularly in our historical analysis. The terms for gender nonconformity also changed over time, as you have learned in Chapter 4: the term transsexual was first used by doctors in the early part of the 20th century, while the term transgender is a self-identifier that gained popularity in the 1990s. In this chapter, I will use the clinical terms (heterosexual, homosexual, transsexual) when discussing the processes of **classification**, and the temporally relevant self-identifiers when talking about the people themselves.

The Invention of Heterosexuality

Why do we use gender as the defining feature of our sexuality? It's not the only option. For instance, one of the most common problems in sexual compatibility is difference in intensity of sexual desire (e.g., how frequently you want to have sex). Imagine a society where instead of primarily identifying ourselves on the basis of gender (e.g., straight, lesbian, bisexual), we identified ourselves based on how frequently we desire sex (perhaps "dailies," "weeklies," "monthlies"), making it easier to find partners with the same intensity of desire. How would that change how we understand ourselves, and how the world is structured? Why the focus on gender?

Sexuality was not always conceptualized with gender as the fundamental organizing structure. Heterosexuality and homosexuality are strikingly recent concepts: the terms were first used in the United States in 1892 (Katz, 1995). Earlier in the 19th century, the primary **dividing practice** in sexuality was between procreative sex within a marriage and all other forms of sex. Only vaginal intercourse that could produce a child within a marriage was seen as legitimate; all other forms of sexual activity (e.g., adultery, masturbation, oral sex, anal sex) were seen as sinful. Same-gender sexual activity was included within the category of sinful behaviour: it was seen as a behaviour equivalent to the other kinds of sinful behaviour.

Then, in the late 19th century, this began to change. Sexual scientists started to study people's sexual interests and created the categories of heterosexual and homosexual. Instead of sex simply being either sinful or not, scientists began presenting it as a way of defining a certain kind of person (Foucault, 1988).

Foucault (1988) identified this invention of new categories of people as an important part of a broader societal shift from religious to scientific authority. He saw the heterosexual/homosexual binary as a new form of **discourse** about sexuality. He argues that inventing the categories of heterosexual and homosexual didn't just describe the world as it was, but rather created a new kind of knowledge about a person: their sexual orientation. The invention of the categories of heterosexual and homosexual didn't reveal an already existing natural truth: instead, they invented a new kind of truth. Sex between people of the same gender went from being seen as a (sinful) behaviour that anyone could take part in to being seen as the defining feature of a certain kind of person: a homosexual. Alongside this came the invention of a new kind of **normal**: the heterosexual. The invention of the heterosexual/homosexual binary also functioned to invisibilize other kinds of sexual identity. While the term bisexual was also invented in the same period as homosexual and heterosexual, it took longer to be scientifically and culturally recognized as a category.

To be clear, when we discuss the "invention" of heterosexuality and homosexuality, we do not mean that people of the same gender weren't having sex prior to this time, nor people of differing genders. We are discussing the social categories through which we make sense of our world (e.g., heterosexual, homosexual) and associated social formations (e.g., nuclear families, white weddings, gay villages), rather than just erotic practices (e.g., sex between people of different genders and between those of the same gender). The social categories and social formations were new; the erotic practices were not.

The invention of these sexual categories wasn't unprecedented, but rather was part of a larger project of **science** at the time. Scientists drew upon new forms of **statistics** to define and measure **norms**: ways of being that they considered to be normal, from which other ways of being were seen as deviating. These classification processes weren't neutral: assigning one category as the norm was a process that assigned higher value to that category. In particular, when the concept of homosexuality was invented it was viewed by many as a psychiatric disorder—and was classified as such until 1973. Likewise, assigning other categories as "deviations" devalued these categories, presenting them as lesser ways of being than the norm. Other kinds of norms (masculinity, **whiteness**, physical ability) were being created alongside heterosexuality, all using similar, mutually reinforcing scientific logics of classification.[2]

In particular, when heterosexuality and homosexuality were invented, the concepts of sex, gender, and sexuality were much more integrated than they are today: a common belief of scientists in the late 19th century was that a homosexual man was a person with a male body and a feminine gender presentation and spirit, which caused the desire for sex with men. This category was also referred to as an "invert."[3] This term was counterposed to the category of the heterosexual, who was both **gender normative** and only attracted to people of another gender.[4] Within this model of sexuality, when two men had sex, only the man who was the receiver was seen as homosexual, as the other man was understood to be attracted to his partner's femininity (Chauncey, 1994).

In contrast, from the early to mid 20th century, the scientific understanding of the category of "homosexual" changed to mean only a sexual desire for those of the same gender regardless of gender presentation, which meant that both men in a sexual act were considered to be homosexual (Chauncey, 1982, 1994). However, the relationship between homosexuality and gender non-**normativity** continued to be researched by scientists, and the two are often still mixed together in popular understanding. This association began to shift in the mid-20th century in conjunction with the invention of the category of transsexuality to describe difference between sex and gender identity (Meyerowitz, 2004; Prosser, 1998). The categories of **cisgender** and **transgender** later followed at the end of the 20th century (Valentine, 2007).

These changes in how experts understood sexuality from the mid-19th to mid-20th century were happening alongside changes in material living conditions. As industrial **capitalism** rose in prominence and agricultural societies diminished, people moved from small, close-knit communities to larger, more anonymous cities. The necessity of children to one's livelihood also diminished, as people began farming less and working in more factory and office jobs. All these changes helped enable the creation of gay (and later, lesbian) communities (D'Emilio, 1997). While sex between people of the same gender had always been possible, it was now feasible to live as a part of an often-hidden community of gay people within a large city. These changes happened differently for women and men: men's greater independence enabled them to establish gay communities earlier. Women were less able to leave the confines of their homes and parental authority to establish lesbian communities—but due to the devaluing of female sexual desire through the discourse of female passionlessness, women were also freer to pursue romantic friendships with other women without necessarily being labelled homosexual (Cott, 1978).

The Consolidation of Heterosexuality

As gay, lesbian, and transsexual communities[5] began to become more visible, gender normative heterosexuality began to be seen as less of an inevitability and more the outcome of what was portrayed as the "correct" process of development. Freud's (1905/2011) psychoanalytic theories were an important part of this transition: Freud argued that everyone has bisexual potential, and that it is only through the "correct" navigation of multiple psychosexual stages that a person's erotic impulses will be channelled into gender normative, heterosexual adulthood.[6] This led to both more attention being paid to the cultivation of gender normative heterosexuality, and increased repression of gender and sexual non-normativity.

By the middle of the 20th century, heterosexuality had become a strongly valued cultural ideal. The 1950s are often portrayed as the epitome of traditional family values: they are idealized as a time when the heterosexual nuclear family was at its strongest. However, the ideals associated with sexuality and family at that time were quite new and quite fraught with tension (Adams, 1997; Coontz, 2005). White middle-class women who had been able to work for pay during World War II were pressured to return to the home and take on the role of mother as their primary identity. These changes limited these women's autonomy and were based on a narrow set of gender normative expectations for both women and men. Heterosexual relationships also changed in focus, with non-procreative sex for pleasure between married women and men becoming more highly valued. Norms for youth also began to change, particularly dating norms. Youth were encouraged to socialize with the other gender in order to foster their heterosexual interests (Adams, 1997; Bailey, 1989). New expectations for appropriate gender development for youths were created, which led to their development becoming more closely scrutinized.

One important moment in the process of the solidification of the concepts of heterosexual and homosexual in the broader North American public imagination was the publication of the Kinsey Reports (Kinsey, Pomeroy, & Martin, 1948; Kinsey, Pomeroy, & Gebhard, 1953). Alfred Kinsey was an American biologist who conducted one of the first large-scale quantitative studies of sexuality. Through interviews where he took detailed sexual histories from men and women, he found that many sexual practices that had been framed as deviant and non-normative were in fact engaged in by large numbers of Americans. These included practices such as premarital intercourse, masturbation, and sex between people of the same gender.[7] The finding that some behaviour that was considered non-normative (e.g., framed as deviant) was actually the statistical norm (e.g., more than half of people participated in it to some degree) revealed that the cultural norms were hegemonic ideals of behaviour as opposed to natural categories. However, this revelation did not eliminate the cultural norm of heterosexuality: in contrast, homosexuality was codified as a form of mental illness at nearly the same time as the Kinsey studies. The American Psychiatric Association listed homosexuality as a disorder in its first *Diagnostic and Statistical Manual*, which was published in 1952.

Alongside the rise of awareness of same-gender sexual activity came the increased repression of gay, lesbian, bisexual, and transsexual communities. For example, in the late 1950s, the RCMP began a program to monitor these communities and search for members of the military and public servants who were homosexual (Kinsman & Gentile, 2010). Police conducted surveillance at gay bars and other locations; those identified were often forced to resign from their jobs and often faced great public shame if their sexual identities became known. The RCMP invented a device known as the "fruit machine" that purported to be able to "detect" homosexual people based on their eye movements when shown photos of naked women and men; however, the device was based on faulty assumptions and never reliably sorted individuals (Kinsman, 1996). This repression was framed as a critical part of national security within the Cold War, with the argument that Soviet spies could blackmail gay, lesbian, and bisexual public servants. However, the hunt for homosexual public servants itself created the most pressure for these individuals to hide their identities and behaviours.

FIGURE 5.1 This 2018 vigil for the victims of a serial killer who primarily targeted gay men of colour in Toronto is a reminder that queer communities are not yet free from persecution, and their relationship with police remains fraught. Despite years of suspicion from both police and community members that a serial killer was operating in the Toronto gay village, queer communities argue that police were slow to take their concerns seriously and then did not sufficiently warn them of the danger. THE CANADIAN PRESS/Christopher Katsarov.

Foucault (1988) states, "where there is power, there is resistance": this is certainly true of the response to the repression of gender and sexual non-normativity. While the creation of the category of heterosexual produced new, discriminatory standards of normality that were used to police gender and sexual expression, the invention of new kinds of "deviants" such as the homosexual, bisexual, and transsexual also created categories around which many could organize their opposition. Further, while the Kinsey study's findings about the unexpected prevalence of same-gender sexual activity fuelled scrutiny of gay, lesbian, and bisexual people, it also spurred these communities to organize, as they had often previously assumed they were alone in their struggles. Kinsey's report, combined with the growth of gay, lesbian, and bisexual communities following World War II as well as the rise of other social movements, led to gay, lesbian, bisexual, and trans people beginning to publicly identify their sexual and gender identities and starting to organize as homophile activists in the 1950s, and then as gay liberation and gay rights activists in the 1970s. These movements spurred considerable change in both public perception of same-gender sexuality and legal rights, including the overturning of discriminatory laws and policies (e.g., decriminalizing sex between people of the same gender), and eventually the establishment of anti-discrimination laws and marriage rights in Canada and beyond. Some of the key moments in this history are outlined in the textbox.

Important Moments in LGBTQ History in Canada

1952—The *Immigration Act* passes, prohibiting homosexuals from immigrating to Canada.

1969—George Klippert becomes the last Canadian to be imprisoned for having consensual sex with another man.

1969—Homosexual sex is decriminalized in Canada following Pierre Trudeau's statement that "there's no place for the state in the bedrooms of the **nation**."

1971—*The Body Politic*, a prominent gay publication, is founded.

1971—We Demand, Canada's first public gay protest, is held in Ottawa.

1976—A protest is held in Toronto after 2 men are arrested for kissing on a street corner.

1977—Quebec becomes the first province to create legal protections against discrimination based on sexual orientation.

1978—Police raid the offices of *The Body Politic* for the distribution of obscene material.

1978—A new *Immigration Act* is passed, removing the restriction of homosexual immigration.

1981—More than 300 men are arrested in a series of police raids on gay bathhouses in Toronto. The next day, 3,000 people marched in protest.

1982—The first case of AIDS is reported in Canada.

1991—Delwin Vriend is fired from King's University College for being gay. He appeals to the Supreme Court, who rule that homosexuality is protected under the Charter of Rights and Freedoms.

1992—Canada lifts its ban on gay and lesbian people serving in the military.

1995—Ontario becomes the first province to make it legal for same-sex couples to adopt children.

1996—After being blocked multiple times earlier in the decade, sexual orientation is added to the Canadian *Human Rights Act*.

2000—Male police officers raid and strip-search lesbian, bisexual, and queer women attending a female bathhouse in Toronto.

2005—Bill C-38 passes, giving same-sex couples the right to marry in Canada.

2017—Trudeau apologies and pledges compensation for the purge of gay public servants during the Cold War.

2017—Gender identity and expression are added to the Canadian Human Rights Code.

2018—Police announce that a serial killer had been targeting gay men in Toronto. A suspect is charged with 8 murders.

For more on Canadian gay, lesbian, bisexual, transgender, and queer history, see Ganev and Gilmour (2016), Gentile, Kinsman, and Rankin (2017), and Warner (2002).

"Born This Way": Nature and Nurture

Scientists' interest with homosexuality did not end with the invention of sexual categories or the designation of homosexuality as an illness: the labelling of the category of the homosexual created the possibility for considerable research on the nature of sexuality. A major area of research in the later part of the 20th century concerned the origin of sexuality, specifically investigating what causes homosexuality.

This debate is largely between two perspectives: nature and nurture. Those advocating nature approaches argue that homosexuality is a physical condition rooted in the body that is present at birth. Thus, they use techniques of bodily truthing (Hegarty, 2003) to attempt to detect homosexuality: methods such as relative finger length, brain scans, and twin studies. Those advocating nurture approaches argue that sexuality is a learned behaviour that is influenced by one's upbringing and **culture**. Their research focuses on twin studies, parenting approaches, and birth order.

These nature and nurture perspectives do not line up neatly with pro-gay and anti-gay **ideologies**: gay rights activists have used both within their arguments, as have anti-gay activists. For examples: the "nature" position argues that homosexuality is an inborn condition that cannot be changed. This approach is helpful for demonstrating that sexuality should be a protected ground for civil rights as it is an immutable attribute, but has also been used as an argument that scientists should attempt to find a "cure" for homosexuality.

Some social theorists (e.g., Kinsman, 2003; Sedgwick, 1991; Stein, 2001) reject this debate outright: they argue that searching for the cause of homosexuality is not a useful question because it is based on the heteronormative assumption that homosexuality is a deviant category whose existence needs to be explained, whereas heterosexuality is simply accepted as the default. Why do scientists not question what causes heterosexuality? The scientific question of what causes heterosexuality is just as valid a research question but is rarely investigated. The category of heterosexuality is presumed to be natural while homosexuality is presumed a deviation, and thus the causes of this "deviation" are extensively questioned. Further, this debate reinforces the heterosexual/homosexual binary, examining only these two categories while disregarding people with interest in multiple genders.

The Production of Heterosexuality

Changing our approach to heterosexuality from a normative judgement (where it is assumed to be the natural, normal way of being) to a sociological judgement (where we see it as a set of practices that are specific to a certain time and place) enables us to ask new questions about heterosexuality. If heterosexuality is actually a relatively new social formation rather than simply a natural way of being, how has it become so common?

A key part of the answer is the system of **heteronormativity**,[8] which Martin (2009) defines as "the mundane, everyday ways that heterosexuality is privileged and taken for granted as normal and natural" (p. 190). Heteronormativity functions to obscure the role that heterosexuality plays in the production and maintenance of systems of power, enabling heterosexuality to seem like an inevitable, natural occurrence (Ingraham, 1994). Remember, heterosexuality does not just mean sexual relations between a woman and a man; heterosexuality is a culturally and temporally specific set of social, cultural, and institutional ideologies and practices such as white weddings (Ingraham, 2008) and nuclear families (Adams, 1997).

A crucial component of heterosexuality is the idea that gender is the most fundamental component of sexuality. Ideas about gender are thus key components of heteronormativity, as gender is based on the male/female, masculine/feminine binary that frames men and woman as opposite yet complementary components of a relationship (e.g., the idea that a strong, protective man complements a sensitive, nurturing woman). Sexuality, gender, and sex are all mutually reinforcing binaries: queer theorist Judith Butler refers to their connection as the "heterosexual matrix" (1990). Further, the masculine and the feminine are not understood or treated equivalently. A primary difference concerns **agency**: men are portrayed as the sexual "doers" who evaluate women's sexual attractiveness and decide which women to approach, while women are portrayed as the passive recipients of these decisions. Thus, "what confirms masculinity is being (hetero) sexually active; what confirms femininity is being sexually attractive to men" (Jackson, 2013, p. 30). The manner in which heterosexuality serves to create and reinforce gender asymmetries has long been an interest of feminist thinking. Second wave feminists noted that in addition to repressing women's sexual agency, heterosexuality serves to reinforce the division of labour between women and men (e.g., men work outside the home while women are responsible for housekeeping and childrearing) as well as unequal pay between men and women. Feminists have highlighted the manner in which heterosexuality was made to be compulsory for women, as it has often been difficult for women to live economically stable lives without male partners (Rich, 1980). Feminists today note the continued pressure on women to do the majority of childcare and housework, as well as the continued **inequality** of pay between men and women, as outlined in Chapter 4.

Heterosexuality is an active process: it doesn't simply occur, but rather is purposefully cultivated, institutionalized, and normalized. Adams (1997) describes how, when heterosexuality was becoming culturally dominant in the mid-20th century, explicit education was aimed at creating appropriate heterosexuality in youth and young couples. Marriage manuals, teen dating advice, teen delinquency programs, and sex education all helped to communicate and create norms for heterosexuality, including that it should be marital, intraracial, monogamous, and normatively gendered. Ideas and interpersonal "scripts" for heterosexual relationships and marriage continue to be communicated through magazines, movies, television shows, and other cultural products (e.g., Gansen, 2017; Maher, 2004; Martin, 2009).

One particularly visible cultural practice of heterosexuality is the white wedding. Consider some of the typical components of a wedding: a diamond engagement ring, a white wedding dress, the father "giving the bride away," and a first dance. These may

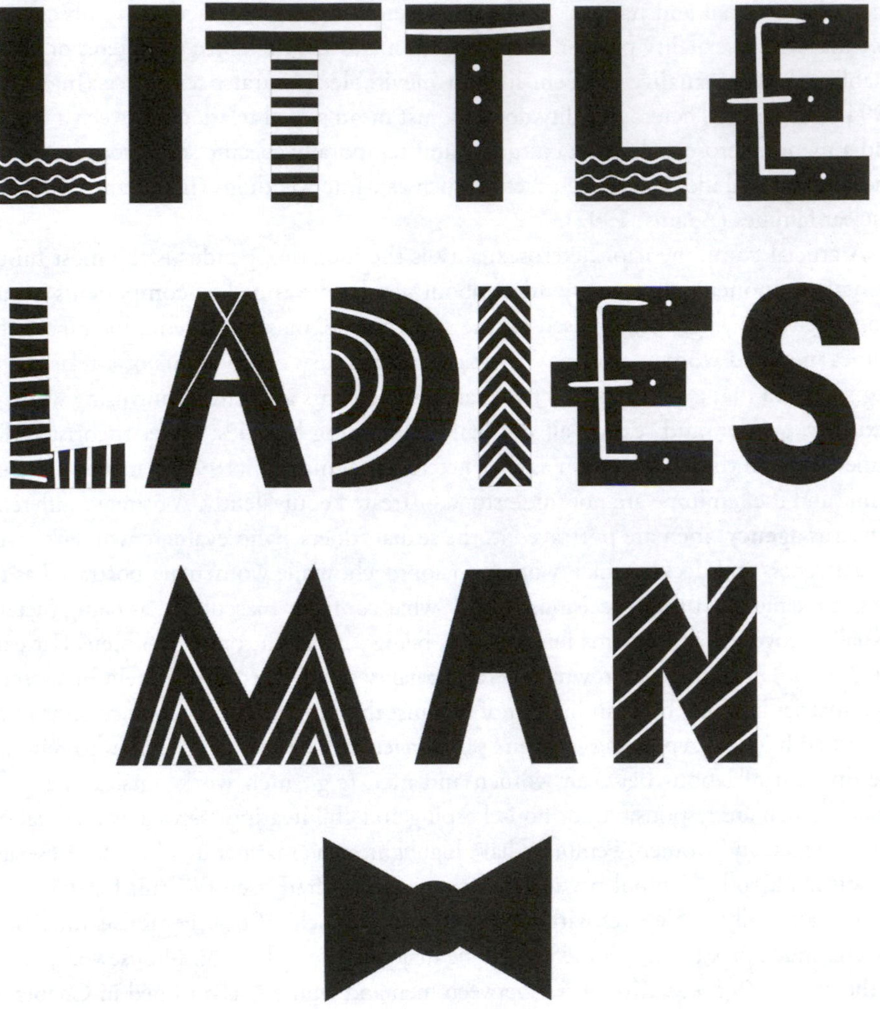

FIGURE 5.2 Small instances of heteronormativity surround us. This nursery poster may seem like it is simply a joke, but that joke reinforces the idea that all children assigned male at birth grow to identify as men, and that all men are sexually interested in women. This product is also an example of how heterosexuality functions as an unmarked centre: a similar product asserting that a child is gay or lesbian would be seen as making a political statement, whereas this product's assertion of heterosexuality is not. Oksana Stepova/iStock.

seem simply to be traditional, romantic, normal ways of getting married. However, these practices all have a history and reproduce certain celebrated forms of gender and heterosexuality, and some have a very recent history (Ingraham, 2008). For example, diamond engagement rings are the product of a 1930s marketing campaign by DeBeers, and white wedding dresses didn't come into fashion until the wedding of Queen Victoria in the 19th century. Prior to the elevation of the white wedding dress, wedding dresses used to become part of the bride's regular wardrobe after the wedding and, for most women, became the dress they wore for special occasions. The idea of the normal woman's wedding dress as an elaborate gown that is only worn once is a more recent phenomenon. While Victoria's choice of white material was primarily a **sign** of wealth (as white material is difficult to keep clean), the symbolism of whiteness as purity developed into the concept of white wedding dresses symbolizing the bride's virginity.

Marriage is idealized as a site of unconditional love, a way for that love to be culturally validated as appropriate, and a mechanism through which husbands and wives will have all their emotional and erotic needs met, with weddings as the most visible and ritual-laden celebration of marriage. The romanticism surrounding weddings helps obscure the ways in which marriage does not always live up to these promises, and indeed often has disappointing, stressful, and even violent effects, particularly on women. Some of the rituals of weddings, such as the father of the bride walking her down the aisle to "give her away" to her husband, romanticize the **patriarchal** roots of marriage as an exchange of property between families. The romanticism of weddings also obscures the role of the state in regulating these exchanges, including the Canadian government's practice of removing **Indigenous** women's **Indian status** if they married a non-Indigenous man, a practice that only ended in 1985. Further, many wedding practices glorify excessive consumption and marginalize other kinds of relationships. Other cultural practices of heterosexuality include Valentine's Day (Ingraham, 1994), prom (Best, 2000), and certain dating norms (Bailey, 1989; Farvid & Braun, 2013).

But what about same-gender weddings (or Valentine's Days, proms, and anniversaries)? Can we reconcile the increasing social acceptance of the participation of same-gender couples within these rituals with the idea that these are fundamentally heteronormative institutions? The answer to this question has two parts. The first is that ideologies like heteronormativity aren't fixed and they aren't totalizing: they can change and they don't determine all aspects of people's behaviours. People have agency and can act in opposition to norms, and in so doing can change the norms. The institution of marriage existed prior to the concept of heterosexuality: the cultural meaning of marriage changed as heterosexuality was consolidated, and it is now changing as same-gender marriage becomes normalized. The second part is that some types of advocacy for the inclusion of same-gender relationships within heteronormative institutions—such as marriage—can actually strengthen those systems, an idea that we will explore in greater depth below.

I Just Want What I Want … Don't I?

The cultivation of heterosexuality (and other sexual identities) doesn't happen only at the level of institutions, such as through the law or corporate media practices; it also happens within individuals. Our sexual identities feel like a natural, intrinsic part of who we are as people; however, that part of ourselves is constructed in relationship with our culture's ideas about sexuality. Just as we bring our genders into being through our actions, we also bring our sexualities into being through our actions. Some of these actions are very obvious: for example, a woman selecting to view only women's profiles in a dating app. But many of these actions are much more subtle.

We can turn to Foucault's concept of **governmentality** to help understand this process. Remember that governmentality refers not to political organizations, but rather to the processes through which we make ourselves and are made into particular kinds of people. When heterosexuality and homosexuality became the culturally hegemonic way to understand sexuality, individual people began understanding and producing themselves (and others) as heterosexuals and homosexuals (and bisexuals and queers). This isn't to say that sexuality is "a choice"—we don't exist separately from our sexuality, and sexuality is not as simple as someone deciding to be straight or gay. Instead, we should think of this as a kind of project of the self that is embedded within a certain socio-historical location: we make decisions like what to wear, what establishments we go to, what kinds of media to consume, who to befriend, and whose gaze to return in a bar within the process of fashioning ourselves into people who are straight or lesbian or bisexual or so on.

Heterosexuality Questionnaire

1 How did you first know you were a heterosexual?
2 What do you think caused your heterosexuality?
3 Is it possible that your heterosexuality is just a phase you will grow out of?
4 Our religion does not approve of "the heterosexual" lifestyle, so why can't you reject your heterosexuality on that basis?
5 Do you think you're heterosexual because of something your parents did?
6 Did you have a bad experience with a person of the same sex? Were you perhaps abused as a child?
7 If you've never had a relationship with a person of the same sex, how do you know you wouldn't prefer that?
8 Is it possible that you just haven't met the right person of the same sex?
9 It's practically impossible to watch a TV show, read a book, or watch a movie without heterosexual relationships being presented or emphasized. Why do heterosexuals place so much of an emphasis on sex?
10 Why do you insist on being so obvious and displaying your heterosexuality in public? MUST heterosexuals hold hands and kiss in public? Can't you just be what you are and keep it private?
11 So many heterosexual marriages end in divorce—why is it so few heterosexual relationships are stable?
12 Do you consider it safe to expose your children to heterosexual teachers, considering that statistics indicate that the majority of people found to be guilty of child abuse are heterosexual?

Because homosexuality, bisexuality, and queerness are considered deviant, marked categories, while heterosexuality is the unmarked centre, we're used to thinking that only gay, lesbian, bisexual, and queer people make decisions about how to negotiate their sexual orientations. See, for example, the textbox, a satirical questionnaire adapted from one created by Martin Rochlin in the 1970s that was designed to demonstrate the absurdity of questions that were frequently asked of gay people. However, heterosexual people also negotiate their sexual orientations. One recent study (Dean, 2014) examined the ways that heterosexual people construct boundaries between themselves and gay and lesbian symbols, social spaces, and people in order to signal their sexual orientations. Notably, Dean found that one of the central ways that people communicate their heterosexuality is through their gender presentation, such as through body language, clothing, haircuts, and other styling choices. For example, one man stated that he didn't cross his legs when sitting as he viewed this as a feminine behaviour that could lead to him being perceived as gay.

Intersections

Sexuality is never just about sexuality—it is always also about sex, gender, **race**, **class**, ability, religion, and age. All these different dividing practices intersect and co-constitute one another. We tend to discuss them separately in this textbook to reflect on their individual roles in structuring **power relations**, but they don't exist in isolation from each other.

This intersection has two effects: one is that distinct dividing practices (such as gender and sexuality) have a relationship with each other: the logic of gender draws upon the logic of sexuality, and vice versa. In this instance, sexuality (e.g., the hegemonic heterosexual/homosexual division) is predicated on a particular model of gender (e.g., the hegemonic masculine/feminine division). These two systems work in conjunction with another. For example, the term "fag" refers to a sexual orientation but is actually primarily used to police gender. In an ethnography in a high school, Pascoe (2012) found that teen boys don't primarily use the term "fag" to label a boy as desiring sex with boys, but rather to label that boy as incorrectly enacting their masculinity, for example by acting too emotionally. Rather than being used to label a specific individual as having a particular sexual identity, it is used as a way of policing all boys' gender presentations. These two systems of division (gender and sexuality) give meaning to one another.

The second effect of the intersection of multiple dividing practices is that the experiences within one category of division differ depending on membership in other categories of inequality: for example, the way that sexuality is policed is different for white women than for Black women. Due to the racist discourses of whiteness and purity, and blackness and animalism, Black women are seen as more sexually aggressive and sexually promiscuous than white women for the same actions (Collins, 2000). The intersection of racial, sexual, and class-based discourses can have severe consequences for women of colour: many of Canada's murdered and missing Indigenous women were labelled "high risk" by police and media due to their poverty and involvement in sex work (Jiwani, 2008), reinforcing the innocent/guilty binary and thus de-emphasizing the problem of violence against these women.

Homonormativity

The 1990s through to the 2010s included many gains for gay and trans rights in Canada, including the passage of Canadian anti-discrimination laws that included sexuality and gender as protected categories, the lifting of bans on gays and lesbians in the military, and the legalization of same-gender marriage. Following these gains, some suggest that the struggle is over and that sexuality is now a private matter for each individual. This idea was expressed in a cover story titled "Dawn of a New Gay" published in *The Grid*, a short-lived alternative weekly newspaper published in Toronto:

> A new generation of twentysomething urban gays—my generation—has the freedom to live exactly the way we want ... To be a twentysomething gay man in Toronto in 2011 is to be free from persecution and social pressures to conform. It's also, in most ways, not about being gay at all. (Aguirre-Livingston, 2011)

This sentiment contrasts with another quote, which is from a homosexual man who lived in Montreal in 1954, who felt he had to hide his sexuality in order to hold a job:

> I know a few people who don't care [if people know that they are homosexuals]. Those who don't care are really pitiful. They are either people who are very insignificant in position or they are in good positions but are independent ... I have to care a lot. (Leznoff, 1954, quoted in Kinsman, 1996, p. 163)

How did perception transition so quickly across half a decade? And are all gay and lesbian people really now free?

A crucial concept to understand this transition is **homonormativity**, a play on the concept of heteronormativity. Homonormativity was introduced as a concept at two distinct points in time. It was first used within gay, lesbian, bisexual, transgender, and queer communities in the 1990s to describe the phenomenon where primarily gay individuals attempted to distance themselves from transgender activism and individuals. They did so by emphasizing the division between sexual non-normativity and gender non-normativity, thus framing homosexuality as distinct from gender non-normativity. This approach sought to undermine the connections[9] that existed between transgender, gay, lesbian, and bisexual communities by positioning homosexuality as being more "normal" and thus less threatening to prevailing social structures, unlike being transgender, which was framed as radically deviant.

Homonormativity was introduced a second time in 2002 by Lisa Duggan, who described it as "politics that does not contest dominant heteronormative assumptions and institutions but upholds and sustains them while promising the possibility of a demobilized gay constituency and a privatized, depoliticized gay culture anchored in domesticity and consumption" (p. 179). Duggan's definition is broader and more directly critical, reflecting the ways in which some kinds of gay activism work to uphold rather than challenge fundamental **social institutions** such as marriage, the military, prisons, and capitalism. A central component of this form of homonormativity is its interconnection to whiteness: these institutions have traditionally and continue to disproportionately benefit white people (Ferguson, 2005). Puar (2006) has extended this discussion to create the concept of **homonationalism**, which describes the ways in which rhetorical support for gay rights is used by the state as a way to construct other countries, particularly predominantly brown[10] Middle Eastern countries, as backwards, uncivilized, and savage. This construction is then used to justify military involvement in these countries.

For example, in 2012, Jason Kenney, then the federal Conservative Immigration Minister, sent a mass email regarding Iranian gay and lesbian refugees at the same time as the Conservative party was speculated to be contemplating military action in Iran. Kenney wrote,

> I believe that Canada should always be a place of refuge for those who truly need our protection … We are proud of the emphasis our Conservative Government has placed on gay and lesbian refugee protection, which is without precedent in Canada's immigration history … In particular, we have taken the lead in helping gay refugees who have fled often violent persecution in Iran to begin new, safe lives in Canada.

Kenney's comment reinforces a binary that frames Canada as a safe, civilized nation in contrast to Iran's danger, which could then be used to justify military involvement in that country. The sincerity of Kenney's interest in actually cultivating Canada as a safe country for gay, lesbian, bisexual, transgender, and queer people is undermined by his history of fighting against the legalization of same-sex marriage, and his decision to remove references to gay rights from the guide for new immigrants to Canada.

All these concepts work together to highlight tactics that position a subgroup of gay, lesbian, and bisexual people as good, proper citizens that are deserving of being included in the current system, in contrast to a **radical** approach to politics, which strives to fundamentally change the current system in order to benefit all. It's not a coincidence that the main struggles the homonormative approach highlights, such as marriage, military involvement, and anti-discrimination laws, don't challenge the role of the state in the management of gay, lesbian, bisexual, transgender, and queer lives, but rather strengthen it. These approaches contrast dramatically with radical queer activism that challenges the current hegemonic family formation and its associated gender norms, resists the **neocolonial** role of the military, refutes approaches to discrimination that frame sexuality as being primarily an individual-level issue, and rejects the racially unjust prison system as an appropriate tool to use to better gay, lesbian, bisexual, transgender, and queer lives (e.g., INCITE!, 2016; Spade, 2015; Sycamore, 2008). Radical approaches highlight the intersections of issues such as poverty, **racism**, immigration, **neocolonialism**, and gender non-normativity with sexual non-normativity. Further, they recognize broader forms of sexual non-normativity, including sex work, BDSM, semi-public sex (such as in bathhouses), and polyamory.

We can apply a similar analysis to the claims made earlier by Aguirre-Livingston (2011) that today gay people are free to live how they want. His approach only considered the experiences of gay people at the centre—e.g., who are cisgender, wealthy, white men living in a large urban environment—who are fortunate enough to be able to live with minimal concerns about their sexuality. When we broaden the scope to include gay people with other intersecting identities, the story looks different. When Aguirre-Livingston's story was published, an outpouring of criticism came from Toronto's gay, lesbian, bisexual, transgender, and queer communities, including from some of the individuals he quoted in his original story (Elie, 2011). There was such a reaction that *The Grid* subsequently published a selection of readers' comments on the story, many of whom stated that the author's experience did not match their own. One stated, "Having grown up in a town of 2500 I literally was the only out gay (we had a lesbian couple) in the village. Mind you I am 29 so slightly outside of his 'enlightened generation' but my experience was quite different. I had a beer bottle thrown at me from a passing car. Hearing homophobic slurs, and language, and threats people would make if they met a 'fag' was a common occurance [*sic*]" (*The Grid*, 2011).

In Canada, lesbian, gay, and bisexual youth are between 1.6 and 15 times more likely to consider or attempt suicide than straight youth (Blais, Bergeron, Duford, Boislard, & Hébert, 2015), LGBTQ youth are approximately twice as likely to be homeless (City of Toronto Street Needs Assessment, 2013), and 34 per cent of gay men and 40 per cent of lesbian women have experienced discrimination at work (Angus Reid, 2011). In the United States, there are no federal anti-discrimination protections for homosexuality, which means that in a number of states it is currently legal to be fired for being gay, lesbian, bisexual, or queer. While homonormativity allows some gay people who are otherwise in the centre to feel like there are no restrictions on their lives, there clearly remains work to be done to enable all gay, lesbian, bisexual, transgender, and queer people to feel the same.

Conclusion: Beyond Acceptance

We're often encouraged to see sexuality as a private matter that is unconnected to politics, institutions, or public life. However, Foucault argues that sexuality is an enormously important area for social research because it has intimate connections both to our bodies (and their pleasures and dangers) and to our populations (and their reproduction and composition). As sexuality is a matter of governance both of the self and of life itself, it should be no surprise that is has been an important area for social struggle and change.

The goal of this chapter has been to denaturalize the heterosexual/homosexual binary: to show that this is not the inevitable way of organizing and understanding sexuality, but rather one particular way that emerged from a specific cultural context. Further, heterosexuality is a recent organizational form and one that could potentially change. By denaturalizing heterosexuality, we can see that "how heterosexuality develops" is just as valid a research inquiry as how other forms of sexuality develop, and we can observe that the development of heterosexuality is an active process carried out through media **representation**, social norms, and cultural practices. Further, people take on the project of having sexual identities and sculpt their actions to match those identities. Finally, we reflected on how forms of gay advocacy can themselves reinforce dominant norms through homonormativity.

Homonormative approaches to gay advocacy assume that the current organization of power within society is fundamentally correct, with the exception of the treatment of same-sex sexuality. This approach doesn't challenge institutions, but rather seeks for same-sex sexuality to be accepted within them. Homonormative approaches can have important beneficial effects, but they affect gay, lesbian, bisexual, transgender, and queer people unevenly: people who are marginalized only by their sexual identity benefit most, while those who are multiply marginalized benefit less. In contrast, we could imagine a system of "bottom-up" advocacy (Spade, 2015) that centres the needs of people most marginalized while benefiting all.

Study Questions

1 What does it mean to argue that heterosexuality was invented in the 19th century? Why is that important to how we should approach the sociological study of sexuality?
2 Define heteronormativity and homonormativity. Do these two systems work in opposition to each other or in coordination with each other? How?
3 Why does Foucault think sexuality is such a fertile ground to study the arrangement of power? Describe how Foucault's different types of power apply to the regulation of sexuality.

Exercises

1 Find a bridal magazine. What is communicated about gender and marriage through its articles and advertisements? Think about the different intersections with sexuality (sex, race, class, age, ability): who is represented within the magazine? How are they represented?

2 Consider your own sexual orientation. What do you do to communicate your sexual orientation? Have you ever been criticized for acting in a way that isn't gender or sexually normative?
3 Watch a few episodes of your favourite television shows, and pay attention to how they portray erotic activities between women and men. Do you notice any commonalities in the "scripts" for how these sequences play out? Are there similarities between how the men act? How the women act? Do they show any erotic activities between people of the same gender? If so, do they follow the same "script"?

Notes

1 The 1990s revival of queer as a self-identifier was related to the formation of a type of social theory (queer theory) rooted in the work of Eve Sedgwick and Judith Butler, as well as an American activist group (Queer Nation).
2 While Foucault discusses the impact of race science on the production of heterosexuality, he has been critiqued on his description of the process and chronology of processes of colonialization and racialization (e.g., Stoler, 1995; McWhorter, 2004).
3 What exactly defined a homosexual/an invert was debated at the time. Some considered homosexuality/inversion to be purely defined by feminine gender expression and saw same-gender sexual desire as incidental to the category of homosexuality.
4 The change from a division based on procreation to one based on gendered desire wasn't immediate. Indeed, when the term "heterosexual" was first coined, it meant someone with a "perverted" interest in non-procreative sex with the other gender (Katz, 1995), in contrast to someone only interested in procreative sex.
5 While the scientific categories of homosexuality and transsexuality were being disentangled at this time, the gay, lesbian, and transsexual communities were still tightly interwoven, with many people's self-understandings merging together the categories of gender and sexuality.
6 While Freud believed homosexuality to be an unfortunate consequence of an incorrect upbringing, he did not condemn homosexuality and didn't see it as either an illness or a crime (Abelove, 1986).
7 The most well circulated fact from the Kinsey studies (that 1 in 10 people are homosexual) is apocryphal: Kinsey strongly argued that it was impossible to separate individuals into the categories of heterosexual and homosexual. Instead, he viewed sexual desire and behaviour as a spectrum, and invented a new kind of system to conceive of sexuality (the Kinsey scale).
8 Sometimes "**homophobia**" is used to denote the centering of heterosexuality within society. This term was first coined by activists as a reaction to the medical

category of "homosexual": it was a way to reverse the argument that homosexuality was an illness, saying instead that the hatred of homosexuality was the real illness. While initially useful, this language individualizes heteronormative processes, making their social structural patterns harder to see (for more, see Kinsman, 1996, p. 33).

9 While sexual and gender non-normativity were largely combined in both community and public understanding up to this time, power inequalities existed within this coalition. Lesbian, bisexual, and transgender people have all protested their marginalization within movement organizing, as have racialized, sex-working, and poor individuals.

10 "Brown" refers to a social categorization of race that is primarily based on skin colour and is used in some places, including North America, to refer to people from certain African, Asian, and South American countries.

References

Abelove, H. (1986). Freud, male homosexuality, and the Americans. *Dissent, 33*(1), 59–69.

Adams, M.L. (1997). *The trouble with normal: Postwar youth and the making of heterosexuality.* Toronto, ON: University of Toronto Press.

Aguirre-Livingston, P. (2011, June 9). Dawn of a new gay. *The Grid.* Retrieved from https://web.archive.org/web/20110611224330/; http://www.thegridto.com:80/city/sexuality/dawn-of-a-new-gay/

Angus Reid. (2011). *Most LGBT working Canadians experience tolerance but some discrimination persists.* Retrieved from http://angusreid.org/most-lgbt-working-canadians-experience-tolerance-but-some-discrimination-persists/

Bailey, B.L. (1989). *From front porch to back seat: Courtship in twentieth-century America.* Baltimore, MD: Johns Hopkins University Press.

Best, A.L. (2000). *Prom night: Youth, schools, and popular culture.* New York, NY: Routledge.

Blais, M., Bergeron, F.-A., Duford, J., Boislard, M.-A., & Hébert, M. (2015). Health outcomes of sexual-minority youth in Canada: An overview. *Adolescencia & Saude, 12*(3), 53–73.

Butler, J. (1990). *Gender trouble.* New York, NY: Routledge.

Chauncey, G. (1982). From sexual inversion to homosexuality: Medicine and the changing conceptualization of female deviance. *Salmagundi,* (58/59), 114–146.

Chauncey, G. (1994). *Gay New York: Gender, urban culture, and the makings of the gay male world, 1890–1940.* New York, NY: Basic Books.

City of Toronto. (2013). *Street needs assessment.* Retrieved from https://www.toronto.ca/legdocs/mmis/2013/cd/bgrd/backgroundfile-61365.pdf

Collins, P.H. (2000). *Black feminist thought: Knowledge, consciousness, and the politics of empowerment* (Rev. 10th anniversary ed.). New York, NY: Routledge.

Coontz, S. (2005). *The way we never were: American families and the nostalgia trap.* New York, NY: Basic Books.

Cott, N.F. (1978). Passionlessness: An interpretation of victorian sexual ideology, 1790–1850. *Signs: Journal of Women in Culture and Society, 4*(2), 219–236.

Dean, J.J. (2014). *Straights: Heterosexuality in post-closeted culture*. New York, NY: New York University Press.

D'Emilio, J. (1997). Capitalism and gay identity. In R.N. Lancaster & M. di Leonardo (Eds.), *The gender/sexuality reader: Culture, history, political economy* (pp. 169–178). New York, NY: Routledge.

Duggan, L. (2002). The new homonormativity: The sexual politics of neoliberalism. In R. Castronovo & D. Nelson (Eds.), *Materializing democracy: Toward a revitalized cultural politics* (pp. 175–194). Durham, NC: Duke University Press.

Elie. (2011, June 10). Why I am ashamed to be on the cover of the grid. *The Gaily*. Retrieved from http://thegaily.ca/editorials/why-i-am-ashamed-to-be-on-the-cover-of-grid/

Farvid, P., & Braun, V. (2013). Casual sex as "not a natural act" and other regimes of truth about heterosexuality. *Feminism & Psychology*, *23*(3), 359–378.

Ferguson, R.A. (2005). Race-ing homonormativity: Citizenship, sociology, and gay identity. In E.P. Johnson & M. Henderson (Eds.), *Black queer studies: A critical anthology* (pp. 52–67). Durham, NC: Duke University Press.

Foucault, M. (1988). *The history of sexuality*. New York, NY: Vintage Books.

Freud, S. (2011). *Three essays on the theory of sexuality* (J. Strachey, Trans.). Mansfield Centre, CT: Martino Publishing.

Ganev, R., & Gilmour, R. (Eds.). (2016). *Queers were here: Heroes & icons of queer Canada*. Windsor, ON: Biblioasis.

Gansen, H.M. (2017). Reproducing (and disrupting) heteronormativity: Gendered sexual socialization in preschool classrooms. *Sociology of Education*, *90*(3), 255–272.

Gentile, P., Kinsman, G., & Rankin, L.P. (Eds.). (2017). *We still demand! Redefining resistance in sex and gender struggles*. Vancouver, BC: UBC Press.

The Grid. (2011, June 15). Dawn of a new gay: The response. Retrieved from https://web.archive.org/web/20110618051157/http://www.thegridto.com:80/city/sexuality/dawn-of-a-new-gay-the-response/

Hegarty, P. (2003). Pointing to a crisis? What finger-length ratios tell us about the construction of sexuality. *Radical Statistics*, *83*, 16–30.

INCITE! (Ed.). (2016). *Color of violence: The INCITE! anthology*. Durham, NC: Duke University Press.

Ingraham, C. (1994). The heterosexual imaginary: Feminist sociology and theories of gender. *Sociological Theory*, *12*(2), 203–219.

Ingraham, C. (2008). *White weddings: Romancing heterosexuality in popular culture* (2nd ed.). New York, NY: Routledge.

Jackson, S. (2013). Sexuality, heterosexuality and gender hierarchy: Getting our priorities straight. In C. Ingraham (Ed.), *Thinking straight: The power, promise and paradox of heterosexuality* (pp. 20–42). Abingdon, UK: Routledge.

Jiwani, Y. (2008). Mediations of domination: Gendered violence within and across borders. In K. Sarikakis & L.R. Shade (Eds.), *Feminist interventions in international communication* (pp. 129–145). New York, NY: Rowman & Littlefield.

Katz, J. (1995). *The invention of heterosexuality*. New York, NY: Dutton.

Kinsey, A.C. (Ed.). (1953). *Sexual behavior in the human female*. Philadelphia, PA: Saunders.

Kinsey, A.C., Pomeroy, W.B., & Martin, C.E. (1948). *Sexual behavior in the human male*. Philadelphia, PA: Saunders.

Kinsman, G.W. (1996). *The regulation of desire: Homo and hetero sexuality*. Montréal, QC: Black Rose Books.

Kinsman, G.W. (2003). Queerness is not in our genes: Biological determinism versus social liberation. In D. Brock (Ed.), *Making normal: Social regulation in Canada* (pp. 262–284). Toronto, ON: Nelson Thomson Learning.

Kinsman, G.W., & Gentile, P. (2010). *The Canadian war on queers: National security as sexual regulation*. Vancouver, BC: UBC Press.

Maher, J. (2004). What do women watch? Tuning in to the compulsory heterosexuality channel. In S. Murray & L. Ouellette (Eds.), *Reality TV: Remaking television culture* (pp. 197–213). New York, NY: New York University Press.

Martin, K.A. (2009). Normalizing heterosexuality: Mothers' assumptions, talk, and strategies with young children. *American Sociological Review*, *74*(2), 190–207.

McWhorter, L. (2004). Sex, race, and biopower: A Foucauldian genealogy. *Hypatia*, *19*(3), 38–62.

Meyerowitz, J. (2004). *How sex changed*. London, UK: Harvard University Press.

Pascoe, C.J. (2012). *Dude, you're a fag: Masculinity and sexuality in high school*. Berkeley, CA: University of California Press.

Prosser, J. (1998). Transsexuals and the transsexologists: Inversion and the emergence of transsexual subjectivity. *Sexology in Culture: Labelling Bodies and Desires*, 116–131.

Puar, J.K. (2006). Mapping US homonormativities. *Gender, Place & Culture*, *13*(1), 67–88.

Rich, A. (1980). Compulsory heterosexuality and lesbian existence. *Signs: Journal of Women in Culture and Society*, *5*(4), 631–660.

Sedgwick, E.K. (1991). *Epistemology of the closet*. Berkeley, CA: University of California Press.

Spade, D. (2015). *Normal life: Administrative violence, critical trans politics, and the limits of law* (Rev. and expanded ed.). Durham, NC: Duke University Press.

Stein, E. (2001). *The mismeasure of desire: The science, theory, and ethics of sexual orientation*. Oxford, UK: Oxford University Press.

Stoler, A.L. (1995). *Race and the education of desire: Foucault's history of sexuality and the colonial order of things*. Durham, NC: Duke University Press.

Sycamore, M.B. (Ed.). (2008). *That's revolting! Queer strategies for resisting assimilation* (New rev. and expanded ed.). Brooklyn, NY: Soft Skull Press.

Valentine, D. (2007). *Imagining transgender: An ethnography of a category*. Durham, NC: Duke University Press.

Warner, T. (2002). *Never going back: A history of queer activism in Canada*. Toronto, ON: University of Toronto Press.

6 Whiteness Invented

MELANIE KNIGHT

"White people—they run the court system."
"Enough," she said. "We're going to fight back … Enough killing our people."
– Debbie Baptiste (McKeen, 2018)

On 9 February 2018, a jury in North Battleford, Saskatchewan, acquitted farmer Gerald Stanley of second-degree murder in the death of a Red Pheasant Cree Nation man, Colten Boushie. The case has fuelled racial tensions throughout the country. It will be interesting as time passes to see how the media frames this tragic event, although we can already see glimpses of where opinion is heading. Some report that deaths like Boushie's can only be prevented by "breaking the cycle of violence" (Kheiriddin, 2018). We are not sure which cycle of violence is meant in these media reports. Prime Minister Trudeau's response to the family has been met with harsh criticism. Some question why, unlike Obama during the shooting of Trayvon Martin,[1] Trudeau did not "call for calm" or "defend the system that underpins the very rights and freedoms his own father enshrined in the Charter of Rights" (Kheiriddin, 2018). Many in support of Stanley assert that the verdict had nothing to do with race, but with crime: a crime was in progress, and a farmer defended his family and property. A slew of racist comments, many from white farmers, surfaced after Boushie's death. An anonymous RCMP officer in Western Canada wrote this Facebook post:

> Too bad the kid died but he got what he deserved … Crimes were committed and a jury found the man not guilty of protecting his home and family. … It should be sending a message to the criminal element that his crap is not going to be tolerated and if you value your life then stay away from what isn't yours. (Isai, 2018)

For the Boushie family and supporters, the case was all about **race**—specifically, about **whiteness** at work. The Boushie family has called into question the conduct of Royal Canadian Mounted Police officers on the night of Colten's death: the officers had entered their home without permission and with weapons drawn. When Colten's mother lay on the floor in disbelief, she was told to "get herself together," and asked whether she had been drinking (Friesen, 2018). An internal investigation cleared the Mounties of any wrongdoing. The RCMP's initial news release about the killing said that the **Indigenous** youth present on the farm were the suspects in a theft investigation, thereby framing the shooting in relation to the stereotyped criminality of Indigenous youth. Media picked up on this, describing Boushie as a suspect and not a victim (Warick, 2018). They sometimes discussed the "Colten Boushie trial" instead of the "Gerald Stanley trial." A slew of anti-Indigenous hate posts online, for which no one was held responsible, also followed.

Saskatchewan Farmers Group

Public Group • 4115 Members

a group made for farmers of all generations to share stories, pictures, fuck ups, how to's, reviews, questions, and for sale adds.

Mark Huck
He should have shot all 5 of them and given a medal.

Jason Finley
Mark Huck Check out this comment lol.

[illegible screenshot of Facebook post]

Mark Huck
Wow!!

Scott Dickson
Wtf!

(no name visible)
Fucking indian

FIGURE 6.1 Racism exposed in the public "Saskatchewan Farmers Group" on Facebook following Colten Boushie's death. Piapot, N. (2016, August 13). Sask. RCMP 'fueled hate' after Indigenous man shot dead, say chiefs. Vice. https://www.vice.com/en_ca/article/xdmpq4/sask-rcmp-fueled-hate-after-indigenous-man-shot-dead-say-chiefs

Jason Jones
Is he one of the chugs that was in the car?

Jason Finley
Yeah He was the one killed.

Michael Rempel
one native on another part of Facebook claims this was a song lyric, but either way...

Jason Finley
Michael Rempel i really hope that is true. Terrible situation for both parties, but something surely needs to change.

Michael Rempel
yeah, sure would be nice to hear from the farmer himself instead of all the natives spreading the victim crap

Paul Drew
Whatever, he's brown bread now.

Lucas Kriger
His only mistake was leaving three witnesses

FIGURE 6.1 (Continued)

This case is about race. For many, a white, settler, **colonial**, so-called justice system forced thousands of Indigenous children into **residential schools**, continued with the **Sixties Scoop,**[2] and is present in the racist child welfare system today. This same system has yet to provide justice for many missing and murdered Indigenous women, and incarcerates Indigenous people at a rate exceedingly higher than that of non-Indigenous people. The question of whether Gerald Stanley as an individual is racist is not the right question to ask. To focus on Stanley, as an individual, individualizes and dehistoricizes the issue.

Whiteness, as does other systems of oppression, has a history. In this chapter, I begin with a focus on history and rely on the work of critical race theorist Cheryl I. Harris (1993) and her article, "Whiteness as Property," which encapsulates and articulates many questions we have about whiteness and **power**. The article largely focuses on the context of the US, details the social construction of race and emergence of whiteness, its boundedness in law, and its power as property. In addition to my focus on Harris,

I also integrate a Canadian frame of reference even though research on whiteness from a socio-historical legal lens in Canada is sparse in comparison to that of the US. In the second half of the chapter, I examine the plethora of studies that have focused on whites' understanding of whiteness. The overall imperative of the chapter is to expose whiteness and the strategies/practices that sustain and reproduce its normalcy and centrality in order to "deconstruct it as the locus from which Other differences are calculated and organized" (Nakayama & Krizek, 1999, p. 95). After showing the ways in which whiteness was organized and legally established in the colonial history of North America, I shift to ways in which patterns of everyday language and thinking among whites in the present work to deny and obscure that history, thereby preventing adequate redress and further entrenching **white supremacy** as the rightful social order.

Whiteness as Property

As a way of entering discussions on whiteness, some speakers or writers begin by overtly putting whiteness or **white privilege** at the forefront or at the onset of conversations, almost as a disclaimer, e.g., "Let me first say that I'm a white heterosexual male …" I see this as a politics of self-disclosure, a strategy that misses the mark. Ahmed (2004) discussed a politics of declaration which is enacted when institutions or individuals "'admit' to forms of bad practice, and … the 'admission' itself becomes seen as good practice" (para. 11). This happens when we hear apologies, for instance, for past injustices against marginalized communities. She argued that declarations are "non-performative" in that they conflate "saying" and "doing" (Ahmed, 2004, para. 54). The "saying" serves to transcend historical injustices. Self-disclosures, unless accompanied by restorative action, are non-substantive. Adding this racial disclaimer ensures that one does not have to do any of the work required to unpack/undo systemic power. Power is rendered individualized, and there is a veneer of accountability. The imperative to make visible networks of power in the hope of democratizing them cannot happen through self-disclosure. We must instead enter any conversation about whiteness through a legal, historical lens.

Harris's (1993) story begins with her grandmother's experience of passing for white in the 1930s while living in Chicago. Although not unique, her grandmother's experience speaks of the benefits and privileges—highly sought after and legally protected by whites—that accompanied the status of being white. Historically, under various systems of slavery and **colonialism**, white identity became the basis of privilege that was "ratified and legitimated in law." Much later, this evolved into the expectation of white privilege as "a legitimate and natural baseline" (Harris, 1993, p. 1714).

The origins of whiteness as property, Harris (1993) argues, lie "in *the parallel* systems of domination of Black and Native American peoples out of which were created racially **contingent** forms of property and property rights" (p. 1714). She argues that in the historical oppression of both Black and Native Americans, race and property[3] established economic subordination, albeit in different ways. Perhaps surprisingly to some, racial lines as we know them today were not heavily entrenched in the 1600s in what later became Canada and the United States. Captured Africans sold in the Americas were distinguished from white **indentured servants**, but not all Africans were "slaves." A racial hierarchy and the distinction between Africans and white **indentured labourers** intensified with the rapid expansion of **chattel slavery**.[4] The economic and political interests defending Black slavery were more powerful than that of indentured labour.[5] According to Harris (1993), by 1660 "the especially degraded status of Blacks as chattel slaves was recognized in law" (p. 1718). In 1661, the Maryland legislature enacted a bill providing that "All Negroes, and other slaves shall serve Durante Vita [for life]" (Gossett, 1963, as cited in Harris, 1993, p. 1718).

Although slavery in Canada is often described as less harsh and pervasive than in the United States and the Caribbean, it consisted of the same principle: the ownership of humans. Under French and British rule, the two largest groups of slaves in Canada were Pawnees and Africans owned by colonists, wealthy landowners, the military, and some clergy (Donovan, 1995; Elgersman, 1999). In terms of law, certain aspects of Louis XIV's Code Noir (1685), which defined conditions of slavery in French colonies in the Caribbean, in particular that the child of a slave mother would also be a slave, applied in Canada (Lawrence, 2016). In 1709, *Ordinance Rendered on the Subject of the Negroes and the Indians called Panis* legalized slavery in New France (the area colonized by France in North America). Indigenous and Black slaves brought to the colony "would be considered *the possession* of those who purchased them" (Lawrence, 2016, para. 6, emphasis mine).

The powerful move from "slave" and "free" to "Black" and "white" as *polar constructs* marked an important step in the social construction of race (Harris, 1993, p. 1718, emphasis mine). Here is where whiteness, as a shield from slavery and symbol of freedom, became a demarcated and highly coveted form of property. By *property*, Harris here means *attribute*. The absence of whiteness means "being the object of property," "a thing." This marked the beginning of a distinction. Despite tensions between property and humanity, slavery as a legal institution treated slaves as property that could be "transferred, assigned, inherited or posted as collateral" (Harris, 1993, p. 1720).

The attribute of whiteness as superior and distinct took shape in Canada through the instituting of a white settler-colonial regime. Colonial encounters between Britain and France and Indigenous peoples over territory and trade rights date back centuries. Once Britain proclaimed victory over France in 1763, for which France ceded land it did not own, Britain laid claim to much of Eastern North America. The Royal Proclamation of 1763 "recognized Aboriginal title to all lands not ceded and acknowledged a *nation-to-nation relationship* with the Indigenous Nations" (Lawrence, 2003, p. 6, emphasis mine). As time went on, the nation-to-nation relationship between British and Indigenous peoples began to change. In 1850, legislation was passed that allowed for the creation of **Indian** reserves, thereby restricting "Indians" to specific territories/areas and for the first time defined, albeit extremely loosely, who should be considered to be an Indian (Lawrence, 2003, p. 7). The Canadian government began limiting the number of people entitled to Indian status through the enfranchisement process (a legal process for terminating a person's Indian status). In 1857, the *Gradual Civilisation Act* was passed, which "made provisions for the conversion of reserve land into alienated plots in the hand of men who would *cease to be Indian* upon enfranchisement" (p. 7, emphasis mine). The European settler government now had the ability to expel/deny one from being Indigenous. In 1869, the *Gradual Enfranchisement Act* was passed, which stipulated that an Indian woman who married a white man would lose her Indian status and any right to band membership. What this Act did was legally identify who was "white," who was "Indian," and which children were legitimate progeny, citizens rather than subjugated "Natives" (p. 8). The offspring of a white man and Native woman was no longer Native, whereas a white woman who married a Native man became a "status Indian."[6] A **blood quantum** stipulation was also added at the time in which the only people eligible to be considered Indian were those who had "at least one-quarter Indian blood" (p. 9).

With the passing of the *Indian Act* in 1876, the exertion of more control over who was Indian was made explicit. Now, the process of differentiating between Indian and "halfbreeds" was intensified. Bonita Lawrence (2003) describes how in the 50 years during which the numbered Treaties (1–11) were negotiated across Western Canada (1870–1920), treaty officials would set up locations where individuals would present themselves to be judged by white officials. Factors such as lifestyle, language, and residence were used to judge criteria of eligibility. Individuals who were "living like Indians" were taken into the treaty and classified as "**status Indians**," which meant that one was recognized as having signed treaties that established provisions for reserves, annuities, hunting and fishing rights, and allowed one to live on reserve land and participate in one's community. Many, however, who were away when registration was first carried out, were deemed to not be "Indian enough" and were registered as halfbreed. As "halfbreed," one was not recognized as part of a treaty or as being a "status Indian." In other parts of Canada where treaties did not explicitly separate the two categories, Indigenous peoples were often listed as non-status Indians.[7] Much like the legal category of slave, the *Indian Act* legitimized the category of white settler Canadian citizen in opposition to that of "Indian"—in some ways through the **classification** of "halfbreed" or non-status Indian. To become enfranchised, to lose one's status, and become a British subject with a chosen Christian name was a form of assimilation and "civilization" but not an invitation into the category of whiteness. The idea that white identity was simply one of personal choice, that one could choose it at will, fails to capture other powerful discourses that enabled its assent. Whiteness had a strong ally: **science**.

The Classification/Science of Race

Racial classification was a task taken on by settler-colonial rule in the Americas, which accepted then-current theories of race as biological fact. As such, the law was able to "parcel out social standing according to race" and to facilitate systemic discrimination by articulating "seemingly precise definitions of racial group membership" (Cottrol, 1988, as cited in Harris, 1993, p. 1737). Dominant and subordinate positions within the racial hierarchy "were disguised as the product of natural law and biology rather than naked preferences" (Harris, 1993, p. 1738). In the US, attempting to legally define what constituted being white was of importance when considering the legal rights attached to it (voting, owning land, carrying a firearm, and so on). Claiming a white appearance or having a white community vouch for one did not guarantee that one was legally white. *White identity*, as defined in law, was tied to blood quantum. According to Harris (1993), "case law that attempted to define race frequently struggled over the precise fractional amount of Black 'blood'—traceable Black ancestry—that would defeat a claim of whiteness" (p. 1738). For categories of Black, Negro, or Coloured, the law in the US followed the hypodescent rule, a system of racial classification in which the subordinate status is assigned to the offspring if there is one "superordinate" and one "subordinate" parent, similar to the Code Noir in Canada.

Let me deviate briefly from the implications of having a subordinate status to describe how that subordination came to be. The legal assumption of race as blood-borne was predicated on the then-authoritative but since debunked sciences of **eugenics** and craniology (for more on scientific fact-making, see Chapter 10). Within the discipline of craniology, skull measurement was used to rank races according to intelligence, morals, and aptitude (see Horsman, 1981).

The leaders of such theories were Samuel Morton, Samuel A. Cartwright, and John H. van Evrie. Baynton (2001) has demonstrated how a **discourse** of disability for various groups was used to further their **inequality**. The legal institution of slavery was rationalized as ethical and essential, since Blacks were said to lack moral character and an ability to care for themselves, largely because of "a deficiency of cerebral matter in the cranium, and an excess of nervous matter distributed to the organs of sensation and assimilation, [causing] that debasement of mind, which has rendered the people of Africa unable to take care of themselves" (Cartwright, 1851, p. 693, as cited in Baynton, 2001, p. 37). Freedom for Blacks was said to result in an ailment Cartwright named *Dysaesthesia Aethiopis*, whose symptoms included a desire to avoid work and cause mischief—universal symptoms among free Blacks (Cartwright, 1851, pp. 707–710, as cited in Baynton, 2001, p. 38). Medical journals reported that deafness and blindness were far more common among free Blacks than among slaves; even after emancipation, some inquired into the mental and physical health of freed Blacks. One study, conducted by J.F. Miller and published in a North Carolina medical journal, found "more congenital defects, and a dramatic increase in mental illness and tuberculosis," and overall a "harvest of mental and physical degeneration" in freed Blacks (as cited in Baynton, 2001, p. 39). A belief in Blacks' inability to govern themselves, and white paternalism, continued long after slavery. Even during the post-emancipation period in the United States, "Southern planters could not reconcile themselves to the fact of emancipation; they believed that 'free Black labor' was a contradiction in terms, that Blacks would never work of their own free will" (Jones, 1985, p. 45).

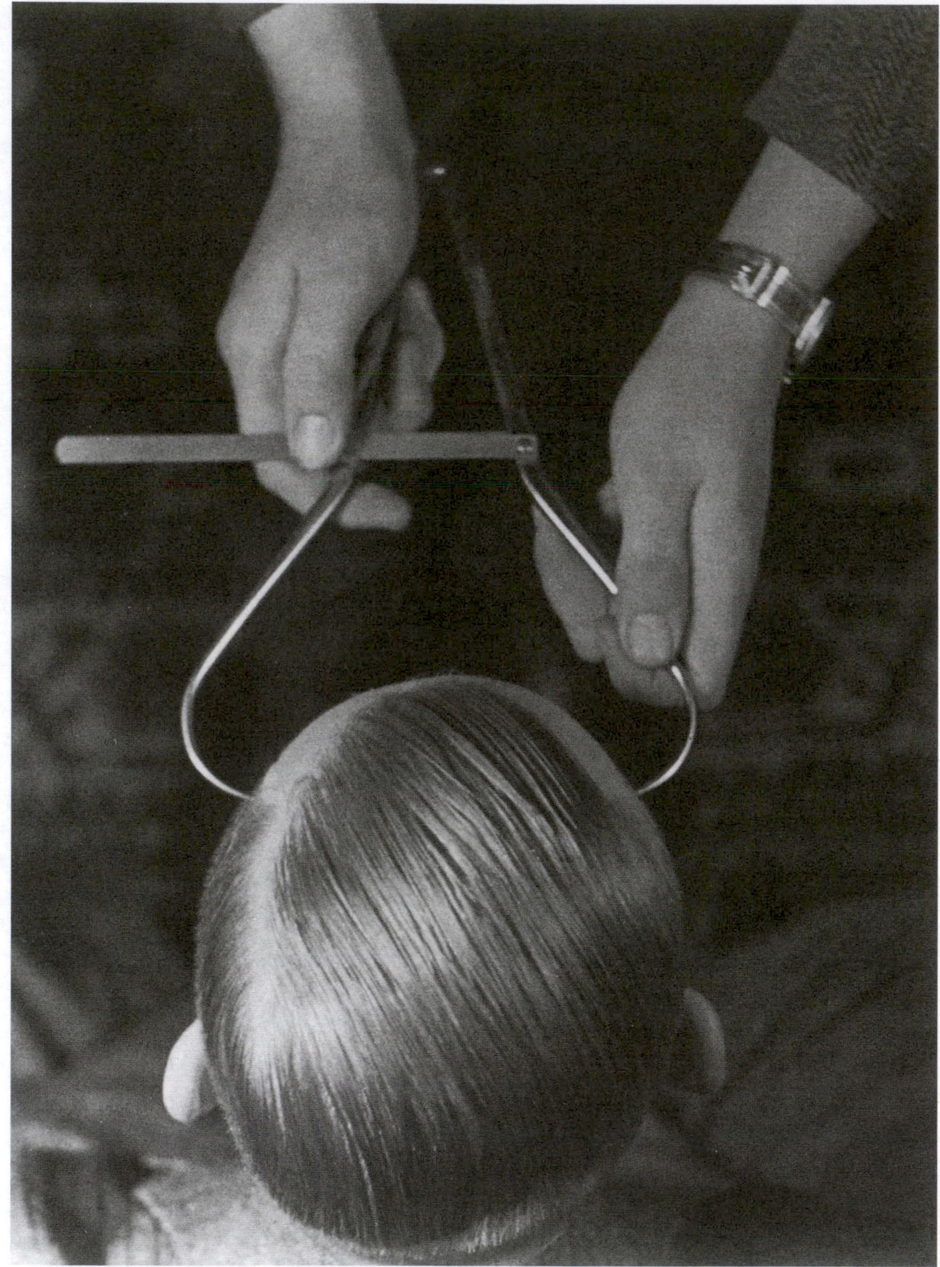

FIGURE 6.2 A racial hygienist measures the forehead of a young man with calipers, 1937. bpk Bildagentur/Fritz Carl/Art Resource, NY.

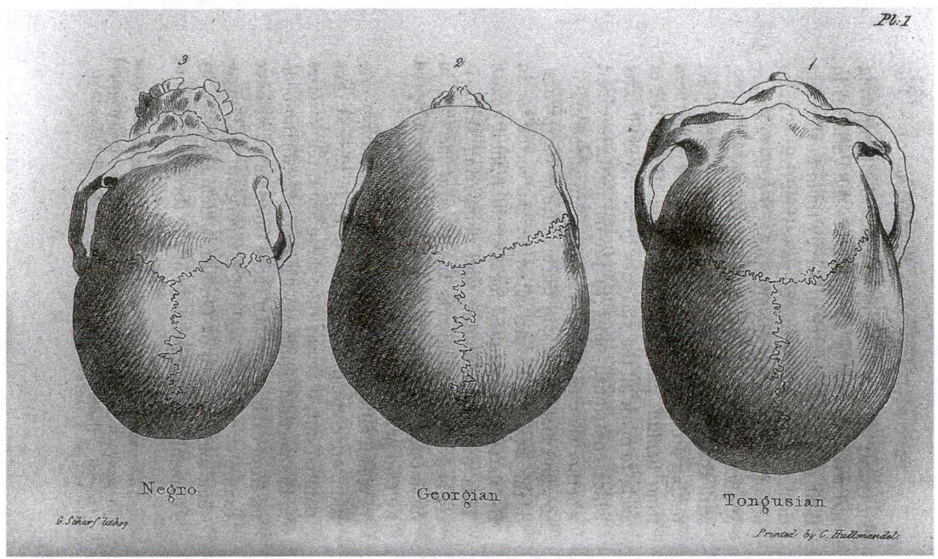

FIGURE 6.3 The work of James C. Prichard depicting skulls from different races, 1826. J.C. Prichard: skulls from different races; 1826. Wellcome Collection. CC BY 4.0.

Returning to the implications of that subordinate status: essentially, any minute fraction of "Black blood" (what was called the "one-drop rule") found in one's ancestral racial logbook expelled one from the category of whiteness. For this, according to Harris (1993), whiteness as privilege was "legitimated by *science* and was embraced in legal doctrine as '*objective fact*'" (p. 1738, emphasis mine). The law, in relation to slaves in the US, did not question whether documents noting racial ancestry or the racial category of ancestors had been appropriately recorded, or that "race mixing" or a "métissage" was most likely true of all people's histories. The concept of racial purity existed. Whiteness as identity—that is, not having "Black blood"—carried privileges that were entrenched in the legal system. To be found out or called out as anything but racially pure was perilous. Only those who could lay "legitimate" claims to whiteness could be legally recognized as "white" because, according to Harris (1993), "allowing physical attributes, social acceptance, or self-identification to determine whiteness would diminish its value and destroy the underlying presumption of exclusivity" (p. 1741).

Similarly, self-serving European science contributed to the classification of Indigenous peoples as "savage," "uncivilized," and "heathen," which worked to justify not only the taking of land but also the policies/laws to "civilize" that followed. Being a "status Indian" was distinct from being white. Unlike the category of slave, white colonial officials looked to limit identification of this category so as to legitimize the white settler encroachment on land and denial of rights to Indigenous peoples.

Although capitalist expansion and economic **exploitation** are at the centre of the making of whiteness, **gender** and **class** complicate racial politics and one's relationship to whiteness (e.g., "Indian status" as legitimized through the male line or imposing slave status on all children born of slave women). How do we understand white women's place in the politics of whiteness, or the white working class? Although doing a historical analysis of race, gender, and class in relation to whiteness is difficult in such a short chapter, there are some key concepts that need to be at the forefront of this debate. Class and gender are not separate from race/whiteness but intrinsic to its workings.

Whiteness, White Women, and White Working-Class Men

Relying on Foucault's work, Higginbotham (1992) has discussed race, gender, class, and **sexuality** as "technologies" (a **concept** that you were introduced to in Chapter 1), that operate through elaborating and implementing discourses that sustain the oppression of one group over another. However, it is race's power and overdeterminacy in Western **culture** that has allowed it to function as a **metalanguage**[8] over other social categories. Thus, gender and class struggles are not only linked but determined by race. So where is whiteness in gender and class politics?

Perhaps surprisingly, from the early 1600s to 1800s, the white **working class** and minorities had close relationships (Roediger, 2007). However, with the advent of chattel slavery, racial lines were increasingly drawn, separating people. White workers saw advantages in distinguishing themselves from their fellow Black and other non-white workers. In some instances their wages were higher, but even when they were not, they benefited socially from being white. For example, unions routinely denied membership to Black workers. One might assume that white labourers would see commonalities with **racialized** workers and unite against capitalist forms of exploitation. But historically and now, in the post-Trump-election era, we can most certainly see evidence that whiteness trumps class—no pun intended.

Similar trends were evident in the Canadian context. Sugiman (2001) examines the politics of race and gender in the auto-manufacturing sector in Ontario between 1939 and 1949. The auto industry had a largely white male workforce, with the exception of a few Black men who primarily worked as janitors or in the foundry (area of a factory that produces metals)—a lower-tier, harsher employment seen as best suited for Black males. Management contributed greatly to the construction of a racial hierarchy among workers. Unlike in the US, however, these white workers did not feel threatened by Black men because of their small numbers. Creese (1988–89), meanwhile, examines the white working class and the increasing anti-Asian sentiment in early 20th-century British Columbia. Asian male workers were brought to Canada to work on the Canadian Pacific Railway to fill the demand for cheap labour. "Asian competition" was regarded by unions as the cause for poor labour conditions. Unions saw threats in the garment, laundry, and restaurant sectors. The unions' rationale for excluding Asian workers was not only because of competition but explicitly racist views. Asian male workers were depicted as "docile," "unorganizable," "foreign," and therefore not considered the "real" (white) working class whose interest organized labour sought to represent.

Race and class have also intertwined with gender to reveal whiteness/race for white women as superior to gender. Going back to Jones (1985), not only was free-Black labour seen as a contradiction during post-emancipation, but Black families faced great hostility when they attempted to remove wives and mothers from the workplace. The cult of domesticity was expected and deemed natural for white women, but it was evil and offensive for Black women to "play the lady" (Jones, 1985, pp. 58–60). In looking at paid work, race most definitely informed class politics. Race fractured the gendered division of labour. Racist policies enforced by factory managers continued to position Black women in the lower tier of factory work. Regardless of class status, education, income, or morals, the majority of Black men and women were forced into low-status, low-pay positions.

Jones (1985) recounted the experiences of 15 Black female tobacco workers in Durham, North Carolina, between 1908 and 1930. Black women were forced to take the dirtier, more dangerous, jobs as stemmers, sorters, hangers, and pullers—positions that white women were never considered for. Extreme wage differentials between Black and white women, Jones (1985) noted, "also forced many into the labour force at an early age. Black women thus worked for a longer part of their lives, and henceforth were more vulnerable to diseases and other health problems" (p. 446). White women would occupy the less hazardous positions, positions deemed "suitable for ladies," all in the name of protecting white women's "racial honour" (Janiewski, 1987, as cited in Higginbotham, 1992, p. 260).

Similar examples can be found in the Canadian context when looking at the immigration and settlement of Blacks in Canada. The large majority of Caribbean women who immigrated during the 1970s and 1980s worked as nurses. Those who were allowed in came under what Calliste (1993) calls "exceptional merit." The immigration department admitted nurses and nursing students under four categories, which streamlined Black nurses into particular low-waged nursing positions. Canadian immigration officials justified restricting the entry of professional and skilled workers from the Caribbean on the grounds that Canadians were not accustomed to seeing Black people in "positions which would place them on the same economic and social levels with their white neighbours" (Calliste, 1993, p. 90). This attitude reflected the stereotypical perception that Blacks were better suited, even inherently suited, to service jobs or those that required heavy physical labour, rather than skilled and supervisory positions.

Histories of white women's elevation above that of Other women show us that race (whiteness) superseded class and gender groupings. What is important to retain here is that this history has informed the present. It is with us now. I now shift to studies that focus specifically on how whites understand whiteness in the current context.

Whiteness at Work in Language and Practice

Much of the research to date that looks to **denaturalize** whiteness and white privilege does so by interrogating whites' understandings of these systems. Rather than search for an essentialized nature attributed to whiteness, Nakayama and Krizek (1999) look to understand "the ways that this rhetorical construction makes itself visible and invisible, eluding analysis yet exerting influence over everyday life" (Nakayama & Krizek, 1999, p. 91). For these authors, "within everyday discourses, there is a central contradiction at work within the 'white' discursive formation that produces its functional invisibility, yet importance" (Nakayama & Krizek, 1999, p. 95). Exposing whiteness's universality can be accomplished by looking at its everydayness, since "experiences and communication patterns of whites are taken as the norm from which Others are marked" (Nakayama & Krizek, 1999, p. 91). Because of this "functional invisibility," in discussions of race it is only when confronting whites about their whiteness that we are able to make visible the ways in which whiteness is sustained and reproduced. Works such as Nakayama and Krizek's are essential, since

> we have yet to chronicle how those who oppress make sense of their power *in relationship* to those they have injured … We lack an elaborate language to speak about those who oppress—how they feel about, think about, react to, make sense of, come to terms with, maintain privilege over, and ultimately renounce the power to oppress. (Hurtado, 1999, p. 226, emphasis in original)

In what follows, I approach this topic from three angles: the **myth of sameness**, **white solipsism**, and **bourgeois decorum**. I provide concrete examples of how theorists have discussed the everydayness of whiteness. I start with a **trope** familiar to many critical race theorists and pervasive in Canada: colour blindness.

Colour Blindness/Myth of Sameness

Whites often believe that fostering a notion of sameness will produce better race and ethnic relations and contribute to the disappearance of racism. A chapter of mine (Knight, 2008), "'Our School Is Like the United Nations': An Examination of How Discourses of Diversity in Schooling Naturalize Whiteness and White Privilege," examined this concept as discussed by white teachers in elementary and secondary schools in Ontario. To provide a bit of context, I analyzed data collected from a five-year national project entitled *Current Trends in the Evolution of School Personnel in Canadian Elementary and Secondary School* (Gérin-Lajoie, 2008). Although a variety of data existed from this project, I focused on interviews collected from 73 white teaching personnel in Ontario schools. For the semi-structured interviews, researchers asked specific questions pertaining to ethnocultural diversity: what characterized this diversity (if existent), what helped in dealing with diversity in the classroom, what pedagogical resources were at the teachers' disposal, and whether they had adapted any practices to deal with this diversity.

For whites, seeing or identifying difference can be an uncomfortable thing. To highlight difference serves to single someone out or to further marginalize them. This was no more evident than when participants were asked how they dealt with diversity in the classroom. The question startled some, and many explained that dealing with diversity was an unnecessary practice. It was unnecessary because racial or ethnic diversity was non-existent in their eyes. What supersedes is a liberal belief in a universal **subjectivity** that we are all simply part of the human race. The belief, very often, is that this liberal philosophy will lessen racial tensions and racist practices. Whiteness is therefore deeply invested in what hooks (1992) described as "the **myth of 'sameness'**" (p. 167). One participant expressed it this way:

> I think most teachers will tell you, you've got a class in front of you, you don't have a class of Asian kids, you don't have a class of Sri Lankan kids, you don't have a class of Korean kids, you've got a class of kids, and maybe you have to sometimes sit back and say, well what backgrounds do you have in there? Well let me think for a second. There's Chris, there's John, there's Thomas, there's Doug, that's how you go … It's a routine. It's a routine. You know there's no categorization. (Interview #4163 / W-M)

For this participant, sameness is having a classroom with "just kids" with "no categorization." You may sometimes "sit back and think" about differences, but aside from that "it's a routine." It is essential to consider difference, but to do so by historicizing, contextualizing, and politicizing it, especially as it relates to racialized groups in Canada. It may be difficult for whites to understand that equal treatment can be discriminatory. On the other hand, recognizing difference by contextualizing its socio-political history is not necessarily showing a preference or prejudice but may in fact be correcting a legacy of historical injustices (Sue, 2004). It is important to distinguish between race as innate biological difference—which is a dangerous myth that has been shown to be without scientific merit—and racism as historical, structural, and everyday commitments to that myth which, as we have seen above, was foundational to the colonial project in the Americas.

Investment by whites in the myth of sameness absolves one from being associated with injustices. Why criticize someone who espouses a common existence? Because it renders any discussion of race and difference a highly contested struggle (hooks, 1992). The myth of sameness also systemically glosses over and erases history. Many are quick to utter such words as "race is socially constructed and irrelevant," or, even more disturbing, that race has now been overly exhausted. Perceived as innocent claims, they negate Canada's colonial history and its history of slavery and indentured labour as well as their demonstrable daily legacy in the lives of non-white groups.

White Solipsism

Another example of whiteness at work is seen in Rich's (1979) concept, white solipsism, a perceptual practice that implicitly takes a white perspective as universal. White universality can be seen in our understanding of women's oppression under **patriarchy**. In particular, an important goal of the 1960s' women's movement was to liberate women from the home. This narrative was one that was seen as universal to all women. What many feminists of colour have aptly noted for decades is that the experience of the oppressed housewife looking to be liberated was that of white, middle-to-upper-class women. Examining Black, Mexican American, and Chinese American women, Glenn (1985) asserted that three concepts needed to be reformulated: the private/public divide, gender conflicts in the family, and divisions of reproductive labour.

Prior to industrialization, productive and reproductive work were organized around the home. With industrialization, reproductive work remained the responsibility of households, and there was a clear ideological separation between men's productive work in public and women's work in private. Examining the interplay between race and gender and the public/private divide, Glenn (1992) questioned the assumption that industrialization created a greater separation between the private and public spheres for all classes and groups. This claim is shattered when looking at the lives of racialized women. The division of labour was "largely illusory for working-class households, including immigrant and racial-ethnic families, in which men seldom earned a family wage; in these households women and children were forced into income-earning activities *in and out of the home*" (Glenn, 1992, pp. 4–5, emphasis added). During the late 19th to mid 20th centuries, poor and working-class women worked in their own homes and for middle-class families. In the latter half of the 19th century, the gap between white and racialized women grew.[9] The public/private divide—often conceptualized as relegating women to the private realm and men to the public—does not hold up in the case of Black women. As hooks (1984) contended, "middle class women shaping feminist thought assumed that the most pressing problem for women was the need to get outside the home and work—to cease being 'just' housewives" (p. 95). Meanwhile, Black women struggled to recover from overwork in exploitative and underpaid jobs, often as sole breadwinners in their households (Mama, 1995). The combination of economic conditions and **ideologies** of race and gender positioned them as less suited for the home and better suited for public work. Poor Black and Latina mothers "were deemed to be 'employable,' and not requiring or deserving of charity" (Glenn, 2002, p. 75). The experience of the public/private divide is clearly one most often told from a white perspective.

In terms of the family, it is often formulated as a "locus of gender conflict" (Glenn, 1985, p. 103), oppressive to women in terms of division of labour and dependence on men. Glenn, however, challenges this assumption, noting that, for women of colour, the family has also been a source of resistance to oppression and is "a bulwark against the atomizing effects of poverty, legal and political constraints" (p. 103). As for reproductive labour, historically, racial ethnic and immigrant women performed much of this labour for white families, which made the "woman 'belle' ideal for white middle class women" possible (p. 104). When examining the lives of racialized women and reproductive labour, we see that the division is more than a mere sexual division of reproductive labour—it is also a racial one.

Bourgeois Decorum

In her article "White Enculturation and Bourgeois Ideology," Dreama Moon (1999) examines how whiteness is performed through bourgeois decorum, a term she extends from hooks (1994) to describe a practice in which whites present a publicly united racial front, performed in two ways: euphemizing[10] white racism and hyperpoliteness. I focus on the former in the following section.

Euphemizing white racism—or whitespeak—is a type of coded speech, a "racialized form of euphemistic language in which what is *not* said—or the absences in language … is often far more revealing than what *is* said" (Moon, 1999, p. 188, emphasis in original). There are three manifestations of whitespeak: the subjectification of racism and race, the erasure of **agency** (**passive voice**), and the disembodiment of subjects. "Subjectification allows white people to disengage in discussions of race and racism. This disengagement allows white people to *deny* their own complicity in relations of racial dominations as well as any awareness or understanding of the historical legacy of white supremacy" (Moon, 1999, p. 189). Agency is bestowed on race and racism, "forcing them to perform as the 'subject,' and at the same time, removes human agency and responsibility from the discussion" (Moon, 1999, p. 188). The erasure of agency enables white people to recognize historical events and thereby demonstrate their empathy for racial others, while repressing any connection to them. The disembodiment occurs when "an anonymous agent is made ultimately responsible for the perpetuation of racism. These unmarked bodies make life difficult for the rest of us good whitepeople" (Moon, 1999, p. 191).

For a good example of the above, let me go back to the *Current Trends in the Evolution of School Personnel* project (Gérin-Lajoie, 2008). Although student diversity was most often described as harmonious, some participants in the survey did speak of racial conflicts that had emerged in their schools:

> Last year we had this conversation [on diversity and conflicts]. I think I would probably have had a certain amount to say because *it* was an issue. There was a group of five or six girls who really stuck together and really thought and looked for areas where *perhaps* they *might* have been treated differently. And *it* was a very public thing all the time with them. And they were all part of the community center that was, children with, probably mixed backgrounds, but South American or the Islands or, who really stuck very closely together and had a bit of a chip on

> their shoulder and maybe *went looking for it*. With the group this year *it's* just, *it's* such a non-issue ... They'd [the girls from the previous year] also gone through a very, very tough year, it probably stemmed after an incident at the community center where one of their counsellors was gunned down. And somebody who was very close to their hearts and it was in the media a great deal and the fact that he was Black played into it. So I think that it was sort of a beginning with the kids questioning more of that and noticing differences perhaps or *looking for differences* and *tried to use*, this particular group, kind of used their colour to question everything or to try to explain why things happened for them or didn't happen. (Interview #4146 / W-F, emphasis added)

The quotation above speaks to the practice of subjectification, which is the idea of disengagement, denial of complicity, and lack of awareness. The word "it" comes to stand for a great deal. We are not quite sure, however, what "it" means, especially when the participant says that the girls went looking for "it." Does "it" here mean conflict, trouble, or looking to identify racism? The participant not only displays a lack of awareness but **pathologizes** experiences and accounts of racism, rendering them as student misunderstandings with words like "perhaps" or "might have been treated differently." There is a lack of awareness of how racism works with the comment that students are "looking for difference" or "went looking for it," as ways for students to gain attention. Distant, anonymous agents are responsible for the perpetuation of racism. As such, whatever may or may not have happened in the past does not reflect on the good relationships that are present now. The burden of racism is not fully understood by those who are able to escape the stigma (Hurtado, 1999). Whites, who are able to live their lives knowing very little of the experiences of people of colour, enjoy the privilege of being able to move on from racism as opposed to having it be a central part of their lives.

The disembodiment of subjects, meanwhile, is apparent with the mention of the killing of a counsellor. This event is completely removed from the daily realities of the violence Blacks experience as a result of systemic racism (e.g., from police officers). Whites understand racism and their role in sustaining it differently than do the recipients of racism (Frankenberg, 1993). Finally, there is once again a temporality here as well as a specificity and particularity that is given to racism. It is not persistent and pervasive but during a particular year and experienced by a particular group of five or six girls. If it is understood as being the result of a few bad white people, it must therefore only be subjected toward a few racialized people at discrete times with an identifiable motive and harm legible to white people. Racism in the lives of racialized students goes largely unnoticed or unacknowledged in its complexities. As we saw with Colten Boushie and Gerald Stanley at the beginning of this chapter, the law is ill-equipped to think beyond the individual when addressing harm and accountability.

When we (researchers from the Current Trends project) asked participants whether they could talk about a recent event in which they adapted curriculum to represent a more racially and ethnically diverse student body, most described substituting events and practices with non-white **norms** and traditions or mixing students of different backgrounds to work with one another. Apart from substitutions and commingling, the performance of whiteness manifested itself in two specific ways when asked about adaptation of practices: the euphemizing of white racism and the use of a passive voice.

Euphemisms, Moon (1999) contended, "are commonly utilised in everyday white discourse around racialized issues such as affirmative action, welfare reform, family values, reverse discrimination, and immigration" (p. 187)—for example, when whites say that African Americans attended "separate" as opposed to segregated schools, or that the Japanese were "relocated" as opposed to interned during WWII. Teachers shared several examples, including this one:

> You know what, no. I don't think I have [adapted teaching or lesson] because as long as I've been here, I've had a very multicultural classroom in front of me so I think you're always aware of who's in front of you. And, you know, if you're teaching history, you're trying to draw attention to maybe a group of people that have been *put down* or, you know, *discriminated against*, and show them that it *happens to everybody* and you have to learn from that and not repeat it. So, you know what, I don't think I've changed anything just because of who's in my room. (Interview #4141 / W-F, emphasis added)

For Moon (1999), euphemisms "work to mask the facts of domination, rendering them 'harmless or sanitized,' thereby obscuring the 'use of coercion' … [and] cloak racist expression with a veneer of 'bourgeois civility/gentility,' while enabling white people freely to express racism—in coded ways—as a signal of white solidarity" (p. 188). Euphemisms in the comment above come in the form of groups being "put down" or that "it" happens "to everybody." The comment is open-ended in that "it" happens to everyone, negating the fixity and specificity of oppression against Indigenous peoples. This oppression is ongoing, ever present, and specific in nature. White people, when discussing issues of race, often linguistically shift, according to Moon (1999), into a kind of "white code" that allows them to discuss race issues in ways that maintain the status quo, removing them from complicity while also securing approval from other whites.

The use of passive voice is another strategy utilized by participants, which coincides with the larger strategy of bourgeois decorum, and in particular whitespeak. Moon (1999) defined passive voice as white people detaching themselves from historical oppressions and their legacies. There is a slight level of empathy and tolerance but nothing more. When discussing issues facing marginalized communities, Moon's participants struggled to explain the challenges and obstacles that are faced by racialized communities. The focus was on personal attributes and character traits as opposed to historical explanation. She gave this quote as an example: "I had a group of Native American kids come to campus for a tour. They were relatively intelligent kids, but had been cloistered on the reservation to the point that they were afraid to come to campus" (Moon, 1999, p. 190). When defining the Native American reservation system, the term "cloistered" negates the responsibility of the agent in addition to the history of **settler colonialism.** We see something similar in the quote above with the use of the words "put down" or "discriminated against" as opposed to "oppressed" or "marginalized."

In my research focusing on teachers (Knight, 2008), it also became evident that the use of a passive voice was a pervasive strategy deployed in discussions of what I call "racialized student dysfunctions," that is, from discussions on racialized students' academic achievement or level of performance:

> Their [racialized students'] environment at home, most of the time, contradicts the environment in the school. So at school there's a lot of structure in place, at home there seems to be, because parents are maybe working late shifts, and they don't get to see their children anymore so. Who knows, whatever it is, but this is what I'm hearing, that there's a lot of, for a lack of a better word, dysfunction within the family home life. (Interview #4125 / W-M)
>
> I think it's just a manifestation of something that these students have witnessed in their own culture. But, now there are some difficulties that manifest more with parents. I mean it's almost like real major difficulties, and again, this is a gross generalization, but the Portuguese, a major issue we have there with Portuguese students is family break-up, divorce, and with Filipinos the major issue we have with them is the real difficulty of the family and/or the individual student making the transition from moving from the Philippines to Canada. (Interview #4138 / W-M)

Later on, Moon provided another example where empathy was the only perspective given: "You're in a ghetto and nobody works because they are all on welfare. This is a broad generalization, but you're used to people in gangs, on dope, hanging out, and that's all you see. Would you get out of it? How would you get out of it?" (Moon, 1999, p. 190). A similar comment was expressed from a participant quoted above:

> It's difficult. When I see a child come in with, I'll just give an example here, a piece of pizza that was obviously eaten before, wrapped up in a Canadian tire flyer, like your jaw just drops and your heart just wants to be out there for that child and the family, if that's what you can do. That's why our school was very instrumental in getting a breakfast program in here really quickly, and doing something to help these families … Our hearts go out to these children. We know where they're coming from. (Interview #4125 / W-M)

Responses reveal a lack of a critical focus on the complex socio-historical circumstances and material conditions that create students' failure and success. On the one hand, teachers were often empathetic to the students' situation but never pointed to any of the historical and present conditions that had structured and continued to structure these situations. Contextualized "dysfunction" forces us to think about racist immigration policies, issues of settlement, denial of proper housing, and precarious work; all contribute to community and family structures.

The participants in Moon's (1999) study recognized the existence of reservations and ghettos. How such sites came into existence, however, did not factor into their frame of reference. The power that created such spaces in the first place were obscured. Comments like the child eating out of a paper flyer, or one's inability to leave the ghetto, or one's fear of coming to campus, on the one hand, allow participants to show concerns, empathy, and tolerance. On the other hand, this framing individualizes social problems and enables one to remove or distance onself from any involvement. Both women quoted from Moon's study were described as using the passive voice to indicate that "'something' happened to 'someone' (e.g., 'they' somehow ended up on a reservation or in a ghetto), without identifying the historical agents who conspired in these events" (pp. 190–191). The issue illustrates how the conditions with which racialized people live are dehistoricized and decontextualized. Much like Moon, I question the lack of agency and responsibility on the part of many whites, and their lack of understanding of how white privilege secures benefits and privileges not available to all.

Conclusion

The studies discussed above point to how subjectivity is in part constructed through difference—"I am not you," so to speak. The myth of sameness, white solipsism, and bourgeois decorum demonstrate a subject that attempts to transcend by glossing over complex histories that implicate whites, including themselves.[11]

Let us not forget that whiteness has a history. Its making, anchored in law, came to be through powerful economic and social forces that were engineered by whites (a class that did not predate these forces, but came into being as not-Black). It is in the dispossession of non-white humans that whiteness was deemed free and worthy. It is in the dispossession of a group that white people were deemed the rightful civilized inhabitants. It is not only the characteristic of whiteness that gave privileges to some and not others. In the present day, one might assume that the election of Barack Obama to the US presidency rendered us into a "post-racial" state, a state where race is no longer relevant and racism no longer existent. We fail to see a white settler-colonial system that kills or incarcerates a high proportion of Indigenous and Black peoples, that neglects to provide resolutions to the cases of many missing and murdered Indigenous women, and that dismisses Indigenous land rights/claims based on the perceived lack of Indigeneity, that concentrates economic wealth disproportionately in white hands. If we are to heal, there must be an account of whiteness's history and present manifestation. If the system is not dismantled, outside in and inside out, there remains little hope for change.

Study Questions

1. When and how historically did white supremacy come to be? Through what systems of oppression?
2. What does Harris mean when she describes whiteness as property?
3. How did colonial science contribute to the creation of a racial hierarchy?
4. How do everyday forms of whiteness manifest themselves in the everyday?

Exercises

1. Although evidence of the legacy and current workings of a white settler-colonial framework is apparent in our society, we often hear from non-Indigenous peoples that we were not taught about our history of colonialism. What everyday examples of racism against Indigenous peoples are visible in media and public life?
2. How do historical, racialized economic disparities (e.g. access to housing, schooling, savings, and land) continue intergenerationally?

Notes

1. Martin was an unarmed Black youth who, on his way home from a corner store in Sanford, Florida in 2012, was shot and killed by George Zimmerman, a neighbourhood watch captain who had reported Martin as "suspicious."
2. During the Sixties Scoop, occurring between 1960 and 1980, the federal government (child welfare services) took an estimated 20,000 Indigenous children from their homes and placed them with mostly non-Indigenous foster families across Canada and beyond, often without the consent of their parents (Sinclair, 2007).
3. Harris uses the concept of property in different ways. Relying on Minogue (1980), she defines property as things/objects, which can be transferred, assigned, and inherited, and includes in the definition things that are recognized in terms of their attributes or properties.
4. An indentured servant/labourer is a worker who is bound by a contract to work for a particular employer for a fixed time and often enters into indenture because of financial obligations, such as a debt (Jones, 1998). Chattel slavery is distinguished from other forms of slavery in that much of the slave labour force was obtained through reproduction, imposing slave status on all children born of slave women. The same was not true for the children of indentured servants.
5. Historians disagree as to why the distinction occurred but the focus should still remain on the fact that it did occur. Many other scholars cite the importance of the change from indentured labour to slavery (see Degler, 1959; Jordan, 1968; Wood, 1997).

6 This would remain part of the *Indian Act* until 1985.

7 A Native person could also be enfranchised for serving in the Canadian armed forces, gaining a university education, or leaving reserves for long periods—for instance, for employment.

8 For Higginbotham, "we must expose the role of race as a metalanguage by calling attention to its powerful, all-encompassing effect on the construction and representation of other social and power relations, namely, gender, class, and sexuality" (1992, p. 252). To understand race as a metalanguage, "we must recognize its historical and material grounding" (p. 256).

9 The family wage, essentially higher wages that were paid to white middle-class men, ensured that white middle-class women did not have to work, prompting their withdrawal from paid work over the course of the 20th century. It extended in some cases to white working-class men (e.g., the auto sector in Canada) and therefore white working-class women (Jones, 1985; Sugiman, 2001).

10 A euphemism is a mild or neutral word substituted for something that, while more accurate, may seem too harsh or graphic to the speaker, such as "collateral damage" instead of "civilians killed in a military operation against an enemy." Euphemisms do political work of downplaying violence and responsibility.

11 For further examples of how white subjectivity uses guilt and/or claims of innocence to disaffiliate from white supremacist practices, see Applebaum, 2010; Bush, 2011; Kowal, 2011; and Wiegman, 1999.

References

Ahmed, S. (2004). Declarations of whiteness: The non-performativity of anti-racism. *Borderlands, 3*(2). Retrieved from http://www.borderlands.net.au/vol3no2_2004/ahmed_declarations.htm

Applebaum, B. (2010). *Being white, being good: White complicity, white moral responsibility, and social justice pedagogy*. Lanham, MD: Lexington Books.

Baynton, D.B. (2001). Disability and the justification of inequality in American history. In P.K. Longmore & L. Umansky (Eds.), *The new disability history: American perspectives*. New York, NY: New York University Press.

Bush, M.E.L. (2011). *Everyday forms of whiteness: Understanding race in a "post-racial" world.* Lanham, MD: Rowman & Littlefield Publishers.

Calliste, A. (1993). Women of exceptional merit: Immigration of Caribbean nurses to Canada. *Canadian Journal of Women and the Law, 6*(1), 85–102.

Cartwright, S.A. (1851, May). Report on the diseases and physical peculiarities of the negro race. *New Orleans Medical and Surgical Journal, 7*, 693.

Cottrol, R.J. (1988). The historical definition of race law. *Law and Society Review, 21*(5), 865–869.

Creese, G. (1988–89). Exclusion or solidarity? Vancouver workers confront the "oriental problem." *BC Studies, 80*, 24–51.

Degler, C.N. (1959). *Out of our past: The forces that shaped modern America.* New York, NY: Harper and Brothers.

Donovan, K. (1995). Slaves and their owners in Ile Royale, 1713–1760. *Acadiensis, 25*(1), 3–32.

Elgersman, M.G. (1999). *Unyielding spirits: Black women and slavery in early Canada and Jamaica.* New York, NY: Garland Publishing.

Frankenberg, R. (1993). *White women, race matters: The social organization of whiteness.* Minneapolis, MN: University of Minnesota Press.

Friesen, J. (2018, February 14). The night Colten Boushie died: What family and police files say about this last day, and what came after. *Globe and Mail.* https://www.theglobeandmail.com/news/national/colten-boushie/article32451940/

Gérin-Lajoie, D. (2008). *Educators' discourses on student diversity in Canada: Context, policy and practice.* Toronto, ON: Canadian Scholars' Press.

Glenn, E.N. (1985). Racial ethnic women's labor: The intersection of race, gender and class oppression. *Review of Radical Political Economics, 17*(3), 86–108.

Glenn, E.N. (1992). From servitude to service work: Historical continuities in the racial division of paid reproductive labour. *Signs: Journal of Women in Culture and Society, 18*(1), 1–43.

Glenn, E.N. (2002). *Unequal freedom: How race and gender shaped American citizenship and labour.* Cambridge, MA: Harvard University Press.

Gossett, T.F. (1963). *Race: The history of an idea in America.* Dallas, TX: Southern Methodist University Press.

Harris, C.I. (1993). Whiteness as property. *Harvard Law Review, 106*(8), 1707–1791.

Higginbotham, E.B. (1992). African-American women's history and the metalanguage of race. *Signs: Journal of Women in Culture and Society, 17*(2), 251–274.

hooks, b. (1984). *Feminist theory: From margin to centre.* Boston, MA: South End Press.

hooks, b. (1992). *Black looks: Race and representation.* Toronto, ON: Between the Lines Press.

hooks, b. (1994). *Outlaw culture: Resisting representations.* New York, NY: Routledge.

Horsman, R. (1981). *Race and manifest destiny: The origins of American racial Anglo-Saxonism.* Cambridge, MA: Harvard University Press.

Hurtado, A. (1999). The trickster's play: Whiteness in the subordination and liberation process. In R.D. Torres, L.F. Mirón, & J.X. Inda (Eds.), *Race, identity, and citizenship: A reader* (pp. 225–243). Malden, MA: Blackwell.

Isai, V. (2018, February 15). RCMP investigating post in officers' Facebook group claiming Colten Boushie "got what he deserved." *Toronto Star.* https://www.thestar.com/news/gta/2018/02/15/rcmp-to-investigate-internal-facebook-post-that-said-colten-boushie-got-what-he-deserved.html

Jones, J. (1985). *Labour of love, labour of sorrow: Black women, work and the family from slavery to the present.* New York, NY: Basic Books.

Jones, J. (1998). *American work: Four centuries of black and white labour.* New York, NY: W.W. Norton & Company.

Jordan, W.D. (1968). *White over Black: American attitudes toward the negro, 1550–1812.* Chapel Hill, NC: University of North Carolina Press.

Kheiriddin, T. (2018). *Justice for Colten requires breaking the cycle.* Retrieved from https://ipolitics.ca/2018/02/16/justice-colten-requires-breaking-cycle/

Knight, M. (2008). "Our school is like the United Nations": An examination of how discourses of multiculturalism uphold Whiteness and White privilege. In D. Gérin-Lajoie (Ed.), *Educators' discourses on student diversity within the Canadian educational policy context* (pp. 103–153). Toronto, ON: Canadian Scholars' Press.

Kowal, E. (2011). The stigma of white privilege: Australian anti-racists and Indigenous improvement. *Cultural Studies, 25*(3), 313–333.

Lawrence, B. (2003). Gender, race, and the regulation of native identity in Canada and the United States: An overview. *Hypatia, 18*(2), 3–31.

Lawrence, B. (2016). Enslavement of Indigenous people in Canada. *The Canadian Encyclopedia*. https://www.thecanadianencyclopedia.ca/en/article/slavery-of-indigenous-people-in-canada

Mama, A. (1995). *Beyond the masks: Race, gender, and subjectivity*. London, UK: Psychology Press.

McKeen, A. (2018, February 10). "We're going to fight back"—Colten Boushie's mother delivers emotional message. *Toronto Star*. https://www.thestar.com/news/gta/2018/02/10/were-going-to-fight-back-colten-boushies-mother-delivers-emotional-message.html

Minogue, K.R. (1980). The concept of property and its contemporary significance. *NOMOS, 22*, 3–27.

Moon, D. (1999). Whiteness in U.S. contexts: White enculturation and bourgeois ideology: The discursive production of "good (white) girls." In T.K. Nakayama & J.N. Martin (Eds.), *Whiteness: The communication of social identity* (pp. 177–197). Thousand Oaks, CA: Sage Publications.

Nakayama, T.K., & Krizek, R. (1999). Whiteness as a strategic rhetoric. In T.K. Nakayama & J.N. Martin (Eds.), *Whiteness: The communication of social identity* (pp. 87–106). Thousand Oaks, CA: Sage Publications.

Rich, A. (1979). Disloyal to civilization: Feminism, racism, and gynephobia. *Chrysalis, 7*, 9–27.

Roediger, D.R. (2007). *The wages of whiteness: Race and the making of the American working class* (Rev. ed.). New York, NY: Verso.

Sinclair, R. (2007). Identity lost and found: Lessons from the Sixties Scoop. *First Peoples Child and Family Review, 3*(1), 65–82.

Sue, D.W. (2004). Whiteness and ethnocentric monoculturalism: Making the "invisible" visible. *American Psychologist, 59*(8), 761–769.

Sugiman, P. (2001). Privilege and oppression: The configuration of race, gender and class in Southern Ontario auto plants, 1939–1949. *Labour/Le travail, 47*, 83–113.

Warick, J. (2018, February 13). The long list of problems Colten Boushie's family says marred the case. *CBC*. https://www.cbc.ca/news/canada/saskatoon/colten-boushie-family-list-problems-gerald-stanley-case-1.4532214

Wiegman, R. (1999). Whiteness studies and the paradox of particularity. *Boundary, 26*(3), 115–150.

Wood, B. (1997). *The origins of American slavery: Freedom and bondage in the English colonies*. New York, NY: Hill and Wang.

7 Being "Middle Class"?

MARK P. THOMAS

In his 2015 campaign strategy to become Canada's prime minister, Justin Trudeau announced that a key component of his platform would include tax cuts for the middle **class**, with the promise that middle-class voters would benefit immediately (Weber, 2015). The middle class was also the prime focus in US President Donald Trump's tax reform bill in 2017. When it passed in December 2017, Trump described the bill as a "Christmas present to the middle class" (Reuters, 2017). Both leaders invoked a refrain frequently heard from politicians across Western capitalist democracies: the importance of the "middle class." Their promises reflected the fact that, throughout the second half of the 20th century and into the 21st century, the ideal of "middle class" became a normalized **centre**, exerting influence over social and economic policies, as well as the everyday class experiences of many in the West. Indeed, beginning in the 1950s, there was significant growth in North America and parts of Western Europe in the numbers of people who were associated with the middle class: those with stable employment, income security, and disposable earnings for leisure and consumption. The ideal of achieving (at least) a middle-class lifestyle was supported by the social and economic policies of the Keynesian welfare **state**. The middle-class ideal emerged in relation to the formation of the nuclear family and exerted a profound normalizing influence over people's identities and aspirations.

For the last several decades, however, there has been an erosion of the middle class, with a growing economic polarization evident in many Western capitalist economies (Gordon, 2016; Piketty, 2014). This growing polarization was brought to the forefront of the public's attention during the financial crisis of 2008, the biggest economic crisis since the Great Depression of the 1930s, as stock values plunged, financial institutions failed, and unemployment increased dramatically. The financial crisis also sparked the emergence of a major protest movement—starting with Occupy Wall Street—that brought attention to the ever-growing disparity between the wealthy 1 per cent and the remaining 99 per cent of the **population**. The irony of Trump's "Christmas present to the middle class," with its disproportionate tax benefits to corporations and wealthy individuals, was that it was part of the neoliberal policy framework contributing to this polarizing pattern. Yet despite the erosion of the middle class, discourses of middle classness persist and continue to orient many toward this normalized centre.

This growing economic polarization raises many profound questions about the world we live in and the social relationships that shape our lives. What is it about **capitalism** that creates such opportunity for some and such insecurity for many? What are the social relations that simultaneously produce such wealth and such profound **inequality**? It is no accident that references to the works of Karl Marx began to appear in commentaries emerging in the years following the 2008 financial crisis (Brown, 2009). Marx wrote of capitalism as a system that is inherently prone to inequality, conflict, and crisis. One hundred and fifty years later, his writing on the class relations of capitalism continues to provide a compelling account of the social organization of class.

This chapter introduces the sociological **concept** of class and illustrates ways in which class—as a social relation—may have profound connections to many aspects of our daily lives. Beginning with the writings of early sociologists Max Weber and Karl Marx, the chapter distinguishes between the understanding of class as a system of **socio-economic stratification** and a "**relational**" approach to understanding class. The chapter then focuses on Marx's writing in greater detail, suggesting that Marx's work provides great insight into the profound ways in which class relations are fundamentally connected to the social organization of **power** (Lukes, 1986). Despite the erosion of the middle class in a material sense, the chapter also points to the ways in which the notion of "middle class" becomes an organizing principle of everyday life in ways that normalize and help to reproduce the class system of capitalism.

As with other chapters in this volume, this chapter situates class in the context of "everyday" **power relations**. By unpacking the everyday object of the *pay stub*, the chapter identifies the importance of recognizing class as a social relation that disconnects many people from the ability to control their labour and that accords power to those who own the economic resources in society. The chapter also identifies the ways in which class relations contribute to and intersect with forms of power covered in other chapters, such as those shaped by **race** and **gender**, in order to begin to think about the ways in which a wide range of social relationships, practices, and everyday experiences may have class dimensions. Overall, the chapter presents an analysis of class that seeks to disrupt the normalized assumption that life in the "middle class" insulates one from these deeper power relations, and points to the ways in which class relations constitute a key element of social organization in contemporary Canadian society.

Beginning with the End (of Class Analysis)

The emphasis on class analysis in this chapter runs against some currents of sociological thinking that have developed over the past several decades. Patrick Joyce (1995) notes that profound economic, political, and social change in the latter half of the 20th century led to the belief that class may be "unequal to the task of explaining our present reality" (p. 3). For example, in writing about the economic growth and "post-industrial" transformation of industrialized economies in the decades following World War II, prominent social theorist Daniel Bell (1973) suggested that the **exploitation** of industrial factory work would give way to the more favourable work environments of white-collar offices, and that new technologies would give people greater leisure time. This "post-industrial" society would lead to a reduction of class-based inequalities and conflicts. Taking a related approach, Alain Touraine (1988) argued that as "post-industrial" society emerged, the class experiences and conflict of the industrial era would disappear and the traditional institutions that represented **working-class** interests—specifically trade unions—would fade. Without the class inequality of industrial capitalism, working-class movements would be replaced by a wide range of "identity-based" social movements. According to Touraine, while working-class movements were predominant in the early and mid 20th century, as class relations faded other kinds of social movements were more likely to reflect the conditions of inequality and social conflicts of the late 20th century.

Similarly, in *The Death of Class*, Jan Pakulski and Malcolm Waters (1996) argued that economic and social transformation of the late 20th century created the need to fundamentally decentre class as a sociological concept. More specifically, they stated that class divisions are eroding in the industrialized economies of the capitalist West to the point where these societies are "no longer class societies" (p. 4) and that class identities and **ideologies** are dissolving as a basis for political movements. They did not suggest that these societies are becoming egalitarian or free from social conflict, but rather that class should no longer be considered the basis for inequality or conflict.

Certainly, these authors draw attention to the need to understand how capitalist societies may have changed in the late 20th century, as compared to the early years of industrial capitalism. And certainly, they point to the need to understand the wide array of social relationships that shape patterns of social organization and inequality. But rather than assume the end of class relations, this chapter instead asks *how* class relations may have changed and *what form* they may take in the present day.

Class, Status, and Stratification

When asked "What is your class identity?," many students will answer "middle class." In a survey conducted by Ekos Research, 50 per cent of Canadians identified as "middle class" (though only 41 per cent of those under 35 did so; Graves, 2017). This reflects a common understanding of class as a position within a socio-economic hierarchy. Seen in this way, one's class position is generally taken to refer loosely to one's income level, with people often identifying upper (wealthy), middle, and lower (poor) class as the range of "class positions," with those who are neither extremely poor nor extremely wealthy placed somewhere in the "middle." This approach to class has been widely accepted and developed within sociology, and has been very influential in studies of socio-economic inequality.

Understanding class as a system of stratification has its roots in the work of German sociologist Max Weber (1864–1920), though Weber's writing on class is ultimately more multidimensional and complex than stratification theory (Wright, 1997). In *Economy and Society: An Outline of Interpretive Sociology*, Weber (1978) developed the concept of "class situation" to describe the social organization of 19th-century capitalism. This term, "class situation," refers to the likelihood of "(i) procuring goods; (ii) gaining a position in life; and (iii) finding inner satisfactions" (p. 302). He considered the likelihood of achieving a particular class situation to be determined "from the relative control over goods and skills and from their income-producing uses within a given economic order" (p. 302). What this means is that people who may have similar levels of ownership and control over things like property (land) or a business, or who had similar levels of skill and/or education, would have a similar class situation.

Weber then used the term "class" to describe those who held a set of shared interests that emerge through their class situation. One's class, for Weber, was determined through a wide range of situations defined by ownership of property, individual assets, occupation, and skills. For example, property owners were a class, as were commercial investors, as were skilled artisans, as were industrial factory workers. But Weber did not see class as a singular experience, as an individual could experience different class situations through their lives, as well as upward mobility between different class situations (Breen, 2005). While one's class was rooted in a set of shared interests with others of the same class, Weber's understanding of class was that there was little potential for broad-based uniformity and unity in class situations, because of the wide variety of class situations and potential for class mobility.

While class situations were quite variable, Weber nonetheless identified four major social class groupings: (a) the working class; (b) the petty bourgeoisie (small business owners); (c) propertyless intelligentsia and specialists (white-collar employees, civil servants, etc.); and (d) classes "privileged through property and education." But consistent with his view of the complexity of class, he saw great potential for differentiation within these groupings. For example, different skills could create differentiation amongst the working class, and different levels of education could create variation in class situation amongst white-collar workers. For those with property, there could be differentiation based on whether or not wealth was hereditary or built up through business ownership. So overall, while he identified four major social classes, he saw a great deal of diversity within these major groups.

Making this picture of social hierarchies even more complex, Weber also introduced the concept of **status**, which he used to denote a form of "social esteem" (p. 305).

Status was not simply associated with income, but could come through formal education or training, or from more traditional means like family background. Status may be connected to class, but was not directly determined by class. Owning property may not necessarily produce high status in and of itself, though it could if it enabled access to higher education. One could belong to a very privileged class (due to wealth and property, for example) but as an individual have very low status if they held an occupation that was of low esteem or if they did not pursue higher education. Thus, the idea of status further complicates the levels of differentiation that may exist between individuals and social groups, according to Weber.

Elements of the Weberian approach to understanding class became quite influential in 20th-century sociology as a way to understand patterns of social and economic stratification, though as stated above Weber's own writing on class cannot be reduced to stratification theory. Stratification theorists built on Weberian concepts to study the ways in which income, education, and occupation become connected to patterns of socio-economic inequality between individuals and social groups (Crompton, 2008; Fantasia, 1988). Because the stratification perspective draws attention to different levels of class and status markers, it is sometimes also referred to as a "gradational" approach to class (Edgell, 1993). Sociologists working from this perspective have made many attempts to break down these categories into detailed class schemes that reflect different class positions, including primary groups of upper, middle, and lower class, as well as subgroups within these, such as upper-middle class and lower-middle class. These class groupings are defined by income levels as well as status indicators such as education credentials, occupational categories, and formal measurements of skill (Edgell, 1993). Within this approach to studying class, the category of "middle class" is often taken as the norm, as it is meant to capture those who are neither extremely wealthy nor poor. Thus, when asked about our class position or class identity, many automatically respond with "middle class."

From this "gradational" approach, we are able to see levels of inequality that may exist between different class groupings, where class is understood as "collections of individuals with shared social characteristics, or in possession of similar amounts of a scarce resource" (Fantasia, 1988, p. 13). However, because of its emphasis on class as a position within a grid or hierarchy, this approach tells us very little about the social relationships that may exist between these classes. More specifically, and in relation to our interests in this textbook, seeing class in a system of stratification tells us very little about the power relations that produce and reproduce class, and the social conflict that may result from those relations (Aronowitz, 2003).

Toward a "Relational" Concept of Class

> "The history of all hitherto existing societies is the history of class struggle."
> Marx and Engels (2002, p. 219)

What does it mean to say class is a social relation and not simply a position in an income hierarchy? And why might this be an important distinction? If we see class as a social relation, we can begin to understand how classes are produced in relation to one another, rather than existing independently of one another. And more importantly, given the aim of this text to explore the social organization of power, we can see how the production of power in an economic form emerges through class relations. It is through critically examining these class relations that we can begin to see how the privilege experienced by some is directly related to the marginalization of others.

To understand class as a social relation we first look to the writing of the German political economist Karl Marx (1818–1883), who argued that classes, as social groups, are defined through their relationships with other classes. In the highly noted statement from *The Communist Manifesto* above we see that, for Marx, class is a fundamental social relationship within human societies and social conflict is a primary aspect of the social relations that exist between classes. David Stark (1980) explains:

> a class … is not a collection or aggregation of individuals. Classes, like the social relations from which they arise, exist in an antagonistic and dependent relation to each other. Classes are constituted by these mutually antagonistic relations. In this sense … the object of study is not the elements themselves but the relations between them. (p. 97)

Framing class analysis in this way moves beyond simply examining levels of difference (inequality, stratification) between different classes or between individuals within class groupings.

Class Relations in Capitalism

As discussed in Chapter 1, Marx developed the method of **historical materialism** to explain class relations. From the perspective of historical materialism, understanding class as a social relation begins with looking at how people produce and reproduce themselves in their daily lives. Canadian sociologist Dorothy Smith (1987) explains:

> [Marx and Engels] insist we start in the same world as the one we live in, among real individuals, their activities, and the material conditions of their activities. What is there to be investigated are the ongoing actual activities of real people. (p. 123)

With this as a beginning, Marx suggested that human history is divided into identifiable periods, each of which is characterized by a particular **mode of production**. The mode of production refers to the economic organization of a society: the ways in which people produce, distribute, and consume goods. Capitalism, for example, is a mode of production. Within capitalism, the social relations of production, exchange, and consumption are very different from those in other modes of production, such as **feudalism**. Keith Faulks (2005) identifies four primary features of capitalism:

- the **means of production** are owned and controlled by relatively few people (capitalists);
- the "primary objective of capitalists is to maximize profit by producing and selling goods and services for as little cost as possible, and selling them on to consumers for as much profit as possible";
- "[p]rofits are achieved largely through the exploitation of **wage labour**"; and
- goods and services (commodities) are exchanged on a 'free' market, "where they are bought and sold according to the laws of supply and demand, and for a value determined not by their intrinsic worth but by their market value." (p. 29)

To better understand capitalism Marx first looked at feudalism, the predominant mode of production that existed in Western Europe before capitalism (Naiman, 2008). Feudalism was an agricultural system where land was held by feudal lords and worked by serfs, who produced for the feudal lord. In exchange for this production, they were allowed a small portion of land on which to produce for themselves. In Western Europe by the 1500s, these peasants were increasingly being expelled from feudal lands so an emerging landed aristocracy could use the lands for new and profitable purposes like raising sheep for wool manufacture. In other words, a new class—capitalists—was emerging in this context and was seizing control over land to put it to use for profit making. Meanwhile, peasants were cut off from the land—their means of production. This transition was aided by legislation that allowed for the expropriation of land and severe violence against those who resisted.

Marx termed this process **primitive accumulation**: the expropriation and enclosure (privatization) of land. Two key interrelated developments resulted from the process of primitive accumulation: (a) the establishment of private control over land so that it could be used for capital accumulation; and (b) the creation of landless masses of people. The masses of people had no means to support or reproduce themselves, since their access to land and livelihood had been eliminated. As capitalism developed, this process of expropriating land spread to other parts of the world, in particular through European colonization. **Colonial** expansion—whether in Asia, Africa, or the Americas—was a means by which European powers secured additional wealth to finance the development of capitalism in Western Europe. So the birth of capitalism is rooted in both the violent expropriation of land and resources and the exploitation of labour in many parts of the world. In Marx's words, "capital comes [into the world] dripping from head to toe, from every pore, with blood and dirt" (1976, pp. 925–926).

These processes were central to the formation of Canada as a **nation-state**, through the **colonialism** of the British and French, as they settled in North America and established control over land that **Indigenous** peoples had lived on for centuries (Coulthard, 2014; Satzewich & Wotherspoon, 2000). Through treaty arrangements, large amounts of land were exchanged for very small amounts of money. Moreover, white European settlement continued to expand even in areas where there were no treaty agreements. This process of appropriation dispossessed Indigenous peoples of land and natural resources, securing these for the growing European settlement and the expansion of a capitalist economy. This primitive accumulation also produced conflicts over land, natural resources, and political **sovereignty** that continue to this day.

In Chapter 15, Margot Francis explores some of the cultural legacies of these processes manifested in contemporary Canada, by looking at the ways in which the colonization of First Nations peoples also produced racist **stereotypes** and myths. As we critically examine the everyday cultural practices that Francis raises, we must also remember that they are very much a part of longstanding historical processes of primitive accumulation that are deeply connected to ongoing struggles over land and natural resources. In other words, the history of colonization remains present in these present-day practices and struggles.

While in Marx's writing primitive accumulation was something that happened a long time ago, we can still see many ongoing examples of this process today. According to the economic geographer David Harvey (2005), who uses the term "**accumulation by dispossession**" to refer to the introduction of market forces into spaces that were previously non-capitalist, we can see the results of primitive accumulation in a wide range of settings. This includes the dispossession of peoples of their land in the search for resources (for example, oil or minerals), or the development of factories in export-processing zones in the Global South. This may also include the privatization of public services—for example in healthcare or education—through **neoliberalism**, which is discussed in the chapter on "**financial fitness**" by Mary-Beth Raddon.

Primitive accumulation created the basis for the emergence of private ownership over land, labour, and capital, and thereby the class relations of capitalism. According to Marx, this process produced two fundamental classes: the bourgeoisie, or **capitalist class**, and the proletariat, or working class. Rather than simply looking at inequality between these classes, Marx argued that these classes are each defined through their *relationship to the means of production*—the materials, infrastructure, and natural resources needed to produce goods and provide services (including factories, technology, tools, etc.). Specifically, the capitalist class are those who own and control the means of production, while the working class are those who do not own means of production and therefore must sell their **labour power**—their capacity to labour—in order to earn wages and ensure their subsistence. It is through the sale and purchase of labour power that these two classes are brought into relation to one another. For Marx, the class relations between the capitalist class and working class constitute the central driving force within capitalist societies (Marx & Engels, 2002).

While Marx saw the working class and capitalist class as the primary classes within this system of class relations, he also recognized intermediate classes, such as the petite bourgeoisie—small business owners, independent farmers and craftspeople, and self-employed professionals. Building on the relational approach to class that Marx developed, sociologist Erik Olin Wright (1997) refined this approach to incorporate those in the middle class. For Wright, the middle class includes those in managerial or supervisory roles (who exercise domination over workers), as well as those with higher levels of skills and/or expertise. Wright noted that since supervisors/managers and higher skilled workers do not own the means of production, they are not part of the capitalist class; however, they may have authority over the work of others, or may experience greater levels of autonomy over their own work than do other members of the working class. Wright argued that this places them in unique—and, more specifically, contradictory and privileged—class locations vis-à-vis the rest of the working class: contradictory for those who exercise managerial/supervisory power, which sets them apart from (and against) other members of the working class; and privileged in that they may retain a higher level of the surplus produced through their labour (i.e. receive higher levels of employment income). However, while Wright's typology is based on recognizing the unique class locations of the middle class, it does so through the lens of the relational approach to class: the middle class is situated in relation to the larger dynamics of exploitation and competing interests between capitalist and working classes. They are not simply a middle layer in a system of stratification based on hierarchical income or status differences.

Another key dimension of the class relations of capitalism can be seen in the link between class power and political institutions. More specifically, Marx saw *the state*—the set of political institutions that encompass governments and their

FIGURE 7.1 James E. Cayne, former Chairman and CEO of Bear Stearns, and Alan D. Schwartz, former CEO, appear before the Financial Crisis Inquiry Commission, 2010. ZUMA Press, Inc./Alamy.

agencies (the police, military, courts, legislature, and public service (Miliband, 1969))—as a source of political power for the dominant class in capitalist society. Thus, "[t]he executive of the modern State is but a committee for managing the common affairs of the whole bourgeoisie" (Marx & Engels, 2002, p. 221). The dominant class utilizes state institutions, whether through laws, the courts, or the police, to establish the political and legal conditions necessary for capitalist production and to repress working-class resistance.

What are the connections between Marx's analysis of class and the social organization of **everyday practices**? Marx wanted to understand one of the most normalized and taken-for-granted everyday practices many people experience in capitalism—wage labour. On the surface, wage labour may appear as an equal and fair exchange: being paid a wage for the number of hours you work at a job. But what underlies this exchange?

Recall that the first step in the emergence of the working class was the process of land expropriation. This created the condition of landlessness needed to produce the industrial workforce of early capitalism. Thus, primitive accumulation created masses of "**free wage labourers**": those who are (a) freed (separated) from the means of production and who must sell their labour power to survive; and (b) freed from any legal constraints that would prevent them from selling their labour power (for example, slavery; Lebowitz, 2003). This is the essence of the class relations of capitalism: the working class sells their labour power in order to survive; and capitalists buy this labour power to generate capital through the production and exchange of commodities (goods or services).

As mentioned above, the system of wage labour may appear as a fair exchange between two parties where each party—worker and capitalist—gets something out of the exchange. The worker gets their wage and the capitalist gets the labour power of that worker to produce something. It is assumed to be mutually beneficial and is generally defined by the everyday term "employment." Marx rejected the view of this as a fair exchange, however. Instead, he saw it as profoundly unequal. More specifically, Marx's theory of class presents these relations as highly exploitative, whereby exploitation is defined as occurring through the appropriation of surplus produced through labour (Wright, 1997). Marx's framework reveals the hidden power dynamics that underpin the social relations that facilitate this appropriation.

Commodification and Alienation

Underlying this analysis of class relations is Marx's concept of the **commodity** (Albo, 2010; Fine & Saad-Filho, 2004). Marx argued that capitalism is ultimately a system of commodity production, where commodities are "**use values** produced by labour for exchange" (Fine & Saad-Filho, p. 19). Use values are goods like food, clothing, and houses, and services like education and healthcare. These are all things that we use (or want) as we reproduce ourselves. A commodity also has an **exchange value**, which is "an equivalence relationship between objects" (Fine & Saad-Filho, p. 17). The exchange value is a quantitative measure that can be used in the process of commodity exchange. In a capitalist market, the exchange value of a commodity is represented through money. So commodities in capitalism have both use values (based on an ability to meet a human need or want) and exchange values (a representation of its value in the form of money—in other words, what something costs).

How does this help us understand the class relations of capitalism? Looking at the organization of wage labour, we can see that the labour power of the working class is itself treated like a commodity. Its use value is its ability to create new value, for example by creating products or providing services. Its exchange value is represented in a wage: the monetary compensation for time spent at work (generally calculated as an hourly rate). This is really just a very abstract way to describe the everyday experience of going to a job. Think of these terms by looking at a job you may have had, like working at a coffee shop, at a call centre, as a swim instructor, or in a clothing store at a shopping mall. Your use value is your capacity to pour cups of coffee, deal with customers over the phone, teach others to swim, or sell a pair of jeans. Your exchange value is the wage you are paid to do these things. This exchange is captured in the everyday object of the pay stub, which provides a record of hours worked and pay received, as well as any deductions made over the course of the pay period.

On its surface, employment appears in our everyday experiences as a fair exchange, as symbolized in the pay stub received so regularly. Wage labour becomes normalized first in the sense that we do not question (or even recognize) the power relations that underlie this exchange, and second in the ways that we contribute to its reproduction through our everyday activities (Burawoy, 1979).

Employer Name and Address		**EARNINGS STATEMENT**
Employee Name		
EMPLOYEE ID	**PERIOD ENDING**	**PAY DATE**

INCOME	**RATE**	**HOURS**	**CURRENT**	**DEDUCTIONS**	**CURRENT**	**YTD**
REGULAR OVERTIME				CPP EI CIT UNION DUES		

YTD GROSS	**YTD DEDUCTIONS**	**YTD NET PAY**	**CURRENT TOTAL**	**DEDUCTIONS**	**NET PAY**

FIGURE 7.2 Sample pay stub.

The lens of **governmentality** (and **poststructuralism**) provides further insight into how these processes become normalized. Employee self-identification with work, the workplace, or even the company can support the adoption of patterns and routines that reinforce and reproduce the authority of management (O'Doherty & Willmott, 2001). When working in the service sector, this takes the form of the **normalization** of conduct oriented toward the principles of good customer service—"service with a smile"—as discussed further below. With regards to "being middle class," this becomes an idealized goal where employment is viewed as an opportunity to become upwardly mobile, through an income that will enable a higher status. In these ways, the class relations of labour exploitation become normalized and reproduced through a variety of everyday activities.

If capitalism is producing such conditions, why do they remain so deeply hidden? What about the (exploitation of the) working class? To help explain why these class relations remain unseen, Marx developed the concept **commodity fetishism**, whereby we tend to associate the value of a commodity with its price, rather than the human labour that produced the commodity. Through this process, the labour, conditions of production, and extraction of **surplus value** connected to a commodity are made invisible: the commodity becomes a "thing" that is separate from the

FIGURE 7.3 Chinese high-tech factory workers assembling components of LCD display boards by hand. SDBBusiness/Alamy.

relationships that exist between capitalists and workers. Thus, this great working-class "rip off" is not recognized. In Chapter 14, Gavin Fridell and Erika Koss look further into this concept, to unravel the labour and production processes that create the cup of coffee.

By recognizing the ways in which our own labour power is treated as a commodity, we are able to begin to unpack the power relations that shape the social organization of the capitalist workplace and that underlie the exchange captured in the pay stub. According to Marx, when we work for a wage, we create surplus value—profit—for our employer based on the fact that wages paid are less than the value of the commodities produced or the services provided. Think about this in terms of the hourly wages of a barista in a coffee shop as compared to the price of all of the cups of coffee that a barista serves in an hour. What this means is that wage labour is inherently a system of exploitation based on the **commodification** of people's labour power that occurs unseen at the "point of production" in the capitalist workplace (Burawoy, 1979). Defining class through relations of exploitation that are rooted in production is a fundamental point of distinction between Marx's approach to class relations and "gradational"/stratification and Weberian approaches (Wright, 1997, 2005).

What are the consequences of these kinds of class relations? Certainly, levels of economic inequality between two major classes are a primary result, as reflected in the discourses of Occupy Wall Street that highlighted the disparity between the wealthy 1 per cent and the remaining 99 per cent. In addition to inequality, Marx and others who have been influenced by his ideas about class relations argue that these social relations produce profound conditions of **alienation** within capitalist society (Braverman, 1974). Since working for a wage entails giving up control over the ability to decide what kind of work one will do and how that work will be carried out, Marx suggested we lose much of our creative capacity through engaging in wage labour. When we look at the class relations of wage labour, we can see multiple dimensions of alienation: from the products of labour (what is created); from the tasks of work (how they are determined and carried out); from creative capacities for expression through work; and from one another (we are positioned in competition with each other, and thereby lose the collective capacity to control work) (Marx, 1964).

We can see examples of alienation—to varying degrees—in a wide range of jobs (Braverman, 1974). The easiest examples that come to mind are factory assembly lines. But what about other kinds of workplaces? Fast food workplaces, for example, are also characterized by high degrees of management control over workers, with the labour process deskilled much like in a factory (Barndt, 2008; Royle, 2000). Working in fast food production typically includes a general routinization of jobs (food preparation, order taking, food serving), a high degree of repetition of simplified tasks, little opportunity for decision-making, and the use of technology to minimize worker knowledge and discretion (for example, cash registers to organize orders and prompt order takers with phrases). What this means is that in addition to receiving low wages and little job security, workers are easily replaced and have little autonomy. What we can see from this example is that the experiences of alienation that may be common on a manufacturing assembly line may also be present in a range of service economy workplaces.

Interaction between customers and workers in the service economy introduces another dimension to how alienation may occur, creating more subjective and less obvious forms of labour control (McDowell, 2009; Pupo, Duffy, & Glenday, 2017). Specifically, in the context of the service economy, a new dimension of alienation occurs through control over **emotional labour**: "the conscious manipulation of the workers' self-presentation either to display feeling states and/or to create feeling states in others" (Leidner, 1996, p. 30). Customer interaction alters the relations of the labour process in service work, whereby the customer becomes an important factor in a system of labour control (Ritzer, 2008). Customers become a part of the process by expecting cheerful service, and they play a key role in establishing control over service work through channels for customer input and assessments of service provision. "Service with a smile" becomes normalized not only as part of the skill set of service work, but also as a form of self-governance for service-sector workers.

This is not to say that all forms of work are equally alienating, or that the conditions of alienation experienced by people today are exactly the same as during the time when Marx was writing. But we can use these ideas that were developed a long time ago to begin to better understand the so-called "fair exchange" of our labour power for a wage in many kinds of workplaces in today's economy. We can also use these ideas as a beginning to understand dimensions of class conflict that play out in the workplace and beyond, in terms of both collective and individual responses to alienation and exploitation. For Marx, the dynamics of working-class resistance to exploitation are a central driving force in capitalist society. As the polarization between classes increased, according to Marx, so too would mass movements against capitalist power (Marx & Engels, 2002). We can see the emergence of trade unions as one example of a collective response to labour exploitation. Trade unions formed as a way to provide working-class people with a collective voice in determining wages and working conditions, and they act to counter the absolute power of employers in the workplace (Jackson & Thomas, 2017). In recent years, we can also see the emergence of mass movements like Occupy Wall Street and the Fight for $15 and Fairness as collective responses to capitalist-class power. In addition, at the individual level, we can see many forms of "everyday" acts of resistance to alienated labour—what Robin D.G. Kelley (1996) refers to as "**infrapolitics**." These can include things like slowdowns, sabotage, absenteeism, altering standardized labour processes, and personalizing workplace uniforms. While exploitation and alienation are key dynamics of the class relations of capitalism, resistance to these social relations is undoubtedly present in many individual and collective forms.

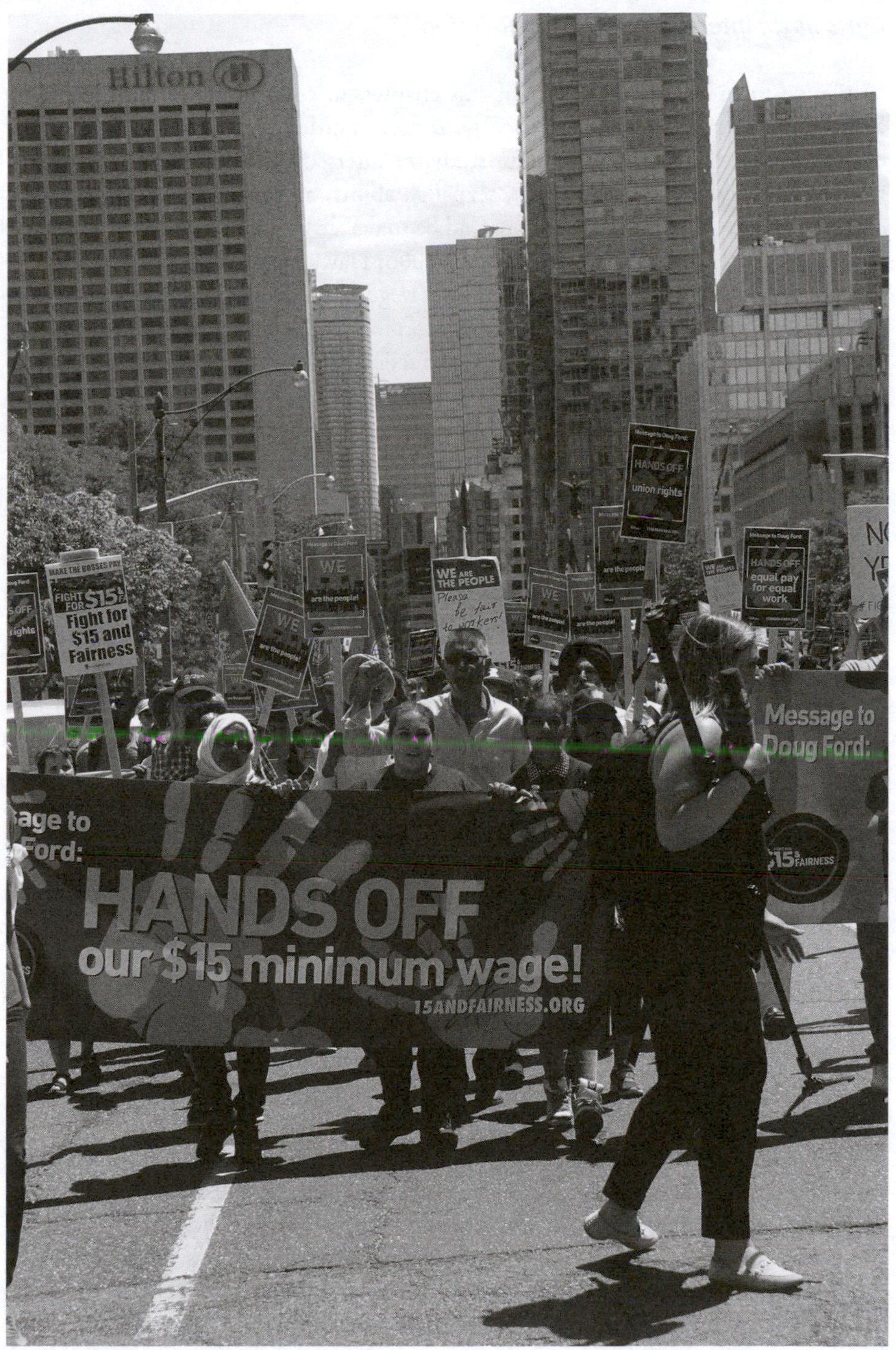

FIGURE 7.4 Fight for $15 and Fairness demonstration. CC BY 2.0/OFL Communications Director.

Class as an Intersectional Social Relation

While we focus on class relations in this chapter, in conjunction with the holistic approach of this textbook we must recognize that in order to understand the everyday dimensions of class relations, we must study the intersection of class with other social relationships including race, gender, sexuality, ability, and citizenship. To treat class separately from other social relations would be to detach it from its material, historical, and social context (Acker, 2006; Bannerji, 2006; Hawkesworth, 2006). So while the work of Marx emphasized the organization of wage labour as central to the class system of capitalism, taking an approach that is informed by the **intersectional analysis** of Crenshaw (1989, 1991) outlined in the Introduction means we cannot understand wage labour unless we seek to uncover the ways in which class relations are simultaneously shaped by other social relations. It means we cannot consider the working class or the capitalist class as simply large, homogeneous groups. We must also pay equal attention to other processes of social differentiation both within and between classes.

As just two examples, we can look at both racialized and gendered divisions of labour in contemporary capitalism. **Racialization** is deeply embedded in the social organization of paid and unpaid work and is central in shaping patterns of labour market inequality in capitalist economies. A prime example of this is through immigration policies that limit the participation of racialized workers in a labour market, such as the temporary foreign worker programs that create systems of low-wage "unfree" **migrant** labour, as discussed in the chapter on citizenship and borders by Nandita Sharma. We can see discourses of "desirable" and "undesirable" work forming in racialized terms and contributing to class dimensions of **whiteness** as a relation of privilege. For example, in the Seasonal Agricultural Workers' Program that brings foreign workers to Canada for seasonal harvesting work, Mexican and Caribbean men are considered to be physically well-suited for agricultural harvesting, work that most Canadians are unwilling to do because it is very physically demanding, with long hours and low pay. But because of racist conceptions of Canadian citizenship, these same workers are socially constructed as "undesirable" future citizens, thereby justifying the government policy that requires them to leave the country once the harvesting season is complete. Thus, class, race, and citizenship are profoundly intertwined through government policies and employer practices that facilitate the exploitation of migrant labourers.

We can also see connections between class and gender, specifically through the organization of **social reproduction**—"the activities required to ensure day-to-day and generational survival of the population" (Luxton & Corman, 2001, p. 29). Discourses and practices of masculinity and femininity become part of the class relations of capitalism through gendered **norms** about women's responsibilities in the home and men's role as "breadwinners," which produce feminized and masculinized norms of employment and gendered occupational structures (Creese, 1999; Steedman, 1997). Similarly, racialized ideologies have contributed to the construction of domestic work as a key site of employment for women of colour, where discourses about the "natural" abilities of women from racialized groups have legitimized further racialized divisions of reproductive labour (cooking, cleaning, caring) (Brand, 1999; Glenn, 1992). In private households, women from racialized groups have long been employed as servants to assist upper- and upper-middle-class white women in the completion of household work, thereby absolving white women of the most onerous aspects of this work. As reproductive labour has been increasingly commodified during the economic expansion of the service sector, women from racialized groups have been employed in a variety of "lower-level" forms of reproductive labour, such as nurses' aides, kitchen workers, maids in hotels, or cleaners in offices, while white women are more likely to be employed as supervisors, professionals, or administrative support staff. Building from an intersectional framework informed by Crenshaw's (1989, 1991) approach, it can be seen through these examples how racialized and gendered norms interact both with and through class to produce the normative practices of wage labour that are premised on hidden but highly exploitative and alienating social relations.

This intersectional approach to understanding class relations also adds to our understanding of state power. For example, feminist political economists have identified the state as a site involved in organizing not only the social relations of economic production, but also social reproduction (Bezanson & Luxton, 2006; O'Conner, Orloff, & Shaver, 1999). This occurs specifically through state interventions that affect the organization of both the family and women's work, in ways that reproduce **patriarchal** relations (Ursel, 1992). While Canada's social safety net was being developed in the decades after World War II, economic policies such as Unemployment Insurance, as well as labour laws that set minimum employment standards, were premised upon the social norm of the male breadwinner. These policies explicitly and implicitly promoted a gendered division of labour that was dependent upon women's unpaid labour in the home by creating different and unequal levels of social security for male and female workers (Porter, 2003; Pulkingham, 1998). Similarly, critical race theorists have shown how state policies have created many forms of racialized inequality. In Canada, this can be seen in immigration policies that discriminate against non-white immigrant groups, as discussed by Nandita Sharma in this volume, or through government policies of land appropriation and forced assimilation for Indigenous populations in white settler societies.

What about the Middle Class?

While the middle class grew through the course of the 20th century in many industrialized countries, in recent times there is much evidence of growing economic polarization that is contributing to an erosion of the middle class. For example, in Canada between 2005 and 2012 the median net worth of the top 10 per cent rose by 42 per cent, while the median net worth of the bottom 10 per cent dropped by 150 per cent (due to growing debt levels). In 2012, the top 10 per cent of Canadians accounted for nearly half of all of the wealth in the country, while the bottom 30 per cent accounted for less than 1 per cent of the country's wealth (Broadbent Institute, 2014).

This growing gap has been enhanced by the growth in low-wage and insecure employment that has occurred during this same time period (Jackson & Thomas, 2017). When we see the predominance of low-wage jobs in the service sector, we must remind ourselves again of the labour that goes into a cup of coffee or the selling of designer jeans. The people brewing and pouring our "everyday" cup of coffee at places like Tim Hortons, Timothy's, Starbucks, and Second Cup, or stocking shelves at The Gap, Loblaws, and Walmart are very much a part of this growing low-wage workforce. The conditions of low-wage work and the experiences of low-wage workers are thus a key part of the everyday practices of buying a cup of coffee or going shopping discussed in other chapters of this textbook.

Moreover, these employment patterns reflect the racialization of low-wage work in Canada's labour market, whereby racialized groups are disproportionately represented in low-income occupations (Galabuzi, 2006). This racialized segmentation is reflected in a persistent earnings differential, whereby the median annual income of racialized men is approximately 30 per cent lower than that of white Canadian men, while the median annual income of racialized women is 21 per cent lower than that of white Canadian women (Jackson & Thomas, 2017). These figures are similar for Indigenous peoples, who have a median income of nearly 30 per cent less than the Canadian workforce overall, with an income gap of 37 per cent for Indigenous men and 22 per cent for Indigenous women. Overall, when we look at the growing gap, we see that the economic polarization in Canadian society includes high levels of racialized inequality.

The growing gap has also been exacerbated by neoliberal state policies, a phenomenon discussed in detail by Mary-Beth Raddon in her chapter on financial fitness. As governments have brought neoliberal principles into public policy, we see an increasing benefit to private capital, legitimated through the popular **discourse** of mutual prosperity through individualized competitiveness. When we look closely at neoliberalism, as Raddon does in her chapter, we can see that while in principle it calls for a reduction of state intervention in the economy, neoliberal policies are in fact about reorienting the way in which governments operate by developing policies that are increasingly favourable to the interests of capitalists (Connell, 2010; Harvey, 2005). This has involved eliminating policies and programs that provide social and economic security (unemployment insurance), increasing the user costs of public services (university tuition), and intensifying the ways in which people's labour power is treated as a commodity by lowering standards that regulate working conditions. In these ways, neoliberal governments undermine social safety nets that were developed over decades to mitigate social and economic insecurity and inequality.

Conclusion

This chapter developed a discussion of class that is grounded in Marx's analysis of the class system of capitalism, a perspective that received a renewed interest in the years following the 2008 financial crisis. The fact that there has not yet been a sustained and revolutionary working-class movement that has fundamentally transformed capitalism has led many to reject Marx's ideas. This chapter, however, has identified ways in which we can use this analysis of class relations to understand power relations that shape important aspects of our everyday lives. While focusing primarily on class analysis, the chapter also pointed to ways in which we can begin to understand interrelationships between class and other forms of everyday power. As class relations remain central to our lives in many ways, we can build on the analysis presented in this chapter to see its connections to the organization of multiple forms of power operating throughout our everyday world.

Study Questions

1 How does Marxist theory conceptualize power? How does this approach to power remain relevant and important?
2 What is the value of our labour? What factors shape its value? How is value differently understood for different kinds of jobs?
3 What are some other examples of ways in which class analysis could be developed through an intersectional approach to power? In what ways is class gendered and racialized?
4 Why and how does class matter in the contemporary economy? How can the **materialist** analysis of class relations be integrated into the Foucauldian analysis of power relations?

Exercises

1 Take notes on the social organization of your workplace. Who has control and decision-making power? Map out your own labour process. How much control

do you have? Over what aspects of your work? Use this exercise as a way to evaluate Marx's theory of alienation and the labour process.

2 Think about the last major purchase you made. What is its use value and exchange value? Where did it come from? Deconstruct this commodity by mapping out the stages of its development from production to consumption. Use this exercise as a way to explore Marx's concept of "commodity fetishism."

3 How is middle class represented in popular culture? Make a list of recent TV shows, movies, and songs that may convey class themes. What assumptions about class are present? Do they reinforce ideas of middle classness? Do they question/challenge this norm? How?

References

Acker, J. (2006). *Class questions, feminist answers.* Toronto, ON: Rowman & Littlefield Publishers.

Albo, G. (2010). The "new economy" and capitalism today. In N. Pupo & M. Thomas (Eds.), *Interrogating the new economy: Restructuring work in the 21st century* (pp. 3–20). Toronto, ON: University of Toronto Press.

Aronowitz, S. (2003). *How class works: Power and social movement.* New Haven, CT: Yale University Press.

Bannerji, H. (2006). Reflections on class and race: Building on Marx. *Social Justice, 32*(4), 144–160.

Barndt, D. (2008). *Tangled routes: Women, work and globalization on the tomato trail.* Lanham, MD: Rowman & Littlefield Publishers.

Bell, D. (1973). *The coming of post-industrial society: A venture in social forecasting.* New York, NY: Basic Books.

Bezanson, K., & Luxton, M. (Eds.). (2006). *Social reproduction: Feminist political economy challenges neo-liberalism.* Montreal, QC: McGill-Queen's University Press.

Brand, D. (1999). Black women and work: The impact of racially constructed gender roles on the sexual division of labour. In E. Dua & A. Robertson (Eds.), *Scratching the surface: Canadian anti-racist feminist thought* (pp. 83–96). Toronto, ON: Women's Press.

Braverman, H. (1974). *Labour and monopoly capital: The degradation of work in the twentieth century.* New York, NY: Monthly Review Press.

Breen, R. (2005). Foundations of a neo-Weberian class analysis. In E.O. Wright (Ed.), *Approaches to class analysis* (pp. 31–50). Cambridge, UK: Cambridge University Press.

Broadbent Institute. (2014). *Have and have-nots: Deep and persistent wealth inequality in Canada.* Toronto, ON: Broadbent Institute.

Brown, I. (2009, June 13). The 18th Brumaire of Barack Obama. *The Globe and Mail.*

Burawoy, M. (1979). *Manufacturing consent: Changes in the labor process under monopoly capitalism.* Chicago, IL: University of Chicago Press.

Connell, R. (2010). Understanding neoliberalism. In S. Braedley & M. Luxton (Eds.), *Neoliberalism and everyday life* (pp. 22–36). Montreal, QC: McGill-Queen's University Press.

Coulthard, G. (2014). *Red skin, white masks: Rejecting the colonial politics of recognition.* Minneapolis, MN: University of Minnesota Press.

Creese, G. (1999). *Contracting masculinity: Gender, class, and race in a white-collar union, 1944–1994*. Toronto, ON: Oxford University Press.

Crenshaw, K. (1989). Demarginalizing the intersection of race and sex: A Black feminist critique of antidiscrimination doctrine, feminist theory, and antiracist politics. *University of Chicago Legal Forum, 14*, 538–554.

Crenshaw, K. (1991). Mapping the margins: Intersectionality, identity politics, and violence against women of color. *Stanford Law Review, 43*(6), 1241–1299.

Crompton, R. (2008). *Class and stratification* (3rd ed.). Cambridge, UK: Polity Press.

Edgell, S. (1993). *Class*. London, UK: Routledge.

Fantasia, R. (1988) *Cultures of Solidarity: Consciousness, Action, and Contemporary American Workers*. Berkeley, CA: University of California Press.

Faulks, K. (2005). Capitalism. In G. Blakeley & V. Bryson (Eds.), *Marx and other four-letter words* (pp. 28–45). London, UK: Pluto Press.

Fine, B., & Saad-Filho, A. (2004). *Marx's capital* (4th ed.). London, UK: Pluto Press.

Galabuzi, G.E. (2006). *Canada's economic apartheid: The social exclusion of racialized groups in the new century*. Toronto, ON: Canadian Scholars' Press.

Glenn, E.N. (1992). From servitude to service work: Historical continuities in the racial division of paid reproductive labor. *Signs, 18*(1), 1–43.

Gordon, R.J. (2016). *The rise and fall of American growth: The U.S. standard of living since the Civil War*. Princeton, NJ: Princeton University Press.

Graves, F. (2017). *Understanding the shifting meaning of the middle class*. Toronto, ON: Ekos Research.

Harvey, D. (2005). *The new imperialism*. London, UK: Verso.

Hawkesworth, M. (2006). *Feminist inquiry: From political conviction to methodological innovation*. New Brunswick, NJ: Rutgers University Press.

Jackson, A., & Thomas, M. (2017). *Work and labour in Canada: Critical issues* (3rd ed.). Toronto, ON: Canadian Scholars' Press.

Joyce, P. (Ed.). (1995). *Class*. Oxford, UK: Oxford University Press.

Kelley, R.D.G. (1996). *Race rebels: Culture, politics, and the black working class*. New York, NY: The Free Press.

Lebowitz, M.A. (2003). *Beyond capital: Marx's political economy of the working class* (2nd ed.). New York, NY: Palgrave MacMillan.

Leidner, R. (1996). Rethinking questions of control: Lessons from McDonald's. In C.L. Macdonald & C. Sirianni (Eds.), *Working in the service society* (pp. 29–46). Philadelphia, PA: Temple University Press.

Lukes, S. (1986). *Power*. New York, NY: New York University Press.

Luxton, M., & Corman, J. (2001). *Getting by in hard times: Gendered labour at home and on the job*. Toronto, ON: University of Toronto Press.

Marx, K. (1964). Alienated labour. In T. Bottomore (Ed.), *Karl Marx: Early writings* (pp. 120–34). New York, NY: McGraw Hill.

Marx, K. (1976). *Capital: A critique of political economy* (Vol. 1, B. Fowkes, Trans.). Harmondsworth, UK: Penguin.

Marx, K., & Engels, F. (2002). *The communist manifesto*. London, UK: Penguin.

McDowell, L. (2009). *Working bodies: Interactive service employment and workplace identities*. Chichester, UK: Wiley-Blackwell.

Miliband, R. (1969). *The state in capitalist society*. New York, NY: Basic Books.

Naiman, J. (2008). *How societies work: Class, power and change in a Canadian context* (4th ed.). Black Point, NS: Fernwood Publishing.

O'Conner, J., Orloff, A., & Shaver, S. (1999). *States, markets, families*. Cambridge, UK: Cambridge University Press.

O'Doherty, D., & Willmott, H. (2001). Debating labour process theory: The issue of subjectivity and the relevance of poststructuralism. *Sociology, 35*(2), 457–476.

Pakulski, J., & Waters, M. (1996). *The death of class*. London, UK: Sage Publications.

Piketty, T. (2014). *Capital in the 21st century*. Cambridge, MA: Harvard University Press.

Porter, A. (2003). *Gendered states: Women, unemployment insurance, and the political economy of the welfare state in Canada, 1945–1997*. Toronto, ON: University of Toronto Press.

Pulkingham, J. (1998). Remaking the social divisions of welfare: Gender, "dependency," and UI reform. *Studies in Political Economy, 56*, 7–48.

Pupo, N., Duffy, A., & Glenday, D. (2017). *Crises in Canadian work: A critical sociological perspective*. Don Mills, ON: Oxford University Press.

Reuters. (2017, December 16). Trump defends tax plan as "great Christmas gifts" to middle class. *Reuters*. Retrieved from https://www.reuters.com/article/us-usa-tax-trump/trump-defends-tax-plan-as-great-christmas-gifts-to-middle-class-idUSKBN1EA0OO

Ritzer, G. (2008). *The McDonaldization of society*. Los Angeles, CA: Pine Forge Press.

Royle, T. (2000). *Working for McDonald's in Europe: The unequal struggle?* London, UK: Routledge.

Satzewich, V., & Wotherspoon, T. (2000). The state and the contradictions of Indian administration. In *First Nations: Race, class and gender relations* (pp. 15–41). Regina, SK: Canadian Plains Research Center.

Smith, D. (1987). *The everyday world as problematic: A feminist sociology*. Toronto, ON: University of Toronto Press.

Stark, D. (1980). Class struggle and the labour process. *Theory and Society*, 9(1), 89–130.

Steedman, M. (1997). *Angels of the workplace: Women and the construction of gender relations in the Canadian clothing industry, 1890–1940*. Toronto, ON: Oxford University Press.

Touraine, A. (1988). *Return of the actor: Social theory in postindustrial society*. Minneapolis, MN: University of Minnesota Press.

Ursel, J. (1992). *Private lives, public policy: 100 years of state intervention in the family*. Toronto, ON: Women's Press.

Weber, B. (2015, October 9). Trudeau: Middle-class tax cut will be 1st Liberal bill. *Huffington Post*. Retrieved from http://www.huffingtonpost.ca/2015/10/09/liberal-government-would-introduce-middle-class-tax-cut-in-first-bill_n_8269392.html?utm_hp_ref=ca-justin-trudeau-middle-class-tax-cut

Weber, M. (1978). *Economy and society: An outline of interpretive sociology* (Vol. 1). Berkeley, CA: University of California Press.

Wright, E.O. (1997). *Class counts: Comparative studies in class analysis*. Cambridge, UK: Cambridge University Press.

Wright, E.O. (2005). Foundations of a neo-Marxist class analysis. In E.O. Wright (Ed.), *Approaches to class analysis* (pp. 4–30). Cambridge, UK: Cambridge University Press.

8 Growing Up, Growing Old

REBECCA RABY

Introduction

In 2018, *Black Panther* movie star Michael B. Jordan shocked Americans because he was still living with his parents at age 31. Many commentators in North America see moving out as a key step toward adulthood, and they have worried about a rise in "boomerang kids"—young people who have had to move back home with their parents, often because of economic pressures (Davidson, 2014). Others suggest that we have seen a recent extension of youth, as young people are taking longer to figure themselves out. But why should moving out be seen as a sign of adulthood in the first place? Commenting on the American reaction to Jordan's revelation, Hamlett (2018) points out that in most of the world it is quite normal to live with your parents well into adulthood, reminding us that adulthood is culturally defined.

While age categories such as teenager, adult, and senior are generally understood to be natural, they are socially constructed, reflecting a specific time and place. And like other normative categories, they reflect and reproduce relations of **power**. This chapter deconstructs dominant assumptions about growing up and growing old, including "unpacking" adulthood, to argue that a certain understanding of adulthood as rational, productive, and independent marginalizes many others, including children, seniors, and many adults. After first introducing and evaluating some relevant sociological concepts, I discuss how specific life stages are both normalized and situated in historical, economic, and political contexts. I then consider some dimensions through which the normative **life course** is disrupted, including intersections with other unequal social identities, processes of production and consumption, interdependency, and advocacy.

The Life Course: Norms, Stages, and Transitions

In the study of growing up and growing old, scholars have developed concepts that are both useful and problematic. The life course refers to our lives, from infancy to death, and considers "the way in which **social institutions** shape and institutionalize individual lives" (Settersten & Mayer, 1997, p. 234). Sociologists have tended to prefer the term "life course" over "life cycle," as the latter implies an inevitable repetition of a pattern and a return at the end of life to an organism's beginnings, much as we see in the *Ages of Man* woodcut shown in Figure 8.1, leaving little room for change or diversity (Settersten, 2003).

FIGURE 8.1 *Dégrés des Ages*, a woodcut from early 19th-century France, provides a historical representation of growing up and growing old. This image makes intuitive sense to many of us as the body goes through initial growth, midlife, and eventual waning, with very old age represented as a return to the dependency of infancy. Yet our aging bodies, while relevant, are not the whole story, for they are interpreted through and affected by culture and hierarchy. For instance, midlife, shown at the peak of the arc, is described as "maturity" and "discretion," while both infancy and old age are associated with *enfance* and the oldest phase is negatively represented as "decline" and "decrepitude." The images are also notably gendered and show affluent, heterosexual couples. World Archive/Alamy.

Many discuss the life course in terms of stages, transitions, and norms. Our lives are frequently thought to unfold through concrete stages, each of which is assumed to come with certain features and/or crises. For example, social psychologist Erik Erikson's well-known life stages (1968) are based on having to complete specific tasks of **identity development**.

Erikson's Stages

Infancy. Basic trust is acquired.
Early childhood. Autonomous will develops.
Childhood. Anticipation of roles, display of initiative, and gradual influence of gender, guilt, and morality.
School age. Task identification, development of a sense of industry.
Adolescence. Gradual acquisition of independent identity.
Adulthood. Crisis of intimacy.
Old age. Development of integrity.

Stage approaches focus on how we develop through sequential stages of morality, emotion, physicality, cognition, and so forth, especially in childhood and adolescence. From this perspective, a certain developmental trajectory is ideal. For instance, Erikson focused on the need to develop into an adulthood based on active mastery of the environment, unity in personality, and a correct perception of ourselves and the wider world (1968), and he raised concerns about failure to appropriately move through particular stages. Stages are similarly defined and framed by transitions, or pivotal points of change from one stage to another. Transitions such as graduation, starting work, marriage, and parenthood have often been of interest to sociologists as common steps toward mature, independent adulthood.

Stages and transitions are the scaffolding for **age norms**, which are shared ideas and expectations about what is "typical" behaviour at certain ages (Lawrence, 1996). Much of the early sociological research in this area was influenced by **structural functionalism**. As you may have learned in courses covering classical sociological theory, this approach argues that social structures and shared values foster consensus in society. Structural functionalists consider shared age norms as valuable to the functioning of society, and necessarily enforced through **social control** (Settersten & Mayer, 1997).

Concepts such as stages, transitions, and age norms have usefully informed a wide body of research and debate about the life course. They have also been important for identifying necessary supports when people are "off time." For example, if a young person is not meeting expected stages of physical or cognitive development, educators can be alerted to their need for help. However, work with these concepts has also been problematized for neglecting diversity, power, and **inequality**. A more critical perspective on development suggests that while there is great diversity and inequality across life courses, dominant groups reinforce narrow age norms or ideals, especially around adulthood, that are then used to evaluate and marginalize others.

When individual and group patterns do not fit normative models of stages or transitions (e.g., by dropping out of school), they are often problematically defined as deviant, whereas in fact their actions are frequently logical, patterned variations arising as people from diverse backgrounds engage with their environments across their lives. Alternative stages and transitions can also be shaped by oppression (e.g., through **colonialism**, poverty, **gender** diversity, **racism**, geographical displacement, minority cultural traditions, single parenthood, **queerness**) (Settersten & Mayer, 1997). For example, Erikson's broad stages favour independence, a trait particularly valued within Western capitalist society but not central to many collectivist societies (see also Chapter 7 on **class** and Chapter 12 on consumption).

To provide a more specific example, Geronimus (2003) presents the provocative argument that American campaigns against teenage childbearing tacitly privilege middle-class, European Americans for whom late childbearing brings rewards. While teenage childbearing is often hard on teenagers, on their families, and on broader social supports, Geronimus argues that for some African American communities in high-poverty, urban areas, early childbearing may be a logical choice as poverty and racial inequality can lead to a shortened healthy life expectancy. For these communities, teen pregnancies, alongside grandparents' childcare involvement, can have better social outcomes than later pregnancies. Geronimus contends that in this context, resources invested in negative categorization of early childbearing reflect how middle-class European Americans educate their own youth for success in ways that may marginalize and problematize others.

We thus need to consider how dominant assumptions about the life course are produced and who benefits from them. We need to ask what interests are served by certain norms, stages, and transitions, and how might they be used to negatively evaluate and regulate certain groups of people? Consider the **everyday practice** of asking someone's age, and how the answer contributes to how they are categorized and evaluated based on social expectations, for example about schooling, work, partnering, and parenting. In today's society, we are deeply invested in locating others and ourselves within age-based markers and expectations, providing solidarity, pleasure, security, self-understanding, but also pressure, self-regulation, judgement, division, and exclusion.

Through **disciplinary power**, we are all participants in the normative regulation of age, even though it can marginalize people whose lives do not fit comfortably into dominant age-based expectations. Joanna Gregson's (2009) ethnographic study into the lives of American teenage mothers provides another, related illustration. Because of their youth, the moms in her study found their mothering to be under constant critical scrutiny and comment from healthcare professionals and the public. While these negative comments sometimes fostered self-doubt, the girls often responded with what Gregson calls "competitive parenting," trying to show how they were better parents than both their peers and older women who had their babies "on time." Thus these young mothers both internalized normative critique and sought to surmount it.

Adulthood

Central to the formation of dominant age norms is the Western, 20th-century understanding of "modern adulthood," a **concept** that is both discursive and material. Modern adulthood is

- presented as the stable endpoint of growing up, associated with attaining stability, completeness, self-knowledge, and self-possession (Blatterer, 2007);
- associated with rationality, maturity, and a command of emotions, as contrasted to the irrationality and emotionality of other age groups (Blatterer, 2007; Walkerdine, 1993);
- linked to middle-class benchmarks such as completed education, a career, economic security, marriage, parenthood, and property ownership (Blatterer, 2007);
- defined through independence, in contrast to both childhood and the dependence often associated with old age (Lee, 2001; Hockey & James, 1993).

These benchmarks might seem to reflect common sense; yet they unravel in the face of personal histories, shifting economic conditions, diverse life experiences, and a focus on the contrasting categories of childhood, youth, and old age.

The concept of **recapitulation** provides an example of how the development of our current beliefs about childhood, adolescence, and adulthood are not benign. Recapitulation, popular in the late 19th and early 20th centuries, posited that the development of human beings from children into adults mirrors the evolution of "the **race**"—"a term that variously meant the human race or the white or civilized race" (Adams, 1997, p. 44). From this perspective, children, animals, and "savages" were equated (Gould, 1977), and all considered incompletely developed, and therefore in need of care and control. This presupposition problematically positioned "normal" white, adult, European men as the pinnacle of development, while non-whites (and women, lower classes, and those with mental disabilities) were considered "arrested" at earlier stages of both evolutionary and human development (Adams, 1997; Lesko, 2001). The attribute of rationality was also used to contrast white, bourgeois men from Others (Alsop, Fitzsimons, & Lennon, 2002). These problematic, hierarchical portrayals were backed by **contingent** scientific evidence of the time (see Chapter 10). One of the starkest examples is that of Canada, where the racist portrayal of **Indigenous** peoples as unruly savages facilitated the **colonial** occupation of their lands, their displacement to reserves, and the forced, traumatic removal of Indigenous children to schools to "improve" and "civilize them" (De Leeuw, 2009), resulting in trauma across generations (Nutton & Fast, 2015; see also Chapter 15).

Notions of modern adulthood also emerged around certain economic and political structures of the mid 20th century, including the availability of stable careers (Kohli, 2007; Lee, 2001). Of course, linking adulthood with paid work excludes others, including women working in the home, for instance, and adults who are unemployed. This marker of adulthood has been undermined by the erosion of solid, long-term careers through an explosion of contract work and a decline in provisions of the welfare state including pensions (see Chapter 13). Some argue that the modern understanding of adulthood as grounded in a career in now unmoored (Lee, 2001), making definitions of adulthood more flexible. Blatterer (2007) contends that adulthood has shifted from fulfilling preset social roles toward individual self-reflexivity and self-control, for instance. Such unbounded possibilities might seem exciting, but they are also uncertain and risky, masking structural inequalities that undermine people's security (Blatterer, 2007; Cartmel & Furlong, 1997). The precarious "gig economy," for instance, is much more easily tolerated by someone with the safety net of family wealth.

Others oppose the idea that age norms defining adulthood are weakening. Kohli (2007) argues that 20th-century life course norms, such as marriage and long-term work until retirement, have persisted for many into the 21st century. Further, new economic life course markers have developed, as we see in expectations that young people must participate in low or unpaid internships or volunteer work before finding a "real" job (Cairns, 2017), and upward shifts in expected ages for childbearing as young people must extend their postsecondary education (Roberts, Clifton, & Ferguson, 2005). In these instances, the assumed trappings of adulthood continue to hold ideological sway, with people still judged as "successfully" adult (or not) on the basis of having a stable career, home, and family, even if these have become elusive benchmarks.

Childhood and Adolescence

Adulthood is in part defined against childhood and adolescence. Psychology and sociology became established in the 19th century as social sciences intent on measuring, scrutinizing, evaluating, and regulating large populations (Foucault, 1978; see Chapter 11), including young people. However, while seeking to manage populations, these approaches also construct knowledge about them (Walkerdine, 1993), including ideas around what is considered "normal" and what is not.

Through developmental psychology, normative and non-normative paths of development are commonly identified to support young people as they grow up and to facilitate intervention when there are abnormalities or problems. A developmental framework has also granted many young people important leeway in their behaviours, as their emotional and thinking processes are undergoing growth and change. This is why children are treated differently than adults in courts of law, and why there is a United Nations Convention specifically addressing children's protection rights. However, while traditional developmental psychology is often considered a neutral, scientific system, uncovering what already exists, critical psychologists have countered that these approaches are "produced in particular circumstances, for particular reasons, and perhaps in the interests of particular persons or groups" (Morss, 1996, p. 48; see also Burman, 2008; Walkerdine, 1993). Developmental discourses, in turn, have effects. They are performative, shaping how we think about childhood, including what children are capable of, how they should be raised, and what to do when they fail to meet normative expectations.

An example of how developmental approaches reflect and produce certain understandings of childhood is illustrated when we look at children's play. Within a developmental approach, play is currently considered a vital, primary way in which children learn, and parent-child play is encouraged to maximize childhood development. Yet Lancy (2007) draws on anthropological work to argue that this position reflects a privileged Western, middle-class conceptualization of childhood and parenting. He notes that in many societies parents do not play with their children and play is in fact discouraged. These contrasting orientations arise from cultural beliefs that resonate with necessity, where parents, especially mothers, do not have the time to play and children make early contributions through work. Lancy suggests that by exporting an ideal of mother-child play based on Western privilege and ideals, parenting (and poverty) are problematized across many cultural settings.

Within sociology, **socialization** has been the more dominant lens than developmental for thinking about childhood and youth, with a focus on how young people learn their socio-cultural environments. Socialization approaches have been criticized for being similarly linear, however, and for conceptualizing young people as passively absorbing their social world rather than participating in creating it (Lesko, 2001). Many sociologists of childhood and youth are concerned that when we focus on development or socialization we only see young people in terms of what they will become in the future and may thus disregard who or what they are in the present (James & Prout, 1990). Lesko (1996) argues that this focus on young people as always becoming prevents them from knowing and representing themselves, with presumably fully developed and rational adults always knowing them better. Young people's views and concerns are thus easily discounted. For instance, when young people speak out on political issues (e.g., Raby & Raddon, 2015), on abuse (e.g., Nybell, 2013), and on how their institutions such as schools are organized (e.g., Raby, 2012), they are often problematically dismissed as innocent, unknowing, incompetent, and/or manipulated. Finally, when children and youth are primarily considered undeveloped, irrational, and peer-focused, adulthood is positioned as developed, rational, independent, and complete (Castaneda, 2002; Davies, 2002; Lesko, 1996).

Childhood

The modern, Western conceptualization of childhood is primarily based on innocence and dependence. For many, innocence is so central to childhood that children exposed to sexual **exploitation**, war, or exploitive labour are seen to have lost their childhoods. This emphasis on childhood innocence has been crucially important for championing children's rights to protection (e.g., from abuse). However, the protections of childhood are sometimes selectively applied to children. For instance, Black children in North America are often interpreted as older, and therefore less likely than white children to receive the protections of innocence (Epstein, Blake, & González, 2017; Ferguson, 2000). In one example, Goff et al. (2014) found that Black boys are more vulnerable to police violence when they are thought to have committed a crime as police overestimate their age. Beliefs about childhood innocence can also re-marginalize children. For example, a focus on childhood innocence can, ironically, be deployed to avoid protecting certain young people because they are no longer considered children due to sexual experiences (Kitzinger, 1988), to deny young people education about **sex** (Davies & Robinson, 2010), or to suggest that the protection they seek is inappropriate, for example in the case of young people seeking contraceptives adults do not wish them to have (Pilcher, 1997). These examples suggest that childhood innocence is not a straightforward idea, but a **discourse** with varying ramifications.

People have not always understood childhood through ideas like development or innocence. Current understandings of childhood are historically and contextually specific. The classic yet controversial text on the history of childhood in Western society is Phillipe Ariès's *Centuries of Childhood* (1962), in which Ariès argues that the modern conception of childhood as a separate stage of life emerged in Europe between the 15th and 18th centuries, together with bourgeois notions of family, home, privacy, and individuality. Ariès asserts that prior to this time, childhood as a unique category requiring special provisions did not exist, with individuals from across the life course sharing in games and work. Young people were integrated participants in society and were afforded no special protection (Qvortrup, 2005). Ariès contends that only in the 1700s did artistic and literary representations begin to mark childhood as a unique domain set apart from the everyday life of adult society. Even now, conceptions about when it ends are widely variant across cultures.

Ariès's viewpoint has not gone unchallenged. Albanese (2009) cites various authors who contend that in other non-Western societies a concept of childhood predated medieval Europe's "invention" of it. Karen Calvert (1998) and others have also criticized Ariès's methodology, including the way he generalized from limited, bourgeois sources such as paintings. Calvert nonetheless argues that Ariès's work illustrates that the form childhood takes and whether age differences are prioritized changes over time.

In fact, modern Western conceptualizations of the child largely emerged through social, economic, and political changes in the late 19th century, when shifts from rural farming to urban industry led to a separation of the private home from the public

FIGURE 8.2 *Madonna and Child*, Duccio di Buoninsegna, ca. 1284–1286. Historian Phillipe Ariès observed that until the 12th century, medieval art tended to portray children with adult-like features, as illustrated in this image. The Print Collector/Alamy.

workplace (Gleason & Myers, 2017). Bourgeois beliefs were promulgated, valuing innocent childhood and domestic motherhood (Chunn, 2003). Social reformers allied with this vision of childhood sought to protect young people, gradually removing them from the workforce through laws preventing children from participating in most forms of work and introducing compulsory education. These reform projects promoted Anglo-Saxon, middle-class understandings of childhood, including ideas about children as innocent and subordinate (Chunn, 2003), which in turn fostered children's protection, but also dependence.

Teenagers

While we commonly hear concerns about "natural" teenage risk-taking and rebelliousness, the concepts of adolescence and teenager are, like childhood, also historically and culturally specific. While white, primarily male, upper-class youth had formed recognizable groups that were subject to public worries prior to this time (Kett, 2003), the term adolescence emerged in the late 19th century in the West, fostered through industrialization and the gradual removal of young people from the workplace and into age-graded schooling. Pivotal to popularizing the concept was Stanley G. Hall's book *Adolescence*, published in 1904. While previously advice to young people "urged the early cultivation of adult responsibility" (Kett, 2003, p. 357), Hall drew on recapitulation theory, arguing that adolescents were in an instinctual, "primitive state" of "storm and stress" and that their development required careful management. Hall's concerns sought to address broader worries about emasculated adulthood and the needs of the American **nation**, so his advice was primarily directed toward white boys and the development of their masculinity through organizations such as the YMCA and Boy Scouts (Kett, 2003).

Concerns linking this time of life to the state of the nation were again prominent across North America in the mid 20th century when the new concept of teenager became popularized, largely as a consumer group (Adams, 1997). Uncertainty permeated the North American psyche after World War II, particularly with the rise of the Cold War with the Soviet Union; teenagers, embodying the future of the nation, were of specific concern. People worried that children had not been supervised enough during the war and now were being drawn into a teen consumer culture. They were increasingly considered a social problem, and the solution was thought to be in fostering the ideal nuclear family with a stay-at-home mom, and channelling young people's developing **sexuality** through moral hygiene films such as *Dating Do's and Don'ts* (Coronet Instructional Films, 1949).

We can see the concepts of adolescence and teenagehood as primarily Western, 20th-century categories, developed through social **science**, schooling, and political concerns. Over the course of the later 20th century, these categories became more rigorously linked to high school peer cultures, dating, marketing, and fears of delinquency. The mid-century advent of television brought home formative **stereotypes** of teenage life.

While there was criticism of Hall's approach when it was first introduced, it still influences how we think about adolescence today, for example in the notion that adolescence is a time of explosive, dangerous sexuality in need of special investigation and guidance by experts (Adams, 1997; Kett, 2003).

Is Youth the New Centre?

This chapter positions adulthood as the commonly unproblematized **centre** of the life course, suggesting that it is the dominant position against which other age categories are defined; yet youthfulness is idealized in marketing, media, and consumption practices (Danesi, 2003). Could it be youth who are really in the dominant life course position today? With rampant marketing of youthfulness and preferences for flexibility, adaptability, and changing technologies, youth may indeed be the new "centre." But while many people may want to look and feel young, young people themselves hold very little power in society generally. As students, they are subjected to a wide range of disciplinary tactics (Raby, 2012). Economically they are excluded from relations of production due to extended schooling and short-term, part-time, low-wage work (Cairns, 2017; Côté & Allahar, 2006). And discursively they are marginalized because they are understood as irrational, unstable, and incomplete compared to adults (Lesko, 2001).

Teenagers are frequently problematized as turbulent, irresponsible, and sexualized, in contrast to stable, rational, and sexually restrained adults (Adams, 1997; Lesko, 1996). Recent, popularized "teen brain" literature similarly argues that even young adults lack a fully mature brain and therefore the ability to think rationally, manage their emotions, and be empathetic, suggesting that they require surveillance and supervision well into their twenties (Payne, 2009). These portrayals are framed as natural, without attention to cultural and institutional context. For instance, by framing teenagers as inherently peer-focused, they are homogenized and dismissed as dangerous others, without regard for how peer culture has developed through intense school segregation (Lesko, 1996). For **racialized** teenagers, consequent surveillance and exclusion are even more marked, contributing to their disproportionate regulation and criminalization in schools and more broadly (Salole & Abdulle, 2015).

The 20th-century removal of young people from the workforce and into long-term, age-segregated schooling has also reinforced the idea that young people are incomplete and preparing for adulthood. Marxist theorists have focused on how schools bolster capitalist hierarchies as they "sort and select" young people into future workers

(Bourdieu & Passeron, 1977; Oakes, 1985) and as age is used to legitimize their inferior wages (Tyyska, 2009). Today we can see young people's extended dependence through the lengthening of necessary postsecondary education, and their exploitation through required volunteer work, low or unpaid internships, and flexible work contracts (Cairns, 2017). Ironically, as young people navigate limited employment opportunities and a stark environmental future, they are nonetheless dismissed as "entitled" (Cairns, 2017).

In this section I have illustrated that while adolescence and teenagehood arose as social categories only within the past century and a half, they are frequently defined through naturalizing discourses and institutionalized inequalities. These processes in turn lead to the regulation, surveillance, and marginalization of young people, while reinforcing the idea of a separate, stable, rational, and independent adulthood (Lesko, 2001).

Post-Adulthood? The "Third" and "Fourth" Ages

Just as conceptualizations of childhood have emerged and changed across time and place, so have conceptualizations of old age. Stephen Katz (1996) argues that in Western, premodern thought, aging was considered spiritual and physical. Age was considered a decline but not a disease, and there was optimism about overcoming old age. In contrast, early modern **gerontology** (the study of aging) tended to focus on uncovering innate characteristics of aging, separating the aged body from other parts of life (a **dividing practice**), and framing age in terms of disorder, disability, and eventual death. Miraculous possibility was replaced by biological certainty as "**modernity**'s forms of calculation, division, and hierarchy separated it as a distinct, developmental stage" (Katz, 2005, p. 32). Conventional gerontology arose, making an ordinary part of life subject to expert understanding and intervention, to evaluate and treat.

In contrast, social gerontology "focuses on what it means to age in society" (Markson, 2003, p. 12). This perspective encompasses a wide range of approaches that share a focus on social rather than biological factors. Social gerontologists tend to recognize how aging is affected by context, personal experiences, and social structures, including class and gender. Social gerontology includes critical gerontology, which looks at power and inequality in naturalized age relations, which in turn legitimize social hierarchy (Baars, Dannefer, Phillipson, & Walker, 2006).

Katz (2005) documents modern governmental and disciplinary processes that have constructed the elderly as a homogeneous group. For example, the introduction of pension plans in many Western nations in the 20th century was an important, positive move by the labour movement and governments to support workers in their old age, one that especially impacted men as they were more likely to be employed. Yet pension plans that based mandatory retirement on age, not incapacity, also contributed to a single view of the life course and created a new **subject position**, or social category, through which to define oneself and be defined by others as distinct from the middle-aged: retired. On the one hand, this subject position of being a retired senior is vulnerable to negative stereotyping about old age, which can contribute to elder abuse (Chappell, McDonald, & Stones, 2008). On the other hand, it can be used to request services unique to an older population. Old age is not a fixed subject position, however. Through diversity in experiences, contexts, and potentials of what it is or can be, Katz suggests that old age itself "undisciplines," or disrupts, generalizations about aging. Might the current increase in working seniors (Statistics Canada, 2017) due to the erosion of pensions, a rise in poverty, and an end to mandatory retirement lead to greater valuation of older people based on their work? Perhaps, but this possibility is complicated by other social forces, including poverty. Today, the ability to spend is as important as the ability to work.

In the late 20th century, it was argued that a longer lifespan in the West, and an increase in post-retirement wealth, produced a fulfilling "Third Age" of choice and "active leisure" (Bury, 1995, p. 22) before a "Fourth Age" of very old age, decline, and dependence (Laslett, 1989). The "Third Age" was considered a time of "**agency**, autonomy, and empowerment" (Wray, 2003, para. 2.4) that continues to be available to some older people today. However, the idea of a "Third Age" has been troubled by critical gerontologists who argue that it is really a consumer category and a bourgeois possibility that is largely available to healthy, upper-class men and couples and that problematizes older, poorer, and less active bodies (Marshall, 2015). Katz and Laliberte-Rudman add that the "Third Age" formulation of aging bolsters neoliberal erosion of state support because it "maximizes individual responsibility in the service of meeting political goals of minimizing dependency and universal entitlements" (2004, p. 146). Poverty in old age is read, in this vein, as an individual failure to invest and plan (rather than an inequitable political and economic scheme over which individuals have little control).

These shifts in senior employment and consumption suggest that, like other parts of the life course, ideas about old age are not rigid and natural, but reflect conditions linked to history, culture, economy, health, and people's political demands. These conceptualizations promote current dichotomies of independence and dependence, bodily health and frailty, and productivity and retirement. They also have unequal effects.

What about the Baby Boomers?

Perhaps it is not youth or adulthood that occupies the centre but a specific group of seniors: the Baby Boomers. Baby Boomers, born in the two decades just after World War II, reaped the benefits of state and career supports over the second half of the 20th century. Commentators argue that their sheer numbers, electoral power, and economic security have shaped social policy in their favour, shifting resources away from other generations. Such a generational analysis notes that specific cohorts, or groups of people born around the same time, can influence how resources are distributed, and consequently how age is understood and experienced. We can thus explore how our conceptualizations of adulthood and older age are shifting not only through the advance of **neoliberalism** and the decline of the welfare state, but as Baby Boomers age.

Disrupting the Centre Stage

Over the 20th century, certain life course stages and their associated traits emerged contextually and became normalized, with modern Western adulthood as the seemingly stable, untroubled centre. As I have noted, life course norms can provide familiar expectations for growing up and growing old, but these normative expectations also produce hierarchies of value, authority, and influence. Life course norms are also undermined and challenged by shifts in discursive and cultural conditions, and by people's diverse, unequal lives. The next section focuses on four areas that problematize clear life stages and especially the "adult centre": intersections, production and consumption, interdependency, and advocacy.

Intersections

An emphasis on homogeneity in life course stages downplays their internal diversity, particularly around the multiple and unequal intersections of gender, class, culture, race, sexuality, and disability. For example, an adult centre premised on labour force productivity is complicated by the many adults outside the labour force because they are unemployed, raising children, or disabled, and by children who work in the labour force. Similarly, those who do not marry and/or are not heterosexual complicate the historical centrality of heterosexual marriage, and linking adulthood to the traditional nuclear family is complicated by teenage childbearing, single-parenting, extended families, preferred childlessness, and infertility.

Intersections can also have profound ripple effects across our lives due to the interdependence of earlier and later life, particularly around class. As populations age they become more heterogeneous, which some attribute to strengthening individuality, but which Dannefer (1987) considers a feature of the **Matthew effect**, or the accumulated consequences of inequalities across the life course. Patterns of education and employment increase differences between people over time in terms of health, resources, and economic and **cultural capital** (the values, beliefs, habits, attitudes, and skills deemed valuable by the dominant members of society). Consequently, as a cohort ages, income inequality within it increases, often exacerbated by gender and racial inequalities.

For example, the standard model of the modern life course has been premised on the trajectory of a male breadwinner. Yet as Mandell, Wilson, and Duffy (2008) discuss, Canadian women at midlife are particularly susceptible to the Matthew effect. Women's economic inequality increases with age due to their propensity to be in lower-paying and/or part-time jobs, and to have spent time outside of the labour market while raising children. In Canada in 2014, 30 per cent of single elderly women were considered low income compared to 12.5 per cent of all seniors (Grant, 2016). Visible minority women who have experienced discrimination in the workplace are particularly vulnerable to poverty in old age (Calasanti, 2008; Evans, 2010). Gendered beauty standards also make women susceptible to ageism, negatively affecting their employment prospects (Hurd Clarke, & Griffin, 2008).

Class and gender are just some of the intersections that complicate and **denaturalize** normative age-based categories, expectations, and transitions, and that are neglected when we laud the freedom and consumption of the "Third Age," for instance.

Production and Consumption

Recall that modern conceptualizations of adulthood have been linked to entry into a stable career, with retirement signalling a transition into a new life stage (Lee, 2001). This conceptualization neglects to address work inside the home, largely undertaken by women. Stable careers are also now under threat as they are being replaced by so-called "flexible" employment arrangements such as short-term contracts. These shifts potentially unmoor an adult centre and disrupt clear transitions between youth and adulthood, and between midlife and old age (Lee, 2001). For both young people and adults, extended education and precarious employment create uncertainty. For older people, unease is intensified with decreasing assurance of state or workplace financial support through pensions (Settersten & Trauten, 2009).

Finally, shifts in emphasis from production to consumption create new opportunities for young and old people who are more affluent. For instance, Western children's disposable income has risen substantially, and children now significantly influence their families' spending choices (Pugh, 2009; Schor, 2004). Similarly, the emergence of Third Agers has been largely based on consumerism extending well beyond retirement (Katz, 2005). Yet while consumption practices decentre adulthood, consumption and marketing strategies often reinforce age categories and construct new, ever more age-graded ones. New terms and consequent identities include toddlers, pre-tweens, tweens, preteens, teens, young adults, boomers, empty-nesters, and "Third Agers," all of which Katz (2005) defines as segmented target markets for businesses.

Ironically, as part of this trend toward age-segmented marketing, we have seen the rise of a powerful marketing culture around anti-aging products, which problematizes age by promising to stretch middle age forever, reminding us of premodern hopes for miraculous longevity. Meanwhile, children are exposed to a force called "kids getting older younger" which sells adulthood (e.g., through sexualized clothing) to young children (Linn, 2004). On the one hand, age stages are blurred through marketing and consumption that promote youthfulness. On the other, age stages are created and exploited. Both suggest the social nature of these categories alongside political and economic investments in them.

Interdependence

A key Western distinction between childhood, adulthood, and old age is based on the assumption of adult independence, through work, personal autonomy, and able-bodiedness. An emphasis on these features in turn distinguishes normative adulthood from the physical and financial dependence of both childhood and old age.

While links between dependency and marginality in childhood are considered acceptable and even idealized because they are transitory, this is not so for the elderly. British scholars Hockey and James (1993) point out that, sadly, the link between adulthood and independence frequently results in the infantilization of older people, especially in retirement facilities. They wonder whether the tendency to treat older people as if they were children might help adults to shore up the "ideological dominance of adulthood" (1993, p. 37) and to distance themselves from their own potential dependency. Infantilization may help middle-aged adults maintain life course boundaries; however, it is experienced by many elderly and those with disabilities as insulting and marginalizing, as they are not taken seriously and are prevented from making their own decisions (Hockey & James, 1993). Of course, infantilization can be difficult for children, too, especially when they are treated as incompetent and their views thus disregarded, as discussed earlier in this chapter.

Nick Lee (2001) counters the underlying belief that adults are independent, autonomous agents by arguing that all people rely on social supports, language, technology, and so forth in order to accomplish goals. Indeed, the idea that we can be separate, independent individuals reflects a narrow, colonial Western history of personhood that invests value in individualism (Hockey & James, 1993). Sharon Wray (2003) provides cross-cultural examples to uncouple the Western conflation of old age, dependency, and powerlessness. She argues that "it is possible … to remain a powerful agent despite the threat or presence of potentially debilitating illness, a change in appearance or a loss of physical functionality" (para 2.9). She supports her position by citing interviews with Pakistani and Bangladeshi immigrant women in England who explained that it was in old age that they felt most in control of their lives, supported through interdependence with family, friends, and, for one, deferment to God. Further, the women saw good health, including health of interrelationships and surrounding community, as key to their empowerment. Hockey and James (1993) similarly cite various non-Western contexts in which social interconnection and cohesion are actively created through interdependence, disrupting the Western obsession with individual independence.

Advocacy

Advocates for children's participation, recognition, and rights have challenged the construction of children as incomplete, immature, and irrational. They counter that children are to be valued as different from adults but not inferior to them. Advocates in the sociology of childhood, for example, prioritize children's agency and emphasize the need for research with, rather than on, children (Berman & MacNevin, 2018). Acharya (2009) documents a compelling example from Orissa in India, where children reported on the conditions of their villages to top decision-makers. In another example, Nybell (2013) draws on in-depth interviews to emphasize the need to listen to young people in foster care. A prominent advocacy tool has been the United Nations *Convention on the Rights of the Child* (1989), signed by all nations except the United States, which emphasizes children's rights not only to health, family, education, and safety but also to participation in decisions that will affect them. Yet the Convention has also been criticized for reinforcing and globalizing a specifically Western definition of childhood based on dependency and protection, and for failing to address underlying political and economic causes of inequality in children's lives. Children's protection and participation can also come into conflict. For instance, many strive to protect children from early work, but various child workers' organizations argue that in some contexts children must work to survive and that it is more important that they have rights to health and safety in that work (Saadi, 2012).

For older people, various movements have sought to create positive images and experiences. While Katz (2005) and Settersten and Trauten (2009) are concerned that these movements may remarginalize those who are dependent or frail, they also recognize that these forms of activism, often initiated by older adults, can politicize and redefine their collective identities. Katz and Laliberte-Rudman cite, for example, the Universities of the Third Age in the United Kingdom, a mutual-education movement of "lifelong learning cooperatives of older people" (www.u3a.org.uk). Another example is the Raging Grannies, started in Canada in 1987, a nonviolent protest group that is part of the women's movement. As their website (https://raginggrannies.org) states, one of their strategies involves embracing popular stereotypes of older age through "dressing like innocent little old ladies so we can get close to our 'target.'"

Further advocacy involves denaturalizing life course stages and their features, just as this chapter has done. Such disruptions involve recognizing diversity, deconstructing life course categories or stages, and recognizing moments of disruption and resistance. Lesko, for example, challenges divisions created between teen, adult, and old by recognizing that each life stage simultaneously embodies "mature and immature, old and young, traditional and innovative" (2001, p. 196).

Such projects raise crucial questions about how we understand growing up and growing old. What might be gained or lost, for example, in denaturalizing our assumptions about childhood? While those in the sociology of childhood advocate for a focus on young people as beings in the present to recognize their voices as worthy, others are

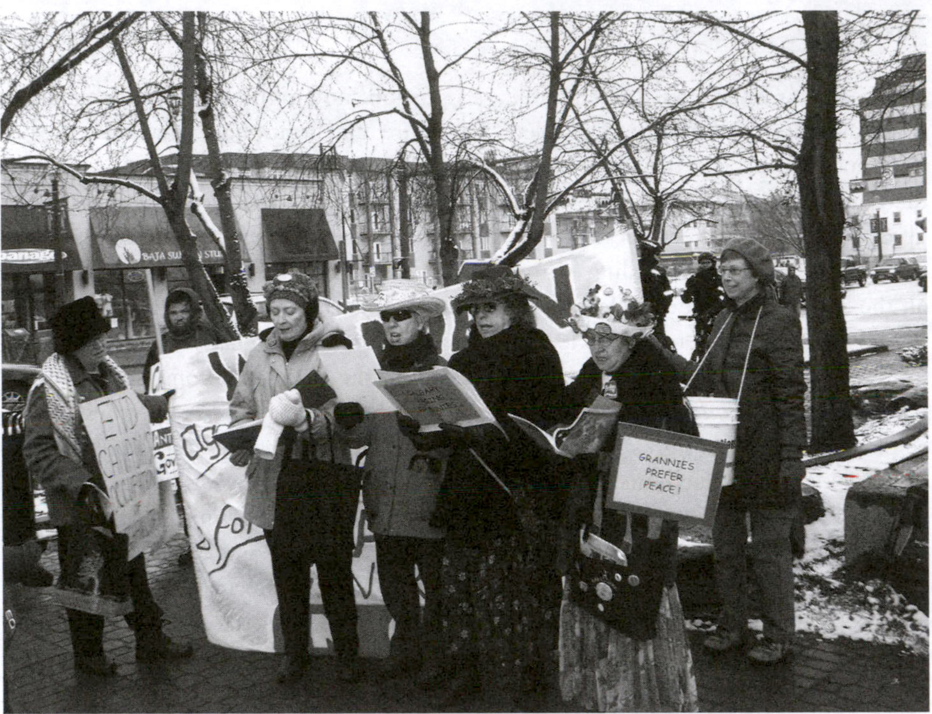

FIGURE 8.3 The Raging Grannies, who first emerged in Victoria, BC, in the 1980s. CC BY 2.0/Robert Thivierge.

concerned that it is only by considering young people as incomplete "becomings" that they are deemed worthy of important social investment (Giroux, 2003). Can we accept that young and older people are distinct from adults in some ways, while at the same time dismantling a normative adult centre that is used to marginalize not just young and old but also many adults? Can young people and those in old age have a legitimate, equal voice to that of able-bodied, "independent" adults? Finally, what priority should be given to the body itself, as it too plays an active role in how we understand, represent, and experience the life course (Castaneda, 2002)?

Conclusion

With the ascent of modern institutions such as the factory, the school, and the nuclear family alongside the categorizing and normalizing embedded in disciplines such as psychology and sociology, modern Western ages and stages emerged, as well as their normative boundaries, assumptions, and hierarchies. This process created new identities based on age, identities that have allowed for the protection of the young and old, but have also marginalized them in relationship to the dominant adult centre.

Many believe that modern age-based categories and norms, including a stable, adult centre, have been eroding in response to neoliberalism, changing family forms, lifelong consumerism, displaced stable careers, and decreasing pensions. At the same time, old and new age norms continue to be asserted, with significant consequences including whose voice is heard, who earns money, who has influence, who is protected, and who is marginalized. Martin Kohli (2007) suggests that what is really at the centre is a life course regime, with the modern Western life course remaining an evaluative benchmark, despite its narrow reflection of Western, middle-class, 20th-century ideals (Katz, 2005). Normative adulthood remains at the centre, produced in part by how we think about and treat younger and older people.

Study Questions

1. With the erosion of many standard markers of adulthood and a deepening embrace of youthfulness, is youth displacing adulthood as the dominant "centre" of the life course? Why or why not?
2. Identify three potential areas of distinction between childhood and adulthood or between midlife and old age. Identify concrete examples that disrupt these distinctions.
3. Identify several examples of behaviour that you feel challenge age norms. Do these norm-breakers face sanctions? What kind? What resources might enable some people to disrupt age norms without consequence?

Exercises

1. *Freaky Friday*, *17 Again*, *Big*, and *The Curious Case of Benjamin Button* all play with disruptions to temporal aging. How do movies such as these normalize certain beliefs about age-appropriate behaviour? Do they also challenge them?
2. Write a personal reflection on your own life course position in relation to adulthood. Do you consider yourself an adult? Why or why not? What assumptions are you making about adulthood in your assessment? How might your self-location be influenced by structural categories such as class, race, or gender?

References

Acharya, L. (2009). Child reporters as agents of change. In B. Percy-Smith & N. Thomas (Eds.), *A handbook of children and young people's participation: Perspectives from theory and practice* (pp. 204–214). London, UK: Routledge.

Adams, M.L. (1997). *The trouble with normal: Postwar youth and the making of heterosexuality*. Toronto, ON: University of Toronto Press.

Albanese, P. (2009). *Children in Canada today*. Don Mills, ON: Oxford University Press.

Alsop, R., Fitzsimons, A., & Lennon, K. (2002). *Theorizing gender*. Malden, MA: Blackwell Publishers Inc.

Ariès, P. (1962). *Centuries of childhood: A social history of family life*. New York, NY: Knopf.

Baars, J., Dannefer, D., Phillipson, C., & Walker, A. (2006). Introduction: Critical perspectives in social gerontology. In J. Baars, D. Dannefer, C. Phillipson, & A. Walker (Eds.), *Aging, globalization and inequality: The new critical gerontology* (pp. 1–14). Amityville, NY: Baywood Publishing.

Berman, R., & MacNevin, M. (2018). Adults researching with children. In X. Chen, R. Raby, & P. Albanese (Eds.), *The sociology of childhood and youth in Canada*. Toronto, ON: CSP.

Blatterer, H. (2007). *Coming of age in times of uncertainty*. New York, NY: Berghahn Books.

Bourdieu, P., & Passeron, J.C. (1977). *Reproduction in education, society and culture*. London, UK: Sage Publications.

Burman, E. (2008). *Deconstructing developmental psychology* (2nd ed.). East Sussex, UK: Routledge.

Bury, M. (1995). Ageing, gender and sociological theory. In S. Arber & J. Ginn (Eds.), *Connecting gender and ageing: A sociological approach* (pp. 12–25). Buckingham, UK: Open University Press.

Cairns, J. (2017). *The myth of the age of entitlement: Millenials, austerity, and hope*. Toronto: University of Toronto Press.

Calasanti, T. (2008). Theorizing feminist gerontology, sexuality and beyond: An intersectional approach. In V. Bengston, M. Silverstein, N. Putney, & D. Gans (Eds.), *Handbook of theories of aging* (pp. 471–486). New York, NY: Springer.

Calvert, K. (1998). Children in the house: The material culture of early childhood. In H. Jenkins (Ed.), *The children's culture reader* (pp. 67–80). New York, NY: New York University Press.

Cartmel, F., & Furlong, A. (1997). *Young people and social change: Individualization and risk in late modernity*. Buckingham, UK: Open University Press.

Castaneda, C. (2002). *Figurations: Child, bodies, worlds*. Durham, NC: Duke University Press.

Chappell, N., McDonald, L., & Stones, M. (2008). *Aging in contemporary Canada* (2nd ed.). Toronto, ON: Pearson Education Canada.

Chunn, D.E. (2003). Boys will be men, girls will be mothers: The legal regulation of childhood in Toronto and Vancouver. In N. Janovicek & J. Parr (Eds.), *Histories of Canadian children and youth* (pp. 188–206). Don Mills, ON: Oxford University Press.

Coronet Instructional Films. (1949). *Dating: Do's and don'ts*. Retrieved from http://archive.org/details/DatingDo1949

Côté, J.E., & Allahar, A.L. (2006). *Critical youth studies: A Canadian focus*. Toronto, ON: Pearson Prentice Hall.

Danesi, M. (2003). *Forever young: The teen-aging of modern culture*. Toronto, ON: University of Toronto Press.

Dannefer, D. (1987). Aging as intracohort differentiation: Accentuation, the Matthew effect and the life course. *Sociological Forum, 2*, 211–236.

Davidson, A. (2014, June 22). It's official: The boomerang generation won't leave. *The New York Times Magazine*. Retrieved from https://www.nytimes.com/2014/06/22/magazine/its-official-the-boomerang-kids-wont-leave.html

Davies, B. (2002). *Shards of glass: Children reading and writing beyond gendered identities.* Cresskill, NJ: Hampton Press.

Davies, C., & Robinson, K. (2010). Hatching babies and stork deliveries: Risk and regulation in the construction of children's sexual knowledge. *Contemporary Issues in Early Childhood, 11*(3), 249–262.

De Leeuw, S. (2009). "If anything is to be done with the Indian, we must catch him very young": Colonial constructions of Aboriginal children and the geographies of Indian residential schooling in British Columbia, Canada. *Children's Geographies, 7*(2), 123–140.

Epstein, R., Blake, J., & González, T. (2017). *Girlhood interrupted: The erasure of black girls' childhood.* Retrieved from https://ssrn.com/abstract=3000695

Erikson, E. (1968). *Identity: Youth and crisis.* New York, NY: W.W. Norton.

Evans, P. (2010). Women's poverty in Canada: Cross-currents in an ebbing tide. In G.S. Goldberg (Ed.), *Poor women in rich countries: The feminization of poverty over the life course* (pp. 151–173). Oxford, UK: Oxford University Press.

Ferguson, A.A. (2000). *Bad boys: Public schools in the making of black masculinity.* Ann Arbor, MI: University of Michigan Press.

Foucault, M. (1978). Governmentality. In G. Burchell, C. Gordon, & P. Miller (Eds.), *The Foucault effect: Studies in governmentality* (pp. 87–104). Chicago, IL: University of Chicago Press.

Geronimus, A.T. (2003). Damned if you do: Culture, identity, privilege, and teenage childbearing in the United States. *Social Science and Medicine, 57,* 881–893.

Giroux, H.A. (2003). Racial injustice and disposable youth in the age of zero tolerance. *Qualitative Studies in Education, 16*(4), 553–565.

Gleason, M., & Myers, T. (Eds.). (2017). *Bringing children and youth into Canadian history: The difference kids make.* Don Mills, ON: Oxford University Press.

Goff, P.A., Jackson, M.C., Allison, B., Leone, L.D., Culotta, C.M., & DiTomasson, N.A. (2014). The essence of innocence: Consequences of dehumanizing Black children. *Journal of Personality and Social Psychology, 106*(4), 526–545.

Gould, S.J. (1977). *Ontogeny and phylogeny.* Cambridge, MA: Belknap Press of Harvard University Press.

Grant, T. (2016, July 12). Incomes of Canadian seniors, singles stagnant, data show. *The Globe and Mail.* Retrieved from https://www.theglobeandmail.com/news/national/incomes-of-canadian-seniors-singles-stagnant-data-show/article30895481/

Gregson, J. (2009). *The culture of teenage mothers.* Albany, NY: State University of New York Press.

Hamlett, M. (2018, February 28). Why do we still shame adults who live with their parents? *The Guardian.* Retrieved from https://www.theguardian.com/commentisfree/2018/feb/28/michael-b-jordan-live-with-parents-millennials-shame

Hockey, J., & James, A. (1993). *Growing up and growing old: Ageing and dependency in the life course.* London, UK: Sage Publications.

Hurd Clarke, L., & Griffin, M. (2008). Visible and invisible ageing: Beauty work as a response to ageism. *Ageing and Society, 28,* 653–674.

James, A., & Prout, A. (1990). *Constructing and reconstructing childhood: Contemporary issues in the sociological study of childhood.* Basingstoke, UK: Falmer Press.

Katz, S. (1996). *Disciplining old age.* Charlottesville: University Press of Virginia.

Katz, S. (2005). *Cultural aging: Life course, lifestyle, and senior worlds.* Toronto, ON: Broadview.

Katz, S., & Laliberte-Rudman, D. (2004). Exemplars of retirement: Identity and agency between lifestyle and social movement. In S. Katz (Ed.), *Cultural aging: Life course, life style and senior worlds* (pp. 140–160). Toronto, ON: Broadview.

Kett, J.F. (2003). Reflections on the history of adolescence in America. *History of the Family, 8*, 355–373.

Kitzinger, J. (1988). Defending innocence: Ideologies of childhood. *Feminist Review, 28*, 77–87.

Kohli, M. (2007). The institutionalization of the life course: Looking back to look ahead. *Research in Human Development, 4*(3/4), 253–271.

Lancy, D. (2007). Accounting for variability in mother-child play. *American Anthropologist, 109*(2), 273–284.

Laslett, P. (1989). *A fresh map of life: The emergence of the third age*. London, UK: Weidenfeld and Nicolson.

Lawrence, B. (1996). Organizational age norms: Why is it so hard to know one when you see one? *Gerontologist, 36*(2), 209–220.

Lee, N. (2001). *Childhood and society: Growing up in an age of uncertainty*. Maidenhead, UK: Open University Press.

Lesko, N. (1996). Past, present and future conceptions of adolescence. *Educational Theory, 46*(4), 453–472.

Lesko, N. (2001). *Act your age! A cultural construction of adolescence*. New York, NY: Routledge.

Linn, S. (2004). *Consuming kids: The hostile take-over of childhood*. New York, NY: New Press.

Mandell, N., Wilson, S., & Duffy, A. (2008). *Connection, compromise, and control: Canadian women discuss midlife*. Don Mills, ON: Oxford University Press.

Markson, E.W. (2003). *Social gerontology today: An introduction*. Los Angeles, CA: Roxbury.

Marshall, B. (2015). Celebrity, ageing, and the construction of "Third Age" identities. *International Journal of Cultural Studies, 18*(6), 577–593.

Morss, J.R. (1996). *Growing critical: Alternatives to developmental psychology*. London, UK: Routledge.

Nutton, J., & Fast, E. (2015). Historical trauma, substance use, and Indigenous peoples: Seven generations of harm from a "big event." *Substance Use and Misuse, 50*, 839–847.

Nybell, L.M. (2013). Locating "youth voice": Considering the contexts of speaking in foster care. *Children and Youth Services Review, 35*, 1227–1235.

Oakes, J. (1985). *Keeping track: How schools structure inequality*. New Haven, CT: Yale University Press.

Payne, M.A. (2009). Teen brain science and the contemporary storying of psychological (im)maturity. In H. Blatterer & J. Glahn (Eds.), *Times of our lives: Making sense of growing up and growing old* [e-book]. Oxford, UK: Interdisciplinary Press.

Pilcher, J. (1997). Contrary to Gillick: British children and sexual rights since 1985. *International Journal of Children's Rights, 5*, 299–317.

Pugh, A.J. (2009). *Longing and belonging: Parents, children and consumer culture*. Berkeley, CA: University of California Press.

Qvortrup, J. (2005). Varieties of childhood. In J. Qvortup (Ed.), *Studies in modern childhood: Society, agency, culture* (pp. 1–20). Houndsmills, UK: Palgrave Macmillan.

Raby, R. (2012). *School rules: Obedience, discipline and elusive democracy*. Toronto, ON: University of Toronto Press.

Raby, R., & Raddon, M.B. (2015). Is she a pawn, prodigy or person with a message? Public responses to a child's political speech. *Canadian Journal of Sociology, 40*(2), 163–187.

Roberts, L.W., Clifton, R.A., & Ferguson, B. (Eds.). (2005). *Recent social trends in Canada, 1960–2000*. Montreal, QC: McGill-Queen's University Press.

Saadi, I. (2012). Children's rights as "work in progress": The conceptual and practical contributions of working children's movements. In M. Liebel (Ed.), *Children's rights from below: Cross-cultural perspectives* (pp. 143–161). Houndsmills, UK: Palgrave Macmillan.

Salole, A.T., & Abdulle, Z. (2015). Quick to punish: An examination of the school to prison pipeline for marginalized youth. *Canadian Review of Social Policy, 72–73*, 124–168.

Schor, J. (2004). *Born to buy*. New York, NY: Scribner.

Settersten, R.A., Jr. (2003). Propositions and controversies in life-course scholarship. In R.A. Settersten, Jr. (Ed.), *Invitation to the life course* (pp.15–48). Amityville, NY: Baywood Publishing.

Settersten, R.A., & Mayer, K.U. (1997). The measurement of age, age structuring, and the life course. *Annual Review of Sociology, 23*, 233–261.

Settersten, R.A., Jr., & Trauten, M.E. (2009). The new terrain of old age: Hallmarks, freedoms, and risks. In V. Bengston, M. Silverstein, N. Putney, & D. Gans (Eds.), *Handbook of theories of aging* (2nd ed., pp. 455–471). New York, NY: Springer.

Statistics Canada. (2017). *Working seniors in Canada, census population of 2016*. Retrieved from http://www12.statcan.gc.ca/census-recensement/2016/as-sa/98-200-x/2016027/98-200-x2016027-eng.pdf

Tyyska, V. (2009). *Youth and society: The long and winding road* (2nd ed.). Toronto, ON: Canadian Scholars' Press.

United Nations. (1989). *Convention on the rights of the child* [treaty]. Geneva, Switzerland: Office of the United Nations High Commissioner for Human Rights. Retrieved from http://www2.ohchr.org/english/law/crc.htm

Walkerdine, V. (1993). Beyond developmentalism? *Theory and Psychology, 3*(4), 451–469.

Wray, S. (2003). Connecting ethnicity, agency and ageing. *Sociological Research Online, 8*(4), 1–11.

9 Citizenship and Borders

NANDITA SHARMA

Introduction: The Trouble with Borders

Making and maintaining national **borders** through **citizenship** and immigration policies is an important part of the **everyday practices** of **power**. Questioning their **normal**-ness—and seeing how it has been constructed—is an important way to unpack the **centre**. The existence of national borders and their fortification affect how—and if—people cross into territories marked as possessions of nationally sovereign states. The immigration and citizenship policies of individual **nation-states** determine who can—and cannot—move into **state** territories, as well as the type of **status** people are given once they enter. The state's bifurcation of people into either citizens or migrants, along with the state's allocation of different kinds of immigration status (for example, from permanent, to temporary, to undocumented or "illegal") profoundly affects people's lives. Whether one can bring family members with them, the types of jobs available, the wage levels on offer, the type of housing or education they can access, whether they will become targets for intense state or public scrutiny, even whether they can plan for a better future, all depend on a person's citizenship and immigration status.

National borders, then, establish certain kinds of social relations by regulating and restricting people's ability to enter nation-state territories, as well as shaping their lives once across. Such relationships are institutionalized in state laws, capitalist markets that influence the movement of goods and people (**labour power**), and expressed every day through ideas of exclusionary national belonging accepted by many people who imagine themselves as members of "nations." **Nationalism**, the belief that some specified group of people have a moral claim to sovereign control over certain territories, is the focus of this chapter. Yet, it is important to know that all "nations" imagine themselves through racialized, gendered, and **heteronormative** assumptions of who its members are—and are not.

Although "nations" and national borders are thought to be eternal and fixed, they are not. Changes in global and national politics create new "nations" and new nation-states, while leading to the dissolution of others. Since the 1990s alone, numerous nation-states have ceased to exist, while new ones have been recognized by the United Nations, a key governing institution of the international order of nation-states. The world's newest nation-state, South Sudan, was formed on 9 July 2011, as was its accompanying nationality of South-Sudanese. These processes show that there is a constant reorganization of "national homelands," nation-states, their borders, and the "national community" they claim to "represent."

It is because national citizenship is highly consequential that borders are in constant flux and more and more people try to cross them. Today, when people's displacement and subsequent **migration** is occurring at an historically unprecedented level—the United Nations (2017) estimates that every year over 244 million people migrate across national borders and live in national societies as non-citizens—nationalism, with its normalizing of highly differential treatment for citizens and foreigners, has become a motor force both for further capitalist expansion and for the further intensification of national exclusions. Indeed, almost three-quarters of inequalities in

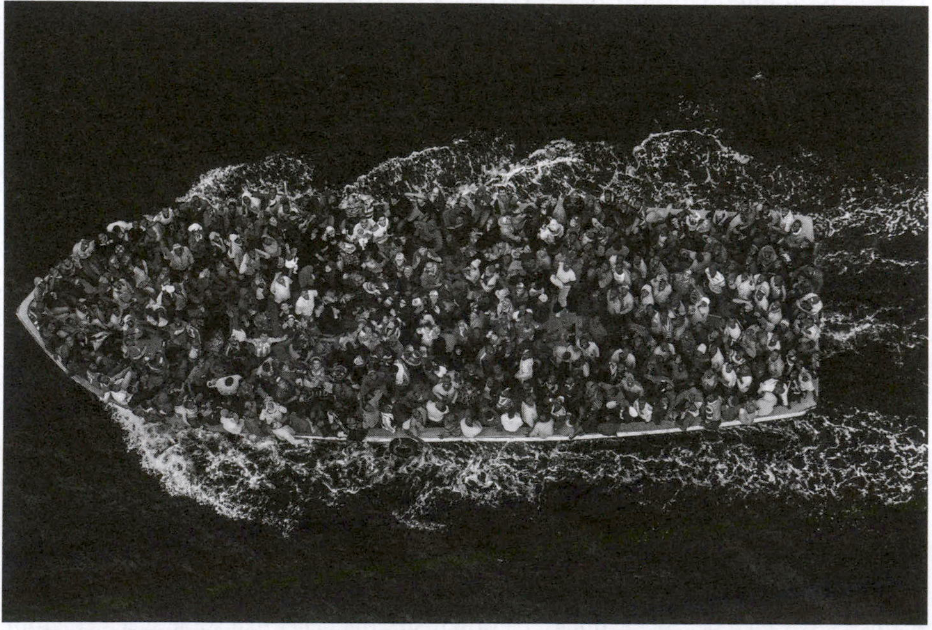

FIGURE 9.1 *Bergamini* ship on the Mediterranean Sea carrying people moving from Africa and trying to land in Italy, 7 June 2014. World Press Photo 2015. © Massimo Sestini.

the world are determined by which nation-state one is a citizen of (Milanovic, 2011). In today's world, one's *nationality* is the greatest determinant of one's income, wealth, and even life expectancy. As Branko Milanovic (2016, p. 132) says, nationality in a Rich World nation-state provides one with a "citizenship rent." Disparities within the global system of nation-states are shaped by how easy it is for someone to cross national borders.

Borders do not affect everyone in the same way. For a small select group of the world's people, they are a mere formality. Business elites, people working for international and national non-governmental organizations (NGOs), and holders of Rich World nationalities (like Canada's), for example, cross national borders with very little forethought (see Chapter 16, "Being a Tourist"). Conversely, borders constantly cast a shadow on other people's lives. Holding a Poor World nationality makes lawful border crossings next to impossible, except for a handful of the most wealthy citizens. For people who are able to cross, but are assigned subordinated state categories such as **migrant** worker or illegal migrant, borders follow them to school, to work, indeed into every aspect of their lives. In our globalized world, the simultaneous existence of a more-or-less borderless world for some and a world of difficult-to-cross national borders for others confronts even those who stay put. People, knowing that their escape routes away from joblessness, poverty, violence, or ecological destruction have been made dangerous and that their chances to improve their futures are limited, often have little choice but to stay.

The Home Economics of Nationalism(s)

The topic of this chapter is national borders, and how they make some people feel at home while rendering others homeless in the very places where they live. I argue that a type of *home economics* is at play in the process of stratifying groups of people according to their nationality and their immigration status (Sharma, 2006). This stratification results in significant material differences between people categorized by nation-states as "citizens" or "migrants," differences that affect every aspect of people's lives. These institutionalized differences are normalized by discourses of nationalism(s), which always-already interact with those of **racism**(s), **gender/sex**, and **class**. In short, I argue that nation-states with their borders against free human mobility exist in part because those who make themselves at home in the "nation" accept the differential treatment accorded to those regarded as "migrants." The result is not necessarily the physical exclusion of all those seen as "foreign," but rather their exclusion from "national society."

Within national forms of **ruling**, "society" is undifferentiated from the nation-state. First, it is assumed that all those living in any given nation-state are—or ought to be—its citizens. Second, the state is portrayed as little more than a vehicle for the demands of its "citizenry." Together, these two ideas create a sense of identification between members of the "nation" and the sovereign or state. This group of nationals, supposedly unified across social relations of class, racism, gender, or **sexuality**, come to believe that the state (or sovereign) rules *for* them. Nationalists don't stop at producing some people as "belonging," but they also produce others as *not*-belonging.

In the process of making nationals, "foreigners" are also made. The **normalization** of the existence of "nations" produces the idea that "foreigners" are external to the "national body." Thus, the quintessential "foreigner" within a world of nation-states becomes the *figure* of the migrant. In nationalist thought, "foreign elements" within the "national body" are a dis-ease that must be eradicated. This makes the potential or actual violence nation-states perpetuate against migrants seem "everyday," "commonsensical," or "normal." Nationalist violence can range from denying migrants the multifold rights associated with citizenship, to expulsion from national membership and territory, to **genocide**.

I discuss three examples to make this clear: first, Canada's various "temporary foreign workers" programs, which legally immobilize most so categorized by tying them to work for specific employers and in specific geographical locations in Canada; second, the Mohawks' (recently outlawed) 1981 *Kahnawà:ke Mohawk Law and Moratorium on Mixed Marriages*, which declared that any Mohawk marrying a non-Mohawk must leave Mohawk territory (along with their non-Mohawk spouse and children); and third, the current genocide in Myanmar (formerly Burma), where Rohingya people have had their Myanmar citizenship taken away and have been represented as "illegal migrants," effectively rendering them stateless with no inherent right to enter or reside in Myanmar's territories. Facing four decades of ever-escalating violence, from late August 2017 to January 2018, two-thirds of all Rohingya people in Myanmar—an estimated 688,000 people—fled Myanmar for Bangladesh to escape the violence of Myanmar's military forces (Ibrahim, 2018; UNHCR, 2018).

While each of these examples involves a distinct set of circumstances, they share in common the idea that "nations" have a fundamental right to determine who is admitted into "their" territories and the status, if any, they will be granted. This internationally recognized right of national **sovereignty** organizes as well as normalizes lawful discrimination—and persecution—of anyone classified as "not-belonging" to the "nation." In analyzing how nationalism(s) produce exclusionary and hierarchical categories of belonging/not-belonging, it is useful to utilize both a Marxist understanding of power to understand the processes by which people's labour power is made available for **exploitation** and a Foucauldian understanding of power that sees it as producing an entire *way of life* that, together, normalize both **racialized** and ethnicized national **subjectivities** and the demonization of anyone categorized as a "migrant" to the "nation." I thus show that the contemporary world order of nation-states not only institutionalizes our ideas of "belonging," but also shapes our consciousness about the character of human social relations.

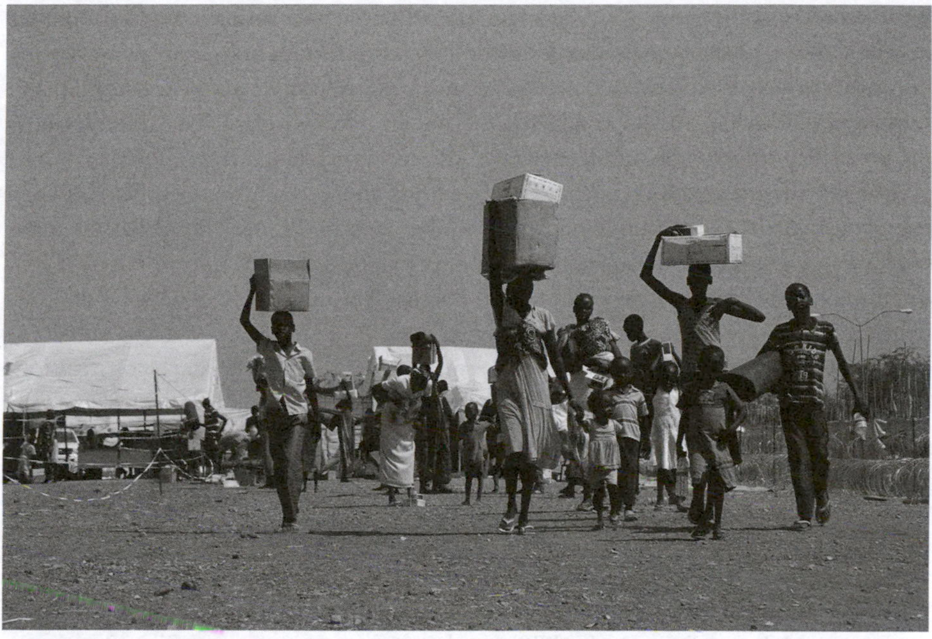

FIGURE 9.2 Tong Ping United Nations Base, South Sudan. Families in Tong Ping displaced persons settlement carry their newly received non-food items back to where they are staying.

Credit: Anita Kattakuzhu/Oxfam

Citizenship and the Making of Difference

Canada's various "temporary foreign workers" programs existed in piecemeal fashion until 1973, when they were consolidated into the Non-Immigrant Employment Authorization Program. The shift from admitting migrants as permanent residents to "temporary foreign workers" started a few scant years later. The timing is relevant because it was only in 1967 when non-white people, denied the ability to lawfully enter Canada because they were deemed to be "non-preferred races" or "non-preferred nations" by its immigration policies, were first deemed admissible to Canada as permanent residents. Shortly after this opening up, the process of closing down avenues of obtaining permanent resident status began. The shift to "temporary foreign worker" programs defined people subject to its conditions as a "foreign" workforce in Canada, even though they lived, worked, and paid taxes in Canada.

The Canadian nation-state has successfully shifted people out of migration statuses such as permanent resident, which provided migrants with some significant rights and entitlements, into statuses such as "temporary foreign worker," where such rights are *legally* denied. In 2011, out of the 350,000 people admitted to Canada for their labour-market skills, about 156,000 were granted permanent residency, while a greater number, about 192,000, were placed in the category of "temporary foreign worker," a status that usually limits their labour market and geographical freedom (Citizenship and Immigration Canada, 2012; Canada, n.d.). For the vast majority, such a status precludes the possibility of permanent residency (and citizenship) status.

Putting such restrictions on people's freedoms and access to citizenship has been enormously beneficial to both employers and the Canadian state. Those given "temporary foreign worker" status are generally cheaper to hire than people with citizenship or permanent resident status. Indeed, their relative "cheapness" is *legislated* by the state to the benefit of employers. "Temporary foreign workers" are also often subjected to working conditions that citizens or permanent residents, who have constitutionally guaranteed labour market and geographical freedoms, would find unacceptable. Moreover, even as these workers pay taxes, the Canadian state refuses social welfare benefits to the vast majority of "temporary foreign workers," thus saving substantial monies they would have to expend if these workers were given the status of permanent resident or citizen.

While almost all "temporary foreign workers" are legally tied to their employer, some, like those regulated by Canada's Live-in Caregiver Program (LCP), the Seasonal Agricultural Worker Program (SAWP), or the even more restrictive Pilot Project for Occupations Requiring Lower Levels of Formal Training program introduced in 2002, face even further restrictions on their freedom and mobility within Canada. All these programs are employer-driven. The LCP legally requires "temporary foreign workers" (mostly non-white women) to live in the same residence as their employers. Not only have there been well-documented cases of abuse arising from this condition, but such a stipulation constitutes a clear violation of Section 6 of the *Charter of Rights and Freedoms* that protects the mobility rights of Canadian citizens, and to a lesser extent that of permanent residents. People regulated by the SAWP often have curfews imposed upon them, are prohibited from receiving visitors of the opposite sex, and are often fired if they become pregnant (Preibisch, 2010). Moreover, the SAWP is organized as a revolving door for "temporary foreign workers" who depart and are readmitted to Canada according to the cycles of the farming industry.

The Pilot Project for Occupations Requiring Lower Levels of Formal Training program, used by firms such as Tim Hortons, stipulates that "temporary foreign workers" must depart Canada at the end of their employment (see Chapter 14, "Let's Get a Coffee"). With this program, the Canadian state has written itself out of its responsibility to intervene in the conditions of work for those recruited through it. This leaves workers with no official recourse if their employer reneges on their part of the contract. Moreover, the contract that is drawn up (by employers with the assistance of the International Organization for Migration) and that potential recruits must sign contains terms for employment that, again, would be considered unconstitutional if applied to permanent residents or citizens. For example, workers are told they should "avoid" joining any group or association, showing any signs of what the employer considers "disrespect," or having sexual relations. The contract even contains a clause regarding the length of the person's hair (UFCW, 2010)! Clearly, Canada's "temporary foreign workers" programs create extra conditions to control workers and their entire personhood that are unavailable to the state or employers to act against "citizens" and "permanent residents."

Canada's immigration and citizenship controls thus allow it to reorganize the nationalized labour market in ways that make it much more hospitable to capitalist investors and employers—and much more dangerous for migrants. Indeed, national citizenship and immigration controls have created a system of **apartheid**, both across the world and in Canada specifically. A system of apartheid exists when at least two different legal systems operate within any given state. Today's **global apartheid** is an apartheid that has one set of laws for nation-states' citizens and another set of laws governing those classified as migrants. In Canada, those with subordinated immigration statuses, such as "temporary foreign worker," live in a segregated legal zone of precarity and relative right-less-ness. While it is clearly the legal system that puts the coercive force of the state behind such classifications, it is important to recognize that it is how we think of non-citizens within Canada that makes such a system appear to be perfectly normal. Nationalism, with its legitimization of nationalized borders and exclusionary practices of granting or denying citizenship, is an everyday practice that organizes discrimination.

For instance, many in Canada believe that if migrant agricultural workers were not forced to work for specific employers and were instead granted the freedom to work for whomever they choose, they would leave agricultural work altogether and look for better-paid and less dangerous, backbreaking work. This is undoubtedly true, since this is precisely what those with Canadian citizenship status have done. To argue that one group (citizens) should have such rights while others (migrant workers) should not is, in part, what produces agricultural profits for farm owners and lowers the cost of agricultural commodities. We tend not to see our support for farm owners or the relative cheapness of our food as directly related to the low wages and lack of rights given to its direct producers because this relationship has been hidden through nationalist **ideologies** that organize our belief in the right to do unto "foreigners" what we would not do to "citizens."

At the same time, there are virulent anti-immigration politics at play in Canada. Those deemed to be legally as well as *socially* migrants (large numbers see non-white co-Canadian citizens as not "really" Canadian) are often represented as the source of problems for "Canadians," be it crime, terrorism, unemployment, competition for housing or university placements, and general anxiety about "Canadian identity" (Wilkes, Guppy, & Farris, 2008). However, the simultaneous presence of anti-immigration political rhetoric and actual increases in the number of people migrating to Canada is not contradictory. In fact, as Ghassan Hage (2000, p. 135) puts it, "anti-immigration **discourse**, by continually constructing the immigrants as unwanted, works precisely at maintaining [their] economic viability to … employers. They are best wanted as 'unwanted'" (see Mark P. Thomas's Chapter 7 on "Being 'middle class'").

FIGURE 9.3 An asylum claimant and her two-month-old baby are taken in custody by RCMP officers in Hemmingford, Quebec, after crossing the border into Canada on 28 March 2017. THE CANADIAN PRESS/Paul Chiasson.

In summary, those categorized as migrants live within each and every nation-state (and in each and every territory imagined as "national"). This demonstrates that national border controls in fact do very little to halt people's movement across national borders. Nor are they intended to. Restricting immigration is not tantamount to restricting people's migration. What border controls do, instead, is make human movement much more dangerous and costly than it otherwise would be. Border controls—and the differential immigration statuses granted migrants—also intensify competition within nationalized markets (for goods, labour, housing, education, etc.). Ironically, then, the stronger the anti-immigrant movements are, and the more restrictive a nation-state's immigration controls are, the more likely there will be greater competition within nationalized markets as people continue to enter, but do so with fewer and fewer rights. Together, these processes shift responsibility for problems in the "nation" onto migrants and away from the underlying institutions of controls and structures of power. It is *because* national borders are imagined as natural that the ways they create migrants *as subordinated beings* within nation-states are normalized and, thus, made un-political.

Mohawks' "Marry Out, Get Out" Policy

My second example of how nationalism—with its assumption that national sovereigns have the power and recognized right to determine membership and, therefore, exclude those deemed to be "foreign"—involves events that take place in Canada, but within territories claimed by the Mohawk Nation. Mohawks, along with hundreds of other human societies, were colonized by British and French imperial-states starting in the late-15th and early-16th centuries respectively. As in other empires, the people who were colonized were categorized as Natives (or Indians). With Canada's "independence" from Great Britain, jurisdiction and power over Natives within Canada's now-national territories was largely transferred to it. Through the 1876 *Indian Act*, Canada defined who was—and was not—an Indian and defined the *content* of what being an Indian meant (Tobias, 1976). The *Indian Act* also established separate reservations for Indians, with legal title over them vested in the British Crown (not Canada). Separate "Band Councils," which Canada retained power over, were created to govern **Indians**. The *Indian Act* defined the rules for political membership in "Indian Bands," including participation in Band Council elections. Moreover, the right to reside on reserves was governed by these Band Councils, with the oversight of Canadian state officials.

The *Indian Act*—and the practices of the Band Councils charged with enforcing it—were significant aspects of racializing and **gendering** Indian membership as well as political status in Canada. *Indian Act* rules institutionalized **patriarchal** social relations, as only children whose mother was married to someone Canada recognized as an Indian would themselves be considered Indian. A woman's status prior to marriage was irrelevant, as Indian women marrying men defined as non-Indian lost their—and their children's—status. Children born to unmarried Indian women were denied Indian status. This had serious and long-lasting material, political, and affective outcomes for all concerned, and profoundly shaped people's subjectivities. The patriarchal practices embedded in Canada's *Indian Act* were finally overturned in 1985 after decades of legal challenges pursued by women who had had their Indian status stripped from them because of their marriage to non-Indian men. With the passing of Bill C-31, the *Indian Act* was brought into line with gender equality provisions of the *Canadian Charter of Rights and Freedoms*. It addressed patriarchal discrimination, restored Indian status to those from whom it was denied as a result, and it allowed Bands to control their Band membership.

Prior to that time—but within the context of several women challenging the *Indian Act*—the Mohawks of Kahnawà:ke in Quebec implemented the 1981 *Kahnawà:ke Mohawk Law and Moratorium on Mixed Marriages*. It declared that "any Mohawk who married a non-native lost the right to residency, land allotment, land holding, voting, and office-holding in Kahnawà:ke" (in Alfred, 2005, p. 165). The Membership Department of the Mohawk Band Council of Kahnawà:ke's further stipulated that "any Mohawk who married a non-native would leave the community" (see Mohawk Council of Kahnawà:ke, 2014). It defined a Mohawk as someone "whose name appeared on the Band list and Reinstatement list and who had 50 per cent or more **blood quantum**" (in Mohawk Council of Kahnawà:ke, 2014). While several evictions of non-Mohawks took place in 1981, a long hiatus ensued until February 2010 when the Mohawk Band Council restarted the practice of issuing eviction letters. A sign seen at a 2016 protest outside the home of a non-Mohawk person read: "Our Lands. Our Rights. Our Blood. Forever" (Shivji, 2016).

Such sentiments are in keeping with all nationalist discourses of **sovereignty**. Indeed, although the Mohawks' "marry out, get out" policy, recently overturned by a 2018 decision by the Quebec Superior Court (and which will not be appealed), is *not* akin to Canada's citizenship and immigration policy in either scope or scale, it is similar in the discourses of nationalism that mobilize it. Struggles over membership in **Indigenous** "nations" are viewed as both an existential issue and a practical issue of allocating rights and resources. As these are all imagined within the framework of nationhood, it works to reproduce an opposition of Mohawks to non-Mohawks. Mohawk scholar Audra Simpson (2014), for example, represents struggles of Indigenous people over who should and should not have membership as a legitimate "national" matter for "nations" to decide amongst themselves. Conversely, the calls by those defined as not-Mohawk for rights are portrayed as an *intrusion* upon Indigenous national sovereignty.

Myanmar Nationalism and the Genocide of Rohingya

The work that nationalisms do is also evident in Myanmar (formerly Burma), where observers argue the "world's next genocide" is currently taking place (Human Rights Watch, 2012). In 1974, Rohingya people, who live primarily in borderland regions of Western Myanmar, were reclassified—and registered—as "foreigners" and, thus, migrants in Myanmar. This effectively rendered them stateless with no inherent right to enter or reside in Myanmar's territories. Having been cast as a vilified group, the homes, livelihoods, and lives of Rohingya people have been under assault ever since. In 2012, approximately 140,000 Rohingya people were moved to 67 camps erected by the state, which many observers see as nothing less than concentration camps (Fortify Rights, 2015). From late August 2017 to January 2018, two-thirds of all Rohingya people in Myanmar—or an estimated 688,000 people—were forced to flee to Bangladesh to escape the enormous violence unleashed against them by Myanmar's military forces (Ibrahim, 2018; UNHCR, 2018). Simultaneously victims of the citizenship regimes of the Myanmar nation-state and the "paper walls" set up by the immigration controls of other nation-states that deny them entrance, Rohingya people have been left in a highly precarious—and murderous—situation.

The situation of Rohingya people needs to be placed in the context of Myanmar's colonization by the British (Burma was made a province of British India starting in 1824) and Burma's declaration of independence in 1948. In the nation-building project preceding and following the formation of Burma as a nation-state, a conflicted process of both "place-making and claim-staking" ensued (Zarni & Cowley, 2014, p. 697). Immediately after "independence," the new national leaders began to sort out who was—and was not—eligible for Burmese nationality. In Chapter II of its founding Constitution (1948), the criterion of "Indigenous race" (in Burmese: *Taiyintha*, or the "original children of the soil") was selected over residency or birth in the nation-state's territory as the basis of citizenship. Initially, Rohingya people were included as one of the "Indigenous races" and granted national citizenship rights as a result.

However, one of the legacies of British **imperialism** was a simmering resentment of anyone viewed as "Indian" (some, but not all, of whom had been positioned in a "middle" position in British Burma and who had become prominent in commercial activities or the British security forces, and had also entered the parliament set up by the British). Active state mobilization against "Indians" began after the 1962 military coup led by General Ne Win and his Burma Socialist Programme Party (BSPP). Recasting Rohingya as migrants from India or East Pakistan/Bangladesh, one of the junta's first acts was to dissolve Rohingya social and political organizations. In 1964, the shops and stores of people popularly referred to as "Indian" or "Chinese" were targeted for nationalization (Zaw et al., 2001). Soon thereafter, anti-Rohingya racism began to be encoded in the law. By 1974, when Rohingya people's citizenship was removed, the situation had deteriorated significantly. Throughout Myanmar society, Rohingya people were (and are) commonly referred to as "Bengali" or "Kalar" (meaning "Black"), both of which are used as racist pejoratives. In keeping with a basic nationalist "truth" that nation-states owe nothing to people they categorize as "foreigners" or migrants, Myanmar has consistently normalized the persecution of Rohingya by referring to them as such.

In contrast, Buddhist citizens of Myanmar consistently refer to themselves as "Indigenous" people. U Oo Hla Saw, a major political figure, proclaimed in 2013 that "this is our native land; it's the land of our ancestors" (in Fuller, 2012). Not only state officials, but also prominent Buddhist monks, voice hostility to Rohingya people. U Nyarna, head of an association of young monks in Sittwe, was quoted as saying that Rohingya were "invaders, unwanted guests and 'vipers in our laps'" (in Fuller, 2012). Buddhist monks' leader Ashin Htawara encouraged the government to send Rohingya people "back to their native land" (in Hindstrom, 2012). The monk leading the economic boycotts and social shunning of Rohingya people did so, he said, because "the Muslim people are stealing our land and drinking our water and killing our people. They are eating our rice and staying near our houses. So we will separate" (in Human Rights Watch, 2012, p. 46).

Nationalizing Homelands

The normalcy attached to the exclusionary ideas and practices of nationalism rests on ideas of "national homelands," which organize people's ideas of themselves, their family, **culture**, and community, including the political community that is the bearer of rights granted by the sovereign/state. Nationalism is, I believe, among the most naturalized and, consequently, most dangerous ideas of our time. In Canada or in Kahnawà:ke or in Myanmar, differences between people **constituted** as Indigenous, citizens, migrants, and temporary foreign workers are all organized through ideas of each of these nationally organized places being the home of some but not **Others**. With the overlaying of the idea of home onto nation, some people are easily understood as belonging in Canada or in Kahnawà:ke or in Myanmar, while others are rendered as foreigners/migrants even though they live and work there—or many may actually hold formal citizenship status but are still negatively evaluated as not "really" belonging.

Indeed, *home* acts as a conceptual bridge between contemporary ideas of family and nation—so much so that the **nation** is understood to be a "magnified version of the family and the circle of close friends" (Johansen, 1997, p. 171). In this, "the National family is a symbolic home" (Morley, 2000, p. 104). This is well captured by former British Prime Minister Margaret Thatcher (1989), who proclaimed, "the family and its maintenance really is the most important thing, not only in your personal life, but in the life of any community, because this is the unit on which the whole nation is built." While "society cannot belong to us as individuals," notes Eric Hobsbawm (1991, pp. 67–68), we are encouraged to imagine that it can still belong to those of us imagined as a "nation." For this reason, "a house identified with the self is called a home, a country identified with the self is called a 'homeland'" (Tabor, 1998, p. 218).

With the modern family's emphasis on biological connection, **hegemonic** conceptions of home are based on the idea that there exist communities of *racialized* similarity. "Its territory is our home; its people is marked by a common 'character,' much like the members of a family; its past is a 'heritage' passed down from our 'forefathers'" (Johansen, 1997, p. 171). Thus, we talk of the "family of nations" and of "native" lands. The ties between family, nation, and state are further elaborated on by Anne McClintock (1995, p. 357), who observes, "the term 'nation' derives from *natio*: to be born—we speak of nations as 'motherlands' and 'fatherlands' so foreigners 'adopt' countries that are not their 'native homes' and are nationalized into the 'national family.'" Having a home within a "nation" is therefore not just a geographical signpost but part of the discourse of nationalism. Through it, home becomes an idea that masquerades as a place. Because of this, it profoundly shapes our consciousness of the relationship between people, place, and "belonging."

The power of nationalism rests in its ability to project ideas of national homelands back through human history so that we see "nations" as eternally existent. In this, some people are portrayed as having "roots" in the "nation" while others—especially migrants—are represented as being "rootless." Looking at how European colonizers made themselves at home in particular colonies is instructive in this regard. The **colonial** doctrine of Terra Nullius asserted the idea that land not held either as private property or as state territory was simply sitting "empty" and awaiting "improvement" by European colonizers. Within non-European colonies, this doctrine informed the large-scale transfer of land to the imperial state and to investors.

Later, lands expropriated from colonized Natives were offered as private property to European workers to garner their support for imperial projects, projects that had forced them to leave Europe. Indeed, it is well worth remembering that starting in 1604 and continuing to 1914, more than 5,200 enclosure Bills were enacted by the British Parliament. Some 6.8 million acres—over a fifth of the total area of England—was enclosed (Turner, 1980). In addition to mass land confiscations in Ireland, a further 1.17 million acres were enclosed in Wales (Chapman, 1987). The Scottish Clearances enclosed millions more acres (Richards, 1985). These enclosures and confiscations were a critical part of the capitalist process of "**primitive accumulation**" and "improvement" that began in the English countryside and spread over the entire face of the earth. The consequence was massive dispossession, the transformation of common lands into imperial territory and private property, and the **commodification** of the labour power of the displaced (Wood, 2002). As a result, many workers in Britain were pressed into service, transported as felons, or kept in unfree employment relations as **indentured servants** under the control of their masters in British colonies in the New World. Here they joined other members of the largely unfree labour force, which included people defined by the imperial-state as Natives or Negroes.

Yet, by the late 17th century, although brutally subjugated, workers from Europe were elevated above all other workers through racist laws that invented the "White Race" (Allen, 1975). In the process, **whiteness** became a crucial aspect of destroying labour solidarity. Through this process, imperial colonies, such as Canada, were refounded as "white settler societies." The understanding was that not only European capitalists, but now also European workers, were colonizers with privileged standing. Conversely, the idea that the diverse people living on these lands for millennia prior to the arrival of European colonizers were never at home on these lands worked to depoliticize their homelessness after the advent of **colonialism** and the official redistribution of land to those who imagined themselves as part of the imperial regime. These ideas profoundly shaped the emergence of nationalist thought in the late 18th century and throughout the 19th.

Racializing and Ethnicizing National Belonging

Indeed, as the above examples demonstrate, attributing "racial" or "ethnic" criteria to membership in human societies has greatly informed the idea of "nations" as natural "homelands" for some (Morley, 2000, p. 212). Our imagination of contemporary "nations" has entailed the dividing of humanity along *racialized* or *ethnicized* lines and arguing that each person belongs to one—and only one—such group. Doreen Massey (in Mackay, 1997) argues that "in that process the boundaries of the place, and the imagination and building of its 'character,' [become] part and parcel of the definition of who is an insider and who is not; of who is a 'local' and what that term should mean, and who is to be excluded" (p. 204). Practices of exclusion are organized through such imaginations.

Attached to ideologies of nationalism, ideas of "race" or "**ethnicity**" tie human cultures to particular places. Being at home in the "nation" is based on "mythic narratives, stories the telling of which has the power to create the 'we' who are engaged in telling them," as well as constructing the idea that "we" have a natural "right to a space (a country, a neighbourhood, a place to live) that is due us … in the name of the 'we-ness' we have just constructed" (Bammer, 1992, pp. ix–x). Such a discourse "allows us to imagine that we do not have to share our space with anyone else unless they are of exactly our own kind by virtue of **consanguinity**" (or relationship by descent from a common ancestor) (Morley, 2000, p. 217). What such a conflation allows is the identification of family-as-"nation"-as-"race." This has had a particularly damaging effect on people categorized as Migrants, especially those who are negatively racialized and separated from those imagined to be members of any given "nation."

Indeed, acceptance of nationalist ideologies of racialized or ethnicized "homelands" changed understandings of people's geographical movements. As discourses of nationalism expanded in the mid-1800s, migrants were increasingly portrayed as trespassers. In other words, as the "nation" became more "homey" to some (the national subjects), Migrants were made homeless. To be a migrant became tantamount to being a vagrant. Since vagrancy was portrayed as a moral (and often a criminal) offence, migrants came to be strongly associated with losing not only their homes but also their moral standing (Anderson, 2013). Together, such normalized ideas worked to define the "national homeland" as that which stands *against* Migrants.

Over time, the naturalization of **xenophobia** mobilized the idea that "nations" have some sort of right to preserve their presumed purity. Thus, unsurprisingly, discourses of anti-**miscegenation** (or prohibitions against "racial mixing") have, today, become the basis of asserting national identities and have often led to virulent and highly violent forms of "homey racism." Such discourses are "a reactionary vocabulary of the identity politics of place and a spatialised politics of identity grounded in the rhetoric of origins, of exclusion, of boundary-making, of invasion and succession, of purity and contamination … [in short,] the glossary of **ethnic cleansing**" (Keith & Pile, 1993, p. 20).

Increasingly, goals of maintaining supposed national homogeneity are fought for not just in the name of "race purity" but also in the name of preserving "cultural integrity." Indeed, contemporary practices of racism rely less on ideas of "race" separation and more and more on ideas that uphold and sanctify "cultural differences." An impoverished view of "culture," one that sees each "culture" as unchanged and unchanging, has come to overlay notions of biological "race" so that what connects *identity to place* is said to be the historical existence of certain "traditions." In this, "tradition [becomes] the cultural equivalent of the process of biological reproduction" (Morley, 2000, p. 65). This "new racism" has been called a "differentialist racism" (Taguieff, 1990) or, simply, "**neo-racism**" (Balibar, 1991).

Significantly, neo-racism separates—and attempts to segregate—people *spatially* so that each "national culture" has "its own" place in the world. Indeed, with pseudo-scientific ideas of "race" discredited after news of the Nazi holocaust (against Jewish, Romani, Sinti, and Black people) circulated, the mutual constitution of nationalism and racism has shifted to the naturalization of "national " difference. The "rooting" of culture in particular geographical places makes immigration a political threat to national identity and the integrity of "national culture" (Malkki, 1992). Immigrants thus become "national security" risks because of their "cultural diversity." In the process, human mobility itself comes to be seen only in the context of crisis—as both caused by crisis and producing crisis for the "national subjects" of the places they move to (Sutcliffe, 2001). It is for this reason that "the common experience of the homeless and the migrant is to be made to feel *out of place*" even as they often live in the *same place* (Bird, 1995, p. 119, emphasis added).

At the same time, however, the very mobility of migrants should call into question the idea of national belonging. This is because migrants "make our taken-for-granted identities visible as specific identities and deprive them of their assumed naturalness" such that "once we start thinking about them, becoming aware of them, we cannot feel 'at home' any more" (Rathzel, 1994, p. 91). A comment by a woman refugee from Cambodia living in Paris puts it succinctly: "We are a disturbance.… Because we show you in a terrible way how fragile the world we live in is" (in Morley, 2000, p. 152).

Discourses of nationalism are crucial for the normalization of nation-state power. Michel Foucault's (1991) **concept** of "government of the self" helps us better understand the crucial importance of nationalism in creating particular kinds of subjectivities, or *sense of self* as a form of self-governance, in mobilizing state power. The proper national subject is constructed through the simultaneous construction of its **binary** opposite; those people who "threaten" national life. Indeed, using insights from the **psychoanalytic theories** of Jacques Lacan, Hage (2000, p. 37) argues that nationalist discourses would fall apart if there were not Others against whom the nation could be defined.

For this reason, Hage (2000, p. 28) argues that nationalists "assume, first, an image of a national space; secondly, an image of the nationalist himself or herself as master of this national space and, thirdly, an image of the racial or ethnic 'other' as a mere object within this space." In this way, nationalism allows those who see themselves as members of "nations" to assume the role of the sovereign/state for themselves, including the right to determine who else does—and does not—belong. This is evident in the fact that "in every [epithet of you] 'go home,' there is an 'I want to and am entitled to feel at home in my nation'" (Hage, 2000, p. 40).

Nationalism as a Legacy of Colonialism

The supposed similarity of "members of the nation" with one another and the extraordinary "strangeness" of those imagined as their opposite ("migrants") is, ironically, an idea formed out of the *global* flow of capital, goods, and people. As I've discussed above, the gross inequalities organized by colonialism and **capitalism** were mapped onto racialized and, later, nationalized ideas of Us and Them. It is no coincidence that passports—the crucial document now needed to lawfully cross national borders—were invented after the end of slavery across the British Empire in the 1830s as a way to control and cheapen the labour of people now categorized as Migrants (Mongia, 2018; Torpey, 2000). Many of today's nation-states came into existence by their own forced dispossession, displacement, violent assimilation, and, sometimes, outright genocide of those they deemed to be strangers to the "nation." This is perhaps most clearly seen in the "New World" nation-states of the Americas, in which the path to nationhood taken by some of the world's first nation-states was paved by the severe reduction, and at times elimination, of diverse groups of people through war, slavery, and disease. Similar processes occurred in Africa, Asia, and even Europe, as nation-states were violently erected by destroying pre-existing societies.

In recognizing the important colonial genealogy in today's nationalisms, however, we must not confuse the process of colonization with migration (see Mongia, 2018). This is what happens in current arguments that all non-Natives are "settler colonists," a position that includes, for example, kidnapped slaves forcibly transported from Africa and indentured "coolie" labourers from Asia (see Fujikane & Okamura, 2000; Lawrence & Dua, 2005). Unlike migration, colonization is *inherently* a relationship of exploitation and oppression, one that results in people's dispossession and their displacement. The problem with colonization is not the "strangeness" or "foreign-ness" of the colonizers, but their destructive practices and the grossly unjust social relations they put into place. Migration, on the other hand, is a quintessential human practice, one long associated with freedom or, at the very least, with escape from untenable situations (war and poverty) or, simply, adventure.

Even more so, the migrations of people are *not* the equivalent to the migration of colonizers. Displaced commoners from around the world (including Europe), African slaves, indentured labourers from China or India, or, today, professionals, families, "temporary" or "illegal" migrant workers, and refugees fleeing political persecution are, instead, shaped by the asymmetrical relationships that European imperialism imposed on the world's people. Migration continues at an unprecedented rate today because of the long-term legacies of such spatial asymmetries in power and wealth. Migration and citizenship controls, and the severe limits they place on free human movement and rights, are a defining feature of what I call the **Postcolonial New World Order of Nation-States**.

This international system was put into place after World War II not to ensure the end of colonialism, but to *contain* the aspirations of colonized people struggling for their liberty. Instead of securing peace, prosperity, and global equality, as demanded by people in the colonies, "national liberation" movements established "independent" sovereign nation-states that controlled both territories and people now re-imagined as *national*. Moreover, not only the colonies but also European metropoles of empires nationalized their sovereignty, so that by the late 1960s, the two largest empires at the start of World War II—Britain and France—had become nation-states.

This Postcolonial New World Order of nation-states implemented severe—and ever-intensifying—restrictions on both political membership in national societies and in free movement into nation-states. This Postcolonial New World Order has gross inequalities and injustices no less—and oftentimes more intense—than those organized by European imperialism. As Samir Amin (2001, p. 7) has noted, there has been an increase in "the **inequality** between peoples from a maximum ratio of two to one around 1800, to sixty to one today." People's inability to move to where the wealth and resources are held is one of the main ways that such inequalities are produced and maintained. In our world, national borders are a major aspect of how the inequalities between what Stuart Hall (1992) has called "the West and the rest" are secured.

In this way, ideas of the "nation" as a home *conceal* the fact that the exclusions organized through national citizenship policies are integral to the nation-state, not simply coincidental or something that can be done away with through bureaucratic reform. In short, nation-states are not capable—structurally or in their structures of nationalist thought—to produce just societies. In this respect, Avner Offer's (1989, p. 235) argument that racist practices are *part* of the liberal "virtues of democracy, civic equality, and solidarity" takes on greater relevance, as does John Holloway's (1994, p. 32) argument that because national sovereignty is constructed through the organization of racialized differences between Us and Them, "the very existence of the [nation-]state is racist."

With regard to national styles of ruling, then, we must pay more careful attention to Kobena Mercer's (1994) question: "Why the need for the nation?" Examining "who needs it, who manufactures the 'need' for it, and whose interests it serves" is an even more urgent task (Burton, 1997, p. 234). In this sense, it is useful to understand that the state, like the nation, is imagined. This does not mean that the state does not exist. Rather, the state, like the nation, is a form of social relations. The legitimacy—and power—of the nation-state in particular is reliant upon the existence of the "imagined community" of the "nation" on whose behalf it is said to rule (Anderson, 1991). That is, the nation-state—and the set of social relationships organized through it—requires the existence of a group who understand themselves to be a "nation" to continue to make common sense to people. Equally so, it relies on the existence of Others—migrants—to bring the "nation" into being.

Concepts of citizenship are the ideological glue that hold such nationalist ideas in place. Together the ideas and practices of citizenship provide legitimacy to the state to legally subordinate those imagined as "foreigners." Indeed, denying the rights, entitlements, and protections that citizens have to migrants is a crucial feature of how dominant ideas of nations-as-homes operate within today's world. This is why it continues to be onto the bodies of migrants that a "foreign" identity can most easily be grafted. In this process, citizenship plays a crucial part. Indeed, the closely related powers wielded by contemporary nation-states and capitalists rest precisely on our (everyday) acceptance of the citizenship divide.

Conclusion

The nation-state system has severely limited our sense of self and left us with an impoverished ability to empathize and connect to people beyond national borders and identities. The very practices that purportedly affirm the belonging of citizens in the nation are the same ones that allow the Canadian nation-state to legally mark some Others who live there to be socially and legally inscribed as foreign bodies.

Challenging nationalized forms of "difference" and reconnecting to people across the boundaries created by national citizenship regimes, therefore, is one of the greatest political challenges of our time. This is because, today, nationalism provides one of the primary modes of self-identification, both for oppressed and oppressing people. Challenging the legitimacy of national forms of discrimination, then, is a direct challenge both to the forms of subjectivity we hold and to the material organization of our lives. Doing so may lead us to ways of organizing human societies at the scales in which our lives are actually lived and with the affinities required to combat many of the major social problems we face, be they ecological disaster, growing poverty, wars over territory, or hatred of the myriad Others who are left out of dominant **norms** of national belonging. The challenge is clearly great. However, the fact that human societies are fundamentally social provides us with the hope for non-national forms of organization.

Study Questions

1 There is a deep relationship between ideas of "nation" and the power of states over people within the national territories it claims. Discuss the ways that the different identities of "national subject" and "foreigner" affect people's everyday lived experience of life in Canada.
2 What are some of the reasons that the Canadian nation-state gives different legal and illegal statuses to people who move to Canada?
3 How are these different statuses legitimized (or normalized) within Canadian society?
4 What does it mean to contend that national border controls are ideological?
5 Do you think that national borders that empower states to regulate and limit people's mobility are ethical?

Exercises

1 Ethical responses to global displacement: There are a number of factors that cause people to migrate. These include war, persecution, abuse, famine, inhabitability of a place (as a result of floods, earthquakes, tsunamis, droughts, etc.), loss of land and/or livelihood, poverty, a sense that there are better opportunities elsewhere, and the excitement of travel and a new life. How is the Canadian state at least partially responsible for the existence of these conditions in a number of places around the world? What is the ethical responsibility of a country like Canada to people who migrate as a result of its activities? Can we separate Canadian policy on immigration from its military policies, its international trade policies, or its policies on greenhouse gas emissions?

2 Migrating to another nation-state: Think about the factors that might cause you to move from Canada to another nation-state. How would you get there? What would you need? What legal channels would you have to follow? What would you do if you were not granted official permission to enter and reside in this new place? What would you miss about your life in Canada? How would you make a living in the new place? Remember, you need to find a place to live, food to eat, water to drink.

3 Rights: Go the websites of international bodies, such as that of the International Labour Organization (http://www.ilo.org/global/lang-en/index.htm) or the United Nations (www.un.org). Think about some of the other already existing ways that rights and entitlements are allocated and distributed in the world today. How do they compare to the rights granted "citizens" (and therefore denied "foreigners")? Are there even less exclusionary (or even non-exclusionary) ways to organize rights and entitlements? What are some other ways that we could allocate rights and entitlements to ensure that all human beings are able to live healthy and dignified lives?

References

Alfred, T. (2005). *Wasase: Indigenous pathways of action and freedom.* Toronto, ON: Broadview Press.

Allen, T.W. (1975). *Class struggle and the origin of racial slavery: The invention of the white race.* Boston, MA: New England Free Press.

Amin, S. (2001). Imperialism and globalization. *Monthly Review, 53*(2), 6–24.

Anderson, B. (1991). *Imagined communities: Reflections on the origin and spread of nationalism.* London, UK: Verso.

Anderson, B. (2013). *Us and them? The dangerous politics of immigration control.* Oxford, UK: Oxford University Press.

Balibar, É. (1991). Is there a neo-racism? In É. Balibar & I. Wallerstein (Eds.), *Race, nation, class: Ambiguous identities* (pp. 17–28). London, UK: Verso.

Bammer, A. (1992). Editorial. *New Formations, 17*, vii–xi.

Bird, J. (1995). Dolce domum. In J. Lingwood (Ed.), *Rachel Whiteread's house.* London, UK: Phaidon Press.

Burton, A. (1997). Who needs the nation? Interrogating British history. *Journal of Historical Sociology, 10*(3), 227–248.

Canada. (n.d.). *Fact sheet: Temporary foreign worker program.* Retrieved from https://www.canada.ca/en/immigration-refugees-citizenship/corporate/publications-manuals/fact-sheet-temporary-foreign-worker-program.html

Chapman, J. (1987). The extent and nature of parliamentary enclosure. *Agricultural History Review, 35*(1), 25–35.

Citizenship and Immigration Canada. (2012). *Annual report to Parliament on immigration 2012.* Retrieved from https://www.canada.ca/content/dam/ircc/migration/ircc/english/pdf/pub/annual-report-2012.pdf

Fortify Rights. (2015, November 27). Ethnic minorities in Myanmar denied vote as Aung San Suu Kyi claims power. Retrieved from http://www.fortifyrights.org/commentary-20151127.html

Foucault, M. (1991). Questions of method. In G. Burchell, C. Gordon, & P. Miller (Eds.), *The Foucault effect: Studies in governmentality* (pp. 73–86). Chicago, IL: University of Chicago Press.

Fujikane, C., & Okamura, J.Y. (2000). Whose vision? Asian settler colonialism in Hawai'i, a special issue. *Amerasia Journal*, *26*(2).

Fuller, T. (2012, December 1). Ethnic hatred tears apart a region of Myanmar. *The New York Times*. Retrieved from http://www.nytimes.com/2012/11/30/world/asia/muslims-face-expulsion-from-western-myanmar.html

Hage, G. (2000). *White nation: Fantasies of white supremacy in a multicultural society*. New York, NY: Routledge.

Hall, S. (1992). The West and the rest: Discourse and power. In R. Maaka & C. Andersen (Eds.), *The Indigenous experience: Global perspectives* (pp. 165–173). Toronto, ON: Canadian Scholars' Press.

Hindstrom, H. (2012, July 25). Burma's Monks call for Muslim community to be shunned. *The Independent*. Retrieved from http://www.independent.co.uk/news/world/asia/burmas-monks-call-for-muslim-community-to-be-shunned-7973317.html

Hobsbawm, E. (1991). Exile. *Social Research*, *58*(1), 65–68.

Holloway, J. (1994). Global capital and the nation-state. *Capital and Class*, *52*(Spring), 23–50.

Human Rights Watch. (2012). "The government could have stopped this": Sectarian violence and ensuing abuses in Burma's Arakan State. Retrieved from https://www.hrw.org/report/2012/07/31/government-could-have-stopped/sectarian-violence-and-ensuing-abuses-burmas-arakan

Ibrahim, A. (2018, February 7). The genocide in Burma continues: Yet the international community is still sitting on its hands. *Washington Post*.

Johansen, A. (1997). Fellowmen, compatriots, contemporaries. In J.P. Burgess (Ed.), *Cultural politics and political culture in postmodern Europe* (pp. 169–212). Amsterdam, Netherlands: Editions Rodopi.

Keith, M., & Pile, S. (1993). The politics of place. In M. Keith & S. Pile (Eds.), *Place and the politics of identity* (pp. 1–21). London, UK: Routledge.

Lawrence, B., & Dua, E. (2005). Decolonizing antiracism. *Social Justice*, *32*(4), 120–143.

Mackay, H. (Ed.). (1997). *Consumption and everyday life*. Milton Keynes, UK: Open University Press.

Malkki, L. (1992). National geographic: The rooting of peoples and the territorialization of national identity among scholars and refugees. *Cultural Anthropology*, *7*(1), 24–44.

McClintock, A. (1995). *Imperial leather*. London, UK: Routledge.

Mercer, K. (1994). *Welcome to the jungle: New positions in Black cultural studies*. New York, NY: Routledge.

Milanovic, B. (2016). *Global inequality: A new approach for the age of globalization*. Cambridge, MA: Harvard University Press.

Mohawk Council of Kahnawà:ke, Membership Department. (2014). Kahnawà:ke membership law project: Communications package for community information sessions. Retrieved from http://www.kahnawakemakingdecisions.com/promo/KMLBinder1.pdf

Mongia, R. (2018). *Indian migration and empire: A colonial genealogy of the modern state.* Durham, NC: Duke University Press.

Morley, D. (2000). *Home territories: Media, mobility and identity.* London, UK: Routledge.

Offer, A. (1989). *The first world war: An agrarian interpretation.* New York, NY: Oxford University Press.

Preibisch, K. (2010). Pick-your-own labor: Migrant workers and flexibility in Canadian agriculture. *International Migration Review, 44*(2), 404–441.

Rathzel, N. (1994). Harmonious Heimat and disturbing Ausländer. In K.K. Bhavani & A. Phoenix (Eds.), *Shifting identities and shifting racisms* (pp. 81–98). London, UK: Sage Publications.

Richards, E. (1985). *A history of the Highland clearances.* London, UK: Croom Helm.

Sharma, N. (2006). *Home economics: Nationalism and the making of migrant workers in Canada.* Toronto, ON: University of Toronto Press.

Shivji, S. (2016). Mohawk Council of Kahnawake hands out more eviction letters. *CBC News* Montreal. http://www.cbc.ca/news/canada/montreal/mohawk-kahnawake-marry-out-stay-out-eviction-notice-1.3658202

Simpson, A. (2014). *Mohawk interruptus: Political life across the borders of settler states.* Durham, NC: Duke University Press.

Sutcliffe, B. (2001). Migration and citizenship: Why can birds, whales, butterflies and ants cross international frontiers more easily than cows, dogs and human beings? In S. Ghatak & A.S. Sassoon (Eds.), *Migration and mobility: The European context* (pp. 66–82). New York, NY: Palgrave MacMillan.

Tabor, P. (1998). Striking home: The telematic assault on identity. In J. Hill (Ed.), *Occupying architecture* (pp. 217–228). London, UK: Routledge.

Taguieff, P.A. (1990). The new cultural racism in France. *Telos, 83,* 109–122.

Thatcher, M. (1989, May 4). Interview with Julie Cockroft. *Daily Mail.*

Tobias, J.L. (1976). Protection, civilization, assimilation: An outline history of Canada's Indian policy. *Western Canadian Journal of Anthropology, 61,* 12–30.

Torpey, J. (2000). *The invention of the passport: Surveillance, citizenship, and the state.* Cambridge, UK: Cambridge University Press.

Turner, M.E. (1980). *English parliamentary enclosure: Its historical geography and economic history.* Hamden, CT: Archon Books.

UFCW (United Farm and Commercial Workers Union). (2010). Guatemalan migrants. *UFCW website.* Retrieved from http://www.ufcw.ca/index.php?option=com_content&view=article&id=2161&Itemid=291&lang=en

UNHCR (United Nations High Commissioner for Refugees). (2018, January 23–February 5). Operational update: Bangladesh. Retrieved from https://data2.unhcr.org/en/documents/details/61917

United Nations. (2017). International migration report. *Department of Economic and Social Affairs.* Retrieved from http://www.un.org/en/development/desa/population/migration/publications/migrationreport/docs/MigrationReport2017_Highlights.pdf

Wilkes, R., Guppy, N., & Farris, L. (2008). No thanks, we're full: Individual characteristics, national context, and changing attitudes toward immigration. *International Migration Review, 42*(2), 302–329.

Wood, E.M. (2002). *The origin of capitalism: A longer view.* London, UK: Verso.

Zarni, M., & Cowley, A. (2014). Slow-burning genocide of Myanmar's Rohingya. *Pacific Rim Law & Policy Journal, 23*(3), 683–754.

Zaw, A., Arnott, D., Chongkittavorn, K., Liddell, Z., Morshed, K., Myint, S., & Aung, T.T. (2001). Challenges to democratization in Burma: Perspectives on multilateral and bilateral responses, report for the international institute for democracy and electoral assistance, Stockholm, Sweden. Retrieved from http://www.idea.int/asia_pacific/myanmar/upload/challenges_to_democratization_in_burma.pdf

PART THREE
Everyday Practices

DEBORAH BROCK, ARYN MARTIN, REBECCA RABY, and MARK P. THOMAS

While chapters in the previous section illustrated how our everyday practices are embedded within broader structural categories and patterns of **inequality**, in this section we focus directly on how **power** permeates our everyday choices and practices: through what we do, the conversations we have with each other, the guidance we seek, and the common "truths" that guide us. We locate what often feel like personal, everyday, decisions and practices in a broader context, drawing from the approaches of Marx and Foucault to understand both the political-economic processes that shape these practices and the ways in which they are organized through (expert and popular) discourses and relations of governance. Analyzing everyday practices such as reading about a scientific study online, seeing a therapist, going shopping or for coffee, or engaging in **tourism** in this way reveals how our personal lives are deeply connected to broader social relations, and how our personal decisions and practices reflect, produce and reproduce wider processes.

With a focus on how **science** pervades everyday life, from the way we think about how the world works to decisions about bodies, Aryn Martin examines how the social shapes the naming of scientific "truths" and how this process suggests the need to turn a critical eye to contemporary scientific truth-making. In their chapter on going to a therapist, Heidi Reimke and Deborah Brock examine how psychological expertise—a form of scientific truth-making—has permeated our lives, how people's problems are increasingly located within the individual, and how the individual is increasingly **pathologized**.

The next three chapters explore relations around commerce. Dennis Soron looks at shopping, a practice that most of us undertake at least every week. While shopping is often presented to us as offering seemingly limitless options and choices, Soron explores how these "free choices" are really practices of governing, as they are constrained and guided by marketing experts. These processes also tend to bolster corporate profit. Also looking at what we do with our money, Mary-Beth Raddon's chapter on finance explores the increasing influence of financial institutions and experts over our everyday lives, and looks at strategies for "**financial fitness**" that have become normalized and perpetuated in our **neoliberal** context through advice and decision-making regarding people's personal finances and estimations of people's financial health. Gavin Fridell and Erika Koss then turn our focus to a very specific social and consumer practice: going for coffee. In this chapter, Fridell and Koss ask what **power relations** are embedded in a cup of coffee. They demonstrate how the production of coffee is embedded within a complex set of economic, political, and social relationships, pointing toward how our own consumption of coffee is thereby connected to such relations.

The remaining two chapters in this section address everyday practices that involve producing **the other**. In her chapter, Margot Francis illustrates ways in which "Imagining Indians," as constructed through **stereotypes**, are connected to longstanding relations of power and inequality that are central to the organization of Canada as a **nation**. Central to her chapter is Francis's discussion of an Anishinaabec-led theatre project through which **Indigenous** youth challenge stereotypes about Indigenous people. Looking at practices of tourism, Gada Mahrouse demonstrates how tourism is a global industry that is profoundly classed, **racialized**, and gendered, and is reproduced through our own "everyday" practices as tourists.

While these chapters cover a wide range of practices, processes, and social relations, they all aim to develop integrative frameworks for understanding the social organization of power within everyday practices. Together, they aptly illustrate that through such everyday practices as buying a self-help book or groceries, going for coffee, or posting travel photos on social media, we are not only embedded in a wide range of power relations, we also participate in their reproduction. Thus, power is not simply exercised "out there," as an abstract, structural, and coercive force but is also reflected in our own daily activities.

10 Science and the "Matter" of Power

ARYN MARTIN

Introduction

Whether we are aware of it or not, science and technology pervade our everyday activities, experiences, choices, and possibilities. We sometimes hear about scholars, activists, or policy makers who study the effects of science on society. This is certainly important work, especially when areas such as genetics, medical research, climate science, and information technology (IT) are changing so rapidly. However, when we pose the question this way—what effects are science and technology having on human lives and communities?—we mistakenly perpetuate the idea that science and technology operate in a sphere separate from society. An alternative view, which sees science and society as inextricably wound together, has developed in the social sciences and humanities disciplines in the last several decades. Gathering under the rubric of "science and technology studies" (STS), sociologists, anthropologists, philosophers, historians, and activists have turned their attention to science as it is actually done. For example, their studies describe how scientists build social consensus using persuasive rhetorical practices (such as writing, arguing, and drawing) and how scientists are embedded in, and influenced by, their economic, religious, political, or social convictions.

Because it is done by humans, science cannot *not* be social. Importantly, exploring science as a social practice is not the same as saying it is bad, misguided, or morally wrong (though particular bits of knowledge or technologies may be). We will see that the social is a source of **contingency** in shaping what becomes scientific knowledge and what does not. Contingency is an important **concept** throughout this chapter. In this context, it means that a specific scientific discovery or invention is dependent on the chain of events that preceded it, including social ones. If the historical sequence leading up to the scientific event were different, the science would be different, too. Even what questions are asked of science and what answers are deemed meaningful to human knowers would be different. This insight isn't meant to debunk science but to better characterize the gradual, creative, sometimes ambiguous, extremely expensive and, yes, powerful set of practices that occupy the top rung on the knowledge ladder in our time. As philosopher Bruno Latour argues, we study the myriad components of science-in-the-making—including human ones—not to get further away from facts, but to get closer to them (2004). Science is more or less like other ways we get reliable and predictive knowledge about the world. The very notion that science has unique access to something called "**objectivity**" is an accomplishment that can be approached historically (Daston & Galison, 1992). And this illusion of objectivity has everything to do with power.

Science and Power

Building on theories of power you encountered in Chapters 1 and 2, you will recognize both Marxist and Foucauldian themes in this chapter. Because science emanates from elite, mostly Western, institutions closely allied with capital, a Marxist conception of power is sometimes invoked. More central, though, is Foucault's influence. Science is implicated in how institutions govern individuals and populations. Genetics, for example, is increasingly playing a role in how people are defined and administered by medical and legal institutions. Moreover, science is a dominant **discourse** at work in the minutest aspects of our self-conduct: what we eat, how we control our sexual and reproductive lives, what our children weigh, how we treat pain and disease, how we care about the environment (or don't), what behaviours we see as "unnatural," and on and on.

One key insight in the work of Michel Foucault (1980) is that whatever is taken to be "truth" in a given time or place has an important relationship to power. Foucault writes:

> Each society has its **régime of truth**, its "general politics" of truth: that is, the types of discourses which it accepts and makes function as true; the mechanisms and instances which enable one to distinguish true and false statements; the means by which each is sanctioned; the techniques and procedures accorded value in the acquisition of truth; the status of those who are charged with saying what counts as true. (p. 131)

Notice how the phrase "whatever is taken to be truth" already modifies the concept of truth, and what it is capable of. We know that what people consider to be true has changed over time and varies in different places according to local ways of making sense of the world. It is not a fixed entity. Nor does it make sense to think of scientific knowledge as arbitrary cultural fabrication (this is how social constructionism is often, erroneously, understood by its detractors). There is a middle ground between saying science generates absolute truths (except for rare instances of fraud or error) and saying that whatever becomes truth in a time and place is merely made up, or an outcome of whoever is in power and speaks the loudest. Particular scientific evidence—such as the consensus that humans are contributing to a dangerously warming planet—can be carefully collected, reproducible, convincing, and useful.

Three centuries of experience has shown us that the scientific method produces enormously useful facts and artifacts, but bracketing their inevitability and authority allows us to ask questions like: Useful for whom? Who practices science, who is excluded, and why does it matter? Which occupations and activities become understood as "scientific," and which are denied this label and the resources it confers? How do economic and global considerations play into what questions are asked of science, and what answers are offered? How do classifications that get called "natural" shape our everyday behaviours and possibilities, and reproduce patterns of **inequality**? What are the sources of ambiguity that get in the way of scientific or medical facts becoming solid or certain, and how are these resolved?

This chapter explores the social dynamics of science by attending to aspects of scientific practice that we (ordinary people) do not normally get to see. We tend to encounter facts after they are already packaged up into certainties—"black-boxed"—and we can't easily tell where they came from. Instead of taking scientific facts for granted when they are already solidified, we will look at the human labour and decision-making that goes into their solidification (in STS, this is sometimes called "opening black boxes"). First, foregrounding observation—a cornerstone of the scientific method—we will look at what sociologists and philosophers have noted about human perceptions of nature. Next, we explore how scientists exist always and only in communities. They inevitably work as part of a team, but in addition, their work is enabled and constrained by the necessity of persuading the larger official collective—the institution(s) of science—of the reliability and usefulness of their knowledge claims. Scientists belong to the same larger society that we all do, with multiple identities and allegiances (gendered, raced, religious, political) that find their way into fact-making. Finally, we ask the question: how does scientific knowledge exert its power effects not just in "ideas" but in everyday socio-material[1] **representations** (such as language and classifications) and in objects (such as technologies and built environments)?

Finding the Social in Science

It is useful to begin a consideration of the humanness of scientists with a brief account of the history of science. It is generally considered that **science** as we now understand it (a method for acquiring knowledge about nature's regularities, certified by a community of experts) began during the **Scientific Revolution**, stretching from the mid-16th century to the end of the 17th century, in Europe. Observations and theories that we now consider "scientific"—about planetary motion and the workings of the human body, for example—long predated this period and come, most notably, from Ancient Greece and later the Islamic world (though we can't fully recover what has been known and lost to official record in the course of human history, a theme addressed in Chapter 2). During the Scientific Revolution, however, the scientific method was self-consciously consolidated by early practitioners and promoted as a way of obtaining certain knowledge about nature.

Observation is critical to the scientific method. The earliest proponents of this method urged their fellow investigators to build careful accounts of phenomena in nature by collecting observations yielded by their own senses. These senses alone were to be trusted, rather than appeals to superstition or religion. This prominence accorded to human observation in the foundations and practice of science implies an important assumption: Because the laws of science are meant to be universal, any two human perceivers ought to make the same observations, given the same sensory stimulus. Does this assumption hold up? Well, what do you see in Figure 10.1?

Do you see stairs? Are they on the ground going up to the left, or on the ceiling? Can you switch back and forth between these? A.F. Chalmers (1999) uses this simple optical illusion to show that even when exactly the same visual content hits our retina at the same time as someone else's, we may make sense of it differently. The content of these

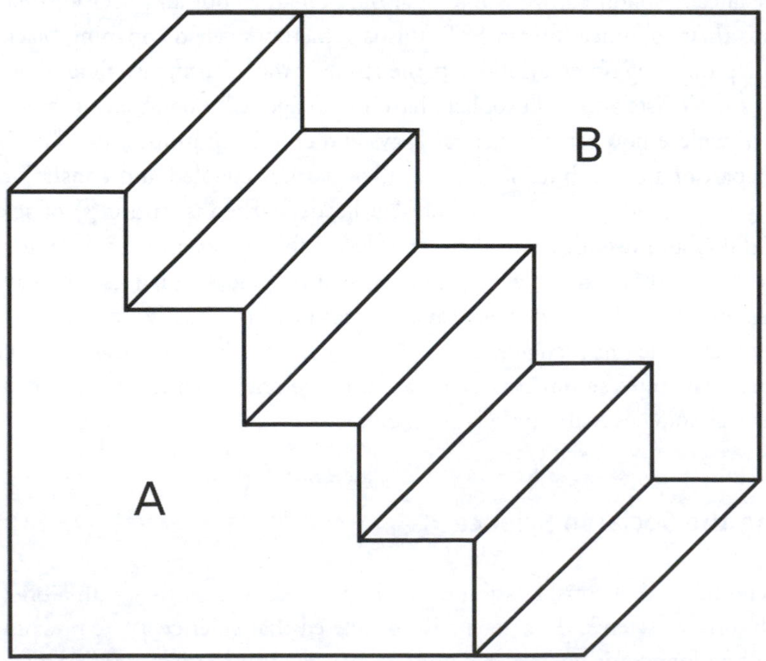

FIGURE 10.1 "Schroeder Stairs," an illustration of interpretive flexibility.

differences is dependent on our own prior experiences, **culture**, and language. If you see stairs in this figure, it is likely because you belong to a culture in which it is common to render 3D objects on 2D flat space. This is not inevitable, and was in fact an innovation that came about at a particular time in the history of art (Edgerton, 2009). When Figure 10.1 is shown to members of a community whose **representational practices** do not include rendering 3D objects in 2D space, let alone staircases, they do not see a staircase at all (Chalmers, 1999). They simply see a geometric design.

The concept that different people see different things despite the same visual information is called **interpretive flexibility**. An example from the history of anatomy illustrates this well. Until the early 18th century, it was uncommon to see a female skeleton in an anatomical atlas; the male form represented the generic human, and women were thought to be less perfect specimens (Schiebinger, 1986). Anatomist Marie Thiroux D'Arconville (a rare woman practising the art) produced one of the first paired illustrations. Compared both to the male skeleton and to present-day measurements of female skeletons, D'Arconville's female skeleton had an unusually small skull and rib cage, yet an unusually large pelvis. Presumably D'Arconville drew what she saw; what she saw depended on prevailing cultural expectations about womanhood that included emphasis on reproduction over intellect (Schiebinger, 1986). When scientists use pre-existing convictions and intuitions about what the world ought to be like to make sense of data, this is called **theory-laden observation**. Theory precedes the observation, and it is embedded in the seeing. "People, not their eyes, see" (Hanson, 1958, p. 6).

Often the expectations that viewers bring to their observations come from existing paradigms in their research domain. When Isaac Newton said, "If I have seen a little further it is by standing on the shoulders of Giants," he was acknowledging that science is a deeply cumulative and social endeavour; no one can start from scratch and trust only his or her own senses, or science would get stuck in rudimentary and repetitive insights. However, this means that at any given time in any given specialty, certain **norms**, expectations, and theories prevail. These norms (be they cultural, like male superiority or **racism**, or more commonly understood as "scientific," like **genetic determinism**) shape what humans are able to see and know.

In this section we have seen that differing experiences and interpretations of sensory observations can co-exist legitimately. These differences open up spaces of ambiguity and uncertainty in science and its applications. How these are resolved has a relationship to power, a theme that will be elaborated upon below.

You Can't Make a Fact Alone in Your Basement

When sociologists and anthropologists started looking closely at scientific practices, they found something surprising: except in the movies, loner geniuses rarely exist. Scientists are fundamentally members of institutions and communities whose work is deeply collaborative. Laboratories and field sites are intensely social places. University scientists are far more likely to work in close-knit groups with an almost familial hierarchy (lab director, post-docs, graduate students, and undergraduates) than are scholars in the social sciences or humanities. The webs of interaction—in which training, labour, ideas, and friendship flow freely—are represented by the fact that most scientific publications have multiple authors. Moreover, many other workers are involved in scientific labour who don't get official credit as authors, or even as scientists. These include family members and "invisible technicians" (Shapin, 1989).

Hence, we see a great deal of collaboration in science, in which workers are in a shared physical space, negotiating what questions to ask, interpretations of evidence, and how to write up experiments. Beyond face-to-face collaboration, scientific knowledge must be certified by a wider community of colleagues. In more simple terms, you cannot make a fact or a discovery alone in your basement. No matter how convinced you are of your own ground-breaking discovery, without community approval the fact will not exist as knowledge in the world. Hence, a great deal of scientists' time is spent communicating—in writing, at conferences, and through teaching—in order to persuade their peers of the correctness and significance of their claims.

Bruno Latour and Steve Woolgar call all this writing **inscriptions** (1986). They observe that scientists spend much of their time producing inscriptions. Scientists move inscriptions from preliminary forms (scribbles in a laboratory notebook, counts, readouts from a machine) to text that is tentative and, combined with many texts that have come before (reference manuals, calculations, others' published articles), to more certain statements of fact that are polished and ready to submit for publication along with one or two cherry-picked illustrations. As statements move from tentative to certain, transformations in language occur. "It is possible that the substance we found is X" becomes "X was found." The most successful fact statement loses any marks of the scientist(s) who first championed it: eventually something becomes so taken for granted that a citation to the source of the claim drops out of the picture.

There is an irony at the heart of this. More than any other genre of writing, scientific writing removes the observer/persuader from view. By relying on the **passive voice** ("the experiment was done ...," "results were observed ..."), the impression is created that the humans who made the observations are irrelevant. It seems that anyone would have come up with the same ideas, experiments, and observations; they were just there in nature waiting to be decoded. Donna Haraway calls this "the view from nowhere" since objectivity denies an embodied knower (1991; see Chapter 2). Historians Steven Shapin and Simon Schaffer (1985) trace the history of this "modest" and "naked" way of writing to Robert Boyle, a prominent early experimental philosopher in the 17th century. As Boyle explains in a letter to his nephew, the deliberate erasure of the writer from the text is meant to be a persuasive rhetorical style—Shapin and Schaffer call it a **literary technology**—that makes the writer seem more trustworthy and the evidence more objective. In other words, when it comes to communicating science, the less you seem to be trying to be persuasive, the more persuasive you are.

Facts acquire greater power as they are moved along the chain from tentative observations to conjectures to facticity; whether they successfully make this translation depends on social and institutional processes that function both as quality control and as gatekeeping. Peer review is a mainstay of scientific institutions. It is the process by which ideas, conference submissions, funding applications, and publications are considered by already successful scientists in the relevant specialty before they are accepted or published. In order to be in a position to be reviewers, these peers will have passed through the training and accreditation required to become experts. Alongside building expertise and skills in a specialized field, this training has the shadow function of producing and rewarding like-minded scholars. Data on the demographics of practicing scientists show us that the vast majority of scientists (especially in senior positions) are English-speaking white men (Guterl, 2014). People with similar social locations will also have some overlap of experiences, interests, and backgrounds. Camaraderie and mentorship is also important to flourishing as a scientist, and women and students of colour (particularly women of colour) often lack this informal but requisite support (Sands, 1986). Recent efforts by universities and other organizations aim to diversify scientific training, advancement, and representation, but the loneliness of marginalized groups in scientific life, and the discrimination they face, causes many who begin in science careers to leave them (Blickenstaff, 2006; Sands, 1986).

As a fact-in-the-making moves toward bona fide knowledge, it might be believed, but it might also be contested or ignored. Recognized researchers from elite scientific institutions and universities have a greater likelihood of ushering a fact to widespread belief than those with lesser university accreditation (for example, degrees outside the UK and US, those without university accreditation, activists, farmers, patients, etc.). Although there are exceptions, this is so even when the relevant group of lay people have a great deal of lived expertise about the topic at hand (Wynne, 1992). Thus, while scientific knowledge purports to operate equally everywhere, free from politics, it usually emanates from the elite and well-funded **centre**. Despite this stratification of knowledge-makers, the illusion of universality and disinterestedness can shield science from critique and scrutiny.

Exclusion of certain members of society because of their identity or group membership unfairly curtails people's possibilities for success in meaningful and lucrative professions. However, there is another cost that spreads beyond individuals. This cost is **epistemological**—it has to do with the content of scientific knowledge. Recall the discussion in Chapter 2 of **situated knowledge** and **partial perspective**. Knowledge always comes from somewhere, with questions and answers contingent on prior experience, expectations, interests, and goals. The greater homogeneity there is among scientists (and their funding sources), the narrower the view. The flipside of this argument is that diversity makes science better by expanding the questions, methods, passions, and perspectives that get built into extant knowledge.

Material Forms of Knowledge

Thus far this chapter's focus has been on who scientists are and how they go about their jobs. In this section, we will look at the product of their work: knowledge. What do we mean, specifically, when we talk about scientific knowledge? We often think of knowledge as something that resides in people's brains: I know the alphabet; I know the formula to calculate the circumference of a circle. But in order to do anything with our knowledge, we must give it material form: to articulate it outside of our brains and bodies in the form of language, symbols (such as numbers), and images (such as graphs). Power/knowledge can also become material through tools for administering people and populations, such as genetic tests, disease classifications, and numerical standards. These tools are vital to Foucauldian **governmentality** (see Chapter 1) whereby institutions (including, but not limited to, governments) produce certain kinds of citizens amenable to control. Finally, power becomes hardened through science into things (such as technologies), which continue to act upon us, even when their human creators are long separated from them. For example, Richard Dyer makes the case that photographic media and movie lighting were constructed in a way that privileges **whiteness**: "It may be—certainly was—true that photo and film apparatuses have seemed to work better with light-skinned peoples, but that is because they were made that way, not because they could be no other way" (Dyer in Johnson & Wetmore, 2009, p. 259). Each of these types of material power—language, images, and things—are fundamental to scientific practice and are its effects. Because of their physicality, they are sturdier than beliefs and more difficult to change. We will examine each category in turn with examples from technoscience.

Language

While scientific language may seem dry and technical, it is remarkably rich in metaphors and figurative expressions. How would you describe **DNA** (deoxyribonucleic acid)? Chances are, even with a rudimentary education in biology, you can come up with some descriptions like "the blueprint for building a body" or "a hereditary code." Both "blueprint" and "code" are metaphors that evoke a whole set of associations from everyday objects to better understand abstract concepts. Some of these descriptions are especially prevalent when scientists talk to non-scientists or to students, but many are deeply embedded in the technical language of science itself. Scientists draw on the analogy between DNA and information when they write about genetic code, messages, transcription, and copying. This particular set of representations has worked very well to bring molecular biology to the forefront of the sciences in the late 20th century, and much use has come from them. However, it is because of a historical collision in the late 1950s and 1960s of early molecular biology and a thriving interdisciplinary field of study called ***cybernetics*** (the study of regulatory systems) that information theory found its way into biology and has stayed there (Kay, 2000). Had different people been involved, with different influences, DNA might have been described and understood through very different metaphors, which might have led to different uses and theories. In other words, the overlap of molecular biology and cybernetics was historically **contingent**; it could have been otherwise.

A very well-known example of the contingent and culture-bound nature of scientific language is the tale of fertilization. Emily Martin, an anthropologist of science, observed that when biological textbooks described the activity of the egg and the sperm leading up to, and at the moment of, fertilization, their language drew heavily on "fairy-tale" **stereotypes** of gendered behaviour (1991). For example, Martin (1991) found the phrases in quotations below in scientific textbooks and journal articles:

> It is remarkable how "femininely" the egg behaves and how "masculinely" the sperm. The egg is seen as large and passive. It does not move or journey, but passively "is transported," "is swept," or even "drifts" along the fallopian tube. In utter contrast, sperm are small, "streamlined," and invariably active. They "deliver" their genes to the egg, "activate the developmental program of the egg," and have a "velocity" that is often remarked upon. Their tails are "strong" and efficiently powered. Together with the forces of ejaculation, they can "propel the semen into the deepest recesses of the vagina." For this they need "energy," "fuel," so that with a "whiplashlike motion and strong lurches" they can "burrow through the egg coat" and "penetrate" it. (p. 489)

The sperm are also depicted as being on a "quest," a "perilous journey," at the end of which the victor might expect to find a damsel in distress. While this imagery seems to make sense at first, because we are so accustomed to it, it is telling to step back from our expectations and remember that neither sperm nor eggs have a **gender**. We ought not to expect them to behave as "masculine" or "feminine," not only because they are non-cognizant cells, but also because the kinds of behaviours deemed masculine or feminine are socially constructed and have changed radically over time, while presumably the mechanics of fertilization haven't. In spite of Martin's well-known critique, these tropes are still widely available (see Figure 10.2).

Martin argues that the contingency of this particular way of describing and seeing fertilization is becoming apparent as some alternative investigators describe a very different sort of encounter. According to these scientists, the egg is very active. It uses a biochemical lasso to "capture" the sperm it chooses. Arguably, the representation of this aggressive egg plays on a different set of gendered **tropes** (the femme fatale), but the

FIGURE 10.2 Romance between egg and sperm, a common motif. Akiradesigns/Shutterstock.

point is that evidence may be available for a variety of different cultural expectations. Because we are never outside of culture, it may be impossible to sort out what the egg and sperm are "really" up to. Instead, we do the best we can, recognizing that all knowledge is provisional and every choice to say something about nature is simultaneously a choice not to say something else. Metaphors are inescapable, because communication of observations and ideas requires human language. It may not even be desirable to escape metaphors altogether, for they can generate novel research directions. However, the specifics of language do matter, because descriptions of what is "natural," rendered in the authoritative voice of science, structure uneven and hierarchical patterns of human relationships. Gender is not only imposed from culture onto descriptions of fertilization; in a circular manner, these descriptions then naturalize an assumed gender hierarchy.

A more recent representation from a scientific publication relies instead on well-established conventions for depicting protein folding at a molecular level (see Figure 10.3). At the outermost junction of sperm and egg, one molecular structure makes contact with another. This illustration shows that the asymmetrical relation (sperm penetrates egg) is not an inevitable takeaway from the observables.

FIGURE 10.3 Biochemical recognition between egg and sperm protein folds. Adapted from Isha Raj, et al. (2017), "Structural Basis of Egg Coat-Sperm Recognition at Fertilization," *Cell 169*(7), 1315–26. Reproduced by permission of Luca Jovine.

Images and Inscriptions

Images are extremely persuasive tools for convincing people of your viewpoint. As such, they are important places to look in trying to understand how some people gain power over others, and how some facts become established as knowledge and some fall away from view. Maps are a good example of how important drawings are to the success of technoscience. Bruno Latour (1990) asks us to imagine an early explorer who stops on land in the Pacific and wants to bring a map back to Paris. He encounters a Chinese inhabitant of the island, who knows the geography of the land well. The Chinese man picks up a stick and draws a very good map of his island, to scale and with important identifying details, in the sand. Seeing that the tide is rising, the explorer quickly makes a copy of the map with pencil in his notebook. This simple difference—an object of communication with a brief existence (the map in the sand) vs. something solid, mobile, and reproducible (the map on paper)—makes all the difference to the subsequent relations of colonization on this island. Latour (1990), who tells this story, writes:

> Commercial interests, capitalist spirit, **imperialism**, thirst for knowledge, are empty terms as long as one does not take into account Mercator's projection,

> marine clocks and their makers, copper engraving of maps, rutters, the keeping of "log books," and the many printed editions of [previous voyage] that [the explorer] carries with him. (p. 25)

These inscriptions aren't simply powerful on their own, but they acquire power in particular contexts where they are used to "muster, align, and win over new and unexpected allies ... they bear on certain controversies and force dissenters into believing new facts and behaving in new ways" (Latour, 1990, p. 25). Let us return to the depiction of the protein structure of egg and sperm above. While I chose to republish it in black and white, with a particular caption and for a particular purpose, in the original the artist-scientist has artificially coloured the egg protein structure pink and the sperm blue. The article refers to the mechanics of "sperm penetration through the egg coat." Science shows us what to see, not (always) through a purposeful filtering, but because knowledge is inescapably situated.

Classifications such as diagnoses are special kinds of inscription in science that figure prominently in how we understand natural-social worlds. Classification is a means by which to carve up the world into non-overlapping categories, to bring order to what might otherwise seem like unmanageable chaos (Bowker & Star, 1999). Examples of prominent classification tools in science and medicine are phylogenetic trees (depictions showing species and evolutionary origins), the periodic table in chemistry, and disease classification systems such as the DSM (*Diagnostic and Statistical Manual of Mental Disorders*), which will be discussed in Chapter 11. Rather than being simply found in nature, classification systems represent collective human decision-making through processes of negotiation and codification. They have histories and often change over time. Despite lacking inevitability, classifications have "material force" (Bowker & Star, 1999). Whether they begin arbitrarily or purposely, whether they have political underpinnings or are politically benign in their origins, they act in and on the world and the people and things in it. Classifications form identities and physical space (think of everyday spaces such as **sex**-specific bathrooms, for example). Their power-laden consequences, intentional or not, are long-lasting and difficult to change.

Things

A final modality through which power becomes material goes by a number of words in sociological theory: technology, artifacts, objects, things. This is the "hardware" portion of technoscience, and it has been integral to scientific work since its inception. Instruments were, in the foundations of the scientific method, seen to both extend and to correct the human senses, and to accomplish things beyond the limits of our senses. Early examples are the air pump and the telescope, while today we hear more about superconducting supercolliders or DNA-sequencing machines.

Instruments simulate conditions of the unwieldy natural world in the laboratory under circumstances carefully controlled by humans. Outside of the lab, phenomena are often too large (an ecosystem), too small (bacteria), too far away (the planets), too dangerous (an atomic reaction), or just too complex (depression) for easy observation. When specific areas of research are studied closely, one finds many disputes about whether the laboratory test or "field site" is close enough to the "real world" to count as viable or useful knowledge. For example, a particular industrial pollutant is tested in isolation in the laboratory and declared to be safe. In the real world, however, one only ever finds this pollutant in combination with others in industrial parks (often in low-income and **racialized** neighbourhoods) where the cumulative toxicity is hazardous, but the producer of the single pollutant cannot be held accountable. **Reductionism** is the name often given to this problem inherent in scientific and technical knowledge, where the messy world (in which nature is never separated from culture "out there") is studied in tiny, isolated, manageable parts. Sometimes it can make science very effective, but sometimes reductionist approaches can be inadequate and even dangerous.

It is an important insight that technologies are fundamental to almost all kinds of science, because when we mistakenly assume that science is just about ideas or statements of facts, we forget the tremendous human and machine labour that goes into stabilizing those facts and making them believable to relevant communities. Instead, the instruments, like the people, disappear from view and the fact stands alone. We place enormous trust in these instruments and in their lack of bias. Historians of science Lorraine Daston and Peter Galison (1992) call this **mechanical objectivity** and locate it historically:

> "Let nature speak for itself" became the watchword of a new brand of scientific objectivity that emerged in the latter half of the nineteenth century. At issue was not only accuracy but morality as well: the all-too-human scientists must, as a matter of duty, restrain themselves from imposing their hopes, expectations, generalizations, aesthetics, even ordinary language on the image of nature. Where human self discipline flagged, the machine would take over. (p. 81)

While mechanization has assumed the burden of removing human bias, it does not guarantee objectivity. Instruments are crafted by humans, and particular theories are built into their possibilities. Moreover, their output (a photograph from a camera, for example) is always a selection from among alternatives and requires human interpretation.

One way objects can become social actors is by embodying the discriminatory assumptions of their designers. While this is sometimes a deliberate strategy to maintain certain alignments of power, it is often a result of the blindness associated with being in the centre and not seeing how technologies and knowledge affect those on the margins. In his article "Do Artifacts Have Politics?," Langdon Winner describes a classic case of the deliberate kind. Robert Moses was a city bureaucrat and public works giant in New

York in the mid-20th century. Moses built overpasses and highways with specifications that would discourage or prevent buses from using them.

> [T]he reasons reflect Moses' social **class** bias and racial prejudice. Automobile-owning whites of "upper" and "comfortable middle" classes, as he called them, would be free to use the parkways for recreation and commuting. Poor people and blacks, who normally use public transit, were kept off the roads because the twelve-foot-tall buses could not handle the overpasses. (Winner in Johnson & Wetmore, 2009, p. 212)

One purposeful outcome of this plan was to limit access of minorities and low-income groups to Moses's great outdoor park on the ocean, Jones Beach.

Winner's story is a parable about technological discrimination, of which there are unfortunately many examples. One of the main lessons of these stories has to do with the longevity of hardware: socio-technical apparatuses keep producing their effects long after they have become divorced from the humans and institutions who made them. Moreover, in a short time, responsibility becomes hard to locate. The discrimination is delegated to objects and machines, and humans are let off the hook. While Moses is long since deceased, "many of his monumental structures of concrete and steel embody a systematic **social inequality**, a way of engineering relationships among people that, after a time, became just another part of the landscape" (Winner in Johnson & Wetmore, 2009, p. 212). Relations of power are also implicated in what isn't in the world—such as the male contraceptive pill (Oudshoorn, 2003)—and what facts or knowledge don't exist. Every experiment not done or design path not taken is also a result of social, economic, and political pressures (in addition to feasibility) that act in conjunction with "nature" to constrain what we know of the world, and what exists in it.

Conclusion

This chapter complicated the ideal of science as a sacred space outside of time and culture that simply holds up a mirror to allow nature to speak for itself. Instead we have seen that the very perceptual activities at the heart of the methods used in science are subject to individual and cultural contingency. Second, we have looked at how science is a social institution much like the other institutions that have long undergone sociological scrutiny. As in other social milieus, we find elitist gatekeeping mechanisms, rhetorical and political strategies for persuading colleagues, economic considerations, and informal exclusion of certain gendered, raced, or classed bodies from full participation. Finally, we explored the **materiality** of scientific knowledge. Paying attention to language, images, charts, and objects complicates the notion that science is composed of ideas and theories and happens in geniuses' brains. It also allows us to see how products of science exert regulatory power in the social world.

Because this chapter has aimed to problematize received notions of scientific facticity, my examples are weighted toward rather flagrant uses and abuses of science and technology in the interests of upholding or justifying privilege. Many examples we could have explored are much more subtle, and many may be free of the markers that we often think of as "social context," such as gender, **race**, class, and global location. However, all the products of technoscience are social accomplishments to some degree, and the methods that have evolved in the past 300 years—as much literary and representational as experimental—work to obscure the contingent origins of facts and things, and in the process fortify the cultural privilege of the scientific worldview.

What do we gain by opening up the "black boxes" of facts and technologies? Sometimes a more shaky and uncertain worldview that isn't entirely reassuring. In the end, we have to live inside the existing world that, at the moment, is deeply scientific and technological. No matter how critical we are, most of us live with medical diagnoses, we get on airplanes, we use email, we believe in global warming, and we trust that our tap water is safe (except in places where, because of social and political neglect, it isn't). We want better science to make personal and societal decisions in the face of uncertainty and of patently false claims. Science is often a useful resource for social movements aiming to challenge inequalities, as it has been in demystifying harmful ideas about biological race (see Chapter 6). But science is one social resource among many, a skillful and effective craft. The insights of this chapter suggest that we can live better in critical relation to technoscience if we draw on the kinds of tools outlined in Chapter 2 to replace the view that facts are inviolable and instead ask where they come from.

Study Questions

1. Explain, in your own words, what Donna Haraway means when she calls science "the view from nowhere."
2. Think of a classification system you encounter in your own life (for example, computer files, university departments). Are the categories fixed or arbitrary? How did they get to be the way they are? What are the effects of the ways in which they are organized?
3. Using the story about Robert Moses's bridges as an example, come up with another case in which discriminatory politics become built into technologies.

Exercises

1. Watch the film *A Theory of Everything* (2014). How is this portrayal of Stephen Hawking consistent with the stereotypical scientific persona described in this

chapter? What aspects of the story challenge the idea that scientists work in social isolation?

2 Find a newspaper or journal article that reports on a new scientific finding. Examine the "literary technology" adopted in this article: Is it written in the first person or the third? Are there any graphs or images, and what are these meant to do? Can you locate any incidences of reductionism?

Note

1 The phrase "socio-material" draws attention to the fact that these entities are symbolic parts of cultural communication (socio-) and *at the same time* they have substance (material).

References

Blickenstaff, J.C. (2006). Women and science careers: Leaky pipeline or gender filter? *Gender and Education, 17*(4), 369–386.

Bowker, G., & Star, S.L. (1999). *Sorting things out: Classification and its consequences*. Cambridge, MA: MIT Press.

Chalmers, A.F. (1999). *What is this thing called science?* Indianapolis, IN: Hackett.

Daston, L., & Galison, P. (1992). The image of objectivity. *Representations, 40*, 81–128.

Edgerton, S.Y. (2009). *The mirror, the window, and the telescope: How renaissance linear perspective changed our vision of the universe*. Ithaca, NY: Cornell University Press.

Foucault, M., & Gordon, C. (1980). *Power/knowledge: Selected interviews and other writings, 1972–1977*. New York, NY: Pantheon Books.

Guterl, F. (2014). Diversity in science: Where are the data? *Scientific American*. Retrieved from https://www.scientificamerican.com/article/diversity-in-science-where-are-the-data/

Hanson, N.R. (1958). *Patterns of discovery: An inquiry into the conceptual foundations of science*. Cambridge, UK: Cambridge University Press.

Haraway, D.J. (1991). *Simians, cyborgs, and women: The reinvention of nature*. New York, NY: Routledge.

Johnson, D.G., & Wetmore, J.M. (2009). *Technology and society: Building our sociotechnical future*. Cambridge, MA: MIT Press.

Kay, L.E. (2000). Who wrote the book of life? A history of the genetic code. *Writing Science*. Stanford, CA: Stanford University Press.

Latour, B. (1990). Drawing things together. In M. Lynch & S. Woolgar (Eds.), *Representation in scientific practice* (pp. 19–68). Cambridge, MA: MIT Press.

Latour, B. (2004). Why has critique run out of steam? From matters of fact to matters of concern. *Critical Inquiry, 30*(2), 225–248.

Latour, B., & Woolgar, S. (1986). *Laboratory life: The construction of scientific facts*. Princeton, NJ: Princeton University Press.

Martin, E. (1991). The egg and the sperm: How science has constructed a romance based on stereotypical male-female roles. *Signs, 16*(3), 485–501.

Oudshoorn, N. (2003). *The male pill: A biography of a technology in the making*. Durham, NC: Duke University Press.

Sands, A. (1986). Never meant to survive: A Black woman's journey. An interview with Evelyn Hammonds. *Radical Teacher, 30*, 8–15.

Schiebinger, L. (1986). Skeletons-in-the-closet: The first illustrations of the female skeleton in 18th-century anatomy. *Representations, 14*, 42–82.

Shapin, S. (1989). The invisible technician. *American Scientist, 77*(6), 554–563.

Shapin, S., & Schaffer, S. (1985). *Leviathan and the air-pump: Hobbes, Boyle, and the experimental life*. Princeton, NJ: Princeton University Press.

Wynne, B. (1992). Misunderstood misunderstanding: Social identities and public uptake of science. *Public Understanding of Science, 1*, 281–304.

11 Are You "Normal"?

HEIDI RIMKE and DEBORAH BROCK

Jasmine is swiping through the latest postings on her social media accounts when an ad grabs her attention. It is a mental health and wellness questionnaire aimed at postsecondary students. She has been hearing a lot lately about mental health concerns faced by students her age, so she pauses to read it. The questionnaire asks if the reader has been experiencing any one of a long list of concerns. It asks:

> Do you have trouble getting out of bed in the morning? Have your sleep patterns changed unexpectedly? Have you experienced changes in your appetite for food or for activities that you enjoy? Have others expressed concern about your mental or emotional state? Do you wonder if your sexual desires are normal? Do you experience feelings of helplessness, meaninglessness, worthlessness, or powerlessness? Are you worried about having an addiction to something, such as television, video or computer games, the internet, social media, sex, food, alcohol, shopping, a relationship, texting, pornography, sports, or anything else?

Jasmine is feeling okay about herself, because she has been putting a lot of effort into improving her attitude and thinking positively, despite the disappointment of not being admitted into her first choice of program at university. Still, she is unsettled by the questions. One morning she accidentally left her phone at home, and she felt lost and on the verge of panic all day.

You have probably encountered questionnaires with questions similar to these while reading a magazine or browsing the Internet. Perhaps a medical or psychological association, pharmaceutical company, or government agency has posted them. The questions are meant to act as a set of identifiable warning signs for the reader's self-reflection. These might then create a crisis in the reader's sense of "normalcy," suggesting to the reader that they may be suffering from a treatable mental or emotional disorder requiring professional help. However, far from referring to exceptional conditions, such lists include common feelings and practices, some of which all of us may experience at some points in our lives. Indeed, as this chapter will discuss, virtually every form of human behaviour has been classified within the normal/abnormal spectrum—and there appears to be no end in sight to the growing index of human dysfunctions, disorders, and diseases that might limit us in some way. At the same time, the list of potential self-improvement projects seems to keep growing: to be fitter, eat healthier foods, be better educated, improve our job prospects, be financially successful, increase confidence, become well-informed and socially skilled, live clutter-free lives, travel more, do yoga, be mindful, and, most of all, be happier.

Whether you choose to see a therapist or take up any of a myriad of self-improvement projects, you are engaged in what Foucault named **techniques of the self**, something that we will return to shortly. But have people not always wanted to feel good, impress others, and succeed in whatever tasks they take on? Presumably, yes. But the idea of the self that we know now has a history. In particular, the self has changed markedly since the rise of **psy discourses**, a term for the interlocking web of psychiatric and psychological ideas that have gained ground throughout the 20th century. North American selves are hyper-individualized, relentlessly self-reflexive, and engaged in constant improvement. The idea that the self is shaped foremost from within the person (psyche, willpower, etc.) rather than from without (communities, cultures, etc.) has created a being that is unique to our time.

As modern Western subjects, we have at our disposal an immense medicalized vocabulary for speaking about our inner selves. Modern individuals reflect internally and with others about their thoughts, memories, beliefs, emotions, and the like through psy discourses. Convinced that we should understand our selves in psychological terms of adjustment, empowerment, fulfillment, good relationships, personal growth, the attainment of happiness and so forth, we actively seek the wisdom of experts and cling to their promises to assist us in the quest for self-change that we "freely" undertake (Rose, 1999). The popularity of psy discourses reflects a deeply held belief that psychology in one way or another can provide the answers that will make us happy, and that at the root of our difficulties are psy problems that can be treated with professional therapy (most recently, the techniques of **positive psychology**, self-help, and/or prescription drug use). Our goal in this chapter is to disrupt the narrative that this striving for an optimal self is a natural or inevitable way to be in the world.

This chapter explores how modern subjects and **subjectivities** have been shaped through the cultural authority of the **psy complex**—which itself is derived from the reigning **culture** of **science**, as you have just explored in Chapter 10. As psy expertise increasingly distinguished itself from the wider category of medicine in the late 19th century, it simultaneously generated a knowledge base about what it meant to be a normal individual through the study of the abnormal individual. We apply Foucault's conceptual and historical approach to understand the social production and effects of psy knowledge. Using brief examples, we show how social factors such as **gender**, **racialization**, **class** relations, and sexual orientation were used in the construction and **classification** of individual **pathology** by psy institutions and discourses. These will be linked to what Heidi Rimke (2000, 2010, 2016, 2018) refers to as **psychocentrism**: the dominant cultural belief that a plethora of human problems—the troubles with which we as people struggle—are due to intrinsic pathologies of the individual mind and/or body. For example, a dominant **discourse** about addictions such as alcoholism is that some people have an "addictive personality," an argument that lets the addictive nature of alcohol, its marketing, and its cultural pervasiveness off the hook by focusing the problem on the individual consumer. Some groups, such as **Indigenous** peoples, are regarded as particularly vulnerable to addiction. Genetic and psychological factors are held responsible, although evidence suggests that Indigenous peoples are no more likely to use drugs and alcohol than other groups living in similar economic conditions (CBC News, 2014). Moreover, a self-report study by Statistics Canada (2012) indicates that Indigenous youth (ages 12–24) are more likely to be non-drinkers than their non-Indigenous peers.

We continue our task of interrogating the **centre** by revealing some of the **power-knowledge** relations that permeate our everyday, taken-for-granted world. We want you to think about how particular knowledges acquire the status of truth, and how people or subjects are "made up" (Hacking, 1986) or **constituted** through **expert knowledge** claims that purport to rely upon scientific rationality to understand, explain, and control human conduct. These experts include the psy disciplines (psychiatrists, psychologists, psychotherapists, etc.), physicians and other medical workers, public health and social workers. Moreover, psy research findings and explanations, often oversimplified, become intertwined with mainstream media representations and popular discourses about mental health.[1] Subjects thus come to see themselves through this interpretive framework, and understand themselves as particular kinds of people. This applies as much to those who regard themselves as normal as it does to those who acquire a diagnosis of illness.

Of course, the issues, discourses, and debates surrounding mental distress, mental illness, or psychological problems are complex. Many therapeutic practices have been enormously beneficial to a great number of people, at least some of the time. Mental processes have biological or physical components, but these are, in most cases, impossible to tease apart from the social meanings we attribute to those deemed "not normal." The analysis here is not meant to downplay human suffering but to enrich our ways of understanding its causes and solutions while casting a critical gaze on the extent to which the production and governance of our innermost thoughts and feelings encroaches on everyday life. In order to understand and think critically about the social and historical development of the psy complex, we will turn our attention to the discourses, institutions, and practices that have made psy knowledge among the dominant forms of knowledge of our time, and also consider their effects. In what follows we draw attention to the specificities of a psychocentric culture and make visible a way of thinking and being we often take for granted.

Normal and Abnormal Have a History

Critical scholarship on the psy complex has benefited from Michel Foucault's books on the history of madness (*Madness and Civilization*, 1961/1988) and on the emergence of medical treatment regimes (*The Birth of the Clinic*, 1963/1994), as well as the **governmentality** approach's insight that **normalization** is a key feature of contemporary social **regulation**. As you learned in Chapter 1, distinguishing between the normal and the abnormal is an expression of **normalizing power** (Foucault, 1979). By encouraging certain ways of life over others, discourses of normalization offer implicit conceptions of who and what constitutes a good self or normal person. They serve as **dividing practices** in that they create distinctions between people, groups, belief systems, and actions in a manner that is value-laden, hierarchical, and unequal.

The hypothetical questionnaire at the beginning of this chapter is a starting point for not only diagnosing people, but for classifying them according to "signs" or "symptoms." The psy disciplines, like other human sciences, have developed an ever-expanding **system of classification**, making distinctions between and among people. This process is not neutral. As Turner and Edgley (1983) have demonstrated, the very core of psychiatric categories and diagnosis can work to **pathologize** people based upon subjective social and moral values. They argue that it is not possible to identify, medically or chemically, "imbalances" that result in behaviours that are socially defined as acceptable or unacceptable. The seemingly "neutral" language of psychiatry masks value judgements about good and bad or right and wrong. In the previous chapter, you read that no scientific test can determine morals and morality; such determinations are always already cultural. In other words, these are social decisions.

The DSM

The ever-expanding *Diagnostic and Statistical Manual of Mental Disorders* (DSM) provides the best example of how systems of psy classification have proliferated such that most social behaviours of concern can now potentially fall within its scope. The DSM was first published in 1952 by the American Psychiatric Association (APA), and intended to provide a comprehensive account of mental illness in American society. The DSM-I was 130 pages long, listing 106 disorders. By its fourth edition, published in 1994, the DSM-IV was 886 pages long and listed 297 disorders, thus nearly triple the volume. Today it acts as the "psychiatric bible" by defining the criteria for an ever-increasing number of mental illnesses and disorders (Kutchins & Kirk, 1998). The latest edition, the DSM-V (2013), raises further concern because it significantly expands classifications of abnormality to include, for example, grief, temper tantrums, and behavioural concerns such as overeating (Frances, 2012). In 1978, the professor of psychiatry and well-known author Thomas Szasz noted that our culture has witnessed "the transformation of ordinary behaviours of ordinary persons into the extraordinary awe-inspiring symptoms of mental diseases" (Szasz, 1978, p. 194), an argument that has been well supported in the intervening years.

It should be clear by now that our purpose is to question the assumptions and certainties about our cultural attitudes, beliefs, desires, and practices concerning the normal and the pathological, and instead ask how these have been incited, produced, and maintained or resisted. Foucault referred to this historical approach as the **history of the present**. Rather than understanding historical developments as inevitable or determined by universal laws, we consider history as **contingent**, because for any event other directions and outcomes were also possible. For example, while it may be commonly assumed that the development of psychiatry and institutions to house the insane were practical, humane, unavoidable, or even evolutionary, Foucault provides us with a detailed way of investigating how they came into being, through a complicated array of discourses and practices that foreclosed alternative understandings and possibilities. Using his **genealogical method**, Foucault provided counter-histories written against the taken-for-granted or dominant histories. This method begins with the present to ask how it has come to be constituted as it is. The aim is to challenge the "naturalness" of dominant ways of thinking by studying the historical relationship between forms of knowledge and the exercise of power.

As you read in previous chapters, Foucault explored power-knowledge relations emerging from the **Enlightenment** onwards that were to have a profound effect on how people were understood. Before the human sciences began to develop in the 19th century, ideas about human nature and human conduct were predominantly derived from a religious framework determined by Church authorities. Humans were understood in religious terms of evil or virtue, rather than medically and scientifically. Behaviours we would now associate with mental illness were understood to have divine origins. With the Enlightenment, scientific theories began to claim that human nature was the result of biological, physiological, and/or psychological factors. By the end of the 18th century, Western theories shifted toward scientific rather than theological explanations. Positivists insisted that through systematic observation, human behaviour could be explained in the same **objective** manner as the physical sciences explained the natural world. They "discovered" that insanity or mental illness, therefore, was not the result of demonic possession or a punishment from God, but rather a disease that required medical attention and treatment. This new discovery became the catalyst for the formation of the medical model of **deviance**. The scientific search for endogenous (internal) causes rooted in the person thus became a hallmark of **modernity**.

By the end of the 19th century, modern society rested upon the new Enlightenment ideals of science, reason, and progress. Human differences were increasingly viewed as scientific problems that could be studied, known, categorized, regulated, and treated or cured. The modern claim that deviance or madness was a scientific matter, rather than a religious matter rooted in evil or sin, dramatically altered how we interpreted and perceived the self and others in everyday life. This was not simply a matter of religious authority being displaced by the scientific; rather, a hybrid discourse of Christian theology and Western science were woven together (Rimke & Hunt, 2002). So, for example, religious discourses held that the "sodomite" (today, the "gay male") was a sinner who engaged in immoral sexual practices with other men. The invention of the more medicalized category of the **homosexual** still relied on a notion of "perversion" derived from this earlier notion of sin, but sought to explain it using biomedical causes (Foucault, 1976). This example demonstrates the influence wielded by two dominant discourses—religion and science—in the making of the idea of the homosexual as an abnormal **subject**. Today in the West, same-gender **sexuality** has been largely de-pathologized (making the psychiatric designation of "homosexual" appear dated and insulting), yet it has not disrupted the assumption that **heterosexuality** is the normative centre, as you read in Chapter 5.

Let's step back in time again to 17th-century Europe, when institutions were newly being designed and built to discipline and regulate certain populations of people, in asylums, prisons, workhouses, and so on. People considered mad or insane were initially confined in the same institutions as the poor, the criminalized, the unemployed, and the idle; specific institutions, such as the asylum and the prison, were later developed to manage, investigate, and treat specific populations. Foucault referred to this as the **great confinement** where those labelled as mad, bad, indigent, and so on were separated from their communities, both conceptually and often physically. These **spaces of exclusion** were both a cause and an effect of the growth of the **disciplinary society** that you first read about in Chapter 1. A diagnosis of madness and institutionalization allowed for the observation of significant numbers of people under controlled conditions, making them prime objects of scientific study and experimentation. In the name of "treatment," patients were subjected to practices that included the frontal or icepick lobotomy, clitoridectomy, physical restraints, involuntary drugging, and electroconvulsive shock therapy (Valentin, 1986). Some of these practices have been denounced and ended, while others (like electroshock) continue, although not without controversy. We will now turn to some more specific examples, keeping in mind that rather than using these examples as indicators of how much we have progressed, we can use them to reflect on what similar dynamics might exist now.

You are already familiar with how early European scientists of the human body created the hierarchical and self-serving idea of distinct racial types, each with its own morphology and character. Early psy disciplines built on this model by attributing to the races distinct psychological characteristics and maladies. A powerful historical example of psychiatric or **scientific racism** is the medical term Drapetomania, invented by a Dr. Cartwright in 1851, defining a slave's desire for freedom as a mental pathology causing slaves to attempt escape. We find here another example of how both religious and

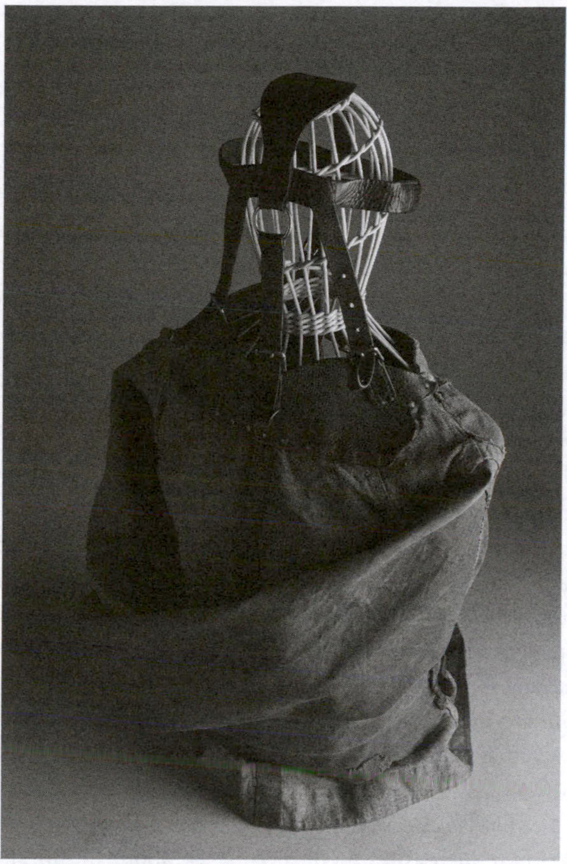

FIGURE 11.1 Benjamin Rush (1745–1813), considered the father of American psychiatry, wrote the first American psychiatric textbook and invented the "tranquilizing chair" in 1811 to immobilize the patient using the "treatment" of restraint and sensory deprivation. Strait jacket, Europe, 1925–1935. Science Museum, London. Wellcome Collection. CC BY 4.0.

scientific discourses have been used simultaneously to justify and perpetuate prevailing inequalities. Dr. Cartwright (1851) explained his findings as "medical fact":

> The cause in the most of cases, that induces the negro to run away from service, is as much a disease of the mind as any other species of mental **alienation**, and much more curable, as a general rule. With the advantages of proper medical advice, strictly followed, this troublesome practice that many negroes have of running away, can be almost entirely prevented.... If the white man attempts to oppose the Deity's will, by trying to make the negro anything else than "the submissive knee-bender," (which the Almighty declared he should be) ... the

> negro will run away; but if he keeps him in the position that we learn from the Scriptures he was intended to occupy, that is, the position of submission; and if his master or overseer be kind and gracious … the negro is spell-bound, and cannot run away.

Contemporary readers will have no difficulty identifying the absurdity of this diagnosis. However, it should remind us to consider more closely how, in our own time, **racialized** people are pathologized as an explanation for the "social problems" of their communities. For example, the claim that there is an "epidemic" of single mothers and absent fathers among African Americans not only identifies the single-parent family as non-normative, but alleges—in the absence of evidence—that male irresponsibility and family instability are integral features of Black communities. Everyday racism is camouflaged or neutralized through biomedical discourse.

Our second historical example shows how psy diagnoses can develop to explain the conditions arising from rapid social change, here in the development of industrial **capitalism**. As discussed in Chapter 7, capitalism did not simply evolve naturally; it was introduced through dispossession of people from their lands and livelihoods, so that they would provide a cheap and plentiful supply of **wage labour**. Marx explained how the transition from agrarian to urban life created conditions of alienation from the products of people's labour, their species-being, and themselves. He was critical of the growing social division and **inequality** that was part of capitalist production and fostered this alienation. In contrast, the emerging psy disciplines individualized and pathologized the conduct of people who were compelled to live in this new and often brutal social reality. For example, Dr. James Prichard (1837) created the diagnosis of **moral insanity** in the context of an increasing medical concern about immoral or disrespectable conduct in rapidly changing and uncertain times. Rapid industrialization, urbanization, and **migration** of people in search of work and a survivable life led to alarm about an expanding urban underclass, one that was thought to threaten the **norms** of respectable society. Moral insanity would later be codified by the psy disciplines as "defects of character," and eventually as "personality disorders" and other "mental and emotional disturbances" (Rimke, 2003). There are similar contemporary examples of psy diagnoses for experiences rooted in economic and class issues. For example, an unemployed person might be prescribed an antidepressant to cope with their inability to find work, and the profound stress this causes in their lives. This solution individualizes the problem of unemployment, rather than challenging the political and economic conditions that create a shortage of good jobs.

Foucault uses the **concept** of the "gaze" to highlight and explain the process of surveillance and the growing influence of expert knowledges. The gaze of the expert attempts to define who people are, without direct input from those under observation. It thus reflects relations of power in which those at the centre can define, categorize, and sometimes even institutionalize those on the margins. For our final historical example, we discuss how feminist scholars have identified many of the ways in which this gaze has been deployed to inculcate "proper" standards of behaviour in women. For instance, in the late 19th and early 20th centuries, women who displayed so-called "masculine" traits such as independence, assertiveness, and sexual self-confidence might have found themselves classified as "morally insane," because such conduct contradicted cultural conceptions of females as essentially weak, chaste, and passive.

By the 1960s, feminists were critiquing the role of psy disciplines in pathologizing women, stating that women's mental health would be best addressed by trying to change women's social, political, and economic conditions rather than attempting to change women themselves by coercing them to conform to traditional roles and expectations. Women's collective frustration exploded as they confronted unequal wages; lack of access to birth control, abortion, and child care; lack of opportunities for advancement in the paid labour force; limited educational opportunities; the double duty of child care and elder care; and sexual degradation and harassment. They spoke against the pathologization that resulted when women consciously or unconsciously refused the limited gendered scripts imposed upon them.[2] An **intersectional analysis** of women's oppression also reminds us that racialized, Indigenous, **working class**, **queer**, and trans women may be uniquely pathologized, the strictures of "normal" femininity in the West being tacitly or overtly defined as middle-class white womanhood.

In summary, scientific and medical discourses can carry with them some highly gendered assumptions. The persecution of women alleged to be witches, and the invention of hysteria, moral insanity, and now "female" personality disorders—borderline, dependent, and histrionic—demonstrate an ongoing pattern of gendered regulation. Each respective era has proclaimed an official category for women who in one way or another defied socially prescribed behaviour according to patriarchally imposed gender rules (Rimke, 2003; Ussher, 1991; Wirth-Cauchon, 2001).

Rosenhan's "On Being Sane in Insane Places"

A Foucauldian approach interrogates the assumptions and certainties embedded in our cultural attitudes, beliefs, desires, and practices concerning the normal and the pathological. Yet scholarly critiques of beliefs and practices about mental illness by no means began with, or are limited to, Foucault and those whom he has influenced. For example, Rosenhan's (1973) classic sociological study, "On Being Sane in Insane Places," also demonstrates the subjective nature of psychiatric medicine. Rosenhan had eight "pseudo patients" present themselves at a psychiatric institution as mentally ill. The actors did not display any form of symptomatic behaviour yet were nevertheless diagnosed and treated as if they were indeed mentally ill. The study demonstrated that even psy professionals cannot always distinguish the sane from the insane because of the subjective nature of judging human conduct.

This section has introduced some historical examples that challenge rather than confirm the notion of linear progress in the histories of medicine and psychiatry. We argue that rather than marking a new respect for the needs of humanity, the success of the psy complex involved the establishment of more finely tuned mechanisms of surveillance and a more effective web of power governing everyday life (Foucault, 1979).

By the mid-20th century, the psy disciplines had achieved a level of respectability in the West that conferred upon the experts significant authority in public and political

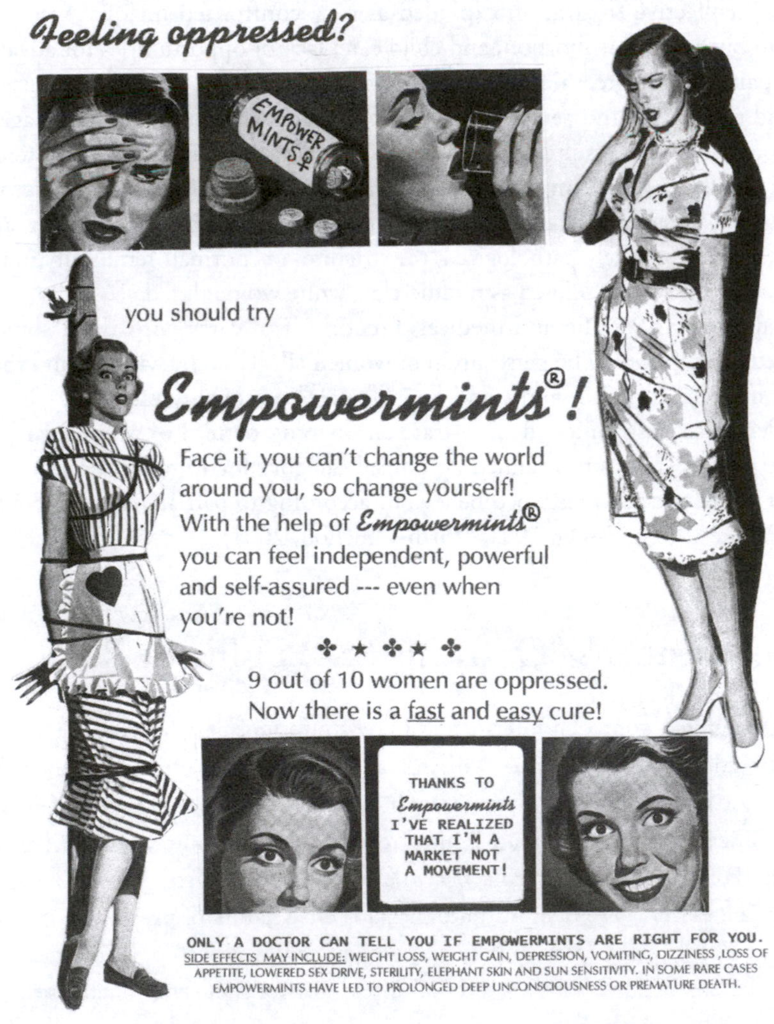

FIGURE 11.2 Empowermints®! by Carly Stasko. Reproduced by permission of Carly Stasko.

affairs. In particular, the physician and the psychiatrist (who, unlike the psychologist, is required to hold a medical degree to legally prescribe drugs) experienced growing social recognition and authority. Psy experts increasingly were called upon to analyze and intervene in a growing array of social, scientific, and legal developments. Their roles ranged from forensic psychology and legal psychiatry (linking certain criminal acts to psychiatric illness), to education and welfare reform, to shaping domestic and foreign policy, to commenting on TV-watching habits. Psy knowledge has now been so popularized that it pervades contemporary Western social life, to the point where we now live in what some have referred to as a **therapeutic culture**.

Our Own Best Selves

Direct therapeutic intervention is only a small part of the social reality that we are making visible here. First, we have become "confessing animals," in the words of Foucault (1976, p. 59). The therapist's office, the self-help group, and an expanding array of social media platforms are all examples of settings in which the **modern confessional** takes place. Rather than turning to the priest to confess and absolve our sins, modern individuals rely on psy analyses for guidance, comfort, and direction. Today people may go to their therapists' offices or their support group to confess—but the important point for Foucault is that it is in the process of confessing that the self is *created* in a particular way rather than *revealed*. One of the main tenets of therapeutic discourses is the assumption that there is an inner core or "truth" about ourselves that therapeutic techniques can help us to reveal to ourselves. However, rather than "discover" the self, self-help discourses help construct different possible narratives about the self: it is in this sense that the self is not uncovered but rather constructed.

Second, to engage with self-help, to seek therapy, and to strive for happiness[3] are exactly what psychocentric culture prescribes and expects instead of a critical discussion of the social bases of struggle and unhappiness. For example, the self-help industry forms an important part of the modern therapeutic culture. It provides a dizzying array of groups, books, experts, shows, podcasts, and so forth to guide us in our exploration of our inner selves and our relations with others, all in the aim of self-improvement, or becoming our "own best selves." If you make a visit to the self-help section of any bookshop or online retailer, you will find that self-help literature comes in numerous different forms of advice: spirituality, how-to manuals, personal change, dealing with loss, relationship advice, and more. There is something for everyone, but what the self-help genre shares in common is that techniques of the self (explained early in this chapter) require individuals to find themselves inadequate and to act upon themselves as a form of self-governance. But governing how?

This leads to a third important aspect of our new social reality: therapeutic culture and self-help perfectly complement and facilitate the **neoliberal** ethos of our times. The increasing focus on individual responsibility and accountability has been occurring simultaneously with the dismantling of public services, including healthcare, forcing individuals to absorb structural deterioration. You have already learned in Chapter 1 that neoliberalism is predicated on the valorization of **free markets**, limiting state powers for the regulation of capital, and **competitive individualism** in economic affairs. Neoliberalism also depends on the creation of new kinds of people, who are "**entrepreneurs of the self**" (for example, see Miller & Rose, 2008). From the 1970s onward, the simultaneous rise of neoliberalism and the **culture of therapy** had a common theme: a focus on the "I" over the "we." Moreover, the apparent remedy to a defective self is consumerism—of therapy, books, TV shows, tests, and drugs—a fact not coincidental but essential to neoliberalism. Therapeutic culture has been an enormously profitable enterprise.

Our critique of therapeutic culture is therefore also a critique of neoliberal values. How can improving your self-esteem be the answer when your anger or depression is a direct result of the systemic racism that you face every day? How will positive thinking help you to secure clean water and adequate housing for your Indigenous community, in the face of **colonial** occupation and neglect? What if no amount of self-help will help you pay the bills?

The sociological insistence that the personal is also social and public, as C.W. Mills teaches us, highlights the fact that the latter is inextricably intertwined with the former. For example, the unemployed person is often without work not because they lack skills or initiative, but rather because local and national economic arrangements have increased joblessness. While some economists claim that a certain unemployment rate is "healthy for the economy" because it drives competition, what of that percentage of the population that suffer the harsh realities of unemployment? Should they feel proud for contributing to the health of the economy? Or is it more likely that they will feel personally inadequate or otherwise psychologically inferior to those who are in advantageous social and economic positions? Prozac may chemically help some individuals cope with the negative personal impact of unemployment, but it is the creation of new jobs that will resolve personal crises resulting from depression, stress, and anxiety resulting from job loss. From this example, you can see how Marx's analysis of capitalism and its class structure as well as Foucault's approach to government both contribute to our understanding of how people, as neoliberal subjects, are constituted through a therapeutic culture that serves to secure relations of domination while claiming to liberate the self. The growth of neoliberalism has resulted in the increasing de-**responsibilization** of social authorities such as municipal and other levels of government. Moreover, social and political systems are rarely taken into consideration, while individuals alone are often blamed and held responsible and accountable for social, political, and economic problems they did not create.

What Needs to Change?

The notion of "the self" as knowable, and as a work in progress, is now as taken for granted by us as brushing our teeth. Perhaps through continually working to improve ourselves we will become "better" people, but according to whose definition and evaluation? By defining human normality, and thus by extension, abnormality, therapeutic culture presumably offers strategies and truths to achieve the good life, and indeed the good self. So should you go to see a therapist? Or buy a self-help book? Or engage in self-improvement? These practices may indeed benefit you, but bringing a **sociological imagination** and awareness of the big picture can help you to be selective and reflexive about external and internalized pressures to work on yourself.

Struggling with the self has become a dominant cultural theme, if not a social expectation, in modern life. All aspects of human experience have been transformed by so-called experts into various dysfunctions, addictions, disorders, illnesses, pathologies, or destructive behaviours that require psy treatment above all else. Furthermore, while human differences certainly exist, psychocentrism does the work of dividing practices (discussed earlier) because it classifies these differences into **binary** categories of good/bad, healthy/sick, normal/abnormal, moral/immoral, and so forth. Indeed, the psy industry has infiltrated and categorized almost all ways of being, and it permeates parents' relationships to their children. It is also one of the most profitable capitalist markets on the planet. That no one is ever really good enough is an infinitely renewable market for **exploitation** and **commodification**. Rather than address and highlight the socially structured bases of human suffering, we are pacified and incited, directed, and instructed to blame and fix ourselves. Consistent with the political rationalities of neoliberalism, psychocentrism masks the negative effects of structural inequalities and injustices on human health and well-being. Instead, we live in a society in which our search for meaning has shifted away from critiquing the public sphere and policy toward one that fetishizes the atomized, privatized self.

The anti-psychiatry movement emerged in the 1960s as part of the larger anti-establishment movement, which included the collective struggles aimed at achieving women's liberation and civil rights. Leading anti-psychiatrists include Michel Foucault, Peter Sedgwick, R.D. Laing, David Cooper, Felix Guatarri, and Thomas Szasz, all of whom received formal training in medicine and psychiatry. Hostile to the fundamental assumptions and practices of the discipline, anti-psychiatry advocates have challenged the modern assumption that confinement in a hospital or other institutional setting is necessary for the majority of those diagnosed as mentally ill, going so far as to say psychiatry itself is a harmful discipline.

Today those critical of psychiatry also challenge the exponential growth of psychopharmaceutical drug use or "chemical restraints" for those targeted as at risk, dangerous, disorderly, disruptive, and so forth, which has become commonplace in the West. Patients and ex-patients have challenged and resisted traditional assumptions and labels by embracing and celebrating their differences as strengths rather than weaknesses—as evident in a growing social movement that includes "psychiatric survivors," ex-patients, user-centred approaches, neurodiversity advocates, and "mad pride" celebrants (Crossley & Crossley, 2001; Curtis, Dellar, Leslie, & Watson, 2000; Shaughnessy, 2001).

The Foucauldian approach to mental health and distress unpacks the psychocentricity of the human sciences. After all, the purpose and promise of the sociological imagination is to produce analyses useful for understanding the link between private troubles and public issues. A critique of the expanding umbrella of psy discourses, practices, and markets is a means to keep this narrative in check and allow for other, less individualized, explanations of human experience to emerge.

Study Questions

1 In what ways has the classification and treatment of mental illness changed over the past 100 years? How does a Foucauldian approach explain these shifts?
2 How does the distinction between normality and abnormality contribute to social regulation? Provide examples.
3 How does this chapter contribute to a critique of neoliberalism?
4 How have counter-discourses challenged psychocentrism? What alternatives to psychocentrism have been proposed? Try to think of some examples that are not discussed in this chapter.

Exercises

1 Go to a bookstore or online retailer to investigate the titles in the self-help genre. Check sections such as health and wellness, business, travel, biography, spirituality, new age, women, lesbian and gay, and sociology. What themes emerge from your investigation?
2 Research a criminal legal case in which a psychiatric diagnosis has been an important component of the evidence and sentencing. How have psy discourses been deployed in the construction of legal evidence?
3 Take note of how many times in a given day you encounter or make use of psy discourse or psy terms such as "normal." How does this exercise contribute to your comprehension of Foucault's notion of government?

Notes

1 For example, the ways in which abnormalized subjects have been constituted or created by expert discourses can be seen in critical social studies on anxiety (Tone, 2008), suicide (Marsh, 2010), personality disorders (Rimke, 2003), shyness (Lane, 2008), stuttering (Petrunik & Shearing, 2002), depression (Horowitz & Wakefield, 2007), ADD/ADHD (Conrad & Schneider, 1980), and hysteria (Didi-Huberman, 2004).
2 As Dorothy Smith and Sara David titled their 1975 collection of papers challenging psychiatry, *I'm Not Mad, I'm Angry* (Smith & David, 1975).
3 Learning how to be happy is a relatively recent theme of the self-help genre. For a critique of the happiness literature, see Ahmed, 2010; Binkley, 2014; and Ehrenreich, 2009.

References

Ahmed, S. (2010). *The promise of happiness*. Durham, NC: Duke University Press.

American Psychiatric Association (APA). (2013). *The diagnostic and statistical manual of mental disorders* (5th ed.). Arlington, VA: APA.

Binkley, S. (2014). *Happiness as enterprise: An essay on neoliberal life*. New York, NY: State University of New York Press.

Cartwright, S. (1851). Diseases and peculiarities of the Negro race. *Africans in America Resource Bank*. Retrieved from http://www.pbs.org/wgbh/aia/part4/4h3106.html

CBC News. (2014, May 30). Aboriginal people and alcohol: Not a genetic predisposition. *CBC News Audio*. Retrieved from http://www.cbc.ca/news/Indigenous/aboriginal-people-and-alcohol-not-a-genetic-predisposition-1.2660167

Conrad, P., & Schneider, J. (1980). *Deviance and medicalization: From badness to sickness*. St. Louis, MO: C.V. Mosby Company.

Crossley, M.L., & Crossley, N. (2001). Patient voices, social movements and the habitus: How psychiatric survivors speak out. *Social Science & Medicine*, *52*(10), 1477–1489.

Curtis, T.R., Dellar, R., Leslie, E., & Watson, B. (2000). *Mad pride: A celebration of mad culture*. London, UK: Spare Change Books.

Didi-Huberman, G. (2004). *Invention of hysteria: Charcot and the photographic iconography of the salpetriere*. Cambridge, MA: MIT Press.

Ehrenreich, B. (2009). *Bright-sided: How positive thinking is undermining America*. New York, NY: Metropolitan Books.

Foucault, M. (1976/1978). *The history of sexuality: An introduction* (Vol. 1). New York, NY: Random House.

Foucault, M. (1979). *Discipline and punish: The birth of the prison*. New York, NY: Vintage Books.

Foucault, M. (1988). *Madness and civilization*. New York, NY: Vintage Books.

Foucault, M. (1994). *The birth of the clinic*. New York, NY: Vintage Books.

Frances, A.J. (2012, December 2). DSM 5 is guide not bible: Ignore its ten worst changes. *Psychology Today*. Retrieved from https://www.psychologytoday.com/us/blog/dsm5-in-distress/201212/dsm-5-is-guide-not-bible-ignore-its-ten-worst-changes

Hacking, I. (1986). Making up people. In T. Heller, M. Sosna, & D. Wellbery (Eds.), *Reconstructing individualism* (pp. 222–236). Stanford, CA: Stanford University Press.

Horwitz, A.V., & Wakefield, J.C. (2007). *The loss of sadness: How psychiatry transformed normal sorrow into depressive disorder*. Oxford, UK: Oxford University Press.

Kutchins, H., & Kirk, S. (1998). *Making us crazy: DSM: The psychiatric bible and the creation of mental disorders*. New York, NY: Free Press.

Lane, C. (2008). *Shyness: How normal behavior became a sickness*. New Haven, CT: Yale University Press.

Marsh, I. (2010). *Suicide: Foucault, history and truth*. Cambridge, UK: Cambridge University Press.

Miller, P., & Rose, N. (2008). Introduction: Governing economic and social life. In *Governing the present: Administering economic, social and personal life* (pp. 1–25). Cambridge, UK: Polity Press.

Petrunik, M., & Shearing, C. (2002). Stutterers' practices. In E. Rubington & M. Weinberg (Eds.), *Deviance: The interactionist perspective* (8th ed., pp. 384–396). Toronto, ON: Allyn and Bacon.

Prichard, J.C. (1837). *A treatise on insanity and other disorders affecting the mind.* Philadelphia, PA: Carey & Hart.

Rimke, H. (2000). Governing citizens through self-help literature. *Cultural Studies, 14*(1), 61–78.

Rimke, H. (2003). Constituting transgressive interiorities: Nineteenth-century psychiatric readings of morally mad bodies. In A. Aldama (Ed.), *Violence and the body: Race, gender and the state* (pp. 403–428). Bloomington, IN: Indiana University Press.

Rimke, H. (2010). Consuming fears: Neoliberal in/securities, cannibalization, and psychopolitics. In J. Shantz (Ed.), *Racism and borders: Representation, repression, resistance* (pp. 95–112). New York, NY: Algora Publishing.

Rimke, H. (2016). Mental and emotional health/distress as a social justice issue: Beyond psychocentrism. *Studies in Social Justice, 10*(1), 4–17.

Rimke, H. (2018). Sickening institutions: A feminist sociological analysis and critique of religion, medicine, and psychiatry. In J. Kilty & E. Dej (Eds.), *Containing madness: Gender and "psy" in institutional contexts* (pp. 15–39). New York, NY: Palgrave MacMillan.

Rimke, H., & Hunt, A. (2002). From sinners to degenerates: The medicalization of morality in the 19th century. *History of the Human Sciences, 15*(1), 59–88.

Rose, N. (1999). *Inventing ourselves: Psychology, power, and personhood.* Cambridge, UK: Cambridge University Press.

Rosenhan, D.L. (1973). On being sane in insane places. *Science, 179*(4070), 250–258.

Shaughnessy, P. (2001). July 9th: Day of action: Mad pride view. *Asylum: The Magazine for Democratic Psychiatry, 13*, 7–8.

Smith, D., & David, S. (Eds.). (1975). *Women look at psychiatry.* Vancouver, BC: Press Gang Publishers.

Statistics Canada. (2012). Aboriginal peoples: Fact sheet for Canada. Retrieved from http://www.statcan.gc.ca/pub/89-656-x/89-656-x2015001-eng.htm

Szasz, T. (1978). *The myth of psychotherapy.* New York, NY: Syracuse University Press.

Tone, A. (2008). *The age of anxiety.* New York, NY: Basic Books.

Turner, R.E., & Edgley, C. (1983). From witchcraft to drugcraft: Biochemistry as mythology. *Social Science Journal, 20*(4), 1–12.

Ussher, J. (1991). *Women's madness: Misogyny or mental illness?* Amherst, MA: University of Massachusetts Press.

Valentin, E.S. (1986). *Great and desperate cures: The rise and decline of psychosurgery and other radical treatments for mental illness.* New York, NY: Basic Books.

Wirth-Cauchon, J. (2001). *Women and borderline personality disorder: Symptoms and stories.* New Brunswick, NJ: Rutgers University Press.

12 Going Shopping: The Politics of Everyday Consumption

DENNIS SORON

In the aftermath of the September 11 attacks in 2001, a number of prominent US politicians, including George W. Bush, famously made appeals to the American people to do their bit for the national recovery effort by going out and shopping more. In the intervening years, and particularly since the financial crisis of 2008, such appeals for consumers to shop for the greater good have become more ubiquitous, as politicians and central bankers across the world have sought to restore "consumer confidence" and encourage accelerated private spending as a means of recession-proofing the precarious global economy.

Such appeals offer a vivid illustration of the contradictory ways in which consumer activity is now understood in affluent regions of the world. Today, shopping and consuming serve as powerful symbols of individual **agency**, market democracy, and a "Western" way of life that seems threatened on all sides by violent conflict, economic instability, and other dangers. At the same time, they also figure in our everyday lives as cultural and economic imperatives, as activities in which we are constantly pressured to participate. In different instances, heightened consumption is regarded both as the best solution for economic stagnation and as the primary driver of environmental destruction and escalating private debt. We are encouraged to take up civic and moral responsibilities through our consumer choices, and yet such choices strike many as an inadequate substitute for genuine democratic **power**. While the commercial media continues to glamourize consumerism as a gateway to fulfillment, this vision of the good life has run up against a growing counter-current of dissatisfaction with the negative and often unjust effects of consumption-intensive lifestyles.

Picking up on this rising popular disenchantment, this chapter challenges some dominant assumptions about the nature and implications of everyday consumer behaviour in today's world. In contrast to the common-sense view that consumption is largely innocent, apolitical, and driven by the needs and preferences of individuals, the chapter emphasizes that consumer behaviour is socially embedded, institutionally organized, and enmeshed with prevailing structures and relations of power. Adopting a hybrid theoretical perspective that draws upon insights from both Foucauldian and Marxist theory, this chapter aims to highlight some of the ways in which power operates in and through consumer behaviour and, accordingly, how consumption has also increasingly become an important site for the expression of popular opposition and resistance.

Free to Choose?

It has become commonplace in much popular and academic debate to claim that consumption is central to the operation of contemporary Western societies. It is for this reason that otherwise diverse nations are often grouped together under the broad banner of "**consumer society**." In a quantitative sense, this widely used term points to the unprecedented volume of material consumption in such societies, and to the expansive range of goods and commercialized messages that have become a dominant feature of our everyday lifeworld. In a more qualitative sense, this term highlights the unparalleled degree to which consumption practices in affluent nations have become a crucial site for broader processes of social integration, public communication, and identity-formation. As Stuart Hall (1984, p. 18) has argued, the dramatic growth of mass consumption in the postwar period did not by any means erase **class** or other key social divisions, but it "did profoundly modify everyday life-patterns, the social experience and expectations and the lived universe of the majority of ordinary people."

While the notion of "consumer society" by its very nature implies that the everyday consumption practices of individuals reflect a broader social logic, conventional conceptualizations of consumer behaviour often ignore their social context. Prevailing ideas about consumer freedom hold that everyday consumer decisions are not and should not be regulated by social influences external to the individual. As sociologist Zygmunt Bauman (1988, 2007) has emphasized, the ideal of unconstrained consumer choice has become an almost sacred value in capitalist society, providing the template for our cultural understanding of freedom itself. The capitalist marketplace is typically celebrated not only for its cornucopia of consumer goods, but for its seeming absence of top-down authority, its ostensible willingness to grant people the freedom to choose what to buy, how to live, and—consequently—who to be.

This ideal of unconstrained marketplace freedom is at the heart of the **concept** of "**consumer sovereignty**," which has established itself as a key part of mainstream economic theory and of neoliberal political **discourse**. This formulation holds that, to the extent that consumers have the power to rationally determine which goods and services match with their own preferences, consumer demand is the force that determines an

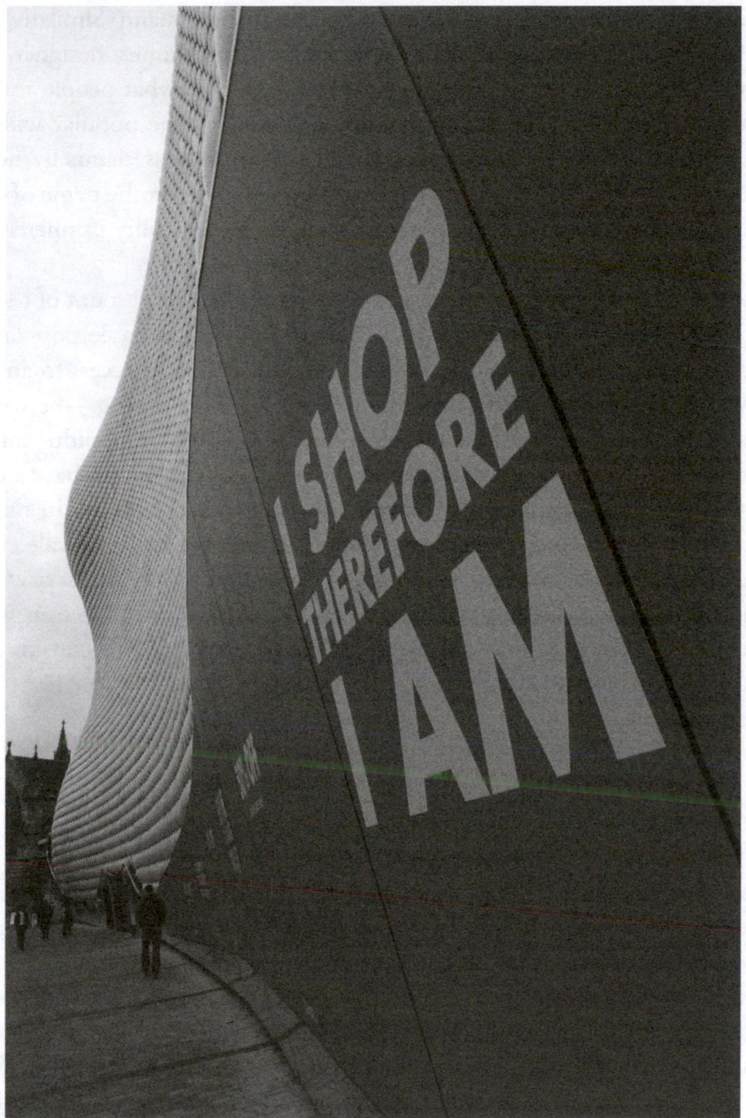

FIGURE 12.1 In the affluent world today, our prevailing notions of freedom, personal identity, and agency are all closely entwined with shopping and consuming. Photo Central/Alamy.

economy's production priorities and regulates its allocation of resources. Accordingly, markets act as highly responsive mechanisms for communicating consumer demand to producers, who function simply to provide people with the goods and services they desire. In this version of marketplace democracy, the power and success enjoyed by giant corporations like Walmart, McDonald's, Microsoft, Time-Warner, and Exxon Mobil only derive from their capacity to grasp and serve consumer demand. Similarly, products such as fast food, SUVs, celebrity gossip magazines, smartphones, designer clothing, and so on only exist in such abundance because they reflect what people really want. This familiar equation of the market with democracy and the popular will—which Thomas Frank (2000) calls "**market populism**"—is what fuels claims by **neoliberal** ideologues that any effort to regulate private economic activity in the name of collective principles such as equality, justice, and environmental sustainability is inherently elitist and authoritarian.

While the ideal of consumer sovereignty offers an inadequate account of the dynamics of consumer behaviour, it does possess a certain understandable popular appeal. Many consumers in affluent regions of the world today do have access to an unparalleled range of choices, even though the significance of these choices—between Coke and Pepsi, for instance—may often not be momentous. Indeed, the undue importance ascribed to often trivial consumer choices in contemporary society can have a desperate and compensatory quality. Most people may not have much freedom in their workplaces and other institutional settings, exert much influence over large-scale events like wars, financial meltdowns, and oil spills, or have much say over the major decisions that affect their futures, but they do exert some measure of direct control over what they eat, drink, wear, and so on. The heightened value now accorded to consumer choice is, at least to some extent, perhaps indicative of the desire many people feel for greater autonomy and control in other spheres of their social lives.

Consumption Is Social

Whatever cultural meanings it may embody, the notion of consumer sovereignty offers a dubious model of consumer behaviour in which—as Juliet Schor argues—"consumption is largely stripped of its social dimensions, becoming reduced to the question of goods and the functionality they provide to the individual" (in Soron, 2004). This view of the rational, utility-driven consumer downplays the extent to which consumption decisions are enmeshed in a wide variety of non-instrumental motivations and desires. Similarly, it fails to consider how class, **gender**, **ethnicity**, age, and other key determinants of socio-cultural identity can all differentially influence consumer behaviour and pattern our choices in particular ways. Most crucially, it fails to appreciate that consumption practices are always socially and institutionally embedded, and they are shaped and constrained by a variety of social forces that the individual does not immediately control and may not even comprehend.

Such insights carry us into the terrain of the **sociology of consumption**, a field of inquiry whose primary concern is with the complex social dynamics that drive consumer behaviour. Refusing to accept that consumer behaviour is either entirely "free" or strictly determined by external forces, Don Slater argues that the sociology of consumption has attempted to approach the everyday consumption of ordinary people with respect for the varied meanings they invest in it, while at the same time seeing it as "a valid starting point from which to map the networks of power in which they are enmeshed" (2005, p. 175). To "map" the diverse forces shaping consumer behaviour in this manner, we need to first develop a working conception of power that goes beyond the theoretical limitations of the consumer sovereignty model.

In line with the tradition of economic **liberalism**, the consumer sovereignty model is oriented toward curbing the **state**'s arbitrary power to interfere with the choices of individual economic actors (whether consumers, investors, or businesses). In this sense, it is vulnerable to Foucault's critique of the broader intellectual tendency to simply equate power with intentional, overt repression and coercion by state institutions and other dominant social actors. Clearly, contemporary consumer behaviour is not strongly subject to power in this narrow sense—insofar as our routine purchasing choices are not directly subject to top-down control. That said, it would be wrong to infer from this that people's ongoing choices over what and how to consume are somehow independent of power and the complex web of social relations, practices, and institutions in which it manifests itself.

Historically speaking, consumption practices (around food, clothing, alcohol, tobacco, etc.) have always been subject to some degree of communal regulation and sanction, but such controls have waned to an unprecedented degree in consumer society. We thus need a more subtle understanding of power itself to understand the manner in which it continues to shape contemporary consumer behaviour. Recall that for Foucault, power is not a finite substance that is simply "possessed" by the powerful few and applied externally onto the powerless many, but is something that is dispersed widely and embedded into the impersonal operations of a variety of institutions, social relations, and everyday life settings. Instead of just functioning in a "repressive" manner by explicitly prohibiting and punishing certain types of unapproved consumer behaviour, power acts in a "productive" manner, helping to engender and discipline our very consumer desires, motives, and **subjectivities**.

In contrast to the consumer sovereignty model, which assumes that consumers rationally seek to maximize their own welfare by choosing the goods and services that best fulfill their self-defined needs, the sociology of consumption has concerned itself with how prevailing consumption patterns are socially produced. While work in this field has been diverse, much of it has attempted to "re-socialize" consumption by underlining that consumer goods are not valued for their instrumental attributes alone, but for their ability to act as means of social communication. Across a range of recent studies, Sylvia Reif writes, the "common ground is that goods are not simply consumed for their function or **use value**, but for their symbolic and communicative qualities that help express and mediate social relations, structures, and divisions" (2008, p. 562). Within sociology, one focus of this communicative model of consumer behaviour has been how commodities can help to symbolically map out the relative social positions of those who own and use them. The earliest and perhaps most famous example of this tradition can be found in Thorstein Veblen's (1934) analysis of "**conspicuous consumption**"—that is, the ostentatious display of expensive and often frivolous goods by the wealthy in order to communicate their superior **status** and to arouse the envy of those below them on the socio-economic hierarchy.

While some aspects of Veblen's analysis of the "leisure class" in 19th-century America may now seem dated, its basic insights about the symbolically competitive and comparative nature of consumer behaviour are still highly relevant. If anything, such competitive pressures have intensified over the past few decades as personal identity has been increasingly drawn into the vortex of consumer **culture**, as everyday life has become ever more saturated with advertising imagery and brand symbolism, and as socio-economic inequalities have continued to widen. Today, with the rise of suburbanization, the decline of face-to-face community interaction, and the growing influence of mass media and its glamourized depictions of wealth and celebrity, consumers of even relatively humble means tend to be drawn into the process of "**upscale emulation**" (Schor, 1999), deriving their material aspirations by looking not to their immediate neighbours and friends, but to the extravagant lifestyles of the "rich and famous."

Such processes reflect how consumer **capitalism** continually fosters new desires, encouraging impulsive purchasing choices that are economically profitable for producers but detrimental to consumers' own well-being. To this extent, they highlight the complex dynamics underlying consumer behaviour and prompt reconsideration of the deeper forces driving economic life in capitalist society. From the perspective of Marxist theory, insofar as capitalism is an economic system driven by the pursuit of private profit and not the satisfaction of collective human needs, consumption patterns tend to be shaped to serve the imperatives of producers first and foremost. In this view, capitalist markets are not democratic, nor are they responsive to what people in general need. Because the only "votes" that count in the marketplace are those that are backed with money, resources, and labour, in capitalist society, they get allocated toward forms of production that yield the greatest profit for producers, even when this leaves the basic needs of many people unsatisfied, compromises the health and happiness of workers and consumers, and generates an array of externalized social and ecological costs.

Understanding the undemocratic tendencies of the so-called "**free market**" requires grappling with the subtle ways in which economic power operates in capitalist society. As discussed in Chapters 1 and 7, in contrast to previous systems in which political and economic power were unified in the hands of an overt **ruling class** (a hereditary aristocracy, for example), capitalism has tended to decouple economic and political power, such that the economy becomes a private, contractual sphere relatively free of direct political control, and those who own the **means of production** have no formal, legal authority over those who do not. It is precisely because capital cannot command our product-related activities through direct, political means, Michael Dawson argues, that it has had to develop indirect forms of control that are effective yet "subtle enough to avoid recognition and resistance" (2003, p. 54). To the extent that consumers are largely free of overt restrictions on their daily behaviour, power operates by generating the conditions in which we come to govern ourselves and express our will in socially approved, system-supportive ways that don't require external coercion. Over the past several decades in particular, as Assadourian (2010, p. 11) has suggested, business interests have been engaged in a constant struggle to "coax more consumption out of people"—for instance, by liberalizing consumer credit, designing products for quick physical and stylistic obsolescence, and undermining the state provision of collective goods that cut into the demand for private commodities.

Advertising: "A Constant Background Hum"

One key sphere of contemporary social life in which the effort of producers to induce and shape consumer desire and behaviour for their own ends is particularly evident is that of corporate advertising and marketing. Global marketing is now an enormous, multi-billion-dollar industry that saturates commercial media and other everyday domains, drawing upon huge stores of demographic and psychological research to develop intricate strategies for shaping our mental or informational environment in ways that "coax" more consumption out of us.

Advertising, as Annie Leonard has argued in *The Story of Stuff* (2010), has become such a massive and influential industry today that it has effectively become "a constant background hum in our lives." Advertising has saturated not only the commercial mass media, but increasingly insinuates itself into the Internet, especially through social media, and even non-commercial public spaces and institutions such as schools and hospitals. As a consequence of this blanketing of everyday life with commercial messages, the average North American now spends roughly an entire year of his or her life encountering advertisements (p. 163).

Ironically, as Sut Jhally (2017) acknowledges, even though advertising is a now a massive global industry whose blandishments to consume have colonized extensive domains of our everyday lives, most people feel personally immune to its messages. While this may suggest that many people are in denial about what really motivates their behaviour, it may also suggest that we often have too narrow of a conception of how advertising exerts its influence. As Jhally argues, advertising's power does not simply pertain to its ability to increase the consumption of specific products or services, but to "how advertising as a storytelling system shapes the perceptions, values and priorities of those of us who live in consumer capitalist societies." As our culture's primary storyteller, Jhally insists, advertising inculcates us with the idea that happiness comes from the individual acquisition and consumption of commodities. It does so not by offering detailed information about consumer goods, but by symbolically linking them to valued human qualities—acceptance, love, empowerment, belonging, freedom, connection to nature, sensuality, and so on—that many individuals today feel that their lives lack.

Jhally and others highlight the ways in which advertising, far from providing us a passport to a land of happiness and abundance, tends to aggravate people's sense of dissatisfaction with life and sharpen their social insecurity. This insight has been well-developed by feminist critics, who have grappled with the ways in which commercial advertising can perpetuate dominant gender **ideologies** and deepen the oppression of women in society more generally. Idealized, airbrushed, and eroticized images of women's bodies and faces are pervasive in contemporary advertising, Kilbourne (2010) notes. One effect of this has been the entrenchment of a narrow cultural definition of femininity premised upon women's appearance alone, and oriented toward the pursuit of highly exclusionary standards of thinness, beauty, and idealized **whiteness**. While this fruitless pursuit comes along with a variety of painful physical and psychological costs for many women themselves, it has also proven to be extremely profitable for various industries (from cosmetics to dieting and plastic surgery) that feed on women's underlying sense of not measuring up to the culture's approved standards of femininity. Indeed, across a wide range of ads targeted at women, Kilbourne provocatively asserts, the message is clear: "you're ugly; you're disgusting; buy something."

Driven to Consume

Advertising is merely one of the many institutional factors that have rendered the imperative to spend and consume a pervasive part of people's everyday lifeworld. Understanding the social organization of consumption today, as George Ritzer has argued, requires us to confront "the almost dizzying proliferation of settings that allow, encourage, and even compel us to consume so many … goods and services" (2005, p. 2). The paradigmatic environment for the contemporary shopper is not the bustling, face-to-face setting of the open-air market or the main street, but huge, enclosed, corporate-controlled milieux such as shopping malls, which bring together an array of goods, brands, services, and attractions in a single location to create an ideal environment to induce consumption. Today, Ritzer argues, not only shopping malls, but theme parks, hotels, cruise ships, casinos, sports facilities, airports, and other hypercommercialized settings have become "**cathedrals of consumption**" that provide magical settings for people to experience the plenitude of their desires and participate in the rituals of acquisition. In spite of their seemingly "enchanted" character, Ritzer suggests, "these places do more than simply permit us to consume things; they are structured to lead and even coerce us into consumption" (2005, p. x). While such public places remain an important part of the contemporary cultural landscape, the decline of the traditional shopping mall in recent years, alongside the dramatic rise in online shopping, has extended powerful new inducements to consume impulsively into the home and other private settings.

Such analyses indicate the degree to which individual consumer behaviour is subtly shaped by the social and material environments that encircle us. Beyond the influences exerted by "enchanted" retail settings, a much wider range of contextual factors underpin prevailing consumption patterns. Consumers do not define and pursue their preferences in a vacuum; indeed, their individual aspirations and actions are always influenced by the institutions, relationships, material settings, and patterns of power in which they are embedded. Such factors can often quietly but powerfully steer us into particular types of routine consumption habits that are to some degree involuntary or "locked-in" rather than freely chosen.

Automobile Dependency and Consumer "Lock-in"

The issue of transportation provides a compelling illustration of the "locked-in" quality of many forms of contemporary consumption. While environmentalists and urban planners may decry our current overreliance on inefficient modes of transportation such as the private automobile, they often fail to recognize that the roots of this problem go deeper than the commuter's personal values and preferences. Indeed, it grows out of a whole range of contextual social influences—urban zoning laws, commercial land-use patterns, incentives for low-density suburban housing, state subsidies for the petroleum and auto industries, underfunded or non-existent public transit systems, growing distances between nodes of daily activity, the growth in exurban employment, inflexible work routines, inadequate child-care arrangements, and so on—that make energy-intensive car use the most practical option for many people as they navigate their way through their complicated daily responsibilities. In turn, such transportation patterns help to engender modes of consumption—drive-through services, fast-food strips, greenfield housing developments, peripheral big box stores rimmed by oceans of free parking, and so on—that reinforce automobile-dependent lifestyles, while further marginalizing and excluding those who don't or can't drive.

The range of influences on our daily transportation choices provides an apt illustration of what the Organisation for Economic Co-operation and Development (OECD, 2002) has labelled the "**infrastructure of consumption**"—that is, the whole contextual matrix of social, material, political, and economic constraints and pressures that effectively compel ordinary people into adopting particular patterns of consumption. To this extent, the OECD and others have suggested, we cannot really understand the "software" of everyday individual consumer behaviour without giving proper consideration to the infrastructural "hardware" in which it operates.

For instance, a great deal of media attention in Canada and the US in recent years has been paid to the growth of diet-related health disorders (such as diabetes and obesity) among poor and socially disadvantaged groups. While it may be tempting to simply dismiss such problems as a "software" defect related to the impulsive choices of disadvantaged individuals themselves, the "hardware" dimension of this issue often remains unexplored. Quite often, poor and marginalized people live in urban areas that are effectively "food deserts," lacking grocery stores and containing high concentrations of unhealthy food sources such as fast-food outlets and variety stores. Beyond the issue of geographical availability, our current food system ensures that healthy items such as fresh produce tend to be more expensive—and hence less financially accessible—than unhealthy, processed, and nutritionally empty items. Such issues are evident in Canada's northern regions, particularly among **Indigenous** communities, where the prevalence of diet-related health disorders is clearly linked to the practical inaccessibility of healthy, nutritious, and affordable food (Dillabough, 2016). Even when healthy food is not entirely inaccessible, poor and marginalized citizens live in a cultural environment where knowledge about food is heavily influenced by corporate marketing and industry-sponsored junk **science**, often lacking alternative information sources and educational opportunities that could help them reframe their food practices. So, while public health officials may bemoan the unhealthy food choices disadvantaged people often make, in practice such choices are heavily shaped and constrained by social circumstances beyond their immediate control.

As the cases of shopping malls, automobile-dependent landscapes, and "food deserts" suggest, the influences that subtly condition our consumption choices have an

FIGURE 12.2 Food deserts that contain a dense clusters of fast-food establishments and few if any sources of healthy food have a strong influence on the food choices of residents. CC BY ND 2.0/ Beaumontpete.

important spatial dimension. We should not forget that such influences also include a crucial temporal dimension. Indeed, time distribution and daily routine are also crucial factors that contribute to the reproduction of particular consumer behaviours. Although we tend to associate private consumption with "free time" or leisure, many consumption patterns today arise from stressful daily schedules in which people experience a chronic sense of "time poverty." This sense of time scarcity makes speed and convenience cardinal virtues, predisposing consumers toward time- and labour-saving goods and services. While they bear down on all of us to some degree, such pressures have increasingly acquired a gendered dimension. In the past few decades, as feminist thinkers have argued, the mass entry of women into the full-time workforce has sapped the domestic sphere of its traditional source of **labour power**, intensifying the **commodification** of household goods and services traditionally provided by the unpaid efforts of women. While shopping tends to be disparaged as a superficial "feminized" pastime, it is in many cases inseparable from vital forms of domestic care-giving. Feeding and clothing one's family, furnishing one's home, purchasing toiletries and medical supplies, finding appropriate gifts for friends and relatives, and so on are all forms of domestic labour that place notable time demands on those who take responsibility for them. Beyond the domestic sphere, the time constraints associated with **wage labour** also influence how and what we consume. By directing the major share of our daytime energies toward paid work and limiting the time we have for self-chosen activities, wage labour in capitalist society tends to deplete our practical skills and creativity, making us increasingly dependent upon the consumer marketplace for our varied social, psychological, and material needs.

Transforming Consumption: A Collective Challenge

Shifting our attention from the individual consumer to the varied social factors that shape consumer behaviour generates new understandings of why people today consume the way they do, and of why certain problematic, unjust, and unsustainable consumption patterns are slow to change. As considered earlier in this chapter, notions of consumer sovereignty assume that consumers, within the limits of their buying power, are free to choose the goods and services they please, as long as they are not encumbered by intrusive regulations and prohibitions. In a Foucauldian vein, this "repressive" conception of power fails to address the "productive" nature of power—that is, the ways in which it creates the conditions in which we form our identities and come to spontaneously govern ourselves in a manner compatible with dominant social prerogatives. In this sense, the infrastructure of consumption is a key part of the disciplinary architecture of everyday life, crystallizing many different power-laden processes operating at multiple scales—from the unequal structures of the global capitalist economy, to state and municipal policy, financing and consumer credit, marketing strategy, retailing practices, urban planning, the intricate dynamics of family life, and beyond.

As discussed in Chapter 14, consumer behaviour can be said to be "political" not simply because it is passively shaped by external structures and relations of power, but because such behaviour is actively involved in maintaining and reproducing unjust and unsustainable social and ecological conditions. Since the Rio Earth Summit in 1992, for instance, environmental activists have advanced a powerful critique of the devastating impact of overconsumption in the affluent world. Worldwide, per capita material consumption has skyrocketed over the past several decades, placing strain upon both renewable and non-renewable resources, generating tremendous amounts of waste, fraying local ecosystems, and helping to accelerate problems such as global warming, deforestation, drought, desertification, and toxic air and water pollution. While such problems are often attributed to the wayward habits of humanity as a whole, they are largely the responsibility of the world's wealthiest countries, which have enjoyed the overwhelming share of the historical consumption boom. Ironically, it is often the poorest regions of the world that bear the brunt of the environmental effects of First-World overconsumption, and that supply the cheap labour and resources that provide affluent nations with an endless stock of affordable consumer goods. In ecologically constrained

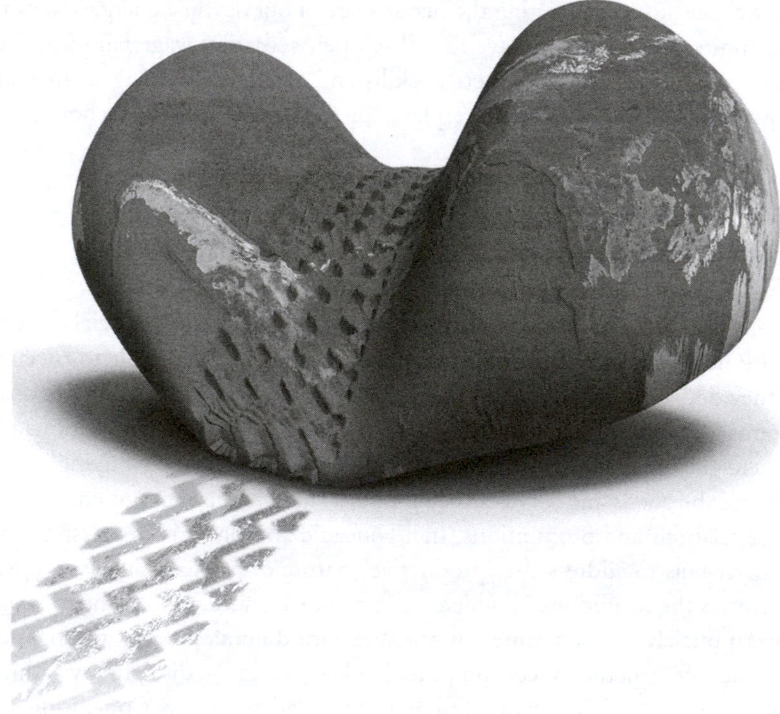

FIGURE 12.3 As this image from the magazine ***Adbusters*** suggests, we are often only dimly aware of the devastating effect current consumption patterns are having on planetary ecology. Reproduced by permission of Adbusters Media Foundation.

conditions, achieving a decent standard of living for all global citizens will require a substantial reduction in the material intensity of lifestyles in affluent nations, alongside consumption increases in poor regions now suffering from shortfalls in basic needs such as food, water, housing, clothing, education, and medical care.

In recent years, a growing popular recognition of the need to reckon with the heavy environmental and human toll of consumer society has been evident in the mounting popularity of anti-consumerist discourses, of ethical and "green" consumption practices, of fair trade and "no sweat" consumer products, and so on. While the political effectiveness of such responses to the social and environmental repercussions of overconsumption in the affluent world is ultimately in doubt, such developments should not simply be dismissed out of hand. They represent at least a partial challenge to what Marx famously referred to as "**commodity fetishism**," whereby the economic value and cultural meanings of everyday commodities are detached from any critical awareness of the exploitative conditions in which they were produced. Many people have little sense of the animal suffering behind our cutely packaged and marketed burgers and chicken nuggets, for instance, or of the exploitative conditions of the sweatshop workers who made the athletic shoes we wear with such pride at the gym. While conscientious purchasing decisions on their own cannot fundamentally reorient the global economic system, ethical and green consumerism represents at least a provisional effort to bridge the psychological and geographical distance that now divides the point of production and the point of consumption, and to ensure that the human and ecological costs of production are factored into our understanding of a product's value.

To the extent that prevailing consumption patterns are entwined with a variety of social and institutional forces, they cannot be challenged on the plane of individual consumer behaviour alone; indeed, they can only be transformed through a broad societal renegotiation of cultural values and through collective action aimed at systemic economic and political change. Insights about the value of solidarity, community-building, and collective action are an implicit part of a range of contemporary anti-consumerist social movements oriented around issues as diverse as **culture jamming**, fair trade, voluntary simplicity, downshifting, **freeganism**, slow food, media literacy, community barter systems, and beyond. As Michael Maniates (2002) and others have argued, "individualizing responsibility" for the social and ecological fallout of consumer society (by asking us to recycle more, or drive less, or buy ethically sourced goods, and so on) may offer a practical and immediate way of putting our values into action, but it ultimately steers clear of a necessary confrontation with the powerful institutions and vested interests that underpin consumption-intensive ways of life. In this sense, steering consumption practices in the direction of social justice and environmental sustainability will require us to transcend our very **subjectivity** as individuated consumers in the pseudo-democratic marketplace. Indeed, it will require us to embrace a new understanding of ourselves as active democratic subjects working together to transform the broader economic, political, and cultural conditions that underpin our consumer behaviour, restricting the fullest development of our capacities, perpetuating **exploitation**, and offering us only a pale, commodified substitute for what human fulfillment can ultimately be.

Study Questions

1. After reviewing the notion of "consumer sovereignty" and the critique advanced of it in this chapter, analyze some of the ways in which aspects of your own daily consumer behaviour are socially shaped and constrained.
2. After reviewing this chapter's discussion of the role and influence of advertising in contemporary capitalist society, develop your own analysis of a current television advertising campaign that has recently caught your attention.
3. Explain and provide examples for the assertion that consumer behaviour is unavoidably "political" in nature.

Exercises

1. Take a 3–4 day "fast" from a familiar consumer good in your everyday life (computer, phone, car, fast food, cosmetics, etc.) and reflect carefully on your experience of going without it. Did this experience give you a better "sociological" understanding of the variety of influences that condition your typical use of and relationship to this good?
2. Using the "**communicative model of consumption**" as a starting point, analyze your relationship to one particular consumer good that has traditionally carried a lot of symbolic meaning and importance for you. How and why has this good acquired the importance it has for you?
3. In your view, does transcending the problems of consumer society simply mean relinquishing all pleasure and enjoyment in life? Develop a list of qualities that define what you consider to be a satisfying, fun, and meaningful life, then try to imagine the ways in which consumer society actually impedes this kind of life. How could a post-consumerist social order actually improve our quality of life?

References

Assadourian, E. (2010). The rise and fall of consumer cultures. In *State of the World 2010: Transforming Cultures* (pp. 3–20). New York, NY: W.W. Norton.

Bauman, Z. (1988). *Freedom*. Milton Keynes, UK: Open University Press.

Bauman, Z. (2007). *Consuming life*. Cambridge, UK: Polity Press.

Dawson, M. (2003). *The consumer trap: Big business marketing in American life*. Chicago, IL: University of Illinois Press.

Dillabough, H. (2016). *Food for thought: Access to food in Canada's remote north*. Thunder Bay, ON: Northern Policy Institute. Retrieved from http://www.northernpolicy.ca/upload/documents/publications/commentaries/commentary-dillabough-food-en-print-16.0.pdf

Frank, T. (2000). *One market under God: Extreme capitalism, market populism, and the end of economic democracy*. New York, NY: Doubleday.

Hall, S. (1984). The culture gap. *Marxism Today*, *28*(1), 18–24.

Jhally, S. (Writer, Producer, Editor). (2017). *Advertising at the edge of the apocalypse* [Motion picture]. Northampton, MA: Media Education Foundation.

Kilbourne, J. (Creator). (2010). *Killing us softly 4: Advertising's image of women* [Motion picture]. Northampton, MA: Media Education Foundation.

Leonard, A. (2010). *The story of stuff*. Toronto, ON: Free Press.

Maniates, M. (2002). Individualization: Plant a tree, buy a bike, save the world? In T. Princen, M. Maniates, & K. Conca (Eds.), *Confronting consumption* (pp. 43–66). Cambridge, MA: MIT Press.

OECD. (2002). *Towards sustainable consumption: An economic conceptual framework*. Paris, France: Organisation for Economic Co-operation and Development.

Reif, S. (2008). Outlines of a critical sociology of consumption: Beyond moralism and celebration. *Sociology Compass*, *2*(2), 560–576.

Ritzer, G. (2005). *Enchanting a disenchanted world: Revolutionizing the means of consumption* (2nd ed.). Thousand Oaks, CA: Pine Forge Press.

Schor, J. (1999). *The overspent American: Why we want what we don't need*. New York, NY: Harper Perennial.

Slater, D. (2005). The sociology of consumption and lifestyle. In C.J. Calhoun, C. Rojek, & B.S. Turner (Eds.), *The Sage handbook of sociology* (pp. 174–187). London, UK: Sage Publications.

Soron, D. (2004). The politics of consumption: An interview with Juliet Schor. *Aurora: Interviews with Leading Thinkers and Writers*. Retrieved from http://aurora.icaap.org/index.php/aurora/article/view/13/24

Veblen, T. (1934). *The theory of the leisure class: An economic study of institutions*. New York, NY: Modern Library.

13 Are You Financially Fit?

MARY-BETH RADDON

A Cartwheeling Businessman

Along a bustling corridor at Brock University, a row of tables displays glossy pamphlets about personal money management. Seated behind the tables, representatives of student loan programs, credit counselling agencies, and the university's student financial services watch as students stream by on their way to classes. A poster mounted in the hallway shows workshops available at today's **Financial Literacy** Fair. Commonplace at other universities, especially during Financial Literacy Month, this November fair is an instance of widespread campaigns of year-round financial education, which are thought to improve ordinary citizens' "financial fitness."

This chapter critically examines **financial fitness** as both a policy agenda and an everyday **discourse** that promotes certain orientations toward financial life and marginalizes alternatives. On the campaign table of Brock's Financial Literacy Fair, financial fitness is visually represented on the largest brochure as an athletic white man in a dark suit turning a cartwheel on the grass beneath a cloudless sky (Credit Counselling Society, n.d.). The banner image suggests that lessons in money management provided in the brochure will prepare students to move gymnastically through life. But will they? Can learning to make a budget or select a credit card help students acquire the financial agility and sunny prospects implied by the image of the cartwheeling businessman? To help answer this question, this chapter explores where the concern for financial fitness comes from and what critics say about these programs' effectiveness. The chapter delves into the key criticism that financial literacy initiatives mainly cultivate dispositions of individualism, personal responsibility, and entrepreneurialism that reinforce the workings of neoliberal **capitalism**. The overall effect of financial literacy programs is to legitimize the dominant financial system, as financial crises and extremes of wealth and poverty are attributed to the shortcomings of ordinary people. The chapter goes on to argue that financial education needs to be much broader than lessons about personal money management. Financial education should encompass studies of the history and politics of capitalism, cultural studies of financial life, and exploration of cooperative strategies for achieving economic well-being.

The Push for Financial Fitness

Financial fitness campaigns, including university fairs, in some ways appear to be an outgrowth of the financial advice industry, to which people have turned for decades in ways befitting their financial **status**. For example, professional wealth managers have long served affluent families, while popular TV or radio personalities pitch their message to everyone wishing to attain new levels of consumption, retire from paid work, or simply get out of debt and make ends meet (Harrington, 2016; Ramsey, 2013). However, contemporary financial fitness is now a crowded field with governments and financial institutions joining professional financial experts and self-help guides, promoting financial education in more coordinated and concerted ways.

Financial literacy emerged as a policy agenda in the mid-2000s through the orchestration of international institutions such as the World Bank and Organisation for Economic Co-operation and Development (OECD, 2005; Santos, 2017). The general idea was that governments would partner with major financial corporations such as Visa Inc. to develop primary and secondary school curricula and adult education programs (Pinto & Coulson, 2011). National outcomes would be measured and survey results compared internationally. This policy agenda caught on globally as heads of **state** and finance ministers endorsed financial literacy recommendations at successive high-level meetings of the OECD, G-20, Asia-Pacific Economic Cooperation, and others. By 2015, more than 50 countries, including Canada, had followed through by adopting a national strategy for financial literacy (Financial Consumer Agency of Canada, 2015).

The Canadian government claims to be a world leader in promoting financial literacy. Canada's National Strategy for Financial Literacy—*Count Me In, Canada*—aims to "strengthen the financial well-being of Canadians and their families by empowering them to manage money and debt wisely, plan and save for the future, prevent and protect against fraud and financial abuse" (Financial Consumer Agency of Canada, 2015, p. 6). The strategy relies on partnerships between corporations, non-profit organizations, community groups, and all levels of government to deliver financial literacy programs to citizens at all life stages and financial circumstances through workshops and various media, and specifically to Canadian children through the education system. Seniors, new Canadians, social assistance recipients, **Indigenous** people, employees in large workplaces, the self-employed, people getting by on low incomes, and people struggling with debt are all among the target audiences, as are people with specific financial goals such as buying a house, saving for a child or grandchild's tuition, or saving for retirement. In other words, the policy considers financial literacy to be a universally required, lifetime process.

Officially, the impetus for national financial literacy strategies is the perception that ordinary people do not have the financial knowledge, skills, motivation, and confidence to participate effectively in the changing economy (Remund, 2010). Canadians are indeed struggling financially as indicated by the record-setting ratio of household credit market debt (credit card balances, mortgages, consumer loans, and unpaid bills) to household disposable income. By late 2017, for every dollar of household disposable income, the average household owed $1.71 (Canadian Press, 2017). This degree of indebtedness, say financial experts, is a serious warning sign about the declining strength of the national economy, which needs to be fixed by teaching people better money management (Carrick, 2017).

A second rationale for national financial literacy strategies is to help ordinary consumers keep pace with innovations in the financial sector (Financial Consumer Agency of Canada, 2015). From the early 2000s, advocates of financial literacy began to point out that people now have more financial options than in previous generations, and also more exposure to the complexity and risk of managing debt, budgeting, saving, borrowing, investing, buying insurance, making a will, and avoiding financial fraud (Remund, 2010).

At the international level, the instigators of financial literacy policy gave another reason for their push: to avoid another financial crisis like that of 2008, which wiped out trillions of dollars' worth of financial assets and plunged the global economy into prolonged recession. For senior policy advisors to the OECD, the lesson of the 2008 financial crisis was this: "At a global scale, inappropriate financial decisions, when they are generalized to a large proportion of households, can have ripple effects and may even jeopardize the stability of the whole economic and financial system" (OECD, 2009, p. 6). According to these financial experts, a basic problem at the centre of the US subprime mortgage crisis in 2008, which triggered the collapse of major financial institutions worldwide, was simply "a lack of individual financial awareness and responsibility," which needs to be remedied by making citizens financially literate (OECD, 2009, p. 4).

Fit for What?

Not everyone agrees that national financial literacy strategies are the right policy solution for individual troubles or global crises. Critics of the policy say the global financial crisis of 2008 was caused by the failure of governments to set and enforce rules on financial industries (Santos, 2017). In the first place, governments did not do enough to prevent many large financial institutions from engaging in risky, predatory, and fraudulent lending, especially mortgage lending. What made matters worse was that investment banks were allowed to sell risky financial products made up of repackaged mortgages and consumer debt. When an inflated US real estate market crashed, these investments lost their value and a cascading effect took place in financial markets around the world. To pin responsibility on the ordinary borrowers who lost their homes and life savings, critics say, is to blame the victims (Pinto, 2013; Santos, 2017).

A related, powerful critique of financial literacy programs is that they simply do not have much impact. As Pinto (2009) explains, "Overwhelmingly, research refutes the assumption that financial literacy education can shape behaviour" (p. 126). Studies of people in financial hardship confirm the lack of relevance of financial literacy programs. For example, Buckland's (2012) study of financial exclusion and poverty in Canada found that poor people may not pass standard tests of financial literacy but they are knowledgeable about the financial matters most germane to their lives. They are also just as likely as other income groups to budget (Buckland, 2012, p. 28). In another UK study, researchers explored how people with low or precarious incomes participate in payday lending, a form of high-cost, short-term credit, also known as fringe finance, which often causes debt to spiral, significantly worsening financial difficulties (Rowlingson, Appleyard, & Gardner, 2016). Qualitative interviews with customers of payday lending showed that people were quite aware that the cost of payday loans was exorbitant but felt they had little choice. Some even reasoned that it was worth it to borrow anonymously and preserve their dignity rather than borrow from family. Overall, their narratives showed that reliance on fringe finance was driven by poverty, not a lack of financial literacy.

Similar findings emerge from a quantitative study of the relationship of indebtedness to financial literacy by Statistics Canada (Chawla & Uppal, 2012). Canada's Financial Capability Survey tracks Canadians' financial characteristics, such as their income, debt, and assets, as well as their attitudes toward money management and knowledge of financial principals and practices. It turns out that household debt is statistically associated with financial literacy in a surprising way: those who score highest on a financial knowledge quiz, and also rate their money management skills most highly, tend to be those with the *most* debt. This finding holds true even when the researchers take into account demographic characteristics such as income, age, and education. It follows that financial literacy programs are not likely to solve the problem of Canadians' high debt-to-income ratio.

Critics of financial literacy argue that financial decisions are determined more by psychology and circumstances than by knowledge (Santos, 2017). Even if financial literacy did guide people toward wise decisions, literacy would not guarantee personal or social security. Increasingly, ordinary people are exposed to the volatility of financial markets: changes in interest rates, real estate prices, stock market values, and the cost of living can result in lost savings, bankruptcy, foreclosure, and eviction through no fault of the individual (Santos, 2017). People have little control over financial risks stemming from events like job loss, relationship break-up, illness, and disaster. For these reasons, skeptics of the national strategy worry that resources are going toward financial literacy at the expense of more urgent government initiatives for financial well-being such as improved regulation of financial industries, poverty reduction, labour protections, and mental health services (Pinto, 2013; Pinto & Coulson, 2011).

Marginalizing Other Ways of Being Economic

Looking more closely at standard financial literacy approaches, critics argue that such training marginalizes the very vulnerable groups that the policy promises to help. This is because financial risks and opportunities differ systemically according to **gender**, religion, and **culture**. By purporting to be value-neutral, gender-blind, and culturally universal, financial literacy programs end up casting blame on people who cannot conform to financial fitness ideals.

Most apparently, the image of the cartwheeling businessman illustrates the lack of fit with financial fitness of women as a group. Statistically, women do not have equal choice and opportunity to earn income and build equity given the gender pay and wealth gaps, which are significantly due to women's occupational segregation into fields and positions that pay less than those primarily held by men, and women's disproportionate family care responsibilities, which compel them to take time away from careers and to work fewer hours. Consequently, women are at a disadvantage when it comes to saving for retirement and benefiting from tax-reducing retirement savings programs. By not taking into account these systemic financial barriers, financial literacy programs paper over gender inequities in financial life and normalize men's financial privilege (Pinto & Coulson, 2011).

Financial literacy programs also tend to ignore cultural and religious difference. For example, much standard financial advice excludes observant Muslims who follow Shariah law as an ethical way of life. Shariah prohibits paying or receiving interest, following the Islamic teaching that Muslims should live on earned income, not seek to accumulate excessive financial wealth and not exploit others financially (Pinto & Chan,

FIGURE 13.1 Financial fitness is commonly represented as an athletic, middle-aged, white businessman. Zone Creative/iStock.

2010). As a result, commonplace financial guidance regarding conventional loans, credit cards, mortgages, and investments that are not Shariah-compliant put many observant Muslims in conflict with their faith.

Levon Ellen Blue's research of financial literacy education practices in Indigenous communities in Canada, including her own, reveals that many Indigenous people, likewise, have difficulty reconciling financial literacy with "Indigenous ways of knowing, being and doing" (Blue & Pinto, 2017, p. 59). Conventional financial literacy lessons, with their individually oriented advice about goal setting, budgeting, saving, and investing, are in tension with the value Indigenous cultures tend to place on generosity and reciprocity. Standard financial literacy texts show "a lack of understanding ... concerning family obligations, sharing of resources and other currencies, besides money, that exist in Aboriginal communities such as the exchange of natural resources" (Blue & Pinto, 2017, p. 57). Financial literacy training, with its emphasis on individual wealth accumulation and neglect of holistic decision-making, ignores these vital resources and values. The most serious implication of these gendered, religious, and cultural exclusions and departures from conventional financial literacy prescriptions is that many people, due to their nonconformity, acquire the appearance of personal failure or group pathology (Pinto & Chan, 2010).

Cultivating the Financial Citizen-Consumer

The goals of financial literacy strategies are so misplaced, critics suggest, it makes sense to understand the policy as really about an ideological project: to give legitimacy to the economic dominance of the financial sector and to shape citizens into consumer-investors (Santos, 2017). In other words, the financial literacy policy agenda appeals to governments, not because it necessarily enhances economic security, but because it cultivates the kind of citizens that best fit within finance-led neoliberal capitalism: the financially fit.

To explain this position requires a few definitions. Introduced in Chapter 1, **neoliberalism** commonly refers to the doctrine that societal arrangements are best determined by the action of markets within a capitalist system. Neoliberals oppose the kinds of government action that would limit capital accumulation, such as environmental or labour regulations on businesses, or tax-funded social programs that presumably reduce people's incentive to work. Ironically, the neoliberal **free market** creed provides a rationale for state interventions (such as **migrant** worker programs, surveillance, and policing) that enable markets to work in ways favourable to business interests (Roberts & Soederberg, 2014).

Coinciding with neoliberalism, **financialization** is another large-scale historical process. Financialization refers to the ascendancy of financial sectors of the economy over manufacturing and service sectors. More broadly, financialization draws attention to the increasing **power** of financial institutions and discourses of finance to shape and govern everyday realities. A Marxist analysis would point out that, presently, the dominant **class** interests are those of large private investors and bankers. Finance-led neoliberalism engages state power to facilitate financial markets on behalf of this financial class. Massive government bailouts of failing financial entities provide the most dramatic examples (Guard & Antony, 2009). Through such interventions, financial risks and costs are transferred from private financial firms onto governments and citizens. However, financial literacy may be understood as another, more subtle form of state intervention in the economy in order to increase participation in financial markets and to make financialization culturally acceptable, despite the growth of wealth disparities and volatility it brings (Santos, 2017).

While a Marxist lens foregrounds how neoliberalism concentrates economic power in a financial elite, as shown in Chapter 1, a Foucauldian perspective reveals how **governmental power** works through personal **agency**. The Foucaudian **concept** of **responsibilization** describes the process of constructing people as responsible, self-managing moral agents (Shamir, 2008). Financial literacy programs cultivate financial fitness primarily through such an emphasis on personal responsibility. For example, the introduction to Canada's National Strategy for Financial Literacy emphasizes a message of personal responsibility:

> Just as being able to read opens a world of possibilities, financial literacy enables you to better understand financial matters on both a personal and large scale. It enables you to apply that knowledge and *assume responsibility for financial decisions now and in the future*. That's what this strategy is about. (Financial Consumer Agency of Canada, 2015, p. 5, emphasis added)

Governance by responsibilization comes about, not through the top-down exercise of power such as the enforcement of legal or bureaucratic rules, but through self-regulation. Responsibilized people act as though whatever befalls them is a consequence of their own action or inaction. Financial literacy responsibilizes when it teaches that individuals must pay their credit card balance in full each month, grow a nest egg for retirement, and avoid relying on state income supports. Failing to be responsible in these ways reflects individual weakness and immorality, while other significant explanations are set aside.

The discourse of financial fitness also activates an ethic of constant self-improvement coupled with an empowered, confident attitude toward personal finance. *Count Me In, Canada* offers this challenge to everyone: "As an individual Canadian, you are invited to make financial learning a lifelong endeavour" (Financial Consumer Agency of Canada, 2015, p. 16). Thus, financial fitness produces the image of its practitioners as "**entrepreneurs of the self**" (du Gay, 2000). Du Gay explains that fulfilling this image means acting toward oneself as though one's life is a business enterprise and oneself is the owner and manager: "Once a human life is conceived of primarily in entrepreneurial terms, the 'owner' of that life becomes individually responsible for their own self-advancement and care; within the ideals of enterprise, individuals are charged with managing the conduct of the business of their own lives" (du Gay, 2000, p. 120). Financially self-managing, entrepreneurial people are in turn seen to sustain and enlarge the financial economy.

Unpacking the discourse of financial fitness, we can see how financial literacy produces financialization by creating responsible, entrepreneurial subjects who are expected to serve the national economy by actively seeking individual, knowledge-based solutions to financial vulnerability throughout their lives. Laura Pinto (2013) observes that financial literacy policy does not call upon the financial sector to be responsible for its contribution to economic instability and crisis.

Financial literacy programs teach limited forms of financial knowledge. The remainder of this chapter recommends three broader arenas for financial education: historical knowledge of finance-led neoliberal capitalism, cultural analysis of shifting patterns within our everyday financial lives, and practical knowledge of financial alternatives in the present.

Financial Education: Beyond the Personal

First, financial education should pay attention to how the present neoliberal economic order arose through the dismantling of the previous governmental arrangement, known as **Keynesianism**. Keynesianism got its name from the British economist John Maynard Keynes (1883–1946), who was concerned with the widespread unemployment of the 1920s and 1930s. Keynesian theory holds that full employment is possible if governments act to stimulate economic demand through social spending during times of recession. Following World War II, the advanced capitalist states were spurred to adopt models of Keynesianism, partly under pressure from **working class** movements for economic justice, and partly due to competition with the Soviet Union, which represented an alternative economic model. These governments' common **objective** was achieving economic growth by actively managing the economy and providing stable conditions for industry and employment within a capitalist framework.

Keynesian policies did achieve steady economic growth and enable rising standards of living for the general population from 1945 to the early 1970s. These policies were designed to foster high wages, decent working conditions, stable employment, predictable pensions, and a social safety net of unemployment insurance, welfare, and disability benefits. In Canada, it was during this period that labour-friendly legislation was passed and major social programs, such as state-provided universal health insurance, were introduced.

Keynesian fiscal policy encouraged governments to go into deficit during times of recession when people lacked money or were reluctant to spend. In such times, governments would spend public money on programs that were considered of broad social benefit. This injection of new money would encourage consumer spending, which would create demand for goods and services, stimulating production. As growth ensued, Keynesian theory directed governments to reduce spending and pay off debt, thus withdrawing money from the economy in order to avoid inflation. However, in the early 1970s, the Keynesian economies encountered a significant wave of inflation to which they could not easily respond, especially after the world price of oil spiked in 1973 and again in 1978.

The economic troubles of the 1970s opened the way for pro-business activists, working through well-funded policy think tanks, to aggressively challenge the Keynesian model with neoliberalism (Carroll & Shaw, 2001). Neoliberal governments came to power with the goal of radically transforming the Keynesian welfare state, restoring political power to elites and instituting new rules of capitalism that would favour the financial sector (Dumenil & Levy, 2005).

Studies of neoliberalism often emphasize privatization, which describes the policy of transferring public-sector, tax-funded, government-provided services to private-sector organizations who bid for government contracts or charge user fees to deliver these services. Privatization also refers to governments selling public assets to private businesses to be commercialized. In an illuminating analysis, Colin Crouch (2008) identifies the neoliberal financial system as another form of privatization. Crouch explains that, under neoliberalism, the economic stimulus function of government was increasingly privatized when individual consumer debt grew into an instrument for maintaining consumer demand and smoothing out market instability. Whereas under Keynesianism, governments took on debt to stimulate the economy, low- and middle-income individuals increasingly came to perform this function through their record levels of borrowing. In the 1990s, governments permitted financial institutions to make it easier for people to qualify for credit cards, personal lines of credit, consumer loans, student loans, and home mortgages. Only since the 2008 financial crisis has the Canadian government gradually introduced tighter mortgage qualifications to protect borrowers who are vulnerable to even a moderate rise in historically low interest rates. However, throughout the neoliberal period, in the face of stagnated or falling real wages, low- and middle-income households have maintained their standard of living by going into debt. In doing so, their consumer spending has provided economic stimulus to combat recession (Buckland, 2012; Crouch, 2008).

In the process of privatizing financial stimulus, risks associated with non-repayment of debt have also been privatized or, in other words, transferred from the state onto households. In a short video for *The Guardian*, anthropologist David Graeber (2015) explains that this rebalancing of debt from public to private ends up saddling people who have little alternative but to buy on credit, take out student loans, or turn to payday lenders. Compared to public debt owned by governments, such private household debt is a boon to financial institutions, which charge individual borrowers much higher interest rates and fees.

The Poor Pay More

"The Poor Pay More," a field project for sociology students created by Kimberly Folse (2002), adds a twist to mainstream financial literacy programs by demonstrating that financial **exploitation** is a penalty of poverty no matter what your level of financial literacy. You may complete the field project independently, with a partner, or in a small group.

To examine how the poor pay more, comparison shop for a large appliance such as a refrigerator, washing machine, or electric range by visiting a rent-to-own store such as Rent-A-Center or EasyHome. Ask about payment options, fees, and interest charges. What happens if the appliance breaks before it is paid off? What if the customer misses a payment or is unable to keep making payments? Do your best to calculate how much the appliance costs, keeping track of any assumptions.

Next, find the same appliance at a major retail outlet. This time, determine the cost of the appliance if you could afford to purchase it with cash or with a credit card that you paid in full before the end of the month.

Finally, estimate your costs if you decided to delay the appliance purchase for six months in order to save enough to buy it without store credit or renting-to-own. For example, how much would you spend if you had to rely on take-out food rather than cooking at home? How does the cost of a coin-operated Laundromat compare with using your own washing machine? Could you afford to live without a refrigerator and freezer? Reflect on what you learned from your investigation into how the poor pay more.

Financial Education: The Financialization of Everyday Life

A second need is for financial education to teach how financial culture has come to pervade everyday life. We have seen how neoliberal policies have eroded economic supports and led people to go into debt or attempt to invest for their future retirement, health needs, or children's education. In addition, more people have a direct stake in the performance of global financial markets through share ownership, mutual funds, or occupational pension plans. The extent of our routine financial participation has required that we shift our thinking from finance as a system that acts upon us from "out there" to finance as a discursive domain threaded through everyday life (de Goede, 2005). What might seem like technical theories of bankers, investment brokers, or economists come to shape how we speak and think about finance, our financial decisions, and actions, and what we then take as objective financial reality (Pryke &

Du Gay, 2007). For example, daily news media reports of stock market indexes are presented as more significant measures of national economic health than increases in employment or wage levels. Stock market performance is less tangible or immediate to most people compared to rates of joblessness, housing costs, or food bank use, yet when analysts report on financial market upticks, many take this as a meaningful signal to spend, borrow, or invest (Martin, 2009).

Changes in financial discourses over time have also shaped the impetus to spend, borrow, and invest. For example, cultural understandings of savings and debt underwent a shift, beginning in the 1980s in the United States and the United Kingdom (Langley, 2008). Prior to that time, depositing earnings in savings accounts and purchasing insurance were seen to demonstrate the virtues of hard work, thrift, and prudence associated with deep-rooted Puritan culture. More recently, financial products for the everyday investor have proliferated and people are advised to prioritize investing over saving. At the same time, consumer credit has become available to groups with increasing risk of default, including members of low-income households, those with precarious employment, seniors, and students. The acceptability of consumer credit, in the form of credit cards, lines of credit, rent-to-own financing, auto loans, and so on, has required a break with Puritan morality and a severing of the connection of earning to spending (Langley, 2008; Manning, 2000). Financial culture has habituated people to debt so that decision-making about borrowing, debt consolidation, and repayment is considered an ordinary activity that builds financial fitness.

In another example over a longer timeframe, people's everyday investment emerged through a historical process of making investment seem rational, trustworthy, and morally legitimate (Preda, 2009). Writing about the history of financial morality, Marieke de Goede (2005) illustrates this perspective "of financial discourse as performatively constructing the reality it is supposed to measure and analyze" (pp. 179–180). She traces moral discourses over two centuries in Europe and the United States to understand how modern finance gained its current reputation as an economically necessary, scientifically respectable, natural reality. In the 19th century, the principled way of gaining wealth was through industry. Financial investment was considered immoral because it was seen to be like gambling, and swindling was widespread. Dissociating finance from the vices of gambling and fraud occurred through a slow process of rewriting anti-gambling laws, conceiving of risk as calculable, and establishing professional legitimacy for financial speculators. This moral and political struggle to create a domain of normal finance is ongoing because there are still connections between gambling and financial investing, as we see in the common depiction of financial transactions as taking place in a "high-speed electronic casino" (Roberts & Soederberg, 2014, p. 659). However, in everyday life, a new financial ethos has emerged in which investment appears as the most rational and responsible way to provide for future needs. These examples of changes to financial morality illustrate how cultural interpretations of everyday borrowing and investing are integral to financialization. The growth of global financial markets, in other words, cannot operate without discourses about finance such as financial fitness.

Financial Education: For the Solidarity Economy

The third arena where education is needed instead of literacy is in thinking about alternatives to finance-led neoliberal capitalism. Financial literacy programs teach that economic security depends on how skillfully we act as personal investors and consumers of financial services, yet the financialization of the economy in recent decades has generated insecurity as well as dramatic **inequality** (McNally, 2009). Whereas financial literacy programs seek to instil confidence about borrowing and investing, enmeshment in financial markets has *undermined* confidence that other kinds of economic politics are possible (Castells, 2017; Gibson-Graham, Cameron, & Healy, 2013). Fortunately, many groups are working together and educating each other on how to create ethical systems of production, exchange, and consumption outside or alongside the dominant economy (Miller, 2010). These diverse initiatives may be described under the umbrella term "**solidarity economy**" because they tend to share values of mutual support, cooperation, ecological sustainability, equity, and social justice.

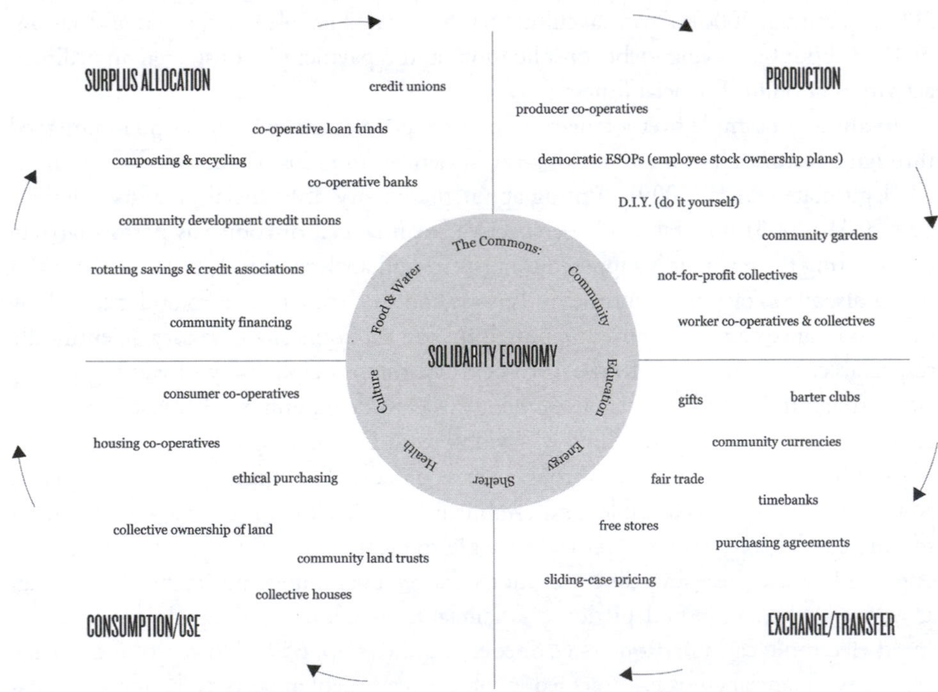

FIGURE 13.2 Many types of economic activity foster social values such as cooperation and community well-being. Taken together, these projects and practices make up the solidarity economy. They contrast with the dominant economy's singular emphasis on financial wealth accumulation. Reproduced by permission of SolidarityNYC and Ethan Miller.

One such movement that represents a departure from financial fitness and exemplifies the solidarity economy is called **slow money**. An outgrowth of the "slow food" movement, slow money is a model of community financing (Tasch, 2010). Investors want to know where their money goes when it is invested, so they put it into diversified, sustainable local food systems, among other types of local enterprises. They reject the dictate of financial fitness that high monetary rates of return should be the primary criteria for financial decisions. Reflecting on enterprises that have attracted slow money investors in the US, Jane Collins (2017) explains, "As an investment strategy, Slow Money … encouraged investors to think of a thriving local economy, a beloved landscape, or meaningful community relationships as part of their return" (p. 87). In other words, these investors understand that their long-term financial interests cannot be separated from their interest in food security, ecological health, and local economic vitality. Seeing that global capital markets undermine these interests, slow money investors instead support small food enterprises, organic farms, farmers' markets, and restaurants that serve locally grown food.

Another movement within the solidarity economy is the movement for local currencies. Local currencies can circulate parallel to the national currency and reduce people's dependence on scarce dollars. The national currency flows to where it may be invested for the highest return, but a **local currency** keeps wealth circulating within intentionally designed exchange networks (North, 2007). A basic form of local exchange is an organized gift-giving arrangement. Swap meets where people are invited to come with goods to give away are an example. Mutual credit schemes are a more highly organized local currency, which often operate as online barter networks with a system of points for keeping track of value. Paper currencies are yet another model. Local currencies are commonly exchanged for personal services, but many independent businesses also agree to accept and spend them because "community bucks" connect the business with a pool of potential customers, workers, and other compatible businesses. The significance of local currencies is that they increase the buying and earning power, mutual support, and economic agency of the people that circulate them.

In summary, financial education with this triple focus—on large structures of financialized capitalism, on everyday life, and on practical alternatives—goes well beyond financial literacy by examining how economic power works and the possibilities for change. This chapter has shown how the growing rate of personal debt among Canadians is a structural feature of the economy that has partially replaced government debt-stimulus programs in the transition from Keynesianism to neoliberalism. This shift in the debt burden, which Crouch (2008) termed "privatized Keynesianism," would not have been possible, however, without a change in our everyday morality of spending, borrowing, and investing, and a new orientation to financial fitness. Financialization is not a stable or complete process, not only because of the recurrent crises that arise, but also because of the dependence of financial authority on tenuous discourses such as financial fitness, which can be broken down and resisted by practicing alternatives to financialization. Movements within the solidarity economy such as slow money and local currencies represent other avenues to financial security than the individual practices of financial literacy. Solidarity economy initiatives involve people meeting a variety of needs through organizing. They demonstrate that economic life can be organized around different values to those of mainstream financial literacy, including the value of cooperation.

Study Questions

1 How have strategies for financial fitness come to be normalized and come to have such a prominent social value? As we practice financial fitness, how are we inside of power?

2 Visit two or three financial literacy websites such as the following:
http://prospercanada.org
https://www.getsmarteraboutmoney.ca
http://www.practicalmoneyskills.ca
http://finfit.ca
How do these sites represent people as self-responsible consumers of financial services and as "entrepreneurs of the self"? What is missing in these approaches to financial literacy? How would you imagine financial education as broader than these lessons in financial literacy?

3 What attitudes and orientations toward education, work, social relationships, and the purpose of life does financial fitness promote? See the 18th-century aphorisms of Benjamin Franklin for an illustration of Puritan morality at <https://www.poorrichards.net>. How does the morality of financial fitness diverge from the Puritan virtues of frugality, thrift, prudence, and hard work? How would you describe the relationship between these shifting cultural conceptions of economic virtue and transformations in global financial markets?

Exercises

1 Learn about the solidarity economy through an interview by Esteban Kelly with Farah Tanis and Jessica Gordon Nembhard about cooperation in African American communities: https://www.youtube.com/watch?v=EpsZw6vsH4A

Next explore a series of short videos created for SolidarityNYU called "Portraits of the Solidarity Economy": http://solidaritynyc.org/#/videos.

How are the people featured in these videos pursuing economic security through cooperation? How do such collective practices represent a form of everyday resistance to discourses of financial fitness? How is such resistance a potential resource in movements for economic justice? Which of the projects showcased in the videos seem the most promising to you?

2 In a group of 5 to 20 people, make a list of group members' resources and skills. Next make a second list of resources and services that members want. If the items on the first list were "offers" and those on the second list "wishes," how many matches might be made? Can you think of a method to keep score of the value of exchanges in your group so that fairness in giving and receiving does not require equal two-way barter? In other words, invent some form of currency so that exchange does not depend on two people offering items of equal value and each wanting what the other has. Research a local currency project online, such as LETS (mutual credit exchange systems), Time Dollars (community service credits), or a paper currency. How did your exchange system compare to one of these models? How might such projects invite us to re-imagine money?

3 Financial literacy training relies on assorted online calculators to help people predict their future financial status: loan and mortgage calculators, savings calculators, budget calculators, retirement income calculators, and so on. Sociologists Mark R. Rank and Tom Hirschl have turned the standard tool kit of financial literacy on its head by creating the Poverty Risk Calculator, <https://confrontingpoverty.org/poverty-risk-calculator/>. This tool estimates an individual American's risk of experiencing near-poverty, poverty, and extreme poverty over the next 5, 10, and 15 years. To use the calculator, submit a profile with five key sociological variables: your age, race, gender, education, and marital status. What do you learn about the risk of poverty when you create different profiles?

4 The Poverty Risk Calculator <https://confrontingpoverty.org/poverty-risk-calculator/> shows that poverty is pervasive and systemic, and the root cause is not the personal deficiencies of poor people. Explore the discussion guide on the website to help you think about possible solutions to poverty. What importance do you place on financial literacy strategies? What other individual, collective, and political actions would you advocate?

References

Blue, L.E., & Pinto, L.E. (2017). Other ways of being: Challenging dominant financial literacy discourses in Aboriginal context. *Australian Educational Researcher, 44*(1), 55–70.

Buckland, J. (2012). *Hard choices: Financial exclusion, fringe banks and poverty in urban Canada*. Toronto, ON: University of Toronto Press.

Canadian Press. (2017, December 14). Canadians now owe $1.71 for every $1 of disposable income they earn: That's a new high. *Financial Post*. Retrieved from http://business.financialpost.com/personal-finance/debt/debt-to-household-income-ratio-rises-in-third-quarter-to-171-per-cent

Carrick, R. (2017, March 25). The ticking time bomb: Financial literacy must tackle our borrowing behaviour. *The Globe and Mail*. Retrieved from https://www.theglobeandmail.

com/globe-investor/investor-education/financial-literacy-strategy-must-tackle-canadians-borrowing-behaviour/article24866625/

Carroll, W.K., & Shaw, M. (2001). Consolidating a neoliberal policy bloc in Canada, 1976 to 1996. *Canadian Public Policy, 27*(2), 195–217.

Castells, M. (Ed.). (2017). *Another economy is possible: Culture and economy in a time of crisis.* Cambridge, UK: Polity Press.

Chawla, R.K., & Uppal, S. (2012). Household debt in Canada. *Perspectives on Labour and Income, 24*(2). Statistics Canada Catalogue no. 75-001-XIE. Retrieved from https://www.statcan.gc.ca/pub/75-001-x/2012002/article/11636-eng.pdf

Collins, J.L. (2017). *The politics of value: Three movements to change how we think about the economy.* Chicago, IL: University of Chicago Press.

Credit Counselling Society. (n.d.). Money management basics: 7 steps that will help you build a budget that works. New Westminister, BC. Retrieved from https://www.mymoneycoach.ca/_Library/docs/CC_MMB_WEB2.pdf

Crouch, C. (2008). What will follow the demise of privatised Keynesianism? *Political Quarterly, 79*(4), 476–487.

De Goede, M. (2005). *Virtue, fortune and faith: A genealogy of finance.* Minneapolis, MN: University of Minnesota Press.

Du Gay, P. (2000). Representing "globalization": Notes on the discursive orderings of economic life. In P. Gilroy (Ed.), *Without guarantees: In honour of Stuart Hall* (pp. 113–125). London, UK: Verso.

Dumenil, G., & Levy, D. (2005). The neoliberal (counter-)revolution. In A. Saad-Filho & D. Johnston (Eds.), *Neoliberalism: A critical reader* (pp. 9–19). London, UK: Pluto Press.

Financial Consumer Agency of Canada. (2015). *National strategy for financial literacy: Count me in, Canada.* Retrieved from https://www.canada.ca/en/financial-consumer-agency/programs/financial-literacy/financial-literacy-strategy.html

Folse, K. (2002). The poor pay more. *Teaching Sociology, 30*(3), 342–347.

Gibson-Graham, J.K., Cameron, J., & Healy, S. (2013). *Take back the economy: An ethical guide for transforming our communities.* Minneapolis, MN: University of Minnesota Press.

Graeber, D. (2015, October 28). Britain is heading for another 2008 crash: Here's why. *The Guardian.* Retrieved from https://www.theguardian.com/commentisfree/2015/oct/28/2008-crash-government-economic-growth-budgetary-surplus

Guard, J., & Antony, W. (Eds.). (2009). *Bankruptcies and bailouts.* Halifax, NS: Fernwood Publishing.

Harrington, B. (2016). *Capital without borders: Wealth managers and the one per cent.* Cambridge, MA: Harvard University Press.

Langley, P. (2008). *The everyday life of global finance: Saving and borrowing in anglo-America.* Oxford, UK: Oxford University Press.

Manning, R.D. (2000). *Credit card nation: The consequences of America's addiction to credit.* New York, NY: Basic Books.

Martin, R. (2009). The twin towers of financialization: Entanglements of political and cultural economies. *Global South, 3*(1), 108–125.

McNally, D. (2009). Inequality, the profit system and global crisis. In J. Guard & W. Antony (Eds.), *Bankruptcies and bailouts* (pp. 32–45). Halifax, NS: Fernwood Publishing.

Miller, E. (2010). Solidarity economy: Key concepts and issues. In E. Kawano, T. Masterson, & J. Teller-Ellsberg (Eds.), *Solidarity economy I: Building alternatives for people and planet* (pp. 25–41). Amherst, MA: Center for Popular Economics.

North, P. (2007). *Money and liberation: The micropolitics of alternative currency movements*. Minneapolis, MN: University of Minnesota Press.

OECD. (2005). *Recommendation on principles and good practices for financial education and awareness*. Retrieved from http://www.oecd.org/daf/fin/financial-education/35108560.pdf

OECD. (2009). *Financial education and the crisis: Policy paper and guidance*. Retrieved from http://www.oecd.org/finance/financial-education/50264221.pdf

Pinto, L.E. (2009). Is financial literacy education the solution to credit crises? *Our Schools/Our Selves, 18*(4), 123–133.

Pinto, L.E. (2013). When politics trump evidence: Financial literacy education narratives following the global financial crisis. *Journal of Education Policy, 28*(1), 95–120. https://doi.org/10.1080/02680939.2012.690163

Pinto, L.E., & Chan, H. (2010). Social justice and financial literacy. *Our Schools/Our Selves, 19*(2), 61–77.

Pinto, L.E., & Coulson, E. (2011). Social justice and the gender politics of financial literacy education. *Journal of the Canadian Association for Curriculum Studies, 9*(2), 54–85.

Preda, A. (2009). *Framing finance: The boundaries of markets and modern capitalism*. Chicago, IL: University of Chicago Press.

Pryke, M., & du Gay, P. (2007). Take an issue: Cultural economy and finance. *Economy and Society, 36*(3), 339–354.

Ramsey, D. (2013). *The total money makeover: A proven plan for financial fitness*. Nashville: Thomas Nelson.

Remund, D.L. (2010). Financial literacy explicated: The case for a clearer definition in an increasingly complex economy. *Journal of Consumer Affairs, 44*(2), 276–295. https://doi.org/10.1111/j.1745-6606.2010.01169.x

Roberts, A., & Soederberg, S. (2014). Politicizing debt and denaturalizing the "new normal." *Critical Sociology, 40*(5), 657–668.

Rowlingson, K., Appleyard, L., & Gardner, J. (2016). Payday lending in the UK: The regul(aris)ation of a necessary evil? *Journal of Social Policy, 45*(3), 527–543. https://doi.org/10.1017/S0047279416000015

Santos, A.C. (2017). Cultivating the self-reliant and responsible individual: The material culture of financial literacy. *New Political Economy, 22*(4), 410–422. https://doi.org/10.1080/13563467.2017.1259302

Shamir, R. (2008). The age of responsibilization: On market-embedded morality. *Economy and Society, 37*(1), 1–19.

Tasch, W. (2010). *Inquiries into the nature of slow money: Investing as if food, farms and fertility matter*. White River Junction, VT: Chelsea Green.

14 Let's Get a Coffee

GAVIN FRIDELL and ERIKA KOSS

If you drank a cup of coffee today, it probably seemed like a normal thing to do. And in many ways it was. Coffee drinking is pervasive in Canada. While patterns do vary based on such things as age, **class**, **ethnicity**, or **gender** (men, for example, tend to drink more coffee than women), in general, all social groups have embraced coffee. Among adults 18 to 79, coffee is the most consumed beverage in Canada, more than tap water, bottled water, tea, alcohol, milk, juice, or pop.[1] The French social theorist Michel Foucault, however, might challenge this **normalization**, viewing it as an effective means of social **regulation** in contemporary Western societies that masks the operations of **power**. After all, for the majority of human history one could not just drop by a local café and buy a coffee, or make a cup of coffee at home. If you lived in a place where coffee is grown in abundance today (like Brazil, Vietnam, or Colombia), you'd be hard pressed to find any coffee at all. If you lived in a non-tropical region (like Canada, the United States, Sweden, or the United Kingdom), the chances of being able to buy a coffee would be extremely low. Five hundred years ago, the world did not have millions of coffee farmers and workers, and coffee was not processed, shipped, stored, roasted, and sold on a massive scale in restaurants, cafés, and retail stores (which did not exist). Therefore, a deeper look into the history of coffee reveals a web of social relations that reproduce **capitalism** and power. Such relations include the consumer's choice of where to purchase and drink one's coffee, which may—however unconsciously—reinforce class **status** and formulations of identity.

These social organizations of power did not emerge through a random process. Today, it's hard to imagine a more everyday global **commodity**, produced in more than 75 countries and consumed in even more, that links the daily routine of millions of people often thousands of kilometres apart. This linkage is not a simple one where a farmer sells a coffee bean to a consumer; it's unlikely that most Northern consumers will ever meet a coffee farmer. This is because the global market masks the relationship between producers and consumers and everyone in between. On supermarket shelves, consumers are faced with abstract commodities, packed with marketing messages that say little about who specifically produces the product. This is what Karl Marx famously termed "**commodity fetishism**"—the commodity itself becomes fetishized as an independent object with its own intrinsic value—a "bag of coffee"—rather than being the end result of the work of other people (Fridell, 2007; Hudson, Hudson, & Fridell, 2013; Marx, 1978, pp. 319–329).

One way to look beyond commodity fetishism is to recognize that millions of producers and consumers, as well as retail and restaurant workers, traders, shippers, processors, investors, financiers, marketers, and powerful CEOs, are linked together through what Ben Fine and others have termed a global "**system of provision** (SOP)" (Bayliss, Fine, & Robertson, 2013; Brooks, 2015; Fine, 2013). Through the SOP, coffee travels from multiple sites of production and consumption to then be transformed into a global commodity. Key to this process is the complex "material culture" embedded in coffee beans (Bayliss et al., 2013). While it is common to consider consumer decisions as rooted in individual, rational economic calculations, individual consumption patterns are embedded in wider collective **norms** and cultural meanings. Similarly, what we choose to consume is not solely cultural, but also material, involving questions of production along with distribution, transportation, and retail. To buy coffee, it must first be available, and then it must be affordable or accessible.

So how did we get to a situation where coffee is as widely consumed as it is today? To understand this, and to challenge what may be considered "normal," let's look back at hundreds of years of historical change that links to today's world of coffee. In this chapter, we do this by first examining the history of coffee production, interwoven with histories of **colonialism** and capitalism, and by then exploring the rise of coffee's consumption and mass marketing. Finally, we conclude by highlighting three instances where historically and socially rooted inequalities in the coffee industry have been contested and changed.

Part I: Coffee Production from Colonialism to Capitalism

For hundreds of years, coffee production and trade was dominated by Yemen and Ethiopia, where it was cultivated for a variety of purposes and traded on a regional basis (Topik, 2009). It was not until the second half of the 17th century that coffee emerged as a significant globally traded commodity as part of the expansion of European colonialism and slavery. The Dutch Empire took the lead in growing coffee in its conquered colonies in South and East Asia, where they violently enslaved native populations. The **exploitation** of slave labour allowed Dutch colonizers to sell coffee beans cheaply on European markets, sparking increasing demand, which in turn led to expanded production and the growing use of slaves (Pendergrast, 2010, pp. 7–21). Rising demand for coffee attracted the interest of other European empires and provided further impetus to the Atlantic slave trade, which had originally been initiated by the Portuguese but by the 18th century was dominated by the British and the French. From 1701 to 1810, European **colonial** powers drove a massive expansion of the slave trade, involving the systematic dehumanization, kidnapping, and forced transportation of more than six million people from Africa, more than in the previous two and a half centuries. So terribly were the enslaved captives treated that millions died on the journey itself and never made it across the Atlantic (Dicum & Luttinger, 2006, p. 196; Pendergrast, 2010, pp. 22–23; Wolf, 1997, p. 196).

In the 19th century, the growth of industrial capitalism transformed the world coffee trade, initiating an unprecedented increase in demand for coffee and other tropical crops (such as sugar, tea, bananas, and cocoa) to meet the consumption needs of the growing **working class**. Previous forms of agricultural production, which frequently involved largely self-sufficient economic units, big or small, were replaced by monoculture plantations dependent on growing goods for sale on the international market (Fridell, 2014; Wolf, 1997). At the same time, many coffee-producing countries gained political independence from colonial powers—much of Latin America gained formal independence from Spain and Portugal in the 1820s. Neither the expansion of capitalism nor the emergence of national independence, however, altered the brutal working and living conditions of workers. In Brazil, for example, the growth of production on giant plantations gave way to an unprecedented increase in slavery. By 1850, Brazil produced nearly half of the world's coffee supply with its enslaved population of more than two million people (Pendergrast, 2010, pp. 21–24).

In Central America, where many self-sufficient **Indigenous** populations did not need or desire waged labour, the political and economic elite coerced them into debt peonage or onerous tenant relations, stripped them of their communal lands, and forced them to work on coffee plantations under the barrel of a gun (Fridell, 2014; McCreery, 2003; Topik, 2009). Throughout much of the coffee world, capitalist social relations (including private property, **wage labour**, and a culture of possessive individualism) expanded through the dispossession and exploitation of Indigenous peoples. This is similar to the Canadian context (discussed in Chapters 1, 2, and 15), except that by the second half of the 19th century the Canadian settler-state placed growing emphasis on dispossession, determining that it "required first and foremost *land*, and only secondarily the **surplus value** afforded by cheap, Indigenous labour" (Coulthard, 2014, p. 12). In Latin America, both labour and land were essential to the spread of the coffee economy, involving forced labour on plantations alongside widespread smallholder cultivation from communities with claims to the land prior to the coffee boom. Owners of small farms often provided forced or waged labour for the plantations (Samper, 1994). In the 20th century, waged labour gradually became predominant, although under highly exploitative and unequal conditions.

Gross inequalities of class, **race**, and gender frequently led to resistance, rebellion, or demands for reform, which the elite often fiercely and violently suppressed (Fridell, 2014, pp. 37–43; Handy, 1994).

Today, despite changing political landscapes in several coffee countries that have carried out some liberal democratic reforms since the 1990s, coffee farmer-producers continue to toil at the bottom of a highly unequal global social class hierarchy. They get very little of the wealth created by the **commodification** of coffee beans, since the bulk flows to local middle agents (who often monopolize local transportation and credit), powerful plantation owners (who employ low-paid workers and possess significant economic and political resources), and, above all, massive transnational coffee companies who make enormous profits by dominating higher "value-added" activities (roasting, trading, processing, distribution, packaging, marketing, retailing). After farmers sell their coffee cherries, they receive only a small proportion of what will be sold as a bag of roasted beans or liquid beverage (Daviron & Ponte, 2005; Fridell, 2014; Talbot, 2004). In 2015, of the final share of the end consumer price, Northern supermarkets received $8.11/kg for coffee beans, while Colombian farmers received only $1.10/kg—meaning the supermarket share was over 700 per cent more than what coffee farmers received (Oxfam International, 2018, p. 76).

While the global coffee industry generates immense wealth at the top, rural workers compete in saturated labour markets for low-paid, seasonal jobs. In 2016, investigative journalism from the independent Danish group Danwatch reported that some plantations in Minas Gerais, Brazil's largest coffee-producing state, rely on a low-paid, **migrant** labour force. Many workers end up in debt bondage, tied to the plantation, or faced with significant health risks—although Brazil legally requires workers to wear protective gear when spraying toxic pesticides, plantation owners do not adhere to this law (Hansen, 2016a). Such conditions also exist in Guatemala, where women and Indigenous migrants remain particularly vulnerable. Migrant workers often have their identity papers confiscated by plantation owners, forcing them to remain tied to the plantation. At times under the watch of armed guards, workers have been forced to mix dangerous pesticides or include their children in the picking of coffee cherries, since the daily pay is based on volume (Hansen, 2016b). Such illegal violations—alongside challenges of food insecurity, the lack of clean water, and deplorable sleeping arrangements—lead to conditions for some coffee workers that are analogous to slavery (Hansen, 2016a, 2016b).

Part II: Coffee and Mass Consumption

As with coffee production, consumption patterns today emerged from a long historical process characterized by unequal wealth and social power. Coffee's centrality to Northern diets was by no means inevitable or "natural" (Topik, 2009). In major Northern coffee markets, coffee was not introduced on a significant scale until the 17th century

FIGURE 14.1 A branch of unripe (green) and ripe (red) coffee cherries from a coffee plantation in the Kona coffee region of Hawai'i's big island. © Erika Koss.

and did not really take off until the 18th and 19th centuries. Several interrelated historic factors helped drive mass coffee consumption.

First, increased coffee consumption required expanded production on a mass scale, to drive up supply and drive down prices. As indicated in the previous section, coffee production has been kept cheap through highly exploited labour. This has not only been the case on farms where coffee cherries are picked, but also at processing stations or mills, where workers are employed to clean, de-shell, and classify green beans prior to export, or where workers roast, package, market, and distribute the beans to coffee markets. Historically, coffee companies have utilized a variety of methods to keep the wages low, such as drawing on piecework and seasonal employment, where wages and benefits are typically lower than with permanent jobs. Due to gendered inequalities and the gendered division of labour, women workers in both the Global North and Global South have often disproportionately held informal, seasonal, or casual jobs; have been paid much less than male counterparts for the same work; have endured sexual harassment on the job; and have been faced with the "double burden" of working outside of the home while still being disproportionately responsible for reproductive, unpaid work in the household (Dore, 2003; Food Chain Workers Alliance & Solidarity Research

Cooperative, 2016; Fowler-Salamini, 2002; Kurian, 2003; McCreery, 2003; Samper, 1994; Tallontire, Dolan, Smith, & Barrientos, 2005).

Non-farm jobs in coffee may now be improving, especially in specialty roasteries or cafés. Yet, while some companies like Starbucks have a reputation for providing better wages and benefits than their competitors, the food industry in general remains among those sectors with the lowest wages and least benefits (Kelly, Electris, Lang, & Bhandal, 2012). A recent report from the Food Chain Workers Alliance and Solidarity Research Cooperative (2016) documents the jobs of 21.5 million workers in the food system (in production, processing, distribution, retail, and service), the largest employment sector in the United States. Despite stressful and demanding jobs, food chain workers frequently lack benefits such as healthcare, face unpredictable and erratic schedules, receive the lowest hourly median wage for frontline workers of all industries, and rely on public assistance to meet basic needs—nearly 2.8 million food workers received food stamps in 2016. The situation is even worse for women and people of colour, with Black women earning 42 cents for every dollar earned by white men working in US food chains (Food Chain Workers Alliance & Solidarity Research Cooperative, 2016, p. 19).

Second, the emergence of a new urban working class, initially in England where industrial capitalism first developed, played a major role in the expansion and normalization of coffee consumption. The working class became the basis for a mass consumer market in cheap everyday goods, such as clothing and food. Under the new factory system, men, women, and children were employed outside the home for long hours, leaving little time to prepare and eat meals. Coffee could be brewed quickly, would not spoil easily, and was seen as a replacement for alcohol. While alcohol can lead to "idle" or aggressive behaviour, coffee contains caffeine, a stimulant than works on the brain to provide temporary energy and alertness, something welcomed by capitalists for its compatibility with the emerging work discipline of the factory (Pendergrast, 2010, p. 16; Topik, 2009). Coffee consumption grew steadily in the 18th and 19th centuries, particularly in rapidly industrializing Western Europe and North America. Per capita coffee consumption in the United States increased from three pounds per year in 1830 to eight pounds by 1859 (Pendergrast, 2010, p. 44).

Coffee sales continued to expand throughout the 20th century amidst the rise of a mass **consumer society**. Social life became increasingly dominated by mass-produced commodities that were standardized and sold at chain stores that were part of vast international distribution networks targeting a consumer base with generic tastes (as opposed to tastes rooted in local ethnicity, class, or geography). Coffee could be drunk easily while on the go, and became one of many commodities of "petty consumption" that was cheap, convenient, and affordable to people from many social classes (Penfold, 2008).

Third, low bean prices and mass consumption fuelled the interests of powerful private companies who used their economic power to promote both. In particular, large, often Northern-based, coffee companies manipulated prices in their favour and promoted widespread consumption through their domination of core markets, economies of scale, massive marketing budgets and "brand power," and access to new technologies and innovations. The original expansion of the global coffee trade, from the 17th to the 19th centuries, occurred during the colonial era and was dominated by mercantilist corporations granted official monopolies by colonial **states**, and often possessing their own private armies. But beginning in the 20th century and to this day, most of the world's green (unroasted) coffee beans have been purchased by transnational food and beverage corporations. Since then, the story of countless mergers and acquisitions, between coffee companies and of coffee brands, tells a complex tale of corporate expansion and profit, replacing the official monopolies of the past with market-driven, corporate oligarchy.

Today, the world's two dominant coffee companies are Nestlé and Jacob Douwe Egberts (JDE). The Swiss corporation Nestlé, founded in 1905, is the world's largest food and beverage company. In 2016, it boasted 442 factories in 86 countries. Since it created the coffee brands Nescafé (in 1938) and Nespresso (in 1986), it has become the world's most profitable coffee company. In the fiscal year 2016, Nestlé's total sales exceeded $86 billion (over $88 billion Swiss francs), with around $9 billion of that in coffee sales (Nestlé S.A., 2017). JDE was formed in 2015 when Mondeléz International, Inc. and D.E. Master Blenders 1753 merged their two coffee corporations to create one of the world's largest coffee companies. A privately held company based in the Netherlands, JDE holds a leading market position in more than 25 countries and serves consumers in more than 100 countries. With a yearly revenue of more than five billion euros, it employs more than 12,000 people worldwide. In 2017, JDE bought the Asian coffee brand Super Group, which added to their expanding coffee portfolio, including many of the world's leading brands such as Douwe Egberts, Gevalia, Maxwell House, Café Pele, Tassimo, Café Noir, and Senseo.[2]

The world's other top roasters include the J.P. Smucker Company (which bought Folgers, Dunkin' Donuts, and Millstone Coffee in 2015), Starbucks, Strauss, Tchibo, UCC Coffee, and Lavazza. Together, these eight businesses roast and sell approximately 40 per cent of the entire world's coffee (Panhuysen & Pierrot, 2014, p. 6). Their promotion and development of cultural values around coffee might now seem "natural," but they have created massive marketing campaigns to help engineer consumer tastes toward increased consumption (Dawson, 2003). For example, in 1949, when Kraft General Foods owned the Maxwell House coffee brand, an unprecedented $2.5 million was spent on TV commercials and magazine ads, promoting their instant coffee as "Good to the last drop." Competitors responded with their own jingles and slogans (Folgers was "the best part of waking up"), propelling further competition for consumers' brand loyalty (Pendergrast, 2010, p. 222).

Far from just informing people about possible consumption options, these corporations have shaped popular culture by constructing consumer identities and brand loyalties around beliefs, values, insecurities, and symbols rooted in gender, class, race, identity, and **nationalism**. Such messages range from the patriotic to the sexist. To give an example of each: in the 1940s, World War II marketing campaigns admonished US civilians of their patriotic duty to adhere to the coffee ration and drink less coffee, to

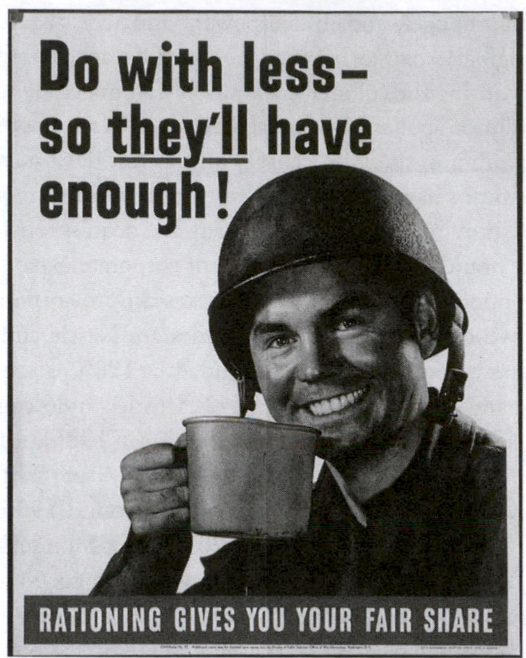

FIGURE 14.2 Cheerful, coffee-drinking American soldiers were popular on a series of World War II posters as part of marketing efforts to encourage rationing on the home front. US National Archives and Records Administration, Records of the Office of Government Reports, 1932–1947, World War II Posters, 1942–1945, 513838.

ensure that there would be enough for soldiers fighting in Europe. In the 1960s and 1970s, many North American coffee commercials featured a middle-class husband who would punish his wife if she couldn't make a perfect cup of coffee, which was considered her "duty" (Pendergrast, 2010, pp. 185–206).

In the 21st century, marketing in the Global North draws on tropical, distant, and romantic imagery of the coffee lands. This is an increasingly dominant approach for marketers who promote specialty or "third wave" coffee, aimed at liberal, urban, or middle-class consumers. Anthropologist Paige West (2012) has conducted extensive research with coffee communities in Papua New Guinea, exploring the gap between the actual lives of coffee farmers and the exotic fantasies drawn on by specialty coffee marketers and retailers. Far from revealing anything substantive about coffee communities, she demonstrates the ways that specialty coffee marketing reinforces colonial notions of a "modern primitive" based on a dual image of "poverty and primitivity," with liberal consumers assigned the role in guiding the poor toward **modernity** (West, 2012, pp. 23–25). Along similar lines, Michael Goodman (2010) has explored the evolution of fair trade (discussed in the final section) by charting the changing nature of its UK marketing strategies. Whereas originally focused on the everyday lives of coffee producers and their relative poverty, over time marketing strategies have shifted toward an upbeat, sexy, romantic imaginary, often focused on tourist landscapes or celebrity endorsements. In this way, fair trade has gained consumer loyalties, but also eroded its ability to pursue its initial goal of "shining daylight on the global spaces of poverty, **inequality** and injustice however limited on coffee bags and websites" (Goodman, 2010, pp. 111–113).

Importantly, Southern coffee countries have played a significant role in the expansion of coffee consumption, not solely through the production of cheap coffee, but also through the creation and promotion of new ways to drink coffee. Often, Southern governments or parastatal institutions were central to this. The iconic fictional coffee figure of "Juan Valdez," for instance, was created by the marketing efforts of the parastatal National Federation of Colombian Farmers (Federación Nacional de Cafeteros, FNC). The idea of a "coffee break," rather than being something that emerged spontaneously out of popular culture in the North, was first created in 1952 as part of a $2 million marketing campaign funded by the Pan American Coffee Bureau—an organization comprising several Latin American governments (Pendergrast, 2010, p. 220).

Marketing has also played a major role in fuelling coffee consumption in Southern countries. Brazil has long been the world leader in coffee production, and Brazilians have consumed significant amounts of coffee since the 1960s. Starting in the 1990s, however, coffee consumption began to soar, so that today Brazil is the world's third largest coffee-consuming economy, after the European Union and the United States (USDA, 2017). Growing consumption is partly driven by Brazil's expanding middle class and growing economy; Brazil is today the world's sixth largest economy. But the choice among urban populations to choose to consume more *coffee* is fuelled by a marketing campaign launched by an association of Brazilian private coffee roasters, the Brazilian Coffee Roasters' Association (Associação Brasileira da Indústria de Café, or ABIC). From 1989 to 1998, the association spent $26.7 million in advertising and total coffee consumption increased by nearly 65 per cent (Fridell, 2014, pp. 131–136; ITC, 2011, p. 27). As with the North, Brazil's coffee consumption connects with a complex interplay of cheap beans and massive marketing efforts.

Part III: Contesting Coffee

Just as the global coffee industry has been built around a web of unequal social relationships that are reproduced daily through the actions of millions of participants, so too has resistance to the dominant **power relations** within the industry formed a central part of its history. Battles against inequality and injustice have been driven by a variety of actors, including Southern governments, Northern-based non-governmental organizations, and civil society groups. The manifold forms of these battles cannot be easily summarized since so many countries with distinctive national histories are involved in the global coffee industry. Three cases of resistance, however, are relevant for understanding the challenges faced by the world's farmers and workers: the International Coffee Agreement (ICA); the fair trade network; and the union drive led by Starbucks Coffee Chile Trade Union.

The ICA was developed in the postwar era by Southern coffee-producing and Northern coffee-consuming countries in an attempt to combat the low prices and extreme price volatility of green beans. This combination had long haunted coffee farmers, in particular smallholders and workers, but it was not until the 1960s that Southern countries, led by Brazil and Colombia, were able to bring enough pressure to bear on Northern countries to begin to address the issue. Driven by Cold War fears that plummeting prices would drive Southern states into communism, the United States and its allies agreed to sign the first ICA in 1963 (Talbot, 2004). The ICA was a quota system designed to stabilize and increase coffee prices by holding a certain amount of green beans off the global market to avoid oversupply. It was renewed several times until 1989, when a group of participants, led by the United States, withdrew their support as part of the movement toward **free trade** reforms.

As a result of the ICA, sociologist John Talbot (2004) calculates that most coffee farmers received higher prices and more income was retained in the South. The ICA did have its challenges, as the global market continued to struggle with oversupply and unpredictable price swings, and signatory nations perpetually disagreed over the quota amounts per country. Moreover, the ICA proved to have a minimal impact on the distribution of coffee income within countries. Countries that pursued social reformist projects that distributed greater resources to small farmers and workers, such as Costa Rica and Colombia, attained better development gains than countries with highly unequal distributions of land and resources, such as El Salvador, Guatemala, and Brazil (Dicum & Luttinger, 2006, pp. 135–136; Fridell, 2013, 2014, pp. 37–43). Yet, as Talbot (2004) has argued, overall, the ICA improved the living standards of broad sectors in the South. In contrast, the decades since the collapse of the ICA have been characterized by increased market volatility and stagnant bean prices: the real value of coffee bean prices in 2016, taking into account inflation, was similar to 2000, when prices plunged so low that the industry was in a global crisis (ICO, 2016). In terms of meeting the needs of coffee producers, the ICA appears to have offered a more successful model than the unregulated, free trade coffee market that dominates today.

In the mid-1980s as the promises of the ICA began to falter, new market-driven alternatives emerged that sought to harness consumer power to attain the integration of poor producers into global markets under better conditions. One such movement has been the **fair trade network**, which connects farmers and craftspeople in the South with organizations and consumers in the North through a system of "fair trade" rules and principles: democratic organization (of cooperatives or worker committees), no exploitation of child labour, environmental sustainability, a guaranteed floor price, and social premiums paid to producer communities to build community infrastructure. Fair trade consumerism has grown significantly in the past decade with more than 812,500 coffee farmers certified.[3]

Despite growing enthusiasm for a variety of certification projects, significant barriers remain to their overall growth and impact. Currently, fair trade only reaches around 3 per cent of the world's coffee farmers, and on average certified farmers can only sell around 35 per cent of their beans on fair trade markets (C&CI, 2014; Fridell, 2014).

Perhaps most significantly, while many instances of specific fair trade projects have made important gains for specific communities, recent assessments question the depth of its overall impact (Cramer, Johnston, Oya, & Sender, 2014; Hoebink, Ruben, Elbers, & van Rijsbergen, 2014; Nelson & Martin, 2013). For example, a systematic review by Oya, Schaefer, Dafni, McCosker, and Langer (2017, p. 183) of 179 studies looking at a range of third- and second-party (industry-led) certification schemes, including fair trade, determined that the overall impacts were mixed, with "a dominance of weak or statistically non-significant effects": prices and access to schooling increased, but the impact on total household income was low or unclear, and wages on fair trade farms were often lower than on noncertified plantations. The fair trade network is highly diverse, with a range of actors who have responded to its limits differently. Southern producer groups, for instance, have demanded, and received, greater say in the management of fair trade standards in the North, and have developed their own standards; in 2005, the Latin American and Caribbean Network of Fair Trade Small Producers and Workers (Coordinadora Latinoamericana y del Caribe de Pequeños Productores y Trabajadores de Comercio Justo, CLAC) launched its own small producers' symbol, with standards developed and overseen by small farmers themselves, aimed specifically at promoting smallholder livelihoods and including such things as higher prices and

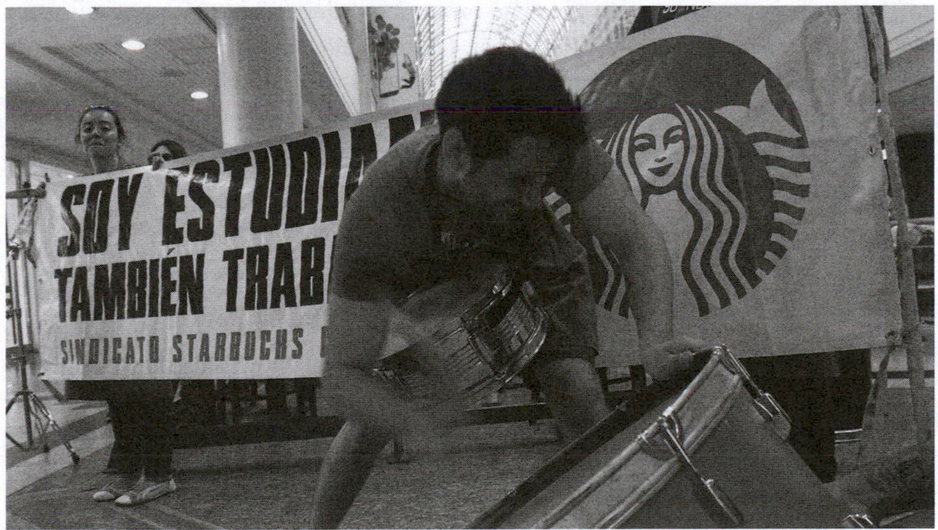

FIGURE 14.3 President of the Starbucks Coffee Chile Trade Union, Andrés Giordano Salazar, leading a protest for workers' rights. Photo used courtesy of Starbucks Coffee Chile Trade Union.

greater purchasing commitments on the part of Northern importers than with previous fair trade standards (Coscione, 2014).

Remember that the global coffee industry depends not just on the labour of millions of coffee farmers and workers, but also on the labour of millions of workers throughout the supply chain, employed in everything from retail, restaurants, cafés, and roasters, to distributors, processors, traders, and dozens of suppliers (from paper cups to espresso machines, from dairy to sugar). Starbucks Coffee Company, the world's leading specialty roaster, marketer, and retailer, now operates 27,339 stores in 75 countries, employing more than 254,000 people worldwide (170,000 in the USA) and making $21 billion in net revenue in 2016 (Starbucks Corporation, 2016). Starbucks provides better benefits to its workers (called "partners") than other restaurant chains. Yet Starbucks remains fiercely opposed to unionization. In 2009, workers at Starbucks's 57 stores in Chile successfully unionized, forming the Starbucks Coffee Chile Trade Union. Following a pattern of cases from North America, Starbucks refused to negotiate with the new union. In response, union members organized two legal strikes and a 12-day hunger strike involving three union leaders, and won four legal disputes in Chilean court against Starbucks for interfering with union activities, intimidating and retaliating against union members, and providing misleading information about the union (Fridell, 2016).

Starbucks remained firm until the union brought the case before the Organisation for Economic Co-operation and Development (OECD) under its "Guidelines for Multinational Enterprises" in 2015. When the OECD representative issued a non-binding ruling against the company, criticizing its failure to recognize the union's valid role, Starbucks backed down and agreed to collective bargaining. On this six-year battle with Starbucks, union leader Andrés Giordano Salazar reflects, "multinationals tend to forget that being socially responsible also means respecting freedom of association and the right to collective bargaining; to this day, I know of no 'socially responsible' company that defends these rights in practice." To counter this, Starbucks Coffee Chile Trade Union sees itself as part of a new movement grounded in global solidarity, communication, and unity. "We've got to go global in new ways," says Giordano Salazar. "Strategy, perseverance, innovation and solidarity are the keys to a new labour movement."[4]

Conclusion: The Future of Coffee

In this chapter, we've highlighted coffee's colonial history, the rise of its consumption, and examples of coffee rebellions. But we've only scraped the surface regarding coffee's future challenges. Gender injustice, including laws that prohibit women from owning their land, is rife in the coffee lands. Of the world's 25 million coffee farmers, most are age 60 or older, so their working days are numbered. Young adult **migration** to urban centres is growing, as children of coffee farmers can't imagine a profitable future in coffee.

Such challenges of human sustainability are matched only by the immense challenges of environmental sustainability and climate change. An ominous prediction from research supported by World Coffee Research (WRC) predicts that half of the land currently suitable for Arabica coffee may no longer be suitable by 2050 (Davis, Gole, Baena, & Moat, 2012). In 2012, researchers of the UK's Royal Botanic Gardens and Ethiopia's Environment and Coffee Forest Forum predict that before 2080, "70 per cent of the world's coffee supply might disappear due to climate change" (Davis et al., 2012; National Geographic, 2014).

The United Nations is deeply concerned about climate change, including its impact on agriculture. In the Intergovernmental Panel on Climate Change's 2014 synthesis report, the authors predict that throughout the 21st century, "heat waves will occur more often and last longer, and that extreme precipitation events will become more intense and frequent in many regions" (IPCC, 2014, p. 10). This threatens coffee because the tree requires consistent sunlight for photosynthesis and cool temperatures that won't parch its cherries. Such an essential combination will be increasingly rare because "most plant species cannot naturally shift their geographical ranges sufficiently fast to keep up with current and high projected rates of climate change in most landscapes" (IPCC, 2014, p. 13). Mitigating climate change will take resources that many smallholder coffee farmers won't possess since the challenges at origin are already disastrous (Fridell, 2014, pp. 143–148).

The rapid acceleration in the rise in global temperature in the past 35 years has led to coffee pests, diseases, and defects unfamiliar to most coffee drinkers, but that are known well to coffee farmers. Among the worst are "coffee rust" (*la roya*), a fungus that attacks the leaf and destroys the branch (and therefore the coffee cherry), the "coffee borer beetle" (*la brocha*), and a coffee defect called the "potato cup." These are only three that have destroyed thousands of acres of coffee trees or cherries in the past decade, particularly in Central and South America. Some of these challenges may be minimized through new pesticides or climate-resistant coffee varietals. But erratic weather conditions pose the most pernicious effects, including severe droughts (negatively impacting Brazilian, Ethiopian, and Kenyan coffee yields in 2014–16) and hurricanes, like Hurricane Maria, that destroyed Puerto Rico's entire coffee sector in September 2017 (Bromwich, 2016; Kennedy, 2017).

Given all these challenges, the future of coffee may be precarious. What remains is an opportunity for North American and European consumers to consider that drinking a cup of coffee has complex political, social, and economic histories that impact the earth and the people behind the cup.

Study Questions

1 What does the term "**commodity fetishism**" mean? How can it be applied to coffee?
2 To consumers in the North, coffee is a drink. But to Southern producers, coffee is a seed, a tree, a cherry, and a "green bean." Consider your drinking habits

and purchasing patterns of coffee. How might these be linked to values that are economic, social, emotional, or symbolic? What does coffee mean to you? (If you don't drink coffee, consider its value to your family or friends.)

3 Imagine the journey of a coffee bean from seed to cup. How many pairs of hands can you count as it travels from Latin America, Asia, or Africa to get to you?

4 When was the last time you asked someone, or someone asked you, to grab a coffee? Consider the rituals of coffee meetings. Where did you meet, and what did that conversation entail? Do you imagine the same conversation would have happened if you had met in your dorm, at a pub, or at an ice cream store? Why or why not?

Exercises

1 Have you ever heard yourself saying "I need coffee"? When did this "need" in your life begin, and why? Is there a pattern to the moments that you feel this "need"? Choose one coffee-producing country and learn about why that country and its people might "need" coffee. How much coffee does your chosen country produce and export? (Check out the data at the International Coffee Organization: http://www.ico.org/new_historical.asp?section=Statistics). How important is coffee compared to other industries? (Explore your country's "Economy" overview at the CIA's World Factbook: https://www.cia.gov/library/publications/the-world-factbook/)

2 Sustainability may be one of the most popular words in the coffee industry, yet the future of coffee is precarious. The National Coffee Association provides a list of global initiatives that seek sustainability. Choose one and explore if the profits are going to coffee professionals in the Global North or to smallholder coffee farmers in the Global South: http://www.ncausa.org/Sustainability/Sustainability-Showcase.

3 Visit your local supermarket's coffee shelf. How many of the coffee brands on the shelf are marked "fair trade" with symbols such as "Fairtrade International," "Fairtrade USA," or "Fairtrade Canada." Can you tell how many of these are distributed by small businesses, not-for-profit organizations, or cooperatives? From the words to the images, what different stories do various kinds of coffee bean packaging tell?

4 Visit different cafés in your area, such as a locally owned café, a corporate café that targets upscale and urban clientele (Starbucks, Second Cup), and a corporate chain that targets blue collar or drive-in customers (Tim Hortons, McCafe, Dunkin' Donuts). Compare the imagery on the walls and ads on the windows. How do these chains market to their respective core customers?

5 Imagine that you could go to a North American café with Karl Marx and Michel Foucault. What might they debate regarding the **everyday practice** of power

embedded in the act of purchasing and consuming coffee? How would their views on **historical materialism** and **postmodernism** differ? What would you contribute to the discussion based on your own perspective after reading this chapter? (You may wish to review the Introduction and Chapter 1 to help answer these questions.)

Relevant Internet Sources

Equal Exchange
http://equalexchange.coop
Fairtrade Labelling Organizations International
www.fairtrade.net
Fair Trade Canada
fairtrade.ca/en-CA
Fair Trade USA
www.fairtradecertified.org/
Food and Agricultural Organization of the United Nations
http://www.fao.org/home/en/
International Coffee Organization
www.ico.org
JustUs! Coffee
https://justuscoffee.com
Oxfam
www.oxfam.org.uk/
Planet Bean
http://www.planetbeancoffee.com
Rainforest Alliance
www.rainforest-alliance.org/
Specialty Coffee Association
https://sca.coffee/
United Nations Conference on Trade and Development:
http://unctad.org/en/Pages/Home.aspx

Notes

1 See the Coffee Association of Canada's "Canadian Coffee Consumption 2017" infographic at https://www.coffeeassoc.com/wp-content/uploads/2018/02/CanadianCoffee2017infographic_whitebkd-2.pdf.

2 JDE is a privately held company. For more information, see the press releases, "A Defining Moment," May 7, 2014, https://www.jacobsdouweegberts.com/

company-news/a-defining-moment/, and "JDE Completes the Acquisition of Super Group LTD," June 6, 2017, https://www.jacobsdouweegberts.com/company-news/jde-welcomes-super-group/.

3 Fairtrade International (FLO), *Coffee*, https://www.fairtrade.net/products/coffee.html.

4 Andrés Giordano Salazar, President of the Starbucks Coffee Chile Trade Union, interview with author, December 2015. See Fridell (2016).

References

Bayliss, K., Fine, B., & Robertson, M. (2013). From financialisation to consumption: The systems of provision approach applied to housing and water. *Financialisation, Economy, Society and Sustainable Development (FESSUD), Working Paper Series*(2), 1–46.

Bromwich, J.E. (2016, September 22). Climate change threatens world's coffee supply. *The New York Times*. Retrieved from https://www.nytimes.com/2016/09/23/science/climate-change-threatens-worlds-coffee-supply-report-says.html

Brooks, A. (2015). *Clothing poverty: The hidden world of fast fashion and second-hand clothes*. London, UK: Zed Books.

C&CI. (2014). Certifiers claim key role in response to fluctuating prices. *Coffee & Cocoa International (C&CI)*, *40*, 26–27.

Coscione, M. (2014). *CLAC and the defense of the small producer*. Black Point, NS: Fernwood.

Coulthard, G.J. (2014). *Red skin, white masks: Rejecting the colonial politics of recognition*. Minneapolis, MN: University of Minnesota Press.

Cramer, C., Johnston, D., Oya, C., & Sender, J. (2014). *Fairtrade, employment and poverty reduction in Ethiopia and Uganda: Final report to DFID*. Retrieved from http://ftepr.org/wp-content/uploads/FTEPR-Final-Report-19-May-2014-FINAL.pdf

Daviron, B., & Ponte, S. (2005). *The coffee paradox: Global markets, commodity trade and the elusive promise of development*. London, UK: Zed Books.

Davis, A.P., Gole, W.G., Baena, S., & Moat, J. (2012). The impact of climate change on Indigenous arabica coffee (*coffea arabica*): Predicting future trends and identifying priorities. *PLoS One*, *7*(11), e47981. https://doi.org/10.1371/journal.pone.0047981

Dawson, M. (2003). *The consumer trap: Big business marketing in American life*. Urbana, IL: University of Illinois Press.

Dicum, G., & Luttinger, N. (2006). *The coffee book: Anatomy of an industry from crop to the last drop* (Revised ed.). New York, NY: New Press.

Dore, E. (2003). Patriarchy from above, patriarchy from below: Debt peonage on Nicaraguan coffee estates, 1870–1930. In W.G.C. Smith & S.C. Topik (Eds.), *The global coffee economy in Africa, Asia, and Latin America, 1500–1989* (pp. 209–235). Cambridge, UK: Cambridge University Press.

Fine, B. (2013). Consumption matters. *ephemera*, *13*(2), 217–248.

Food Chain Workers Alliance & Solidarity Research Cooperative. (2016). *No piece of the pie: U.S. food workers in 2016*. Retrieved from http://foodchainworkers.org/wp-content/uploads/2011/05/FCWA_NoPieceOfThePie_P.pdf

Fowler-Salamini, H. (2002). Women coffee sorters confront the mill owners and the Veracruz revolutionary state, 1915–1918. *Journal of Women's History, 14*(1), 34–65.

Fridell, G. (2007). Fair trade coffee and commodity fetishism: The limits of market-driven social justice. *Historical Materialism, 15*(4), 79–104.

Fridell, G. (2013). *Alternative trade: Legacies for the future*. Halifax, NS: Fernwood.

Fridell, G. (2014). *Coffee*. Cambridge, UK: Polity Press.

Fridell, G. (2016, January 20). The battle to unionize Starbucks in Chile: An interview with Andrés Giordano Salazar. *Counter Punch*. Retrieved from http://www.counterpunch.org/2016/01/20/the-battle-to-unionize-starbucks-in-chile-an-interview-with-andres-giordano-salazar/

Goodman, M.K. (2010). The mirror of consumption: Celebritization, developmental consumption and the shifting cultural politics of fair trade. *Geoforum, 41*(1), 104–116. https://doi.org/10.1016/j.geoforum.2009.08.003

Handy, J. (1994). *Revolution in the countryside: Rural conflict and agrarian reform in Guatemala, 1944–1954*. Chapel Hill, NC: University of North Carolina Press.

Hansen, J.H. (2016a). *Bitter coffee I: Slavery-like working conditions and deadly pesticides on Brazilian coffee plantations*. Retrieved from https://old.danwatch.dk/wp-content/uploads/2016/03/Danwatch-Bitter-Coffee-MARCH-2016.pdf

Hansen, J.H. (2016b). *Bitter coffee II: Guatemala's coffee plantations are marked by child labour, threats to union organisers, and signs of forced labour*. Retrieved from https://old.danwatch.dk/wp-content/uploads/2016/09/Bitter-coffee-Guatemala-2016.pdf

Hoebink, P., Ruben, R., Elbers, W., & van Rijsbergen, B. (2014). *The impact of coffee certification on smallholder farmers in Kenya, Uganda and Ethiopia*. Retrieved from https://www.ru.nl/publish/pages/721725/final_report_solidaridad_impact_study_east_africa_290114.pdf

Hudson, M., Hudson, I., & Fridell, M. (2013). *Fair trade, sustainability and social change*. New York, NY: Palgrave MacMillan.

ICO. (2016). *Assessing the economic sustainability of coffee growing*. Retrieved from http://www.ico.org/documents/cy2015-16/icc-117-6e-economic-sustainability.pdf

IPCC. (2014). *Climate change 2014: Synthesis report: Contribution of working groups i, ii and iii to the fifth assessment report of the intergovernmental pane on climate change*. Retrieved from http://www.ipcc.ch/report/ar5/syr/

ITC. (2011). *The coffee exporter's guide* (3rd ed.). Retrieved from http://www.intracen.org/The-Coffee-Exporters-Guide-Third-Edition

Kelly, M., Electris, C., Lang, H., & Bhandal, G. (2012). *Worker equity in food and agriculture*. Retrieved from http://www.sustainalytics.com/sites/default/files/workerequity_october2012.pdf

Kennedy, M. (2017, October 10). "This was a beautiful place": Puerto Rico's coffee industry devastated by Maria, heard on *All Things Considered*. *NPR*. Retrieved from https://www.npr.org/sections/thetwo-way/2017/10/10/556657967/-this-was-a-beautiful-place-puerto-rico-s-coffee-industry-devastated-by-maria

Kurian, R. (2003). Labor, race, and gender on the coffee plantations in Ceylon (Sri Lanka), 1834–1880. In W.G.C. Smith & S.C. Topik (Eds.), *The global coffee economy in Africa, Asia, and Latin America, 1500–1989* (pp. 163–190). Cambridge, UK: Cambridge University Press.

Marx, K. (1978). Capital, volume one. In R.C. Tucker (Ed.), *The Marx-Engels reader* (2nd ed., pp. 294–438). New York, NY: W.W. Norton.

McCreery, D. (2003). Coffee and Indigenous labor in Guatemala, 1871–1980. In W.G.C. Smith & S.C. Topik (Eds.), *The global coffee economy in Africa, Asia, and Latin America, 1500–1989* (pp. 191–208). Cambridge, UK: Cambridge University Press.

National Geographic. (2014). Too hot for coffee. *National Geographic*. Retrieved from https://news.nationalgeographic.com/news/special-features/2014/05/140507-too-hot-for-coffee/

Nelson, V., & Martin, A. (2013). *Final technical report: Assessing the poverty impact of sustainability standards*. Retrieved from https://www.standardsimpacts.org/sites/default/files/NRI%20Assessing-The-Poverty-Impact-Of-Sustainability-Standards%20-%20Final%20Technical%20Report.pdf

Nestlé, S.A. (2017). *Annual review*. Retrieved from http://www.nestle.com/asset-library/documents/library/documents/annual_reports/2016-annual-review-en.pdf

Oxfam International. (2018). *Ripe for change: Ending human suffering in supermarket supply chains*. Retrieved from https://policy-practice.oxfam.org.uk/publications/ripe-for-change-ending-human-suffering-in-supermarket-supply-chains-620418

Oya, C., Schaefer, F., Dafni, S., McCosker, C., & Langer, L. (2017). Effects of certification schemes for agricultural production on socio-economic outcomes in low and middle-income countries: A systematic review. *Campbell Systematic Reviews, 3*. https://doi.org/10.4073/csr.2017.3

Panhuysen, S., & Pierrot, J. (2014). *Coffee barometer*. Retrieved from https://hivos.org/sites/default/files/coffee_barometer_2014_report_1.pdf

Pendergrast, M. (2010). *Uncommon grounds: The history of coffee and how it transformed our world* (2nd ed.). New York, NY: Basic Books.

Penfold, S. (2008). *The donut: A Canadian history*. Toronto, ON: University of Toronto Press.

Samper, M.K. (1994). Café, trabajo y sociedad en Centroamérica (1870–1930): Una historia común y divergente. In V.H. Acuña Ortega (Ed.), *Las Repúblicas agroexportadoras: Tomo IV: Historía General de Centroamérica* (2nd ed.). Costa Rica: FLACSO-Programa Costa Rica.

Starbucks Corporation. (2016). *Fiscal 2016 annual report*. Retrieved from https://investor.starbucks.com/financial-data/annual-reports/default.aspx

Talbot, J.M. (2004). *Grounds for agreement: The political economy of the coffee commodity chain*. Oxford, UK: Rowman & Littlefield.

Tallontire, A., Dolan, C., Smith, S., & Barrientos, S. (2005). Reaching the marginalised? Gender value chains and ethical trade in African horticulture. *Development in Practice, 15*(3/4), 559–571. https://doi.org/10.1080/09614520500075771

Topik, S.C. (2009). Historicizing commodity chains: Five hundred years of the global coffee commodity chain. In J. Bair (Ed.), *Frontiers of commodity chain research* (pp. 37–62). Stanford, CA: Stanford University Press.

USDA. (2017). *Bi-annual report: Coffee: World markets and trade*. Retrieved from https://www.fas.usda.gov/data/coffee-world-markets-and-trade

West, P. (2012). *From modern production to imagined primitive: The social world of coffee from Papua New Guinea*. Durham, NC: Duke University Press.

Wolf, E.R. (1997). *Europe and the people without history*. Berkeley, CA: University of California Press.

15 Indigenous Youth: Representing Themselves

MARGOT FRANCIS

It's the spring of 2009, and I'm up in northern Ontario in the communities of Garden River and Batchawana First Nations, just outside Sault Ste. Marie, to witness a new play called *Treaty Daze* by Alanis King (Anishinaabe), who is working with a team of **Indigenous** and white youth actors. The focus of the play will be on the history of treaties, or land agreements, between white settlers and Anishinaabe people in this region. The team has mapped out the main characters and is now looking for a hook, an opening scene to grab the attention of the audience and signal that we "know" how this history plays out in the taken-for-granted interactions between contemporary Indigenous and white youth in schools.

One of the actors, Teddy Syrette, starts to talk about his own very recent experiences. Like roughly 70 per cent of Indigenous youth on northern reserves, he dropped out of secondary school—but his reasons had nothing to do with apathy. For the past three years, Teddy's been the lead actor in this local summer theatre company, and he's someone we've all come to know as bright, funny, and uber-responsible. So he talks about his secondary-school experience: about being on the receiving end of nasty comments about "Indians getting special privileges"; about social events where white people were getting drunk and being told they were acting "just like Indians"; and about not knowing how to respond when white friends said that "Indians get things for free."[1]

I'm using the term "**Indian**" because I want to signal that I am referring to the imaginary ideas that many non-Indigenous Canadians—such as Teddy's high school friends—have taken up as the "truth" about Indigenous people. This chapter will explore how Indigenous youth challenged these stereotypical ideas through an Anishinaabe-led theatre project (2009) that dramatized the contemporary impact of land dispossession on the north shore of Lake Huron. My interest is to explore how the actors and audience members (Anishinaabe and white youth) negotiated the "contact zone" of intercultural theatre. If "contact zones" constitute "social spaces where disparate cultures meet, clash, and grapple with each other, often in highly asymmetrical relations of power" (p. 4) as Mary Louise Pratt (2008) argues, then this chapter explores the work of emotions in navigating the cultural politics and material inequalities of **colonial** relations.

This research responds to a significant strain in feminist and anti-racist movements that stresses the importance of *not* making white people "feel bad" on the assumption that this makes white **racism** worse, or simply intensifies white guilt, which can often be narcissistic. My interviews with Anishinaabek and white youth, however, highlighted the inevitability of confronting what my interviewees named as "shame" in relation to the Canadian **state** dispossession of Indigenous land. In this chapter I will explore how these "bad feelings" worked, sometimes to acknowledge settler *un*belonging, while at other times covering over the violence of contemporary colonial relations. My aim is to interrogate the limits and possibilities of intercultural theatre that attempts to witness Indigenous–settler conflict in the colonial *present*.

Prior to reflecting on this theatre performance, however, I explore how the ideas that Teddy Syrette faced in secondary school originated and unpack how discourses normalized through colonization continue to pervade our everyday ideas and practices.

Setting the Scene

Prior to Confederation in 1867, all of the area now called Canada was Indigenous territory belonging to many different Indigenous nations. The shift in governance structures and ownership signalled by the arrival of new settlers was not benign; it was violent and deeply contested (Lawrence, 2002). Early colonial powers and then the Canadian state exercised legal and military force to negotiate land agreements, seize huge tracts of land, and relocate Indigenous communities to isolated reserves. Over two centuries of European invasion and Indigenous resistance, Indigenous people were deprived of a sustainable economic and political base and excluded from participation in the new Canadian **nation**. For example, Indigenous people were the last group to be included in the federal franchise, only gaining access to the vote in 1960. It was this long and fraught process of entrenching material and spacial **inequality** that allowed Canada to come into being (Stasiulis & Jhappan, 1995).

Integral to this colonial land grab, 1876 marked the passage of the *Indian Act*, legislation that provided a coercive and **patriarchal** set of "cradle to grave" directives governing Indigenous **culture** and education, while also setting arbitrary standards for who was, and was not, a "**status** Indian." In particular, the *Indian Act* profoundly undermined local self-governance and marginalized women's spheres of authority and leadership within communities (Lawrence, 2003). For example, until Bill C-31 changed how Indigenous people were granted status in 1984, Indigenous women who married white or non-status men lost their legal "status" as Indigenous people. As a result, they were compelled to leave their communities, and all of their descendants lost their status and were, for the most part, permanently alienated from their Indigenous kinship networks, land, and culture. As Bonita Lawrence has argued, "the damage caused, demographically and culturally, by the loss of status of so many Native women for a century prior to 1985, whose grandchildren and great-grandchildren are not no longer recognized—and in many cases no longer identify—as Indian, remains incalculable" (Lawrence, 2003, p. 9).

While Bill C-31 (1984) allowed some Indigenous people to regain status, it also put in place new rules that will likely ensure there are no federally recognized Indigenous people left in Canada within six or seven generations (Cannon, 2008). More specifically, Bill C-31 established a cut-off point of two or three generations, after which *any* Indigenous person who marries a white or non-status person will no longer be able to pass on their status (Lawrence, 2003). Once Indigenous people are no longer legally recognized by the Canadian state, they will have no legal right to their land and territories, thus freeing the government and private corporations from having to negotiate for use of Indigenous land (for example, in the tar sands or along the Trans Mountain Pipeline route). Hence, "status" and land agreements have become central areas of advocacy and resistance for many Indigenous communities, activists, and scholars (Lawrence, 2003; Simpson, 2017).

The *Indian Act* (1876) also outlawed Indigenous religions, cultural practices, and languages, and distorted the integrity of familial and community structures by legally compelling several generations of children to attend residential or day schools where the goal was to assimilate them into the lowest rungs of settler society. The Conservative government-appointed *Truth and Reconciliation Commission* has now confirmed that these children were subject to pervasive physical, cultural, and sexual abuse, and that it is likely, according to government figures, that at least 25 per cent of the children who attended died there (TRC, 2015; Milloy, 2017). As a result of the profound impacts of these schools, in 2008 Prime Minister Stephen Harper made a formal apology for the actions of the Canadian government, which he acknowledged constituted a **cultural genocide**—the effects of which continue today.

As a result of this history, the United Nations Department of Economic and Social Affairs noted in 2006 that the situation of Indigenous peoples remains "the most pressing human rights issue facing Canadians" in the new millennium, and this judgement remains relevant today. For just one example, we can look to the Canadian Human Rights Tribunal 2016 decision which ruled that the federal government is continuing to discriminate against Indigenous children on reserves by providing 38 per cent less funding to child welfare services than exists elsewhere. The decision compares on-reserve child welfare to the **residential schools** system, and notes that "the fate and future of many First Nations children is still being determined by the government" (Fontaine, 2016).

Indeed, Indigenous people are the only group in Canada who continue to live in conditions more commonly found in former colonies in the Global South, despite being in a country that consistently rates among the top ten in the United Nations Human Development Index. (See text box, "Poverty Amongst Canada's Aboriginal Peoples"). Foucault's ideas of **normalization** can provide a conceptual framework to help understand this contradiction. The everyday **stereotypes** about Indians as "savage," "noble," "lazy," or "primitive" work to portray Canada as an exemplary and tolerant nation, and help to normalize Canada's continuing colonial relationship with Indigenous people. In so doing, they obscure contemporary material inequalities, thus allowing the "**centre**"—or the existing relations of power—to survive unquestioned and intact.

Poverty amongst Canada's Aboriginal Peoples[1]

Research indicates that "at best, the health situation of Indigenous peoples mirrors that of the world's poorest, but is made worse by their social and cultural marginalization."[2] The 1996 Royal Commission on Aboriginal Peoples (RCAP) noted that: Aboriginal people are at the bottom of almost every available index of socio-economic well-being, whether [they] are measuring educational levels, employment opportunities, housing conditions, per capita incomes or any of the other conditions that give non-Aboriginal Canadians one of the highest standards of living in the world.[3] Poverty amongst Canada's Aboriginal population has seen only slight improvements since RCAP. Recent data indicates that:

- One in four First Nations children live in poverty as compared to one in six for non-Aboriginal children.[4]
- Approximately 40% of off-reserve Aboriginal children live in poverty.[5]
- Aboriginal people living in urban areas are more than twice as likely to live in poverty than non-Aboriginal people. In 2000 for example, 55.6% of urban Aboriginal people lived below the poverty line compared with 24.5% of Canada's non-Aboriginal urban residents.[6]
- Rates of poverty for Aboriginal women are double that of non-Aboriginal women.[7]

As a result of living under conditions of poverty:

- More than 100 First Nations communities are currently under boil water advisories and have little or no access to clean water for drinking and sanitation.[8]
- Nearly one in four First Nations adults live in crowded homes and 23% of Aboriginal people live in houses in need of major repairs.[9]

- First Nations suffer from "**Third World**" diseases such as tuberculosis at eight to ten times the rate of Canadians in general.[10]
- Aboriginal people in Canada were found to be four times more likely to experience hunger as a direct result of poverty.[11]
- More than one quarter of Aboriginal people off reserve and 30% of **Inuit** children have experienced food insecurity at some point.[12]
- Aboriginal children are drastically overrepresented in the child welfare system. Physical neglect as a result of poverty, poor housing, and substance abuse is a key factor in child apprehension.[13]

In Canada, a key strategy for reducing Aboriginal poverty is to close the gap in government funding between Aboriginal and non-Aboriginal Canadians. Between 1996 and 2006, the Aboriginal population increased by 45%, nearly six times faster than the 8% rate of increase for the non-Aboriginal population.[14] Despite this increase, per capita spending on First Nations (based on a growth rate of only 23%) is half the amount of average Canadians: $7000–$8000 compared to $15,000–$16,000.[15] As a result, First Nations governments are unable to keep up with the socio-economic demands of a growing population, particularly with respect to programs and services. The budget cap on services to Aboriginal communities must be removed and fiscal arrangements must be developed based on real costs.[16] Bottom-up approaches are equally important in alleviating Aboriginal poverty in Canada. It has been widely argued that "unless the particular situation and voices of Indigenous peoples are taken into account, [there may be] … accelerated loss of land and natural resources, and accelerated assimilation, thus prolonging and even worsening the marginalization, discrimination and further impoverishment of Indigenous peoples."[17]

---

1 Poverty as a Social Determinant of First Nations, Inuit, and Métis Health, available from the National Collaborating Center for Aboriginal Health (2009–2010), https://www.ccnsa-nccah.ca/docs/determinants/FS-PovertySDOH-EN.pdf. This text box reproduces verbatim a section from the online article (pp. 2–3) and includes the original formatting for endnotes. "Aboriginal" throughout this fact sheet refers collectively to the Indigenous inhabitants of Canada, including First Nations, Inuit, and Métis peoples (as stated in section 35(2) of the Constitution Act, 1982). Wherever possible, we provide names and data for distinct groups/communities. Reprinted by permission of the National Collaborating Centre for Aboriginal Health.

2 Stephens, C., Porter, J., Nettleton, C., & Willis, R. (2006). Disappearing, displaced, and undervalued: A call to action for Indigenous health worldwide. *The Lancet, 367*: 2023.

3 Royal Commission on Aboriginal Peoples (1995). *Choosing life. Special report on suicide among Aboriginal people*. Ottawa, ON: Supply and Services, p. 24.

4 Campaign 2000. Oh Canada! Too many children in poverty for too long: 2006 Report card on child and family poverty in Canada, http://www.campaign2000.ca/rc/rc06/06_C2000NationalReportCard.pdf [accessed January 16, 2009], p. 4.
5 Ibid, p. 4.
6 Canadian Council on Social Development. (2003). Social challenges: The well-being of Aboriginal people, 2003, www.ccsd.ca/cpsd/ccsd/c_ab.htm [accessed January 16, 2009].
7 Townson, M. (2005). Poverty issues for Canadian women. Ottawa, ON: Status of Women Canada, Government of Canada, 2005, hwww.swc-cfc.gc.ca/cgi-bin/printview.pl?file=/resources/consultations/ges09-2005/poverty_e. html [accessed January 28, 2009].
8 Assembly of First Nations. (n.d.). The reality for First Nations in Canada: Fact Sheet, www.afn.ca/article.asp?id=764 [accessed January 16, 2009].
9 Ibid.
10 Public Service Alliance of Canada. PSAC Statement on National Aboriginal Peoples Day June 21, 2008: Making Aboriginal poverty history, www.psac.com/what/humanrights/june21factsheet1-e.shtml [accessed January 16, 2009]
11 McIntyre, L., Connor, S., & Warren, J. (1998). A glimpse of child hunger in Canada . Ottawa, ON: Applied Research Branch, Strategic Policy, Human Resources Development Canada.
12 Office of Nutrition Policy and Promotion. (2007). Income related household food security in Canada. Ottawa, ON: Health Canada.
13 Trocmé, N., et al. (2004). Canadian Incidence Study of Reported Child Abuse and Neglect (CIS). Final report. Ottawa, ON: Minister of Public Works and Government Services Canada, p. 10.
14 Statistics Canada. (2008). Aboriginal peoples in Canada in 2006: Inuit, Métis and First Nations 2006 Census. Ottawa, ON: Ministry of Industry, Catalogue no. 97-558-XIE.
15 Assembly of First Nations. (2007). Make Poverty History presentation, http://www.afn.ca/cmslib/general/mph2006101893457.pps#276,3, Truth About Spending on First Nations [accessed January 16, 2009].
16 Assembly of First Nations. The $9 billion myth exposed: Why First Nations poverty endures, www.afn.ca/cmslib/general/M-Ex.pdf [accessed January 16, 2009]
17 UN Permanent Forum on Indigenous Issues. (2005) as cited in Stephens, C., Porter, J., Nettleton, C., & Willis, R. (2006), p. 2026.

"The Rest" in the "West"

In the context of these profound colonial inequities within Canada, Stuart Hall's conception of "the West *and* the rest" (1992) must be considered for the ways he emphasizes that "the West" has always relied on "the rest" to consolidate the political imaginary of **modernity** over and against those who are characterized as primitive by contrast. Indeed,

British and French colonizers claimed entitlement to land through the "doctrine of discovery," a **race**-based idea that was used as the legal and moral justification for colonial dispossession of sovereign Indigenous nations.[2] In short, Canada relies on Indigenous dispossession for our very existence. "The rest" are indeed *in* the "West."

This ongoing colonial structure (Wolfe, 2006) has resulted in Indigenous lands by and large being reduced to "postage stamp" reserve communities removed from urban centres. This spacial marginalization profoundly influences the context in which Indigenous youth live as they bear the weight of land dispossession as well as cultural genocide in Canada. These contemporary realities continue to injure the social, economic, educational, and kinship relations within Indigenous communities and circumscribe the possibilities for a dignified life—resulting in a wide range of hardships now characterized as individualized risk factors, despite their origin in dispossession and state-sanctioned violence (Styres, Haig-Brown, & Blimkie, 2013).

In response to this context, Anishinaabe scholar Leanne Simpson (2014, 2017) argues that Indigenous theory cannot simply be generated as an academic pursuit, but instead must be produced by Indigenous scholars engaged in building resistance movements "on the ground" and fostering Indigenous-specific resistance and intelligence. Many Indigenous activists, artists, and scholars are indeed working from this perspective, and re-imagining specifically Indigenous epistemologies through story, cultural production, engagements with multi-generational kinship networks, and, most importantly, by foregrounding a reciprocal relationship to land. This conceptualization of theory resituates intellectual production within a broader project that aims to question coercive educational institutions, capitalist consumer culture, and alienated relationships to the natural world. Indeed, Simpson's analysis sketches out an enormous undertaking; as she herself puts it, "it's not just pedagogy; it's how to live a life" (2014, p. 18). This theorization of "how to live a life" is both an ambitious re-imagining of new worlds lived out despite the continued colonial context, and also an invitation to very different forms of research than are typical within white academic contexts.

In keeping with Simpson's analysis, the Anishinaabe-led theatre project described below attempted to use cultural production to make theory through on-the-ground life practice. The research described in this chapter emerged from my six-year collaboration with the Anishinaabe scholar Karl Hele writing about Anishinaabe-led youth summer theatre productions in his home community of Garden River First Nation in northern Ontario (2007–2012). This project could be considered an example of how researchers might work collaboratively with artists and community members to "do sociology" through supporting on-the-ground projects with direct benefits to local communities. Informed by Simpson's analysis, this project supported Anishinaabe youth to work with local artists and develop their own responses to debates about land, **sovereignty,** and status—in their own voices, and through their own creative processes.

The *Treaty Daze* project started with a script development workshop in April 2009, and brought together elders, Indigenous and white youth actors, academics (my colleague Karl Hele and myself), and theatre professionals including the Anishinaabe script writer and director Alanis King (former Artistic Director of the Saskatchewan Native Theatre Company) and the allied director Sue Barber from Shot in the Dark Productions in Sault Ste. Marie. This discussion provided the context for participants to talk about the implications of early land agreements for present-day land conflicts. For example, one elder recounted the story of the *first* Indigenous protest on the Trans-Canada Highway in 1963, led by Alice Corbiere, which pressured the federal government to recognize the community's right to compensation for Indigenous lands confiscated for the highway. This early lobby with then Minister of Indian Affairs, Jean Chrétien, was a crucial moment in the long process of trying to influence the government to recognize that Anishinaabe communities would not tolerate living with little access to clean water, paved roads, electricity, and municipal services. These conversations with early activists and elders like Alice Corbiere were crucial to script-building, and after that initial workshop, the team of actors met regularly for rehearsals and to learn more about the contemporary implications of land disputes and the intergenerational impacts of residential schools.

In the final production of *Treaty Daze*, the central character is a contemporary Anishinaabe teenager, Didjamawyn, whose name is a humorous pun on the phrase "did your ma win," implicitly referencing the popularity of bingo amongst communities living on reserve territory. Didjamawyn learns about the historical struggle for land and resources through a wry series of flashbacks to key moments in the treaty negotiations between Anishinaabe leaders, mining interests, and the colonial state. *Treaty Daze* was performed on August 14–16, 2009, during the Garden River Powwow. I was a participant/observer for the script workshop, for periods during rehearsals, and for the week prior to and after the Powwow. I attended all the shows and interviewed the cast and selected youth in the audience the week after the production.

I start my analysis of the *Treaty Daze* play by highlighting the discursive themes that emerged from my interviews about this production. The first theme, "informed ignorance," comes from a phrase coined by one of the Anishinaabe youth audience members, and refers to the ways *all* of the youth, including the Anishinaabe and white interviewees, described their knowledge of Indigenous land dispossession. We hear two different perspectives on this "informed ignorance" in the following excerpts. The first is from a young white woman in the audience:

> I mean, everybody's heard … the "white man came and stole the land" sort of thing, [it's] even in … Disney movies for heaven's sake, but I didn't know where that came from … [or] have any examples to fall back on. But now that I learned about them [from the play], they were really, I mean, it affected me. It made me think about it a lot. And, you know, feel guilty [laughs] for a minute there. I was like "Wow, we suck." [laughs][3]

The second excerpt is from a mixed-race[4] Anishinaabe youth actor who lived off-reserve, and who, until his involvement with the play, had had little knowledge of

Indigenous politics: "I just didn't realize how actually crazy and disorganized it was. How everything was just totally, totally up in the air, you know? White settlers just came in and just started settling on Indian land and there were no treaties or anything, they just kind of came in and took over. It was … psycho."

For all the interviewees, the impact of the play came, first, from learning the specific process through which "race" had come to be naturalized as "place," and through understanding how land dispossession was accomplished locally. In other words, the Canadian colonial land grab used material, social, and legal processes in the local arena to limit Indigenous peoples' connection to place. The performance, in contrast, provoked a move from the banal and easily disregarded references to "land theft" (like those found in Hollywood films) to a more difficult engagement with the racial politics of colonial relations. Attending to this knowledge produced the possibility of an encounter that broke through a primary defence that many use to protect themselves from a felt awareness of genocide: namely, the prolonged indifference to the Canadian dispossession of Indigenous land.

This move from "informed ignorance" into a confrontation with racial and colonial power was facilitated, however, not only by new knowledge, but also by the dramatic "container" provided by the *Treaty Daze* performance. Audience members said that they were engaged by the script, music, and especially the Anishinaabe humour. Some Anishinaabe audience members commented that humour was particularly important, as the contents of the play were too "overwhelming" to endure without laughter. Here the white audience members occasionally found themselves on the "outside" of the action. As one white audience member noted: "Watching it, I knew that there were some jokes that I didn't get. I was like, 'OK, that was a joke, right?' … Some of the dialogue was hilarious, but there were jokes where I was like, 'What's going on?' It's kind of like a role reversal … when you think about it, you're on the outside when you're with them … [so it made me wonder] how do they feel when they're with you?"

Partly as a result of the ability of this production to promote laughter and self-reflexivity, many suggested that *Treaty Daze* should be incorporated into the curricula in local schools. As one white actor put it: "This stuff should be pumped into the kids—especially because … it's like 'Oh, this happened right here,' that's pretty cool." But when I asked the youth cast why they thought this material was not already taught in public schools, the response by the white actors was emphatic—and here I quote from the group discussion:

Shame.
Yeah, it's shame.
Yeah, it's always as peacekeepers, that's the only history that we even learn …
When you look at the concept that Canada was pretty much killing off this culture … like it's hard to grasp that … I think a lot of high school teachers don't touch that because … they'd be asking so much more of the students.

Interestingly, cast members noted that it was not genocide itself that was difficult to speak about. Instead, it was the acknowledgement that racially motivated forms of land displacement and attempted genocide had happened in Canada. In this context, the commentary from some of the Anishinaabe youth is particularly startling. For example, one actor whose heritage was Anishinaabe and Hungarian noted that within his family, stories of his grandfather's traumatic flight from Hungary prior to World War II were well known. In contrast, although he had five uncles and aunts who were in residential schools, he knew nothing of that legacy. Indeed, after a cast workshop on residential schools he commented that it was "a huge eye opener … it just kind of boggles my mind that it's not openly talked about even today."

While the discursive and emotional contests I have chronicled so far speak to the promise of the *Treaty Daze* performance to facilitate a politics of ethical engagement to challenge white settler dominance, a second set of reflections suggests its opposite: namely, the limits of some white participants' willingness to acknowledge the ongoing violence of colonial relations. In particular, some white actors argued that with present-day human rights legislation, land dispossession could not happen today. Indeed, often their sense of distress was about how ignorant white people "used to be." This **discourse**, which says in essence, "times have changed … things are not like that anymore," disavows the harsh material and social consequences of present-day power arrangements, many of which I outlined at the beginning of this chapter. Consequently this "times have changed" discourse works primarily to rearticulate the **Enlightenment** narratives of progress and white racial "innocence" and through these to refuse the opportunity to testify to or witness injustice and material inequality. Put differently, this response refuses to acknowledge the ongoing effects of colonial dispossession of Indigenous territory in the present day.

In the context of this resistance it was the Anishinaabe actors and audience members who repeatedly challenged white settler denial. Here I will highlight just one example of an Anishinaabe actor confronting white racial "innocence."

> It's still a lot … the hurt is still there. Which we're not going to get over it in a century or two … [like] African American people, who still have that hurt, from their ancestors' slavery. It's basically like, we understand that we're not gonna get all of our land back, we understand that we're not gonna get all the minerals that were extracted … we're not going to get back all the trees that were cut down on our reserves … they're not just gonna grow back because there's cities and towns and other people living on that land. As an Aboriginal person, I understand that now, so I … just hope that, for future generations that nobody else forgets about it as well.

Despite these efforts by Anishinaabe youth to challenge others, comments from some white actors repeatedly suggested reactivity and resistance in ways that confounded movement toward a **testimonial encounter**.[5] Here something was at work that was more complex than the smooth assimilation of new knowledge. Amidst dramatic swings between defiance and engagement, all the white cast members were unanimous about at least one aspect of their emotional discomfort: they named it shame. Consequently, I want to suggest that one way to take seriously the youth commentary emerging from this project would be to engage in a more sustained analysis of the **epistemology** of shame.

I start with an imaginative definition of shame provided by Margaret Werry and Roisin O'Gorman (2007) in their writing on pedagogy and emotion.

> Shame, noun & verb—1 noun a) *predominant … [emotion] at work in the learning process*. b) a taut delicate thread drawn between two persons, a ghost of the past waiting to haunt, taint, animate the present.…
> 2 verb a) to wound, to punish … b) [irregular usage] to connect, to acknowledge, to register, to know … a state experienced in the aftermath of thwarted interest; a contingency of desire, passion. (p. 213, emphasis added)

Most common associations with the word shame, then, understand it as a *relational* experience.

The history narrated at the start of this chapter highlights that shaming tactics have most often been systematically employed against Indigenous people in the regulation of Indigenous communities (through residential schools and legal sanctions against Indigenous languages, ceremony, and culture). It is striking that for the Anishinaabe actors and audience members, the play worked precisely *through and against* this legacy. As Eve Sedgwick (2010) argues, shame is not a distinct and toxic part of a group or individual identity that can simply be excised, but it *can* be available for the work of metamorphosis and transformation (p. 51). That is, we cannot just locate and "get rid of" the shame we feel about who we are, or how people imagine us, but we can use that shame as fuel to challenge societal assumptions.

Some of the youth participants in *Treaty Daze* engaged in this potentially transformational process through wanting to "do the research" and "nail the role," others through performing Anishinaabe humour, and still others through continuing to assert the "gravity" of present-day **colonialism**, in the face of repeated refusals. In this context, the actor who avowed that "we're not going to get over it in a century or two" is articulating an Indigenous-specific claim to the necessarily unfinished work of land-based connection. That is, they are claiming Indigenous peoples' right to the ongoing process of (re)connecting to the land, and their sovereign relationship to their territory.

But how might we understand the perspectives of the white youth who took up the language of "shame," but then quickly moved on to assert that "times have changed" and disavowed the present-day colonization? Here youth moved from engaging with a collective sense of shame to sense of a *national* identity as inevitably focused on positive attributes. Indeed, several argued that Canada "is a 'kick-ass' country." This move, from the individual to the national, is telling. As Sarah Ahmed (2005), in her analysis of discourses of reconciliation between white settlers and Indigenous people in Australia suggests, "what is striking is how shame becomes not only a mode of recognition of injustices committed against others, but also a form of nation building" (p. 102).

Drawing on Ahmed (2005), I want to explore how quickly some youth moved from acknowledging a collective sense of "shame" to asserting that this legacy makes no demands on the present. I highlight aspects of Ahmed's (2005) analysis in order to reflect on how shame and pride, shame and dignity, and shame and performativity are "different interlinings of the same glove" (Sedgwick, 2010, p. 51). As I noted earlier, shame is a relational experience. In her analysis, Ahmed takes up the *sticky* nature of national shame, as the very ideals that have been violated are the ones that "stick" members of a community together. Here the failure of a nation to live up to its ideals becomes a mode of identification and a form of recuperation—we feel ashamed of "our past" as a way of convincing ourselves we, as a nation, are better in the present. In Ahmed's (2005) words,

> Those who witness the past injustice through feeling "national shame" are aligned with each other as "well-meaning individuals"; if you feel shame, you are "in" the nation, a nation that means well. Shame "makes" the nation in the witnessing of past injustice, a witnessing that involves feeling shame … *By witnessing what is shameful about the past, the nation can "live up to" the ideals that secure its identity or being in the present.* In other words, our shame means that we mean well. (p. 109, emphasis added)

For Anishinaabe youth the play provided a language to articulate and dramatize the multiple displacements that have violated Anishinaabe territory and knowledge practices over almost two hundred years. In this context, Anishinaabe youth did not overcome the "bad feelings" brought up by the discursive contests mapped out here, but some of them began, at least, to establish a different relationship to them, by asserting a new understanding of this legacy. But for some white youth, the project raised deeply unsettling questions about whether or not times *have* changed. These misgivings were often resolved through a recuperation of the nation as only momentarily shame-faced, so that **whiteness** was retrieved as not so bad anymore, while Canada was imagined as having moved into a new era where colonial violence was not a continuing event.

What interests me most about the *Treaty Daze* production is how it invited all its participants to look shame in the eye. Here I return to Werry and O'Gorman's analysis of shame as integral to pedagogy, as cited earlier: "Shame: a) predominant emotion in the learning process; b) a delicate thread drawn between persons, a ghost of the past waiting to haunt, taint and animate the present" (2007, p. 213).

I argue that productions such as *Treaty Daze* are one way through the "bad feelings" that inevitably "haunt, taint, and animate the present" when confronting white invasion, settlement, and colonial dispossession of Indigenous people in the land now called Canada. However, there is no guarantee that this form of decolonial resistance will have the intended effect. While feelings like "shame" can be transformed, as the Anishinaabe actors demonstrated so clearly in their efforts to name the violence of dispossession and "nail the role," others only acknowledged a collective sense of "shame" in order to re-assert that this legacy makes no demands on the present. Indeed, their very acknowledgement of "past" injustice quickly transformed to nationalist boosterism. Even for the white participants who did not disavow inequality in the present, their use of shame to cast themselves as "good" white witnesses became a form of recuperation.

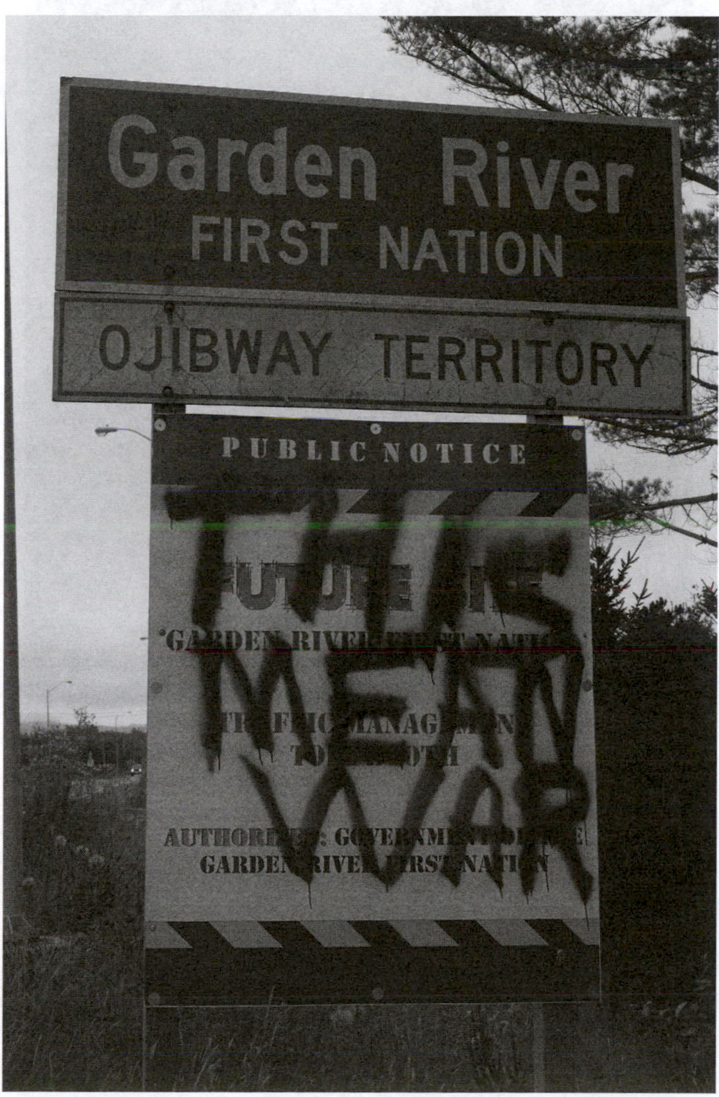

FIGURE 15.1a Retaliation against Garden River First Nation protest of HST. © Margot Francis.

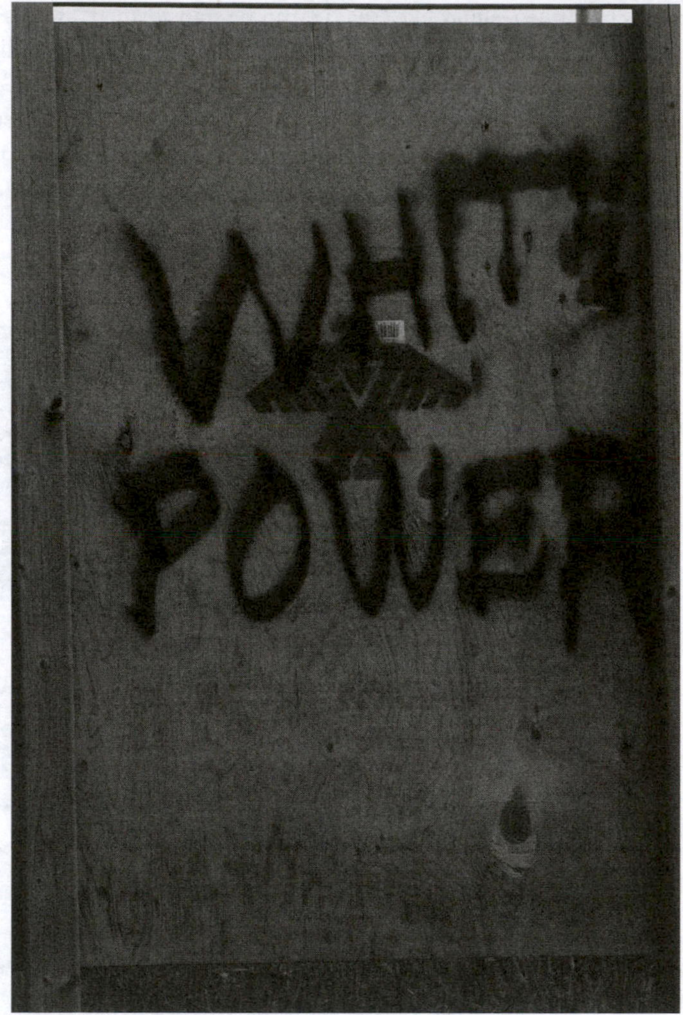

FIGURE 15.1b Retaliation against Garden River First Nation protest of HST. © Margot Francis.

The resistance of some white actors who participated in the *Treaty Daze* project is not accidental. Despite their working side-by-side with an Anishinaabe-led team and portraying the corrupt dealings of the Canadian government and mining interests in land and treaty negotiations in this performance, the cast was not uniformly supportive of the analysis presented in the play. For some actors, their sense of distress was about "how ignorant white people *used* to be." This narrative that "times have changed … things are not like that anymore" worked both to re-assert national pride and also to preserve white racial "innocence" and through these to refuse a testimonial encounter.

Afterwards ...

As the summer theatre project described here extended over six years, I was back in Garden River and Batchewana First Nations in the spring of 2010. This time the youth collective were working on a new play called *Reservations* developed by the same Anishinaabe-led youth team, but this time in collaboration with Debajehmujig Theatre Group on Manitoulin Island (*Debajehmujig* means "storytellers" in the Cree and Ojibwa languages). The production highlighted the conflict sparked by the then-new Harmonized Goods and Services Tax (HST). Local tensions between Anishinaabe and white settlers came to a head in May 2010 when the Garden River band council erected a sign on the Trans-Canada Highway just outside the reserve notifying travellers they would be charged a poll tax for crossing Anishinaabe territory if the HST was levied against people on the reserve, which they argued contravened their treaty rights. Within 24 hours vandals had retaliated by spray-painting the sign with their own message: on one side "White Power" and on the other "This mean war" (Figure 15.1a, b). During this same period local Indigenous children in elementary school reported being harassed by white boys, who were also responding to conflict regarding the HST. They taunted, "Why don't we just kill all the Indians?"[6]

Once again, these actions highlight the stakes implicit in the colonial relationship; racist graffiti and school bullying are not simply random acts by individuals with no relationship to the larger structure of Canadian society, they are connected to the normalized violence that shapes Indigenous–settler relations. Nevertheless, perhaps the most important legacy of this project comes from observing the ways Anishinaabe youth worked, over several years, to reclaim their history and lead a process of cultural resistance which challenged the Canadian state policy of dispossession. This "on-the-ground" resistance through cultural production articulated Anishinaabe leadership and intelligence, despite the resistance by some white actors. While the corrosive legacy of Canadian state dispossession will never be "overcome," the Anishinaabe youth in this theatre project did establish a different relationship to that legacy and created space for articulating new ways to make sense of this inheritance. As Lawrence and Dua (2005) argue, it is only settlers' contemporary negation of the contested legacy that allows many of us not to see the "colonial project that is taking place around us" (p. 124). I hope this critique will contribute to new forms of solidarity to challenge that ongoing shameful legacy.

Study Questions

1 What stereotypes of "Indians" have been part of your experience? Has reading this chapter changed any of your perceptions?
2 This analysis invites us to "unpack the centre." What is "the centre" in colonialism? Has it changed over time? How did Indigenous youths' theatre performances help them to unpack the centre?

3 In this chapter, white participants in the theatre project felt ashamed of their past, but they used the fact of that shame to make themselves feel better about the present. Can you think of other examples of times when white people make themselves feel good now by feeling bad about the past? What could they do instead?

Exercises

1 A survey by the Coalition for the Advancement of Aboriginal Studies done in collaboration with the Canadian Race Relations Foundation found that 80 per cent of first-year university and college students had gained little exposure to Indigenous issues and felt unprepared to address contemporary conflicts between Indigenous and non-Indigenous peoples (Coalition for the Advancement of Aboriginal Studies, 2002). What is known in your family about Indigenous–Canadian relationships? How does this compare to the analysis in this chapter?

2 Choose one area from the following list to explore how Indigenous people are being portrayed or discussed: Hollywood film; television; magazines; newspapers; advertising; comic books, graphic, and mass-market novels; public art; outdoor/nature organizations; and educational materials and textbooks.

3 Are popular culture references to Indigenous people hard to find? In the media you see every day, are issues such as land and treaty negotiations, health, poverty and the rights of Indigenous people referred to or discussed? What stereotypes appear? Who created the images and what version of history is being presented? How do you tell the difference? Do the images feel different to you than they would have before reading the chapter?

Notes

1 Teddy Syrette, interview with the author, April 2009.

2 Assembly of First Nations, *Dismantling the Doctrine of Discovery*, January 2018. See: http://www.afn.ca/wp-content/uploads/2018/02/18-01-22-Dismantling-the-Doctrine-of-Discovery-EN.pdf

3 This quote and all subsequent material from the actors and audience members are taken from interviews with the cast and selected members of the audience, in Garden River First Nation and Sault Ste. Marie, August 17–18, 2009.

4 This references an actor who was of mixed Indigenous and European heritage. The term is not meant to reference any "essentialist" meaning for "race," but rather to acknowledge how actual people use colloquial terms to describe their mixed heritage.

5 The testimonial encounter can be thought of as a space where people listen, acknowledge, and take responsibility for trauma or violence recounted by a survivor, and become ready to respond.
6 Teddy Syrette, interview with the author, August 2010.

References

Ahmed, S. (2005). The politics of bad feeling. *Australian Critical Race and Whiteness Studies Association Journal, 1*(1), 72–85.

Cannon, M. (2008). Revisiting histories of legal assimilation, racialized injustice, and the future of Indian status in Canada. In J.P. White, S. Wingert, D. Beavon, & P. Maxim (Eds.), *Aboriginal policy research Volume 5: Moving forward, making a difference* (pp. 35–48). Toronto, ON: Thompson Educational Publishing.

Coalition for the Advancement of Aboriginal Studies. (2002). Learning about walking in beauty: Placing Aboriginal perspectives in Canadian classrooms. *Canadian Race Relations Foundation.* Retrieved from http://www.crrf-fcrr.ca/images/CRRF_Policy_and_Research_projects/cover_page-ISBN.pdf

Fontaine, T. (2016, January 26). Canada discriminates against children on reserves, tribunal rules. *CBC News.* Retrieved from http://www.cbc.ca/news/Indigenous/canada-discriminates-against-children-on-reserves-tribunal-rules-1.3419480

Hall, S. (1992). The West and the rest: Discourse and power. In S. Hall & B. Gieben (Eds.), *Formations of modernity* (Vol. 1, pp. 275–331). Cambridge, UK: Polity Press in Association with the Open University Press.

Lawrence, B. (2002). Rewriting histories of the land: Colonization and Indigenous resistance in Eastern Canada. In S. Razack (Ed.), *Race, space, and the law: Unmapping a white settler society* (pp. 21–46). Toronto, ON: Between the Lines Press.

Lawrence, B. (2003). Gender, race, and the regulation of Native identity in Canada and the United States: An overview. *Hypatia, 18*(2), 3–31.

Lawrence, B., & Dua, E. (2005). Decolonizing anti-racism. *Social Justice, 32*(4), 120–143.

Milloy, J. (2017). *A national crime: The Canadian government and the residential school system.* Winnipeg, MB: University of Manitoba Press.

Pratt, M.L. (2008). *Imperial eyes: Travel writing and transculturation* (2nd ed.). London. UK: Routledge.

Sedgwick, E.K. (2010). Shame, theatricality, and queer performativity: Henry James's *The art of the novel.* In D.M. Halperin & V. Traub (Eds.), *Gay shame* (pp. 49–62). Chicago, IL: University of Chicago Press.

Simpson, L.B. (2014). Land as pedagogy: Nishnaabeg intelligence and rebellious transformation. *Decolonization: Indigeneity, Education & Society, 3*(3), 1–25.

Simpson, L.B. (2017). *As we have always done: Indigenous freedom through radical resistance.* Minneapolis, MN: University of Minnesota Press.

Stasiulis, D., & Jhappan, R. (1995). The fractious politics of a settler society: Canada. In D. Stasiulis & N. Yuval-Davis (Eds.), *Unsettling settler societies: Articulations of gender, race, ethnicity and class* (pp. 95–131). London, UK: Sage.

Styres, S., Haig-Brown, C., & Blimkie, M. (2013). Toward a pedagogy of land: The urban context. *Canadian Journal of Education/Revue Canadienne de l'éducation*, *36*(2), 34–67.

Truth and Reconciliation Commission of Canada (TRC). (2015). *The Truth and Reconciliation Commission's final report* (chapter 2). https://www.rcaanc-cirnac.gc.ca/eng/1450124405592/1529106060525

United Nations, Department of Economic and Social Affairs, Division for Social Policy and Development, Secretariate of the Permanent Forum on Aboriginal Issues, International Expert Group Meeting on the Millenium Development Goals, Aboriginal Participation in Good Governance, New York, January 11-13, 2006) available at: http://un.org/esa/socdev/unpfii/documents/workshop/_MDG_chartrand.doc. https://undocs.org/E/C.19/2006/7

Werry, M., & O'Gorman, R. (2007). Shamefaced: Performing pedagogy, outing affect. *Text and Performance Quarterly*, *27*(3), 213–230.

Wolfe, P. (2006). Settler colonialism and the elimination of the native. *Journal of Genocide Research*, *8*(4), 387–409.

16 Being a Tourist

GADA MAHROUSE

Introduction: Exploring Power in Tourism

In August 2017, at the peak of the summer holiday season, anti-tourism protests took place in Barcelona, Dubrovnik, Rome, and Venice (McLaughlin, 2017; Peter, 2017). At around the same time, graffiti with the words "Tourist go home" started appearing near popular tourist attractions in several European cities. These negative publicly displayed commentaries about tourism puzzled many and provoked a lot of debate. In general, **tourism** is regarded as economically beneficial, and growth in the tourism industry is seen as positive. Furthermore, if we consider the profits that the tourism industry generates, it becomes difficult to understand why some local residents want to reduce or end it. Profits aside, many believe that tourism is good insofar as it creates opportunities for people to interact with others who live far away, sometimes in very different conditions. Why, then, would there be so much dislike of tourism? What would provoke local residents to call for the expulsion of tourists and take to the streets to protest their presence? The starting point for answering these questions is to understand tourism as an **everyday practice** that is shaped by many complex and overlapping **power relations**.

Of course, not all agree with the graffiti and the protests. Some residents of those cities passionately argue that tourists should be welcomed, and business owners compete to draw them into their hotels, package tours, souvenir shops, and restaurants. In addition, increasing numbers of tour operators are offering "eco" tours or opportunities to "give back" through volunteer tourism. How then do we make sense of this push-pull reaction to tourism? Are tourists wanted, or not? This chapter explores some of these questions. The goal is not to suggest less tourism, or more of it. Nor is the goal to judge

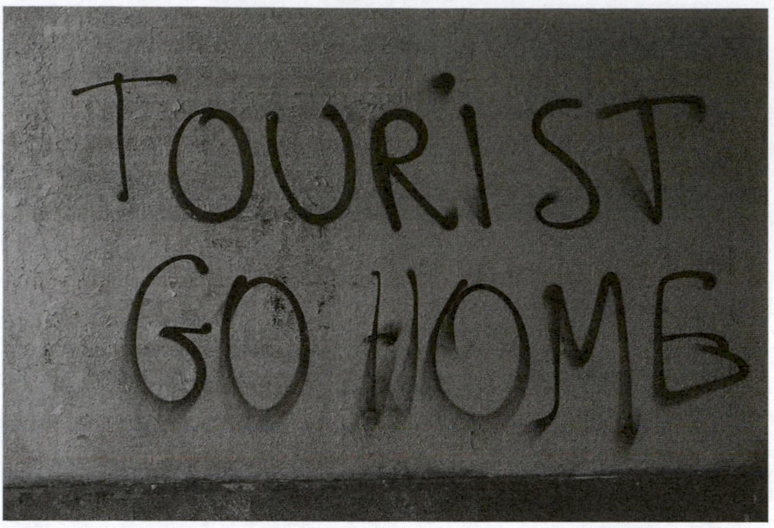

FIGURE 16.1 Graffiti in Barcelona, Spain. bestjeroen/Shutterstock.

some forms of tourism as good and others as bad. Rather, the goal of this chapter is to reveal how everyday power relations are at the heart of tourism.

Definition, Frameworks, and Overview

Tourism has existed for centuries and is therefore not new. Records show that it was well established by the Roman era. However, it is in the early 20th century that mass-scale tourism became possible because of advancements in transportation infrastructure (Raby & Phillips, 2012). Whereas it was once only the elite classes who could afford to travel, today affordable fares have made it possible for working-class people to travel. Tourism currently represents the largest movement of people ever across national **borders**, and therefore has enormous impacts on all parts of the world. At the environmental level, it depletes natural resources and creates pollution, including harming the ozone layer through air travel (Gmelch, 2010).

Although many varying definitions exist, in this chapter "tourism" will be defined as the *voluntary* movement of people who have the resources of money, time, and official documents to undertake *leisure* travel (Harrison, 2003; Amit, 2007). Moreover, it will be examined as a practice of power that has economic, environmental, and socio-political impacts. It raises many questions about privilege, access, political economies, consumption, representations, and **subjectivity**. For instance, who can freely, safely, and easily cross borders? Who benefits from the profits of the tourism industry? What types of jobs does it generate? How are destinations commodified and marketed to draw us in? What do the photos and blogs we post about our trips reveal about how we position ourselves in the world?

The chapter homes in on some of these questions. It is not a comprehensive survey of the study of tourism. Instead, it is mainly concerned with the specific socio-political issues and debates that help us better understand everyday power in tourism. To do this, the chapter focuses on three main themes. First, using the example of a typical beach holiday trip to a destination in the Caribbean, we consider some of the ways that **colonial** histories continue to influence contemporary tourism. The second section focuses on the growing niche market of "heritage" tourism to explore how the (relative) privileges of **race**, **gender**, **class**, and **citizenship** come together to produce identities. The third section focuses on the connections between tourism, border controls, and militarism to illustrate how **governmental power** allows geographic mobility for some while restricting the movement of others. The chapter concludes by returning to the motivations behind anti-tourism protests and the push/pull forces of tourism.

In addition to the frameworks for studying power outlined in the Introduction and Chapter 1, this chapter draws heavily from postcolonial, transnational feminist theorists who have been instrumental in drawing awareness to how race, gender, class, and citizenship are shaped and reflected in the taken-for-granted practices of tourism. Some concepts will also be taken from what is now known as *Critical* Tourism Studies. Until relatively recently, the field of Tourism Studies has focused mainly on the business aspects of the tourism industry and ways that it could be increased (Bianchi, 2009, p. 488), so practices of power in tourism have not been considered. Some identify John Urry's publication of *The Tourist Gaze* in 1990 as marking what is referred to the "critical turn" in Tourism Studies. Unlike his predecessors, Urry (1990) drew from Foucauldian thinking on the relationship between power and knowledge and inspired others to shift their attention toward the social, cultural, discursive, and **representational practices** of power in tourism (Bianchi, 2009, p. 489).

Anti-tourism Protests

Although they may have been new to Europe, anti-tourism protests are not uncommon in **Indigenous** communities and some parts of what is considered the "Global South," where many have been tirelessly protesting the damaging effects of tourism on their communities and environments for some time. For example, academic-activist Haunani-Kay Trask (1993) has written strong critiques of tourism in her homeland of Hawaii. She has argued that tourism in Hawaii is a colonial imposition and has challenged the idea that, for Americans, it is "*theirs*: to use, to take, and above all to fantasize about long after the experience" (Trask, 1993, p. 180, emphasis in original). Trask (1993) also juxtaposes the mainstream **representations** of Hawaii as a pleasurable paradise with the harsh political, economic, and cultural conditions most Hawaiians live in, which she describes as "hard, ugly, and cruel"

(p. 180). Another example of anti-tourism protests comes from the beaches of Goa in southern India—known for its all-night dance party **culture** that has made it a favourite destination for young Western European and North American tourists. Yet, many Goans have objected to the impact that tourism has had on their environment, economy, and culture (Sen, 1999). Similarly, a group called *Indigenous Tourism Rights International* has argued that although "ecotourism" is a buzzword used by many governments; many supposed ecotourism activities are carried out in Indigenous communities without their consent or participation (Garcia, 2002).

Tourism as Neocolonialism: The Quest for the Exotic, Authentic, and Low-Cost

In the Introduction we met Jasmine whose friend, Mandy (a woman from Toronto), is getting married in the summer and planning an "exotic" honeymoon. Elaborating on this hypothetical story about Mandy's trip helps to reveal some of the neocolonial facets of contemporary tourism and everyday power.

Mandy and her partner had spent a lot of money on their wedding, so they wanted a honeymoon that would not cost them much. To start planning, Mandy searched "cheap honeymoon in Caribbean" on Google and came upon an article titled "10 Affordable Beach Honeymoon Destinations." The images on it were very enticing. They showed empty beaches with white sand and attractive smiling Black waiters and waitresses carrying trays of elegant plates of food and colourful cocktails. Mandy wanted to go somewhere where English was the official language, and so she started scrolling through the section on Grenada. There she read that it is considered the "Spice Island" because of its nutmeg plantations. The description also stated that many of its towns "maintain a great colonial feel and charm." One of the island's main landmark sights is a beautiful cathedral church that is perched on top of a hill. It sounded perfect.

Mandy wanted to have an authentic experience of the island and wanted to interact with some locals, but at the same time she heard that there is a lot of crime in the Caribbean and was concerned about safety. She went to TripAdvisor and typed in "We do not want to stay in a resort but need a bit of background info about safe areas before booking anywhere." In response, someone named Denis from the UK wrote back recommending they stay in the enclave where a lot of British ex-pats rent out "safe and clean" villas. Denis added that the villas "often include a laundry service and sometimes at minimal cost the maid will prepare meals for you."

Searching further, she also found a blog called "The Real Grenada" written by a Canadian who had been there twice. He described how much it has changed from the time he first visited it ten years ago which, according to him, was before "the island was ruined by mass tourism." Another of his complaints was that the Grenadian people were much friendlier and more welcoming in the past. He also gave tips about where to go for the best-priced meals and souvenirs.

Mandy's approach to planning her trip is familiar and provides us with a good entry point for thinking about tourism, **neocolonialism**, and **micro-processes of power**. To begin with, Alexander and Mohanty's (1997) idea of "colonial legacies" is helpful because it implies that we need to **historicize** tourism as a continuation of colonial relations of power. Many of the very things that drew Mandy to Grenada such as English being the official language, the "nutmeg," and even the beautiful cathedral were direct results of both English and French imperial conquests. Indeed, Grenada's current position as a popular, relaxing, and peaceful tourist destination contradicts its complex colonial history which entailed pillage, destruction, and slavery (Steele, 1974). After the island was "discovered" by Columbus in 1498, both the French and the English claimed the island at various points over the years. By the early 1700s, its sugar industry began to flourish, and African slaves were imported by the French to work the plantations (Steele, 1974). Moreover, Grenada was only granted full independence from Britain in 1974, making it one of the last small outposts of the British Empire (Steele, 1974).[1]

Mandy's desire for an "exotic" location and "authentic" experiences, along with how she understands herself in relation to the place she will be visiting, are also formed by colonial histories, political economies, and **discourses** about what Stuart Hall refers to as "the rest" (as opposed to the West). As many **postcolonial** theorists and writers have shown, when it comes to people from the "Global North" visiting places in the "Global South"—or what has been referred to as "the core-periphery relationship" (Tucker & Akama, 2009, p. 504)—tourism reproduces colonial power relations in several significant ways (Clifford, 1997; Kaplan, 1996).

For example, the travel websites that Mandy visits show how the legacies of colonialism continue in contemporary tourism through the imagery used to market destinations such as the Caribbean (Hall, 1997). The websites reveal how, within late-capitalist **neoliberal** conditions of economic **globalization**, culture is commodified for the consumption of the tourist. As Tucker and Akama (2009) have argued, these images are "a direct continuation of the **racialized representations** that began in the seventeenth century" (p. 506). As noted in Chapter 1's introduction to Stuart Hall's work, discourses produce knowledge about the "West" and the "Rest" in ways that are directly connected to economic and political institutions in the production of systems of power. In this example, the affordable "exotic" location is produced by both a discourse of "the **other**" *and* a **political economy** of poverty and global **inequality** that enables some to *become* tourists while others *serve* tourists.

Mandy's concerns about safety and cleanliness can also easily be traced to these discourses in which othered groups are stereotyped as threatening or dirty. In fact, the blog exchanges about Grenada are a direct extension of earlier forms of "travel writing" in which the Western identity was shaped through the narratives disseminated about encounters with the Other (Kaplan, 1996; Lewis & Mills, 2003; Pratt, 1992; Said, 1978). As Holland and Huggan (1998) argue, although the style and means of circulating travel narratives have changed in recent years, they continue to reinforce the tropes and clichés of their earlier counterparts, including **stereotypes** of danger. Some of the travel bloggers' claims about knowing the "real" Grenada are also examples of colonial knowledge production. The sweeping generalizations about Grenada and its people that these narratives reproduce are validated with the qualifier "I know, because I was there" (Tusting, Crawshaw, & Callen, 2002).

The blogger who complained about the changes in Grenada over the ten years since his first trip is a good example of how what is considered the real or authentic nature of a place is something embedded in a fixed past. This has been referred to as **imperialist nostalgia**—a phenomenon where people mourn the passing of what they themselves have transformed (Rosaldo, 1989). In this example, the blogger's complaints are contradictory because they conceal his complicity with the very things of the past that he yearns for. Specifically, he blames the increases of tourists for the changes in Grenada, but ironically does not consider his own participation in tourism as something that has contributed to the increase.

The travel websites and blogs that Mandy visited did not offer any indication of the negative impacts of tourism from the perspectives of locals. To get a sense of how some people in or from the Caribbean perceive the negative impacts of tourism, it helps to turn to Jamaica Kincaid's creative nonfiction book *A Small Place* (1989). Focusing on the tourism industry in Antigua, Kincaid (1989) reveals the unpleasant, though often hidden, impacts of tourism that the typical tourist is not exposed to. For example, she prompts tourists to question their taken-for-granted privileges and attempts to reverse the **tourist gaze** back onto them:

> Every native would like to find a way out, every native would like a rest, every native would like a tour. But some natives—most natives in the world—cannot go anywhere. They are too poor. They are too poor to go anywhere. They are too poor to escape the reality of their lives; and they are too poor to live properly in the place they live, which is the very place you, the tourist, want to go—so when the natives see you, the tourist, they envy you, they envy your ability to leave your own banality and boredom, they envy your ability to turn their own banality and boredom into a source of pleasure for yourself. (pp. 18–19)

Kincaid's book also challenges the idea that tourism is the means of economic "development" for poorer countries. Others have similarly exposed the "precarious form of dependency and inequality" perpetuated through tourism whereby those "in the South continue to perform menial labour for rich, visiting westerners" (Raby & Phillips, 2012, p. 12). The laundry service and meal preparation services available at minimal costs in the rental villas that Mandy was contemplating are a typical example of this. The affordability of such services hints at the gross discrepancies in wages and income.

The inequalities embedded in the relative affordability of tourism in the Caribbean as a whole is also examined in the documentary film *Life and Debt* (Black, 2001).

Focusing on the example of Jamaica, it reveals that because of debt accumulated through International Monetary Fund (IMF) loans, the country was compelled to develop the tourism industry rather than services that would directly benefit its people. It also shows how the policies of the IMF, the World Bank, and other aid organizations continue to control its economy.

June Jordan's "Report from the Bahamas"

June Jordan's "Report from the Bahamas" gives an account of her experiences as a Black woman tourist going to the Bahamas on a holiday. Written in 1982, it offers a contrasting yet complementary vantage point to Jamaica Kincaid's (1989) book on Antigua, which is written from the perspective of someone from the "host" community. Jordan, who is originally from Jamaica but who lives in the United States, reflects on the encounters she has with the locals in the Bahamas, given her race, class, gender, and diasporic identity. For example, focusing on her complex privileged positioning with the local women in the tourist industry who serve her, she writes, "I notice the fixed relations between these other Black women and myself. They sell and I buy or I don't. They risk not eating. I risk going broke on my first vacation afternoon. We are not particularly women anymore; we are parties to a transaction designed to set us against each other." (Jordan, 2003, pp. 7–8)

In sum, Mandy's honeymoon trip planning offers glimpses into some of the ways that colonial power relations produce contemporary tourism. Certainly, it is easy to see how power operates in cases like Mandy's where people from the Global North travel to destinations in the Global South. But power relations in tourism are not always so clear cut. For example, what if Mandy had ancestral ties to Grenada and wanted to go there to learn about her family history? How would the relations of power differ? In the next section, using the example of what is known as heritage or **diaspora** tourism (when second- or third-generation people in the Global North travel to their ancestral "homelands") we will consider some of the more complicated ways that the micro-politics of race, gender, citizenship, and class can operate in tourism. Through this example, we will also examine more closely how tourism is a site of identity formation.

Race, Citizenship, and Class Privilege in Heritage Tourism

In its May 2017 online issue, *Condé Nast Traveler* featured an article on "heritage" tourism, stating that it is more popular than ever (Lippe-McGraw, 2017). Indeed, heritage tourism (which is sometimes referred to as "diaspora" or "roots" tourism) is a fast-growing niche market. It mainly caters to people from **settler-colonial** countries such as Canada, Australia, New Zealand, and the US, who plan vacations based on a desire to reconnect with their family histories. As a result, countries with large diaspora populations in North America such as Ireland, India, and China are seeing increases in visitors looking for links with their ancestral homelands. The term "diaspora" can refer to those whose ancestors chose to leave their home countries versus those whose departures were forced or coerced (Agnew, 2005; Brah, 1996; Hall, 1997). According to the 2016 census, more than one in five Canadians (21.9 per cent) were born in another country, and Statistics Canada projects that will increase to more than 28 per cent by 2036 (Statistics Canada, 2017), so the growing popularity of the heritage tourism market is perhaps not surprising. In what follows, we will see that heritage tourism is a compelling site for examining questions of racialized power, mobility, multiculturalism, and space. Unlike conventional tourism to "exotic" places discussed in the previous section, heritage tourism is seen as more virtuous because the people who participate in it can claim some personal connection to the destination.

Although heritage tourism is not a new phenomenon, and there are many different types, two relatively recent changes can be attributed to its rapidly increasing popularity. One is a push for people to find their roots, promoted through television shows such as *Who Do You Think You Are?* and *Finding Your Roots* and genealogy sites like *Ancestry.com* (Lippe-McGraw, 2017). The other is that many **nation-states**, recognizing the potential economic benefits of heritage tourism, have now developed sophisticated marketing strategies to increase it. For instance, the Ministry of Overseas Indian Affairs has developed a project whereby people of Indian origin can request to have their roots traced (Newland & Taylor, 2010, p. 7). Scotland's *Homecoming 2009* campaign is another example of an elaborate effort to draw heritage tourists. One component of it was the release of an "I am a Scot" video with people describing what makes them Scottish in a purposeful effort to make diaspora members feel like they "have a stake in the country's future" (Newland & Taylor, 2010, pp. 7–8). One of the most established examples of heritage tourism is the *Birthright Israel* program that was started in 1999. It is an all-expenses-paid 10-day tour for young Jews living outside of Israel to develop a sense of attachment to Israel (Newland & Taylor, 2010, p. 9). Heritage tours to some parts of Africa aimed at Black people living in the US and Canada have also become big businesses (Essah, 2001). The growing interest in these tours can be seen in the fact that UNESCO supported the development of a program called *African Diaspora Heritage Trails*, which links sites in Africa and the Americas associated with the transatlantic slave trade (Newland & Taylor, 2010, p. 8).

Heritage tourism is largely seen as a "vehicle through which transnational identity structures between diasporic communities and homelands are maintained" (Duval, 2003, p. 52), and it is promoted as a way of "bridging" cultures because it creates opportunities for fostering **hybridity** (hyphenated identities) and emotional ties to people and places elsewhere. Some researchers have found that heritage tourism can indeed strengthen emotional ties to one's ancestral identity (Louie, 2010) and can be experienced as an emotionally satisfying "homecoming" (Basu, 2007). For example, Lev Ari and Mittelberg (2008) found that Jewish North Americans do develop emotional attachments to the **state** of Israel on *Birthright Israel* trips.

At the same time, heritage tourism can also give rise to more ambivalent and complicated processes of identification (Bhimji, 2008). For instance, researchers have also found that some heritage tourists experience a sense of **alienation** when they visit their ancestral homelands and are surprised to find that they identify more strongly with their countries of residence, or with fellow diaspora tourists, than with their ancestral homeland (Jamal & Robinson, 2009). For example, travellers might have always thought of themselves as Chinese Canadian, but after going to China and having the locals treat them as they would any other tourists, they can come to think of themselves as more Canadian after the trip. In other words, the encounters facilitated through heritage tourism can disrupt one's sense of having a hyphenated identity (Coles & Timothy, 2004).

As with any type of tourism, we must think about the political economies, processes of citizenship, and complex ways in which nationalisms are implicated in heritage tourism (Ebron, 1999; Hannam, 2004; Mani & Varadarajan, 2005). Recalling Hall's (1997) analysis of "the West and the rest" is helpful here, too, because the economic and political **exploitation** inherent to European colonialism were both connected to *and made possible by* discourses of Western cultural superiority. If we consider marketing strategies aimed at diaspora communities, for instance, we see that they too commodify histories and cultures (Bandyopadhyay, 2008). For instance, writing about the Indian diaspora, Prashad (1996) points out that, to successfully boost its economy with foreign capital by drawing the diaspora to vacation in India, the Indian government relies upon and reproduces **Orientalist** tropes like "maharajas," because this static romantic imagery of the homeland has great appeal. Prashad (1996) also notes that these representations obscure the complexities of modern India, including vibrant political struggles that persist there. Focusing on YouTube videos uploaded by the Ministry of Tourism of India to promote tourism to diasporic Indians located in the Global North, as well as those from elite social classes in India, Patil (2011) similarly found that the images and tropes are Orientalist. According to Patil (2011), some of the videos highlight social and class differences by showing elite Indian and diasporic Indian tourists as having lighter skin tones. These videos, which are produced by the government, therefore perpetuate demarcations of race and class. Patil (2011) argues that this is but one example of why we need to further examine how neoliberal logic is reshaping processes of othering in tourism promotion.

Heritage tourism to parts of Africa has also been found to reproduce **racialization** because it trades in notions of "authentic" claims of being "Black," "African," and/or "African-American/Canadian" (Clarke, 2006). This has led some to question the type of "racial bonding" that is produced through heritage tourism (de Santana Pinho, 2008). In other instances, heritage tours to Africa gloss over racial histories vis-à-vis the social and political forces of economic globalization by using terms like "**ethnicity**" or "culture" instead of "race" (Pierre, 2009). Moreover, the sentimental notion of claiming a "homeland" abroad also needs to be questioned. It has been argued that state-sponsored heritage tourism is driven by political and economic motives, rather than creating personal bonds. For example, one study found that the aim of forging transnational relationships between diasporic Chinese youth and China was to encourage them to consider future economic investment in China or serve as informal spokespeople on the nation's behalf (Louie, 2010).

In sum, while the connections that are facilitated through heritage tourism can be personally meaningful (Lew & Wong, 2004), we have to consider how these connections can also reinforce structural inequalities. As Ishkanian (2004) writes:

> Regardless of whether tourism is part of a roots or heritage tour, both traveler and hosts recognize that this visit is temporary and that the traveler has no intention of settling and establishing permanent residence. These travelers who are "going home" are sojourners and, to some extent, interlopers, searching for particular emotional or spiritual experiences from the homeland that they hope will validate their current identities and choices of residence. (pp. 118–119)

Ishkanian's (2004) views suggest that the "First-World" positioning of the heritage tourist is still a privileged one and therefore should be questioned in terms of asymmetrical power relations and how it converges with the neoliberal economic and political conditions through which it is produced. Therefore, like other types of tourism, heritage tourism is a commodified form of leisure travel—one derived by choice and one deeply implicated in political economies, border nationalisms, and privileged **mobilities**.

Who Gets to Be a Tourist?

Whether it is for the purpose of a honeymoon in the Caribbean or a heritage tour to learn about one's ancestral roots, one of the main issues related to everyday power in international tourism is who gets to freely cross borders. Indeed, the figure of the tourist must be considered alongside two other figures: the person who cannot travel because they do not have the financial resources and the person who is forced to leave, for instance because of war or political conflicts (Ahmed, Castañeda, Fortier, & Sheller, 2003). This last point is especially striking in light of the forced migrations of people in what has recently come to be known as the "refugee/migrant crisis" that Sharma addresses in Chapter 9. In fact, some have argued that tourism can be considered a social phenomenon (as opposed to an industry) in which the access to voluntary travel is paradoxically linked to the increased policing and surveillance of borders (Torabian & Mair, 2017). In other words, the *mobilities* of some (tourists) and the *immobilities* of others (refugees and asylum seekers) are co-dependent and are in fact coproduced (Ahmed et al., 2003; Bauman, 1998).

FIGURE 16.2 Migrants in dinghy about to land at Del Canuelo beach in Tarifa, southern Spain, July 27, 2018. REUTERS/Jon Nazca.

The image in Figure 16.2 highlights the juxtaposition of "two absolutely dichotomous figures—the wealthy tourist from the Global North and the utterly disenfranchised refugee from the Global South—within the same geographical space" (Pugliese, 2010, p. 105). It shows migrants approaching Del Canuelo beach in Tarifa, Spain, in July 2018 after crossing the Strait of Gibraltar from the coast of Morocco. The jarring contrast between these two figures is also the subject of a striking photo essay by Jörg Brüggemann entitled "Tourists vs. Refugees." In the photos, taken in Kos, Greece, in September 2015, a life-vest like those worn by countless refugees who have dangerously crossed the Mediterranean to escape war is pictured next to a flotation device associated with leisure seaside holidays.

The encounters between tourists and refugees show the need to bring together knowledge from the fields of Tourism Studies and Migration/Mobility Studies.

Until recently, differential access to crossing national borders has been the focus of Migration/Mobility Studies scholars and has been overlooked in the field of Tourism Studies. Increasingly, however, scholars are calling for bringing the two fields of study together to create "opportunities to develop critiques of the tensions underscoring the so-called 'right to travel' and to highlight the ways in which tourism relations and processes are ultimately about power" (Torabian & Mair, 2017, p. 18). For example, Torabian and Mair (2017) examine governmental security practices such as "smart technologies" including the biometric-data NEXUS card system (which was created to allow frequent low-risk travellers easier access between Canada and the United States). They point out that although these technologies give the impression of "quasi-borderless" countries, it has in fact become more difficult for people from certain countries to enter Canada and the United States (p. 27). For example, "no-fly" lists and "random" airport searches of people who wear head coverings (i.e., Muslim women) since 9/11 reveal that airport/travel screening systems are becoming stricter for members of certain racialized groups.

While it may have intensified since 9/11, there is a long history of the Canadian state's discriminatory use of surveillance technologies to control movement through entry laws, passports, and different classifications of mobility. For instance, between 1906 and 1915 the government established the "continuous journey" regulation to make it legal to restrict the entry of people from India who were British subjects while allowing white people from other parts of the Commonwealth to come (Mongia, 1999). According to Mongia (1999), these racialized exclusions were central to organizing and securing the modern definition of the Canadian **nation** and state (p. 529), and the passport system in Canada was introduced to allow a selective (i.e., racialized) mechanism for limiting the entry of people from certain countries.

It goes without saying that questions of mobility, surveillance technologies, and border security are highly political. Yet tourism has somehow been set apart as a lighthearted, even frivolous practice, and therefore by extension, seen as being separate from international politics. Cynthia Enloe's ground-breaking book *Bananas, Beaches and Bases* (1990) was one of the first to challenge this perception. For example, Enloe (1990) points out that Hawaiians refer to the large hotel chains owned by Americans and Japanese as the new "plantations" because white men are the hotel managers, Hawaiian men and women entertain tourists, and Filipino women are the chambermaids (p. 34). Others have since similarly dispelled the myth of the political innocence of tourism by exploring the ways in which tourists are implicated in global geopolitics and showing that tourists' presence is highly political because they are "'living symbol[s]' of a foreign **nationalism**" (Phipps, 1999, p. 78). This is best seen in examples where tourists have been kidnapped or taken hostage for political purposes (such as the European backpackers who were kidnapped in Kashmir in 1995).

The connections between tourism and militarism have also been the focus of recent scholarship. For example, Bender, Fabian, Ruiz, and Walkowitz (2017) posit modern tourism encounters as seeping into diplomacy, militarism, and empire-building. Similarly, Lisle (2016) explores the connections between militarized violence and tourism, showing that one of the ways militarism and tourism are linked is through the growing niche market of "war-zone tours." Indeed, an Internet search of the terms "war tourism" and "danger tourism" readily turn up countless guide books, films, and websites of tour operators that promote or sell travel to some of the most troubled places in the world (Mahrouse, 2016). Some attribute the growing market of tourism in war zones to the fact that we live in a time in which combat and military themes permeate leisure practices ranging from television programming to children's toys (Weaver, 2010, as cited in Mahrouse, 2016). Another explanation for its growth ties back to the ideas of privilege and authenticity. For example, it has been argued that those who are motivated to take part in unconventional tourism like going to war zones want to set themselves apart from other tourists and are drawn to such places and experiences because it creates class and social distinction from their tourist peers who cannot take part in it (Adams, 2006; Laderman, 2013; Phipps, 1999).

Reality Tours[1]

Public awareness of the ways in which tourism contributes to the economic and environmental demise of the Global South has become commonplace and, in response, various forms of responsible "alternative," "reconciliation," "eco," or "pro-poor" tourist options are steadily on the rise (Fennell & Malloy, 2007; Higgins-Desbiolles, 2003). One variation of this more responsible type of tourism is offered by a non-governmental organization (NGO) based in San Francisco called "Global Exchange" whose motto is building "people-to-people ties." As their name suggests, these tours seek to expose rather than hide the harsh realities of local people's lives. Typically, these package tours draw middle-class people from the US and Canada and consist of visiting various local communities to see and learn about some of the social conditions they face. The tours are designed to make use of locally owned businesses and stress the resilience and resourcefulness of the local people. Participants are also encouraged to disseminate what they learned when they return to their home countries. Indeed the "exchange" framework that they operate in implies a form of reciprocity, suggesting that participation in such tours is a departure from the unequal relations in ordinary tourism. As such, reality tours are hailed as a socially responsible and promising step toward a more equitable model of tourism.

While these tours are undoubtedly better than conventional ones, upon closer view they nevertheless give rise to several compelling questions about North/South relations of power, bringing to the surface a number of contentious themes and practices that have long been at the fore of critical feminist, postcolonial, and anti-globalization activists and scholars. First, at a very fundamental level, reality tours take as given the privilege of access and mobility of people with the socio-economic means and citizenship status of being a member of the "First World." Second, since tourists are encouraged to disseminate information they collect through audio- or video-recorded interviews with local and Indigenous people, the representational practices of tourists on reality tours also demand careful consideration. Third, these tours are underpinned by the assumption that contact with local communities is a means of bridging differences and shifting power structures. This combining of education with leisure is indicative of a larger trend in the tourist industry (Amit, 2007) and in education (Roman, 2003). Underlying this approach is the idea that by interacting with people from elsewhere, individual awareness of injustice will increase. Yet, critical analyses have suggested there is little evidence that exposure to difference and the development of personal connections will result in social change. For example, Roman (2003) warns that far from being transgressive, global citizenship education discourses and programs tend to reinforce that people from the Global North can freely cross borders, and paradoxically reinforce nationalisms. Fourth, at the heart of the promise of exposing tourists to "reality" is the idea of authenticity—a concept that has been shown to be about the desire to find "real" people and places as a form of Western idealization (Conran, 2006; West & Carrier, 2004).

Some questions that emerge when considering alternative tourism like reality tours:

- What is being taught, how, and from what perspective?
- How do participants of alternative tours understand themselves in relation to the people and places they are visiting?
- How do the tourists negotiate issues of representation in their efforts to document and report on the conditions they witness?

---

1 Adapted from Mahrouse (2011).

Conclusion

The anti-tourism demonstrations described at the start of this chapter may bring to mind the stereotypically loud, arrogant tourist who is rude, entitled, and insensitive to their surroundings. However, as we have seen, it is not just the crass displays of power by the stereotypical obnoxious tourist that ought to concern us. Indeed, every aspect of tourism—buying a cheap flight, showing your passport at a border, buying souvenirs, checking into a hotel, and telling stories about trips after returning—is not only connected to power, but helps to reproduce power.

Surely, there can be cultural, social, and economic benefits to tourism. For example, members of marginalized communities can be self-empowered by conducting their own tours as a pragmatic way of setting the tourist agenda (i.e., narrating their own histories) while at the same time bolstering their economy with the tourist dollar (Alternative Tourism Group, 2005). However, as the protests described at the start of this chapter reveal, the growing opposition to tourism is becoming difficult to ignore. Local residents who are calling for a reduction of tourism in their cities are not merely annoyed by the crowds; their lives have been deeply and adversely impacted by it. Writing about Barcelona, a local resident explains that tourism has driven up rental prices so significantly that lower-income individuals and families are being driven out (López Díaz, 2017). How then do we counter the negative impacts of tourism? Perhaps, as the graffiti suggests, we need to question the assumption that the tourist is welcome and wanted everywhere they go and to throw into question the assumed "right" that some of us have to being tourists.

Study Questions

1. Do you think that tour operators like Global Exchange (see text box) commodify authenticity? Should we be concerned about this?
2. Writing about the women who serve her on her holiday in the Bahamas (see text box), June Jordan (2003) declares, "We are not particularly women anymore; we are parties to a transaction designed to set us against each other" (p. 8). What do you think she means by this?
3. People are now paid to post on social media about their trips to different countries or specific hotels. What are some of the advantages and disadvantages of this trend?

Exercises

1. What was your best experience as a tourist? What was the worst? How do you think race, gender, class, and citizenship impacted these experiences?
2. What places have you called home? What stories of **migration** were told by your families? What do they reveal about class, race, and gender?
3. Some people have argued that posting pictures of yourself enjoying yourself on vacation has become more important than actually enjoying yourself. Do you think that is true?
4. It has been argued that the question of who can travel has to be supplemented by the question of who can stay at home (Ahmed et al., 2003). In your view, what conditions limit some people from leaving their home countries?
5. International tourism is one of the world's largest and fastest growing industries. According to the United Nations World Tourism Organization, in 2016 worldwide earnings from international tourism reached a new record value of $1,220 billion (UNWTO, 2017). Yet, it estimated that only 20–60 per cent of

the revenue remains in the host country (Urry & Larsen, 2011). Discuss some of the reasons for this. What could be done to make sure that local economies benefit from tourism more?

6 Discuss the role of social media (Instagram, Twitter, Facebook) in tourism.

Documentary Film Resources

1 For more on the racialized exclusions in relation to the continuous journey stipulation, see *Continuous Journey* by Ali Kazemi (2004, 87:30 minutes).

Director's description: In 1914, the *Komagata Maru*, a vessel with 376 immigrants from British India, became the first ship carrying migrants to be turned away by Canada. The consequences were felt throughout the British Empire. *Continuous Journey* is a provocative and multilayered film essay that interweaves photographs, newsreels, home movies, and official documents to unravel a complex and little-known story that reverberates to this day. https://www.cbc.ca/radio/ideas/voyage-of-the-undesirables-remembering-the-komagata-maru-1.2914096

2 For more on tourists' representational practices, see *Cannibal Tours*.

Directors' description: Cannibal Tours is two journeys. The first is that depicted—rich and bourgeois tourists on a luxury cruise up the mysterious Sepik River, in the jungles of Papua New Guinea … the packaged version of a "heart of darkness". The second journey (the real text of the film) is a metaphysical one. It is an attempt to discover the place of "the Other" in the popular imagination. It affords a glimpse at the real (mostly unconsidered or misunderstood) reasons why "civilized" people wish to encounter the "primitive." The situation is that shifting terminus of civilization, where modern mass culture grates and pushes against those original, essential aspects of humanity; and where much of what passes for values in Western culture is exposed in stark relief as banal and fake.

O'Rourke & Associates, Institute of Papua New Guinea Studies, Channel Four (Great Britain), & Direct Cinema Ltd. (1988). *Cannibal tours*. Santa Monica, CA: Direct Cinema [distributor].

Note

1 For a more detailed sketch of the island see Steele (1974).

References

Adams, K.M. (2006). Terror and tourism: Charting the ambivalent allure of the urban jungle. In C. Minca & T. Oakes (Eds.), *Travels in paradox: Remapping tourism* (pp. 205–228). Lanham, MD: Rowman & Littlefield.

Agnew, V. (2005). *Diaspora, memory and identity: A search for home*. Toronto: University of Toronto Press.

Ahmed, S., Castañeda, C., Fortier, A.M., & Sheller, M. (2003). Introduction. In S. Ahmed, C. Castañeda, A.M. Fortier, & M. Sheller (Eds.), *Uprootings/regroundings: Questions of home and migration* (pp. 1–19). New York, NY: Bloomsbury Academic.

Alexander, M.J., & Mohanty, C.T. (1997). Introduction: Genealogies, legacies, movements. In M.J. Alexander & C.T. Mohanty (Eds.), *Feminist genealogies, colonial legacies, democratic futures* (pp. xiii–xlii). New York, NY: Routledge.

Alternative Tourism Group. (2005). *Guidebook: Palestine & Palestinians*. Bethlehem, Palestine: Beit Sahour.

Amit, V. (2007). Structures and dispositions of travel and movement. In V. Amit (Ed.), *Going first class? New approaches to privileged travel and movement* (pp. 1–14). New York, NY: Berghahn Books.

Bandyopadhyay, R. (2008). Nostalgia, identity and tourism: Bollywood in the Indian diaspora. *Journal of Tourism and Cultural Change*, *6*(2), 79–100.

Basu, P. (2007). *Highland homecomings: Genealogy and heritage tourism in the Scottish diaspora*. New York, NY: Routledge.

Bauman, Z. (1998). *Globalization: The human consequences*. New York, NY: Columbia University Press.

Bender, D., Fabian, S., Ruiz, J., & Walkowitz, D.J. (2017). Editor's introduction: Unpacking tourism. *Radical History Review*, *2017*(129).

Bhimji, F. (2008). Cosmopolitan belonging and diaspora: Second-generation British Muslim women traveling to South Asia. *Citizenship Studies*, *12*(4), 413–427.

Bianchi, R.V. (2009). The "critical turn" in tourism studies: A radical critique. *Tourism Geographies*, *11*(4), 484–504.

Black, S. (Producer/Director). (2001). *Life and debt* [Documentary]. Kingston, Jamaica: Tuff Gong Pictures Production.

Brah, A. (1996). *Cartographies of diaspora: Contesting identities*. London, UK: Routledge.

Brüggemann, J. (2015). *Tourists vs. refugees*. Retrieved from http://www.joergbrueggemann.com/tourists-vs-refugees/

Clarke, K.M. (2006). Mapping transnationality: Roots tourism and the institutionalization of ethnic heritage. In K.M. Clarke & D.A. Thomas (Eds.), *Globalization and race: Transformations in the cultural production of blackness* (pp. 133–154). Durham, NC: Duke University Press.

Clifford, J. (1997). *Routes: Travel and translation in the late twentieth century*. Cambridge, MA: Harvard University Press.

Coles, T., & Timothy, D.J. (Eds.). (2004). *Tourism, diasporas and space*. New York, NY: Routledge.

Conran, M. (2006). Beyond authenticity: Exploring intimacy in the touristic encounter in Thailand. *Tourism Geographies*, *8*(3), 274–285.

de Santana Pinho, P. (2008). African-American roots tourism in Brazil. *Latin American Perspectives*, *35*(3), 70–86.

Duval, D.T. (2003). When hosts become guests: Return visits and diasporic identities in a commonwealth eastern Caribbean community. *Current Issues in Tourism*, *6*(4), 267–308.

Ebron, P.A. (1999). Tourists as pilgrims: Commercial fashioning of transatlantic politics. *American Ethnologist*, *26*(4), 910–932.

Enloe, C. (1990). *Bananas, beaches and bases: Making feminist sense of international politics.* Berkeley, CA: University of California Press.

Essah, P. (2001). Slavery, heritage and tourism in Ghana. *International Journal of Hospitality & Tourism Administration, 2*(3–4), 31–49.

Fennell, D.A., & Malloy, D.C. (2007). *Codes of ethics in tourism: Practice, theory, synthesis.* Toronto, ON: Channel View Publications.

Garcia, J.J. (Director). (2002). *Voices from the international forum on Indigenous tourism* [Videorecording]. Saint Paul, MN: Indigenous Tourism Rights International.

Global Exchange. (2018, October 22). *Reality tours FAQ.* Retrieved from https://globalexchange.org/realitytours/upcoming-reality-tours/reality-tours-faq/

Gmelch, S.B. (2010). Why tourism matters. In S.B. Gmelch (Ed.), *Tourists and tourism: A reader* (2nd ed., pp. 3–24). Long Grove, IL: Waveland Press.

Hall, S. (1997). The work of representation. In S. Hall (Ed.), *Representation: Cultural representations and signifying practices* (pp. 13–64). London, UK: Sage Publications.

Hannam, K. (2004). India and the ambivalences of diaspora tourism. In T. Coles & D.J. Timothy (Eds.), *Tourism, diasporas, & space* (pp. 246–260). New York, NY: Routledge.

Harrison, J. (2003). Being a tourist. In *Being a tourist: Finding meaning in pleasure travel* (pp. 3–42). Vancouver, BC: UBC Press.

Higgins-Desbiolles, F. (2003). Reconciliation tourism: Tourism healing divided societies. *Tourism Recreation Research, 28*(3), 35–44.

Holland, P., & Huggan, G. (1998). Post script: Travel writing in the millennium. In *Tourists with typewriters: Critical reflections on contemporary travel writing* (pp. 197–217). Ann Arbor, MI: University of Michigan Press.

Ishkanian, A. (2004). Home-coming and goings. *Diaspora: A Journal of Transnational Studies, 13*(1), 111–121.

Jamal, T., & Robinson, M. (Eds.). (2009). *The Sage handbook of tourism studies.* London: Sage Publications.

Jordan, J. (2003). Report from the Bahamas, 1982. *Meridians: Feminism, Race, Transnationalism, 3*(2), 6–16.

Kaplan, C. (1996). *Questions of travel: Postmodern discourse of displacement.* Durham, NC: Duke University Press.

Kincaid, J. (1989). *A small place.* New York, NY: Plume.

Laderman, S. (2013). From the Vietnam war to the "war on terror": Tourism and the martial fascination. In R. Butler & W. Suntikul (Eds.), *Tourism and war* (pp. 26–35). New York, NY: Routledge.

Lev Ari, L., & Mittelberg, D. (2008). Between authenticity and ethnicity: Heritage tourism and re-ethnification among diaspora Jewish youth. *Journal of Heritage Tourism, 3*(2), 79–103.

Lew, A.A., & Wong, A. (2004). Sojourners, *guanxi* and clan associations: Social capital and overseas Chinese tourism to China. In T. Coles & D.J. Timothy (Eds.), *Tourism, diasporas and space* (pp. 202–214). New York, NY: Routledge.

Lewis, R., & Mills, S. (Eds.). (2003). Introduction. In R. Lewis & S. Mills (Eds.), *Feminist postcolonial theory: A reader* (pp. 1–21). Edinburgh, UK: Edinburgh University Press.

Lippe-McGraw, J. (2017, May 11). Why heritage tourism is more popular than ever. *Condé Nast Traveler.* Retrieved from https://www.cntraveler.com/story/why-heritage-tourism-is-more-popular-than-ever

Lisle, D. (2016). *Holidays in the danger zone: Entanglements of war and tourism*. Minneapolis, MN: University of Minnesota Press.

López Díaz, A. (2017, August 9). Why Barcelona locals really hate tourists. *Independent*. Retrieved from https://www.independent.co.uk/travel/news-and-advice/barcelona-locals-hate-tourists-why-reasons-spain-protests-arran-airbnb-locals-attacks-graffiti-a7883021.html

Louie, A. (2010). Crafting places through mobility: Chinese American "roots-searching" in China. *Identities: Global Studies in Culture and Power*, *8*(3), 343–379.

Mahrouse, G. (2011). Feel good tourism: The ethical option for socially-conscious Westerners. *ACME: An International E-Journal of Critical Geographies*, *10*(3), 372–391.

Mahrouse, G. (2016). War-zone tourism: Thinking beyond voyeurism and danger. *ACME: An International Journal of Critical Geographies*, *15*(2), 330–345.

Mani, B., & Varadarajan, L. (2005). "The largest gathering of the global Indian family": Neoliberalism, nationalism, and diaspora at Pravasi Bharatiya Divas. *Diaspora: A Journal of Transnational Studies*, *14*(1), 45–74.

McLaughlin, K. (2017, August 10). Anti-tourism attacks in Spain: Who is behind them and what do they want? *Independent*. Retrieved from https://www.independent.co.uk/voices/spain-attacks-anti-tourism-british-tourists-visit-barcelona-majorca-valencia-san-sebastian-a7886371.html

Mongia, R.V. (1999). Race, nationality, mobility: A history of the passport. *Public Culture*, *11*(3), 527–555.

Newland, K., & Taylor, C. (2010). *Heritage tourism and the nostalgia trade: A diasporic niche in the development landscape*. Washington, DC: Migration Policy Institute.

Patil, V. (2011). Reproducing-resisting race and gender difference: Examining India's online tourism campaign from a transnational feminist perspective. *Signs*, *37*(1), 185–210.

Peter, L. (2017, August 5). "Tourists go home": Leftists resist Spain's influx. *BBC News*. Retrieved from http://www.bbc.com/news/world-europe-40826257

Phipps, P. (1999). Tourists, terrorists, death and value. In R. Kaur & J. Hutnyk (Eds.), *Travel worlds: Journeys in contemporary cultural* politics (pp. 74–93). New York, NY: Zed Books.

Pierre, J. (2009). Beyond heritage tourism: Race and the politics of African-diasporic interactions. *Social Text*, *27*(1), 59–81.

Prashad, V. (1996). Desh: The contradictions of homeland. In S. Maira & R. Srikanth (Eds.), *Contours of the heart: South Asians map North America* (pp. 225–236). New York, NY: Asian American Writers' Workshop.

Pratt, M.L. (1992). *Imperial eyes: Travel writing and transculturation*. New York, NY: Routledge.

Pugliese, J. (2010). *Transmediterranean: Diasporas, histories, geopolitical spaces*. Brussels, Belgium: P.I.E. Peter Lang.

Raby, R., & Phillips, J. (2012). Tourism: Globalization and the commodification of culture. In D.R. Brock, M.P. Thomas, & R. Raby (Eds.), *Power and everyday practices* (pp. 299–320). Toronto, ON: Nelson Education.

Roman, L. (2003). Education and the contested meanings of "global citizenship." *Journal of Educational Change*, *4*(3), 269–293.

Rosaldo, R. (1989). Imperialist nostalgia. *Representations*, *26*, 107–122.

Said, E. (1978). *Orientalism*. London, UK: Routledge.

Sen, G. (Director). (1999). *Goa under Siege* [Film]. New Delhi, India: Magic Lantern Foundation.

Statistics Canada. (2017, October 25). *Immigration and ethnocultural diversity: Key results from the 2016 census*. Retrieved from https://www150.statcan.gc.ca/n1/daily-quotidien/171025/dq171025b-eng.htm

Steele, B.A. (1974). Grenada, an island state, its history and its people. *Caribbean Quarterly: A Journal of Caribbean Culture*, *20*(1), 5–43.

Torabian, P., & Mair, H. (2017). (Re)constructing the Canadian border: Anti-mobilities and tourism. *Tourist Studies*, *17*(1), 17–35.

Trask, H.-K. (1993). *From a native daughter: Colonialism and sovereignty in Hawai'i*. Monroe, ME: Common Courage Press.

Tucker, H., & Akama, J. (2009). Tourism as postcolonialism. In T. Jamal & M. Robinson (Eds.), *The Sage handbook of tourism studies* (pp. 504–521). London: Sage Publications.

Tusting, K., Crawshaw, R., & Callen, B. (2002). "I know, 'cos I was there": How residence abroad students use personal experience to legitimate cultural generalizations. *Discourse & Society*, *13*(5), 651–672.

UNWTO. (2017). Statement by the Secretary-General, General Assembly, twenty-second session, Chengdu, China, 11–16 September 2017. Retrieved from http://cf.cdn.unwto.org/sites/all/files/pdf/a22_04_statement_by_the_secretary_general_en.pdf

Urry, J. (1990). *The tourist gaze: Leisure and travel in contemporary societies*. London, UK: Sage Publications.

Urry, J., & Larsen, J. (2011). *The tourist gaze 3.0* (3rd ed.). Los Angeles, CA: Sage Publications.

Weaver, A. (2010). Tourism and the military: Pleasure and the war economy. *Annals of Tourism Research*, *38*(2), 672–689.

West, P., & Carrier, J. (2004). Ecotourism and authenticity. *Current Anthropology*, *45*(4), 483–498.

Conclusion

DEBORAH BROCK, ARYN MARTIN, REBECCA RABY, and MARK P. THOMAS

We hope that you will have gained an appreciation of the thematic concepts that have guided this textbook—the **centre**, **normalization**, and **power**—and that you have become intrigued by the task of unpacking the relevance of these concepts for everyday life, and for broader social, political, and economic relations.

The Centre

In this book we have drawn attention to the taken-for-granted, everyday order of things, ideas, institutions, and practices. This centre is often visible when we come into conflict with it, because we have been in some way left out, marginalized, or harmed by prevailing social arrangements. However, it is one thing to know that "they" are doing something to "us" (for example, through the rising cost of tuition fees or gasoline, an abrogation of First Nation treaty rights, or police killings of young Black men), and another thing to comprehend all of the forces that make these events possible. Books like this one allow us to learn about the centre and to think about how it operates. How does the centre persist and with what effects? *Power and Everyday Practices* does not attempt to definitively answer these questions, but it does provide you with some theoretical and methodological tools with which to notice patterns, conduct research, ask questions, and formulate alternatives.

Normalization

Second, we have seen how extraordinarily important normalization is as a condition for **governmental power** (as Foucault understood it) to take hold. The idea of **normal** and how it is created and reproduced is something that we may question the least, because social **norms** do not simply occupy the centre; rather, they come to seem natural and help to secure governmental power, the most common expression of power in the West today. For example, the chapters in *PEP* have shown how normalization secures the idea of a two-sex, two-**gender** system. This system homogenizes the possibilities of who people can be and how they can be known, despite the evidence that substantial numbers of people cannot or will not fit into this simple **binary** logic. But normalization is not only homogenizing; it is simultaneously productive of the idea of the "not normal," the deviant, the sick, and the strange. In other words, it also serves to create **other** specific kinds of individuals and populations of people considered beyond the realm of normal, or falling below normal in a hierarchy of belonging. When we challenge norms, therefore, we simultaneously need to suggest a more ethical way of living because, while norms can change, these changes can simply create new hierarchies and exclusions. It is important to think about how we can challenge norms in a way that instead allows for greater inclusivity. What alternative, ethical ways of organizing personal and social life may be possible?

Power

In *Power and Everyday Practices*, we have identified power in the choices that we make, from the cup of coffee that we drink, to the job application forms that we complete, to the gender and **sexuality** that we identify with, to the self-improvement projects that we undertake. Power is everywhere, from our gaze upon one another to the massive changes that surge across societies.

A number of chapters in the book draw your attention back to one particular manifestation of power that has been building over the last half century, and that has reshaped our daily lives: the neoliberal approach to **capitalism**. Although it takes many forms, **neoliberalism** is now a global normative logic (Dardot & Laval, 2014), with a particular concentration in the West. It is premised on discourses of freedom, yet its practices and outcomes reveal something entirely different. We have seen throughout *PEP* how, in order to understand neoliberalism, we must deepen our understanding of the workings of capitalism as an economic system. In this, Marx remains an invaluable guide, and his observations from the early days of capitalism remain remarkably prescient. Like Marx, we can question why an economic system that, through its extraordinary productive engine, is capable of overcoming scarcity and want, yet does not actually accomplish these most fundamental human goals. Instead, while some prosper, others are neglected and abandoned, living their lives in a state of precarity.

Yet we have also seen how ubiquitous and multifaceted the **organization of consent** and flows of power are, and for that we have turned to other theorists, most notably Michel Foucault and Stuart Hall, to try to grasp the everydayness of power, and to explore the interconnections of multiple forms of **social inequality**. This has required going beyond looking at what is done to people and groups by powerful individuals, organizations, and institutions. Inspired by the work of Foucault, we have introduced you to new ways of thinking about power, including sovereign, disciplinary, biopolitical, and (most importantly) governmental power, that we think deepen understanding of power's complexities. A **governmentality** approach to power relies on "how" questions, because asking how things happen provides insights into the history of ideas, discourses, and actions. How do certain discourses come into being, and become able to claim to speak the truth? How do they shape our personal lives and the broader social world?

We have unpacked **colonial** logics, which have been intrinsic to the development and expansion of capitalism, racial ordering, and the dispossession of **Indigenous** peoples. Throughout *Power and Everyday Practices*, we have asked you to consider how the normative centre includes an everyday enactment of colonial relations of power that stretch back centuries, despite all grand social claims to progress and democratic freedoms. *PEP* does not claim to sufficiently address subordinated **Indigenous knowledges** and experiences, but it does frequently nudge readers to think about how these knowledges and experiences have been cast into invisibility, as we go about our lives on **Turtle Island**.

We have offered you some theoretical and methodological tools to tackle many assumptions and questions about the centre, normalization, and power. The tools we have offered are not the only ones available to you, but they are a good beginning, because these tools compel us to take apart, or deconstruct, ideas to see how they were put together. We can then deepen our analysis to understand the **assemblage** of meanings and actions that shape our everyday lives, and begin to consider how, through our everyday lives, we are ourselves connected to broader relations of power.

We remind you again of Marx's assertion that our task is not simply to understand the world, but to change it (Marx & Engels, 1969). This is what resistance is, in its core meaning. What does resistance entail in the context of this book, and the times that we live in? Part of that we leave to you, our readers, to decide. But following the ideas presented in this book, you will be asking where your knowledge comes from, investigating established "truths," questioning the norm, switching the **discourse**, and unsettling the people that we have become. You will embrace change, beginning with your own ideas and practices. This list, which is only a beginning, may sound daunting, but it is firmly rooted in the belief that ordinary people living their everyday lives can make a difference.

References

Dardot, P., & Laval, C. (2014). *The new way of the world: On neoliberal society*. London, UK: Verso.

Marx, K., & Engels, F. (1969). *Karl Marx and Frederick Engels, selected works*. Moscow, Russia: Progress Publishers.

Glossary

accumulation by dispossession: David Harvey's (2005) term for contemporary examples of Marx's concept of primitive accumulation. At its base level, it refers to the introduction of market forces into spaces that were previously non-capitalist. This includes privatization of public resources, usurping foreign resources, and dispossession of land.

affective labour: see **emotional labour**.

age norms: Shared ideas about what is appropriate behaviour at certain times of people's lives.

agency: A capacity to make choices within the frames of reference and possibility available to us, and to act on those choices. Although we employ this basic definition, there are a number of different ways to theorize agency.

alienation: Loss of much creative capacity by workers, and their detachment from true productive capacities through engaging in wage labour, because working for a wage involves giving up control over the ability to decide what kind of work one will do, and how it will be done.

apartheid: The policy or practice of segregation of peoples through political, legal, and economic means. Apartheid is therefore a system of social and economic discrimination that maintains and perpetuates social inequalities. The most well-known system of apartheid was in South Africa, where from 1948 until 1993 the state enforced a system of racial segregation. Some social and political theorists now apply the concept of apartheid to international conflicts such as Israeli state policy toward the Palestinian people. The concept of *global apartheid* has also been developed to describe a global system of political, legal, military, and economic power that restricts the movements of people while facilitating the movement of capital.

assemblage: A collection of things, people, and ideas such that new possibilities and outcomes are produced. Social theorists have developed this concept in numerous ways; in this book we work with this basic definition.

authoritarian populism: A concept developed by Stuart Hall (1988) in his analysis of the rise of conservativism in England during the 1970s. Hall revealed the cultural and policing mechanisms through which the organization of consent is secured, even where it may be against the best interests of many of those who lend their consent. Authoritarian populism is characterized by the attainment of broad public support for authoritarian forms of governing.

binary: A perspective in which being, thought, and action is conceptualized as being made up of a pair or two parts. The division of humans into females and males is one example. Binary categories are often presented as dichotomous, with little to no overlap between them.

biological determinism: The claim that your bodily make-up (genetics and other inherited traits) determines who you are. It further postulates that certain social conditions (for example, poverty and criminal activity) are inevitable due to the inherent characteristics of individuals.

biopower: The name given by Michel Foucault (1978) to a form of power that arose in the 18th century, with the shift from hereditary monarchical rule to elected liberal democracy and the nation-state. Its emergence marked the state's interest in the body and in how people lived. Biopower takes two main forms: disciplining of the body and intervention in the life of the population as a whole. It involves all of the questions, investigations, and governance of bodies and populations to produce what is considered appropriate and necessary for individual and social life.

blood quantum: A method for determining membership in racial groups based on ancestry. Blood quantum assumes that race is an innate, purely biological characteristic and assumes different races to be distinct, non-overlapping groups. Blood quantum is defined as the proportion of one's ancestors who belong to a certain racial group: for example, someone with one "full blood" white parent and one "full blood" Indigenous parent could be said to have a blood quantum of ½ Indigenous. Blood quantum laws were used to determine rights and privileges such as the right to vote, and continue to be used to determine membership in some Indigenous groups.

borders: Used here to denote demarcation lines between nation-states. Borders are more than physical markers; they represent claims to sovereignty by nation-states. Borders are also "fictions" in that they are made up; there is nothing in the material world that suggests that a border should be in one place or another. Rather, borders are constructed by nation-states through military and political rule.

bourgeois decorum: bell hooks's (2000) term for the practices of dominant groups that disguise racism by framing explicit discussion of racism as rude. Instead, the use of euphemism is encouraged, valorizing superficial politeness.

capacity: Refers to the level of mental and physical ability a person has as a result of structural factors such as access to education, wealth, safe working conditions, privilege, power, enhancements, and so on.

capitalism: A system of economic organization and production. It is based on ownership of private property, in which the few who own or control the means of production can accumulate capital through the sale of goods produced for a profit. Most people who live in capitalist societies must exchange their labour power for a wage; they experience exploitation as the values of wages remain below the value of goods produced or services provided. While the exploitation of labour remains a fundamental form of capital accumulation, capital is also increasingly generated through financial speculation.

capitalist class: According to Marx, one of the primary classes in capitalist society. The capitalist class consists of those who own and control the means of production, and through this accumulate capital. See also **ruling class**.

cathedrals of consumption: A term used by George Ritzer (2005) to refer to not only shopping malls, but also theme parks, hotels, cruise ships, casinos, sports facilities, airports, and other hypercommercialized settings for consumption. In spite of their seemingly "enchanted" character, Ritzer suggests, such environments are actually highly rationalized and carefully engineered to entice us to consume.

centre, the: Taken-for-granted, normative features of social organization, distinguished by the ability to confer privilege upon those who occupy it.

chattel slavery: Distinguished from other forms of slavery, in that much of the slave labour force is obtained through reproduction, imposing slave status on all children born of slave women.

cisgender: Derived from a biological term meaning "the same," cisgender refers to individuals whose gender identity coincides with their sexed body and connected gender, for example, individuals assigned a female sex at birth who are socialized as women (or as feminine) and self-identify this way.

cissexed: Derived from a biological term meaning "the same," cissex refers to individuals whose understanding of their sex (i.e., male/female) coheres to their sex as assigned at birth.

citizenship: The attribution of political membership in a nation-state through possession of that state's nationality. It guarantees that one has the right to reside in and return to that nation-state, and is entitled to its benefits.

class: Max Weber used this term to describe those in the same "class situation," which referred to the likelihood of "(i) procuring goods; (ii) gaining a position in life; and (iii) finding inner satisfactions," leading to a set of shared interests. Marx developed a class analysis premised on a "relational" concept of class, defining classes in terms of their relation to the means of production. Within capitalism, the two primary classes are the working class and the capitalist class. The emphasis on class as being defined through exploitation, rather than simply income or status differences, is one of the fundamental points of distinction between Marxist and Weberian approaches to class relations.

classifying/classification: See **system of classification**.

colonial/colonialism: The conquest and control of other people's lands and resources through genocide, enslavement, and resistance; imposition of foreign governing structures and legal systems; immigration and settlement; and binary knowledge systems and representational forms. Colonial expansion and wealth extraction were part of European empire-building, but in later stages coincided with the development of capitalism and the nation-state. Unlike migration, colonization is inherently a relationship of exploitation and oppression, one that results in people's dispossession and their displacement. The problem with colonization is not the "strangeness" or "foreign-ness" of the colonizers, but their destructive practices and the grossly unjust social relations they put into place.

commodification: Expansion of the market, or commercialization, into areas not previously part of the market or commercialized. Not only material goods, but people, cultures, and places are increasingly drawn into the global market.

commodity: Something produced as a generic or universal good specifically for sale on the market. Commodities are "use values produced by labour for exchange." "Use values" are goods such as food, clothing, and houses, and services such as education, and healthcare. In capitalism, commodity production primarily takes place for the purpose of exchange for profit rather than immediate use. Also, people's capacity to labour (labour power) is itself treated as a commodity and is bought and sold through market exchanges (wage labour).

commodity fetishism: A term coined by Karl Marx to refer to a common condition of modern capitalism where a commodity becomes "fetishized" as an independent object with its own intrinsic value. Under capitalism, social relations between producers and consumers are not based on direct contact but are mediated by the market. Individual consumers purchase abstract commodities from store shelves that appear to be without connection to the workers who actually produced them; people's knowledge of the lives of those who consume what others produce and those who produce what others consume is obscured by the market.

communicative model of consumption: A model of consumer behaviour, prevalent in the sociology of consumption since the 1980s, which holds that goods are not simply valued for their material or instrumental qualities, but for their ability to symbolically communicate social status and self-identity.

competitive individualism: The belief that people have equal opportunities to succeed, and that success depends on individual skill and initiative. Those who work the hardest and/or have natural abilities will rise to the top.

concept: A mental representation that groups things that are similar in some way. Concepts enable us to cognitively hold on to the idea of something by giving it a name or a symbol we can incorporate into our thinking. They also give us a context for understanding the many people, objects, and events we encounter every day: she's another student, that's a chair, they are having an argument. We often use concepts to designate specific types of people in our society: deadbeat dads, terrorists, or the mentally ill. These designations are based on the presumption that we have a shared cultural understanding about who belongs in these groups.

consanguinity: The idea of "shared blood," often used to refer to a familial relationship by descent from a common ancestor. Often used by nationalists to refer to co-members of a nation.

conspicuous consumption: A term coined by Thorstein Veblen (1934), it refers to the ostentatious acquisition and display of expensive and often frivolous goods by the wealthy in order to symbolically communicate their status and arouse the envy of those below them on the socio-economic hierarchy.

constitution/constituted: A term for the making up (or social production) of people, beliefs, and practices, as in the constitution of the subject.

consumer society: An umbrella term used to categorize wealthy regions in the postwar world in which material consumption rates have risen dramatically, and in which consumption practices have acquired an unprecedented centrality to social life and personal identity.

consumer sovereignty: A term in wide use in mainstream economics and neoliberal political discourse, whose premise is that the consumer's self-defined needs and wants are what determines an economy's production priorities, regulates its allocation of resources, and decides what is and isn't brought to the market for sale.

contingency/contingent: Something dependent on the chain of events that preceded it.

counter-hegemonic: Said of forces that offer possibilities for resistance due to the fact that maintenance of hegemony is an uneven and difficult process, depending on the balance of social forces at a given time and place.

cultural capital: A concept coined by Pierre Bourdieu (2002) to broaden the notion of capital beyond economic resources. It refers to access to material and symbolic resources, such as education, healthcare, social and intellectual networks, the arts, and languages. Young people who have access to significant cultural capital will be raised in homes that provide them with the conditions for economic and social success. According to Bourdieu, class position is therefore partly reproduced by maintaining and expanding one's cultural capital.

cultural genocide: See **genocide**.

cultural hegemony: In Antonio Gramsci's (1971) thought, power is maintained through a complex and contradictory web of cultural practices. In this way domination can be accomplished without direct authoritarian rule. See also **hegemony**.

culture: The totality of socially transmitted ideas, behaviours, customs, and products of a group of people. There may be different cultures operating in a single place at any one time.

culture jamming: Designates a variety of tactics for subverting some aspect of our cultural environment. By altering billboards and advertisements, engaging in street theatre and other unexpected public performances, and so on, culture jammers aim to disrupt everyday consciousness and get people to think critically about consumerism and other dominant value systems.

culture of therapy: See **therapeutic culture**.

cybernetics: The study of communication systems (both animal and machine) for securing efficient operation, regulation, and control. The study of cybernetics may involve an interdisciplinary approach, involving both the human and the physical sciences.

debility: Refers to the lack or loss of abilities as a result of unjust social relations, such as the way in which capitalist pursuit of profit requires the debilitation of some workers.

deconstruction: Following on the premise that the social world is constructed, deconstruction takes apart, or unpacks, meaning to show that the world is unstable, to show how things have been created, to consider effects of these creations, and to remind us that they could be created differently. A deconstructionist approach often focuses on and challenges choices and structures in language, especially the use of hierarchical binaries such as rational/irrational, adult/child, man/woman. Originating within literary theory, the concept of deconstruction is now used in various ways in a number of disciplines.

denaturalize: To disrupt the presumption that a given idea or belief is natural, absolute, or given.

deviance: Any form of conduct that violates social norms, rules, or laws. To designate a person or a group as deviant is a proscriptive act; that is, it casts a negative judgement on those who engage in beliefs and practices outside of what is considered acceptable, right, and normal. One purpose of the deviant designation, then, is to define and regulate differences.

diaspora: The dispersion of any people from their original homeland. The term can refer to those whose ancestors chose to leave their home countries as well as those whose departures were forced or coerced.

disability studies: Investigates disability as a social, cultural, and political phenomenon, focusing on how disability is defined, represented, and practiced in society. A disability studies approach does not regard disability as an individual characteristic or problem that must be fixed or cured, but rather engages with the ways in which disability creates meaning within social and cultural contexts.

disciplinary power: Foucault traced the beginnings of new forms of discipline back as early as the 15th century, to the first signs of the Enlightenment and scientific reasoning. The authority of sovereign power was gradually displaced by the emergence of new social institutions, such as prisons, schools, and hospitals, that involved new ideas and techniques concerning how to punish, correct, shape, and guide children, households, the poor, armies, and eventually bodies, minds, cities, and states.

disciplinary society: A society characterized by strategies to administer to and regulate populations and individuals through observation, examination, judgement, and direction. This favours normalization and correction over punishment, and reform over revenge. Power is most effective when it is bound with knowledge (see **power-knowledge**), rather than enforced through overt forms of social control.

discourse: Organized systems of knowledge and social practices that produce a particular version of reality. They provide the framework people use to understand and interpret the everyday world. They shape what can be thought, said, and done, and what is understood to be true. Social constructionists argue that the material world only becomes meaningful to us through the concepts and systems of classification provided by language and discourses.

dividing practices: Actions that involve making value-laden distinctions between people, beliefs, and activities, typically in a hierarchical manner. Dividing practices are a key ingredient in the establishment of social inequality.

DNA: A substance located within cells that contains genetic material that instructs the development and maintenance of components of living organisms. Often referred to as "the blueprint for building a body" or "a hereditary code."

documentary evidence: Is used to support knowledge claims. It relies on news reports, policy papers, letters, and so on, as opposed to oral knowledge transmission. One should always critically examine these sources, because the claims may support the perspectives of those with privilege or status, who have greater access to these sources and better representation by them.

double colonization: A concept used in postcolonial theory to refer to the subordination of women in postcolonial contexts through a combination of imperial and patriarchal powers.

economic nationalism: The principle of supporting government intervention in the economy in ways that are deemed to be in the national interest. This often involves developing economic policies that aim to protect domestic industries and workers against foreign competition in a global economy. Economic nationalism may be motivated by feelings of patriotism and/or xenophobia. In practice, it produces systems of trade barriers and tariffs, restrictions on im/migration, and other forms of exclusions related to economic activities.

emotional labour: The manipulation of self-presentation while providing services to others. It is a key dimension of work in service-sector workplaces. Personal interaction with customers makes demands on the emotional energy of workers, since customers expect smiling, cheerful service. Moreover, customers play a key role in establishing control over emotional labour through channels for customer input and assessments of service provision. Thus, service with a smile becomes a form of self-governance for service-sector workers.

Enlightenment, the: A period that was underway in Europe by the late 17th century. Enlightenment thought posed the radical new idea that people could use human reason to shape history, challenging the certainty that God alone was responsible for all creation. Enlightenment thinkers believed that science could be a tool for human progress. Through modernist scientific exploration, it was (and is) believed that we can measure, understand, and control not only the natural environment but also human behaviour. Scientific method was (and is) used to try to identify underlying structures or foundations that shape the organization of social life. Enlightenment thought produced a revolution in knowledge, one that challenged the primacy of the church over social life, and the "natural rights" of the aristocracy, which were based on the perceived certainty that these rights had been ordained by God. This was to open the way for new forms of political rights, based upon notions of individualism and freedom. It also opened the way for scientific critiques of the material and ideological conditions that sustained emerging systems of power, as Karl Marx's life's work did.

entrepreneurs of the self: A neoliberal interpretation of people as self-governing individuals who conduct themselves as though their lives are business enterprises and they are owners/managers responsible for developing their own human capital in order to produce maximal self-fulfillment.

epistemology: A branch of philosophy that focuses on what constitutes knowledge and how we come to know things. Epistemological perspectives inform us about what counts as evidence, what criteria need to be met in order to develop new knowledge, and how knowledge is related to morals or values.

essentialism: Refers to a belief that particular phenomena exists naturally as fact and, therefore, cannot be changed. Essentialism can be rooted within religion (i.e., "God made it/us that way") or scientific (e.g., biological determinist discourse: "there are two sexes, determined in utero and based on chromosomal make-up and genitals").

ethnic cleansing: As the mobilization of the idea of ethnicity wherein people are imagined as being wholly different "types" of people as a result of their different cultural practices. Ethnic cleansing is the violent act of expelling or killing people portrayed as outside of national society.

ethnicity: An arbitrary and socially constructed classification of persons on the basis of their supposed sharing of culture, including customs, traditions, religion, and food. The notion has come to be a way of talking about race without using the term. Like race, it too is a consequence of power relations and has been used to define and reinforce the segregation of people within and across national borders.

ethnocentrism: The belief that one's own nation and culture are superior to those of others.

eugenics: Derived from the Greek word *eugenes*, meaning "well born," eugenics refers to a scientific practice of human betterment. The formal eugenics movement began in the US in the 19th century with a series of laws and policies reliant on the principle of selective breeding, wherein people with traits or characteristics deemed socially desirable (i.e., in accordance with colonial norms privileging white Western European ancestry, physical and intellectual strength, etc.) were encouraged and often incentivized to reproduce. Those with traits deemed socially undesirable were discouraged from reproducing or often prevented outright through state-sponsored practices of segregation, incarceration, sterilization, and/or euthanasia.

euphemisms: Mild or vague words that are used instead of saying something that might be considered offensive or harsh.

everyday practices: The routine, taken-for-granted activities that people engage in on a regular basis.

exchange value: A quantitative measure that can be used in the process of commodity exchange. In a capitalist market, the exchange value of a commodity is represented through money. Commodities in capitalism are both use values (based on an ability to meet a human need or want) and exchange values (a representation of its value in the form of money). To understand how a commodity comes to be exchanged, we need to look at its exchange value.

expert knowledge: Knowledges that are specialized and often exclusive to those who develop and wield them. Dominant knowledges and discourses influence how societies and people are understood. They may be used to explain who people are, without direct input from those under observation.

exploitation: Marx asserted that the system of wage labour is based on the exploitation of the working class by capitalists. More specifically, within capitalism the value of commodities that workers produce is greater than the value that they are paid in wages. Marx referred to this difference as surplus value, otherwise known as profit. Hence, for Marx, capitalists are able to accumulate capital by controlling the labour of the working class.

fair trade network: The fair trade network is a system that links farmers, rural workers, and craftspeople in the Global South with non-governmental organizations, cooperatives, corporations, and consumers in the Global North through a system of "fair trade" rules and principles. Emphasis is placed on democratic organization (of cooperatives or worker committees), no exploitation of child labour, environmental sustainability, a guaranteed floor price, and social premiums paid to producer communities to build community infrastructure. One of the most significant "fair trade" certification bodies is Fairtrade International (FLO), but there are numerous ethical and sustainable certification initiatives with varying standards and systems of accountability.

feudalism: A social, economic, and political system in which lords ruled over "serfs" who were compelled to pay tribute to the latter in the form of labour, military service, food, and other goods.

financial fitness: A neoliberal discourse about the responsibility of individuals to participate in financial culture in prescribed ways, such as by using credit cards and repaying the monthly balance. A form of self-care, similar to diet and exercise, personal money management is thought to be important to individual and national financial health.

financial literacy: Individuals' ability to understand normalized financial concepts (such as money, credit, savings, compound interest, and investment risk) that makes them capable of participating in financial culture. Programs to enhance financial literacy are geared to making people better prepared for and inclined toward self-financing their education, leisure, housing, transportation, retirement income, and so on.

financialization: An economic and cultural shift that has taken place in the latter decades of the 20th century involving the expanding scale of financial markets and institutions (related to accounting, investment, insurance, pensions, savings, and debt) relative to other sectors of the economy; the increasing significance of financial knowledge in everyday life; and the growing importance of everyday financial activity, calculation, and decision-making among widening categories of people.

free market: The notion that in order to be fully competitive capital must be allowed unfettered access to national and global markets.

free trade: Rooted in classical political economy, free trade is the belief that state regulation of the market is inefficient and wasteful. Free trade, in particular the reduction of tariff, quotas, and other trade barriers, sparks competition, leading to technological innovation and specialization. Drawing on the work of David Ricardo (1971), proponents argue that free trade allows nations to find their "comparative advantage": a relative economic advantage compared to other nations for the production of some goods. Since the 1970s, free trade has been revived and often paired with neoliberal reforms calling for the privatization of public assets, deregulation, and government austerity.

free wage labour: The sale of labour power for a wage. According to Marx, wage labour requires two specific forms of "freedom" experienced by the working class in capitalist societies: (a) freedom (separation) from the means of production, and (b) freedom from any legal constraints that would prevent one from selling their labour power (for example, slavery). These conditions create the need to sell labour power in exchange for a wage, which according to Marx leads to the exploitation of the working class. See **exploitation** and **surplus value**.

freeganism: A clever play on the term "veganism," freeganism denotes a lifestyle that aims to refrain as far as possible from the purchase of consumer goods. By engaging in dumpster diving, foraging for wild foods, reusing discarded items, and so on, freegans aim to meet their needs in an ecologically friendly way, outside of the formal cash economy.

gender/gendering: In the West, refers to the label of "feminine" or "masculine" assigned to most of the world, from bodily behaviours and social practices to objects and places. Also refers to labels of "woman" and "man," and the social meanings assigned to them. Many feminists and other critical theorists have argued that "gender" is different from "sex," and that masculinity and femininity are socially constructed rather than biologically based. However, recent theorists turn this approach upside down by suggesting that the social meanings given to gender shape our understanding of anatomical sex, and that binary maleness and femaleness have a history and are socially constructed.

gender fluid: People whose gender identification changes and varies throughout their lifetime. This may include people who are non-binary, trans*, or identify with more than one gender.

gender identity: A classification relating to the gender binary that includes understanding of self and others in terms of masculinity or femininity. Typically, individuals identify as men or women; however, gender identity refers to trans* identities as well (e.g., gender queer, non-binary, agender).

gender normative: See **normative gender**.

gender performativity: A concept developed by Judith Butler (1990) to disrupt discourses of gender authenticity or the notion of one's true gender. There is no original or true gender; rather, through primarily unconsciousness processes, individuals co-create and express particular characteristics of masculinity and femininity. While the way that bodies appear and act seems to be natural, gender is produced through doing or performing and is neither a state nor a genuine state of being. Gender as performative denotes that gender can be challenged and resisted.

gendercide: A term used mainly by decolonial feminist scholars and activists to refer to the prominent role that annihilating Indigenous genders played, and continues to play, in settler-colonialism's definitively genocidal logic. The elimination of two-spirit individuals and violence against women functioned as a strategy to eradicate indigenous cultures and ways of knowing, as well as to establish and naturalize the Western sex/gender binary as superior.

genealogical method: Emphasizes the history of dominant paradigms of thought that pervade our culture and that produce current "truths." The genealogical method starts with the present, not to affirm or deny it, but to interrogate it, asking how the present has come to be constituted as it is, and how we create ourselves according to, or against, those truths. See also **history of the present**.

genealogy: A method that marks the changing relations between knowledge, power, and human activity in society and provides a way to understand how human activity has been shaped by changing historical forces.

generalizability/generalizable: The extent to which knowledge can be extended to understand a group of people (or population) larger than the group (sample) from whom information was collected.

genetic determinism: The idea that genetic material alone (i.e., DNA in the nucleus of our cells) dictates all that an organism is and does, eclipsing other factors such as environment or relationships.

genocide: The intentional and systematic destruction of a people on the basis of their race, ethnicity, religion, or national origin, accomplished through the mass extinguishment of their actual physical beings.

gerontology: The multidisciplinary study of aging, with a focus on late life. For some, gerontology's primary focus is biology; for others, gerontology encompasses a wide range of areas, including the body and social factors such as behaviour, attitudes, and the environment.

global apartheid: See **apartheid**.

globalization: The increasing economic, political, and cultural integration throughout the world as a result of economic, technological, and political forces. Economic globalization describes the increase in global economic integration, characterized by an increase in the flow of goods, services, technology, and labour across national borders.

governing rationality: A form of reasoning through which governmental power (in the Foucauldian sense) occurs.

governmental power/governmentality: An approach first developed by Michel Foucault that is distinct from the idea of the state as government. Foucault's approach addresses the shaping of human minds, desires, and conduct (think Govern-Mentality) by a wide range of expert knowledges and truth claims. Governmental power entails, foremost, the production and organization of knowledge, or how we come to know what we know, and the techniques and strategies that make governance possible. Governance is not simply a top-down process; we are indeed governed, but we also govern others and govern ourselves. This distinguishes governmental societies from disciplinary ones. However, Foucault importantly noted that sovereign, disciplinary, and governmental power can co-exist in the same society.

grand narratives: Sweeping claims or stories about history. Examples are the explanations of history and knowledge provided by Christianity, capitalism, and socialism. Also known as metanarratives, a concept introduced by Jean-François Lyotard (1984).

great confinement, the: An unprecedented program of asylum building that was underway in 17th-century Europe. Foucault regarded the great confinement as a means for disciplining and regulating certain populations of people, in asylums, prisons, workhouses, and so on.

hegemonic/hegemony: As described by Antonio Gramsci (1971), "intellectual and moral leadership" that takes into account "the interests and tendencies of the groups over which hegemony is exercised" through compromises that may benefit many but do not ultimately threaten the rule of the dominant group. This is accomplished through both coercion (military and police) and the manufacture of consent (the production of popular knowledge). In this way, the ruling ideas of a society operate hegemonically through "common sense" shared by everyone but that reproduces dominant interests. See also **cultural hegemony**.

hegemonic masculinity: A ruling or dominant set of practices that shape the ideal, or fantasy, of what defines the proper man within a specific time and particular place. Rooted within patriarchal society, these practices produce a gender hierarchy that legitimizes one form of masculinity as superior, producing difference among men and the subordination of women and other feminine forms of gender expression. As an ideal form of masculinity, hegemonic masculinity is not fully attainable and does not coincide with most men's lived experiences. Within a North American context, hegemonic masculinity intersects with settler colonialism, whiteness, and class.

heteronormative/heteronormativity: The idea or implication that gender normative heterosexual identity is the only normal and natural expression of human sexuality, to the exclusion of all gender and sexual non-normativity. Heteronormativity works in multiple ways, such as by representing heterosexuality as fulfilling and positive, by representing other forms of sexuality as dangerous and negative, and through absences and silences that make non-heterosexual practices seem rare and abnormal or non-existent.

heterosexual/heterosexuality: Said of sexual attraction to a person of the "opposite" sex and "opposite" gender. Based on and intertwined with the binary sex-gender system, which assumes that men and women are complementary opposites. The dominant assumption is that heterosexuality is the natural and normal sexual state of affairs. The term only emerged in the late 1800s when new sexual categories based on gender were created. Prior to that time, sexuality was primarily divided between married procreative activities and all other activities.

historical materialism: The methodology for social research favoured by Marx, based on two essential assumptions. First, social relations can only be understood in historical context. While Marx saw class relations and class struggle as present throughout human history, he believed that the specific form these social relationships may take varied considerably across different historical periods. Second, to understand class relations, we must study the material conditions under which people live. In other words, we must look at how humans produce and reproduce themselves.

historicize: To contextualize social phenomena within specific historical conditions.

history of the present: History is viewed as contingent—meaning that, for any event, other directions and outcomes were also possible—rather than inevitable or determined by universal laws. Foucault developed this approach to interrogate the production of discourses, knowledge, and objects, and the meanings associated with them. Foucault used this method in order to avoid making universal claims, for example, that there is such a thing as "truth" or "human nature." Instead, he undertook an analysis of how we come to believe in universal claims, seeking to discover how particular discourses come to be regarded as "truth." Foucault's later work referred to this as his genealogical method.

homonationalism: Extending the idea of homonormativity, Jasbir Puar (2007) proposed the term homonationalism to describe the ways in which rhetorical support for gay rights is used to foster nationalistic, xenophobic sentiments that in turn construct other countries, particularly predominantly brown, Middle Eastern countries, as backwards, uncivilized, and savage. This construction is then used to justify military involvement in these countries and to enforce exclusionary immigration policies.

homonormative/homonormativity: Describes the approach to advocacy that seeks to have same-gender relationships recognized within current institutions, such as marriage and the military. It is also an approach that frames homosexuality as being compatible with being gender-normative, in contrast to transgender people who are not. This approach doesn't challenge existing power structures beyond attempting to get them to include same-gender relationships.

homophobia: This term was first coined by activists as a reaction to the medical category of "homosexual" to reverse the argument that homosexuality was an illness and to say instead that the hatred of homosexuality was the real illness. The term has since broadened to refer to negative attitudes toward same-sex relationships, and more broadly to refer to the centring of heterosexuality, although there is still concern that this language individualizes heteronormative processes, making it harder to see their social structural patterns.

homosexual/homosexuality: Pertaining to sexual attraction to a person of the "same" sex and "same" gender. The term is based on and intertwined with the binary sex-gender system, which assumes that men and women are each other's opposites, and accordingly treats "heterosexuals" and "homosexuals" as opposing categories. It originated in the medical literature of the 1860s describing "homosexuals" as people who are psychologically of the "opposite" sex. Because the term has a long history of use to describe something abnormal and pathological, and was not chosen by the people it describes, it is seen by many as outdated. Preferred terms include gay, lesbian, and queer.

human capital: An outlook in which people are considered akin to a resource, and we must continually build and maintain our value as if our worth as human beings is dependent on it.

humanism: An outlook predicated on the belief that there are essential inviolable truths about people (the humanist subject), most notably that individual consciousness will shape human understanding and action.

hybridity (also hyphenated-identities): The mixing and blurring of cultures and ideas, creating new ways of being. This may entail the combining of dominant and marginalized forms of knowledge. When used in reference to postcolonial approaches to diaspora studies, it usually refers to a critique of celebratory multiculturalist notions of cultural merging or blending.

identity development: The process of coming to have a coherent inner sense of self, often assumed to develop throughout childhood and to be actively explored and consolidated in adolescence.

ideology/ideologies: A broad prescriptive framework of beliefs, assumptions, and values furnishing people with an understanding of their world, and influencing how they interpret social, cultural, political, and economic systems and structures. The content of ideology is not neutral; it reflects the status quo, or "relations of domination," edging out alternative and competing ideas.

Idle No More: An Indigenous activist organization committed to organizing resistance against neocolonialism through peaceful revolution. Its objectives include asserting Indigenous inherent rights of sovereignty, including a reinstatement of traditional laws and treaties between nations, over land and water, protecting them from destruction by corporate interests. Idle No More began as a series of teach-ins in Saskatchewan and rapidly expanded throughout Turtle Island (the Indigenous name for North America). Women have held the central role in the formation and leadership of INM, honouring and building the central role that women have historically held in Indigenous communities. For more information, see idlenomore.ca.

imperialism: The extension of a nation-state's authority or rule over other national territories through control of their economies. The development of imperialism often superseded direct colonial rule (see **colonialism**), rendering formal political and military control unnecessary for meeting the economic objectives of dominating nation-states.

imperialist nostalgia: A longing for an idealized past, where "tradition" functions as a metaphor for colonial and imperial order.

indentured servant/indentured labourer: Worker who commits to labour for a particular employer for a fixed time and is bound by contract for that time. The worker often enters into indenture because of financial obligations, such as a debt incurred to immigrate to a new country.

Indian: A historically inaccurate term for Indigenous people. Also refers to imagined archetypes regarding Indigenous people, such as "savage," "noble," and "lazy." All these archetypes present the "Indian" as primitive, in (often unspoken) contrast to "civilized" whiteness. The figure of the "Indian" is purposefully disconnected from the lived realities of Indigenous people in order to invisibilize the role of Canadian colonization in creating the current situation for Indigenous people.

Indian status: See **status Indian**.

Indigenous: Peoples considered to be the original occupiers of a land, usually prior to the incursion of a colonizing force.

Indigenous knowledges: Systems of knowledge, meaning, and skills developed by Indigenous peoples throughout their history. Distinct from Western scientific knowledge, Indigenous knowledges are deeply connected to cultural activity and to the natural environment and resources upon which life depends.

inequality: See **social inequality.**

infrapolitics: "Everyday" acts of resistance to alienation and exploitation. In the context of the workplace, infrapolitics include activities/actions such as work slowdowns, sabotage, absenteeism, altering standardized labour processes, and personalizing workplace uniforms. They may also be present in daily conversations, songs, and other forms of everyday cultural expression. Because infrapolitics are often very individualized and outside the realm of formal workplace organizing (for example, through trade unions), they are generally not recognized as forms of resistance. Yet they are often kept "invisible" by design and provide an important way for marginalized individuals and groups to resist and contest power.

infrastructure of consumption: Refers to the social, material, technological, and institutional framework that shapes and constrains the terrain of consumer choice, compelling us into certain types of patterned and predictable consumer behaviour.

inscriptions: Written traces in two-dimensional space. These might be produced by humans or machines, and they might be text, images, graphs, maps, and so on.

interpretive flexibility: The concept that different people see different things despite the same visual information. This concept can include people or groups giving different meaning to the same symbol, object, or experience.

interpretive repertoire: A cluster of terms, descriptions, metaphors, and figures of speech that people use to understand the world around them. They provide a framework that people use to locate their own position in the world relative to others. Our interpretive repertoires help us establish our subject position, which we then use to give meaning to our experiences.

interpretivism: An approach to knowledge that emphasizes how people interpret their environment, assign meanings to things, and then act on the basis of their understanding of each situation. Interpretivism is strongly associated with symbolic interactionism. Interpretivists generally adopt a social constructionist perspective on reality.

intersectional analysis: An analytic perspective that accounts for how factors such as race, gender, class, sexuality, dis/ability, and citizenship (and including social locations and subject positions) intersect, penetrate, and inform one another so that they become mutually constitutive and act together. It recognizes that vectors and patterns of oppression such as racism, classism, and sexism ultimately cannot be separated from one other when examining the organization of power and inequality. See also **relational analysis**.

Inuit: The Indigenous peoples of northern North America and Greenland. The Inuit were for a time referred to as "Eskimos," a name that was derived from the colonizing language of anthropologists and that has been rejected for its colonial origins and failure to acknowledge Indigenous communities' histories, language, and identification.

juridical power: A form of power that includes the rule of law, the techniques of the court, and the practices of policing. Juridical power has its roots in the exercise of sovereign power, and it retains the capacity for domination, repression, and control. However, much of the authority of juridical power is now governmentalized and normalized. There is general support for laws, courts, and policing as necessary aspects of ensuring democratic ordering.

Keynesianism: An economic theory first developed in the 1930s and dominant in Western industrial capitalist countries in the period following World War II, according to which governments should take an active role in managing the national economy, especially through public-sector spending during periods of recession. Keynesian policies aim to achieve stable conditions for economic growth and employment by anticipating and moderating the disruptive effects of market cycles. States that have adopted Keynesianism have also instituted progressive taxation as a mechanism of downward wealth redistribution in order to support social welfare programs such as medical insurance, unemployment insurance, and old age pensions.

labour power: People's capacity to engage in economically productive activity. Karl Marx stated that the working class are those who do not own means of production and therefore must sell their labour power in order to earn wages to ensure their subsistence. The capitalist class purchases the labour power of the working class for a wage in order to generate profits.

liberalism: A philosophical, political, and economic approach that focuses on the primacy of the individual and on individual rights. Liberalism as a belief system was created simultaneously with the growth of capitalism and the notion of democracy. See also **neoliberalism**.

life course: A social understanding of the duration of our lives from infancy to death, shaped by history, social institutions, practices, and beliefs.

literary technology: A way of writing calculated to act on the readers in particular ways.

local currency: Money issued by community-based organizations or municipal governments that is designed to generate new circuits of earning and paying within a specific geographical region or among a particular network of participants. Local currencies may have a number of goals such as reducing dependence on large corporations, buffering local economies from global crises, fostering more personal relationships between producers and consumers, and reducing the separation between production and consumption.

looping effects: The interaction between a classification and those people who are classified. Humans inevitably respond to classification, which in turn alters their conduct, which will have an effect on the classification, and so on.

marked bodies and unmarked bodies: People who are set apart from "normal" in a given social context are considered marked, whereas the normal and expected identity is unmarked. In practice, this marking is sometimes literal, such as make-up on women or the numerical tattoos on Jews during the Holocaust. In discourse, linguistic modifiers like "female" mark a generic category like "scientist," where the unmarked subject is considered normal and without need of description. If a person with a marked identity makes an assertion, it is often read as biased or tainted by their "special interests," whereas the unmarked perspective is popularly understood as objective or without disqualifying prejudices.

market populism: A term coined by Thomas Frank (2000), highlighting the tendency in contemporary society to portray the capitalist marketplace as the ultimate expression of democracy and the popular will.

materialist: In order to understand class relations we must study the conditions in which people actually live, and how humans produce and reproduce their conditions of life. New forms of materialist analysis also account for the importance of discourses, spiritual worlds, bodily experiences, and community life.

materiality: The physical properties of anything (see **matter**). For example, to insist that books have materiality (in addition to symbolic content) is to draw attention to the kind of paper, the typesetting, the font, the ink, and the cover.

matter: Anything that takes up space and has mass. In social theory, drawing attention to matter is usually in contrast to intangible entities like concepts, ideas, forces, feelings, norms, and beliefs.

Matthew effect: The cumulative effects of class-based inequalities over the life course.

means of production: The materials, infrastructure, and natural resources needed to produce goods and provide services (including factories, technology, tools, etc.). Specifically, the capitalist class owns and controls the means of production, while the working class is compelled to sell its labour power.

mechanical objectivity: The notion that machines are disinterested in outcomes and therefore remove the subjective biases of humans.

medicalization: A broad sociological concept that refers to the social processes that define and categorize certain human conduct or experience as a medical problem, usually as an illness or a disorder requiring professional attention.

meritocracy: The assumption in capitalist liberal democracies that people get ahead based on their own merit—because of their abilities, talent, and perseverance. The idea of a meritocracy is challenged by the reality of inherited wealth, as well as various other forms of social privilege, including class, race, gender, sexuality, being a white settler, and citizenship.

metalanguage: Words or symbols used to describe practices, concepts, or objects. For example, the word *noun* is an example of metalanguage—a word used to describe other words.

metaphor: Describing one thing in terms of another in order to imply a comparison.

microaggressions: Statements, actions, or incidents of indirect or subtle discrimination, violence, or negativity directed against members of a marginalized group.

micro-processes of power: The detailed, contextual, contingent, and specific circulation of social meaning and practice.

migrant: Any human being whose movement across space is regulated and restricted by states. In a world of nation-states and their border regimes, the label of migrant is often applied to anyone who is regarded as foreign to the nation and its imagined community.

migration: A quintessential human practice of movement, one long associated with freedom or, at the very least, with escape from untenable situations (war and poverty) or, simply, with adventure.

miscegenation: A term coined in the United States in the mid-19th century to foment the fear of people of supposedly different "races" engaging in consensual sexual relations or marriage, hinging on the idea that "race mixing" would lead to the dilution or elimination of the "white race." Laws based on the idea of miscegenation were passed throughout the US starting in the mid-17th century. The last of these was overturned in 1967. While the idea may appear to be dated, the supposed harms of miscegenation inform contemporary racist ideas and, in particular, the ideology of white supremacy.

mobilities: When used by critical tourism studies, it is often used to draw attention to who has the right to travel and cross borders, given people's relative power and privilege.

mode of production: The economic organization of a society; the ways people produce, distribute, and consume goods. Using the method of historical materialism, Marx suggested that human history is divided into identifiable periods, each characterized by a certain mode of production.

modern confessional: A metaphor coined by Foucault to characterize the use by residents of Western nations of such things as the therapist's office, the self-help group, and the blog, increasingly relying on the psy sciences (psychology, psychiatry, psychotherapy, etc.) rather than turning to the priest to confess our sins. Through the process of confessing we create our "self" rather than reveal it.

modernism: A mode of thought developed in the context of the Enlightenment, underlying which was the belief that through scientific exploration one could measure and understand not only the natural environment but also human behaviour. In other words, the scientific method could be used to identify underlying structures or foundations that shape the organization of social life. Enlightenment thinkers embraced the hope that science could be a tool for human progress.

modernist: The modernist espouses the view that the physical world is not simply the creation of God nor an unsolvable mystery beyond scientific understanding. See also **modernity** and **modernism**.

modernity: Typically, the social, economic, political, and cultural conditions and beliefs that have arisen since the Enlightenment and the rise of capitalism.

moral insanity: A diagnosis introduced in the mid-19th century as part of the growing medical fixation on immoral or disrespectable conduct, particularly in response to what was perceived as increasing vices arising from industrialization and the growth of cities. Moral insanity linked perceived moral flaws to madness, as if one were the cause of the other.

myth of sameness: bell hooks's term for the idea that racism can only be resolved by treating everyone equivalently. hooks argues that this approach makes it impossible to recognize the impact of historical and ongoing institutional racism. Recognizing race—not as an innate biological difference, but rather as a historical and social product—is essential to addressing racism.

nation: A socially constructed political formation of people that is imagined as limited in terms of who its members can be, as having sovereign (exclusive) authority over particular territories, and as a historical community bound together through ideas of race.

nation-state: A form of state power in which the political community is imagined to be a "nation" that is distinct from other "nations." This "nation" is imagined to be a cross-class "community" with a shared, general interest. In addition, ideas of nationhood are often, and perhaps always, dependent on ideas of the "racial" or "ethnic" similarity of separate "nations." Nation-state power is also dependent on the idea that it is not the state, but the "nation" that rules, so that the state is seen to merely represent the will of the "nation." Attaching the idea of "nation" to state power thus helps to obfuscate the relations of ruling within any given nation-state.

nationalism: A modern ideology centred on the shared values and myths of the community of the nation-state. This is a relational process in that the nation-state relies on the complicity of those who make themselves at home in the nation in order to legitimize (or make "common sense" of) the highly differential treatment accorded those classified as the nation's non-citizens, particularly those placed in legal state categories. Nationalism is a discourse central to the production of national forms of sovereign (or state) power. In a discourse of nationalism(s), a certain cross-class group of people, defined by ideas of shared race or ethnicity, are said to form a nation for whom the sovereign/state supposedly rules. Discourses of nationalism thus are productive of racialized ideas of "shared ancestry" or "culture." Nationalisms attempt to institutionalize such ideas through sovereign forms of power over territory (assumed to be "national homelands") and the people on them ("nationals" as well as "migrants"). In the process, the existence of states or classes is concealed.

natureculture: A concept used to assert that nature and culture are not opposites, or even able to be dissociated. Many of the entities humans create, encounter, and give meaning to are both nature *and* culture at once. For example, a garden is a natureculture, as is a dog breed, or a fetal sonogram.

neocolonialism: New kinds of colonialism that have emerged alongside the continuation of historical forms, not through direct political and military control, but through economic domination.

neoliberalism: A set of governing practices that came to rival Keynesianism starting in the 1970s, resulting in the reorganization of capitalist states and social life around the idea of markets as the most efficient and moral mechanisms for allocating social goods and shaping individual and collective behaviour. Neoliberal policies result in, and legitimize, upward redistribution of wealth. Although neoliberal philosophy decries government "interference" in the economy, neoliberal governments take an active role in negotiating the frameworks for global trade and financial activity, protecting private property, and converting public assets into private, for-profit businesses. One measure of the success of neoliberalism is its ability to capture our minds and reshape our sense of self, limiting our ability to even begin to question such a world. In this, we are constituted as neoliberal subjects.

neo-racism: With the delegitimization of the idea that people belonged to differently biologized races, practices of racism have shifted to emphasis on cultural differences understood to correlate to nations. Hence, neo-racists imagine a world where "different cultures" are spatially segregated by immigration controls into "their own" nation-states.

New Right: A philosophy that began in England in the 1970s combining neoliberal economics with conservative social values in order to dismantle the welfare state and replace it with a more punitive, individualistic approach toward both citizens and non-citizens.

normal: Used both as a description of a common or expected quality of a given situation, object, or person, and as an evaluation or judgement about its moral quality.

normalization: Foucault's term for how a certain version of things takes on the label of standard, true, or "normal." Normalization has become a popular theoretical tool for identifying the arbitrariness of assigning "normal" status to many things most of us take for granted. Foucault believed that normalization is among the most effective means of social regulation in contemporary Western societies.

normalizing power: Compares, differentiates, creates a hierarchy, homogenizes, and excludes. It is therefore also a dividing practice, because it clearly involves the making of value-laden distinctions between people.

normative gender: Ruling or dominant sets of practices that shape the ideal, or fantasy, of what defines proper womanhood and manhood in society. These idealized sets of characteristics that influence the ways women's and men's bodies and behaviours ought to be are not fully attainable and create hierarchies amongst women and men, amongst individuals who are feminine- and masculine-identified, and in relation to those who are androgynous. Within a North American context, normative gender intersects with settler colonialism, whiteness, and middle-class ideals.

normativity: Mode of designating some qualities, actions, or outcomes as good, right, and acceptable, while casting others as bad, wrong, objectionable, or even forbidden.

norms: Social expectations about attitudes, beliefs, and values.

objectivity: A research approach that strives to ensure that the researcher's own perspectives, biases, and opinions do not influence the research process. In theory, researchers should be interchangeable. Some researchers argue that objectivity is impossible to achieve.

official statistics: Statistics collected or compiled by a government agency in order to find out more about a national population, usually with the goal of informing policy.

organization of consent: a process through which people come to identify the interests of the ruling group as synonymous with their own, making the exercise of power in Western, capitalist, and formally democratic countries much more effective.

orientalism: Edward Said (1978) used the term orientalism to describe a way that Eastern cultures are problematically represented or depicted in the West as exotic, different, static, backwards, and/or mysterious and to thus position the West as rational and superior.

Other, the: A category of exclusion through which certain groups of people are considered different and inferior. The process of othering simultaneously secures the otherer's own position.

panopticon: A type of prison envisioned by Jeremy Bentham in 18th-century England, which placed guard posts at the centre of a circular containment, so that the watchmen (prison guards) could not be seen and would always be presumed by the inmates to be present and watching. Inmates would thus feel compelled to conduct themselves as if they were under constant surveillance. The panopticon thereby not only constrained prisoners' bodies but reconfigured their minds as well. Foucault adopted the model of the panopticon as illustrative of the growth of the disciplinary society.

partial perspective: This goes hand in hand with situated knowledge. Any individual human knower is capable only of partial perspective, where partial means both biased and incomplete. Combining many partial perspectives leads to better knowledge.

passive voice: A grammatical formation that emphasizes the person who experiences an action (e.g., "Mary was hit"), in contrast to the active voice, which emphasizes the actor (e.g., "John hit Mary"). The passive voice is a tactic of bourgeois decorum that de-emphasizes the active role that white people play in historical and ongoing racism by foregrounding the people affected by racism (e.g., racialized people) instead of the actors responsible for racism (e.g., white people).

pathologize: To regard particular beliefs, feelings, habits, thoughts, and/or behaviours as rooted in physical or mental disease or dysfunction, as determined by scientific ideas.

pathology: Refers to a medicalized abnormality or disease. The pathological approach is the view that some people are abnormal in their bodies/minds/psyches, and that personal problems are individual and caused by biological and/or psychological factors. This is a distinctly Western and recent historical phenomenon.

patriarchy: A system in which social, economic, and political privilege and entitlement is conferred upon men over women and children, regardless of the presence or absence of privilege in other areas of men's lives, and regardless of if/how they act upon that privilege.

political economy: A field of study that seeks to understand the long-term history of, and prospects for, social change, especially the potential of emancipation from unjust and exploitative social relations under capitalism. As a methodology for understanding social organization, it puts emphasis on studying class relations and interactions between capital and states. Many of those taking a political economy approach also adopt an intersectional analysis that recognizes class as inseparable from other social, cultural, and political relations. That is, in order to understand the everyday dimensions of class relations, we have to study the intersection of class with other social relationships, including race, gender, sexuality, and citizenship.

politics of invisibility: Refers to the inseparable relationship between knowledge/power and the ways that knowledge is often created through intentionally suppressing awareness, thereby rendering particular histories, subjects, or communities unseen or unacknowledged. Such invisibility lends itself to the naturalizing or normalizing of particular identities or relations of power because competing realities seem non-existent.

politics of the image/politics of representation: Analysis of how meaning is given to things, an understanding that reveals how knowledge and power intersect. Stuart Hall (1997) urged us to engage in an interrogation of the image and uncover its political aspect. See also **representation**.

polysemy: In semiotics, a single sign can have more than one meaning or be interpreted in multiple ways. See **semiotics**, **sign**, **signified**, **signifier**.

population: Foucault used this term to refer to the biological processes of a society, including health conditions and birth and mortality rates.

populism: The definition of populism has historically referred to the "will of the people," although contemporary usage has veered toward reference to the people vs. the elites. It is typically an ideologically loaded concept because it can be utilized from a range of political perspectives.

positive psychology: An approach that assumes that people want to develop their best selves, for the best life possible. Psychology provides the necessary tools for self-examination and improvement. To live thinking positively and to strive for happiness and personal fulfillment are the goals of this psychological approach, in counterdistinction to approaches that focus on maladjustment, illness, and so on.

positivism: An approach to knowledge that emphasizes the collection of information using the five human senses and the systematic rational analysis of observations to identify general truths. Positivism espouses a clear distinction between scientific facts (good) and religion or superstition (bad). Those who use this approach are known as positivists.

postcolonialism: Exposes and challenges Western European forms of knowledge and claims to truth, showing how this knowledge production serves the advancement of European thought and colonial power. Postcolonial theorists explore histories of thought that provide alternatives to, and often predate, European theory.

postcolonial new world order of nation-states: An international system that was put into place after World War II not to ensure the end of colonialism, but to contain the aspirations of colonized people struggling for their liberty. Instead of securing peace, prosperity, and global equality, as demanded by people in the colonies, "national liberation" movements established "independent" sovereign nation-states that controlled both territories and people now re-imagined as "national." Moreover, not only the colonies, but European metropoles of empires also nationalized their sovereignty, so that by the late 1960s, the two largest empires entering World War II—Britain and France—had become nation-states.

postmodernism: A way of thinking that began to develop by the late 1970s, at a time in history when established truths had possibly never been so quickly and extensively shaken through rapid changes in technology, material life, and meaning. Liberation struggles and social movements that began to flourish in the 1960s—such as anti-colonial liberation struggles (in what was then known as the "Third World" and among Indigenous peoples the world over), anti-racism movements, the women's liberation movement, and the lesbian and gay liberation movements—challenged prevailing hierarchical orders. These social challenges permeated and intersected with the new trends in the arts and design, as well as in scholarly thinking. There were more stories to be told and more truths to be claimed. Postmodernism rejects the Enlightenment belief that, through human reason and research, humanity is on the road of progress. Instead, history is reconceptualized as fragmented, discontinuous, and without a larger purpose. Postmodernism is strongly linked to **poststructuralism**.

poststructuralism: A way of thinking that rejects the belief that there are stable underlying, unifying structures, or rules, shaping social life and communication (known as structuralism), and that these structures can be studied through the objective scientific method. It rejects understanding the world in terms of binary oppositions (which means offering either/or choices or categories), finding that binaries cannot provide sufficient explanation of the nuances of social and material life. "Either/or" choices, such as between bad and good, irrational and rational, black and white, woman and man, or child and adult are deconstructed, or critically taken apart, and replaced by "both/and" in poststructuralist thought. Identities are not considered fixed, but understood as relational, ever-changing, unstable, defined through difference, normalizing, and multiple, across our lives. Research is best pursued through localized studies that reveal the minutiae of social meaning and organization.

power: At its most general level, the ability to put into place the definition of a situation, whether through consent or by force. Karl Marx believed that power is maintained through a system of domination, in which control is exercised by the ruling class over land, labour, and capital. Alternatively, Michel Foucault suggested that contemporary power does not work in one direction, from the top down, through direct coercion or physical violence. Rather, it comes from everywhere, and can have a positive character, creating new conditions of possibility. Nevertheless, the effects of power can also result in domination, and can be experienced by both the dominators and the dominated.

power-knowledge: Foucault linked power and knowledge together in a circular, or co-constitutive, relation because they are the cause and effect of one another. This linkage of power and knowledge is an important feature for the workings of contemporary forms of governance. They are usually inseparable. Discourses are infused with power-knowledge relations. Note that this is different from the idea that knowledge is power.

power relations: A relational approach to power considers how it produces and sustains inequalities between social groups. This requires an exploration of not only causes and effects, but also how power is mobilized in obvious and imperceptible ways.

primitive accumulation: The expropriation and enclosure (privatization) of land that occurred when feudalism was transformed into capitalism. This situation created a mass of people (the working class) who had no means to support themselves, since their access to land had been cut off.

psy complex: A heterogeneous network of agents, sites, practices, and techniques for the production, dissemination, legitimation, and utilization of psychological truths. The psy complex includes a loosely defined group of experts who possess a professional and moral status, such as psychiatrists, psychologists, psychiatric nurses, counsellors, psychotherapists, criminologists, and social workers.

psy discourse: The perspective that all human problems are psychological or psychiatric in origin.

psychoanalytic theory/theories: Claims that individuals are motivated by strong and dynamic unconscious drives and conflicts arising in early childhood rather than biological functions of the brain and central nervous system. Psychoanalysis provides a non-biological theory of emotional and mental life alongside the dominating neurological, behaviourist, evolutionary, or hereditarian paradigms.

psychocentrism: The dominant cultural belief that a plethora of human problems—the troubles with which we as people struggle—are due to intrinsic pathologies of the individual mind and/or body.

queer: Sometimes used as an umbrella term to denote lesbian, gays, bisexuals, and transgender people, the term is more appropriately used to convey the rejection of the sex/gender binary at the heart of the gendered system of sexual identification, and the belief that sexuality and gender are both malleable and fluid. The term reminds us that the boundaries between sexual categories are often blurred, meaning that binary-based categories like gay, lesbian, and heterosexual/straight are too rigid to accurately describe the range of people's sexual curiosities and desires.

race: An arbitrary and socially constructed classification of persons on the basis of real or imagined physical characteristics. Race has no scientific meaning; there is only a singularity known as the "human race." The notion is a consequence of power relations, as it has been used to define and reinforce the unequal relations between dominant and subordinate groups.

racialization: A process through which "race" is attributed to a population of people, facilitating the practice of racism against them.

racialized person(s), group(s), or racialized Others: (An) individual(s) to whom "race" is assigned and to whom the process of racialization is applied. The term may refer to groups, for example "racialized immigrants." It may substitute for related terms that imply racial difference, such as "people of colour," "visible minority," "Asian," "Native," "African Canadian," and so on.

racialized representations: Since the 17th century, discourses have flourished that construct "the other" based on early Western science's ideas about race. Coextensively, these discourses produce knowledge about the "West" and the "Rest" in ways that are directly connected to economic and political institutions in the production of systems of power. See **representations**.

racism: Discrimination accorded to a group of people differentiated and evaluated on the basis of their alleged or real physical or social qualities. It is evident in its effects, as it affirms power relations and structural advantage and disadvantage. Racism is often attributed to institutional procedures, systemic inequities, or structural practices.

radical: An approach to political organizing that seeks to address issues "at the root" by fundamentally altering the dominant social structure, in contrast to approaches that seek to ameliorate or reform the existing structure. For example, consider the issue of the exclusion of transgender people from the US military. An example of an ameliorative approach would be to advocate for transgender people to have the right to join the military; a radical approach might challenge the very existence of the military, as well as the systemic conditions that create economic need and lead to an interest in joining the military.

radical resurgence: There is a history of anti-capitalist ideas and practices in Indigenous thought and communities. Some Indigenous theorists and activists call for the use of Indigenous theory and critique as a means to formulate Indigenous alternatives to settler-colonial logics and the dispossession of Indigenous peoples and lands. This includes organizing in opposition to capitalism, heteropatriarchy, white supremacy, and state control.

realism/realist: Realism is a perspective premised on the idea that there is a single reality that exists independently of human consciousness and is governed by unchanging natural laws. A realist is someone who maintains this perspective.

recapitulation theory: A theory popular in the late 19th and early 20th centuries that posited that the development of human beings from children to adults mirrors the evolution of "the race" (which ambiguously could mean humanity itself or—much more problematically—white people).

reductionism: The practice of explaining complex events or processes in terms of isolated parts of it (for example, explaining crime exclusively in terms of genetics).

régime of truth: A dominant system of knowledge that attempts to establish the limits of what is knowable and possible.

regulation: Certain attitudes, beliefs, and conduct are regarded as normal, right, and proper, while breaches are discouraged or punished. Regulation can take many forms, including through socio-legal relations, truth regimes, and normalizing discourses. A narrow definition of regulation typically refers to legal restrictions established by the state.

relational: A way of explaining one belief or thing in relation to another belief or thing, so that they become constituents of one another.

representation: Traditionally, a re-presentation of something that has already happened or is "standing in" for something. Cultural theorists such as Stuart Hall (1997) argue that representation goes beyond this; it becomes part of the thing itself, that is, representations become constitutive. It is in this wider sense that things are given meaning in the context of our shared culture. See also **politics of the image/politics of representation**.

representational practices: How representations are put to use, with particular aims, objectives, and possible outcomes. See **representation**.

residential schools: A program run by the Canadian government from 1831 to 1996 that removed Indigenous children from their families and placed them in boarding schools run by Christian churches at great distances from their communities. The goal of this program was to separate Indigenous children from their culture and to assimilate them into white Christian society. Children were prohibited from speaking in their ancestral languages. These schools caused great harm to Indigenous children through the disruption of families and Indigenous cultures as well as the exposure of children to physical and sexual abuse. The Canadian government has acknowledged that residential schools constituted a form of cultural genocide.

responsibilization: The process of transferring responsibility for peoples' needs (for education and training, healthcare, retirement income, etc.) from the collectivity, as organized through the state, onto individuals. Responsibilization requires that individuals adopt an ethic of self-improvement and self-care, and that they are provided with information about the risks associated with the choices available to them.

rhetorical devices: Linguistic techniques used to promote a particular understanding of a person, object, or event. Metaphors, alliteration, and hyperbole are commonly used rhetorical devices.

ruling/relations of ruling/ruling apparatus: How power in, or emanating from, Western capitalist nations is held in place. Although "rule" can include violent means, we include Dorothy E. Smith's (1990) notion of relations of ruling to signal that the everyday form of rule in the West is through knowledge production, and its attendant managerial and administrative discourses and practices. This ruling apparatus is secured through the production and circulation of institutional and bureaucratic texts, such as documentary evidence.

ruling class: As Marx defined class in terms of relationship to the means of production, for Marx the ruling class in capitalist society refers to those who own and control the means of production—the materials, infrastructure, and natural resources needed to produce goods and provide services within capitalism. Ownership of the means of production provides the capacity to accumulate capital (profits to be reinvested) and to generate individual wealth, thereby securing the power of the ruling class. See also **capitalist class**.

science: A way of acquiring knowledge that depends on systematic observation and experimentation. Science is often considered to be outside of, and separate from, society and culture. However, it is a thoroughly social institution whose power is often invisible precisely because it is dismissed as extra-social, inevitable, and unchanging.

scientific racism: The use of scientific methods to advance the idea that a hierarchical racial ordering exists in nature, and that racism is therefore justifiable for societies. We do not simply reject this as pseudoscience, because science itself is always influenced by the beliefs and interests of the society in which it is developed. Rather, we highlight the problematic character of its social construction, because this racial ordering reflects prevailing racist assumptions about a people's level of superiority or inferiority, based upon physiological features such as skin tone.

While scientific racism was denounced by the mid-20th century, it continues to inform many scientific, political, and social decisions.

Scientific Revolution: A revolution in meaning that began in the mid-16th century, through which scientific frameworks, analysis, and objectives reshaped how social and material life was understood and lived.

self, the: A general definition of the self refers to people's essential nature or character. However, we use the concept in the manner of Foucault, which, instead of seeking a core meaning, explores how the self is constituted, or socially made, in particular ways.

semiotics: The study of signs in systems of language, communication, and culture.

settler colonialism: Where a population of people seek to dispossess the original inhabitants of a land through occupation and the establishment of sovereignty, and through legal, bureaucratic, administrative, and cultural control of Indigenous peoples. Although widely used to describe how Canada has taken over Turtle Island, Nandita Sharma (Chapter 9) notes a number of limitations. The concept does not really address the fact that the settling of people in Canada was largely a project of the state and the crown, in keeping with the goals of imperialist and capitalist expansion. Nor does it address the conditions of migration for non-white people whose arrival in Canada was less than freely chosen, or the politics of exclusion and lack of true belonging of non-white people that is the other side of Canadian nationalism. In her chapter, Sharma unsettles settler colonialism as she asks, "What becomes the mark of 'belonging' to a place, and the key attribute necessary for claiming rights?"

settler-colonial relationship: See **settler colonialism**.

sex: In the West, the label of female or male assigned to bodies on the basis of supposedly binary genital and reproductive differences. A person's sex is often assumed to be biologically based or naturally occurring. Sex can also denote erotic practices. Since the late 19th century, sex acts have come to be seen as the basis of sexual identity and are treated as who a person is, rather than just what a person does or desires.

sex/gender binary: A system of governance based on the naturalization of an "either/or" dichotomous relationship between two sexes and two genders. The sex/gender binary legitimizes the knowledge that individuals are born either male or female and are socialized masculine or feminine respectively. Sexes and genders that differ from this rigid dualistic logic are rendered as abnormal, deviant, and problematic.

sexual identity: How a person understands their erotic interests. In current Western culture, sexual identities are centred on attraction based on gender. Common sexual identities include straight, gay, lesbian, and bisexual. Some people identify as "queer," rejecting the sex/gender binary at the heart of other forms of sexual identity. Some people identify as "asexual," denoting that they do not have sexual desire. Sexual identity is distinct from gender identity.

sexuality: A broad term encompassing the social meaning given to erotic practices and identifications. The dominant assumption is that sexuality is part of a person's core identity.

sign: Something (a word, gesture, sound, etc.) that means something, and can be communicated to others. In semiotics, signs are historically and culturally produced in relation to both the signifier and the signified.

signified: The concept or idea represented by a signifier.

signifier: A symbol that calls up our conceptual understanding of an object, event, experience, feeling, or action. There is no guarantee that every person will interpret a signifier in the same way.

situated knowledge: A concept introduced by Donna Haraway (1991) to insist that knowledge does not exist in the disembodied abstract, but always comes from somewhere—and someone—specific. Situated knowledge defies neutrality and pure objectivity and insists that the context of the knower is always relevant to what is known.

Sixties Scoop: Between 1960 and 1980, the federal government (child welfare services) took an estimated 20,000 Indigenous children from their homes and placed them with mostly non-Indigenous foster families across Canada and beyond, often without the consent of their parents.

slow money: A social movement for investment in small productive enterprises, especially organic farms, organic food products, heritage seed companies, restaurants that serve local food, and other elements of local food systems. Considerations other than short-term financial returns motivate investors, who may be equally concerned about supporting ecological sustainability, small-scale farming traditions, animal welfare, or social justice aspects of food production.

social constructionism/social constructionist: The idea that what we understand as reality is constructed by, or socially made, through our shared culture. As a result, social constructionists attempt to identify the historically and culturally specific character of social beliefs and practices.

social control: How social structures and beliefs serve to dominate and constrain individuals and collectivities. Critics find that the social control perspective overstates the success of social control while understating the significance of human resistance to all forms of domination.

Social Darwinism: The application of Charles Darwin's research on evolutionary biology to human social life (Darwin himself only studied natural selection). Herbert Spencer (1820–1903) was among the first to do so; he coined the term "survival of the fittest" in his hypothesis that social principles were similar to evolutionary principles.

social deviance: See **deviance.**

social inequality: Unequal access to advantages and benefits among people in a society. Sociologists explore how unequal relations between individuals are linked to unequal relations between groups, with particular attention to inequalities organized by gender, race, class, sexuality, citizenship, and (dis)ability. Sociologists typically regard social inequality as a systemic feature of Western industrialized countries.

social institutions: Complex social forms—such as governments, the family, human languages, universities, and legal systems—that endure and reproduce themselves.

social regulation: See **regulation**.

social reproduction: In the broadest sense, the wide variety of interconnected processes that sustain a given social order over time and perpetuate its characteristic forms of power and inequality. For some feminist sociologists, this term refers to the day-to-day forms of domestic labour, care work, and familial responsibility that sustain the life of a society's current members and enable the emergence of new generations. The concept has been used by feminist political economists to illustrate the interdependent relationship between paid employment and unpaid reproductive labour by framing unpaid labour in the home as more than simply a private service that supports households. It also highlights the ways discourses and practices of masculinity and femininity become part of the class relations of capitalism by producing gendered norms about women's responsibilities in the home and men's role as "breadwinners," thereby sustaining feminized and masculinized norms of employment.

socialization: A key concept in sociology, used to explain the process through which individuals come to acquire social habits, beliefs, and skills. Critics of the concept of socialization are concerned that it assumes a high degree of homogeneity among social groups and underemphasizes difference and resistance that result from people occupying multiple subject positions.

socio-economic (class) stratification: A concept associated with Weberian approaches to "class," whereby class groups are separated/stratified according to economic criteria (wealth, income, property ownership, etc.). Economic stratification is also related to social factors such as education, which may impact income. Theories of stratification present descriptive accounts of economic inequality, but do not necessarily link inequality to relationships between class groupings.

sociological imagination: Coined by C. Wright Mills (1959), the sociological imagination is the idea that we can only understand ourselves and others through considering where we are located in our historical time, geographical place, and political context. It is vital to see how the social world shapes us. However, we can also shape the world around us. By becoming aware of social forces, we can become active participants in making history.

sociology of consumption: A subfield of sociology concerned with the social dynamics that drive consumer behaviour, and the ways in which such behaviour interacts with prevailing structures and relations of power. This field of inquiry challenges the individualistic focus that has prevailed within discussions of consumer behaviour in economics and psychology.

solidarity economy: An umbrella term for various projects and ways of organizing economic life that seek to provide alternatives to capitalism and that are guided by values such as cooperation, social justice, and equity.

sovereign power: Power exercised through direct political rule (for example, the rule over subjects by a monarch or the representatives of the monarch). It can also include other asymmetrical relationships, such as the patriarchal authority of men over their wives, children, and servants. Sovereign power is best described as power over groups and individuals, and it is generally negative and prohibitive ("You must not"). Sovereign power is expansive, and can be exercised as total control.

sovereignty: Power and authority claimed by monarchies and nation-states, giving them the right to rule over or govern a geographical territory, its political system, and its people.

spaces of exclusion: Separate institutions to which, from the 18th century on, people considered mad or diseased, poor, criminal, unemployed, and idle began to be confined, which weakened their ties with their communities and constituted them as outcast groups. See also **the great confinement**.

state, the: Political institutions that encompass governments and their agencies (the police, military, courts, legislature, public service). The state is a political and administrative apparatus that claims legitimacy to manage or rule the affairs of a geographical and political territory. Within capitalist economic systems, it is fundamentally a capitalist state. It ultimately works in the interest of preserving a particular economic order that benefits foremost the owners of economic wealth. The modern state carried forward some of the features of sovereign power, particularly through its juridical authority.

statistics: Aggregate data compiled on births, deaths, morbidity (patterns of illness), income, education, employment, housing, family size, and so on. With the growth of capitalism, industrialization, and urbanization, the administrative apparatus of governments became increasingly detailed and pervasive in producing new techniques of power linked to disciplinary power. As part of this trend, state administrators began to compile data in an increasingly detailed way about political subjects. This "science of the state" could only occur in the context of the production of new knowledges such as medicine, criminology, epidemiology, psychology, and so on.

status: Social position in an economic hierarchy, in which status is connected not only to income, but also to occupation and education. For example, an occupation that affords one a high income and that requires a high level of formal education may be seen to reflect one's position in the "upper class," conferring a high social status. The concept emerged from Weber's writing on class.

status Indians: Canada's federal government passed the *Indian Act* in 1876, with the intention of regulating all aspects of Indigenous life. Notably, a person was only known as an "Indian" by being registered as such under the *Indian Act*. All other people of Indigenous heritage were designated as without status, and not entitled to any of the land or other rights that Indigenous peoples may have held. Until 1985, a woman lost Indian status by marrying a non-Indigenous man, as did the children of that marriage.

stereotypes: Stuart Hall (1997) discusses stereotypes as signifying practices that try to "fix" the meanings attributed to people and groups, thus problematically reducing them to limited, essentialized, naturalized features.

structural functionalism: A theoretical position that conceptualizes society as based on consensus, with all parts functioning to serve the whole.

structuralism: See **poststructuralism**.

subaltern: Those who possess knowledges subordinated by European colonial history and science.

subject, the: People are constituted, or become "knowable" (understood), in the context of the power and knowledge relations of their time and place.

subject positions: Our understanding of who we are, achieved through both conscious and unconscious processes. We absorb social rules and meanings that originate externally to us, and understand who we are through this process. At the same time, we are always negotiating, and possibly reframing, our subject positions according to the distinct composition of multiple social locations that we occupy and according to the ever-changing social world we live in. See also **subjectivity**.

subjectification: The formation of subjects.

subjectivity/subjectivities: Our sense of who we are, premised on the idea that perspectives, experiences, and values shape each person's understanding of the world around them. Thus, our subjectivity is somewhat fluid, rather than a rigidly fixed aspect of who we are. See also **subject positions**.

subjugated knowledges: Foucault's reference to forms of knowledge that are hidden, disqualified, or masked by dominant knowledges.

surplus value: In the wage labour relationship, the difference between wages paid and the value of the commodities produced or the services provided. The production of surplus value is the key to the condition of exploitation experienced by the working class and how the capitalist class generates profit through wage labour.

symbolic system: An interconnected group of symbols that have acquired a widely understood cultural meaning. The most prominent of our shared symbolic systems is language, in which a series of letters stand in for an idea or a concept.

system of classification: Placement of concepts in relation to one another to extend our models of the social world. It tells us what types of things are alike and what types are different. Concepts such as "race" and "gender" rely on complex systems of classification.

system of provision: A term used to explore the historical and socially rooted relationship between consumption and production beyond individual and supposed rational economic considerations. The focus is on how a "material culture" is shaped by both consumption and production.

taxonomy: A system of classification.

techniques of the self: Can also be thought of as projects of the self, because they comprise the ways that we are compelled to be constantly working at self-care and self-improvement, whether that be through our manners, education, employment skills, body image, self-understanding, and so on. Through self-discipline, we can become better people.

testimonial encounter: The testimonial encounter can be thought of as a space where people listen, acknowledge, and take responsibility for trauma or violence recounted by a survivor, and become ready to respond.

theory-laden observation: The action of scientists who bring pre-existing theories about what the world ought to be like to their interpretation of sensory information.

therapeutic culture: The culture of therapy suggests that we live in a time of compulsory self-examination and critique, where the tools offered by psychology are required to make sense of ourselves. We must look inside ourselves for answers to the questions we hold, privileging the private life of the mind over the causality of our social circumstances. It is within each of us that the "truth" of our being can be found.

Third World: An older term first used to refer to the countries that were unaligned with either NATO or the Soviet bloc during the Cold War. It was used to refer to African, Asian, and Latin American countries that were considered less developed or less industrialized.

tourism: The voluntary movement of people who have the resources of money, time, and official documents to undertake leisure travel. Also refers to the whole realm of leisure travel distinct from one's regular work, including the expectations and adjustments made by host residents, the employment of a very large number of people that make such travel possible, the involvement of numerous tourism-related agencies and institutions, the production of particular ways of seeing and understanding the world, and the inequalities embedded in all of these dimensions.

tourist gaze: A specific way of seeing the world that distinguishes a place, thing, or experience from the tourist's everyday experiences. The tourist gaze is fostered by brochures, books, and tour guides that instruct people on what is an important site to examine, how to look at it, and how to interpret it as tourists. Also, tourists often assume the right to "know" all about another culture, and this knowledge in turn becomes a commodity.

trans*: An umbrella term referring to the plethora of existing trans identities. The use of the asterisk is derived from computer-based terminology where, when it is typed after a search term, all results related to the word are made available. Trans asterisk gestures toward scholars' and activists' acknowledgement of both the exclusionary nature of listing all identities belonging to the moniker of transgender, as well as the fact that gender is flexible and new ways of identifying will emerge and must be respected.

trope: A familiar and repeated symbol, pattern, character, or theme used as a shortcut for communicating information.

truth claims: All knowledge is created by people and comes from somewhere. Ideas have a history. Foucault asks us to examine how claims to truth arise, from where, and in whose interests. This has led some critics to state that Foucault is relativist (that everything is relative, and there is no real truth). However, Foucault does not necessarily deny the veracity of some truth claims over others; instead he wants us to think about knowledge as socially and historically constructed, partial, contingent, and subject to change.

Turtle Island: The Indigenous name for North America.

two-gender system: A model of understanding gender as a simple binary, as if there are two and only two genders. See also **sex/gender binary**.

two-spirit: A term coined in the 1990s by representatives from various Indigenous communities across North America attending a conference on HIV/AIDS. This term serves as a reclamation of gender and sexual diversity within so many Indigenous cultures that settler colonialism tried to eradicate. "Two-spirit" acknowledges that many Indigenous societies had enabled the flexibility for individuals to move between gender categories and identities.

upscale emulation: A term coined by Juliet Schor (1998) to describe the comparative process by which consumers come to derive their material aspirations by looking upward to the unattainable lifestyles and consumption patterns of the "rich and famous," as opposed to striving to "keep up with the Joneses" and other reference groups that are closer to their own socio-economic status.

use value: The ability to satisfy a human need (or want). Every commodity—including goods like food, clothing, and houses, and services like education, healthcare, and personal services—has a use value.

wage labour: See **free wage labour.**

white privilege: Whites are able to operate in an economic and racial system that privileges their norms, values, practices, beliefs, and lives over those of non-whites. Because white existence is the norm, whites can partake and operate freely within the system, something denied to those who are non-white.

white solipsism: The assumption that only white values, interests, and needs are important and worthy of attention. It involves the achievement of an emotional and structural distance from its interdependence with racialized Others, creating psychic distance between a population identified as "us" and another identified as "them." It ensures an abdication of responsibility for the problem by dismissing the relevance of economic and cultural inequalities organized on the basis of race.

white supremacy: The privileging of white people in all or most aspects of social, economic, and political life, in relation to cultural recognition and access to material resources. White supremacy is conveyed in both unconscious and conscious ways, from everyday assumptions about racial ordering to the exercise of political, policing, and military power.

whiteness: A social designation and position of systemic advantage and social dominance that accrues to those who are socially determined to be white. The designation of a group as white (for example, the Irish) has varied over time, indicating that the naming of races is indeed a social decision rather than a biological fact. Whiteness is typically unmarked and unnamed in white-dominated societies, which lends itself to non-recognition of white privilege.

working class: A fundamental class in capitalist society, alongside the capitalist class. The working class consists of all those who do not own the means of production and thus must sell their labour power in exchange for a wage in order to survive.

xenophobia: Fear and hatred of assumed "differences" and the inability to see that such "differences," far from being "natural," are socially organized. Often related to nationalism's fear and hatred of migrants.

References

Bourdieu, P. (2002). The forms of capital. In N. Woolsey Biggart (Ed.), *Readings in economic sociology* (pp. 280–291). Malden, MA: Blackwell.

Butler, J. (1990). *Gender trouble*. New York, NY: Routledge.

Frank, T. (2000). *One market under God: Extreme capitalism, market populism, and the end of economic democracy*. New York, NY: Doubleday.

Foucault, M. (1978). *The history of sexuality, an introduction: Volume I*. New York, NY: Vintage Books.

Gramsci, A. (1971). *The prison notebooks*. New York, NY: International Publishers.

Hall, S. (1988). *The hard road to renewal: Thatcherism and the crisis of the left*. London, UK: Verso.

Hall, S. (1997). *Representation: Cultural representations and signifying practices*. London, UK: Open University.

Haraway, D. (1991). *Simians, cyborgs, and women: The reinvention of nature*. New York, NY: Routledge.

hooks, b. (2000). *Where we stand: Class matters*. New York, NY: Routledge.

Lyotard, J.F. (1984). *The postmodern condition: A report on knowledge*. Minneapolis, MN: University of Minnesota Press.

Mills, C.W. (1959, 1967). *The sociological imagination*. London, UK: Oxford University Press.

Puar, J.K. (2007). *Terrorist assemblages: Homonationalism in queer times*. Durham, NC: Duke University Press.

Ricardo, D. (1971). *On the principles of political economy and taxation*. Harmondsworth, UK: Penguin.

Ritzer, G. (2005). *Enchanting a disenchanted world: Revolutionizing the means of consumption* (2nd ed.). Thousand Oaks, CA: Pine Forge Press.

Said, E. (1978). *Orientalism*. New York, NY: Vintage Books.

Schor, J. (1998). *The overspent American: Why we want what we don't need*. New York, NY: Basic Books.

Smith, D.E. (1990). *Texts, facts and femininity: Exploring the relations of ruling*. London, UK: Routledge.

Veblen, T. (1934). *The theory of the leisure class: An economic study of institutions*. New York, NY: Modern Library.

Contributors

Deborah Brock is an Associate Professor in the Department of Sociology, York University. Her research and teaching address social, moral, and sexual regulation. Her publications include *Governing the Social in Neoliberal Times* (sole editor; University of British Columbia Press, 2019); *Criminalization, Representation and Regulation: Thinking Differently about Crime* (co-edited with Amanda Glasbeek and Carmela Murdocca; University of Toronto Press, 2014); *Making Work, Making Trouble: The Social Regulation of Sexual Labour* (sole author; University of Toronto Press, 2009, 1998); and *Making Normal: Social Regulation in Canada* (sole editor; Nelson, 2003).

Margot Francis is an Associate Professor in Women's and Gender Studies and cross-appointed to the Department of Sociology at Brock University. She is the author of *Creative Subversions: Whiteness and Indigeneity in the National Imaginary* (University of British Columbia Press, 2011) and has published in journals such as *Native American and Indigenous Studies*, *Feral Feminisms*, and *Critical Sociology*. Her research interests include Indigenous and decolonializing perspectives on settler societies, community arts for Indigenous resurgence, and BIPOC sexual violence activism.

Gavin Fridell is a Canada Research Chair in International Development Studies at Saint Mary's University and a member of the Advisory Council of the Canadian Fair Trade Network. He is the author of three books—*Coffee* (2014), *Alternative Trade* (2013), and *Fair Trade Coffee* (2007)—and numerous articles on fair trade and free trade. His latest research explores socially responsible trade policy, the political economy of NAFTA, and Caribbean trade.

Kelly Fritsch is an Assistant Professor in the Department of Sociology and Anthropology at Carleton University. As a feminist disability studies scholar and crip theorist, her research focuses on disability, accessibility, and social justice. She is co-editor of *Keywords for Radicals: The Contested Vocabulary of Late-Capitalist Struggle* (AK Press, 2016) and has co-edited special issues of *Somatechnics*, *Feminist Formations*, and *Catalyst: Feminism, Theory, Technoscience*.

Alix Holtby is a PhD candidate in sociology at York University. Her research focuses on the role of quantification in the formation and consolidation of sexual and gender identity categories in the United States in the 20th century.

Dan Irving is an Associate Professor in the Pauline Jewett Institute of Women's and Gender Studies and the Human Rights & Social Justice programs at Carleton University. He is the co-editor of *Trans Activism in Canada: A Reader* (with Rupert Raj; Canadian Scholars' Press, 2014), and has co-edited a special issue of *Transgender Studies Quarterly* addressing trans-political economy (with Vek Lewis, 2017). His work is published in *Sexualities* and *Radical History Review*.

Melanie Knight is an Associate Professor in the Department of Sociology at Ryerson University in Toronto. Her research interests are primarily focused on the history of Black business ownership, racism and the discourse of enterprise, Black activism, and Black collective economic initiatives. She has been published in the journal *Critical Race and Whiteness Studies*, the *Southern Journal of Canadian Studies*, and *Gender, Work & Organization*. She was recently awarded the Viola Desmond Faculty Award and is involved in community initiatives that focus on women and employment.

Erika Koss is a PhD candidate in International Development Studies at Saint Mary's University. Her research on coffee utilizes resilience frameworks to explore the role of the state, climate change policy, and gender policy and practice in East Africa. She has served as a Literature Specialist at the National Endowment for the Arts in Washington, DC, has taught poetry at the US Naval Academy in Annapolis, and worked as an assistant dean at Northeastern University in Boston.

Gada Mahrouse is an Associate Professor at the Simone de Beauvoir Institute, Concordia University. Most of her research focuses on racialized power relations in transnational encounters. She has published articles in *International Journal of Cultural Studies*, *Citizenship Studies*, *Race and Class*, and *ACME: An International E-Journal for Critical Geographies*. Her book *Conflicted Commitments: Race, Privilege and Power in Transnational Solidarity Activism* (McGill-Queens University Press, 2014) won the Women's and Gender Studies et Recherches Féministes 2016 Outstanding Scholarship Prize. Bringing together critical mobilities/migrations, critical tourism, sociology of emotions theories, and critical race feminist and postcolonial frameworks, she is currently examining the dichotomous figures of the tourist and the refugee.

Aryn Martin is an Associate Professor of Sociology at York University. Her works on social and historical studies of biomedicine have been published in prominent journals in the fields of science and technology studies (STS), feminist theory, and sociology.

Anne McGuire is an Assistant Professor in the Equity Studies Program at New College, University of Toronto. Her teaching and research draw on interpretive perspectives in disability studies, cultural studies, and crip/queer theory, and focus on questions of human vitality and precarity. McGuire's monograph, *War on Autism: On the Cultural Logic of Normative Violence* (University of Michigan Press, 2016) was awarded the 2016 Tobin Siebers Prize for Disability Studies in the Humanities.

Andrea M. Noack is an Associate Professor in the Department of Sociology at Ryerson University. She is the author of *Social Statistics in Action: A Canadian Introduction* (Oxford, 2018).

Rebecca Raby is a professor and sociologist in the Department of Child and Youth Studies at Brock University. She studies constructions of childhood and youth, intersecting inequalities in young lives, and theories of participation and agency. Her recent publications include *School Rules: Discipline, Obedience and Elusive Democracy* (University of Toronto Press, 2012), *Smart Girls: Success, School and the Myth of Post-Feminism* (with Shauna Pomerantz; University of California Press, 2017), and *The Sociology of Childhood and Youth in Canada* (with Xiaobei Chen and Patrizia Albanese; Canadian Scholars' Press, 2018).

Mary-Beth Raddon is an Associate Professor of Sociology and is currently serving as Graduate Program Director of the MA in Social Justice and Equity Studies at Brock University. She is a qualitative researcher in the field of economic sociology who writes about the politics of philanthropy, charity, and fundraising in the Canadian welfare state. She also practices community-engaged teaching and research in the study of local, non-profit poverty-reduction efforts.

Heidi Rimke is an Associate Professor in the Department of Sociology at the University of Winnipeg. She specializes in classical and contemporary theory, political sociology, critical self-help studies, and the sociology of medicine and psychiatry. She is broadly interested in questions of power, knowledge, injustice, inequality, and resistance. She is currently working on research that examines the intersectional risks of gendered violence and suffering in Canada, including the role of compassion in the healing process.

Nandita Sharma is a Professor of Sociology at the University of Hawai'i at Mānoa. She is an activist scholar whose research is shaped by the social movements she is active in, including No Borders movements and those struggling for the global commons. She is the author of *Home Rule: National Sovereignty and the Separation of Natives and Migrants* (Duke University Press, forthcoming) and *Home Economics: Nationalism and the Making of "Migrant Workers" in Canada* (University of Toronto Press, 2006). She is also the co-editor (with Bridget Anderson and Cynthia Wright) of a Special Issue of the journal *Refuge* on "No Borders As a Practical Political Project" (26:2, 2009).

Dennis Soron is an Associate Professor of Sociology at Brock University. His current teaching and research interests include social theory, environmental sociology, municipal anti-poverty policy, and the sociology of addiction and mental health.

Mark P. Thomas is an Associate Professor in the Department of Sociology at York University. He is former Director of the Global Labour Research Centre at York, and has been a Visiting Professor at the Institute of Political Economy, Carleton University, and a Visiting Researcher at Institut de Recherches Sociologiques, Université de Genève. He is the author of *Regulating Flexibility: The Political Economy of Employment Standards* (McGill-Queens University Press, 2009), co-author of *Work and Labour in Canada: Critical* Issues, 3rd edition (Canadian Scholars' Press, 2017), and co-editor of several volumes including *Change and Continuity: Canadian Political Economy in the New Millennium* (McGill-Queen's University Press, 2019).

Index

Page numbers in italics refer to figures